CARIBBEAN HANDBOOK

THE VIRGIN, LEEWARD, AND WINDWARD ISLANDS

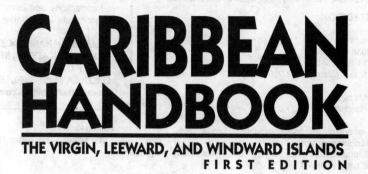

CARIBBEAN HANDBOOK

THE VIRGIN, LEEWARD, AND WINDWARD ISLANDS
FIRST EDITION

KARL LUNTTA

MOON
PUBLICATIONS INC.

CARIBBEAN HANDBOOK
THE VIRGIN, LEEWARD, AND WINDWARD ISLANDS

FIRST EDITION

Published by
Moon Publications, Inc.
P.O. Box 3040
Chico, California 95927-3040, USA

Printed by
Colorcraft Ltd., Hong Kong

© Text and photographs copyright Karl Luntta, 1995.
All rights reserved.
© Illustrations and maps copyright Moon Publications, Inc., 1995.
All rights reserved.

Some photographs and illustrations are used by permission
and are the property of the original copyright owners.

ISBN: 1-56691-027-7
ISSN: 1082-4685

Editor: Gina Wilson Birtcil
Copy Editors: Valerie Sellers Blanton, Deana Corbitt Shields
Production & Design: Karen McKinley
Cartographer: Bob Race
Index: Nicole Revere

Front cover photo: Caribbean Beach by Dave G. Houser
All photos by Karl Luntta unless otherwise noted.

Distributed in the U.S.A. by Publishers Group West
Printed in Hong Kong

Please send all comments,
corrections, additions,
amendments, and critiques to:

**CARIBBEAN HANDBOOK
MOON PUBLICATIONS, INC.
P.O. BOX 3040
CHICO, CA 95927-3040, USA
e-mail:travel@moon.com**

Printing History
1st edition — November 1995

*This one is for Phyllis
and for Kaarlo and for Nikki,
three points on the core compass.*

ACKNOWLEDGMENTS

The chapters of this book are peppered with the wisdom, advice, and support of a great many West Indians and others. Some of these people work in the hotel and tourism industry, some with the various tourist boards of the islands, and some are part of the life. All were helpful in the extreme. My special thanks to: Marty Flaherty and Amoret Bethel in Anguilla; Maryse Romney and Bernadette Davis in Saint-Martin; "Baby" in Sint Maarten; Elise Magras and David Henderson in Saint-Barts; Wilma Hassell in Saba; Pat Riley and Peter Titley in St. Kitts; Dr. Adly Abdel-Megud, Elmeader Prentice, and Fitzroy "Teach" Williams in Nevis; Elizabeth Mason in Antigua; James "Mango" Frith in Montserrat; Guy Claude-Germaine, Sylvia Schwarzer, and "Serge of Gosier" in Guadeloupe; Marie-José Edwards, Glenroy Espirit, and Zoltan Csete in Dominica; Annie Merlande, Georgie Vernes, and Roland Cupit in Martinique; Maria Monplaisir and John Jeremie in St. Lucia; Celia Ross and "Bam" in St. Vincent; Anadene Casimir and Sitah Singh in Trinidad; and Van Richards in San Francisco, once of Barbados.

In the U.S., my appreciation for helping me put my travels together is owed to the diligent Myron Clement, Tim Benford, Lauren Thomas, Marcella Martinez, Frank Connelly, Regina Henry, Peter Rothholz, Joan Medhurst, Catherine van Kempen, Daryl Minsky, and Betty Tahir at LIAT.

The staff at Moon Publications have provided their usual—therefore thoughtful, professional, and superior—support, and I am indebted to them one and all. It's been a smooth ride, and a pleasure.

Finally, to my family and friends, and especially our parents, for whom my erratic lifestyle has on occasion become a testing grounds: Many and deep thanks for seeing us through.

CONTENTS

MAPS

MAP SYMBOLS

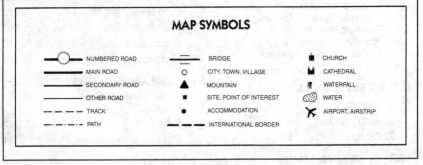

CHARTS

CONTINUED ON NEXT PAGE

CHARTS (CONT.)

SPECIAL TOPICS

IS THIS BOOK OUT OF DATE?

The truth is more important than the facts.
— FRANK LLOYD WRIGHT

Frank Lloyd Wright's sentiment carries a lot of, well, truth. It's a weighty proposition for travel writers; to be sure, the essence of any work is its truth. For travel writing, however, the simple truth about a place may not be enough; facts are what get you there, get you around, and bring you back again.

This book has been carefully researched to provide the most accurate, timely information available, with the hope that it will serve you better, making things easier to discern, and enhance your stay in the Lesser Antilles.

Still, things change—good for the Lesser Antilles, sometimes not so good for a travel guide. Foreign exchange rates fluctuate, hotels raise their rates, restaurants disappear, new governments are elected, and books take months to get into print. While the general information in *Caribbean Handbook* remains constant, specific details may become inaccurate by the time you pick it up. If that's the case, we want to hear from you: about your experiences on the islands and what you've found that can help us in our continuing effort to

revise and update *Caribbean Handbook*. Jot down observations while you're there—information recorded at the source is always most accurate. When you return, send the information to us; we'll check it out. The most helpful letters will receive an acknowledgment in the next edition.

We would especially like to hear from female travelers, hikers, campers, and outdoor adventurists. If you've run into problems you think other travelers should know of, fill us in. We also encourage long-time island residents to submit comments and opinions based on an insider's view. Be specific; comment on maps, area descriptions, and prices. Include sources where appropriate. Hotel owners are welcome to keep us updated on current rates and other information. Of course, if you found *Caribbean Handbook* useful, we'd also love to hear about it.

Address your comments to:

Caribbean Handbook
c/o Moon Publications
P.O. Box 3040
Chico, CA 95927-3040 USA
E-mail: travel@moon.com

BOB RACE

INTRODUCTION

Scenery is fine—but human nature is finer."
—JOHN KEATS (1795-1821), POET

"Travel is fatal to prejudice, bigotry, and narrowmindedness."
—MARK TWAIN (1835-1910), ESSAYIST, WRITER

"I don't even know what side of the street Canada is on."
—AL CAPONE (1899-1947), GANGSTER

Whenever I step off a plane in the Lesser Antilles, I'm surrounded by what at first seems an unnatural air. Whether it's a sweet breeze sweeping steady and fanlike through Saba's airport, or a thick, juiced wind rolling down off Dominica's high mountain rainforests, I'm struck by the difference of it—I come from New England, where ocean winds are often bracing, cause to shudder rather than wonder. The smell, the sense of the Lesser Antilles, is spice and rotting fruit mingled with brine and heat and the pungency of ocean jetsam carried off the sea's surface by the steady northeasterlies. It's a fertile, rich perfume; it carries an energy—you might call it an alarm. Something is going to happen. Whether good or bad, I'm instantly aware of possibilities.

Of course, the air is not unnatural. It's simply distinct, exotic, and ripe, and, like much else about these fascinating islands, takes but a short while to get into your blood.

I seem to be fixated on air, but for good reason. If you've never been to the islands, air is the one element that cannot be portrayed through print imagery, television, film, or music, all of which have given the world dozens of fixed and dependable Caribbean icons. You've known about the limpid blue water and swaying palms, heard the metallic tremors of the steel drum, and seen elegant people of all hues and tongues—the standard pictures, the clichés of the Caribbean. Yet it's that first and constant contact, the air, that leaves an indelible impression.

In places and at times, the Caribbean is all those clichés, all that you imagine it is. Its people—descendants of African slaves and European slavers, the nouveau entrepreneurs of this century, Arawak and Carib Amerindian groups, even buccaneers and pirates—contribute not only to the region's rich and weighty history but also to its current multicultural exoticism. Caribbean languages, likewise, reflect a swirl of the Queen's English, French, Dutch, Portuguese, Spanish, Amerindian and African holdovers—and of course the unique Caribbean creations, the melodious Patois and Creoles that have become the peoples' languages. The cultures, religions, cuisines, and architecture of the Caribbean reflect the rich amalgam of its various conquerors and visitors, and are, in themselves, attractions.

Yet, the antithesis of this complex utopia, the cliché of "trouble in paradise," also rings true. Whether one calls the Caribbean—or, in our case, the Lesser Antilles—a third-world region, a developing area, or a variation thereof, the fact is that it is generally a poor region. On several islands, the average annual per capita income is less than a tourist might spend during a week's stay at a luxury resort. Garment industry workers, for instance, in St. Kitts and Nevis earn about 90 cents per hour (US$); in St. Vincent and the Grenadines the minimum wage is set at 20 Eastern Caribbean dollars (EC$20), or about US$7.40, per day. The region was once the domain of sugar barons and the landed gentry—and slave classes—yet is today a disparate

group of struggling economies, in some cases loosely banded together for economic and regional growth, but in many cases reliant on the tourist dollar for foreign exchange. This situation contributes to a disproportionate economic and class milieu—high-rise hotels and mega-resorts stand alongside the matchbox homes of the near-indigent, and luxury cars pass plodding donkey carts on countryside roads. While economic inequity is not a situation unique to the Lesser Antilles, it does, given the region's notoriety as a fun-and-sun hub, command the attention of even the most aloof visitor.

And there are other modern problems. Social plagues such as racial disenfranchisement, crime, drug use, and sexually transmitted diseases, including AIDS, are threats and threads in the fabric of Antillean life, just as they are in the rest of the world. Political corruption has found its place in some governments, and phrases such as coup d'état and "military intervention" which throughout the 19th century were part and parcel of life in the Lesser Antilles, have again become part of local lexicon—recent incidents include a 1969 British intervention in

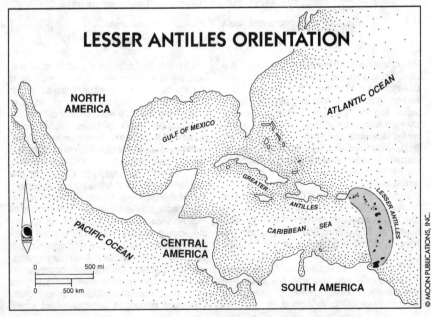

LESSER ANTILLES ORIENTATION

NORTH AMERICA

ATLANTIC OCEAN

GULF OF MEXICO

GREATER ANTILLES

PACIFIC OCEAN

CENTRAL AMERICA

CARIBBEAN SEA

LESSER ANTILLES

SOUTH AMERICA

0   500 mi

0   500 km

© MOON PUBLICATIONS, INC.

Anguilla, the 1983 U.S.-led intervention in Grenada, and the attempted Muslimeen coup in Trinidad and Tobago in 1990.

As well, despite replacement efforts, which for the most part took place during this century, forest depletion has taken its toll; it is estimated that over 50% of the region's virgin forests have been squandered over the last 500 years.

The Lesser Antilles is a very pretty picture with a deeper story to tell—in many ways, probably the same as the place from which you came. Its very human problems mirror the issues faced by the rest of the world. The region is, pound for pound, one of the most intriguing and exquisite places on earth, yet its seductiveness is cloaked by harsh history and persisting afflictions. It's not an easy place to love, nor is it an easy place to leave. To experience it is somewhat like gazing at the magnificence of da Vinci's "Mona Lisa"—the painting's allure is enhanced by that skewed, faintly melancholy smile.

And its promises, carried by a mellow breeze, can be private, even intimate. You can make the Lesser Antilles your place to simply lay down a towel, relax in the sun, maybe eat some fine food. You can dance your own dance. And, you can make it a place to discover something about yourself.

ISLANDS AT A GLANCE

DEFINING TERMS

Geographic Divisions

The geographic region covered herein is called the Lesser Antilles, and that in itself bears explanation.

The terms "West Indies," "Caribbean Islands," and the commonly heard sub-groups—the Greater Antilles, Lesser Antilles, Windward Islands, Leeward Islands, French West Indies, and Netherlands Antilles, among others, represent the myriad political and cultural influences the nations of the world have had on this relatively tiny region. It can be a labyrinth of terminology, difficult to discern which island is where, which island is politically affiliated to whom, or even which languages and currencies are used. For instance, the island of Saint-Barthélémy is designated as a French West Indies island located in the Leeward Islands group of the Lesser Antilles.

To make sense of it, a quick West Indies primer:

The West Indies is an archipelago, or group of islands, some 1,500 miles (2,400 km) in length, comprising a roughly hewn "border" that divides the Atlantic Ocean and the Caribbean Sea. The total land mass of the hundreds of islands in the archipelago is 91,000 square miles (236,000 square km), about the size of Africa's Uganda. Cuba alone represents just under half of the total West Indies' land area, and only some 50 islands of the group are inhabited to any significant degree.

The West Indies comprises the Bahamas and Turks and Caicos Islands in the Atlantic Ocean, and the Greater and Lesser Antilles of the Caribbean. Bermuda, some 570 miles (917 km) east of the Carolinas in the Atlantic, has some of the weather characteristics and cultural similarities of the West Indies, yet is not considered part of the island group. The West Indies lie between 10° and 27° north and 55° and 85° west, generally east and south of the Florida coast, east of Central America, and north of the coast of South America.

The Greater and Lesser Antilles form a sweeping arc; this stretches from Cuba, the northwest tip of which lies between Key West in Florida and Mexico's Yucatán peninsula, to the southeast, creating a necklace-like string of islands that ends north of the Venezuelan coast. The body of water encompassed by these islands is the Caribbean Sea, an area of more than one million square miles (2.6 million square km). The Greater and Lesser Antilles lie south of the Tropic of Cancer, placing these islands firmly in the tropics.

The Greater Antilles are, in order of descending size, Cuba, Hispaniola (Haiti and the Dominican Republic), Jamaica, and Puerto Rico, plus their smaller adjacent islands. The three Cayman Islands also lie in the waters of the Greater Antilles.

The Lesser Antilles, which were called the more lyrical "Caribbee Islands" in the 17th century, are a bit more complicated. Their two main divisions are the Leeward Islands and the Windward Islands—which would be fine if everyone would agree on which islands are which. Agreement often depends on the nationality of the speaker. The Dutch, for instance, refer to Saba, Sint Eustatius, and Sint Maarten, their three islands in the north, as the Netherlands Antilles Windward Islands. The statement is true enough in that they do, in fact, lie windward of Aruba, Curaçao, and Bonaire, the Dutch islands to the southwest. However, they also lie in the island group generally known as the Leeward Islands. For some time the British used the terms Windward and Leeward Islands for administrative purposes, as in British Leeward Islands. Yet the terms applied to their possessions and commonwealth affiliates and not, for instance, the French islands that lie in the same waters. The French do not use the terms at all. Today, the terms leeward and windward are considered to be locative and carry no political significance.

The following Lesser Antilles subdivisions are in general use: Farthest north are the British Virgin Islands and U.S. Virgin Islands. South of the Virgins is the Leeward Islands group, which consists of Anguilla, Saint-Martin/Sint Maarten, Saba, Sint Eustatius, Saint-Barthélémy, St. Kitts and Nevis, Antigua and Barbuda, Montserrat, Guadeloupe, and adjacent islands. Next comes the Windward Islands group, comprising Dominica, Martinique, St. Lucia, St. Vincent and the Grenadines, Grenada, and adjacent islands. The remaining Caribbean islands of Barbados, Trinidad and Tobago, the Venezuelan Islands, and Aruba, Curaçao, and Bonaire, commonly known as the ABC Islands, complete the Lesser Antilles roster.

Political Divisions

The other divisions among the Caribbean islands rely on politics, not geography. The French West Indies, sometimes called the French Antilles, and the Netherlands Antilles define political groups of islands with past and present affiliations to those countries. Great Britain maintains political ties with the West Indies through direct possessions and associations within the Commonwealth. Spain, today, maintains mostly cultural ties with several ex-colonial possessions. The territories of Puerto Rico and the U.S. Virgin Islands have direct political and cultural ties to the United States. All of the West Indies retain varying degrees of autonomy in their associations.

The largest group of politically affiliated islands are those that were the British colonies, at one time collectively called the British West Indies. Today they have become either direct possessions or Commonwealth nations. The direct British possessions, throughout the West Indies, are the British Virgin Islands, Anguilla, Montserrat, Cayman Islands, and the Turks and Caicos. The Commonwealth nations are Antigua and Barbuda, Bahamas, Barbados, Dominica, Grenada, Jamaica, St. Kitts and Nevis, St. Lucia, St. Vincent and the Grenadines, and Trinidad and Tobago. These islands have degrees of independence and associated relationships with Britain. By and large they are distinguished by British influence in their cultures and government, and by the official use of English (unofficially, a wide range of Patois and Creoles is spoken)—and by the fact that one can catch a good cricket game in any of these places. The U.S. Virgin Islands, with United States affiliation, are the other English-speaking islands of the Caribbean.

The French West Indies is a smaller group consisting of Guadeloupe, with its nearby dependencies Marie-Galante, Les Saintes, La Désirade and its northern dependencies Saint-Barthélémy and Saint-Martin (which shares island space with Sint Maarten), and Martinique to the south. French is widely spoken on these islands, and they are administered as *départements d'outre-mer,* or overseas departments of France. Their residents are considered French citizens, and travel between the French West Indies and France is unfettered by heavy documentation. Beleaguered Haiti, the Caribbean's other French-speaking country, has been independent since the mid-19th century and no longer maintains political ties to France.

The Netherlands Antilles is also a small group, consisting of Bonaire, Curaçao, Sint Maarten (which shares island space with Saint-Martin), Sint Eustatius, and Saba. These islands are, as a unit, autonomous parts of the Kingdom of the Netherlands, and Dutch culture is evident. Dutch is the official language, although English and other languages, such as Papiamento, are widely spoken. Aruba withdrew from the Netherlands Antilles in 1986, becoming an autonomous member of the Kingdom of the Netherlands and enjoying the same status as the rest of the Netherlands Antilles combined.

The Spanish have the longest history of Europeans colonizing the Caribbean. It was Christopher Columbus, sailing under a Spanish flag, who came upon the West Indies and set the stage for future Caribbean drama. Cuba, in a state of revolution since Fidel Castro overthrew Fulgencio Batista y Zaldívar in 1959, is an independent nation. The Dominican Republic, which shares the island of Hispaniola with Haiti, is also independent but maintains strong Spanish cultural influences. The Venezuelan islands are Venezuelan possessions. Puerto Rico, a commonwealth territory of the United States since the Spanish-American War, has conducted ongoing referendums to decide the island's political status (Puerto Rico's islanders have been asked to choose among ongoing commonwealth status, statehood, and independence).

It is confusing to many, but perhaps historically understandable, that geographers and various sources classify the islands in a number of different ways: some list the Virgin Islands as part of the Leeward Islands, others list Trinidad and Tobago as part of the Windwards, still others list Barbados as separate from the whole lot. It goes on. How important is it to know which is which? All in all, not very. The semantic permutations of the Caribbean region are less important than your ability to distinguish the islands by location, cultural influences, and other factors related to your Lesser Antilles visit.

The specific area our Caribbean excursion will cover hereafter is called the Lesser Antilles. For our purposes, this area will include the islands from and including the British and U.S. Virgin Islands in the north, through Trinidad and Tobago in the south. Yet in certain instances, since no one island in the Caribbean is completely isolated, nor does any one remain uninfluenced by its neighbors, we will refer to the entire Caribbean region. Our destination chapters—the U.S. Virgin Islands and British Virgin Islands, British Leewards, British Windwards, French West Indies, and Netherlands Antilles—have been arranged for ease of reference and not necessarily due to current political affilia-

tions. The British Leewards and Windwards do not refer to ongoing political associations (although all are members of the Commonwealth of Nations, often referred to regionally as the Commonwealth Caribbean), but rather past relationships and common cultural affiliations. On the other hand, the islands of the French West Indies share both cultural and political lives, as do the Netherlands Antilles.

DEFINING CHARACTERISTICS

Anguilla
Anguilla, the northernmost of the Leeward Islands, lies 190 miles (306 km) east of Puerto Rico and five miles (eight km) north of Saint-Martin/Sint Maarten.

The island is a flat, low-lying coral formation 16 miles (26 km) long and about three miles (4.8 km) wide. The highest point on the 35-square-mile (90-square-km) island is the central **Crocus Hill,** only 213 feet (65 meters) above sea level. The soil is thick with clay and nonarable in many places. The island's coast is irregular, serrated by small coves and bays with powder-white and pink coral sand beaches—some of the finest in the region. With a population of about 9,000, Anguilla sees fewer visitors than its neighbors and is known for its relaxed ambience, low-key tourism facilities, and fine beaches.

Antigua and Barbuda
The state of Antigua and Barbuda comprises the islands of Antigua, Barbuda, and tiny, uninhabited Redonda. Barbuda lies about 27 miles (43 km) north of Antigua. The half-square-mile (1.3-square-km) island of Redonda lies about 30 miles (48 km) southwest of Antigua. Antigua's land area is 108 square miles (280 square km).

The three islands are located at the heart of the Leewards Islands and nearly at the midpoint of the Lesser Antilles archipelago—generally east and south of St. Kitts and Nevis, and northeast of Montserrat. Antigua's airport, V.C. Bird International, is the home base of LIAT, the regional airline.

Antigua is a connection hub for interisland travelers and is a popular destination in itself.

ISLAND PRONUNCIATIONS

Just as some say "toe-may-toe" and some say "toe-mah-toe," the pronunciation of the islands of the Lesser Antilles has varied widely throughout history. After all, to take a word and put it through the ringer of Arawak, Carib, African, English, French, Dutch, Swedish, Portuguese, and a half-dozen pickup languages over the course of 400 years is to give it, at the very least, a subjective pronunciation spin. To begin with, the region's name, the Caribbean, can be heard as both "Ca-RIB-ee-an" and "Ca-ri-BEE-an." Both are correct, but, for the record, most locals use the latter. Below are the widely accepted pronunciations of major Lesser Antilles islands:

Anguilla—an-GWI-lah

Antigua—an-TEE-gah

Barbuda—bar-BEW-dah

Barbados—bar-BAY-dos

Bequia—BECK-way

British Virgin Islands—those in the know say "B.V.I."

Carriacou—CARRY-ah-koo

Canouan—CAN-oo-ahn

Dominica—dahm-in-EEK-ah

Grenada—greh-NAY-dah

Grenadines—GREN-ah-deens

Guadeloupe—gwad-eh-LOOP

Martinique—mar-tin-EEK

Montserrat—mont-ser-AHT

Mustique—mus-TEEK

Nevis—NEE-vis

Saba—SAY-buh

Saint-Barthélémy—"Saint Barts" is most common

St. Kitts—KITS

St. Lucia—LOO-shah

Saint-Martin/Sint Maarten—both are pronounced the same, "Saint Martin"

Sint Eustatius—you-STAY-shus; the common nickname is "Statia," pronounced STAY-shuh

Trinidad—TRIN-eh-dad

Tobago—toe-BAY-go

United States Virgin Islands—usually rendered as "U.S. Virgin Islands" or "U.S.V.I."

The island is one of the most tourism-conscious and developed of the Leewards, and it features several of the Caribbean's most luxurious resorts. Barbuda—flatter, dry, and more sedate—features inexpensive accommodations and the famous Codrington Lagoon, home to many seagoing bird species. The combined population of Antigua and Barbuda is estimated at 75,000.

Barbados

Barbados has had direct British or Commonwealth ties for three centuries, longer than any other island in the region, prompting some to dub it "Little England of the West Indies." The 166-square-mile (430-square-km) island lies about 100 miles (161 km) east of St. Vincent and is the easternmost of the West Indies. Technically, the island is not a Caribbean island, as it is completely surrounded by the Atlantic. Yet in spirit and culture, the island is Caribbean to its core.

Chief among its attractions are fine dining, a wide range of accommodations, preserved historical structures, and a healthy tourism infrastructure.

Barbados is about 21 miles (34 km) north to south and 14 miles (22 km) at its widest point, with a population of 255,000, making it one of the more densely populated islands in the West Indies.

British Virgin Islands

Approximately 60 islands, cays, and tiny volcanic rocks comprise the British Virgin Islands archipelago. The islands feature striking beaches, and the crystal waters of the area are a haven for divers and sailors. No hotels reach higher than two stories, about the height of the tallest palm tree. The islands have no casinos, no large nightclubs, and no large towns.

The four main British Virgins are **Tortola, Virgin Gorda, Jost Van Dyke,** and **Anegada,** lying in a sort of horizontal chain beginning 50

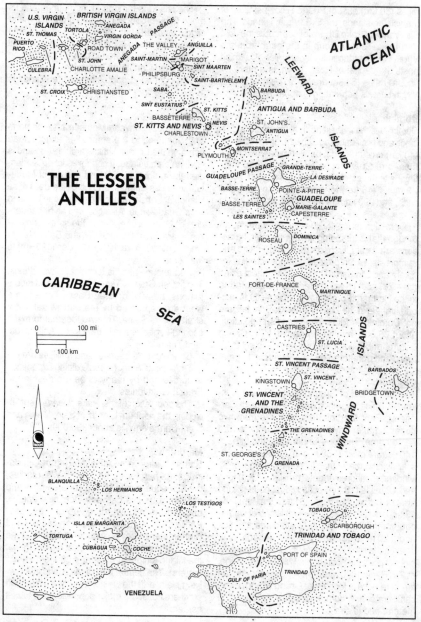

miles (80 km) east of Puerto Rico, just west of their sister islands, the U.S. Virgin Islands. The **Sir Francis Drake Channel** separates the Jost Van Dyke-Tortola group in the north from the Virgin Gorda string in the south. Tortola, which hosts the capital of Road Town, is a mere 21 square miles (54 square km). The total British Virgin Islands population is about 16,000.

Dominica

Dominica is the farthest north of the Windward Islands and lies almost equidistant, about 30 miles (48 km) on either side, between the French territories of Guadeloupe to the north and Martinique to the south. The island is rugged, some 29 miles (46 km) long and 15 miles (24 km) wide, and 290 square miles (750 square km) in area.

Dominica is not frequented by tourists, although that is changing slowly. Its main attractions are its big, lush, dramatic mountains and rainforests, which provide outdoor activities for hikers and climbers. The island's highest point, the 4,747-foot (1,447-meter) **Morne Diablotins** in the Northern Forest Reserve, is also the second highest in the Lesser Antilles. Beaches are not Dominica's forte. The island's population, about 86,000, retains strong ties to its Creole culture, and the experience here is likely to be rustic and unfettered by heavy tourism hype.

Grenada

The lush island of Grenada, also called the Island of Spice, together with the islands of Carriacou, Petit Martinique, and more than two dozen smaller cays, form the country of the same name. The total land area of the three is 140 square miles (362 square km). Grenada itself, slightly smaller than its northern neighbor St. Vincent, measures about 21 miles (34 km) long and 12 miles (19 km) at its widest point, a land area of 120 square miles (311 square km). The 13-square-mile (34-square-km) island of Carriacou is the largest of the Grenadines and lies about 20 miles (32 km) north of Grenada.

Grenada itself is a mountainous island, with its highest point the north-central **Mt. St. Catherine,** at 2,757 feet (840 meters). A national park and forest reserve is located at **Grand Etang,** a volcanic crater now dormant, rising 1,740 feet (530 meters) above sea level.

The island is famous for its nutmeg and its mace (a by-product of nutmeg production) and produces nearly half the world's supply of both spices. The island is infamous for past political troubles that culminated in a 1983 intervention by U.S. and Caribbean forces.

The combined population of the islands is 103,000.

Guadeloupe

Guadeloupe, between Montserrat to the north and Dominica to the south, lies almost dead center in the Lesser Antilles archipelago and is itself an archipelago. It counts as its dependencies the neighboring island groups of Marie-Galante, Les Saintes, and La Désirade. These islands are offshore and close and can be seen from Guadeloupe. Also counted as dependencies of Guadeloupe, and in the same *département,* are Saint-Barthélémy and Saint-Martin, which both lie more than 120 miles (193 km) to the north.

Guadeloupe itself is technically two islands. The flattish Grande-Terre to the east and mountainous, heavily forested Basse-Terre to the west are separated by the narrow saltwater strait Riviere Salée. The two together form the second-largest island in the Lesser Antilles, behind Trinidad.

Guadeloupe's beaches and facilities are excellent, and its French Creole dining experience is considered by many to be the best in the French West Indies.

The population of the entire *département,* including the northern islands of Saint-Martin and Saint-Barthélémy, is about 390,000.

Martinique

Somewhat more sophisticated than Guadeloupe, its partner in the French West Indies, the 425-square-mile (1,100-square-km) island of Martinique lies between Dominica and St. Lucia in the Windwards group of the Lesser Antilles. The northern central part of the island is characterized by a volcanic mountain range that includes the still-active volcano Mont Pelée, the island's highest point at 4,660 feet (1,421 meters). The central part of the island is a low-lying plain, and the western windward side and southern coast are major population and tourist centers.

Martinique is an overseas department of France and offers a highly developed infrastructure, fine dining, good beaches, and an intact French Creole culture. The population is 400,000.

Montserrat

Tiny Montserrat is some 39 square miles (101 square km) in area and about 25 miles (40 km) southwest of Antigua in the Leeward Islands group. The island is dominated by mountain ranges and semi-active volcanic peaks, the most striking of which is the southern range, home of the towering Galways Soufrière. Hikers can walk directly into the volcanic crater and be surrounded by its pungent gases and steaming vents.

Montserrat's beaches are not composed of the striking powdery white sand of nearby islands; rather, the sand is composed of crushed pumice and other volcanic residue, giving it a flinty gray sheen.

Culturally, the 12,000 islanders have African, British, and Irish roots, and Montserrat remains a British crown colony. Accommodations and tourist facilities on the island tend to be simple and adequate for the type of experience one would expect—a nice restaurant here and there, some swimming and hiking, but primarily a good place to relax.

Saba

Saba is a tiny spit of a rock dominated by the 2,855-foot (871-meter) **Mt. Scenery,** part of an ancient volcanic chain in the "inner arc" of the Leeward Islands. The volcano on Saba has been extinct for more than 5,000 years, and no one is even sure where the crater is or was.

Sheer cliffs roll off the mountains into the sea, and a rugged surf is the norm along the island's perimeter. Saba has no beaches to speak of.

Only five square miles (13 square km) in area, the rock is home to four settlements along its east and south sides connected by a seven-mile (11-km) road. Saba's population, about 1,200, is nearly evenly split between descendants of European settlers, who include Dutch, Irish, and Scottish, and descendants of slaves who were brought in to work small farms and to help in construction. Accommodations are simple and inexpensive, and the big attraction of

Saba, other than its unusual shape and striking views, is some of the best scuba diving in the Lesser Antilles.

Saint-Barthélémy

St. Barts, as it is commonly known, is a French West Indies island in the Leeward Islands of the Lesser Antilles, 20 miles (32 km) southeast of Saint-Martin/Sint Maarten and 125 miles (201 km) north of Guadeloupe, of which it is a dependency.

The hilly island is volcanic in origin, ringed by 20-odd beaches set in small coves and bays along its irregular coast. The island itself tends to be dry, and several small lakes and salt ponds dot the valleys and coastline, particularly along the windward and southern coasts.

The St. Barts population numbers just over 5,000, and most residents are French, descendants of French settlers, or descendants of slaves. The tiny island has long been an enclave of either the rich and famous or young and adventurous; accommodation, dining, and tourism facilities tend to reach both sides of the spectrum.

St. Kitts and Nevis

St. Kitts—really St. Christopher—and Nevis have been linked as an entity for more than a century. St. Kitts is where the history of English colonization in the Lesser Antilles began; the first settlement was established in 1623.

The nation is located between Sint Eustatius to the north and Montserrat in the Leewards group. Oblong St. Kitts is the larger of the two, with 68 square miles (176 square km). Nevis, nearly circular, is about half the size—36 square miles (93 square km)—and is dominated by Nevis Peak, some 3,232 feet (985 meters) above sea level. The two islands are separated by a two-mile (three-km) strait, serviced by ferries.

St. Kitts and Nevis are home to dozens of plantation-era "greathouses," evidence of former status as sugarcane-producing islands. Many of the wide-ranging accommodations are centered in these greathouses, and the islands sport several excellent beaches. The mainly African-descent population is a combined 45,000.

St. Lucia

The triangular island of St. Lucia measures roughly 27 miles (43 km) long and 14 miles (22 km) at its widest point, and is 238 square miles (616 square km) in area, which is slightly smaller than Dominica. It lies in the Windward Islands chain, separated from Martinique by the 25-mile (40-km) St. Lucia Channel in the north, and from St. Vincent by the 20-mile (32-km) St. Vincent Channel in the south.

The rugged island is mountainous and volcanic, and is an excellent spot for hiking and diving. The 151,000 people, now members of the British Commonwealth, are descended from African slaves and retain a French Creole culture from early colonial incursions.

Saint-Martin/Sint Maarten

This 37-square-mile (95-square-km) island is located in the Leewards group, 20 miles (32 km) north of Saint-Barthélémy and five miles (eight km) south of its nearest neighbor, Anguilla. It is, unlike its sister Caribbean islands of Antigua and Barbuda or Trinidad and Tobago, not two islands combined to form one nation, but rather two nations within one island. The island shares not only two names, but two cultures, two governments, three currencies, and at least four languages. However, no customs, immigration facilities, or formal borders separate the two countries.

The island's two dominant cultures are French and Dutch, hence the unwieldy name Saint-Martin/Sint Maarten. Saint-Martin is the slightly larger northern French side, and Sint Maarten is the southern Dutch side.

The island is thoroughly discovered and reliant upon tourism. Saint-Martin/Sint Maarten is one of the Lesser Antilles most popular cruise ship stops, so some of the Lesser Antilles' best resorts, restaurants, and shopping are found here—but at a price. It is rarely a quiet place, but rather jamming and congested. The 1950s population of the island, in the pre-tourism boom days, was about 5,000. Today it is calculated at over 60,000, with only an estimated 20% born on Saint-Martin/Sint Maarten.

St. Vincent and the Grenadines

The 20-mile (32-km) St. Vincent Channel separates the Windward island of St. Vincent from its northern neighbor, St. Lucia. Barbados, a major entry point for the island, lies some 100 miles (161 km) to the southeast.

This multi-island nation comprises the main island of St. Vincent and the smaller northern Grenadines, which number 32 islands—or nearly 600, including rocks, sandbars, and islets—that stretch some 45 miles (72 km) to the southwest, ending at Petit St. Vincent.

The Grenadines are recognizable by their names: Bequia, Mustique, Canouan, Union Island, and the Tobago Cays are among the major islands in the small chain, popular with sailors due to their proximity and docking or mooring facilities.

St. Vincent is a rugged volcanic island with an active volcano, characterized by a high central mountain range and a shorter range that stretches diagonally across the southeastern portion of the island. Tourism facilities on the island are limited but growing.

The majority of the 112,000 population is descendant from 19th-century slaves.

Sint Eustatius

Statia, as the island is popularly known, is a Netherlands Antilles entity located 17 miles (27 km) southeast of Saba; Sint Maarten, the probable gateway for getting to the island, lies 38 miles (61 km) to the north.

The island is a mere eight square miles (21 square km) and is dominated by a southern volcanic peak called **The Quill**, a long-extinct crater rising 1,980 feet (604 meters) above the sea. The slopes of the hill and inside its crater are covered by a lush tropical rainforest, host to a wide array of flora and fauna, including hummingbirds, lizards, and towering mahogany trees. The Quill is accessible by trails and is one of the more popular excursions on the island.

Facilities on the island are limited but not unavailable. Once a major shipping and transfer point, Statia has seen its share of rough times in this century. As evidence: the 1790 population was more than 8,000, and today's population numbers just over 1,800.

Trinidad and Tobago

The sister islands of Trinidad and Tobago are the most southerly of the Lesser Antilles, and of the entire West Indies. Trinidad lies just seven miles (11 km) from the north coast of Venezuela, its nearest neighbor. Its land area is 1,864 square miles (4,828 square km), and it is the largest island in the Lesser Antilles.

Tobago, Trinidad's cucumber-shaped neighbor 21 miles (34 km) to the northeast, is roughly 26 miles (42 km) long by seven miles (11 km) wide and has an area of 116 square miles (300 square km). The low-lying island, with several fine beaches and hiking possibilities in a central forest reserve, is the center of the nation's tourism industry.

Trinidad has produced two of this century's most recognizable Caribbean icons: calypso and steel bands. The island's Carnival is known worldwide for its music and its freneticism.

The population of Trinidad and Tobago is approximately 1.3 million, of which about 41% are of African descent and 41% of East Indian descent. The result of the nearly equal divide is a unique mix of uneasiness, energy, and culture.

U.S. Virgin Islands

The United States Virgin Islands group, an unincorporated territory of the U.S., comprises an estimated 70 islands, islets, and cays, of which three, **St. Thomas, St. John,** and **St. Croix,** are significantly large and inhabited. The islands are located 40-70 miles (64-112 km) east of Puerto Rico and 1,100 miles (1,771 km) southeast of the southern tip of Florida.

Each of the three islands has its unique characteristics. St. Thomas, commercially developed and home of the capital, Charlotte Amalie (a-MAHL-yah), measures 13 miles (21 km) by three miles (five km) at its widest point and is 32 square miles (83 square km) in area.

St. John lies some four miles (more than six km) east of St. Thomas and seven miles (11 km) west of Tortola in the British Virgin Islands. It is, at nine miles (14 km) long by five miles (eight km) at its widest point, and 20 square miles (52 square km) in area, the smallest of the U.S. Virgin Islands; it is also the least populated. Nearly 70% of the island is designated as part of the Virgin Islands National Park system.

St. Croix, located some 40 miles (64 km) south of St. Thomas, is the largest of the U.S. Virgin Islands at 84 square miles (217 square km), or 28 miles (45 km) long by seven miles (11 km) wide. It is less dramatic than its sister islands, characterized by gently sloping hills, some semi-rainforest topography to the west, and dry areas to the southeast.

THE LAND

Like giant dollops of whipped crème de menthe floating on a cerulean sea, the Lesser Antilles wend their way along the eastern border of the Caribbean Sea in a sweeping arc from the coast of Puerto Rico to Trinidad and beyond. A glance at a map will confirm that the islands are not sitting haphazardly in their waters; there is, rather, a pattern to the way they've popped up. If one imagines them as stepping stones of the gods, one could imagine the gods strolling, not hopping about in a desultory fashion, from the coast of South America to Florida.

The reason for this pattern, and for the formation of the entire Caribbean region, involves the theory of plate tectonics. Plates are the large, solid land slabs that compose the earth's crust. These plates, estimated at a dozen to 20 worldwide, are affected by the seething, roiling inner masses and pressures exerted at the earth's core, and are therefore in more or less a constant state of flux. That is, they move—as much as several inches per year—and have been doing so since the formation of our earth, some 4.6 billion years ago.

Tectonic plates average 50 miles thick but several have been estimated to be as much as 100 miles thick. Some correspond to the continents and land masses, others to the floors of the great oceans. Plates do not move in a visible way; rather, their changes are slow and constant through entire geological periods. And when they move, they move against each other, bumping and grinding in the geological equivalent of a million-year slow dance.

This relentless pressure causes changes in the earth's surface, particularly along boundaries, the weakest links of moving plates. One such plate roughly corresponds to the area we know as the Caribbean Sea, with its eastern boundary along the Lesser Antilles chain. Throughout this boundary area, earthquakes and volcanoes are not uncommon.

About 50 to 70 million years ago, a series of violent underwater volcanic eruptions thrust mountains from the floor of the sea, many of which broke the surface of the ocean. The peaks of these mountain chains became the islands of the Caribbean. The easternmost islands of the Lesser Antilles are slightly older, having been thrust out of the ocean as part of a series of eruptions that also created the Greater Antilles and Andes mountain range of South America. Gradually, these eruptions subsided, and over the course of several million years marine and other life forms developed and lived and died, leaving layers of limestone and sediment on the islands. By the time a second series of eruptions formed the inner arc of the Lesser Antilles, another several million years later, the first islands had become flattened, dead volcanoes. Today, in the inner-arc group of "younger" islands, active or semiactive volcanoes are still evident.

The result of all this underwater erupting and mountain-building activity yielded a mixed bag of Lesser Antilles, composed of rocky volcanic islands, limestone-based islands, and smaller offshore cays.

By far, the majority of the Lesser Antilles belong to the volcanic group. These islands, roughly from the British and U.S. Virgins in the north to Grenada in the south, are characterized by jagged and breathtaking rises, deep valleys, and the remains of volcanic activity, including the formation of volcanic vents, black-sand beaches, and steaming, primordial sulfur springs. Some volcanoes are more active than that—the massive 1902 eruption of Mont Pelée in Martinique destroyed the then-capital of Saint-Pierre, killing nearly 30,000. An eruption in 1977 of Soufrière (from the French *soufre,* for sulfur) in St. Vincent forced the evacuation of a segment of the island. In Montserrat, one can hike into the active volcanic crater of Galways Soufrière. In the crater of St. Lucia's volcano, near a town also called Soufrière, water bubbles and hisses. In Dominica, both hot and cold water flows from springs at Trafalgar Falls, and you can hike to the areas known as the Boiling Lake and the sulfur-ravaged Valley of Desolation, both reminders of volcanic business at hand.

A wide range of habitats, generally regulated by amount of rainfall, exist on these islands. Tropical rainforests, scrubby savannah-like plains, and mangrove swamps are all found to some degree on most islands. Soil on the islands tends to be leached and relatively devoid of nutrients for two reasons: the high humidity and rainfall of most islands means equally high rates of erosion, particularly in the mountainous regions where runoff is pronounced; and the massive deforestation of the last two centuries has accelerated the pace of erosion and added to the woes of island soil conditions.

The "older" islands on the outer arc of the Lesser Antilles, notably Anguilla, parts of Saint-Martin/Sint Maarten, Antigua and Barbuda, the

the northwest coastal town of Saint-Pierre, Martinique, with the active volcano Mont Pelée in the background

Rocky, rugged Saba, dominated by the towering Mt. Scenery, is volcanic in origin.

northeastern section of Guadeloupe, and Barbados, are relatively flat compared to their volcanic sisters. They are, in fact, noticeably flat in comparison to the newer islands. The primary ingredient in their composition is limestone. Trinidad and Tobago are structurally and climatically similar to the northeast coast of Venezuela, and their mountains are thought to be an extension of the Andes.

CLIMATE

The Lesser Antilles are, to a degree, always warm. Though they are subject to some seasonal changes, all lie below the Tropic of Cancer, where their proximity to the equator limits seasonal temperature changes to less than 10° F (6° C). Moreover, the powerful Caribbean Current (flowing from the juncture of the North Equatorial Current and the Guiana/South Equatorial Current to the Caribbean Sea at its southeast extremity, then northwest) helps to keep the islands surrounded by warm water. Average temperature in the Lesser Antilles is about 78° F (26° C) year-round. The widest variations in temperature occur with elevation, at about 1° F (0.6° C) of cooling for every 300 feet (98 meters) of ascent; or with day-to-night (diurnal) temperatures, which can drop the thermometer an average of 10° F (6° C) or so.

Added to the weather equation, the Lesser Antilles are always humid. That doesn't mean you will always feel the humidity. Constant low-impact winds tend to keep the air moving, which in turn creates the famed balmy breezes of the tropics. Nevertheless, daily humidity averages 65-85%, almost never drops below 50%, and sometimes reaches as high as 90%.

Rainfall and in fact most weather throughout the Caribbean is affected by the region's constant northeasterly trade winds. The northeasterlies (meaning they *come from* the northeast) originate in the high-pressure belts of the Atlantic and work their way across the warm Atlantic and Caribbean on their way to the relatively low-pressure regions of the equator. En route, the winds pick up moisture. When these wet winds encounter the islands, they also encounter elevations, either from mountainous ridges or from the elevation of the island itself. This elevation produces a cooling effect, which in turn condenses moisture in the winds, producing rainfall. Thus, the "tall" islands, or those with mountainous peaks and spines, have the most rainfall. The flatter islands, belying the imagery of the soggy tropics, actually experience drought, a situation in some cases exacerbated by large numbers of water-needy tourists.

Despite the locative monikers Windward and Leeward Islands, each island itself has a windward and leeward side. Windward is the side facing the prevailing northeasterlies, or generally the eastern or northeastern Atlantic Ocean side of the island. Leeward is the side opposite the prevailing winds. Rainfall is heavier on the windward side of the islands than on the leeward, or rainshadow, side.

Mountainous terrain means that average rainfall varies from island to island, and from windward side to leeward side on each island. The Windward Islands are perhaps the wettest, with averages of 40-65 inches (1,016-1,651 millimeters) per year, and up to 200 inches (5,000 millimeters) in the mountains.

Rainfall is most common during the North American summer, roughly May-October. The dry season in the Lesser Antilles is about Feb.-April.

HURRICANES

Despite all this talk of temperate climes and gentle rains, the Lesser Antilles does face the annual threat of bad weather—that is, hurricanes.

A hurricane is a wild, high-pressure storm of intense wind that revolves around a low-pressure center, the placid vortex or "eye" of the storm. The shifting eye varies in diameter but can reach 100 miles (161 km), and generally moves in a westward direction. As high-pressure winds revolve around and move toward the low-pressure vortex, they're whipped into a frenzy by centrifugal force, and can reach speeds of 120 miles (193 km) per hour or more. Severe hurricane winds exceeding 200 miles (322 km) per hour have been recorded. Thunder, lightning, torrential rain, and turbulent seas usually accompany a hurricane.

Hurricanes tend to travel from the east, often as small storms originating near the west coast of Africa. They move relatively slowly, about 10 miles (16 km) per hour, and gather momentum and destructive force as they make their way across the open ocean. An estimated eight hurricanes per year pass through the Caribbean area, but most do not touch land. Those that do, such as 1988's Hurricane Gilbert, one of the worst Caribbean storms recorded, or 1989's Hurricane Hugo, can cause massive destruction and loss of life. Even lesser storms, such 1993's Tropical Storm Debbie, can cause extensive damage. Debbie, which brought 10 hours of steady, driving rain to Dominica and St. Lucia in September of that year, killed four, injured 23, and washed away nearly 80% of St. Lucia's banana crop.

The islands' hurricane season is roughly July-Oct., though June and November have been visited in the past. A simple island ditty has been used to explain it: "June, too soon; July, standby; August, prepare you must; September, remember; October, all over."

A new service offered by the National Oceanic and Atmospheric Administration will update you on hurricanes and whether they're brewing at sea or on top of the area you'd like to visit. The service is available 1 June-30 Nov. at 98 cents per minute, tel. (900) 933-2628.

FLORA AND FAUNA

The face of the Lesser Antilles has changed a great deal since the early days of Arawak and Carib settlement. Since the arrival of Spanish colonials in the 15th century, forays into large-scale agriculture, foresting, light and heavy industry, and even tourism have altered the landscape by reducing large rainforests, partially replenishing others, and introducing new, sometimes life-sustaining, plant and animal species. There are at least a few places on each island, however, that remain untouched.

That much is true, throughout the islands. It is also true that generalizations about the flora and fauna of the Lesser Antilles are difficult to make. The area stretches some 900 miles (1,450 km), from the eastern coast of Puerto Rico to the Venezuelan coast. And, since many of the islands are separated by great bodies of ocean, each has had ample opportunity to evolve its own unique ecosystem and wallow in it for millenniums. As such, endemic plant and animal species are extant on certain islands. This is particularly true of the larger islands such as Guadeloupe, Dominica, Martinique, St. Lucia, and Trinidad. It is less true of the smaller, closer islands such as the British Virgin Islands or the Grenadines.

Having said that, a few gross generalizations never really hurt anyone.

FLORA

Along coastal areas, one is most likely to find sparse woodlands, marshes, and mangrove swamps. Mangroves are the trees that give the "jungle" look to movies and travel videos shot in the tropics. Several species of mangrove drop vertical roots from the branches of the main tree into the mucky swamp, giving it the appearance of a jail cell. As the roots develop, young branches break off from the parent tree to form their own extended growth. Although mangroves support a great amount of life within their own peculiar ecosystems, unchecked mangrove growth can choke the free flow of rivers and streams.

Drier environments, such as the leeward sides of several islands and large parts of the outer, flatter islands, support sparse forests, thorny scrub bushes (such as acacia), and some species of cactus.

Rainforests are characterized by towering ceiba (cotton), lignum vitae, and other large, hardy trees. At elevations of 1,000 feet (305

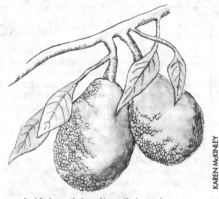

Jackfruit, a relative of breadfruit, produces a yellowish, edible fruit and seeds that resemble chestnuts.

meters) or so, trees are covered with tree ferns, bromeliads, wild orchids, vines, and a variety of epiphytes. This wet and warm environment is self-sustaining and seasonless.

Much of the region's flora has been introduced over the years by various settlers and conquerors. The first imports were maize, cassava, sweet potato, cocoa, and tobacco. These were introduced (as were many words for those crops, such as "tobacco" and "cassava") by the Lesser Antilles' original residents, the Arawaks. The Spanish brought with them several crops that would become the basis for island economies, primarily the banana, sugarcane (originally from the Far East), and pineapple. The islands of St. Kitts, Guadeloupe, Dominica, Martinique, St. Lucia, St. Vincent, and Grenada are still reliant on these crops for much of their export income. Bananas and sugarcane, in particular, weave their way through the archipelago, covering the islands' coastal areas with a lush cloth of familiarity.

The Spanish were also responsible for the introduction of ginger, turmeric, tamarind, oranges, limes, and lemons. Indian laborers brought marijuana, or "ganja," and the British and others contributed flowering plants, garden vegetables, and the ubiquitous breadfruit tree, brought originally to Jamaica and St. Vincent in 1793 by Captain William Bligh. (Bligh's first excursion to India and the South Pacific to retrieve the plant, where it is indigenous, was famously

conch shells for sale

KAREN McKINLEY

THE SUGARCANE STORY

Sugarcane is a common name for several species of grass, actually perennial herbs of the genus *Saccharum*. Sugarcane, a long, thick-stemmed plant, is well suited for cultivating in tropical and subtropical countries and has been an economic bedrock for dozens of emerging nations, particularly the islands of the Greater and Lesser Antilles.

Cane was first brought to the West Indies by the Spanish, who grew it with great success in Brazil and Cuba. After experimentation with other crops such as tobacco and cotton, sugarcane gradually caught on among the French, British and other settlers of the Lesser Antilles.

In the early 17th century, when the Lesser Antilles were emerging as economic entities, sugarcane farming was a slow and labor-intensive endeavor. Instead of plows and animals, slaves provided the backbone of the labor force; they were so inexorably linked to the crop's production that their emancipation throughout the islands during the 19th century ended sugarcane's domination and the plantation society of the day.

Due to the advantageous climate of the Lesser Antilles, sugarcane could be planted year-round but was best planted during the wet season, June-November. New cane was started from cuttings of old cane and took about 16 months to ripen. The cane was harvested during the drier season, Jan.-May, and immediately sent for milling and processing. Because cane would spoil unless processed within hours of being cut, planters had to stagger the harvesting (and, therefore, planting) over several months. A large plantation with a sizable labor force could expect a yield of about one ton of semi-processed sugar per year per acre.

Milling and processing were done on the plantation. Molasses and rum were also produced on the plantation, necessitating mills, boiling houses, distilleries, and storage houses, as well as slave quarters, cooking houses, stables, and a greathouse for the plantation owner. Slaves, in addition to their initial cost, were themselves an expenditure—they needed to be clothed and fed. Yet even given the large initial capital outlays, the whimsies of nature (hurricanes, droughts, and rodent infestations), and human obstacles (market fluctuations, wars, and, of course, slave rebellions), a planter's profit margin was healthy. In the late 17th century, the biggest sugarcane producers on Barbados, then the center of sugar production for the British, could hope to gross as much as £4000 per annum.

---

unsuccessful. During the 1789 voyage, his crew mutinied under the leadership of master's mate Fletcher Christian, reportedly in part because they were denied the very water that was used to nourish the breadfruit seedlings. The crew captured Bligh's ship, the *HMS Bounty,* and cast Bligh and 18 others adrift in a longboat. Bligh survived and went on to successfully transport breadfruit to the West Indies.)

Thousands of flowering plants grow throughout the Lesser Antilles, called by hundreds of different local names. They include several hundred species of orchids, as well as angel's trumpet, monkey tail, bird of paradise, ginger, hyacinth, and lobster claw. Bougainvillea, the ostentatious flowering vine of the tropics, grows everywhere. Its delicate white, rich purple, and orange flowers snake along trees, fences, and other bushes. Added to the scenery are the multicolored hibiscus, frangipani allamanda, and oleander bushes.

Common trees include the famous poinciana, named after a 17th-century governor of the French Antilles. Its flower is bright red, hence another popular name: the flamboyant. Also found are the tropical almond tree, soursop and sweetsop trees (the pulpy, edible fruits are not sour and sweet, but rather sweet and sweeter), and the huge banyan tree. Banyans are easily recognized by their roots, which drop from horizontal branches to take root at the base of the tree, giving them the appearance of dreadlocked evergreens. Calabash trees bear a large round fruit, which, when ripe, can be hollowed out and dried to make, well, a calabash. The mahogany tree is a native of the West Indies, and produces a dark, hard wood. The papaya tree, sometimes called pawpaw, yields a soft fruit rich in vitamin C.

Mango trees yield their sweet fruit, a favorite in the Caribbean, from March to October. Date palms, queen palms, royal palms, and of course, coconut palms, are found throughout the region. The coconut palm is perhaps the most useful of all. The coconut itself produces food, drink, and oil for cosmetics, and the fronds have long been used to weave mats, hats, and even walls for huts.

FAUNA

Mammals

Most mammal life in the Lesser Antilles has been introduced. Early European settlers brought to the West Indies an assortment of domestic animals including dogs, cattle, sheep, goats, horses, donkeys, fowl, and pigs. In some areas, pigs escaped domestication and are now found wild in uplands and rainforests. Rats found their way to the islands, perhaps as stowaways on ships. Vervet monkeys, probably introduced from West Africa, are found in large numbers on St. Kitts, Barbados, and Grenada.

The mongoose, a ferret-like animal introduced by sugarcane farmers in the 18th century to help control the destructive cane rat, became notorious soon after its arrival. The prolific rodent turned to hunting chickens, fish, crab, insects, and other harmless island creatures, and is still the bane of small farmers.

The agouti and the opossum (also, *manicou*) are harmless rodents that feed on fruits and roots and are found in the forests of larger islands such as Guadeloupe, Dominica, Martinique, and St. Lucia. The agouti, in looks similar to a guinea pig's bad date, was once hunted for its meat; its numbers have been reduced over the last century. A species of raccoon is found in Guadeloupe; Trinidad, again following patterns similar to South America, hosts red howler monkeys, sloths, and armadillos.

Of indigenous mammals, bats are the most widespread. More than a dozen species inhabit the islands' caves and the cool shade of mangrove swamps, feeding on fruit, fish, and insects.

Birds

Serious birders are probably aware that the Lesser Antilles host a staggering number of bird species. Casual birdwatchers will soon become aware of a small portion of the thousands of local species, from the large and multicolored parrots to the lanky pink flamingos and nattering gulls that make their homes in the rainforests, flatlands, and shorelines of the islands. A difficulty in identifying birds lies with the custom of using colloquial names for them throughout the islands, but local guidebooks are available that will help identify the more popular species.

Several islands are host to endemic species, some of which have become rare due to rainforest reduction and the international exotic pet trade. Perhaps no other birds symbolize the tropics as succinctly as the parrots, and parrots are the ones that have suffered most in the international trade. St. Lucia and St. Vincent host several species, such as the richly hued St. Vincent parrot. The *sisserou,* or imperial parrot, Dominica's national bird, has seen its numbers decline and is now a protected species. The Grenada dove, another endemic species, is protected as well.

Multishaded and shimmering hummingbirds of the Lesser Antilles are frequently seen flitting over banana blossoms and other nectar-producing flowers. The tiny bananaquit, yellow-breasted with dark plumage, may be your uninvited guest, feeding at the sugar bowl of your cafe table.

The birds of Trinidad and Tobago are related more to birds of South America than to the common birds of the Lesser Antilles. The soaring flight of the scarlet ibis can be seen at the Caroni

egret

tropical flowers

Bird Sanctuary on Trinidad. Rare birds, such as the New Zealand shelduck and the marble teal, are also found on the island.

Seagoing booby birds, or terns, recognized by their forked tails, live the better part of the year at sea and return to land or small outlying cays to lay eggs. An important breeding ground is Little Tobago Island, off the coast of Tobago, which also hosts the Audubon shearwater and the sooty tern.

Other Antillean birds include several species of egret, such as the snowy and cattle egrets. Herons, a related species, are found in swampy areas throughout the islands. Starlings and house sparrows are plentiful. As well, the islands are stopover points for migratory birds, the proverbial North American birds that go south for the winter. They include thrushes, warblers, and orioles.

For a more thorough treatment of the Lesser Antilles' thousands of bird species, refer to the seminal work by ornithologist James Bond (whose name was later borrowed by writer Ian Fleming for his Agent 007), *Birds of the West Indies* (Collins), or *Birds of the Eastern Caribbean* (Macmillan) by Peter Evans.

Amphibians and Reptiles
The snakes, lizards, and frogs of the Lesser Antilles figure into a plethora of local folktales, legends, and dishes. The famous "mountain chicken" (*crapaud*) of Dominica and Montserrat is a large forest frog, similar to a bullfrog,

that reportedly has very tasty legs. *Crapaud* legs are the national dish of Dominica.

Other frogs inhabit the forests. Several varieties of toads, introduced to the islands to control insects and cane rats, are, unfortunately, prolific breeders and have become pests.

The iguana (some theorize that the word may have Arawak origins) is a large, seemingly prehistoric lizard indigenous to the Caribbean. Iguanas, which can grow to lengths of five feet or more, are considered a delicacy by some and have been hunted for centuries. Over the years they have also fallen victim to the miscreant mongoose and their numbers have been greatly reduced.

Other lizards are much more abundant. One of the most common is the gecko. Geckos tend to live around houses and feed on insects. You'll recognize them by their bobbing heads as they run down window screens or across walls, heading for electric lights and moths or other insects. If you find geckos in your room, remember that they are harmless, and try not to hurt them. In fact, they're helpful—they eat mosquitoes.

Snakes, of course, come with their own set of folk legends, yet the snakes of the Lesser Antilles are generally harmless. One of the largest is the boa constrictor, which can be dangerous to small animals but will flee from humans. The fer-de-lance, a venomous snake that also avoids human contact, can be found on Martinique, St. Lucia, and Trinidad.

Several species of sea turtle are common to the Lesser Antilles. Some species can grow to lengths of five feet or more and weigh as much as 1,500 pounds (nearly 700 kilograms). Turtles are found throughout the islands, and females use isolated beaches to lay as many as 125 eggs during the March to August breeding period. Though protected by law, it is here on the beach where the turtles are vulnerable to hunters and poachers. The most common sea turtle is the green turtle, which is actually brown. Other indigenous species include the leatherback, the loggerhead, the olive ridley, and the hawksbill.

Insects

The Lesser Antilles are home to a lively array of insects, and for many of them you are destined to be their meal ticket. Mosquitoes, of course, and some blackflies and sand fleas make sleeping nets and repellent a necessity when hiking or spending time outdoors.

The Lesser Antilles' most notable insects are perhaps their butterflies, of which there are nearly 300 recorded species. The large orange-and-black monarch butterfly is found throughout the region.

The hercules beetle, found in the rainforests of Dominica and other islands, sports an odd claw at the top of its head. It is one of the world's largest beetles and has been known to reach five inches (13 centimeters) in length.

Marine Life

Ocean life originates in and around coral reefs with the smaller, microscopic residents that rank low on the food chain. Coral reefs are actually colonies of living creatures called polyps that exist with the corallite or skeletal remains of past polyps, creating life and death cycles that use past skeletal remains as building blocks. Coral, then, has the appearance of growth. When snorkeling or diving a reef, the brilliant colors seen on coral are provided by zooxanthellae, tiny single-cell algae life-forms that live within the coral structure itself. The polyps also provide color, but their skeletons

are usually white. (The topsoil of some coral atolls is formed, in part, from broken corallite remains.) The organism itself is generally hollow and tubular, with an anterior mouth surrounded by tentacles for gathering tiny food particles. Polyps range in size from microscopic to inches across. The coral polyp life-form has been in existence for over 100 million years.

Always popular with snorkelers and divers, a coral reef is one of nature's most sublime and quietly remarkable structures. The abundance of life in the reef is astonishing, if not always evident. A reef accommodates scores of life-forms including algae, some forms of sea sponge, and sea fans. Small and exotic fish, shrimp, and the spiny lobster make their homes in and among certain coral limbs, taking advantage of the rich fare that passes their way. Predatory animals such as crabs, eels, and some sharks use the reef for shelter and as a hiding place.

Coral grows in warm, clear saltwater, generally no deeper than 100 feet (30 meters) below the surface, and the reef can grow upward at rates of as much as 40 inches (102 cm) per year. In the case of a fringing reef, it often grows in shallow water closer to shore, aided by the sun. Much of the reef in the Lesser Antilles is within sight of shore or just a few minutes' boat ride from shore.

Coral reefs in the Lesser Antilles are generally of three types: common reef, barrier reef, and atoll. A common reef, also called a fringing reef, is actually part of the shore and main body of the island, and extends outward like a shelf from the mainland. A barrier reef rises from the ocean floor farther offshore and is separated from the mainland by open ocean or channels. Coral atolls are in fact entire islands (for example, Anegada in the British Virgin Islands) composed of coral remains; they are typically low-lying, croissant-shaped islands with a shallow lagoon

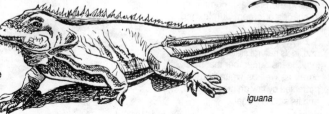

iguana

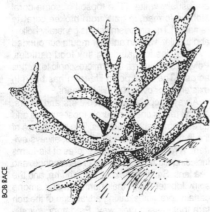

finger coral

on the "inside" of the arc and open ocean on the "outside."

In places, coral brushes the water's surface at low tide. Thus, coral is easily threatened by careless divers and changes in ocean current and weather, particularly hurricanes. Today, the biggest threat to coral reefs is from both local and tourist fishermen and divers.

Coral life found in local waters includes staghorn and elkhorn corals, so named for their resemblance to the horns of those animals.

Cathedral (also called majestic) coral generally thrives as isolated colonies, away from the main reef. Finger coral, small finger coral, and club finger coral are all common, as is brain coral, named for its resemblance to the outer membrane of the human organ.

Soft coral, those with flexible skeletal remains, are mesmerizing as they wave back and forth with the ocean's undulation. Gorgonian coral, named for the snake-hair sisters in Greek mythology, includes sea whips and sea feathers. Gorgonian coral is among the prettiest, commonly in shades of green, purple, and orange.

Black coral is also abundant and, in its natural state, quite striking. Please remember that black coral, as well as white coral, is protected by law on most islands, and its sale is illegal.

Fish and Other Ocean Dwellers

The fish along the reefs of the Lesser Antilles are plentiful and every bit as colorful as their host coral and sponge colonies. About 700 or so species are associated with the coral reef, and while you may not see every one, it'll seem like you have.

Many types of groupers, snappers, and the red squirrel fish (all good eating) feed on the reef. Flounders, including the common peacock flounder, are plentiful. In Barbados, the oddly adapted flying fish is consumed in great quantities. The multicolored parrot fishes, tiny butterfly fish, hamlets, and wrasses fill in the spectrum. Angelfish are among the more recognizable reef fish. In addition, a variety of nocturnal fish including the cardinal fish are visible.

Game fish and larger fish found in deeper waters include the blue marlin, a favorite of deep-sea fishers for its fighting prowess and its value as a food source. Look to the British and U.S. Virgin Islands, Saint-Martin/Sint Maarten, Barbados, and Trinidad and Tobago for well-organized deep-sea fishing charters.

Other large fish, many protected by fishing regulations, include the white marlin, wahoo, tuna, barracuda, and the blunt-nosed dolphin fish (not the mammal). Bonito and kingfish also run in the deep waters.

Eels, rays, and the aforementioned turtles also are common among Antillean ocean fauna. The most common eel is the spotted moray, a creature that seems to be all mouth and teeth. They're generally harmless and tend to feed at night. Still, it's best to stay an arm's length away. Morays should not be eaten—they're known to carry toxins that cause food poisoning. The snake eel resembles a snake and may be handled—but gently. Giant manta rays, known in places as devilfish, have been known to give divers a hitch. Mantas are ocean fish, mesmerizing to watch; their pectoral fins propel them

wahoo

BOB RACE

barracuda

with elegant, wavy swells in a fishy version of a slow-motion ballet.

Sharks are not always common in Antillean waters, but are seen on occasion. Nurse sharks, as long as 14 feet (4 meters), can be observed lying motionless on the ocean floor. They are not particularly aggressive but they are, after all, sharks. If agitated or cornered they will strike. Other sharks found in and around reefs are bull sharks, lemon sharks, blacktips, and sand tigers.

Other reef dwellers are a variety of starfish, sea worms, snails, and shellfish. The conch (rhymes with "honk") is prized for its meat and shell, which can be seen by the hundreds at roadside stands throughout the islands.

HISTORY

PRE-COLUMBIAN HISTORY

Slavers and slaves, owners and the owned: the history of the Lesser Antilles is inexorably linked to Europeans and Africans. For centuries, sugar and slavery drove each other and the economies of these small islands. The human mix formed the basis for the cultures, art, music, food, and the social stratification you'll find in the present-day Lesser Antilles. Yet before the islands had sugar in common, and before Ferdinand and Isabella sent Columbus on his way, the islands had known residents for roughly 4,000 years.

The first were Stone Age hunters and gatherers of whom we know little. We do know, of course, that they hunted and gathered and used tools made of flint and stone. Beyond that, they left no apparent artifacts. We know them today as the Ciboney (sometimes spelled "Siboney"), and that name is reflected in hotel and place names throughout the Lesser Antilles.

The Ciboney were followed by the Arawaks, a daring group of seafarers who crossed the Caribbean Sea in two waves, so to speak—the first estimated sometime between the death of Christ and A.D. 500, and the second approximately A.D. 850-900—from the Amazon River Valley and Orinoco regions of northern Brazil and Venezuela. They settled the Antilles in groups from Trinidad to Cuba, where Christopher Columbus would first encounter them in his late-15th-century voyages. A smaller Arawak subgroup, called the Taino, settled areas of Puerto Rico, Haiti, and eastern Cuba.

The Arawaks appear to have been relatively peaceful. They were a fishing and farming culture, fond of ceremony and organized games, and had little history of attacking others.

They settled in large villages with up to 1,000 huts and 3,000 people, generally by the sea or near rivers, yet skilled Arawak artists left paintings on cave walls that indicate they lived in the central and upland areas of certain islands. They shaped and milled their "canoes" (originally an Arawak word that made its way to English via Spanish). They were expert sailors, and their canoes seemed to vary in size and purpose. Some fishing canoes held only one person; traveling vessels held up to 60.

The Arawaks were a diminutive people (averaging five feet, or one and one-half meters), with dark, Asiatic features. They grew cotton with great success, and from that crop we have adopted the Arawak invention and word "hammock." The Arawaks also crafted jewelry and working implements from stone and shell.

The Arawaks grew "tobacco"—the word derived from the name of their pipe—and used it both socially and ritually. They grew fruit and vegetables including maize and cassava, the starchy staple of the tropics, which they called yuca. The Arawaks grew two types of cassava, commonly known as the sweet and bitter varieties. The now-famous pepperpot stew, popular throughout the Lesser Antilles, is also Arawak in origin. Guava, a fruit that has also taken its name from the Arawak language, was widely utilized. The Lesser Antilles' first inhabitants were also responsible for the introduction of the words "barbecue," "hurricane," and "manatee" into various languages.

Gender roles were clear: men worked at building and fishing, while women cared for children, worked the gardens, and spent time spinning and weaving cotton. Some anthropologists believe that the Arawaks held a concept of an earth mother and sky father, not unlike other Amerindian groups. Their deities were male and female and were involved in all aspects of Arawak life from creation (of life, not of the earth; the Arawaks seemed to believe that the earth had always been in existence), to the interplay of elements, to death. In one creation myth, the male god Iocauna created humans, who emerged from caves and the earth. Later he created the sun, the moon, and the fish in the sea. Some linguists believe that the Arawak word for the staple crop *yuca* is related to the name of the god Iocauna. The female god Attabeira performed other functions, including Mother of Tides and Springs. The Arawaks reached their gods through use of stone idols called *zemis,* believed to be inhabited by spirits of deceased rulers.

In death, the spirits of departed Arawaks, called *opias,* were said to wander around in the bush at night, indistinguishable from the living save for the lack of a navel. The Arawaks buried their dead in caves, sometimes placing the head and other body parts in large pottery bowls. These bowls and preserved skulls are on display today in museums around the islands.

For centuries the Arawaks existed unperturbed until the arrival of the bellicose Caribs, another seagoing indigenous group from the Orinocos region of South America. The Caribs were possibly distant relatives of Arawak groups and had, over the years, made their way from South America to the Lesser Antilles, leaving destruction and conquered islands in the wakes of their fleets of war canoes; it is estimated that as

Arawak figure

many as 100 canoes comprised a raiding party. According to some evidence, they captured and destroyed entire villages. Although it's disputed by some scholars, the Caribs reportedly ate their adversaries. In fact, the word "cannibal" is derived from *Caribal,* or perhaps *Caníbales,* the Spanish word for the Caribs.

By the mid-15th century, the Caribs had reached as far north as Puerto Rico, Cuba, and Hispaniola. Their combative nature, in conjunction with the devastation of early Spanish settlement, would succeed in reducing the indigenous Arawak population of the Lesser and Greater Antilles from two or three million to a few thousand by the early 16th century.

In fact such was the extent of the Caribs' influence that the waters around them, again via the Spanish, acquired their name—the Caribbean Sea.

EARLY EUROPEAN EXPLORATION

Meanwhile, in another part of the world, events were taking place that would change the destiny of the tiny islands of the Lesser Antilles.

In his relentless, largely ego-driven quest for riches and a route to the New World, the Italian explorer Christopher Columbus (Christoforo Colombo, in his native language) sailed into both fame and a bit of infamy on his four voyages to the Americas (1492-93, 1493-96, 1498-1500, 1502-04).

The premise of his daring plan, a plan that inspired the sponsorship of Spanish sovereigns Ferdinand and Isabella, was that the ever-growing European demand for Asian luxuries necessitated a simpler and more efficient route to obtain them. The current overland routes were dangerous, time-consuming, and costly. It was part of Columbus's grand scheme, the "Enterprise of the Indies," to find an ocean route west from Spain to Asia, and to secure land for Spain's empire. He did not know, of course, that the Americas lay uncharted between Europe and Asia. It took years and no small effort for Columbus to convince his

BOB RACE

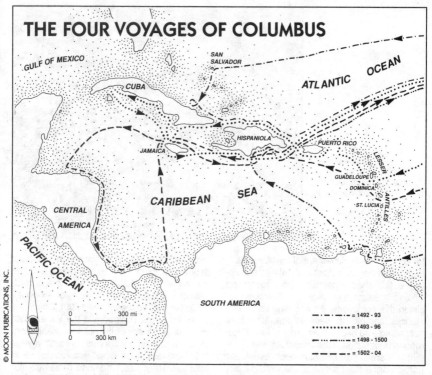

THE FOUR VOYAGES OF COLUMBUS

GULF OF MEXICO

SAN SALVADOR

ATLANTIC OCEAN

CUBA

HISPANIOLA

PUERTO RICO

JAMAICA

LESSER

GUADELOUPE

DOMINICA

ANTILLES

ST. LUCIA

CENTRAL AMERICA

CARIBBEAN SEA

PACIFIC OCEAN

SOUTH AMERICA

0   300 mi
0   300 km

—·—·— = 1492 - 93
············· = 1493 - 96
—···—···— = 1498 - 1500
— — — — = 1502 - 04

© MOON PUBLICATIONS, INC.

patrons that he could find this shorter route and thus enrich the Spanish empire and its sovereigns. When he eventually succeeded in convincing the Spaniards to support his venture, Columbus set sail with the added incentive that, with his success, he was ensured political and property rights for himself and his descendants, as well as 10% of all goods and gold traded or discovered during the voyage.

Columbus, with the title "Admiral of the Ocean Sea, Viceroy and Governor," and his crew of 90 sailed from Palos, Spain, on 3 August 1492 with a fleet of three caravels, the *Niña,* the *Pinta,* and his flagship *Santa María.* Columbus was optimistic that the New World was less than 2,800 miles (4,500 km) to the west. Of course, due to a gross miscalculation of the earth's size and an overestimation of Asia's easternmost point, his calculations fell drastically short. The actual (airline) distance

between Spain and easternmost Asia is about 10,000 miles (16,100 km).

On 12 October 1492 Columbus and his crew sighted land. It was an island the native residents called *Guanahani,* renamed San Salvador or "Holy Savior" by Columbus, and was most likely today's Watling Island of the Bahamas. Later in this first voyage Columbus went on to explore Cuba and Espaniola, or "Little Spain" (today's Hispaniola).

Of the native Arawaks Columbus encountered, he wrote, "They love their neighbors as themselves and their speech is the sweetest and gentlest in the world; and they always speak with a smile." Apparently, this love of neighbors was never adopted by Columbus; he kidnapped six of these sweet and smiling people to serve as guides and to tout as proof of his visit to the New World. His ultimate plan was to both convert and enslave the remainder of the Arawaks

Arawaks often committed suicide rather than submit to European encroachment.

COURTESY OF THE NATIONAL LIBRARY OF JAMAICA

for Spain. The enslavement of the Arawaks in Hispaniola began almost instantly as Columbus established a garrison there to protect Spain's interests in the island. The Arawaks resisted this enslavement by fighting and, in instances, committing mass suicide rather than submitting—so began the history of forced European domination in the Lesser Antilles.

It is a small part of Columbus's eventually heroic (in the strict sense of the word) legacy that when he landed he erroneously believed he was in the Indies, near the coasts of Japan and China. It would be his lifelong belief that he'd discovered islands off the coast of Asia, gateway to the lands traveled by Marco Polo more than two centuries earlier. His lifelong quest was to make contact with the emperor of China, the Great Khan. He would, of course, never succeed. Nevertheless, he collectively named the islands he discovered the "West Indies" and the people who inhabited them "Indians." The momentum of history carries those names today.

In his next voyage (1493-96), now bearing the title "Viceroy of the Indies," Columbus came upon Jamaica, Puerto Rico, Dominica, Guadeloupe, Antigua, and several other Lesser Antillean islands. It was on these trips that he first encountered the Caribs, already settled in the islands. In his journals the explorer wrote: "As for monsters I have found no trace of them except at one point on the second island on the way to the Indies; it is inhabited by a people considered throughout the island to be most ferocious."

On his third voyage (1498-1500), Columbus sailed as far as Trinidad and the Venezuelan coast, charting islands but not necessarily landing on all of them. By the time his fourth voyage (1502-04) took place, his adventures had taken their toll. The Great Khan had remained elusive, and no substantial amounts of gold had been discovered. The sovereigns Ferdinand and Isabella began to question their support and argued over Columbus's compensation. During this last voyage, his old caravels gave way and sank, and he and his crew members were marooned on Jamaica for more than a year. When finally rescued, Columbus returned to Spain a discouraged, broken, and ultimately defeated man. Within two years of his return, on 20 May 1506, he died at Valladolid.

The early discoveries of Columbus opened the floodgates of European exploration. However, all this settlement spelled doom first for the hapless Arawaks, then for the Caribs. During the 16th and 17th centuries, the Caribs were enslaved, murdered, and infected with disease. Many committed suicide rather than submit to European domination. Entire communities were eliminated, and eventually the ruthless process was complete. Today only a handful of these indigenous people survive; most live on the islands of St. Vincent and Dominica.

COLONIES

During the 16th and 17th centuries, the European powers established major ports in the Greater and Lesser Antilles. Tobacco was one of the islands' first cash crops, and small settlements grew larger with the introduction of sugar, cotton, coffee, and other crops. With the absence of Arawak slave labor, African slaves were imported in increasing numbers, thus determining the ethnological and sociological makeup of the Caribbean today.

The European ports and outposts in the Lesser Antilles were, however, by no means permanent. Eager to find footholds in the New World and eager for expansion and commerce (and in some cases religious freedom), principal European countries vied for power and possessions. Spain, which controlled the seas and the major islands of Puerto Rico, Cuba, Hispaniola and, briefly, Jamaica and Trinidad, was the target of French, Dutch, and English ships of war, as well as privateers and assorted scalawags who roamed the Caribbean in search of easy riches. The Danes, who ruled the Virgin Islands for two centuries, and the Swedes, who eventually occupied St. Barthélémy from 1786 to 1878, were also players in the acquisitions game. The rattling of sabers in the Caribbean was part and parcel of the continuing European wars of domination, where treaties were signed and alliances rearranged—and islands changed hands repeatedly.

The late 17th century was also a time of unbridled recklessness with a smattering of heroics perpetrated by some of the Caribbean's more colorful malcontents, the buccaneers (the name evolved from the French *boucan,* for a wooden rack used to dry meat). A loose association of sailors, pirates, thugs, and some truly evil people (outcasts who'd given up their nationalities for the lure of the sea and quick wealth), the buccaneers were bound together by a unwavering distrust for authority and a particular distrust for Spain. With Spain controlling the trade routes of the West Indies, the

buccaneers were also outlaws. They were, then, perfect for the job of harassing Spanish possessions throughout the New World.

Nominally employed as privateers by the likes of England, the mercenary buccaneers waged war on the Spanish Main, particularly in Panama, as well as the Spanish ports of San Juan, Havana, and Cartagena. Names such as Francis Drake, Henry Morgan, Calico Jack Rackham, Edward Teach (also known as Blackbeard), Mary Read, and Anne Bonney rank among the more well-known—and feared—privateers of the time.

The War of Spanish Succession, fought mainly in Europe, was brought to an end by the 1713 Treaty of Utrecht. During that war, France and Spain, then allies, battled and lost to England and the Netherlands in a familiar skirmish over property and trade rights. With Spain divested of its European possessions and England awarded France's Asiento (a contract to supply Spanish New World possessions with slaves), the buccaneers were left without a united front. England no longer needed them, and most buccaneers reverted to their historic roots—they became a small group of marauding pirates, aligned to no one. They were desperate and ruthless, and were hunted down like dogs. Others, such as Sir Francis Drake

---

CREOLE

When the Spanish began their 16th-century colonization of the New World, a new vocabulary accompanied them, springing up from the unusual circumstances of their exploration. As their colonies grew and Spaniards were born in the New World, the word "criollo" came to refer to a native of Spanish America. It was later adapted by English and French colonials during the days of slavery to refer to native blacks, slaves born in the West Indies, and to people of mixed race born in the West Indies. Later, after the colonies emancipated slaves, it came to refer to people of all races who were native-born. Today the word is a catch-all, referring to a wide range of aspects of the West Indian lifestyle originating in the region. Music, cooking, language, beliefs, and the people themselves can all be called Creole, *créole, criollo,* or variations thereof.

and Sir Henry Morgan (at the time of this change of heart they were knighted), astutely sensed that the times had changed, and they changed with them. They disavowed their erstwhile comrades in arms, the pirates and buccaneers, and even helped in their persecution, proving once again that pragmatic hypocrisy has a firm place in world history. Drake and Morgan moved on to become wealthy aristocrats and titled land holders.

It wasn't until the period of the Napoleonic Wars, when the 1815 Treaty of Vienna was signed after the defeat of Napoleon at Waterloo, that the Lesser Antilles settled down into a semblance of orderly rule. Ultimately, the history of the islands demonstrates numerous changed hands. The island of St. Lucia, for example, was discovered and first colonized by Spain, then ruled by France, and eventually changed hands 14 times before finally emerging as a British colony. Present day Saint-Martin/Sint Maarten is half-French, half-Dutch. The U.S. Virgin Islands have known Spanish, Dutch, French, Danish, and U.S. rule, as well as a brief stint under the Knights of Malta.

PLANTOCRACY AND SLAVERY

Emerging from the European rivalries of the 17th and 18th centuries was an Antillean society economically steeped in agriculture and the slave trade. The "triangle" of trade, stretching from West African ports where slaves were bought and loaded onto cargo ships, to various European ports and to the sugar-producing ports of the Antilles (and Brazil), commerce was brisk and profitable. Fortunes were made, often by absentee landholders, and the great plantocracies of the Caribbean created the basis for the multitiered, multiracial society we know today.

During the 18th and early 19th centuries, sugar reigned in the Caribbean. Over 10 million African slaves were imported to the Americas, most from western, central, and eventually eastern Africa Most were brought to the Greater Antilles and Brazil, where large land masses favored the production of sugar. Still, virtually all the islands of the Lesser Antilles produced sugar and other crops, and slaves provided the backbone for building roads, ports, and the infrastructures of the day.

The planter society was characterized by a mishmash of landed plantation owners, overseers, merchants, and, of course, Africans bound by slavery. In white society the ugliness of brutality, ignorance, and illiteracy was rife, and that was in part the result of years of island colonization by European misfits and criminals. The masters were more often than not unrepentant bigots, and their methods of keeping slaves in line were legendary—beheadings, live burnings, and mutilations were not uncommon. Slaves outnumbered their masters by the thousands. In these societies, too few held too much power—a perfect recipe for tension, rebellion, and ultimate failure.

captive slaves led away in yokes

COURTESY OF THE NATIONAL LIBRARY OF JAMAICA

Slave life itself was tragic. Beginning with the infamous Middle Passage from Africa, where captive Africans were chained and relegated to the stench-filled bowels of cargo ships, a slave's lot was one virtually without hope. During the 12-week Atlantic passage, many died of starvation or dehydration. On arrival, slaves were typically stripped, exhibited for sale, and even branded—not nearly the last affront to dignity they would encounter. Labor in the sugarcane fields was the most difficult and grinding possible, and many slaves died from it or were beaten to death by overseers. Still more committed suicide, were killed as retribution for running away, or died during open rebellion. Planters could expect an average of six deaths to occur for every live birth among slaves, and the need to import more Africans increased with the expansion of trade and planter society.

Black slaves consorted—most often by force—with whites to produce a new "brown" layer of society, mixed-race offspring who held the unintentionally peripheral position between the whites and hapless Africans. In some cases, the mixed-race class was called "free coloreds"; many were unable to function in a racist society that considered them inferior to whites, yet superior to black Africans. The emergence of a brown class so fueled the planters' fears that miscegenation would kick in the door of white supremacy that a bizarre and ultimately futile system of racial classification emerged throughout the islands. A person of mixed race would be, in the English-speaking colonies, classified as musteefino, octaroon, quadroon, mulatto, sambo, and so on, depending on the percentage mix of white and black heritage. In the French Antilles, official and presumably complicated gradations of color numbered more than one hundred. Today, though official classifications no longer exist, and though the islands' mottos and tourist brochures proclaim multiracial societies existing in ebony-and-ivory harmony, one needn't look very hard to find that informal color classifications still exist on social and economic levels.

The planter society lived in constant and justified fear of slave uprisings. If the sheer number of slaves wasn't enough cause for concern, the planters found themselves dealing with a people they had clearly misjudged in terms of intellect and ability to organize. Slaves customarily and relentlessly sabotaged their masters' plantations by ruining farm equipment, holding forbidden meetings, and plotting reprisals. Rebellions erupted in Barbados, Jamaica, Trinidad, and Antigua, and were put down with frightening brutality. The black Haitian leader Toussaint L'Ouverture, borrowing philosophy and impetus from the late-1700s French Revolution, led a successful uprising in 1794 and became the first leader of a free black state—home to more than 450,000 newly freed slaves—in the New World. In America, the slave preacher Nat Turner led Blacks on a wide-scale rebellion in 1831.

For years, particularly during the 18th century, many in mainstream European society had been horrified by the spectacle of slavery in the Antilles. Guided by abolitionist movements and the clergy, people commonly protested and called for an end to the practice. Finally, during the early 1800s, the reprisals exacted on rebellious slaves by the plantocracy of the New World reached the ears of an already agitated Europe. Reports of the thousands of slaves murdered by Whites during, for example, the repression of the slave rebellion led by Sam Sharpe in Jamaica, caused massive outcries in Britain. Finally, after much debate (and in the case of America, a civil war) the slave trade in the New World began to disintegrate. The Danes were the first to abolish the slave trade, in 1792. Great Britain banned slave trade in 1808. By 1814, most European countries had followed the lead, and the legal trade in slaves had virtually ended. Twenty years later, slavery as an institution began to disintegrate in the Americas. The British outlawed ownership of slaves in 1834, the French in 1848, the Dutch in 1863, and the U.S. by 1865. The Spanish, who then operated large sugar plantations in Brazil and Cuba, followed in 1886.

POST-EMANCIPATION LIFE

The end of slavery was the death knell for the heyday of West Indian planter society. Many former slaves went on to farm small parcels of land, while others remained on the plantations as indentured, paid laborers. Eventually, planters imported more laborers from West Africa, Europe, East India, and other parts of Asia. In-

After trade in slaves was declared illegal in the early 19th century, profiteers continued to engage in trade and shipping. When British patrol boats approached, they threw the slaves overboard.

COURTESY OF THE NATIONAL LIBRARY OF JAMAICA

dentured laborers, often contracted from existing British colonies elsewhere, were paid passage and either minimal wages or none at all and forced to work for a fixed period of time (three to eight years) with a promise of land at the contract's end.

Yet even this new labor force was not enough to save the large plantations. Rising production costs and competition from other countries, notably from Brazil's massive sugar plantations where slavery remained intact until the late 19th century, forced the hand of the plantocracy. Some plantations gave way to smaller, more profitable farming activity. Some were gobbled up by emerging production companies. In effect, the great plantocracy of the West Indies became a wistful memory in the colonial mind, and its absence paved the way for the islands' turbulent 20th-century battles for racial equality and viable economies.

THE 20TH CENTURY

The late 19th century and early parts of this century saw a worldwide move in agrarian societies toward forms of industrialized activity. In the Lesser Antilles, this shift was first to the industrial centers, the emerging cities of the islands such as Bridgetown in Barbados and Port of Spain in Trinidad. Wage-paying oil refineries

in Trinidad and large sugar production plants fueled the urban move, and the cities soon began to feel the rise of urban tension. Agricultural production had diversified to include coffee, cocoa, bananas, and other profitable crops, and the infrastructures needed for processing and exporting the crops employed thousands.

The influence of the United States in the Caribbean increased in this century, starting with the acquisition of Puerto Rico in the Spanish-American War of 1898. After the completion of the Panama Canal in 1914, the U.S. purchased the Virgin Islands from Denmark, primarily for strategic use.

After WW I, the Lesser Antilles, no longer innocent or isolated and for the most part shunned by their colonial rulers, were caught up in worldwide movements fomenting a wide range of human rights, including the right to vote. Nationalism and universal suffrage were the words of the day. The islands and islanders began to define their emerging national identities, and a growing sense of pride in local cultures emanated from this nascent nationalism. This was in marked contrast with the prevailing European attitude of the time, which saw the islands as little more than pitiable ghettos and ready-made markets for expensive European technologies. By and large, the typical Creole (in this sense, born in the West Indies) islander of the early 19th century was a disenfranchised worker, a source of cheap labor for foreign-owned industries, yet one whose past and future were linked to the island itself. These conditions naturally led to independence movements and conflict between the islanders and former colonial masters.

The worldwide depression of the 1920s and '30s plunged the islands into an abyss of economic despair. Islanders who had migrated in the thousands seeking employment in Central and South America and the U.S. now returned home to find stagnant economies and neglected paradises. Despair and poor working conditions in turn led to widespread worker riots in 1935-38, primarily in the British islands. These riots, in addition to correcting some immediate wrongs within the workplace, resulted in the reformation of child-labor laws, an acknowledgment of trade unions, and the birth of organized and recognized political parties. If nothing else, political parties within the colonies signaled the advent of new, self-governing islands of the Lesser Antilles, if not an independent Lesser Antilles.

Tourism, to an extent, had existed in the islands during the early part of the century; it consisted primarily of cruise ships. In the postbellum '50s, many of the islands, having made a shaky shift from agrarian to industrial activity, took stock of their natural resources and saw the dollar signs written on the wall—those signs spelled "tourism." The crystal Antillean waters and swaying palms were the allure. Aggressive promotion brought tourism to the Caribbean in a way that hadn't been seen previously. Today, in many Lesser Antilles islands, tourism earns more foreign currency than any other industry; it is both the boon and the bane of the local populace.

The '50s and '60s also saw the ripening of inchoate political movements. Clamors for island self-rule and independence became louder than ever, and colonialism finally began to relinquish its strong grip—sometimes grudgingly, sometimes with great relief. For the British in particular, the islands had ceased to be profitable since the emancipation of slaves in 1834, and independence, along with Commonwealth status, came somewhat easily to her islands. Jamaica and Trinidad and Tobago, the two largest states, became independent in the early '60s. The Dutch Kingdom Statute of 1954 gave the Netherlands Antilles islands direct representation in the Dutch government as districts of the Kingdom of the Netherlands. Likewise, laws passed by the Paris National Assembly in 1946 gave the French Antilles status as *départements d'outre-mer,* or overseas departments of France. As such, their residents enjoy all the privileges of French citizenry.

Yet the independence movements of the Lesser Antilles have not always been without discord. Britain, for instance, had in 1825 attached the island of Anguilla to St. Kitts and Nevis for administrative purposes. She granted the three islands internal self-government in 1967. Anguilla objected to the collective agreement, forming instead a breakaway political party that demanded independence from St. Kitts and Nevis. By 1969, in the midst of failed talks and increasingly violent agitation, the situation became dangerous. British troops invaded Anguilla, establishing an interim rule that remained on the island until 1972. Anguilla is now a crown colony of Great Britain.

In 1983, Grenada, faced with continued reliance on Cuba for technical and financial aid and rocked by anarchic internal political strife, was invaded by a U.S.-Caribbean force that restored order to the island. In 1984, the French government in Guadeloupe banned the Caribbean Revolutionary Alliance, a radical independence group, after a series of bombings convulsed the island.

Trinidad was a surprise news item in 1990, when an attempted coup organized by a Muslim fundamentalist group was put down. Over 20 people were killed and scores injured when Port of Spain's main police headquarters was bombed and the parliament building was overtaken. Rioters spilled into the streets. The government subsequently regained control, but trials and legal ramifications for the coup leaders are ongoing. As recently as November 1993, the normally stable St. Kitts was rocked by protest during general elections when an equal number of parliamentary seats were won by the two major parties, necessitating a tie-breaking decision by the governor-general. The governor-general awarded the election to the incumbent party, even though the challenging party had won a majority of the popular vote. Minor rioting broke out in the streets of Basseterre, and the government declared a 21-day state of emergency and instituted curfews.

Today's Lesser Antillean societies still struggle with borderline economies, high unemployment, and social stratification of wealth and power, often related to ethnicity. The concept of "pan-Caribbeanism"—a united Caribbean state or status borne primarily of economic need and similar ethnic and historical backgrounds—has been a recurring theme in discussions of the future of the region. It does not seem to be something the peoples of the Caribbean are interested in, nor does it seem possible today given the evolution of myriad and distinct Antillean cultures. There do exist, however, collective regional organizations that deal with trade, tourism, and culture throughout the Caribbean, such as the Caribbean Community (CARICOM)

nations, the Caribbean Tourism Organization (CTO), the Eastern Caribbean States Export Development Agency (ECSEDA), the Caribbean Development Bank (CDB), and others. A 1994 treaty signed by two dozen Caribbean and Central American states created the Association of Caribbean States (ACS), dedicated, in part, to "establish, consolidate, and augment, as appropriate, institutional structures and cooperative arrangements responsive to the various (regional) cultural identities." According to analysts, the ACS has the potential to become the world's fourth largest trading block, behind the European Union, the North American Free Trade Agreement (NAFTA), and the Association of Southeast Asian Nations (ASEAN).

PEOPLE

With the dawn of the 20th century, the influx of peoples from the world over had turned the Lesser Antilles into a unique amalgam of races, languages, religions, music, cuisines, and cultures. Blacks, Whites, Jews, Asians, East Indians, and smatterings of exotic people from the far corners of the globe formed the new Creole societies that are today our image of the Caribbean. Yet, as we've noted, to characterize the Lesser Antilles as rainbow societies living in multiracial harmony would be ambitious and naive—despite tourism slogans that portray the islands as long limbo lines of ethnic assimilation.

The reason, of course, harkens back to slavery. The bedrock of Antillean society, the literal back upon which nations were built, consisted of displaced and ultimately disenfranchised Africans and their descendants. In the early days of slavery, Africans outnumbered Whites by the thousands, particularly on major sugar-producing islands such as Barbados. By some estimates, over 10 million slaves were brought to the West Indies in the heyday of the planter society, the 17th and 18th centuries. The descendants of those slaves form the current majority population throughout the Lesser Antilles.

As mentioned earlier, the early emergence of a mixed-race class, spawned most often by forced miscegenation, added a layer to society

which to this day maintains a political and economic presence somewhat distinct from those of pure African descent.

After the demise of slavery, planters turned to other sources for labor with which to keep their sprawling plantations alive. Among their first sources of paid laborers were, ironically, more Africans, this time as indentured (ostensibly free) laborers. East Indians (from India, as opposed to West Indians), Chinese, and Europeans all found their way to various islands. In Trinidad and Tobago, East Indians make up nearly 40% of the population, on equal par with African-Trinidadians. In Dominica, some of the few remaining Caribs occupy a territory on the eastern side of the island. Descendants of Scottish Highlanders and the Irish deported in Lord Cromwell's 17th-century purges can be found in Barbados. St. Vincent is host to descendants of Portuguese indentured laborers brought in after the demise of slavery. Descendants of Dutch settlers are found on the tiny island of Saba. Other Europeans, some of whom have resided in the islands for generations, are evident throughout the islands, particularly in the French Antilles.

The people of the Lesser Antilles, in other words, present a diverse and exotic human face that in many ways defines the energy of the islands.

RELIGION

Modern religions in the Lesser Antilles follow patterns similar to those of widely diverse nations. Religious tolerance is expected and practiced to a large degree. On any given Sunday, or Saturday in some cases, the tiny wooden structures of the rural areas and the towering city cathedrals seem to expand with the lung power of the faithful.

Because of widespread proselytizing during the early days of Caribbean settlement, particularly among the slave quarters, organized religion took an early but somewhat tentative hold in the lives of Antillean peoples. It was partially missionary zeal that first drove the converters to the slaves, but later it became an act of self-preservation—it did not take long for the planters to discover that Christian slaves were easier to control than pagan slaves. Yet the religious beliefs of present-day Antilleans reflect a blend of deity-based New World beliefs and ancient, African cosmologies.

Africans, most often from West African areas, had retained their own strong religious beliefs through the dreadful transition from freedom to slavery. Often these beliefs consisted of various spirit- and animist-based tenets, reflected in devotion to ancestors and other revered spirits. The actual practices involved invoking these ancestors through ritual drumming, dancing, offerings, and oral prayer. Europeans (who conveniently ignored the equally spiritual elements attributed to the Christian God, as well as the deeply ritualistic behavior involved in Christian church services and masses) deplored the African religions as paganistic magic and forbade them, driving them quickly underground. So, as the early missionaries began the process of winning souls for the church, the Africans in turn began the process of disguising their ancient beliefs and syncretizing them with the new rules of Western theology.

It remains so today. While Anglican, Roman Catholic, Lutheran, Methodist, and other Protestant religions predominate throughout the region, African-Caribbean peoples are not hedging their bets. Arcane and mystical practices, most commonly described under the umbrella term obeah, literally produce the magic that fills in the gaps where Western religions fall short. The word is thought to have originated with *obayi,* an Ashanti (West African, today primarily heard in Ghana) word meaning priest or sorcerer. The use of obeah and other magic became stronger during the post-emancipation period, when free West Africans were brought to the Lesser Antilles as indentured laborers, and in turn reinvigorated existing African beliefs.

Not everyone in the Lesser Antilles practices obeah, nor does everyone believe in it (nor is

hillside cemetery near Fort-de-France, Martinique

everyone who believes it of African descent). The practice is more widespread on some islands than others and is called by many names. Haiti's voodoo, for example, is a variation on the theme of animism, magic, spirits, and the dark forces of evil. The practitioner in the French West Indies is called the *quinbossier.*

Obeah is, in fact, illegal on most Lesser Antilles islands. Designated practitioners called obeah men (and women, in cases) are both respected and feared, and are certainly sought out. Obeah magic involves rum, tobacco, herbs, fetishes, drumming, chanting, spirits called *jumbies* and *duppies* (among other names)—a literal witches' brew of ingredients. Obeah can be evil, and it can seek to alter the natural courses of the universe by eliminating—or causing—disease, wealth, fortune, or even death. But whatever obeah is or is not, it is seen by many as a vital and dynamic force, the magic that hums below the surface of everyday Antillean life. The use of obeah or other magic forms, combined with traditional Christian practice, is strong in several island cults. The Shango sect of Trinidad utilizes ritual practices of the Yoruba group (in today's Nigeria, Togo, and Benin), including drumming, dancing, and some animal sacrifice. Voodoo, coexisting uneasily with Catholicism, plays a large part in Haitian life.

Meanwhile, on the surface, the Lesser Antilles are peppered with the religions of their various conquerors and settlers. Among the Christian churches are the Anglicans, Roman Catholics, Methodists, Baptists and offshoot Baptist groups, Seventh-Day Adventists, various evangelical movements, Moravians, Society of Friends (Quaker), and Mormons, who have seen their influence grow in the latter half of this century.

Jews are found throughout the islands, though today not in large numbers. The history of Judaism in the Lesser Antilles mirrors that of other religious and ethnic groups of the region—the flight from persecution in Europe and later South America saw Jews settle in small communities throughout the islands.

Not surprisingly, Catholicism is strong in the French Antilles. The Church of England and Protestant sects remain dominant in several of the former British colonies such as Antigua and Barbuda and Barbados. The exception is Montserrat, where Catholicism dominates due to the island's origins as a refuge for Irish settlers fleeing religious oppression in St. Kitts and Nevis. In Dominica, St. Lucia, St. Vincent and the Grenadines, and Grenada, the French influence is evident in the number of adherents to Catholicism, who coexist with several Protestant sects. Trinidad and Tobago host a wide range of religions, from Catholic to Anglican to Hindu to Muslim.

Rastafarianism, the quasi-religious sect that grew out of Jamaica's Kingston ghettos in the 1930s, has attracted an increasing number of adherents throughout the Caribbean and the world since the 1970s, including famous acolytes such as the late reggae musician Bob Marley. Rastafarianism is based on the strong belief that Africa, particularly Ethiopia, is Zion, or heaven on earth, and the rest of the world's countries and systems are the undesirable Babylon. Adherents believe that the late ruler of Ethiopia, Haile Selassie I, whose ordination name was Ras Tafari, was a living messiah, born to lead all displaced Africans back to the promised land. At the very least, Rastafarianism espouses a strong message of African pride and borrows from the teachings of Jamaican Marcus Garvey, an early advocate of pan-Africanism. Rastafarianism has in places become more a fashion statement than a true set of beliefs; heavy identification with the more stylish aspects, such as reggae and the ritual use of marijuana, can overshadow the true spiritualism of the sect. Rastas are recognized by their dreadlocks and symbolic clothing sporting the Ethiopian national colors of red, green, and gold.

LANGUAGE

Two or three minutes on any island in the Lesser Antilles should clear up any worries you'll have about communicating in the local dialect. You won't.

Not that you won't be able to communicate at all. Islanders do speak excellent English and French, the two most common languages in the Lesser Antilles. And they'll speak it readily—with you. But among themselves, you'll most likely hear an accelerated and lyrical version of a language that is at once familiar and indiscernible. It incorporates, again, the history of the region.

The languages of the Lesser Antilles descend from English, French, Spanish, Dutch, African, and various pick-up languages that wove their way through the islands during their wartime exchanges and agricultural heydays. Called Patois, Creole, and Papiamento—a Patois with heavy Spanish and some Portuguese influences—the languages evolved as a practical method for communication among slaves, who had come from numerous West African linguistic groups. Over the years, as islands changed hands, new languages were introduced and incorporated into the local Patois. Today, each island has developed its own distinct version of Patois, yet it would be a mistake to assume that the current political affiliations of the islands also dominate their languages.

French is an official language of Martinique, Guadeloupe, and Saint-Barthélémy, but the lingua franca is French Creole. English is spoken, though a working knowledge of French would greatly enhance your visit. Saint-Martin, a dependency of Guadeloupe, uses French, Creole, and some Papiamento from next-door Sint Maarten. English, however, is widely spoken.

In general, the former British colonies and dependents use English and English-based Patois. Exceptions are St. Lucia, Dominica, and St. Vincent, which, because of numerous political exchanges during the colonial days, use a Patois heavily laced with French Creole and some Spanish. Trinidad's Patois retains some Spanish influences.

In Sint Maarten, Saba, and Sint Eustatius, Dutch is the official language but most everyone speaks fluent English. Papiamento is popular with locals on these islands, but is much more common in Aruba, Bonaire, and Curaçao.

THE ARTS

MUSIC AND DANCE

The music of the Lesser Antilles is, in many ways, the music of the entire Caribbean. Reggae, calypso, soca, and the French beguine and *zouk,* among others, have been made accessible by modern interisland movement and communication, and to an extent by tourism. Grouped, they define an island sensibility by their up-beat tempos and often bawdy and satirical lyrics of love, sex, and politics. But it would be a mistake to categorize any single one of them as a typical West Indian sound.

The origins of Antillean music, folk songs, and dance lie, again, in the syncretic blend of cultures and people that were its first settlers. Today's Caribbean music has evolved through centuries of settlement and is at this point purely Creole—original West Indian music born in the blue-green waters and tropical sun of the islands.

The strongest influence in West Indian music is the African influence, from the universal drumming that recalls ancient (and current) rituals, to the dances of modern day carnivals. African drums, in fact, can claim responsibility for the overtly rhythmic quality of today's calypso and reggae.

Trinidad, not an unlikely candidate for pioneering musical forms due to its large population and the huge attention paid to its Carnival, claims responsibility for two innovations—calypso and the steel band.

Calypso

Calypso may be the most widely recognized island music outside the West Indies. In its original form it is thought to have been a type of rebellious call-and-response song originating in the slave fields of early Trinidad. The name itself is a source of debate, but many posit that it has its roots in *kaiso,* derived from a West African word meaning "well done." Calypsonians today have not only brought their music to the international arena ("All Day, All Night, Mary Ann," or "Day-o" are two examples of calypso songs that found worldwide audiences, the latter popularized by Harry Belafonte) but are an integral part of the Trinidad Carnival celebrations. You'll find

LIMBO

What in the heck is limbo, anyway? I mean, you know what it *is*, at least in the observable sense. It's a dance usually performed at floorshows in tourist enclaves. Lithe, professional limbo dancers slink under a descending crossbar until they're parallel to, even scraping, the ground, accompanied by the beat of drums and the chant of a group leader wondering "How loooow can you go?" Sometimes the bar is on fire to add drama to the dance, and later tourists are invited to limbo away to slightly higher, less dangerous crossbars. It's a sure recipe for fun and lower back pain, but wherein lies the reality of the show?

In truth, limbo has little to do with the Lesser Antilles. There is no evidence to link it to ancient African tribal rites, as is often claimed. It appears to be a wholly invented tourist activity, as is fire-eating, which often accompanies these shows.

calypso competitions in tents throughout the island, with calypsonians belting out their seemingly stream-of-consciousness lyrics laced with ribald sexual innuendo, competing for cash, prizes, and notoriety. The grand prize is that of Calypso Monarch, and the winning song will become the anthem of the year, the Road March. Calypsonians take stage names like Attila the Hun, Lord Kitchener, Cro Cro, and Chalkdust, names that are not a small part of their appeal. The calypso field today is dominated by men, although several women have entered competitions in the past. One of the most popular calypsonians worldwide is the venerable Mighty Sparrow, as of late known simply as Sparrow. In his lifetime, Sparrow has cut an estimated 300 albums, testament to his talent and to the widespread appeal of calypso throughout the world. Throughout the Lesser Antilles, calypsonians are popular; Invader No. 3, a past winner of Barbados' Calypso Monarch crown, and calypso-soca crossover king Arrow, of Montserrat, are two examples.

Tinpanny—the Steel Band

Trinidad also claims responsibility for the development of another ubiquitous island sound, the steel band, also called tinpanny. A steel band is an ensemble group of tuned percussion instruments called pans, or steel drums, which are today made from oil drums. Their development recalls the harsh days of post-emancipation colonial life, when, in their efforts to suppress local gatherings, the British governors of Trinidad banned African and East Indian drumming at street processions and festivals. The aim was to ban the festivals altogether. From this ban evolved tamboo-bamboo bands, where musicians substituted the thumping of hollow bamboo for their drums. In fact, musicians began to bang on just about everything they could lay their hands on—other than the forbidden drums. By the 1930s and '40s, with the growth of Trinidad's oil industry in overdrive, a copious supply of oil drums in the country apparently seemed to beg for artistic expression.

They got what they wanted, and musicians sunk, pounded, grooved, and tuned the tops of oil drums to form the prototype of today's instrument. They then sawed off the barrels to the proper length to create "ping-pongs" (tenor pans), rhythm pans (including double pans and cello pans), and "tuned-booms" (bass pans). Initially used to accompany the Carnival, the unique sound of the steel pans quickly found their way into the mainstream music scene. Trinidadians today claim that the pan is the only musical instrument to have been invented in this century. While that claim may be based more in national pride than in fact, the prevalence of steel bands worldwide may indeed prove that it is one of the few internationally accepted instruments new to the scene. Today, few regional carnivals, hotels, nightclubs, popular music venues, or even schools do not feature the instruments in some form. Players today are highly trained, sophisticated, and adept; in concert halls you might hear tunes from calypso to Tchaikovsky to the Beatles.

Soca

Another popular and hybrid musical form said to have its roots in Trinidad is soca, a combination of the words **so**ul and **ca**lypso. The form is derived from the combination of calypso and an American rhythm-and-blues backbeat. Soca originated with a younger generation of calypsonians who were exposed to R&B, and who merged the sounds and styles of the two musical forms. Soca is also wildly popular throughout the islands and hosts its own competitions and concerts.

Reggae

No one can say for sure when or from what the term reggae originated. Some theorize that it came from the Jamaican slang terms *rege rege,* meaning rags or ragged clothing, or *raga raga,* meaning ragamuffin. According to the official biography of Bob Marley, *Catch A Fire,* by music writer Timothy White, its apparent first appearance in print came in 1968 on a single by Jamaican legends Toots and the Maytals called "Do The Reggay." Some even credit singer Frederick (Toots) Hibbert with originating the form. Whatever the word's origins, however, most would agree that reggae equals calypso as one of the standards of the Caribbean and international music scene.

By the early '70s, the Jamaican scene had already produced the popular ska and "rock steady" forms that were continuing to evolve into reggae. Jamaican singer Millie Small, based in the U.K., had scored a hit with her rock steady tune "My Boy Lollipop." Texan Johnny Nash had hits with his album *I Can See Clearly Now,* which included the Bob Marley tunes "Stir It Up" and "Guava Jelly." Singer Paul Simon traveled to Jamaica to record his reggae-inspired "Mother And Child Reunion." Jimmy Cliff, the then-reigning king of Jamaican pop and today one of Jamaica's best known singers, had put the singles "Wonderful World, Beautiful People," "Wild World," and the popular "You Can Get It If You Really Want" on the charts in 1969 and 1970.

Still, the recognized reggae spokesman and premier performer, without whom reggae might have ended its days as a standard on Jamaica's oldies charts, was Bob Marley. In fact, it still is Bob Marley, more than 10 years after his death from cancer in 1981. Marley's success with the Wailers in the '70s, and with other bands in the late '70s and early '80s, established reggae as an international behemoth, and today the sound is as infused with Antillean life as is the sun and the sea. Also popular throughout the Lesser Antilles are the reggae spinoffs, dub and dancehall, which combine the heavy bass and beat of reggae with the lyric-dense style of rap.

International Influences

Somewhat less universal, the Afro-Spanish sounds of the Cuban congo and rumba, the plena and bomba of Puerto Rico, and the Dominican Republic's merengue still have influence beyond their shores, particularly in the Spanish-speaking world, but can be heard on many of the Lesser Antillean radio stations and in concerts.

The French Antilles gave us *zouk,* which blends the drumming and percussion of West Africa with the lush horn and synthesizer arrangements of Europe, and the energetic beguine, with lavish arrangements and inspired quasi-ballroom dancing styles. The Virgin Islands gave us *fungi* bands, traditional groups consisting of guitars, bass and drums, and bamboo instruments.

Antillean Undulations

Antillean dance styles emulate the distributions of cultures throughout the region. Most Creole dance evolved from traditional African drumming and dancing, later combined with the European planters' dances

steelband

KAREN McKINLEY

QUADRILLE DANCING

Quadrille dancing is a variation on the 18th-century French *cotillion* (petticoat) country dancing. The dance involved partners executing three to five complex sets of movements. Slaves in the West Indies often copied and parodied their owners' customs; they adopted quadrille dancing, as well as reels, jigs, and other European forms as their own. Accompanied by string bands, these dances soon became part of slave culture and ended up in West Indian-African ceremonies and carnivals. Quadrille dancing is a direct predecessor of the popular North American country square dancing.

such as the quadrille, the waltz, and others. These dances were used in celebrations, the most important being the widespread carnivals throughout the islands. In St. Lucia, the *kutumba* drum and dance style was most frequently seen at ceremonies for the recently deceased. On the Grenadian island of Carriacou, the tradition of "Big Drum" dancing continues today; dancers in elaborate costumes parade and sing to the drums and "chac-chac" rattles.

Today, several Lesser Antilles islands, notably Martinique and its Les Grands Ballets de la Martinique, host national dance troupes that perform regularly at carnivals and other festivals.

LITERATURE

The Oral Tradition

Caribbean storytelling has an ancient history. Pre-Columbian groups, primarily the Arawaks and Caribs, left rock carvings and petroglyphs that indicated a strong oral storytelling and folktale tradition. With the virtual elimination of Amerindian groups by Europeans by the 17th century, virtually all traces of this oral tradition—and, for that matter, most traces of their languages—disappeared.

The enslaved West Africans who in turn replenished the New World labor force brought with them stories and folktales that managed to survived the harsh "Middle Passage" across the Atlantic on the slavers' ships. Again, the tradition was verbal, and the African folktales have

since been passed along to succeeding West Indian-born generations, who have kept many of them, or derivations, alive through today.

These folktales, steeped in mysticism and, in many ways, conventional morality, have over the years evolved to incorporate a distinct West Indian environment, but are no less powerful than their African antecedents. The vivid characters in the folktales originate both in the West Indies and in Africa, and are often anthropomorphized animals such as lions, rabbits, turtles, dogs, or spiders. One of the more popular characters in several island folktales is the quick-witted Anancy (also Ananse, Anansi, Anance), a half-human, half-spider huckster that is able to outwit foolish, bumbling, and corrupt humans (not surprisingly, often a harsh plantation master), and who is able to escape from his self-instigated trouble in hilarious ways.

Early Caribbean literature was in many ways not Caribbean at all, but tended to follow the conventions of European narrative traditions from which it flowed. After all, early settlers did not consider themselves "Caribbean" in any real sense, but rather temporary residents of the colonies.

Contemporary Works

Caribbean literature often invokes rich aspects of West Indian life. Patois and other lilting languages, as well as the music, foods, family life, races, and religions are all strong components of Caribbean writing. Some of the best examples of West Indian fiction are in fact better resources than nonfiction textbook treatments for exploring the elements of Caribbean lives.

Conventional wisdom links the emergence of contemporary Caribbean literature with the widespread labor union unrest of the 1920s, unrest that provided the impetus for the birth of political parties and strong nationalist movements. As Caribbean people began to identify themselves as such and embrace their nationalism and regionalism, their literature began to reflect Caribbean values, language, and heritage, often with emphasis on African heritage.

Several themes recur in contemporary Caribbean literature. A major theme is the writer's struggle to understand a multitude of identities—personal, national, racial—within the context of the diverse Caribbean heritage.

Another recurrent and perhaps more contemporary theme explores the ongoing Caribbean diaspora. Since the turn of the century, when industrialism began to replace agriculture as the world's economic base, millions of West Indians have migrated to the U.S., Canada, and the U.K. in search of better opportunities. Entire West Indian communities have been established in foreign cities, and entire generations have never returned to the Caribbean. West Indian writers have created a large body of work exploring that sense of insecurity and anxiety that envelops strangers in a strange land.

Caribbean Authors

The Spanish Caribbean produced many notable writers, among them Christopher Columbus, who documented his ocean crossings and island landings from the period August 1492 to March 1493, his first voyage to the New World. His *Diario de a bordo (The Onboard Log)* is extremely important to the world body of literature in that it contains the first written accounts of the islands that would eventually become the West Indies.

Later, the 16th-century Spanish Bishop Bartolome de Las Casas became an outspoken advocate of the Arawaks and wrote prolifically and passionately about their plight.

The French-speaking West Indies, including Haiti, produced writers who early on embraced the recognition of African and Caribbean cultural heritage in their work. Their literary movement was called *négritude,* a term attributed to the Martiniquan poet, playwright, and politician Aimé Césaire. *Négritude* called for the recognition and advancement of black cultural values and black heritage worldwide—black humanism—and further rejected the French colonial influences.

Césaire, who was born in 1913, studied in Paris among black expatriates of the 1930s. His works, including the epic poem *Cahier d'un Retour au Pays Natal (Return to My Native Land;* 1939), often incorporate a surrealistic style. Césaire once served as mayor of Fort-de-France and is considered an influential political philosopher.

Nationalism and the voice of black culture came somewhat later, during the 1930s and '40s, to the English-speaking Caribbean. With several notable exceptions, a large body of English literature originates from the islands of Barbados, Trinidad, and Jamaica, presumably because of their large, diverse populations, excellent universities, and, now, literary traditions.

Novelist George Lamming, born in Barbados in 1927, often explores the dilemmas of race and culture confronting Caribbean peoples living overseas. Lamming's works include a critically acclaimed first novel, *In the Castle of My Skin* (1953), and *Season of Adventure* (1960).

Frank Collymore (1893-1980), a Barbadian poet and short-story writer, was influential in the Caribbean literary scene during the heyday of 1930s nationalism. Aside from several volumes of poetry, including *Beneath the Casuarinas* (1945) and *Flotsam* (1948), and a posthumous collection of short stories called *The Man Who Loved Attending Funerals and Other Stories* (1993), his major legacy to West Indian writing is the literary magazine *Bim,* which he established in 1942 and edited for most of his life. Over its long life, the magazine has printed and promoted the work of nearly every major West Indian literary talent.

The novelist Jean Rhys (1894-1979) is considered by some to be less Caribbean- than European-influenced, yet she was born in Dominica and used a Caribbean setting for one of her most famous works, *Wide Sargasso Sea* (1966).

BOB RACE

petroglyphs

Trinidad's writers have flourished under a long tradition of literature and publishing that includes a fairly rigorous free press. The multicultural setting of Trinidad is unique with its large numbers of East Indians, Africans, and Asians—a situation Trinidadian writers have found ripe with drama and passion.

V. S. Naipaul, born in Trinidad in 1932 and now living in the U.K., is possibly the most celebrated regional writer, although he is often critiqued as a British rather than a Caribbean writer. His early works, which often incorporate his East Indian roots, reflect Caribbean themes and a sharp wit. Among them: *The Mystic Masseur* (1957) and the famous *A House for Mr. Biswas* (1961), which deals with the breakdown of a West Indian family and its culture in the face of the tedium of colonial life.

Trinidadian Samuel Selvon (1923-94) wrote more than a half-dozen novels and collections of short stories that deal with Trinidadian life and the East Indian experience, as well as works that explore the lives of Caribbean expatriates in Britain. Among his works, the novels *A Brighter Sun* (1952) and *An Island is a World* (1955) are set in the Caribbean.

Jamaica Kincaid was born in Antigua in 1949 and traveled to the U.S. in 1966, where she became a novelist, short story writer, and staff writer for *The New Yorker*. Kincaid has published several works, including the story collection *At the Bottom of the River* (1983) and the novel *Annie John* (1985). The autobiographical *Lucy* was released in 1990.

Two writers of West Indian origin have become Nobel laureates in literature. The 1992 winner, poet and playwright Derek Walcott, ranks among the illustrious writers of this century. Walcott, who was born in St. Lucia, has to date produced nine volumes, including his 1990 epic *Omeros*, a broad narrative that mixes Homeric legend with West Indian themes. As well, in 1959 Walcott established the Trinidad Theatre Workshop in Port of Spain. In his native St. Lucia, he's created an international writers' retreat called the Rat Island Foundation.

The poet Alexis Saint-Léger Léger, who wrote under the pen name Saint-John Perse, was born in Guadeloupe and won a Nobel Prize in 1960. Although not widely translated, Perse's work is well-known in European literary circles.

Among his books: *Anabase* (1924) and *Song for an Equinox* (1971). He died in 1975.

Several island-based literary magazines continue to publish the work of contemporary Caribbean writers. Among them is the aforementioned *Bim*, taken from Bimshire, a nickname for Barbados. *The Caribbean Writer*, started in 1987, is produced by the University of the Virgin Islands. It has published the works of Derek Walcott, poet Marvin Williams, and poet Paul Keens-Douglas, among others.

ART

A good deal of the art found in galleries of the Lesser Antilles is of the handicraft variety, some of it cheap and mass-produced for the tourist market, some of it intricate and truly reflective of the cultures of the artists.

Fine handicrafts can be found throughout the Lesser Antilles. Strawcraft, woodcarvings, dolls, shellcraft, silkscreens and batiks, pottery, and jewelry are the usual suspects and can be found at nearly every hotel or tourist center. For better deals and, in cases, a better exposure to folk art, it's best to go to the source.

A few of the many examples of folk art centers: **Tropicrafts Island Mats** is a weaving center in Roseau, Dominica. The (mostly) women handcraft the mats in the showroom, and you may order one from a chosen design. Ask permission to take a photo, please. Tropicrafts also sells straw hats, spices, local rums, bay rum, and other island crafts.

The St. Barts fishing village of **Corossol** is where you'll find descendants of the early

---

BAY RUM

You'll see it in the markets, on the shelves of cosmetic counters, and at duty-free stores. The aromatic, spicy Bay Rum, often spelled Bay Rhum, is the product of distilled leaves from the tropical tree *Pimenta racemosa* of the family Myrtaceae, or myrtle, which is related to the bayberry. When mixed with sugarcane alcohol, oil of orange, rum, or variations, the concoction is sold as aftershave or for use in other cosmetics.

French settlers selling local strawcraft. The women, in their traditional sunbonnets and long skirts, sell hats, bags, dolls, and other products woven from *lantania* (sabal) palms. Again, ask permission for photos.

Eudovic's Art Studio, just outside Castries, St. Lucia, is an island center for woodcarvings and crafts. On the premises, artisans craft large and small works from mahogany, red cedar, and other indigenous woods. Near the village of Basse-Point, Martinique, the restored **Plantation de Leyritz** has a museum of locally crafted dolls, called *poupées,* made from plant leaves. Inland from the village of Old Road Bay on St. Kitts is Romney Manor, an old plantation greathouse and gardens. The picturesque greathouse itself, a fine example of period architecture, is now home to **Caribelle Batik,** a fabric and clothing shop utilizing original batik designs executed on the property. The workshop is open to the public.

Other sources for local crafts in the islands are the open markets, which, in addition to produce, fish, and meats, will likely have handicraft kiosks and stalls offering locally produced goods such as perfumes, lotions, and, inevitably, rums.

The colors, textures, and lighting of the islands have long inspired painters to reproduce island life on canvas. In 1887, the French artist Paul Gauguin spent five months visiting a friend in Anse Turin, Martinique, and produced several works during his time there (a small museum in the nearby town of Carbet town features Gauguin letters and memorabilia). Other artists, both local and visiting, have been similarly inspired. Today's Caribbean art runs the gamut from intricate, expressionistic painting to "primitive," brightly colored images reproduced on wood, canvas, or cut tin. In particular, paintings from Haiti, which are often categorized as primitive, are popular throughout the islands. The animated pastels and simple imagery and scenes used in the paintings and tin sculptures

have now been imitated by Lesser Antillian artists; if it is at all possible to say that a certain type of art typifies a region, this would be it.

Art galleries are found in every major town in the Lesser Antilles, as well as in hotels. Sidewalk and market-based artists, however, may be selling fine paintings at good prices and will often bargain.

THEATER

Traditional theater and modern theater groups can be found on many, but not all, islands in the Lesser Antilles. Traditional, or folk, theater groups present tales and vignettes through song, dance, drumming, comedy, and narrative, often incorporating elaborate costumes and folk instruments in their presentation. The themes of folk theater often harken back to African life, or to the 18th and 19th century days of plantations and slaves.

Well-known island groups offering regular performances include **Les Grands Ballets de la Martinique, Mayoumba Folkloric Theatre** of Anguilla, the **Folkloric Troupe** of Guadeloupe, **Caribbean Dance Company** of the U.S. Virgin Islands, and the **Barbados Museum** troupe, which presents a historical program called "1627 and All That." Smaller islands have lesser known folk groups, and you can catch them at selected hotels, museums, or cultural events throughout the year. Check local newspapers and radio for listings and events.

Modern theater groups that present plays, either locally written or taken from the international pool, are found in fewer venues. Look to the major towns of the larger islands, particularly Port of Spain in Trinidad, Fort-de-France in Martinique, and Pointe-à-Pitre in Guadeloupe for regular performances (see destination chapters for theater listings).

BOB RACE

OUT AND ABOUT
RECREATION

GREEN TRAVEL

Eco-Tourism in Theory

During the latter part of this century, it became clear that it is important to monitor the world's burgeoning populations and their demands on our natural resources. Thousands of rivers and lakes and entire sections of oceans have been polluted to varying degrees, the air we breathe in our cities has been turned to a sort of sludge, and the world's soil and forest reserves have been taxed to what many consider their limits. Whatever your belief regarding the severity of the problems, this much is true: we have rearranged our way of thinking about how we live on this planet. While conservation groups and societies dedicated to natural preservation have existed for centuries, more recent concerns have spawned highly organized movements (Greenpeace, World Wildlife Fund), political parties (the Greens, of Germany), and other groups dedicated to the somewhat loosely defined cause of saving the Earth.

Never willing to miss opportunities, the tourism industry has jumped on the bandwagon and in-troduced a similarly loosely defined offshoot industry called "eco-tourism," also referred to as "eco-travel" or "nature travel."

No doubt, the awareness generated by an ecology-minded travel industry has benefitted the preservation of delicate natural resources. We now know that unbridled development of any tourist or recreational facility, be it a mega-resort complex or a miniature golf course, can have a deleterious effect on the environment. We now know that wherever tourists go, whether in great numbers or small, they will affect the environment in some way. And we know that local cultures can be most affected by human activity.

We also know that tourism is a major factor in the world economy and is clearly here to stay. Tourism is in fact partially responsible for the revenue needed to preserve a great many natural resources. Throughout the Lesser Antilles, national parks and forest reserves are funded in part by admission fees. It appears that a healthy and mutually beneficial relationship between tourism and conservation is at least possible.

Yet, problems accompany eco-tourism, and these problems often involve the word, not the

DEPARTMENTS OF TOURISM
WITH LESSER ANTILLES ADDRESSES

Anguilla
Department of Tourism, The Valley, Anguilla, West Indies, tel. (809) 497-2795 or 2451, fax 497-2751.

Antigua and Barbuda
Department of Tourism, P.O. Box 363, St. John's, Antigua, West Indies, tel. (809) 462-0480, fax 462-2483.

Barbados
Board of Tourism, P.O. Box 242, Harbour Road, Bridgetown, Barbados, West Indies, tel. (809) 427-2623, fax 426-4080.

British Virgin Islands
Tourist Board, P.O. Box 134, Road Town, Tortola, British Virgin Islands, West Indies, tel. (809) 494-3134, fax 494-3866.

Dominica
Division of Tourism, National Development Corporation, P.O. Box 73, Roseau, Commonwealth of Dominica, West Indies; tel. (809) 448-2351/2186, fax 448-5840.

Grenada
Board of Tourism, The Carenage, St. George's, Grenada, West Indies; tel. (809) 440-2279, fax 440-6637.

Guadeloupe
Office Départementale du Tourisme, 5 Square de la Banque, BP 1099, 97181 Pointe-à-Pitre Cedex, Guadeloupe, French West Indies; tel. (590) 82-09-30, fax (590) 83-89-22.

Martinique
Office Départementale Du Tourisme de la Martinique, Blvd. Alfassa, 97206, Fort-de-France, Martinique, French West Indies; tel. (596) 63-79-60, fax 73-66-93.

Montserrat
Department of Tourism, P.O. Box 7, Plymouth, Montserrat, West Indies; tel. (809) 491-2230/8730, fax 491-7430.

Saba
Tourist Board, P.O. Box 527, Windwardside, Saba, Netherlands Antilles; tel. 599-4-62231, fax 599-4-62350.

Saint-Barthélémy
Office Municipal du Tourisme, Quai du General de Gaulle, Gustavia, 97095 Saint-Barthélémy, French West Indies; tel. (590) 27-87-27, fax 27-74-47.

St. Kitts and Nevis
Tourist Board, Pelican Mall, Basseterre, St. Kitts, West Indies; tel. (809) 465-2620 or 465-4040, fax 465-8794.

St. Lucia
Tourist Board, P.O. Box 221, Castries, St. Lucia, West Indies; tel. (809) 452-4094 or 452-5968, fax 453-1121.

Saint-Martin
Office du Tourisme, 97150 Port de Marigot, Saint-Martin, French West Indies; tel. (590) 87-57-21, fax 87-56-43.

St. Vincent and the Grenadines
Department of Tourism, P.O. Box 834, Kingstown, St. Vincent and the Grenadines, West Indies; tel. (809) 457-1502, fax 457-2880.

Sint Eustatius
Sint Eustatius Department of Tourism, 3 Fort Oranjestraat, Oranjestad, Sint Eustatius, Netherlands Antilles, tel. 599-3-82433.

Sint Maarten
Tourist Board, Walter Nisbet Rd. #23, Philipsburg, Sint Maarten, Netherlands Antilles; tel. (599-5) 22337, fax 22734.

Trinidad and Tobago
Tourism Development Authority, 134-138 Frederick St., Port of Spain, Trinidad, West Indies; tel. (809) 623-1932/4, fax 623-3848.

United States Virgin Islands
Division of Tourism, P.O. Box 6400, Charlotte Amalie, St. Thomas, U.S. Virgin Islands 00804; tel. (809) 774-8784, fax 774-4390.

GREEN TOUR OPERATORS

The following offer specialized tours throughout the Lesser Antilles, though larger islands such as Guadeloupe, Dominica, Martinique, Grenada, St. Vincent, St. Lucia, and Trinidad and Tobago tend to offer a wider variety of eco-tour opportunities. Packages may or may not include flights, but most include lodging or meals, and of course tour activities. Some are all-inclusive.

Caligo Ventures, 156 Bedford Rd., Armonk, NY 10504, tel. (800) 426-7781 or (914) 273-6333, fax 273-6370, specializes in Trinidad and Tobago nature tours, with emphasis on the excellent birding opportunities on the sister islands.

Caribbean Adventures, P.O. Box 1066, Waitsfield, VT 05673, tel. (800) 846-6594 or (802) 496-3305, fax 496-5581, offers hiking, trekking, whalewatching, and individualized tours of St. Vincent, Bequia, Dominica, and Grenada.

EarthCorps, the field wing of the nonprofit Earthwatch organization, sends volunteers, no skills necessary, on two-week scientific and conservation projects throughout the world. Past excursions have included helping endangered sea turtles in the U.S. Virgin Islands. You pay your travel, food, and lodging. Contact Earthwatch, 680 Mt. Auburn St., Box 403, Watertown, MA 02172; tel. (800) 776-0188 or (617) 926-8200, fax 926-8532. On the Internet, direct e-mail to info@earthwatch.org.

Ex-Ec Hikes and Tours of Dominica is the single best source for Dominica tours, specializing in hiking, mountain biking, sea kayaking, and customized tours. The "Ex-Ec" stands for Executive and Ecological. Contact them at 5206 Decarie Blvd., Suite 1, Montreal, PQ H3X 2H9, Canada, tel. (800) 667-3932 or (514) 486-9720, fax 486-1065.

Forever Yours Nature Tours, 1491 West 5th Ave., Eugene, OR 97402, tel. (800) 578-6535, fax (503) 686-3396, specializes in nature tours including birdwatching, fishing, and diving expeditions.

Massachusetts Audubon Society offers natural history trips where you are accompanied by field experts to St. Lucia, Dominica, and other islands. Destinations change every year. For information write to 208 S. Great Rd., Lincoln, MA 01773; or call (800) 289-9504 or (617) 259-9500, fax 259-8899.

---

concept. Eco-tourism, for some unscrupulous or merely uninformed tour operators, has become a hackneyed term, an advertising gimmick. A wide range of activities, including tours, forest excursions, and even basic camping are now touted as eco-tourism activities, simply because they take place outdoors. A recent conversation with a hotelier revealed his plan to convert his resort into an eco-tourism spot—by making it a nudist resort. This, with no regard as to how it would affect the people of the villages located in the area. Such thinking is, unfortunately, not uncommon and does no good to clear the muddied waters of the eco-tourism industry.

Another radical view of eco-tourism is an extension of an extreme concept among some conservationists, the "nature good, man bad" simplification that any human activity on this earth is detrimental to the environment. This seems to be illogical histrionics, and really nothing more.

Having said that, there are certainly legitimate opportunities to hook up with responsible ecology and nature-oriented tours. However, since the industry has spawned large lists of eco-travel operations, some research is in order. Specialty groups exist for birdwatching (for aficionados, not to be missed), biking, hiking, diving, river rafting, whalewatching, and historical awareness tours. In particular, the islands of Guadeloupe, Dominica, Martinique, St. Lucia, St. Vincent, Grenada, and Trinidad and Tobago, with their lush rainforests and mountains, lend themselves to land-based excursions. Good diving can be found from the Virgin Islands to Trinidad and Tobago. Walking tours of Barbados

The Nature Conservancy, a nonprofit organization, sponsors natural history tours worldwide, with in-country naturalists on board. Past trips have included U.S. Virgin Islands cruises and work-trips aimed at creating a conservation education center at the site of an 18th-century sugar estate on St. Croix. The Conservancy can be reached at 1815 N. Lynn St., Arlington, VA 22209, tel. (703) 841-5300, fax 841-4880.

Nature Expeditions International, 474 Willamette St., P.O. Box 11496, Eugene, OR 97440, tel. (800) 869-0639 or (503) 484-6529, fax 484-6531, conducts expert-guided wildlife and cultural expeditions on Trinidad and Tobago and Dominica.

Smithsonian Study Tours and Seminars arranges tour work and study tours worldwide and has in the past included natural history tours of Dominica and cruises in the Grenadines. Tours are led by in-country experts. To be eligible for study tours, you must become a member of the Smithsonian Institution; cost is US$22 for a one-year membership. Contact Smithsonian Associates, Dept. 0049, Washington, D.C. 20073-0049; tel. (202) 357-4700, fax 633-9250.

Special Expeditions offers an annual "expedition cruise," usually in March, aboard their 80-passenger ship. You'll sail from Panama to Antigua in the company of naturalists, with plenty of side excursions on land and sea. Other cruises ply the southern Lesser Antilles. For information write to 720 5th Ave., New York, NY 10019; or call (800) 762-0003 or (212) 765-7740, fax 265-3770.

Unique Destinations, 307 Peaceable St., Ridgefield, CT 06877, tel. and fax (203) 431-1571, specializes in hiking, biking, diving, kayaking, and historical/cultural and other customized tours and unique accommodations in St. Kitts, Nevis, Saba, Dominica, and St. Vincent and the Grenadines, and Trinidad and Tobago.

Victor Emmanuel Nature Tours offers birding tours worldwide, including excursions to Trinidad and Tobago. Contact them at P.O. Box 33008, Austin, TX 78764, tel. (800) 328-8368 or (512) 328-5221, fax 328-2919.

Wonderbird Tours, Inc. offers Caribbean and other regional birding, horticultural, and tailored natural history tours led by field experts. In the Lesser Antilles, the primary destination is Trinidad and Tobago. Their address is P.O. Box 2055, New York, NY 10159-2055, tel. (800) BIRD-TUR (800-247-3887) or (212) 736-2473.

---

are very popular and involve visiting historical buildings and sites.

In-country groups offer the best eco-tours for the obvious reason that their operators are often local and thoroughly familiarized with the environment. The destination chapters in this book will cover those, but the accompanying chart will give you an idea of what's out there. Further, these publications might be worth researching before you depart:

Center for Responsible Tourism is a referral organization and will give recent information on organizations and groups and travel companies that promote what they call responsible travel. Contact 2 Kensington Road, San Anselmo, CA 94960; tel. (415) 258-6594.

Directory of Alternative Travel Resources, by Dianne Brause, covers a wide range of adventure and eco-oriented tours and travel possibilities. Cost is about US$7.50. Contact Lost Valley Educational Center, 81868 Lost Valley Lane, Dexter, OR 97431.

The Green Travel Sourcebook: A Guide for the Physically Active, the Intellectually Curious, or the Socially Aware, by Daniel and Sally Wiener Grotta, is a valuable resource for eco-travel tour and travel opportunities, and discusses eco-travel both philosophically and practically. Ask your local bookseller if it's available; the publisher is John Wiley and Sons.

Specialty Travel Index is a U.S.-based magazine that comes out twice per year and lists over 600 tour operators and outfitters that cater to interests ranging from biking to hiking to diving to archaeology. Entries are thoroughly cross-

DIVING AND SNORKELING SAFETY

Care should be taken to use only certified diving facilities and facilities that will escort only certified divers. Sometimes unqualified operations offer cheap diving packages to neophytes who are unaware of the methods and inherent dangers of scuba diving. They might simply strap a tank on your back and let you have at it, a danger both to you and to the diving world.

If diving isn't your cup of "sea," then snorkeling will do nicely. All hotels and dive centers rent equipment, and it's inexpensive enough to do as often as you like. Snorkeling is generally safe, but remember: test your equipment first. Get used to your mask and snorkel by practicing first in a pool or shallow water, and don't snorkel or swim alone. Some like to wear a T-shirt for both protection against the sun and accidental brushes against coral.

Snorkeling in choppy seas is potentially dangerous and probably futile. Sloshing, murky water greatly reduces visibility, and waves can push you into rocks and coral. Even though coastlines may have minor tides and gentle currents, be aware of the currents when you are snorkeling or diving.

Avoid the porcupinelike sea urchins—unless they're served for dinner—especially the black, long-spined urchin. The strong barbs will pierce the skin and break off, resulting in painful swelling. Remove the fragments immediately and soak the affected area in straight vinegar or a strong ammonia solution—urine will do in a pinch—and treat with antiseptic as soon as possible. Then see a doctor.

Likewise, avoid the green or orange bristle worm, which can also make for a very bad day if you touch its brittle, white whiskers. They detach and become imbedded in the skin. Again, vinegar and medical treatment should follow.

The red fire sponge is nice to look at but will cause swelling and discomfort if touched. Also, try to stay clear of all forms of jellyfish, which are not fish at all, but primordial globs of membrane and primitive intelligence—again, nice to look at but not to touch. Their tentacles have small, stinging organisms that detach when brushed. Splash the affected area with alcohol, but avoid rubbing it or you may activate detached stingers. Talcum powder and other drying agents—sand will work in an emergency—are useful for jellyfish encounters.

Avoid touching any live coral, for the organism's safety and for your own. All corals can be harmful, either by a slow-healing gash or toxins released on touch. Avoid even the smooth-looking coral. Fire corals and stinging corals do what their names suggest and clearly should be avoided. If you accidentally touch them, treat the sting with vinegar and seek treatment. If you want to touch underwater fauna, it's best to wear protective gloves. If you're not wearing fins, wear some sort of protective shoes. Likewise, breaking coral, kicking it with your fins, brushing it with your underwater camera, or other injurious behavior can traumatize the delicate ecological balance of the reef.

Snorkeling with a local who can point out reef life is both rewarding and safe. Many hotels offer guides for snorkelers as well as divers.

---

referenced by geographical region, personal interests, activities offered, and more. This important publication for focused travelers costs US$6 per copy or US$10 for a subscription. Contact 305 San Anselmo Ave., San Anselmo, CA 94960, tel. (415) 459-4900, fax (415) 459-4974.

Eco-Tourism in Practice

So what exactly is eco-tourism? A simplified definition might be this: it is any activity that emphasizes and respects the ecological and human cultural aspects of an environment and that seeks to leave the ecosystems and cultures unaltered by the presence or acts of visitors to that environment.

Whatever you choose to call it—responsible travel, eco-travel, green travel, or simply good travel—it need not be the domain of tour companies and specialized travel outfits. Good travel ultimately starts with personal choice. It is a personal choice to try to leave untainted the natural resources and local cultures of any place you visit. This includes being aware of your attitudes and behavior and having some prior knowledge of the balances that need to be maintained in an environment.

Most countries publish lists of endangered island plant and animal species, usually obtainable at information centers of national parks, preserves, or at regional tourism offices. They offer the dos and don'ts of behavior regarding use of natural resources, and it is in everyone's interest to follow the rules.

Many countries in the Lesser Antilles enforce bans on the consumption of certain sea turtles, which are endangered. Still, confusingly, some restaurants offer turtle meat on the menus. You can help by not buying it. Several countries disallow the sale of spiny lobsters during their reproductive season, roughly April through June. Yet, some roadside vendors and restaurateurs are happily unimpeded by the ban and offer the lobsters for sale. Similarly, many countries enforce a ban on the sale of endangered corals, usually black coral and, in places, white coral. Yet market vendors have these corals and will try to sell them to you. (In fact, any coral accidentally broken or deliberately removed will upset the delicate ecological balance of the life-sustaining reef and thus disturb the food chain.) The choice to buy or not to buy becomes yours.

Even seemingly innocuous behavior can directly affect the environment. Riding motorcycles or dune vehicles on a beach can compact sand and therefore contribute to beach erosion. The popular Jet Skis offered for rent at many resorts can contribute to the environment what many call "noise pollution" and are annoying.

On the cultural front, you will soon note that the people of the Lesser Antilles are often conservative in dress, contrary to brochure and popular poster imagery. Bathing suits, short shorts, and other revealing clothing, for both men and women, are fine for the beach or pool but not in town. You'll also note that nude and topless sunbathing are restricted to certain areas, with the exception of the French Antilles, where topless is acceptable on most beaches. You may offend sensibilities by not heeding local custom.

Many locals throughout the islands object to having their photographs taken without permission. This is true in many developing countries, where the indigenous cultures have been poked, prodded, photographed, and displayed in everything from serious scientific magazines to trendy travel publications. It is always best to ask first. In cases, people may ask you to pay to photograph them—an unfortunate by-product of the times and tourism. But if the photo means that much to you, pay up.

DIVING AND SNORKELING

Excellent diving facilities are available on just about any island in the archipelago. In particular, the U.S. and British Virgin Islands, Barbados, Saba, Anguilla, Dominica, and most of the Grenadines offer relatively untouched environments. Look to hotels for dive centers, which offer diving equipment, diving instruction, and snorkeling equipment.

Certified divers should bring their certification cards. Noncertified divers can receive PADI (Professional Association of Diving Instructors) beginner's training, which will allow a supervised 30-foot dive, a sort of introduction to the world below. If you're interested and have the time and money, certification is available from various dive centers for an average of US$350, which generally includes daily dive fees, manuals, dive tables, a log book, and certification processing fees.

ACCOMMODATIONS

SEASONS

The busy tourist season in the Lesser Antilles lasts, not surprisingly, from mid-December through mid-April, or roughly the equivalent of the Northern Hemisphere's winter. Summer is off-season and priced accordingly. You can count on room rates being less expensive, in cases as much as a 40% reduction. As well, you'll have the added luxury of traveling in uncrowded areas. Some hotels retain the same rate all year, and others have three or more different rates depending on the season. During the summer many small hotels are short of guests, and substantial rate reductions can often be negotiated no matter what your length of stay. Talk to the manager or owner.

Many hotels do not fill up, even during the high season. Rather than letting empty rooms sit, where no money is earned, hotels may shift a certain percentage of their business to hotel wholesalers at bulk rates. Wholesalers in turn offer these accommodations to the public at significant discounts. One such wholesaler is the U.S.-based **The Room Exchange,** tel. (800) 846-7000, fax (212) 760-1013. This exchange will book properties throughout the Lesser Antilles. Some rooms may be available for as much as 25% off in the high season, and up to 50% off in the low season.

A rule of thumb in looking for discounts: it is not *always* best to rely on travel agents; your own research and telephone work will often be rewarded. In many cases it is best to first call the hotel or guesthouse directly and ask if they are offering any deals, discounts, or packages. If not, suggest one yourself.

DISCOUNT PACKAGES

A wide range of discount plans are available at hotels and resorts, including package tours sponsored in conjunction with airlines, honeymoon packages, golf packages, and scuba diving packages, to name a few. Most discount packages include ground transfers, inexpensive hotel arrangements (although the hotel might not be the best of its class), and features relating to the theme of the trip (e.g., champagne and flowers for honeymooners, several "free" dive excursions, discounted greens fees). When reading brochures and information regarding these packages, note the fine print. Some are offered contingent on mid-week travel, Saturday-to-Saturday travel (or, pick the day), or travel during the off-season. Prices are often listed *per person based on double occupancy*, and the single rate, if it exists, may be more than one half of the double occupancy rate.

Of all plans, however, the most common are meal plans. In hotel literature, "EP" means European Plan, and that indicates no meals are offered (except in the case of hotels or bed-and-breakfast inns that provide breakfast, often continental breakfast). "AP" indicates American Plan, or a full three meals offered on the plan. This ought to be at least vaguely disturbing to Americans, but probably is not. At any rate, "MAP" means Modified American Plan and indicates the hotel will provide two meals, usually breakfast and a choice of lunch or dinner.

"All-inclusive" resorts have found their place in the Lesser Antilles. All-inclusives, a concept pioneered by the SuperClubs and Sandals resort chains of Jamaica (both chains also have resorts in the Lesser Antilles), are just what they say they are: resorts that offer the room, all meals, amenities, tips, and extras for one price. The advantage for many is the simplicity of the exchange. You needn't be bothered by tipping, arguing over who pays for dinner, or loose change in your shoes on the beach.

The disadvantage is one of attitude. The incentive to leave the resort for any reason is hardly there. Meals are paid for, which means there is no reason to experience local cuisine elsewhere than the confines of the resort. The same applies to other activities. The choice to go out and explore, to experience the country becomes more difficult, and, ultimately, less cost-effective.

Still, all-inclusive resorts can offer advantageous packages, particularly when offered with airfare and transfers. The concept has without a doubt arrived full force in the Lesser Antilles and can be the right sort of experience for a great many vacationers.

CAMPING

Unfortunately, camping is not widely encouraged throughout the Lesser Antilles. This has as much to do with personal safety as with the predilection of certain tourist boards and governments to encourage spending in higher-priced hotels. Exceptions are found chiefly in the French West Indies, particularly on Martinique, which has a wide array of campgrounds with facilities as well as a number of camping vehicle rental companies. To a lesser extent, camping facilities are found on Guadeloupe and its dependencies. St. John, of the U.S. Virgin Islands, features exceptional campgrounds on Cinnamon Bay and Maho Bay. Some facilities exist in the British Virgin Islands.

VILLA RENTALS

Villa rentals are a good bet for families or groups who have a hankering to retain a greater degree of autonomy than resorts might offer and who want to save money to boot. You can cook, eat, see the sights, and sleep at your leisure. Most come equipped with cooks and household help, which gives you the chance to relax a bit and let someone else do the work, should that be your choice. For a large group, a villa can be cost-effective. The accommodations vary wildly, from apartments to large complexes and near-mansions. And the rates vary according to size, amenities offered, and location. Rates can be as little as US$900 per week to as much as US$12,000 per week in the high season.

Hundreds of companies and private individuals market their villas through publications such as *Caribbean Travel and Life, Islands, Travel and Leisure,* and the U.K.-based *Caribbean World,* as well as other magazines, all available at most magazine stands. Major newspapers,

particularly in their Sunday travel sections, list dozens of Caribbean villa rental possibilities. Several other places to start: **At Home Abroad,** 405 E. 56th St., Suite 6H, New York, NY 10022, tel. (212) 421-9165; **Leisuretime Destinations,** 905 E. Martin Luther King Dr., Suite 600, Tarpon Springs, FL 34689, tel. (800) 704-2233; **Villas and Apartments Abroad,** 420 Madison Ave., Suite 1105, New York, NY 10017, tel. (212) 759-1025; **Villas Caraibe,** tel. and fax (800) 743-8270 or tel. (612) 623-8270; **Villas Caribe,** 9403 E. Chenango Rd., Englewood, CO 80111, tel. (800) 645-7498, fax (303) 741-2520; **Villas of Distinction,** P.O. Box 55, Armonk, New York, NY 10504, tel. (800) 289-0900 or (914) 273-3331, fax (914) 273-3387; **Villas International,** 605 Market St., Suite 510, San Francisco, CA 94105, tel. (800) 221-2260 or (415) 281-0910, **Villa Leisure,** P.O. Box 209, Westport, CT 06881, tel. (800) 526-4244 or (407) 624-9000; or **West Indies Management Company (WIMCO),** P.O. Box 1461, Newport, RI 02840; tel. (800) 932-3222 or (401) 849-8012, U.K. tel. (800) 89-8318, U.S. fax (401) 847-6290.

TAXES, SERVICE CHARGES, AND OTHER MONEY MATTERS

Local government taxes may be added to hotel and restaurant bills. Check to see if the tax is included in the rate or will be added later. This tax, variable throughout the islands, ranges 5-10%.

An additional charge you might see on a hotel bill is a 10-15% service charge, which is meant to be a tip for services rendered at the hotel. Ostensibly, this tip is divided among the hotel staff, but if you feel like giving your chambermaid or porter something more, feel free to do so.

Most hotels and restaurants in the Lesser Antilles will accept major North American and European credit cards. American Express, MasterCard, and Visa are most common; Discover Card is gaining acceptance. Diners Club is still used, though less frequently than during its heyday years ago. Smaller hotels will accept traveler's checks, but for many small guesthouses throughout the region you will have to pay cash.

FOOD AND DRINK

There is an old saying among hoteliers in the Lesser Antilles: "Your stay in the Caribbean is only as good as your last meal." Presumably those who say this might be insecure hoteliers, but there is, as always, some truth to the adage.

Such is the power of food. Your stay in the Lesser Antilles will certainly be enhanced by trying the local cuisines, and you may find that sampling local savories is an end in itself. The combination of imported ingredients coupled with West Indian spices, fruits, vegetables, exotic meats, and of course seafood, creates the exotic Creole mix. The end result is one of the most widespread cultural exports from the Caribbean—you'll find West Indian restaurants and food items in many of the major cities of the world. Into which lounge in the Western world would you walk and not find a daiquiri? Or a piña colada? These rum-based drinks were invented in Cuba and Puerto Rico, respectively.

West Indian cuisine embraces a variety of imports and native foodstuffs. Bananas and plantains, carried by the Spaniards westward from the Canary Islands, are today island dietary staples as well as export crops. Sugar and pineapples were also introduced by the Spanish and are part of island folklore as well as diet (sugarcane provides the basic ingredient of rum). African slaves brought, literally, the seeds of future vegetable and fruit crops. Okra, several types of yams, the ackee, and pigeon peas are African imports. Pigeon peas (also called red peas or gungo peas) play a enormous part in the West Indian diet. When combined with rice, the dish is a staple and side dish in most homes and Creole restaurants. It's often called rice and beans or rice and peas.

The meat dishes, such as goat stew, goatwater, mutton (which may be, confusingly, meat from either goat or sheep) stew, pork, the famous curries of Trinidad, and the exotic *crapaud*

THE STORY OF RUM

Pirates swilled it, slaves distilled it, planters knocked it back with a dash of lime and sugar, and it emerged as one of the Lesser Antilles' most enduring icons. It's rum, and it tastes better here than anywhere else in the world.

Rum is, without a doubt, *the* drink of the West Indies. It's served everywhere and anyhow: with fruity, frothy accoutrements in the glitzy tourist resorts, or with a cool splash of water in the smoky backstreet rum shops of the towns. It's sprinkled in obeah and herbalist ceremonies, or perhaps offered as a gift for redemption in the religious ceremonies of underground sects. And it is, behind calypso and sunburn, the region's most successful export.

The origins of the word are uncertain. Some believe "rum" is derived from the botanical name of sugarcane, *saccharum officinarum,* from which rum is produced. Others believe the word originated among the planters of Barbados, where it was reputedly called "rumbullion" for the escapades it brought on.

During Columbus's third voyage to the West Indies, he planted sugarcane on the island of Hispaniola. The Spanish colonists soon found that a sweet liquor could be made by distilling molasses, the heavy residue of processed cane. Sailors and buccaneers soon discovered the drink. Cheap to produce and easy to transport, it became identified with life on the seas, as in "yo ho ho and a bottle of rum."

In the 1600s, the British began to make excursions into the West Indies, and sugarcane production on massive plantations became a way of life. Rum was produced on a large scale in Barbados and was first produced commercially in Jamaica. Still, rum was first considered a drink of ruffians, of the lower class, and did not gain wide acceptance as proper drink in polite European society for centuries. It wasn't until the early 20th century that rum came into its own as a cocktail ingredient.

The original distilling process is still the basis for rum production today. Sugarcane is pressed and or frog legs, of Dominica, are island favorites. Pepperpot stew, which is claimed by several islands, may originally have been an Arawak dish. Its base is a meat stock with added spices, vegetables, and callaloo, the leafy stalk of the eddoe (or, *dasheen*) plant. Eddoe—the word and plant are native to West Africa—is a starchy tuber that grows throughout the Lesser Antilles.

Seafood dishes are, not surprisingly, specialties in the islands. Large game fish such as mahimahi, marlin, and tuna are common, as are the smaller yet no less tasty grouper and red snapper. Flying fish is considered a delicacy on Barbados and is grilled, baked, or thrust into sandwiches. On most of the islands you can expect traditional French-type rich sauces or the light treatments of nouvelle cuisine and delicate grilling. On others, well, expect the same. Coconut cream, called "run-down" or variations on the phrase, is a favorite sauce on fish. Other sea animals find themselves on West Indian plates no less frequently than fish. Conch may be grilled, deep fried to make fritters, or steeped in chowder. Boiled crabs, stuffed crabs, and even sea urchins, which produce a heavy and gritty sort of meat, are favorite West Indian snacks. Lobster, the clawless variety, and shrimp and crayfish (freshwater shrimp) are served simply grilled with butter and garlic.

Many countries in the Lesser Antilles enforce bans on the consumption of endangered sea turtles; several also forbid the sale of spiny lobsters during their reproductive season, roughly April through June. However, these rules do not stop some restaurants from offering turtle meat on the menus, and some roadside vendors and restaurateurs are happily unimpeded by the ban and offer lobsters for sale. Do your part by not buying these items.

Spices perhaps distinguish West Indian cuisine more than anything else. Red pepper, hot sauces, and curries are frequently featured either in the recipe or as a condiment along with the salt and pepper. Ginger and pimento (a spice from the fruit of the pimento tree that combines the essentials of cinnamon, clove, nutmeg, and pepper, called allspice elsewhere) are common seasonings. Nutmeg is frequently used; it's grown in Grenada, which produces 40% of the world's crop.

As well, restaurants that feature international cuisine exist throughout the Lesser Antilles. Chi-

---

produces cane juice, from which both sugar and by-products such as molasses emerge. Water is then added to the molasses to reduce the sugar content, and the mixture is pasteurized. Yeast is added to the molasses mix, and the fermentation produces alcohol. The alcohol in turn kills the yeast, and the result is called "dead wash," which is then distilled to produce rum.

In some processes, particularly those favored by distillers in the French Antilles, rum is produced from sugarcane juice rather than the heavier molasses.

Traditionally, the rum was aged in oak casks. The casks produced both the colors and flavor of the various rums you see on the market, although caramel is often added to produce the darkest of rums. Today's rum is still aged, but often in vats, for about three years. Premium rums are aged for as long as 20 years.

Rums run the gamut from the smooth, amber drink to the dark, nearly black rums, the richest in flavor. Each island produces its own rum, some for local consumption, some for export. The famous Mount Gay and Cockspur rums of Barbados, Clarke's Court brand of Grenada, Old St. Croix of the U.S. Virgin Islands, and Rhum Vieux of Martinique are just a few of the local brands you'll see in the Lesser Antilles. Export rums are also produced in Puerto Rico (which exports the world's most widely consumed rum, Bacardi, as well as the Don Q brand), and in Jamaica, Guyana, and neighboring states.

The West Indies' famous "overproof" rums, both white and dark, are the strongest of the lot—you've been warned. The 151-proof rums will put the heartiest of imbibers under the table in a New York minute.

Rum drinks are very popular in the tropics, as much for their attendant fruit mixes and foamy daiquiri-style additions as for the rum itself. One of the oldest mixed rum punches originated during the plantation heydays. Its recipe, in this order, was simple: sour, sweet, strong, and weak. Translation: One part sour, or lime juice; two parts sweet, or sugar; three parts strong, or rum; and four parts weak, or water or fruit juice. In the French Antilles the recipe, with slight variations, is called "ti punch."

nese, East Indian, Italian, Vietnamese, and other exotic cuisines are popular on the larger islands. The language of pizza is universal. On several islands, local fast-food restaurants serve fried chicken, hamburgers, and meat patties. Several American fast-food chains have found their way to the Lesser Antilles and are, perhaps ironically, favorites with locals. Among them are Kentucky Fried Chicken, Pizza Hut, and Burger King.

The restaurants of the region run the entire gamut, price- and ambience-wise, from roadside stands to four-star extravaganzas. Roadside stands serve anything from hot dogs to deep-fried crayfish, and the quality can be good. Sanitation is often not so good. Luxury restaurants, however, offer superb settings and presentations, and you pay for it. The food is also superb, even though it appears that "nouvelle" is French for "light sauces, small portions, too much money." Good deals are the smaller, medium-priced restaurants and cafes that serve authentic Creole and Continental cuisine.

Caribbean drinks are a treat—and a surprise. The native *mauby* (rhymes with "Toby"), made from the bark of a tree, tastes a bit like sarsaparilla's wayward cousin. Still, it is said to be healthful for pregnant women and especially helpful for men who are having, well, stamina problems. It's safe to say that *mauby* is an acquired taste. Much the same can be said about sea moss (also, Irish moss), a drink made from gelatin extracted from seaweed. The gelatin is sweetened and combined with milk or ginger and is used as a restorative tonic, particularly in

matters, again, of sexual potency. Coconut water, the clear, potassium-rich liquid from the center of a green nut, is found on virtually every corner and in every market throughout the islands. Coconuts are inexpensive, germ-free, and fun to drink. Coconut water, derived from the meat of the nut, is not to be confused with coconut cream or coconut milk.

Dozens of small soft-drink producers exist throughout the islands, and the drinks range from the thick ginger beers of Trinidad to the ubiquitous Ting, a grapefruit-based sweet drink.

All sorts of alcoholic drinks are available in the resorts and pubs of the Lesser Antilles, many of them oddly colored with those tiny umbrellas that get stuck in your nose. Two beverages are universally available: beer and rum. Several of the islands produce their own beer, and some of it is quite good. Hairoun Lager of St. Vincent stands out, as does the Carib brand, which has breweries on several islands. Banks is the excellent beer of Barbados. Red Stripe, which is brewed in Jamaica, has found its place in the Lesser Antilles, as have several other foreign brands such as Heineken and Miller.

Rum, however, is the beverage of the islands. The drink, which is made from sugarcane, originated in Barbados and was first called rumbullion, presumably for the escapades it induced. Today's rums are dark, amber, white (overproof, deceptively strong), and spiced varieties. Every major island in the Lesser Antilles has one or more distilleries for production of the local spirits. Much of the world's rum is produced in the West Indies.

HEALTH AND PERSONAL SAFETY

In the Lesser Antilles, the problems most visitors encounter are overexposure to sun and over-indulgence in rum and spicy foods—all preventable by common sense. It's always wise to increase your intake of nonalcoholic fluids in a tropical environment—you'll lose quite a bit through sweat. Doctors recommend at least eight large glasses (about eight pints) of water per day. Coconut water is healthy, inexpensive, and a fun alternative to soft drinks.

SKIN CARE

It's hot, the water is inviting, and you'd like to get out of doors as soon as possible. But remember, the tropical sun is extremely strong, even when covered by clouds. If you've got sun-sensitive skin, a wide-brimmed hat and strong sunscreen are in order. Although sunscreen is universally available, it is not always the best brand, and the prices may be more than you'd pay at home. It's best to bring your own brand, and try to take it easy on the tanning process for the first few days. Aloe vera is good for a sunburn, but it doesn't replace the best cure: shade. If you are light-skinned and plan on snorkeling for any length of time, you might want to wear a good T-shirt (ultraviolet rays can penetrate thin clothing) to guard against overexposing your back.

Strange environments and stranger bacteria can affect your skin by contributing to slower healing of cuts and scratches; they become infected more easily, and linger. Scratched mosquito bites are prime offenders, as are small scrapes or other skin breaks. Wash, disinfect, and cover all cuts as soon as possible. Try not to scratch bites. It is not true that salt water is a good healer for cuts, especially cuts in their early stages. Salt water carries enough bacteria to give you a nasty infection.

Mosquitoes

Mosquitoes are carriers of the protozoan infections malaria and dengue fever. Malaria is problematic in parts of Haiti, the Dominican Republic, and Venezuela but has not been reported in the Lesser Antilles for some time. Dengue fever (symptoms include fever, joint and muscle pains, severe headaches) has been reported in all the Lesser Antilles islands but is more prevalent in the Greater Antilles. The only prevention for dengue fever is mosquito prevention. In mosquito-dense areas, use good repellent and wear clothes that cover your arms and legs. Mosquito nets and screened bedrooms will provide protection. If the smoke doesn't bother you, mosquito coils are helpful.

FOOD AND WATER

Drinking water is generally safe throughout the Lesser Antilles, and most is filtered and/or chlorinated. The exceptions to watch out for are periods immediately after hurricanes, floods, or other high-water situations, when contaminants might mix with the drinking water supply. Infectious hepatitis, or Hepatitis A, can be carried by contaminated water. If you are in a situation where you are wary of the water, drink bottled water, which is available in most situations, or coconut water, which is naturally sterilized. Washing or peeling fruit yourself and paying strict attention to personal hygiene will reduce the likelihood of contracting hepatitis. See also "Vaccinations, Prescription Drugs, Insurance" below.

VACCINATIONS, PRESCRIPTION DRUGS, INSURANCE

Smallpox and yellow fever vaccinations are no longer required of North Americans and Europeans when traveling to the Lesser Antilles. Travelers originating from other Caribbean countries, as well as South America, Asia, Africa, and other parts of the world should check regulations before departure. A commonly available inoculation, gamma globulin, is effective against

Hepatitis A. Doctors can prescribe it, and it should be administered as close as possible to your departure date.

If you need prescription drugs don't count on them being readily available—bring enough to last your trip. An extra pair of prescription glasses or contact lenses is also in order.

Check your health insurance to see if you're covered overseas and what the coverage entails. If you want to purchase more, the following offer treatment and evacuation coverage, as well as hard-to-find protection for scuba-diving injuries. Payment is determined by the length of time you travel and the coverage you need. Price is about US$100 per week for a package of medical, evacuation, accident, and loss of life coverage. Some may include trip-cancellation coverage. In the U.S. try **American Express Travel Protection Plan,** P.O. Box 919010, San Diego, CA 92191-9010, tel. (800) 234-0375; or **Access America International,** 600 3rd Ave., New York, NY 10163, tel. (800) 284-8300.

SEXUALLY TRANSMITTED DISEASES

The Lesser Antilles has not escaped the worldwide proliferation of sexually transmitted diseases. Herpes, gonorrhea, and other venereal diseases exist. Condoms are available in all pharmacies and hotel shops. *Check expiration dates.*

AIDS has become a problem throughout the Caribbean, as it has throughout the world. No large-scale studies have been conducted to determine the number of infected persons in the region, but a conference of health officials from Antigua, the Bahamas, Barbados, Cuba, Dominica, the Dominican Republic, Grenada, Guyana, Haiti, Jamaica, and Trinidad and Tobago established that those countries account for more than 16,000 confirmed cases of HIV infections. Confirmed AIDS cases numbered more than 5,000. The actual number is probably far greater. Given the number of tourists who move through the region yearly, as well as the number of West Indians who travel abroad, it would be foolish to engage in unsafe sex. However, be aware that even though greater strides have been made in public education, some taboos still exist regarding condom use and other safe sex practices.

PERSONAL SAFETY

Women who travel alone are taking a chance of incurring some harassment, most of it verbal. This behavior is as common in the Lesser Antilles as it is elsewhere. Men staring, whistling, and approaching a woman are not uncommon behaviors—remember, tourists often represent people out for a good time. That may not be you, but it is true for some, and you'll have to put up with the behavioral flotsam left in their wake. Women traveling in groups or with a companion are in a better position to avoid it.

The Lesser Antilles are more conservative than not, but the proximity of tourist activity lends a looseness to the social atmosphere that may be misinterpreted. Beachwear, for instance, is just that, and wearing bathing suits or other revealing clothing in public places may send the wrong signals.

Avoid walking along deserted beach stretches at night or getting into unmarked cars declaring themselves taxis. Areas in and around large towns may be dangerous, particularly at night, both for locals and for visitors. If you are unsure, ask the hotel staff or a taxi driver whom you trust.

Be street smart as you would in any major city worldwide. Lock your rental car. Carry your wallet or purse in a pouch or front pocket. Avoid basket-type or open handbags; they're easy targets for pickpockets. Pulling large wads of cash out to buy things sends a signal as bright as a lighthouse beacon. Don't leave bags unattended at the beach.

ILLEGAL DRUGS

Parts of the Lesser Antilles have reputations as party epicenters, and with some justification. Marijuana, cocaine, hallucinogens—the usual suspects—are available, in some instances widely available, in the Lesser Antilles. They are, as well, universally illegal. Local authorities are very sensitive to the drug problem, and the police can be sophisticated in detecting drug use and trafficking. Possession and use are punishable by heavy fines, deportation, and jail sentences. The penalties for smuggling are worse, and the bottom line is this: you do *not* want to spend time in a Caribbean jail. Honestly.

INFORMATION AND SERVICES

TIME ZONES

The Lesser Antilles lie in the Atlantic standard time zone, which is four hours behind Greenwich mean time (e.g., 4 p.m. in London on a Wednesday is noon in Barbados on that same Wednesday). The Atlantic standard time zone is directly east of North America's eastern standard time zone and does not make seasonal adjustments; this makes it one hour ahead of eastern standard time during the winter months, and the same as daylight saving time during the spring and summer months. (In the U.S., daylight saving time begins at 2 a.m. on the first Sunday of April and ends at 2 a.m. on the last Sunday of October).

More simply: if it's noon in New York in December, then it's 1 p.m. in Antigua. But when it's noon in New York on a hot day in July, it's also noon in Antigua.

ELECTRICITY

One wonders who dreamed up the confusing business of 110-120 volts alternating current (AC), which dominates North American households and appliances, and the 220-240 volts direct current (DC) that is Europe's mainstay. Whatever. Despite the merits of one system or another, it surely has made international travel a challenge. In the Lesser Antilles, you will be similarly volt-challenged. A 220-240 volts, 50-60 cycles AC system dominates the region, but there are exceptions.

Anguilla, Barbados, Saba, St. Eustatius, Trinidad and Tobago, the British Virgin Islands, and the U.S. Virgin Islands use 110-120 volts. Antigua and Barbuda use 110-120 volts systems in some locations, 220-240 volts in others.

The island of Saint-Martin/Sint Maarten, in keeping with its separate currencies, languages, and cultures, is no different where electricity is concerned. The French side operates on 220-240 volts, while the Dutch side uses 110-120 volts.

The rest of the Lesser Antilles (St. Barts, St. Kitts and Nevis, Montserrat, Guadeloupe, Dominica, Martinique, St. Lucia, St. Vincent and the Grenadines, and Grenada) use the 220-240 volts system, although, again, each island may have hotels or buildings that are exceptions.

When booking ahead, check to see if the hotel will have the proper current to run your appliance. These days, many travel appliances such as hair dryers, shavers, and even computers have voltage converters built in. Larger hotels carry adapters for use by guests, and you can easily buy the proper adapter set at any electrical store at home. The French islands, as well as certain hotels throughout the islands, use European-style round plugs. Plug adapters are available at most electrical stores in the U.S. and Europe.

COMMUNICATIONS

Stamps originating in the Lesser Antilles are bold, colorful, and among the most striking in the world. Philatelists will enjoy them. And they do their job; your letters and packages generally will arrive safely. However, postal service in the region is notoriously slow. Regular post to North America may take ten days or so; to Europe, even longer.

A viable, though expensive, alternative is FedEx (until recently, called Federal Express), which now has offices or representatives on virtually every major island in the Lesser Antilles. FedEx is convenient for packages containing souvenirs, books, or other items too large to carry home.

Telephone communication in the Lesser Antilles is very good and getting better. The English-speaking islands use the area code 809, which makes direct dialing to the Lesser Antilles no more difficult than calling anywhere in North America. The French Antilles and Dutch Antilles use a combination three-digit country code and four- to six-digit telephone number. The country code varies among the islands.

TELEPHONE CARD SURFING

Long-distance telephone calling card holders be warned: a scam called "card surfing" is not unknown in the Lesser Antilles. It involves someone reading your card numbers from over your shoulder or scanning your code as you punch it into a public phone. Then your code is passed along or sold to any number of people who use it to call around the world. For example, this writer's phone card was "surfed" in the Caribbean, resulting in a two-day run of several hundred calls to places such as Monrovia, Hong Kong, and Brooklyn. The resulting bill, before the phone company noticed the run on the number and shut down the service, amounted to more than US$6000. To their credit, the phone company recognized the scam and absorbed the loss—which, of course, was later passed on to us, the consumers. Nevertheless, in any public place you would be well advised to shield your card and dialing procedure while making a call. Avoid writing your code on slips of paper or napkins, which can later be rummaged from garbage bins. If possible, memorize your number.

AT&T USADirect Service operates throughout the islands, particularly in larger hotels and airports. This service is for North American telephone calling card holders and either bills your home telephone number or allows you to call collect.

A majority of the Lesser Antilles' telephone companies have created local phone cards, meant to take the place of coins in public phones. These magnetized cards come in several denominations and may be purchased at the local phone company, post offices, and shops or convenience stores. The concept is simple: insert the card, make the call, and the cost is deducted from the value of the card.

Note that telephone calls made from hotels, whether local or overseas, will usually incur a surcharge.

MONEY AND CURRENCIES

The different currencies used in this relatively small land area may be confusing. This is especially true if you intend to do some island hopping.

The exchange rates given below are as current as possible but are always subject to change. In North America and Europe, exchange rates are often listed in large metropolitan newspapers. In the islands, local papers often list exchange rates of major world currencies.

Several Lesser Antilles islands use currencies related to the countries to which they are politically linked. The French franc is the currency of Guadeloupe, Martinique, Saint-Barthélémy, and Saint-Martin. Exchange rate is F5.50 = US$1.

The Netherlands Antilles florin (or Netherlands Antilles guilder) is the currency of Saba, Sint Eustatius, and Sint Maarten. Exchange rate is NAF1.80 = US$1.

The Eastern Caribbean (EC) dollar, the currency of several former and current British colonies, is used by Anguilla, Antigua and Barbuda, Dominica, Grenada, Montserrat, St. Kitts and Nevis, St. Lucia, and St. Vincent and the Grenadines. The exchange rates are the same throughout these islands, EC$2.70 = US$1.

The U.S. dollar is the currency of both the U.S. and British Virgin Islands.

The Barbados dollar is the official currency in Barbados, trading at an exchange rate of Bds$2 = US$1.

In Trinidad and Tobago, the Trinidad and Tobago dollar is the legal currency. The Trinidad and Tobago dollar has had it rough lately and has fluctuated since a devaluation procedure in the late '70s and subsequent floating in 1993. The current rate is TT$5.70 = US$1.

Realistically, the U.S. dollar is the most widely accepted of all foreign currencies in the Lesser Antilles and the Caribbean at large. Often, it is legally interchangeable at businesses and restaurants with the local currency. This is true on all islands that use the EC dollar, the French franc, and the Netherlands Antilles florin. In some places prices are quoted in the local currency and in U.S. dollars as well as other currencies. Canadian dollars are also acceptable in instances. Aside from the British pound sterling and French franc, most European currencies are not widely accepted. You may find, however, that rather than using U.S. dollars or a eurocurrency, converting your cash to the local currency will be to your advantage. This has to do with the common tendency to "round off" prices, taxis rates, and other fares, usually to the advantage of the vendor, not you.

In countries where foreign currency is not used openly (but, as a practical matter, is used anyway) such as Barbados and Trinidad and Tobago, banks will exchange currencies at the official rate. On the French islands, *bureaux de change* also exchange money, at rates often better than are offered by banks. Some post offices exchange money, but at rates less favorable than banks or *bureaux de change*. Make sure to keep your exchange receipt—there are restrictions on carrying certain currencies abroad, and you may be required to produce proof of exchange. It is always better to reconvert your money to U.S. dollars or your own currency before leaving the island—doing so at home is not impossible but is often impractical.

Black markets exist in certain countries, and you may get much more for your currency by using the illicit market—but beware of its ramifications. By utilizing the black market, you may be inflating the cost of goods and services, especially for locals, because you are essentially paying less for them. As well, it is not unknown for local police to set up sting operations in black market areas, often in collusion with black marketeers themselves. The penalties and fines can be heavy.

Traveler's checks are widely accepted in the islands, but don't expect the little roadside coconut stand to cash one. Major credit cards such as American Express, Visa, MasterCard, Discover and, to an extent, Diners Club and Carte Blanche, are used in frequently traveled, tourist-dense islands, and in large hotels and resorts on smaller islands. It would be wise to check with your hotel or car rental agency before you depart to find out what forms of payment are acceptable.

Tipping is common in the Lesser Antilles. Think 10-20% at restaurants, but check to see that the gratuity hasn't been included in the bill. You are certainly allowed to tip more should you think well of the service. As well, hotels often automatically add a 10-15% service charge to the bill. In general, taxi drivers, porters, chamberpersons, and sky caps are all customarily tipped. For some, this is a major source of income.

LESSER ANTILLES CURRENCIES

The U.S. dollar is widely accepted throughout the Lesser Antilles, Canadian dollars and eurocurrencies less so (with the exception of the French franc, the currency of the French West Indies). Exchange rates below are subject to fluctuation at any time.

CURRENCY	USED IN	EXCHANGE WITH ONE U.S. DOLLAR
Eastern Caribbean dollar (EC$)	Anguilla, Antigua and Barbuda, Dominica, Grenada, Montserrat, St. Kitts and Nevis, St. Lucia, St. Vincent and the Grenadines	EC$2.70
French franc (F)	Guadeloupe, Martinique, Saint-Barthélémy, Saint-Martin	F5.50
Netherlands Antilles florin (or guilder) (NAF)	Saba, Sint Eustatius, Sint Maarten	NAF1.80
U.S. dollar (US$)	U.S. Virgin Islands, British Virgin Islands	
Barbados dollar (Bds$)	Barbados	Bds$2
Trinidad and Tobago dollar (TT$)	Trinidad and Tobago	TT$5.70

Automatic Teller Machines (ATMs) are slowly wending their way onto the islands, and some exist already for local bank account and card holders. In the French Antilles, cash machines are compatible with French systems. For U.S-based ATM cards, such as those compatible with the Cirrus system and others, the going is not good, with machines currently available only in the U.S. Virgin Islands.

GETTING THERE

Getting to the Lesser Antilles is easier than you might think; many major North American and European airlines operate regular routes to Caribbean countries, and these will be dealt with in the appropriate country chapters. Keep in mind that airline routes may change with seasons, and some companies, Northwest Airlines for example, operate Caribbean routes only during the high season. As well, the financial status of several major international carriers is a bit rocky these days; keep a close eye on the operating status of your intended airline.

Getting around the islands presents some interesting logistical puzzles, and several words to the wise would be to plan well ahead, confirm ongoing flights, and have patience. Several of the smaller islands cannot land large aircraft; they rely instead on small, internal airline companies for their transport. Still others have no facilities or erratically available facilities for night landings, so plan your trip around them. Ferries and cargo transports are an option when traveling island to island, but they tend to take time and are more subject to weather conditions than are airplanes.

AIRLINES

International Flights
Major international air arrival points for the Lesser Antilles are on St. Thomas, Sint Maarten, Antigua, Guadeloupe, Martinique, Barbados, Grenada, and Trinidad. Airlines that connect these islands to Europe and North America and their North American contact numbers are: **American Airlines,** tel. (800) 433-7300; **Air Canada,** tel. (800) 776-3000; **Air France,** tel. (800) 237-2747; **British Airways,** tel. (800) 247-9297; **British West Indies Air International,** tel. (800) 327-7401 or (800) 538-2942; **Continental,** tel. (800) 231-0856; **KLM,** tel. (800) 374-7747; **Lufthansa,** tel. (800) 645-3880; and **United,** tel. (800) 241-6522. One of the region's newer airlines is **Antigua Paradise**

sign at Antigua's V.C. Bird International Airport

Airlines, tel. (800) 299-8784, owned by the Antigua and Barbuda government. APA operates twice-weekly flights from Newark, New Jersey to Sint Maarten and Antigua.

San Juan, Puerto Rico, is an important Caribbean hub and the gateway to many of the smaller islands. San Juan can be reached from major cities throughout North America on **Delta,** tel. (800) 241-4141; **US Air,** tel. (800) 428-4322; **Northwest,** tel. (800) 447-4747; and **Trans World Airlines,** tel. (800) 892-4141. Two new outfits, **Kiwi International,** tel. (800) 538-5494, and **Carnival Airlines,** tel. (800) 437-2110, offer connections to San Juan from Newark and Orlando, and Newark and JFK International, New York, respectively.

Charter companies operate a great many flights to the Caribbean, and their fares tend to be less expensive than regularly scheduled airlines. That is their advantage. The disadvantage is that charter flights are often coupled with expensive hotel or resort packages, though you can in many instances opt to buy the flight and not the entire package. A further disadvantage is that many charter companies operate on a once-per-week basis, departing for the islands on, for example, Saturdays only. This means you must return the following Saturday. There are penalties to pay for an added week's stay, and deep-pocket penalties for cancellation. Advance-purchase tickets are often non-refundable. A final and unfortunate disadvantage is that charter companies may reserve the right to cancel the flight if not enough people have signed on. Refunds can be spotty at best. You be the judge.

Interisland Travel

To get to the smaller islands, one enters the murky, somewhat labyrinthine world of Caribbean interisland travel. Several major and numerous smaller airlines operate regular and charter services to the Lesser Antilles islands (see

LEEWARD ISLANDS AIR TRANSPORT (LIAT) QUICK REFERENCE CHART

MAIN OFFICE

V.C. Bird International Airport, P.O. Box 819, St. John's, Antigua, West Indies, tel. (809) 462-0700, fax 462-2682.

REGIONAL OFFICES

Anguilla: Wallblake Airport, tel. (809) 497-5000/2.

Barbados: Bridgetown, tel. (809) 436-6224.

Bequia: Mitchell Airport, tel. (809) 458-3713.

Barbuda: Crown Point Airport, tel. (809) 460-0289.

British Virgin Islands: Road Town, tel. (809) 495-1187/9.

Carriacou: Carriacou Airport, tel. (809) 443-7362.

Dominica: Roseau, tel. (809) 448-2412/2.

Grenada: St. George's, tel. (809) 440-2796/7.

Guadeloupe: Raizet Airport, tel. (590) 82-12-26 or 82-00-84.

Martinique: Lamentin Airport, tel. (596) 51-00-00 or 51-21-11.

Monserrat: Plymouth, tel. (809) 491-2533 or 491-2362.

St. Croix: Fredericksted, tel. (809) 778-9930.

St. Eustatius: Oranjestad, tel. (599) 3-82524.

St. Kitts: Basseterre, tel. (809) 465-2286 or 465-2511.

St. Lucia: Castries, tel. (809) 452-3051/2/3.

St. Thomas: Charlotte Amalie, tel. (809) 774-2313.

St. Vincent: Kingstown, tel. (809) 457-1821.

Sint Maarten: Princess Juliana Airport, tel. (599) 52403.

Trinidad: Port of Spain, tel. (809) 623-1838 or 623-4480.

Tobago: Crown Point Airport, tel. (809) 639-0484.

Union Island: tel. (809) 458-8230.

OTHER OFFICES

Aiken Tours, 1661 Nostrand Ave., Brooklyn, NY 11226; tel. (718) 856-7711, fax (718) 282-1152.

Edenbridge Travel, Edenbridge Plaza, 25 Fontenay Ct., Toronto, Ontario M9A 4W7, tel. (416) 249-8489, fax (416) 249-6436.

E.C. World Wide Travel, 18327 N.W. 7th Ave., Miami, FL, tel. (305) 653-7264/5.

Transatlantic Wings, Kensington, London W8 6NX, tel. 71-602-4021.

U.S. Sales: New York, tel. (212) 251-1717, fax (212) 545-8474.

also "Interisland Ferries" and "Boat Charters" under "Getting Around" later in this chapter). Chief among them is **Leeward Islands Air Transport (LIAT),** which currently operates regular service to 27 destinations throughout the Caribbean. LIAT is owned and operated by 11 English-speaking regional governments, with headquarters at V.C. Bird International Airport in Antigua.

Basically, LIAT flies to just about everywhere in the Lesser Antilles and in some cases is the only carrier. Check for special packages including their Caribbean Super Explorer, which allows unlimited travel for 30 days to any LIAT destination. Cost is about US$367. Other incentives include an Explorer fare, which allows three stopovers within 21 days with return to your point of origin for US$199, and discounts are offered for senior citizens and children. Contact LIAT through your travel agent or: LIAT, New York, tel. (212) 251-1717, fax (212) 545-8474; Alken Tours, Brooklyn, New York, tel. (718) 856-7711, fax (718) 282-1152; Edenbridge Travel, Toronto, tel. (416) 249-8489, fax (416) 249-6436; E.C. World Wide Travel, Miami, tel. (305) 653-7264/5; Transatlantic Wings, Kensington, London, tel. (071) 602-4021.

Additionally, LIAT maintains regional offices in all its Caribbean destinations. Headquarters address is V.C. Bird International Airport, P.O. Box 819, St. John's, Antigua, West Indies, tel. (809) 462-0700, fax (809) 462-2682.

Other regional airlines include **British West Indies Airlines International (BWIA),** pronounced "BEE-wee." BWIA, based in Trinidad, is currently a government-owned airline but is restructuring to become a publicly held company with shares offered on Caribbean stock exchanges. The airline's disadvantage is that it flies large transport jets and does not land on many of the Lesser Antilles' smaller islands. From Miami, New York, Toronto, Frankfurt, London, Zurich, and Georgetown (Guyana), BWIA flies to Antigua, Barbados, Grenada, St. Lucia, Sint Maarten, and Trinidad and Tobago, as well as Jamaica. BWIA does have a 30-day excursion pass—no destinations may be revisited except for connections—for about US$356, and you'll need to fix your itinerary before buying the ticket. Reservations can be made through travel agents or BWIA U.S.A., tel. (800) 538-2942 or (800) 327-7401; BWIA Canada, tel. (800) 283-2942; or BWIA International Airways, P.O. Box 604, Port of Spain, Trinidad, West Indies, tel. (809) 669-3000, fax (809) 669-1865.

Windward Islands Airways (Winair) operates out of Sint Maarten to the islands of Anguilla, Guadeloupe, St. Kitts, Nevis, St. Croix, St. Thomas, Saint-Barthélémy, Saba, and Sint Eustatius. The airline is a good bet when traveling in the Windwards, but offers few incentives and does not have the range of LIAT. Each island mentioned above has a Winair ticketing agent. The main office is at Princess Juliana Airport, on Sint Maarten, tel. (599) 522-313.

A dozen or so smaller, island-based airlines such as **Air Saint-Barthélémy, Air Martinique,**

MAJOR AIRLINES SERVING THE LESSER ANTILLES

NORTH AMERICA AND EUROPE TO LESSER ANTILLES HUBS, WITH TOLL-FREE NUMBERS

American Airlines: tel. (800) 433-7300.

Air Canada: tel. (800) 776-3000.

Air France: tel. (800) 237-2747.

Antigua Paradise Airlines: tel. (800) 299-8784.

British Airways: tel. (800) 247-9297.

British West Indies Air International (BWIA): tel. (800) 327-7401 or (800) 538-2942.

Continental Airlines: tel. (800) 231-0856.

KLM: tel. (800) 374-7747.

Lufthansa: tel. (800) 645-3880.

United Airlines: tel. (800) 241-6522.

NORTH AMERICA TO SAN JUAN, PUERTO RICO

Delta: tel. (800) 241-4141.

US Air: tel. (800) 428-4322.

Northwest Airlines: tel. (800) 447-4747

Trans World Airlines (TWA): tel. (800) 892-4141.

Kiwi International: tel. (800) 538-5494.

Carnival Airlines: tel. (800) 437-2110.

Air Guadeloupe and **St. Vincent Airways** operate regular, though limited, service to various nearby islands. As a rule, your LIAT ticket will be about the same cost as these anyway, and less expensive still if you've bought an excursion fare.

Keep in mind that virtually all Lesser Antilles islands charge an airport departure tax (if you've stayed for 24 hours or more) which may be payable in the local currency. Make sure to have that money put aside when checking in for your departure flight.

CRUISE LINES

First, a thought: If you really want to explore an island, to experience its culture and milieu, you probably won't do it on a cruise ship.

Cruising is a wonderful, relaxing experience and a great idea for a vacation. A cruise recalls the days of elegance and grandeur; the days when traveling was a major and costly undertaking. Today, cruises are within the reach of middle-class incomes, and the ships are teaming with families on holiday. All the better. Yet it is clear that an ocean cruise is not the means to the end, but is, for most, the end itself. The cruise is the thing, the port is the icing on the cake.

Still, having said that, we have to keep in mind that cruising on these floating hotels is a wildly popular way of visiting the Caribbean. Overall, the Caribbean saw more than nine million cruise ship passengers in 1993 (up from 8.2 million in 1991) compared to 12 million stayover visitors. In the Lesser Antilles, cruise ships stop at major ports from the Virgins in the north to Trinidad and Tobago in the south.

Typically, a cruise ship will stop at several ports, up to one per day, on a one- to two-week cruise. The ship visits each port for a few hours or for the day, generally enough time for passengers to disembark and go shopping, have lunch, and maybe visit some sights. (A note of caution: on the days cruise ships pull into port, you can be sure the price of many tourist-related items in the craft shops will be inflated. Ditto with taxi rates and other services. The key to getting your money's worth is to negotiate.)

CRUISE LINES SERVING THE LESSER ANTILLES

Carnival Cruise Lines, 3655 N.W. 87th Ave., Miami, FL 33178, tel. (305) 599-2600 or (800) 327-9501.

Celebrity Cruise Lines, 5200 Blue Lagoon Dr., Miami, FL 33126, tel. (305) 262-8322 or (800) 437-3111.

Clipper Cruise Line, 7711 Bonhomme Ave., St. Louis, MO 63105, tel. (800) 325-0010.

Club Med, 3 East 54th St., New York, NY 10022, tel. (212) 750-1687 or (800) 258-2633.

Commodore Cruise Lines, 800 Douglas Rd. Suite 700, Coral Gables, FL 33134, tel. (305) 529-3000 or (800) 832-1122.

Costa Cruise Lines, World Trade Center, 80 S.W. 8th St., Miami, FL 33130, tel. (305) 358-7352 or (800) 462-6782.

Cunard Line, 555 5th Ave., New York, NY 10017, tel. (800) 221-4770.

Dolphin Cruise Line, 901 South America Way, Miami, FL 33132, tel. (305) 358-2111 or (800) 222-1003.

Fantasy Cruise Lines, 5200 Blue Lagoon Dr., Miami, FL, tel. (305) 262-5411 or (800) 423-2100.

Norwegian Cruise Line, 95 Merrick Way, Coral Gables, FL 33134, tel. (800) 327-7030 or (305) 447-9660.

Princess Cruises, 10100 Santa Monica Blvd., Los Angeles, CA 90067, tel. (310) 553-1770.

Royal Caribbean Cruise Line, 1050 Caribbean Way, Miami, FL 33132, tel. (305) 539-6000.

Royal Viking Line, 95 Merrick Way, Coral Gables, FL 33134, tel. (305) 447-9660 or (800) 422-8000.

Windjammer Barefoot Cruises, P.O. Box 120, Miami Beach, FL 33119, tel. (305) 672-6453 or (800) 327-2601.

Winstar Cruises, 300 Elliott Ave., Seattle, WA 98119, tel. (800) 258-7245.

Cruise ships vary in size and capacity, as well as facilities offered. You know the routine: fine dining, shuffleboard, smiling celebrities, nightly entertainment, romance, et al. The average capacity is about 700 passengers, but in today's world of supercruisers—some so large that they cannot dock in some of the Caribbean's smaller ports—many carry up to 1,300 passengers. One of the Caribbean's most impressive mega-liners, the *Majesty of the Seas* of the Royal Caribbean Cruise Line (the largest line in the world), has 14 decks, 11 bars, a casino, a five-story lobby, and carries over 2,300 passengers—greater than the population of many of the Grenadines' islands.

Cruise ships from North America depart from New York, Florida, New Orleans, San Juan, and other East Coast points, as well as from Los Angeles and San Francisco. Cost varies, of course, with the length of cruise and the cabin chosen. Cabins vary in size and location on board. Another variant in the cruise cost is the addition of roundtrip flights and transfers from your home to the port of departure. An average cabin rate could be as little as US$800 per person based on double occupancy for a seven-night cruise, to as much as US$4000. Check with your travel agent for package deals and costs. It's best to find a travel agent who specializes in cruise packages. For further information on the ins and outs of cruising, send a self-addressed, stamped envelope requesting the pamphlet "Cruising Answers to Your Questions" to the **Cruise Lines International Association,** 500 5th Ave., Suite 1407, New York, NY 10110.

IMMIGRATION AND CUSTOMS

Island immigration regulations vary, but as a practical matter, only slightly. As a general rule most islands will proffer a two- or three-month visitor's visa for those with proper identification and proof of an onward ticket. Proper identification can be a license with photo, a voter registration card, or other solid proof of citizenship. A notable exception is Trinidad and Tobago, which requires a valid passport from everyone who wants to enter. *If you don't have a passport, try to obtain one;* it just makes life easier. In particular, this is true of Americans—when returning

home, U.S. customs officials require that you document your identity and U.S. citizenship. Several countries have been known to refuse to board Americans who do not have sufficient proof of U.S. citizenship. Among them are Barbados and Grenada. Again, a passport is the best documentation of all with which to travel.

Additionally, it is a good idea to make two photocopies of important travel documents such as passports, birth and marriage certificates, and so on. Leave one copy at home and travel with the other. In the event the original is lost or stolen, photocopies will help the process of replacement.

In general, advance entry visas are not necessary for citizens of the U.S., Canada, Britain, and most European countries. Citizens of other countries, including Australia, New Zealand, India, certain African states, and others should inquire well ahead before traveling to the Lesser Antilles.

Customs regulations throughout the islands vary, but as a general rule you will be allowed to bring in one carton of cigarettes and one quart of liquor duty free to most islands. Upon returning home you will, of course, encounter your own country's customs policies. Given the vast number of countries in the world, individual customs policies are too involved to detail here, but will almost always involve the amount of time you've spent in the Lesser Antilles, what you purchased there, and details regarding fruit, animal, and other agricultural products you may want to bring home. The first place to go for information is a reputable travel agent.

Customs regulations for U.S. citizens returning from the Lesser Antilles will vary according to the island from where you are returning, but as a general rule you will be able to return with US$400 worth of purchased items. U.S. citizens will find current information available in the pamphlet *Tips for Travelers to the Caribbean,* U.S. Government Printing Office, Washington, DC 20402, tel. (202) 783-3238. There is a small charge. Or, for a complete list of regulations covering the world, write to the U.S. Customs Service, P.O. Box 7407, Washington, DC 20044 for the free pamphlet *Know Before You Go.*

A note for everyone: The phrase "duty free" applies to the vendor from whom you've bought your perfume, jewelry, or trinkets. It means that the vendor was not required to pay duty on these items, and, ostensibly, has passed on these savings to you. It has nothing to do with your own country's duty requirements.

GETTING AROUND

ON THE ISLAND

Public transport in the Lesser Antilles has its quirks and intricacies, but if you take time to master the system you can travel inexpensively. Beware, however: buses tend to be irregular in places, are often overloaded, and are not always marked by destination. Some depart at regular times, others when it seems as if they've got a full load. Some make one-way trips to far ends of the larger islands, but don't return until the following day. Hence, mastering the system is a necessity.

Taxis are metered on some islands, and on others have government-regulated fares between destinations. Others operate as route taxis, as buses or between set points. It's always best to have a chat with your taxi driver to negotiate and set the price for your trip. Most taxis will rent themselves out by the hour or day for island tours and special trips. Again, negotiate the price before stepping into the taxi. Often, for those arriving by airplane, taxi rates are posted at the local airport for easy reference. Never get into a car where the driver has no identification as a bona fide taxi driver.

For those who prefer independence of movement, hiring a car or motorbike is perhaps the best option. Rates across the islands vary with the type of vehicle and the length of the rental, but you can figure on a range of US$30-60 per

The ferry from Saint-Martin (background) arrives at Blowing Point, Anguilla.

INTERNATIONAL TRAFFIC SIGNS

Curves Ahead

Right of Way Intersection

Stop and Yield

No Parking on left side

No Parking on right side

Yield

Dangerous Crossing

School Zone/ Children at Play

No Waiting

No Entrance

Danger

Right of Way Road

End Right of Way

No right turn

day for a small compact car. For those traveling in a group, splitting the cost of a rental can be an attractive option. A motorcycle or scooter is a bit less, about US$15-40 per day. Requirements for rental also vary, but in most cases you'll need a valid driver's license or international license, and, if you're not using a credit card, a deposit. Many islands require that you purchase a temporary visitor's license—in effect, a local license—at a cost of roughly US$4-8. Several islands won't rent to anyone under 25 years of age, and others won't rent to anyone over 65 years of age.

Driving in former and current British dependencies is on the left side of the road and in the French and Dutch islands is on the right. In Anguilla an odd situation occurs in that cars tend to be U.S.-manufactured with the steering wheel on the left, but people also drive on the left. This puts the driver near the shoulder of the road rather than the center. Practice in the parking lot before taking the car on the road; it will help.

INTERISLAND FERRIES

Traveling through the islands by interisland ferry is, unfortunately, a limited option. Ferries tend to connect selected islands that are in close proximity, such as Saint-Martin and Anguilla, or that are politically affiliated such as St. Kitts and Nevis, or St. Vincent and Bequia. Interisland ferry travel may be less expensive than flying, but the infrequency of departures and the time involved out on the ocean may diminish the allure of any savings. Still, worth mentioning here is the **Caribia Ferries** group that makes twice-weekly runs between Pointe-à-Pitre, Guadeloupe and Roseau, Dominica (four hours one-way), and Fort-de-France, Martinique and Castries, St. Lucia (two hours 45 minutes one-way). It is a big vessel, capable of transporting 1,200 passengers plus cars and trucks. It offers a lounge, cafeteria, sleeping cabins, cinema, and duty-free shops. Simple one-way tariff sans vehicle or sleeping cabin is FF150, about US$27. In Pointe-à-Pitre, contact 7 Rue Saint-John Perse, tel. (590) 89-42-67 or 89-42-69. In Fort-de-France, go to the offices at 31 Rue Lamartine.

BOAT CHARTERS

In many ways, the sea defines the Caribbean. Sailing is a fascinating way to get to know a large part of island living, and options are available for those with a yen to travel on the water. You can charter boats on the U.S. mainland, Puerto Rico, or the Virgin Islands, or from just about any island in the Lesser Antilles. Your options when chartering, which is really nothing more than renting, range from day charters to long-term charters, either with crew or bareboat, and with a group or alone.

Sailors tend to enjoy the British Virgin Islands and the Grenadines because of the relative closeness of the islands—you'll never leave one without seeing the next—and the hundreds of small harbors, inlets, and coves are perfect for dropping anchor for a day. Throughout the Lesser Antilles, however, sailing is popular in the extreme.

Crewed boats come with a professional crew, and have the options of meals, fishing and sporting equipment, perhaps a bar, and other choices. Costs vary with options and with the season, and they can be expensive, from US$2000 per week without provisions. Bareboat charters start at about US$900-1500 and require the renters to have sufficient sailing and anchoring experience to handle the boat. One option is to charter a bareboat and work as crew, but hire on a skipper who knows the ins and outs of the local waters.

Local boat charter companies are listed in the destination chapters, but the following good places to start include **The Moorings,** 1305 U.S. 19S, Clearwater, FL 33546, tel. (800) 437-7880 or (800) 535-7289; **Nicholson Yacht Charters,** 9 Chauncy St., Cambridge, MA 02138, tel. (800) 662-6606 or (617) 661-8174; **Stardust Marine Yacht Charters,** 2280 University Dr., Suite 102, Newport Beach, CA 92660, tel. (800) 634-8822 or (714) 650-0889, fax (714) 642-1318 (luxury, high-end yacht charters); **Virgin Islands Sailing, Ltd.,** P.O. Box 146, Road Town, Tortola, BVI, tel. (800) 233-7936, Florida tel. (800) 382-9666, local fax (809) 494-6774; and **West Indies Yacht Charters,** 2190 S.E. 17th St., Fort Lauderdale, FL 33316, tel. (310) 698-8972.

SPECIAL INTERESTS

DISABLED TRAVELERS

The Lesser Antilles' tourism infrastructure offers a little bit for everyone, but specialized travel situations need some research.

Disabled travelers will not, unfortunately, find much in the way of accessible facilities in hotels and general transport systems throughout the region. In particular, wheelchair-bound visitors will have to plan well in advance to ensure that their needs are met. Some hotels have accessible first-floor rooms, but not all have appropriate doorways, bathroom facilities, or light switches.

For information regarding regional facilities for disabled travelers, the following may be useful: **Society for the Advancement of Travel for the Handicapped,** 347 5th Ave., Suite 610, New York, NY 10016, tel. (212) 447-7284, fax (212) 725-8253; or **Travel Industry and Disabled Exchange,** 5435 Donna Ave., Tarzana, CA 91356, tel. (818) 343-6339. Both organizations charge fees for membership, and the Disabled Exchange publishes a quarterly newsletter (US$15 per year) with information on travel facilities for the disabled. Subscribers to *The Itinerary: The Magazine for Travelers with Physical Disabilities* may find occasional articles about Caribbean travel; contact P.O. Box 2012, Bayonne, NJ 07002-2012, tel. (201) 858-3400.

For an up-to-date regional resource, contact Derrick Palmer, director of **Disabled Persons International,** P.O. Box 220, Liguanea, Kingston 6, Jamaica, West Indies, tel. (809) 929-2073 or (800) 926-6776. Palmer and his organization have worked hard to promote disabled-accessible facilities throughout the Caribbean. Alas, he cannot yet recommend a wide variety of hotels in the Lesser Antilles that are truly accessible. The bottom line: decide on the hotel you would like to visit and call ahead for information on their facilities. Be specific with your questions.

SENIOR TRAVELERS

Older travelers will find most of the Lesser Antilles an easy and rewarding trip. For those who want to relax and stay by the sea, this is where the majority of hotels and other accommodations are anyway. For those who prefer mountain hiking, biking, and the outdoors existence, that experience is also available on almost every island. Since seniors are often retired and unencumbered by job obligations, they can travel at their leisure and take advantage of off-season rates and uncrowded streets. By and large, however, hoteliers and restaurateurs have not adopted the custom of giving discounts to seniors. Some do, but not as a rule. Still, bring identification for proof of age if you intend to seek out senior discounts.

Traveling with senior groups on charters or on special cruises organized by senior travel programs may be helpful. In the U.S., contact **American Association of Retired Persons (AARP),** 601 E St. NW, Washington, DC 20049, tel. (800) 441-2277 or (202) 434-2277 (annual dues US$8). Also try the **National Council of Senior Citizens,** 1331 F St. NW, Washington DC 20004, tel. (800) 322-6677 or (202) 347-8800 (annual dues US$12).

STUDENT TRAVELERS

Full-time students may be eligible for an **International Student Identity Card (ISIC),** which is available to students through colleges and universities, or by application to the Council on International Education Exchange, 205 E. 42nd St., New York, NY 10017, tel. (212) 661-1414. It's a picture identification card with which you can receive discounts at certain museums, theaters, and attractions, and it offers some medical insurance benefits. The use of this card is not widespread in the Lesser Antilles, but it is worth a try. There is a nominal fee, about US$14, for the card.

TRAVELING FAMILIES

Families are generally accommodated without a problem in the Lesser Antilles. Many hotels offer free rooms or discounts to families with children under 12 or so, as long as the child stays in the room with parents. Many offer baby-sitting services and special programs for kids.

Other resorts, particularly some of the all-inclusives, do not accommodate children under 18, or in some cases, under 16. Check the destination chapters for specifics.

Dozens of guidebooks on the market deal specifically with family travel. Recommended is *Best Places to Go,* Vol. I, by Nan Jeffrey (San Francisco: Foghorn Press). A popular newsletter called *Family Travel Times* is published by **Travel With Your Children,** 45 W 18th St., 7th floor, New York, NY 10011, tel. (212) 206-0688. The newsletter does not limit itself to the Caribbean but does have Caribbean features and publishes a Caribbean issue every September. Cost is US$55 per year for 10 issues.

Villa rentals may be advantageous for families because of the autonomy and, if you do your research, affordability. Most come with household help, including baby-sitters and cooks. The accommodations vary wildly, from apartments to large homes, and the rates vary according to size and location (see "Accommodations" above for villa listings).

SINGLE TRAVELERS

Singles have the widest range of possibilities in the Lesser Antilles, for the obvious reasons. Remember, most hotels give rates for single and double rooms, but others give rates per person based on double occupancy, which may not be the same as single occupancy. This is particularly true in the all-inclusive resorts that allow singles. Some all-inclusives will book single travelers into a room with someone of the same sex, unless a "guaranteed single" fee is paid, sometimes as much as US$75 per day. Some all-inclusive hotels allow couples only; singles need not apply. Refer to the specific destination sections of this book.

NATURISTS

Anyone who wants to doff their duds outdoors, either at the beach or on cruises, will find plenty of opportunities to do so in the Lesser Antilles. Clothing-optional beaches are found on Martinique, Guadeloupe, Saint-Barthélémy, Saint-Martin, Antigua, and, in a way, wherever you can find an isolated and safe stretch of beach. Remember, however, that certain cultures in the Lesser Antilles will be offended by public nudity; personal responsibility is important.

Entire resorts, such as the Club Orient on Orient Beach in Saint-Martin, offer clothing-optional living, and several cruise companies offer clothing-optional sailing experiences.

For sanctioned stitchless activities, several groups will be able to provide information and bookings. Start with **Travel Au Naturel,** 35246 US 19 N., Suite 112, Palm Harbor, FL 34684, tel. (800) 728-0185; or the cruise-oriented **Bare Necessities,** 504 Congress Ave., Suite 210, Austin, TX 78701, tel. (800) 743-0405. On the islands, try the Anguilla-based **Travel Naturally,** tel. (809) 497-6007, which represents clothing-optional activities and properties throughout the region.

One of the best single sources for information on worldwide clothing-optional activities, with substantial sections on the Caribbean, is Lee Baxandall's *World Guide to Nude Beaches & Recreation.* Write to N Editions, P.O. Box 132, Oshkosh, WI 54902.

GAY AND LESBIAN TRAVELERS

Gays and lesbians will find in the Lesser Antilles several island cultures that do not embrace homosexuality. While obviously homosexuality does exist in the islands, it is not a lifestyle that is always accepted or even tolerated on a level that would make openly gay visitors comfortable in all situations. This is not to say that gay and lesbian travelers should avoid the Lesser Antilles—the issue, rather, is one of your own comfort level in being open. Some islands are better about it than others—the French Antilles, which are host to large populations of Euro-French, come to mind. Trinidad and Tobago are somewhat more cosmopolitan than other islands and are therefore more tolerant. For more information about specific islands, and for gay and lesbian travel in general, a good source in the U.S. is the **International Gay Travel Association** in Key West, Florida, tel. (800) 448-8550. Call them and they will be able to put you in touch with a travel agent in your area who specializes in gay travel.

SPECIALTY TRAVEL INDEX

It seems worth repeating: an extremely useful publication for all travelers is the U.S.-based *Specialty Travel Index,* 305 San Anselmo Ave., San Anselmo, CA 94960, tel. (415) 459-4900, fax (415) 459-4974. The magazine comes out twice per year and lists more than 600 tour operators and outfitters that cater to special and not-so-special interests. Entries are cross-referenced by geographical region, personal interests and activities. Cost is US$6 per issue, or US$10 per year.

BOB RACE

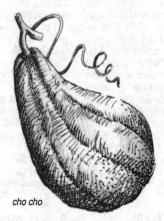

cho cho

BOB RACE

THE U.S. VIRGIN ISLANDS

INTRODUCTION

The U.S. Virgin Islands enjoy instant name recognition among travelers from North America—not surprising, considering the islands are U.S. territories and heavily promoted. They're our natural playgrounds, true tropical islands with all the enticements of exotic oddities, but with the comforts and, depending on your travel needs, trappings of familiarity.

The three main islands of the group, St. Thomas, St. John, and St. Croix, share similar histories and cultures, yet are as different as siblings in a family. St. Thomas, the islands' busy social and economic hub, is as dissimilar to sparsely populated, lush St. John as is a lawn—albeit a nice lawn—to a flower garden. To the south, large and, in some places, desert-like St. Croix is the U.S. Virgin Islands' museum archive, hosting the islands' historic towns of Christiansted and Frederiksted, as well as forts, ancient storage warehouses, and dozens of structures from colonial days.

In the end it's the people of these islands that tie them together, creating the single entity of the U.S. Virgin Islands. With a dual West Indian-American identity, both politically and culturally, you're as likely to see a richly colorful, loud street festival as you are an American fast-food

joint; you're as likely to hear the plaintive plucks and thumps of an island string band as you are the metal-driven wails of a rock-and-roll bar band. And it all makes sense, not like a theme park package dreamed up by Madison Avenue, but rather like the dynamic, fluid culture it is.

THE LAND

The U.S. Virgin Islands group comprises an estimated 70 islands, islets, and cays, of which three, **St. Thomas, St. John,** and **St. Croix,** are significantly large and inhabited. The islands are located just 40-70 miles (64-112 km) east of Puerto Rico, and 1,100 miles (1,771 km) southeast of the southern tip of Florida. Geologically, the U.S. Virgin Islands share origins with the British Virgin Islands, Puerto Rico, and the Greater Antilles; all are part of the extensive underwater shelf called the **Virgin Bank.**

St. Thomas is the hub of the three islands, separated from the Puerto Rican islands of Culebra and Vieques by the **Virgin Passage.** The island is small, measuring 13 miles (21 km) by three miles (five km) at its widest point, and 32 square miles (83 square km) in total area. It is, like the rest of the U.S. Virgin Islands, a volcanic island; hilly, rugged, and dramatic, with a jagged, irregular coast. Both St. Thomas and St. John are touched by the Atlantic on their north coasts, and by the Caribbean Sea on the south. St. Croix, to the south, sits squarely in the Caribbean Sea.

Crown Mountain on the western end of St. Thomas is the island's highest point at 1,556 feet (434 meters). The rest of the densely populated (60,000) island is characterized by lesser hills, lowlands to the south and southeast, and a dented coastline of small bays and inlets. Dozens of cays and islets surround the coast and include the national park entity **Hassell Island** in **St. Thomas Harbor** across from the south coast's **Charlotte Amalie** (pronounced a-MAHL-yah). Charlotte Amalie is the largest town on St. Thomas, the cruise-ship center, and the capital and administrative center of the territory.

St. John—some four miles (about six km) east of St. Thomas and seven miles (11 km) west of Tortola in the British Virgin Islands—is the smallest of the U.S. Virgin Islands, measuring nine miles (14 km) long by five miles (eight km) at its widest point, and 20 square miles (51 square km) in area. Of this, nearly 70%, or more than 10,000 land and offshore acres, is part of the Virgin Islands National Park system. The land, donated by the millionaire Laurance Rockefeller in 1956, is one of the oldest of the U.S. national parks. St. John, the least populated of the islands (2,900), is hilly and lush, with its highest point the central **Camelberg Peak,** at 1,193 feet (364 meters). The coast is lined with quiet bays and long beaches, some of the most compelling in the islands. The far western portion of St. John is home to **Cruz Bay,** the island's main center.

St. Croix, located some 40 miles (64 km) south of St. Thomas, is the largest of the U.S. Virgin Islands at 84 square miles (217 square km), or 28 miles (45 km) long by seven miles (11 km) wide. It is less dramatic than its sister islands, characterized by gently sloping hills, scattered semi-rainforest topography to the west, and dry areas of cacti and scrub in the southern and eastern sections of the island. **Christiansted** on the central north coast and **Frederiksted** on the west coast are home to the majority of the island's 60,000 population.

HISTORY

The U.S. Virgin Islands were settled by prehistoric Stone Age groups, and later Amerindian groups, long before Columbus and his crew made their dramatic, if erroneous, "discoveries" and assumptions about the New World. The Arawaks (also called Taino), the first to make their way from the Orinoco regions of South America, settled islands from Trinidad and Tobago in the southern Lesser Antilles to the northern Greater Antilles; they arrived in the U.S. Virgin Islands about A.D. 500. They were followed by the aggressive Caribs, who arrived not too long before Columbus charted the islands. Important archaeological discoveries at **Salt River Bay** in St. Croix indicate that the area was a major cultural center for various Amerindian groups.

11,000 Virgins

By the time Christopher Columbus came upon St. Croix during his second voyage in November 1493, the Caribs had taken control of the island. They called it Cibuquiera, or "Stony Land." Columbus sent a landing party—the first and only documented landing Columbus was to accomplish on what is now a U.S. territory—that took several Arawak slaves from the Caribs. Hours later, a Carib vessel approached Columbus's flagship, the *Niña,* and a fight ensued in which one Spaniard and one Carib were killed. This, in turn, was the first documented resistance of native peoples to the Old World explorers.

Columbus then thought it prudent to sail off, first to chart the island he called San Tomas, and then on to the larger Greater Antilles, driven by the quest for the gold of El Dorado and for a meeting with the ever-elusive Great Khan. On his departure, he dubbed the island Santa Cruz ("Holy Cross") and called the entire archipelago Las Once Mil Virgenes, or "The 11,000 Virgins," in honor of the British 4th-century Saint Ursula and her 11,000 virgins—yes, 11,000—murdered at the hands of the Huns at Cologne. Some historians contend that the name was actually Las Islas Virgenes; whatever the case, parts of the name stuck and the islands became associated with virgins.

While Columbus claimed the islands for Spain, the Spanish did little to colonize them over the next century. Instead, they used the islands as stopover points and as ready sources for Indian slave labor, which they imported to their mines and plantations in Puerto Rico and the larger islands. By the late 16th century, the conquered Caribs were virtually eliminated in the U.S. Virgin Islands.

The Europeans Arrive

Over the next century, the U.S. Virgin Islands were settled by the Dutch, the English, and the French, often simultaneously. St. Croix proved to be the touchstone, as it was agriculturally profitable and simply one of the larger islands in the vicinity. By 1645, the Dutch had left St. Croix, and by 1650, the Spanish had reclaimed the island and driven off the English. The Spaniards were in turn disposed of by the French, who in 1653 invited the Knights of Malta to settle and manage the island. The Knights then sold the island back to the French. Thus continued the schizophrenic history and cultural and linguistic paths that today define the entire Caribbean region.

During this period the tobacco, cotton, sugar, and indigo plantations of St. Croix begged for labor. The importation of African slaves commenced in 1673 and thereafter accelerated.

Also during this period, in 1666, the Danes, under the Danish West India and Guinea Company, claimed St. Thomas. Charlotte Amalie, first named Taphaus ("Tap House"), was founded in 1691. The name was later changed to honor the Danish queen. In 1694, the Danes claimed St. John, but continuing hostilities with the British on nearby Tortola prevented them from actually inhabiting the island until 1717. Then in 1733, two important events took place. First, the French sold St. Croix to the Danish West India and Guinea Company. Second, a massive slave rebellion on St. John—a result of harsh working conditions, a devastating drought, and a hurricane—put the island in the hands of Africans for six months. The rebellion was put down by the Danes, who were reinforced by French warships and troops. But it would be more than a century later before slavery was finally abolished in the Danish islands in 1848.

Having added St. Croix to their holdings, the Danish formed the Danish West Indies colony, and the islands prospered. St. Thomas, which had been named a free port in 1724, flourished as a center of trade and commerce—and as a center of pirate activities, including those of Edward "Blackbeard" Teach and Captain William Kidd. St. John hosted massive sugarcane and cotton plantations, before and after the slave rebellion, and St. Croix, then host to the Danish West Indies capital of Christiansted, also had an agricultural economic base.

The end of the 18th century was a time of great upheaval in Europe, and, in due course, the Caribbean. Denmark, a longtime ally of France, made the unfortunate but historically inevitable choice of siding with Napoleon against the English during the Napoleonic Wars. The British in the Caribbean saw this as an opportunity to expand their territory, and they attacked St. John in 1801 and occupied it for a year, then attacked again in 1807, holding it this time for seven years.

When the Danes regained St. John in 1815, the demise of the sugarcane industry and the great Lesser Antillean plantocracies was imminent. Sugar extracted from beets rather than the more expensive sugarcane found its way into the marketplace. Additionally, the great sailing cargo ships of the 18th and early 19th centuries were soon obsolete due to the innovation of steam ships. This rendered St. Thomas and other major Caribbean ports less important as stopover points. Agitation from abolition groups continued to undermine the slave trade. In fact, Denmark had already stopped its slave trade in 1802, but the subsequent British occupations had revived it.

The Danes Dump the Islands

After the final emancipation of slaves in 1848, the Danish West Indies, along with most of the Caribbean, entered a period of economic slump and massive migrations that saw freed slaves leave for plantation and construction work in Central America and elsewhere. By the 1870s, the Danes had entered a period of protracted negotiations with the U.S., seeking to unload their unprofitable and weighty Caribbean possessions. In 1917 the U.S., fearful of the sort of massive destruction wrought by the first world war and seeking a base from which to guard their new canal in Panama, bought the islands for US$25 million in gold. It was a good deal.

The U.S. ruled the islands a naval base until 1927, when citizenship was given to the islanders. The navy and army remained on the islands through WW II; today the U.S. Marine Corps still maintains airfields on St. Thomas and St. Croix. Soon after, universal suffrage was granted, roads and infrastructures were built, a university was established, and a national park was created on St. John. In 1932 the Organic Act introduced self-government to the U.S. Virgin Islands, and in 1968 the U.S. Congress passed an act allowing for greater internal rule with a governor elected by popular vote. Four years later, in 1972, the U.S. Virgin Islands sent their first elected delegate to congress.

PEOPLE AND CULTURE

The blend of European and African cultures in the U.S. Virgin Islands prevails in the language, food, place names, and culture of the islands. While the obvious trappings of Americanism are evident on the islands, in most ways this certainly isn't Kansas, Dorothy.

The residents of the U.S. Virgin Islands speak English, but with a Creole (sometimes called Calypso) twist. On St. Croix, pockets of Puerto Ricans speak Spanish. Spanish influences also affect the English of St. Croix to produce a Creole language and culture, called Cruzan (also the name of St. Croix's famous rum).

Place names such as Christiansted, Bonne Esperance, Vluck Point, Cruz Bay, and America Point testify to the wide range of nationalities that have left their mark on the islands. Likewise, predominant island religions include Roman Catholic, Anglican, Moravian, Episcopal, Jewish, and Lutheran, among others. Oddly, a small but significant group of Palestinians, primarily businesspeople, live and work on St. Croix.

West Indian culture, which is to say predominantly African blended with various European customs, is evident in the local foods such as *fungi* (a pasty cornmeal), goatwater (goat soup), *souse* (pig's head soup with lime juice), johnny cakes (fried bread), and the islands-wide *maubi* (tonic made from maubi tree bark with other herbs). Local vegetables include callaloo and okra. Fruits such as soursop, mango, *genip*, and papaya are grown or imported. Seafood is of course important to the U.S. Virgin Islands cuisine and includes various preparations of conch (conch fritters are a favorite), lobster, whelk, grouper, snapper and tuna. Other cultures in the modern U.S. Virgin Islands are also represented through their cuisine. You'll find world-class French, Italian, Chinese, East Indian, and more. American fast-food giants KFC and McDonald's also ply their wares here.

Holidays and Festivals

Holidays that keep cultural traditions strong include St. Thomas's annual post-Easter **Carnival,** held in late April. The Carnival features African customs such as drumming, dancing the energetic *baboula,* and exhibiting devils, *jumbies* (spirits or ghosts), and other figures through masquerades. The *mocko jumbi,* a stock comic-grotesque character likely to be

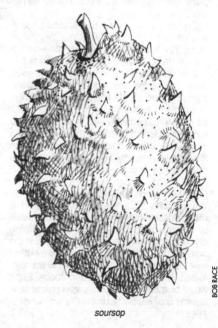

soursop

found on stilts and wearing a mirror, inhabits many an island festival. Carnival also features masquerade parades, feasts, calypso contests, French quadrille dancing, and steel bands.

Emancipation Day is celebrated in July. The sounds-like-a-California-thing **Organic Act Day,** in June, celebrates the granting of internal government to the U.S. Virgin Islands. **Transfer Day** in March celebrates the 1917 transfer of the island from Danish to U.S. possession. St. Croix hosts the two-week **Crucian Christmas Festival,** from Christmas Week through the first week in January, featuring feasts, parades, contests, French quadrille dancing, and Christmas festivities. The U.S. **Independence Day** (Fourth of July) has become St. John's version of Carnival, complete with a week of fireworks and the trappings of the St. Thomas Carnival.

Also celebrated are most U.S. federal and religious holidays such as Thanksgiving Day in November (as well as an additional Thanksgiving Day in October celebrating the end of hurricane season), Christmas, New Year's, Martin Luther King Jr. Day, Presidents' Day, Good Friday, Easter and Easter Monday, Memorial Day, Labor Day, and Columbus Day, as well as a half-dozen boating and other local sports festivals.

Dance and cultural troupes perform regularly on the islands; the **Caribbean Dance Company** can be seen locally and around the islands and at the **Reichhold Center,** tel. (809) 774-4482, of the University of the Virgin Islands in St. Thomas. The **St. Thomas Arts Council** (call the tourist office, tel. 809-774-8784) can be contacted for a full schedule of local folk art companies.

Personal Safety

A note about personal safety in the U.S. Virgin Islands: the current island milieu has not escaped crime such as petty theft and more serious capital crimes. Drugs, poverty, and just regular bad guys are all present, and they can combine to make trouble if you are not aware. Be streetwise: don't venture into unknown areas late at night, lock your valuables in the car or hotel safe, and don't leave items unattended on any beach.

GOVERNMENT AND ECONOMY

The U.S. Virgin Islands group, officially The Virgin Islands of the United States, is an unincorporated territory of the United States. The head of state is the U.S. president, and the islands combine to elect a non-voting representative to the U.S. House of Representatives. Within the internal government structure of the U.S. Virgin Islands, the executive is a governor, elected every four years, supported by a 15-member legislature of senators. The 122,900 citizens of the U.S. Virgin Islands are also citizens of the United States. The Democratic, Independent Citizens Movement, and Republican parties are the dominant island political groups.

There has been agitation in the past regarding the political status of the U.S. Virgin Islands. Some citizens would like to see full independence; some would like greater affiliation with the U.S., even statehood; others are happy with the present form of representation. Ongoing debates or referendums, however, do not seem likely to change the islands' status in the near future.

The economy of the U.S. Virgin Islands is reliant on U.S. aid and remittances from U.S. Virgin Islanders abroad, as well as from tourism. A Hess Oil refinery and an aluminum plant, both on St. Croix, provide some employment, but by far government and tourism are the main employers. The average minimum wage of the islanders is the same as on the U.S. mainland, about US$4.50 per hour, and the standard of living is higher than on most of the neighboring Lesser Antillean islands. Unemployment is low, about three percent at last census, against a labor force of approximately 50,000.

Tourism

Tourism accounts for about 60% of the U.S. Virgin Islands' gross domestic product, from a total of more than 1,900,000 visitors annually. Of this number, 34% are bonafide stayovers, while 66% are day visitors on cruise ships or yachts. St. Thomas is considered to be the number one cruise-ship stop in the Caribbean—an average of nearly two ships per day stop at Charlotte Amalie, while dozens per month also anchor at St. Croix. The islands' hotels have approximately 5,000 rooms available, and this figure is rising. In fact, the government and private sector launched a $250 million investment in 1988 for the upgrading of tourist facilities and islands' infrastructure to meet the growing demand.

Local territorial government and the public sector employ the most people, accounting for about one third of the islands' workforce. Agriculture employs few, but outstanding among them are the Senapol cattle breeders of St. Croix.

In 1989 Hurricane Hugo swept through the islands, rending, in particular, St. Croix. Damage was estimated at US$1 billion, and the islands were declared a disaster area. U.S. troops were sent in to control unrest and looting. With US$272 million spent in government disaster relief to date, the islands have nearly completely recovered.

PRACTICALITIES

WATER SPORTS

It is not easy to go anywhere in the U.S. Virgin Islands without finding water sports facilities. Many hotels have their own activities centers, as well as tennis facilities, which they will let non-guests use for a fee.

Diving and Deep-Sea Fishing

On St. Thomas: **Aqua Action Watersports,** tel. (809) 775-6285; **Coki Beach Dive Club,** tel. (809) 775-4220; and **Underwater Safaris,** tel. (809) 774-1350.

On St. John: **Cruz Bay Watersports,** tel. (809) 776-6234, and **Low Key Watersports,** tel. (809) 776-7048.

On St. Croix: **Dive St. Croix,** tel. (809) 773-3434, and **VI Divers,** tel. (809) 773-6045.

If you're interested in **deep-sea fishing,** start with **St. Thomas Sportfishing Center,** tel. (809) 775-7990, or **Sapphire Marina,** tel. (809) 775-3690. On St. Croix, call **St. Croix Marine,** tel. (809) 773-0289.

Sailing

Sailing the U.S. and British Virgin Islands is huge, and any number of charter companies will rent bareboat or crewed charters, power or sailboats, for day sails to monthly rentals. It is best to reserve this kind of activity before arriving on the island. If you're there already and just get the urge to sail, start with **Avery's Boathouse,** tel. (809) 776-0113, in Charlotte Amalie. As well, contact **VIP Yacht Charters,** 6118 Estate Frydenhoj #58, St. Thomas, U.S. Virgin Islands 00842-1402, tel. (800) 524-2015; or **Blue Water Cruises,** P.O. Box 1345, Camden, ME 04843, tel. (800) 524-2020, for a range of chartering possibilities.

SHOPPING

St. Thomas, more so than the other two islands, offers a wide range of duty-free shopping, art galleries, and so on. There are an estimated 400 shops that carry jewelry, electronic goods, crystal, linens, liquor, the usual suspects. What is more, no sales taxes apply on the islands, so good deals can get even better.

Charlotte Amalie is the main shopping district, particularly along the area bordered by **Main Street** and the **Waterfront Highway.** At **Emancipation Park** you'll find **Vendor's Plaza.** Near the cruise ship dock is **Havensight Mall,** and on the outskirts of town are a half dozen smaller malls and strip malls.

On St. John, shopping is at the **Wharfside Village** in Cruz Bay, near the ferry dock. A short walk from the National Park Visitor Center you'll find **Mongoose Junction,** a small center for artisans' shops and studios.

On St. Croix, Christiansted's **Market Square** on **Company Street,** as well as the rest of Company Street and **Strand Street,** offer dozens of shops.

GETTING THERE

Two airports service the U.S. Virgin Islands: the **Cyril E. King Airport** is located a few miles west of Charlotte Amalie in St. Thomas; the smaller **Alexander Hamilton Airport** in St. Croix is located on the southwest coast of the island. St. Thomas is the entry point for most flights, as well as a stopover for flights heading on to other Caribbean destinations. St. Croix is a stopover for small island-hoppers, particularly for flights from Puerto Rico, St. Thomas, and the British Virgin Islands. St. John is accessible by ferry, private boat, and helicopter.

American Airlines, local tel. (800) 474-4884, flies into St. Thomas several times daily, nonstop, from New York, Raleigh-Durham, Miami, and San Juan. That airline's **American Eagle,** tel. (809) 776-2560, flies to St. Thomas and St. Croix from its San Juan hub. **Delta,** tel. (809) 777-4177, connects to St. Thomas from Atlanta and Orlando. **Continental,** tel. (809) 777-8190, flies nonstop from Newark. The beleaguered and sometimes bankrupt **Sunaire Express,** tel. (809) 778-9300, schedules nonstop flights between St. Croix, St. Thomas, and San Juan, as well as Tortola and Virgin Gorda in the British Virgin Islands. A new airline, **Virgin Islands Paradise Airways,** tel. (800) 299-USVI, offers daily nonstop flights from Miami and Newark to St. Thomas and St. Croix.

There are no nonstop flights from Europe to St. Thomas or St. Croix. Flights have to be made to San Juan, Antigua, Sint Maarten, or any number of islands, with ongoing connections to the U.S. Virgin Islands on smaller airlines. Among those smaller airlines are **Air Anguilla,** tel. (809) 776-5789; **Aero Virgin Islands,** tel. (809) 776-8366; **BWIA,** tel. (809) 778-9372; **LIAT,** tel. (809) 774-2313; and **Winair,** tel. (809) 775-0183.

St. Croix can be reached from St. Thomas by Sunaire or American Eagle; the 25-minute flight costs about US$55 one-way.

A departure tax of US$3 is payable when leaving the U.S. Virgin Islands.

GETTING AROUND

Taxis and Buses

Taxis and buses are widely available on St. Thomas and St. Croix, less so on St. John. Cars can be rented on all three islands.

Taxis identified by a "TP" (St. Thomas) or "JP" (St. John) on the license plate are approved by the government. Beware of taxis without the proper identification; they may just take you for a ride—so to speak. Since taxis are unmetered, rates are set by the government and all drivers are required to carry a rate sheet in the vehicle. Ask for it and negotiate if the driver does not have it. You can pick up a copy of *St. Thomas This Week* or *St. Croix This Week* at the airport, which both contain published taxi rates. Rates in St. Thomas are set per one passenger, with reduced rates per person if the taxi is shared. For that reason, taxis can often take on the same status as buses. In St. Croix, the rates are for one or two persons with reduced rates for a shared vehicle. It is complicated, but not unmanageable. Drivers are generally honest and helpful.

Island tours will cost about US$30 for one or two persons, with US$12 per extra person. Taxi rates increase between midnight and 6 a.m. by US$1.50 per trip, and suitcases will cost about US$.50 per bag.

Your hotel will be able to arrange a taxi for you, but for those late night pickups in St. Thomas call **East End,** tel. (809) 775-6974; **Independent,** tel. (809) 776-1006; or **VI Taxi Association,** tel. (809) 774-4550. On St. Croix, call **St. Croix Taxi,** tel. (809) 778-1088; **Caribbean Taxi** in Christiansted, tel. (809) 773-9799; or **Combine Taxi** in Frederiksted, tel. (809) 772-2828.

Buses, both "country buses" and the shared "taxi-buses," or vans, are less reliable than taxis, but certainly inexpensive and available, most of the time. In St. Thomas the bus system runs more or less east to west, or from the east coast's **Red Hook** to Charlotte Amalie, through the airport and as far west as **Bordeaux Bay.** Cost is a flat US$1 for those big belching touring buses, or US$3 for the taxi-bus-vans. You'll figure it out. City buses run all about Charlotte Amalie and to the airport and university, at a flat 75 cents (US$). Buses start at about 6 a.m. and run until 9 p.m. There are no bus systems on St. John or St. Croix other than the shared vans.

Rental Cars

Rental cars are widely available for those 18 years or older. Some companies require that the driver be at least 25 years old. U.S. drivers will need a valid license, and others will need to obtain a temporary license through the rental company. Credit cards are almost universally accepted, and rates start at about US$30 per day. Most offer free mileage and free pickup and drop-off. On St. Thomas and St. Croix, just about any type of car will do as long as it has a trunk where you can lock up your valuables. On St. John, where dirt and gravel roads are the norm, a jeep or vehicle with high clearance is recommended.

Note: even though the U.S. Virgin Islands are a U.S. territory and use left-hand drive vehicles, driving is on the left—a legacy of the Danish system.

On St. Thomas, contact **ABC Auto,** tel. (809) 776-1222 or (800) 524-2080; **Budget Rent-A-Car,** tel. (809) 776-5774 or (800) 626-4516; **Cowpet Auto Rental,** tel. (809) 775-7376 or (800) 524-2072; **Discount Car Rental,** tel. (809) 774-2253 or (800) 522-3076; **Sea Breeze Car Rental,** tel. (809) 774-7200; or **Sun Island Car Rentals,** tel. (809) 774-3333 or (800) 233-7941.

On St. John, contact **St. John Car Rental,** tel. (809) 776-6103; **Spencer's Jeep Rental,** tel. (809) 776-6628 or 776-7784; or **Sutton Car Rental,** tel. (809) 776-6479.

On St. Croix, contact **Budget Rent-A-Car,** tel. (809) 778-9636 or 778-4663; **Hertz,** tel. (809) 778-1402 or 773-2100; **Midwest Auto Rental,** tel. (809) 772-0438; **Olympic-Ace Rent A Car,** tel. (809) 773-2208 or (800) 344-5776; or **Thrifty Car Rental,** tel. (809) 773-7200.

Ferry Service

Getting around the U.S. Virgin Islands and to the British Virgin Islands by ferry is fun and inexpensive; you'll meet an interesting crowd. And it's not a hassle in good seas—we are not talking long distances here. The passage from Red Hook on St. Thomas to St. John, for instance, takes about 15 minutes.

Ferries depart St. Thomas from Charlotte Amalie or from the National Park Dock at Red Hook, with destinations Cruz Bay in St. John, or Tortola or Virgin Gorda in the British Virgin Islands.

A Red Hook-to-Cruz Bay ferry departs about every hour from 6:30 a.m. until midnight, and the fare is US$3 for the 15-minute trip. Call **Transportation Services,** tel. (809) 776-6282.

The **Native Son,** tel. (809) 774-8685, departs from Red Hook to Tortola three times daily, cost US$31 roundtrip, about 30 minutes one-way.

A ferry from the docks in Charlotte Amalie to Cruz Bay in St. John departs about every two hours, at US$7 for the 45-minute trip. Other ferry runs include Charlotte Amalie to Tortola, Cruz Bay to Tortola, Red Hook to Jost Van Dyke (British Virgin Islands), and Charlotte Amalie to Virgin Gorda (British Virgin Islands). A number of private ferry companies, including **Dohm's,** tel. (809) 775-6501, will take you "anywhere, anytime."

ACCOMMODATIONS

Accommodations in the U.S. Virgin Islands run the full range from large resorts, hotels, guesthouses, and villas, to a couple of stunning campsites on St. John. Hotels and guesthouses will be listed in the island sections below. Prices in the following categories are per person, per night during the 15 December to 15 April high season: **Luxury** US$100 or more, **Moderate** US$50-100, **Budget** US$50 or less.

Rates are reduced by as much as 40% during the summer season. A government resort tax of 7.5% is charged at accommodations, and often a 10-15% service charge is added to the bill. Occasionally, an energy surcharge is also added. Most hotels accept major credit cards, but this is not always the case.

Villas

Private villas, cottages, condos, or apartments—often the best bet for families or large groups—are widely available on all three islands.

On St. Thomas contact **Chateau Dolce Villas,** P.O. Box 12149, Charlotte Amalie, St. Thomas, U.S. Virgin Islands 00801, tel. (800) 843-3566, fax (809) 776-4494; **Byrne Brown Realty,** P.O. Box 7967, Charlotte Amalie, St. Thomas, U.S. Virgin Islands 00801, tel. (809) 774-3300, fax 774-1556; **McLaughlin Anderson Vacations,** 100 Blackbeard's Hill, Charlotte Amalie, U.S. Virgin Islands, tel. (800) 537-6246 or (809) 776-0635, fax 777-4737; and **Ocean Property Management,** P.O. Box 8529, Charlotte Amalie, St. Thomas, U.S. Virgin Islands, tel. (800) 874-7897 or (809) 775-2600, fax 775-5901.

INFORMATION DIRECTORY

TOURISM INFORMATION

In the U.S., call (800) USVI-INFO. In Canada, the number is (800) 465-USVI.

Otherwise, write or call the U.S. Virgin Islands Division of Tourism:

P.O. Box 6400, Charlotte Amalie, St. Thomas, U.S. Virgin Islands 00804, tel. (809) 774-8784, fax 774-4390.

P.O. Box 200, Cruz Bay, St. John, U.S. Virgin Islands 00830, tel. (809) 776-6450.

P.O. Box 4538, Christiansted, St. Croix, U.S. Virgin Islands 00822, tel. (809) 773-0495, fax 778-9259.

225 Peachtree St. NE, Suite 760, Atlanta, GA 30303, tel. (404) 688-0906.

500 North Michigan Ave., Suite 2030, Chicago, IL 60611, tel. (312) 670-8784, fax 670-8788.

3460 Wilshire Blvd., Suite 412, Los Angeles, CA 90010, tel. (213) 739-0138, fax 739-2005.

2655 Le June Rd., Suite 907, Coral Gables, FL 33134, tel. (305) 442-7200, fax 445-9044.

1270 Avenue of the Americas, New York, NY, tel. (212) 332-2222, fax 332-2223.

900 17th St. NW, Suite 500, Washington, DC 20006, tel. (202) 293-3707, fax 785-2542.

33 Niagara St., Toronto, M5V 1C2, tel. (416) 362-8784, fax 362-9841.

2 Cinnamon Row, Plantation Wharf, York Place, London SW11 3TW, tel. (071) 978-5262, fax 924-3171.

EMERGENCY AND OTHER

Ambulance, tel. 922.

Fire, tel. 921.

Police, tel. 915.

Hospital, St. Thomas, tel. (809) 776-8311

Myrah Keating Smith Clinic, St. John, tel. (809) 776-6400.

Hospital, St. Croix, tel. (809) 776-6311.

American Express Representative, St. Thomas, tel. (809) 774-1855.

American Express Representative, St. Croix, tel. (809) 773-9500.

FedEx, St. Thomas, tel. (809) 776-8887.

FedEx, St. Croix, tel. (809) 778-8180.

Virgin Islands National Park Service, tel. (809) 775-6238.

On St. John try **Caribbean Villas,** P.O. Box 458, Cruz Bay, St. John, U.S. Virgin Islands 00831, tel. (800) 338-0987 or 776-6152, fax 779-4044; **St. John Properties,** P.O. Box 700, Cruz Bay, St. John, U.S. Virgin Islands 00831, tel. (800) 848-4397, fax (809) 776-6192; and **Vacation Homes,** P.O. Box 272, Cruz Bay, St. John, U.S. Virgin Islands 00831, tel. (809) 776-6094, fax 693-8455.

On St. Croix get in touch with **American Rentals and Sales,** 2001 Old Hospital St., Christiansted, St. Croix, U.S. Virgin Islands 00820, tel. (809) 773-8470, fax 773-8472; and **Island Villas,** 14A Caravelle Arcade, Christiansted, St. Croix, U.S. Virgin Islands 00820, tel. (800) 626-4512 or (809) 773-8821, fax 773-8823.

Camping

Camping is allowed on St. John, and it could be argued that the two campgrounds there, on Cinnamon Bay and Maho Bay, are among the finest in the Lesser Antilles. The beaches are long and fine and the setting tranquil. The campgrounds themselves offer anything from inexpensive bare sites to luxury tents or cottages with kitchenettes. **Cinnamon Bay Campground,** P.O. Box 720, Cruz Bay, St. John, U.S. Virgin Islands 00831, tel. (800) 539-9998 or (809) 776-6330, fax 776-6458, is the national park campground and has 125 sites along a half-mile white sand beach. The range is from bare sites (US$15 in off-season) to tented sites (US$44 in off-season) to cottages (US$56-60). Water sports, some handicapped facilities, and an open-air restaurant are also found on the facility. Next door is the privately owned **Maho Bay Camps,** P.O. Box 310, Cruz Bay, St. John, U.S. Virgin Islands 00831, tel. (800) 392-9004 or (809) 776-6240, fax 776-6504. The camp features 114 "tent-cottages," sort of the type you might see in a Lawrence of Arabia film, each with wood floors, kitchenettes, furniture, a porch, electricity, and rooms separated by screens. Toilets and showers are communal, and water sports facilities and a restaurant are also available. Cost is US$90 d in the winter season, US$60 d off season, more for each extra person. No credit cards are accepted.

Both campsites are extremely popular, particularly in the winter months, so contact them well ahead for reservations.

More information regarding accommodations is found in the island sections below, or through the **St. Thomas-St. John Hotel Association,** tel. (809) 774-6835, and the **St. Croix Hotel and Tourism Association,** tel. (800) 524-2026 or (809) 773-7117.

MONEY, HOURS, AND COMMUNICATION

The currency of the U.S. Virgin Islands is the U.S. dollar. If you'd like to change traveler's checks, do so at your hotel or at the bank. Banks give better rates and are generally open Mon.-Thurs. 9 a.m.-3 p.m., and Friday 9 a.m.-5 p.m.

Government offices and many businesses are open 9 a.m.-5 p.m., and shops, particularly in Charlotte Amalie and Christiansted, may remain open in the evening if a cruise ship is docked in town.

The area code for the U.S. Virgin Islands is "809" followed by a seven-digit number. Toll-free "800" numbers are also utilized by hotels, car rental agencies, and other businesses.

The U.S. Virgin Islands postal system is no different than that on the mainland. Internal U.S. postal rates apply (US$.32 for a letter, US$.20 for a postcard), as do U.S. postal rates for packages and mail to foreign destinations.

Newspapers from the mainland—New York and Miami for the most part—are available daily, as is *The International Herald Tribune* and local newspapers. The *VI Daily News* is published every day except Sunday. Be sure to pick up its weekend edition, with listings of local goings on, music, shows, and special events. The free tourist papers *St. Thomas This Week* (includes St. John) and *St. Croix This Week* are available at tourist stands and shops throughout the islands.

The literary magazine *The Caribbean Writer,* started in 1987, is a University of the Virgin Islands publication. It has published the works of Derek Walcott and poets Marvin Williams and Paul Keens-Douglas, among many others.

Cable TV is available and includes a local commercial station as well as a local PBS station, or you can tune in to a half-dozen radio stations.

ST. THOMAS

It is not easy, early in a trip to the U.S. Virgin Islands, to overcome the sense that St. Thomas in particular is little more than a large, albeit exotic, side street off the North American vacation boulevard. From the ubiquitous McDonald's to the Hard Rock Cafe to the surgeon general's warning on cigarette packs, it seems as if the U.S. has come to stay. And it has. The U.S. Virgin Islands, as territories of the U.S., are not likely to eschew the accoutrements of that status. For some visitors, this is the appeal.

Yet the island, for all the trappings of North American familiarity, is distinctly West Indian; the people, their language and culture, and their history reflect this.

Of course, the magnificent beaches also count for something. All are reminders that the mainland has indeed been left behind. This is truer the farther one gets from Charlotte Amalie in St. Thomas, and truer still as one leaves St.

Thomas for its sister islands St. Croix and St. John; there is much to recommend here. The distinctions between the major islands, as well as possibilities for exploring the nearby British Virgin Islands, make for a wide array of choices.

BEACHES

All beaches in the U.S. Virgin Islands are open to the public, yet some are fronted by hotels and resorts that offer facilities for guests only. Fees for parking or beach use are charged in some areas, usually no more than US$4 per day.

On St. Thomas, an estimated 44 talcum-white sand beaches make the island one of the better beach islands in the Lesser Antilles. Among the best is **Coki Beach** in the northeast, offering water sports. However, it is often crowded with cruise ship passengers. Next door on the same

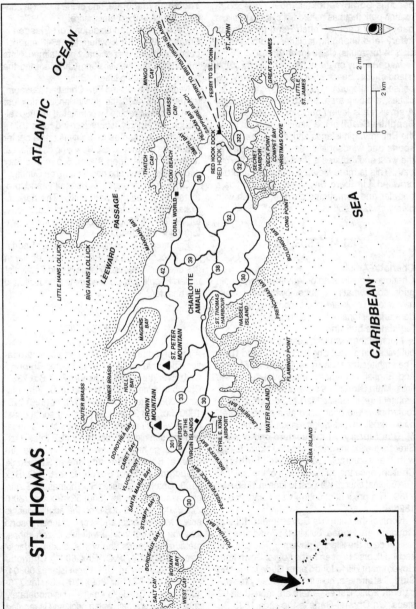

© MOON PUBLICATIONS, INC.

ST. THOMAS

beach is **Coral World**, tel. (809) 775-1555, a marine park that has nature trails, turtle pools, a baby-shark pool, a Touch Pond for kids, an aviary, and changing facilities. Admission is US$14 for adults, US$9 for children.

Magens Bay on the north shore is one of the island's nicer beaches. It's a wide, roomy expanse, with lifeguards, water sports, changing facilities, a picnic area, beach bars, and shops. A small fee is levied per person and per car. **Sapphire Beach** at the island's east end faces the British Virgin Islands and is a popular water sports and windsurfing spot. **Stumpy Bay** at the west end requires a short walk from the car park. This is more isolated, but quiet and uncrowded. **Lindberg Bay**, near the airport, is a popular and sometimes crowded beach with plenty of water sports.

ISLAND SIGHTS

Charlotte Amalie

Charlotte Amalie is an orderly town, laid out in grids, somewhat hilly, but enjoyable and easily navigated. The **Waterfront** is bustling with vendors and historic buildings, including the 1874 **legislature building.**

Much of the town was destroyed—not once, but twice—in devastating fires in 1802 and 1804. The architecture today reflects Danish, French, and English influences, most post-dating the fires. **Main Street** has several examples of this architecture, including **Market Square,** an iron-roofed structure once used as a slave market, now a produce and trinket market, and the **Enid M. Baa Library.** At the eastern end of Main Street is the extension street called **Norre Gade,** with the cream-colored **Frederick Lutheran Church,** once the official church of the islands. The original church was lost to fires in 1750 and 1789. The present structure was completed in 1826.

North of the church is **Government Hill** and **Government House,** built in 1867 and now the residence of the islands' governor. The first and second floors are open to the public. Down from Government Hill to **Lille Tarne Gade** is the **"99 Steps" staircase,** built in the 1700s by the apparently ironic Danes—there are more than 99 steps. On **Crystal Gade** is the circa 1833 **St.** **Thomas Synagogue,** one of the oldest in continuous use in this hemisphere.

South from Norre Gade on **Fort Plasden** is **Emancipation Park,** where the 1848 emancipation of slaves was officially proclaimed. Note the bust of the Danish King Christian and the small replica of the Liberty Bell.

Nearby is the rust-red **Fort Christian Museum,** tel. (809) 776-4566, the oldest standing structure in St. Thomas, reputedly completed in 1680 (although, confusingly, a frontpiece indicates 1671). The fort was used as an administrative center and, more recently, a jail. Now it holds historical displays and is open 9 a.m.-5 p.m. Monday through Saturday, and noon-4 p.m. on Sunday.

Offshore in the harbor is **Hassell Island,** protected as a national park entity. The park includes military ruins and an old shipyard. A ferry, tel. (809) 774-9652, makes runs from the waterfront to the island.

For more on recreation, see "Water Sports" and "Shopping" under "Practicalities" earlier in this chapter. See also "Holidays and Festivals" under "People and Culture" in the Introduction to this chapter.

ACCOMMODATIONS

A few standouts in St. Thomas accommodations deserve special mention here. **Bolongo Club Everything Beach Resort,** P.O. Box 7337, Charlotte Amalie, St. Thomas, U.S. Virgin Islands 00801, tel. (800) 524-4746 or (809) 775-1800, fax 775-3208, is on a great south-coast beach with all amenities and sports. It's huge, and you can elect all-inclusive or EP rates. Luxury. Bolongo has other resorts on the island, another at Bolongo Bay and one at Red Hook. **Frenchman's Reef Beach Resort,** P.O. Box 7100, Charlotte Amalie, St. Thomas, U.S. Virgin Islands 00801, tel. (800) 524-2000 or (809) 776-8500, fax 776-3054, on the south coast is now a Marriott hotel and is one of those resorts that you can get lost in, with two dozen shops, restaurants, sports, the works. Luxury. **Blackbeard's Castle,** P.O. Box 6041, Charlotte Amalie, St. Thomas, U.S. Virgin Islands 00804, tel. (800) 344-5771 or (809) 776-1234, fax 776-4321, is near Charlotte Amalie. This moderately priced resort is small, with a pool, and is reputed

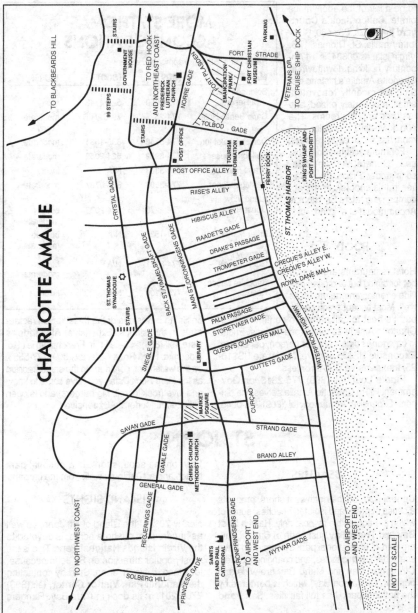

CHARLOTTE AMALIE

© MOON PUBLICATIONS, INC.

to be a lair of the eponymous pirate. **Calico Jack's Courtyard Inne,** P.O. Box 460, Charlotte Amalie, St. Thomas, U.S. Virgin Islands 00804, is a 17th-century building downtown in Charlotte Amalie's historic district; it's recently renovated, small, moderately priced, and features only six rooms. The pub downstairs is popular. One room has handicapped access.

For more accommodations, see "General Accommodations" under "Practicalities" earlier in this chapter, or the accompanying "More St. Thomas Accommodations" chart.

FOOD

Hotel restaurants are a good bet for dining out and often provide evening entertainment as well. Most accept credit cards, but it's best to call ahead to confirm and, in Charlotte Amalie, to make reservations. Prices in categories below are per person, per entree: **Expensive** US$25 or more, **Moderate** US$10-25, **Inexpensive** US$10 or less.

Fiddle Leaf, tel. (809) 775-2810, on Government Hill in Charlotte Amalie serves fine dinners. Expensive. **Romanos,** tel. (809) 775-0045,

MORE ST. THOMAS ACCOMMODATIONS

Rates per s, EP when applicable, winter

NAME	(809)	(800)	TARIFF
Bolongo Beach Villa Resort	775-1000	524-4746	luxury
Carib Beach Hotel	774-2525	79-CARIB	moderate-luxury
Danish Chalet Inn	774-5746	635-1531	moderate
Galleon House	774-6952	524-2052	moderate
Grand Palazzo	775-3333	N/A	luxury
Heritage Manor	774-3003	828-0757	moderate
Island View Guest House	774-4270	524-2023	budget-moderate
Miller Manor	774-1535	N/A	budget-moderate
Ramsey's Guest House	774-6521	N/A	budget-moderate
Sapphire Beach Resort	775-6100	N/A	luxury

on Smith Bay is one of the finest Italian restaurants in the islands. Expensive. **Alexander's Cafe,** tel. (809) 776-4211, in Frenchtown is chic. Moderate. **Hard Rock Cafe,** tel. (809) 777-5555, on the waterfront, continues in the same tradition as the Hard Rock Cafes you have come to know and love (rock 'n' roll, big burgers) and is open until 2 a.m. Moderate-Expensive.

ST. JOHN

BEACHES

Caneel Bay, on the northwest shore, presents a series of pretty and isolated beaches, some of which are accessible by boat only. **Hawks Nest Bay** and **Trunk Bay,** just north of Caneel Bay, are part of the national park system, and have snack bars, picnic tables, and changing facilities. **Cinnamon Bay** and **Maho Bay** are wide and popular. Cinnamon Bay, which is bordered by the national park, has full facilities. **Salt Pond**

Bay, on the south shore, is a national park beach and a 10-minute walk from the carpark.

ISLAND SIGHTS

Nearly 70% of the island of St. John, as well as hundreds of offshore acres, is devoted to the **Virgin Islands National Park.** This is the most popular attraction on St. John because, let's face it, it is St. John. Start by contacting the **National Park Visitor Center,** tel. (809) 776-6201, at its dock in Cruz Bay. Rangers are there and will help in planning hikes, walks, and excursions. The park has 22 trails, all self-guided save for the **Reef Bay Trail,** which starts at the center of the island and heads south to the sea. Along the way you'll see rainforest-like flora, petroglyphs, and old plantation buildings from the Reef Bay Plantation. The ranger is there to explain it all. The visitor center stocks pamphlets that illustrate the trails.

ACCOMMODATIONS

In addition to the campsites, St. John has a few hotels and a handful of guesthouses and cottages. The best are mentioned here. **Caneel Bay,** P.O. Box 720, Cruz Bay, St. John, U.S. Virgin Islands 00831, tel. (800) 929-8889 or (809) 776-6111, fax 693-8280, has 171 luxury rooms—no phones or television, with fans, not air-conditioning—on some of the nicest beaches on the island. This luxury place offers ports, water sports, and a pool. **Hyatt Regency St. John,** P.O. Box 8310, Cruz Bay, St. John, U.S. Virgin Islands 00831, tel. (800) 233-1234 or (809) 693-8000, fax 693-8888, south of Cruz Bay is the largest hotel on the island, with nearly 300 rooms and suites, all amenities, and a pool that could swallow a small country. Luxury. **Cruz Inn,** P.O. Box 566, Cruz Bay, St. John, U.S. Virgin Islands 00831, tel. (800) 666-7688 or (809) 693-8688, fax 693-8590, wins the award for clever names. The small, comfortable inn is in town, good location. Moderate.

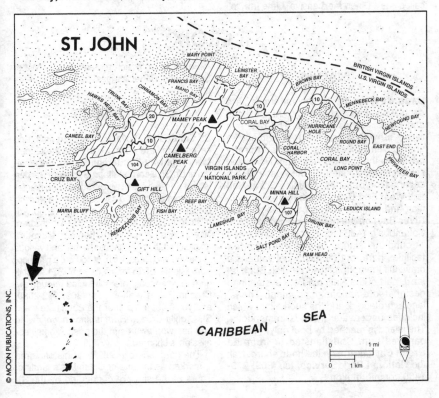

For more accommodations, see "General Accommodations" under "Practicalities" earlier in this chapter and the "More St. John Accommodations" chart here.

MORE ST. JOHN ACCOMMODATIONS

Rates per s, EP when applicable, winter

NAME	(809)	(800)	TARIFF
Cruz Bay Villas	776-6416	N/A	moderate-luxury
Inn at Tamarind Court	776-6378	221-1637	budget-moderate
Raintree Inn	693-8590	666-7449	moderate
Serandip Condos	776-6646	N/A	moderate-luxury

FOOD

The Fish Trap, tel. (809) 776-9817, in downtown Cruz Bay does the seafood thing, and does it well. Moderate. **Joe's Diner,** tel. (809) 776-6888, is uptown from the dock and, whatever you think of the food (and it's just fine), you have to love a place called Joe's Diner. Inexpensive. **Lime Inn,** tel. (809) 776-6425, downtown is open-air, popular. Moderate. **JJ's Texas Coast Cafe,** tel. (809) 776-6908, is the place for Tex-Mex. The small, two-street town of **Hercules** is good for West Indian Creole cuisine.

ST. CROIX

BEACHES

Cane Bay, on the northwest shore, is a popular snorkeling spot with plenty of shade and water sportss facilities. The beach is rarely crowded, and the reef is close to shore. **Sandy Point** is a long and pretty beach on the island's west end. North and south of Frederiksted, on the west end, are several long beaches including **Sprat Hall** and **West End Beach Club,** both with facilities and rentals. **Columbus Beach (Salt River Bay)** on the north shore is the site of Columbus's 1493 landing on St. Croix; see "Around the Island," below. There are few facilities here, but the historical value is a draw. Off the northeast shore, visit **Buck Island,** part of the National Park system and designated a national monument. The island is protected, and the snorkeling, which includes underwater trails, is tremendous. The island is reached by boat only, with departures from Christiansted or from the **Green Cay Marina** on the north shore. Call the **National Park Service,** tel. (809) 773-1460, for information.

For more on beach recreation, see "Water Sports" under "Practicalities" earlier in this chapter.

ISLAND SIGHTS

St. Croix can be covered in a short time, and several sites are worth visiting. On the **Queen Mary Highway (Centerline Road),** the western end's **St. George Village Botanical Garden** is built on the ruins of an old sugarcane plantation. There are trails, a cactus garden, a working blacksmith shop, displays, and a gift shop. Admission is US$4 for adults, US$2 for children. Nearby is the **Whim Plantation and Museum,** an old plantation greathouse, a mill, and various plantation structures. With, of course, a gift shop. Admission is US$5 for adults and US$1 for children. Guided tours are conducted through the **Cruzan Rum Distillery,** tel. (809) 772-2080, and you'll get a nip after the 20-minute walk. St. Croix's Cruzan Rum is known worldwide and has won awards in the past. A small admission is charged.

The north shore's Salt River historic area is marked as the site of Columbus's landing. Tours of the site are conducted by the **St.**

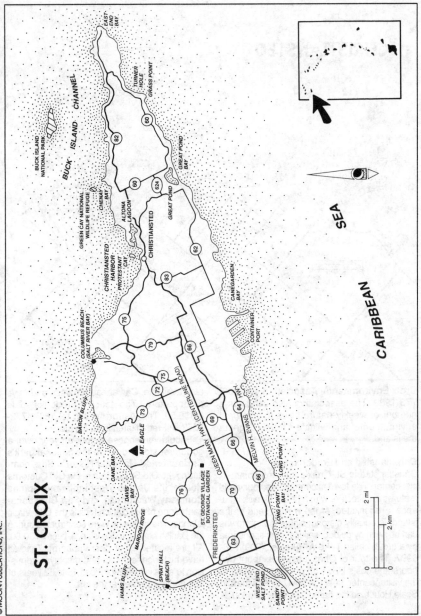

ST. CROIX

© MOON PUBLICATIONS, INC.

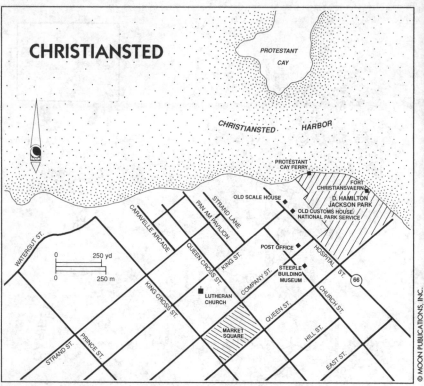

Croix Environmental Association, tel. (809) 773-1989. The association also conducts a number of weekly nature hikes to important environmental and wildlife sites throughout the island.

Christiansted and Frederiksted
Christiansted is St. Croix's hub and commercial center. The town is compact and busy and features architecture with a heavy Danish influence. Frederiksted, at the western end of the island, is equally historic; sights in both towns can be seen by guided walking tours sponsored by a group called **Take-A-Hike,** tel. (809) 778-6997. The tour of Christiansted is about two hours and costs US$5.50 per person; meet at the visitor center, near the post office at the Old Scale House on the harbor. An extended tour is

also available. Call ahead for times and days of departure. The tour of Frederiksted is US$6.50. The **visitor center,** tel. (809) 772-0357, in Frederiksted is on the pier.

Should you choose to tour on your own, a good first stop would be the national park's **Christiansted National Historic Site,** comprising the **Old Scale House,** the **Old Customs House,** the **Danish West India and Guinea Company Warehouse,** and **Fort Christiansvaern,** one of five Danish forts in the U.S. Virgin Islands. The buildings were constructed during the Danish heyday in the islands, circa 1730-80. All are located on or near the harbor, and all have historical exhibits and displays. Admission to sites is US$2 for those 16 to 62 years of age and is collected at the fort.

ACCOMMODATIONS

Most of St. Croix's hotels and resorts are located along the central north shore, east and west of Christiansted. Among the island's best: **Hotel on the Cay,** P.O. Box 4020, Christiansted, St. Croix, U.S. Virgin Islands 00821, tel. (800) 524-2035 or (809) 773-2035, fax 773-7046, is a small resort on an offshore cay in the harbor, great beach, pool, tennis, restaurants, regular ferry service to town. Luxury. **Carambola Beach Resort,** P.O. Box 3031, Kingshill, St. Croix, U.S. Virgin Islands 00851, tel. (800) 333-3333 or (809) 778-3800, fax 778-1682, is just west of town on Davis Bay. It's large and resorty, with two restaurants and a good beach. Luxury.

The Frederiksted Hotel, 20 Strand St., Frederiksted, St. Croix, U.S. Virgin Islands 00841, tel. (800) 524-2025 or (809) 773-9150, fax 778-4009, is a 40-room hotel downtown, the best place to stay, a few blocks from the pier and a block from the water. Moderate.

For more accommodations, see "General Accommodations" under "Practicalities" earlier in this chapter and the "More St. Croix Accommodations" chart, following.

FOOD

Apart from the hotels, St. Croix has a bit less to choose from than St. Thomas. Still, you won't go hungry on the island. **Antoine's,** tel. (809) 773-0263, on the wharf in Christiansted serves fine seafood. Moderate. **Stixx on the Waterfront,** tel. (809) 773-5157, has a raw bar, pizzas, sandwiches, great place to down a few brews or a Cruzan rum punch. Inexpensive-Moderate. **The Chart House,** tel. (809) 773-7718, is also on the wharf, good steaks and seafood. Moderate-Expensive. **The Berlin Wall,** tel. (809) 773-4010, might sound like mortar and barbed wire, but the small deli serves great sandwiches and some—here's a surprise—German specialties. Breakfast and lunch only, no credit cards. **Cheeseburgers in Paradise,** tel. (809) 773-1119, is not owned by Jimmy Buffett, as far as we know, but serves large burgers, burritos, salsa and chips, and, of course, margaritas. It's open until 11 p.m. daily; no credit cards.

MORE ST. CROIX ACCOMMODATIONS

Rates per s, EP when applicable, winter

NAME	(809)	(800)	TARIFF
Anchor Inn Hotel	773-4000	524-2030	moderate-luxury
The Breakfast Club	773-7383	N/A	budget
The Buccaneer	773-2100	223-1108	luxury
Caravelle Hotel	773-0687	524-0410	moderate
Danish Manor Hotel	773-1377	524-2069	moderate
Hilty House	773-2594	N/A	moderate
Prince Street Inn	772-9550	524-2026	budget
St. Croix by the Sea	778-8600	524-5006	luxury
Sprat Hall Plantation	772-0305	843-3584	luxury
Tamarind Reef Hotel	773-4455	619-0014	luxury

BOB RACE

THE BRITISH VIRGIN ISLANDS
INTRODUCTION

The British Virgin Islands, or B.V.I., have been and remain happily unencumbered by what often appears to be a Caribbean-wide scramble for the tourist dollar. This does not mean visitors are unwelcome—the British Virgin Islands receive thousands per year, most of whom are either on yachts or wishing they were. And it does not mean this is the only group of islands in the region that has maintained a relatively quiet serenity in the face of rapid regional growth. It is just that they do it well. The expressed policy of the tourism authorities is to maintain the integrity of the natural environment, which has everything to do with the sea around the 60 or so islands, cays, rocks, and volcanic blips that comprise the striking archipelago. No hotels reach higher than two stories, about the height of the tallest palm tree. The British Virgin Islands are among the last places left in the region where the phrase "getting away from it all" applies more often than not. The main island of Tortola is home to several fine beaches and hotels, and the sleepy capital of Road Town is the extent of the British Virgin Islands hype. The islands host no casinos, no large nightclubs, and, for that

matter, no large towns. It is the sea, the sailing, the diving, and the uncanny beauty of the beaches and shores that attract visitors to the islands.

THE LAND

The British Virgin Islands lie in a sort of horizontal chain beginning 50 miles (80 km) east of Puerto Rico, just east of their sister islands, the U.S. Virgin Islands. A larger archipelago, a "parent" archipelago comprising the U.S. and British Virgin Islands as well as the Puerto Rican islands of Culebra and Vieques, lies on the **Virgin Bank,** a huge underwater shelf that encompasses the islands and waters stretching east of Puerto Rico and the Greater Antilles, to which it is geologically related.

The **Sir Francis Drake Channel** separates the Jost Van Dyke-Tortola group in the north from the Virgin Gorda string in the south. Virtually the entire group is of volcanic origin, save for Anegada, a flat coral formation at the far northeast end of the chain.

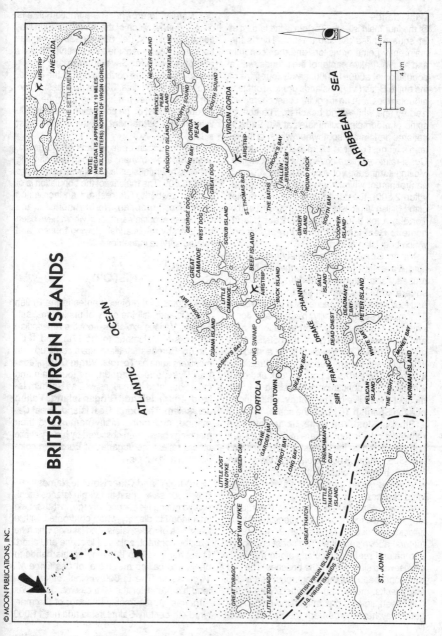

BRITISH VIRGIN ISLANDS

© MOON PUBLICATIONS, INC.

ATLANTIC OCEAN

CARIBBEAN SEA

NOTE:
ANEGADA IS APPROXIMATLY 10 MILES
(16 KILOMETERS) NORTH OF VIRGIN GORDA.

AIRSTRIP

ANEGADA

THE SETTLEMENT

4 mi

4 km

0

0

NECKER ISLAND

PRICKLY PEAR ISLAND

EUSTATIA ISLAND

NORTH SOUND

MOSQUITO ISLAND

LONG BAY

SOUTH SOUND

GORDA PEAK

VIRGIN GORDA

GREAT DOG

GEORGE DOG

WEST DOG

SCRUB ISLAND

ST. THOMAS BAY

AIRSTRIP

CROOK'S BAY

FALLEN JERUSALEM

THE BATHS

ROUND ROCK

SOUTH BAY

GINGER ISLAND

COOPER ISLAND

GREAT CAMANOE

LITTLE CAMANOE

BEEF ISLAND

AIRSTRIP

BUCK ISLAND

SALT ISLAND

DEADMAN'S BAY

WHITE BAY

PETER ISLAND

DEAD CHEST

SIR FRANCIS DRAKE CHANNEL

LONG SWAMP

SEA COW BAY

ROAD TOWN

TORTOLA

BRANDYWINE BAY

GUANA ISLAND

JOSIAH'S BAY

PELICAN ISLAND

THE BIGHT

MONEY BAY

NORMAN ISLAND

CANE GARDEN BAY

CARROT BAY

LONG BAY

FRENCHMAN'S CAY

LITTLE THATCH ISLAND

GREAT THATCH

LITTLE JOST VAN DYKE

GREEN CAY

JOST VAN DYKE

GREAT TOBAGO

LITTLE TOBAGO

ST. JOHN

BRITISH VIRGIN ISLANDS
U.S. VIRGIN ISLANDS

Main Islands

Of the four main islands, **Tortola** is the largest at 21 square miles (54 square km). This is the main entry point for visitors and the economic and administrative center of the islands, with a population of about 13,000, nearly four-fifths of the entire British Virgin Islands group. Tortola is mountainous with an irregular coast characterized by fine white-sand beaches. The central spine of mountains culminates at **Mt. Sage,** a national park in the southwest, which is the island's highest point at 1,780 feet (542 meters). Quasi-rainforest flora covers the mountainside. Moving southeast, you'll come to **Road Bay,** a natural harbor which hosts **Road Town** (population 2,500), the capital and business center of the British Virgin Islands. At the far east end of Tortola, a toll bridge connects **Beef Island,** home to **Beef Island International Airport,** which both islands share.

Virgin Gorda is an extremely irregular island; it's really three islands connected by isthmuses, for a total of eight square miles (21 square km). The eastern section is low-lying and features several beaches and outlying cays. The middle section is hilly, rugged, and dominated by **Gorda Peak,** another national park and the island's highest point at 1,359 feet (414 meters). The southern section is flat and somewhat arid, with several beaches and attractions, including **The Baths,** a popular rock and cave formation. The population of the island is 1,500, most of whom live in **The Valley,** which incorporates **Spanish Town,** in the south.

Smallish **Jost Van Dyke,** named after the reputed pirate, is four square miles (10 square km) of mostly hills, the highest at just over 1,000 feet (305 meters). The settlement at **Great Harbour** is home to most of its 200 inhabitants, who are engaged primarily in tourism and related services.

Anegada, 15 flat square miles (39 square km), is composed of coral limestone and sandy hillocks that rise no higher than 27 feet (eight meters) above sea level. The coast is smooth, and natural reefs, particularly along the western, leeward side, protect the beaches. The reef is not only beautiful, but dangerous; nearly 300 shipwrecks, more than anywhere else in the Caribbean, lie offshore. In fact, the name Anegada may have come from the Spanish *ane-gar,* literally "to drown." The attraction here is diving, clearly. Much of the island, through National Parks Trust (tel. 809-494-3904) regulations, has been set aside as a reserve for birds and other wildlife. Several large salt ponds stretch inland in the northern part of the island. The island is 20 miles (32 km) northeast of Virgin Gorda, somewhat isolated from the main group, and most of the population of nearly 300 lives in **The Settlement,** on the island's west side.

Another dozen or so islands of the group, some privately owned, are inhabited, bringing the British Virgin Islands population up to more than 16,000. The majority of the population is of African descent. The rest are an increasing number of European, North American, and Caribbean expatriates, most of whom have been attracted by the islands' growing tourism and related service industries.

HISTORY

The origins of the place names in the British Virgin Islands tell the story of the islands' settlement. Various explorers, from the Amerindian Arawaks to Columbus to the 17th- and 18th-century European settlers, have come up with monikers such as **Tortola, Virgin Gorda, Jost Van Dyke,** and **Anegada,** the four main and most populated islands, as well as **Norman Island, Peter Island, Ginger Island, Fallen Jerusalem, The Dogs, Beef Island, Great Camanoe,** and more. Many names and their meanings have been obscured by history, while others reflect the vagaries of European colonization and whimsy.

"Fat Virgin" and Other Notable Names

Columbus sailed past the Virgin Islands archipelago during his second voyage, in 1493. One imagines his dismay when confronted with a literal sea of rocks, islets, and islands which he was, by contract, enjoined to name and chart. One imagines him throwing up his hands in panic and calling the entire lot *Las Once Mil Virgenes,* or "The 11,000 Virgins" (others contend his name for the islands was "Las Islas Virgenes"), presumably in honor of the martyred 4th-century Saint Ursula and her 11,000 virgins. He beat a hasty retreat after this christening, however, off to greener and golden shores in search of the Great Khan of the Indies. It is his name, Virgin Gorda, the somehow unseemly "Fat Virgin," that still sticks to the island today.

Over the years the Spanish, the Dutch, and various pirates used the islands for stopovers and as bases for raiding passing ships. In 1595 Sir Francis Drake, the mercenary explorer, passed through the channel that now bears his name. One legend claims that the infamous Edward Teach, or "Blackbeard," once anchored with his crew off Deadman's Bay while splitting the spoils of a successful raid. An argument erupted and Blackbeard set 15 pirates on the island called Dead Chest, providing one bottle of rum and their sea chests for their last days. Hence—and this is where legends always become suspect—the old salts' song with the line "fifteen men on dead men's chest, yo ho ho and a bottle of rum."

Europeans Arrive
By the mid-1600s, the British staked claims on some of the islands, yet remained in a continuous state of altercation with the Dutch and Spanish over territory. In 1672, the British governor of the Leeward Islands claimed Tortola (Spanish for "turtledove") for England and sent settlers from Anguilla to appropriate the island. By 1680, the British had established settlements on Anegada and Virgin Gorda. Soon after, the peripatetic pirates and buccaneers, whose reign in the Caribbean and Americas would soon be over, moved on to better and safer shores.

Modern Times
Throughout the years, the British fought back attempts to oust them from the islands. Most attacks were feeble and short-lived, and the British Virgin Islands have remained a British entity for the entirety of their modern history. They were administered as a colony and part of the Leeward Islands Administration until 1956, when the nascent Federation of the West Indies was in the process of forming. The Federation of the West Indies was the administrative unit comprising British West Indies islands, which collapsed in 1962 due to internecine bickering between, primarily, Jamaica and Trinidad and Tobago. The British Virgin Islands elected not to join the West Indies Federation, instead opting for a form of internal control over their affairs and economic links with the U.S. Virgin Islands. It was the best of both worlds for them, and today that economic link is still seen—the U.S. dollar is the official currency.

During the 1960s and '70s, constitutions were drawn that allowed for greater internal government, including the formation of political parties and local elections of a Legislative Council. The head of local government today is Chief Minister Hamilton Lavity Stoutt, who has held the post since 1967.

PEOPLE AND CULTURE

The British Virgin Islands are still a British Crown Colony and, therefore, dependent territory. The cultural norms are British and African—with, of course, a West Indian twist. English is used by everyone, although West Indian colloquialisms and the lilting lyricism of island language is heard throughout. British Virgin Islands cuisine reflects the West Indian sensibility, using local fruits, vegetables, seafood, and spices. Rum, of course, is the beverage of choice, still produced locally the old way, in copper vats and a still.

Among the locals, the tradition of covering up remains strong. British Virgin Islanders pride themselves on neatness and appearance. Long skirts, uniformed school children, and modesty are the norm; bathing attire or skimpy shorts and shirts will be offensive if worn off the beach.

Holidays and Festivals
Festivals and local events attest to the blending of the cultures. Virtually no month goes by in which no sailing race or regatta is held. These include, and this is a short list, the **Sweet Hearts of the Caribbean Classic Yacht and Schooner Regatta** in February, the **British Virgin Islands Spring Regatta** in April, and **Around Tortola Sailing Race** in November. The **Queen's Birthday** is celebrated (11 July), as is the birthday of the Heir to the Throne (14 November). Yet the **B.V.I. Summer Festival** is

the islands' nod to West Indian and African influences; it amounts to a raucous midsummer carnival. The festival, held in late July, features two weeks of nightly music, steel bands, calypso competitions, Prince and Princess shows, feasts, and arts and crafts shows.

GOVERNMENT AND ECONOMY

The British Virgin Islands are a Crown Colony, with the Queen represented on the island by an appointed governor, who presides over an Executive Council comprising the chief minister, an attorney general, and several ministers of government. The Legislative Council comprises elected members plus a governor-appointed member and a speaker of the council.

The economy of the islands is reliant on British and associated aid, and on the tourism industry; yachting, boating, and chartering play a large role in the latter. Nearly 200,000 visitors fly in or sail through each year, and more than half take up some form of yacht activity for their vacations.

An interesting although small source of local income comes from the recently established B.V.I. Film Commission, tel. (809) 494-4119, which promotes island locations for motion picture and television shoots. Recent commercials for products such as such as Coors beer and Frito-Lay chips have been shot on the island.

PRACTICALITIES

WATER SPORTS

Aside from the sailing opportunities mentioned above, various other water sports activities are a major attraction in the British Virgin Islands. Diving—including resort certification, advanced dives, and night dives—and snorkeling can be arranged by **Baskin in the Sun** in Sopers Hole, Tortola, tel. (809) 494-2858, U.S. tel. (800) 233-7938; **Blue Waters Divers** in Nanny Cay Marine, Tortola, tel. (809) 494-2847; **Dive B.V.I.** at Virgin Gorda Yacht Harbour, Leverick Bay, and Peter Island, tel. (809) 495-5513, U.S. tel. (800) 848-7078; **Island Diver** in Road Town, Tortola, tel. (809) 494-3878; and **Underwater Safaris** also in Road Town, Tortola, tel. (809) 494-3235, U.S. tel. (800) 537-7032. Cost for one-tank dives is US$50-60, night dives US$60-75. Multi-dive packages and hotel packages are available.

Deep-sea fishing is organized through **Charter Fishing** in Road Town, tel. (809) 495-3311, or **Classic** at Biras Creek, Virgin Gorda, tel. (809) 494-3555. Cost is US$650 per day, US$450 per half day.

GETTING THERE

Tortola's **Beef Island International Airport** is the main entry point for those arriving by air.

Virgin Gorda also has an airport and is serviced by light aircraft. St. Thomas, in the U.S. Virgin Islands, and San Juan are the main connectors from North America—there are no nonstop flights to the British Virgin Islands from North America. Several airlines connect to San Juan or St. Thomas, including **Air Canada, American, Continental, Carnival, Delta,** and **Northwest.** From Europe, **British Airways, BWIA, Lufthansa, Iberia, Air France,** and others fly to, primarily, San Juan, St. Thomas, Antigua, Barbados, Martinique, Sint Maarten, and Trinidad and Tobago.

American Eagle, local tel. (809) 495-2559, has seven flights daily from San Juan to Tortola. **Sunaire Express,** tel. (809) 495-2480, has several nonstop flights weekly from San Juan, St. Croix, or St. Thomas to Tortola and Virgin Gorda. **LIAT,** tel. (809) 494-3888, connects nonstop from Anguilla, Antigua, St. Kitts, Sint Maarten, and St. Thomas and has connections from throughout the Caribbean.

You can choose to enter the British Virgin Islands by sea rather than air, and several options exist. Various ferry services operate between St. Thomas and Tortola, St. John and Tortola, and St. Thomas and Virgin Gorda. The port at Road Town on Tortola is the entry point and main port for cruise ships, some yachts, and ferries in the British Virgin Islands. The Government Jetty is the ferry departure point. West End, on Tortola's west end, is also a ferry stop.

Daily service on **Native Son, Inc.,** tel. (809) 495-4617, connects St. Thomas to West End and Road Town. They also make a St. Thomas to Virgin Gorda run Wednesday and Sunday. **Smith's Ferry Services,** tel. (809) 494-4430, 494-2355, or 495-4495, does the same. Between the two you can expect at least four departures every day. **Inter-Island Boat Services,** tel. (809) 776-6597, connects Cruz Bay in St. John with West End at least three times per day.

The **departure tax** upon leaving the British Virgin Islands is US$5 by air, US$3 by sea.

GETTING AROUND

Interisland travel among British Virgin Islands is accomplished by ferries or by flying. Ferries make regular runs from West End, Road Town, or Beef Island in Tortola to The Valley or North Sound in Virgin Gorda, and to Great Harbour in Jost Van Dyke. From Road Town to Virgin Gorda, **Speedy's Fantasy,** tel. (809) 495-5420, operates at least twice daily, and Smith's Ferry Services (see above) has three runs Mon.-Sat., twice only on Sunday. **North Sound Express,** tel. (809) 494-2746, operates between Beef Island and Virgin Gorda's North Sound three times daily. **Beef Island to Virgin Gorda Service,** tel. (809) 495-5240, operates between Beef Island and The Valley twice daily. **Reel World,** tel. (809) 495-9277, makes three runs daily between West End and Jost Van Dyke. The **Jost Van Dyke Ferry Service,** tel. (809) 495-2775 or 494-2997, operates between West End and Jost Van Dyke four times each weekday, three times on Saturday, and twice on Sunday.

As well, the **Peter Island Boat,** tel. (809) 494-2561, operates between Road Town and Peter Island seven times daily.

Daily flights are available between Beef Island and Virgin Gorda or Anegada on several small airlines, including Sunaire Express, (809) 495-2480; **Aero Gorda,** tel. (809) 495-2271; or **Atlantic Air B.V.I.,** tel. (809) 495-2000. Aero Gorda is available for charters as well.

Boat Charters
Of course, many visitors will elect to charter a boat and sail their way around. Not only is this a wonderful way to see the islands, but it is, in some ways, the most convenient. The type of boat and/or crew you charter will depend on your sailing skills and budget. Dozens of charter outfits in the British Virgin Islands offer everything from organized sailing, snorkeling, or diving excursions, to bareboat charters, to crewed charters, or variations (e.g. you hire a skipper and you are the crew). You'll find about 15 marinas scattered around the island group, providing water, electricity, and shopping for boat visitors, as well as anchorages scattered throughout the bays and inlets. Boat charter rates depend on the number of passengers, the size and make of the boat, whether a sail- or powerboat, the size of the crew, and amenities offered. Figure US$1500 per week minimum for a bareboat in high season to as much as US$14,000 per week for a crewed charter for 10 persons. Rates are significantly reduced—by as much as half—during off season. Just a few of the many reputable charter outfits include the original charter company **The Moorings,** Mariner Inn, Road Harbour, Tortola, British Virgin Islands, tel. (809) 494-2331, U.S. tel. (800) 535-7289; and **Virgin Islands Sailing,** Mill Mall, Road Town, Tortola, British Virgin Islands, tel. (809) 494-2774, U.S. Virgin Islands tel. (800) 233-7936 or (800) 272-2566, local fax (809) 494-6774, which may have more boats than anyone else. Others include **Discovery Yacht Charters,** P.O. Box 281, Road Town, Tortola, British Virgin Islands, tel. (809) 494-6026, Canada tel. (416) 891-1999, local fax 494-6035, Canada fax 891-3623; **Marine Enterprises Boat Rentals,** P.O. Box 3069, Road Town, Tortola, British Virgin Islands, tel. (809) 494-2786, fax 494-4744; **Seabreeze Yacht Charters,** P.O. Box 528, East End, Tor-

tuna

BOB RACE

tola, British Virgin Islands, tel. (809) 495-1560, fax 495-1561; and **Tropic Island Yacht Management,** P.O. Box 532, Maya Cove, Tortola, British Virgin Islands, tel. (809) 494-2450 or (800) 356-8938, fax 495-2155. On Virgin Gorda, contact **Euphoric Cruises,** P.O. Box 55, Virgin Gorda, British Virgin Islands, tel. (809) 495-5542, fax 495-5818.

Car Rentals

Driving on Tortola or Virgin Gorda is easy if you're comfortable with driving on the left. There are few traffic jams, no traffic lights, and the views can be breathtaking. You'll need to produce your valid driver's license to purchase a temporary B.V.I. license, US$10; car rental companies handle this. Rental rates start at US$35 per day. On Tortola, most companies are located in Road Town. Try **Alphonso Car Rentals,** tel. (809) 494-3137; **Avis,** tel. (809) 494-3322; **Budget,** tel. (809) 494-2531; **Caribbean Car Rental,** tel. (809) 494-2595; **Hertz,** tel. (809) 495-4405; or **National,** tel. (809) 494-3197. On Virgin Gorda, call **Potter's Car Rental,** tel. (809) 495-5329, or **Speedy's Car Rental,** tel. (809) 495-5235. On Anegada, call **Anegada Reef Hotel,** tel. (809) 495-8002. Motor scooters start at about US$30 per day and are found in Road Town at **DJ's Scooter Rentals,** tel. (809) 494-5071, and in Virgin Gorda at **Honda Scooter Rentals,** tel. (809) 495-5212.

Taxis

You'll find taxis on Tortola at the airport and at the ferry docks in Road Town and West End. Taxi rates are set by the government, and virtually all offer island tours as well as simple transportation. On Tortola, tours start at US$12 per person, on Virgin Gorda US$10 per person. If you need a taxi, either let your hotel recommend one or call: **B.V.I. Taxi Association,** tel. (809) 494-2875; **Style's Taxi Service** on Tortola, tel. (809) 494-2260; or **Mahogany Taxi Service** in The Valley, tel. (809) 495-5542.

Buses on Tortola are inexpensive—fares are no more than US$3—but the schedules not always discernible. Nevertheless, **Scato's Bus Service** in Road Town, tel. (809) 494-2365, is the one to call; they offer island tours as well.

ACCOMMODATIONS AND FOOD

Accommodations listed below fall in the following categories. Prices are per person, per night, during high season. **Luxury** US$100 or more, **Moderate** US$50-100, **Budget** US$50 or less.

Villas

Most accommodations in the British Virgin Islands are located on Tortola and Virgin Gorda and to a lesser extent on Anegada and Jost Van Dyke as well as several of the small, private islands. Accommodation ranges from slick resorts, although not necessarily large resorts, to hotels, guesthouses, apartments, and several approved campsites. Villas are available throughout the islands. The B.V.I. Tourist Board will assist in making contacts and reservations with dozens of property management companies throughout the islands. Or, contact directly: **Property Management Plus,** P.O. Box 1072, The Valley, Virgin Gorda, British Virgin Islands, tel. (809) 495-5867; and **Kanaka Property Management,** P.O. Box 25, The Valley, Virgin Gorda, British Virgin Islands, tel. (809) 495-5201. Cost ranges US$600-2400 per week during the high season. **Virgin Gorda Villa Rentals,** P.O. Box 63, The Valley, Virgin Gorda, British Virgin Islands, tel. (809) 495-5201 or (800) 848-7081, fax 495-7367, deals directly with Virgin Gorda rentals, starting at about US$900 per week in the winter for a one-bedroom villa.

All accommodations add a seven percent government tax, and most add a 10-12% service charge in addition to that.

Camping

Campgrounds offer both prepared sites with tents at US$20-35 per double or bare sites at US$10-15 during the high season. Approved sites are **Anegada Beach Campground,** The Settlement, Anegada, British Virgin Islands, tel. (809) 495-8038; **Brewer's Bay Campground,** P.O. Box 185, Road Town, Tortola, British Virgin Islands, tel. (809) 494-3463, in St. John; and **Tula's N&N Campground,** Little Harbour, Jost Van Dyke, British Virgin Islands, tel. (809) 495-9302.

INFORMATION DIRECTORY

BRITISH VIRGIN ISLANDS TOURIST BOARD

P.O. Box 134, Road Town, Tortola, British Virgin Islands, tel. (809) 494-3134, fax 494-3866.

370 Lexington Ave., New York, NY 10017, tel. (800) 835-8530 or (212) 696-0400, fax 949-8254.

1686 Union St., San Francisco, CA 94123, tel. (800) 232-7770 or (415) 775-0344, fax 775-2554.

110 St. Martin's La., London WC2N 4DY, tel. (44-71) 240-4259, fax 240-4270.

Sophienstrasse 4, D-65189 Wiesbaden, Germany, tel. (49-611) 300262, fax 300766.

OTHERS

Emergencies, tel. 999.

Peebles Hospital, Tortola, tel. (809) 494-3497.

Chief Immigration Officer, Tortola, tel. (809) 494-3701.

National Parks Trust, tel. (809) 494-3904.

Food

Tortola has a wide range of restaurants, Virgin Gorda less so, and the other islands host several beach bars or hotel restaurants. Local specialties include seafood, exotic fruits and vegetables, and West Indian dishes such as *fungi,* a pasty cornmeal starch. Hotel restaurants often accept credit cards, but don't count on it in every case. Smaller restaurants, particularly beach bistros, are not as likely to accept credit cards. The categories used in the British Virgin Islands sections below are priced per person, per entree: **Expensive** US$25 or more, **Moderate** US$10-25, **Inexpensive** US$10 or less.

MONEY, HOURS, AND COMMUNICATION

The U.S. dollar is the **currency** of the British Virgin Islands. U.S. dollar traveler's checks are widely accepted, as is cash. **Credit cards** are accepted in many businesses, but not all, particularly smaller hotels, guesthouses, or restaurants. Currencies are best changed at **banks,** which are located in Road Town and Virgin Gorda and include **Barclays,** tel. (809) 494-2171, and **Scotiabank,** tel. (809) 494-2526, among others. Bank hours may vary but are generally Mon.-Fri. 9 a.m.-2 p.m., with extra hours on Friday afternoon, 3-5 p.m.

Shops and others businesses are open Mon.-Sat. 9 a.m.-5 p.m., and most are closed on Sunday.

The British Virgin Islands use the **area code** "809," followed by a seven-digit number. Phone cards are used in public phones and may be purchased at the offices of **Cable and Wireless,** in Road Town, tel. (809) 494-4444, or The Yacht Harbour in The Valley, tel. (809) 495-5444. Cable and Wireless is available to make phone calls, and to send faxes, telexes, and cables. Hours are weekdays 7 a.m. -7 p.m., Saturday 7 a.m. -4 p.m., and Sunday 9 a.m. -2 p.m.

TORTOLA

Tortola is the British Virgin Islands' population and administrative center and, at 21 square miles (54 square km), is the largest island of the group. The island is also a center of activity, restaurants, and accommodations, and many folks could happily spend their entire vacation just on Tortola.

BEACHES

Tortola's best beaches are found along its north and northwestern shore. Some are accessible by car, others by boat or by short hikes. Some have facilities and yacht moorings in secluded bays, while others have few facilities. All, however, are open to everyone. Among the best is **Smuggler's Cove** at the far west end, accessible by dirt road, a small beach with reputedly good snorkeling. Heading east is **Long Bay,** which is not surprisingly long, and the rougher **Apple Bay,** lined with palm trees and a favorite spot with surfers. This is the site of **Bomba's Surfside Shack,** tel. (809) 895-2148, in turn the site of Bomba's monthly "Full Moon Party," a wildly popular island event. Several other small restaurants and bistros are located on this beach. **Cane Garden Bay** is wide and long,

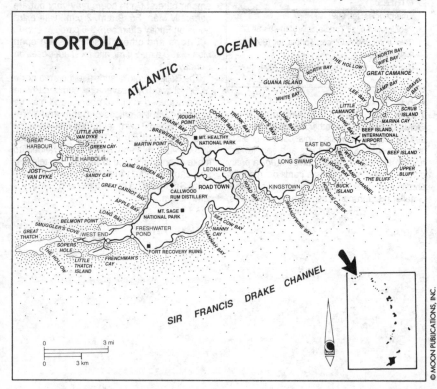

and popular with yachties and swimmers; here you'll find plenty of beach bars and water sports. **Brewer's Bay** was once the site of several sugar mills and distilleries, and now has beach bars and a campground. It is often empty. **Elizabeth Bay,** on the eastern end, is small and secluded. Just north of the airport on Beef Island is **Long Bay,** another secluded beach. The nearby salt pond is home to nesting terns and other sea birds.

For information on beach recreation, see "Sports" under "Practicalities" earlier in this chapter.

ISLAND SIGHTS

You'll find **Mt. Sage National Park** at the island's west end. At 1,780 feet (543 meters), it's Tortola's highest point; the views are stunning. Trails lead from the parking area through the park's 92 acres and up to the peak, an easy walk. The quasi-rainforest hosts a variety of rainforest flora and fauna, including a wide array of birds. Admission is free.

At the far west end of the island is **Sopers Hole,** believed to be the site of the first Dutch landing on the island in 1648. The harbor has a ferry landing with customs and immigration facilities, as well as a marina, restaurants, and shops. Nearby is **Fort Recovery,** in the Fort Recovery Villas complex. The remains of the fort consist of a tower and a few crumbled remains. There are no tours, but you can clamber around.

At **Cane Garden Bay** along the North Coast Road, you'll find the **Callwood Rum Distillery** in an old stone plantation building. It's not a big distillery, but rum is still produced in copper vats and a still, much the same as it was during the plantation era. Bottles of rum are sold here. At **Mt. Healthy,** another small national park, the draw is an old stone windmill, once part of a sugar plantation.

Road Town

Road Town is a small, functional center, with a Main Street, government offices, and busy waterfront. Here you'll find a post office, banks, churches, a prison, the tourist board, Cable and Wireless offices, police station, a museum, shops, the ferry dock, several hotels and, of course, the marinas. The town's style is quaint

and modern West Indian. The style of the brightly painted wooden and stone buildings, particularly along the old **Main Street,** an attraction in itself, is the architecture of the turn-of-the-century Caribbean.

On Main Street is **Sir Olva George's Plaza,** across from the post office and near the ferry dock. The square sits beneath several large ficus trees and is lined with government offices and shops. Nearby is the small, picket-fenced **Virgin Islands Folk Museum,** with stone artifacts from the early Amerindian presence on the islands and displays from the plantation slavery days. The museum also features bits and pieces salvaged from the wreck of the RMS *Rhone,* a British mailship that sunk off the coast of Peter Island in the 1800s. A small gift shop carries several good books about island history and lore. The hours (variable with season) are 9 a.m.-4 p.m. weekdays except Wednesday, when it is closed, and Saturday 9 a.m.-noon. It's closed Sunday. Admission to the museum is free, although donations are accepted.

Near the center of town and the police station is the **J.R. O'Neal Botanic Gardens,** tel. (809) 494-4557, a four-acre garden with a wide array of local and imported tropical plants, a hothouse, a pond, and self-guided walks. The gardens are open daily, and, like the museum, admission is free, but donations are accepted.

Several forts and historic ruins dot the countryside near Road Town. **Fort Burt,** now a hotel, was originally constructed by the Dutch and later rebuilt by the British. The foundation is all that remains of the original structure. The ruins of **Fort George** and **Fort Charlotte,** both built in 1794, can be found on strategic hills overlooking the harbor.

ACCOMMODATIONS

The following hotels are recommended. **Frenchman's Cay Resort Hotel,** P.O. Box 1054, West End, Tortola, British Virgin Islands, tel. (809) 495-4844, U.S. tel. (800) 223-9832, fax 495-4056, offers nine self-contained villas on the beach at the southwestern tip of the island. Luxury. **Tamarind Country Club Hotel,** P.O. Box 509, East End, Tortola, British Virgin Islands, tel. (809) 495-2477, is mainly villas, and it's just a short walk to the beach. Luxury.

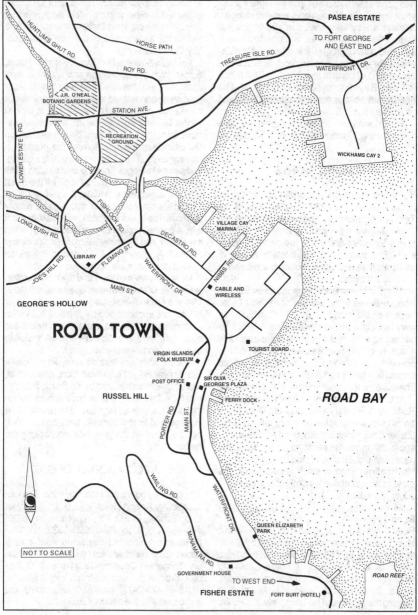

PASEA ESTATE

TO FORT GEORGE
AND EAST END

HUNTUM'S GHUT RD.

HORSE PATH

ROY RD.

TREASURE ISLE RD.

WATERFRONT DR.

J.R. O'NEAL
BOTANIC GARDENS

STATION AVE.

RECREATION
GROUND

WICKHAMS CAY 2

LOWER ESTATE RD.

FISHLOCK RD.

LONG BUSH RD.

VILLAGE CAY
MARINA

DECASTRO RD.

JOE'S HILL RD.

LIBRARY

FLEMING ST.

NIBBS RD.

WATERFRONT DR.

MAIN ST.

CABLE AND
WIRELESS

GEORGE'S HOLLOW

ROAD TOWN

TOURIST BOARD

ROAD BAY

VIRGIN ISLANDS
FOLK MUSEUM

POST OFFICE

SIR OLVA
GEORGE'S PLAZA

RUSSEL HILL

PORTER RD.

MAIN ST.

FERRY DOCK

WAILING RD.

WATERFRONT DR.

QUEEN ELIZABETH
PARK

NOT TO SCALE

MCNAMARA RD.

GOVERNMENT HOUSE

TO WEST END

ROAD REEF

FISHER ESTATE

FORT BURT (HOTEL)

© MOON PUBLICATIONS, INC.

MORE TORTOLA ACCOMMODATIONS

Rates per s, EP when applicable, winter

NAME	(809)	(800)	TARIFF
Admiralty Estate Resort	494-0014	223-9815	luxury
Beef Island Guest House	495-2303	N/A	budget
Cane Garden Bay Beach Hotel	495-4639	N/A	moderate
Fort Burt Hotel	494-2587	835-8530	moderate
Harbour View Guest House	495-4549	N/A	budget
Hotel Castle Maria	494-2553	N/A	moderate
Josiah's Bay Cottages	494-2533	N/A	moderate
Maria's by the Sea	494-2595	N/A	moderate
Sugar Mill Hotel	495-4355	462-8834	luxury
Wayside Inn Guest House	(write Box 258, Road Town, Tortola, British Virgin Islands, West Indies)		budget

Sebastian's on the Beach, P.O. Box 441, Tortola, British Virgin Islands, tel. (809) 495-4212, U.S. tel. (800) 336-4870, fax 495-4466, is medium-sized, with 26 rooms on the surfing beach at Little Apple Bay. Clean and comfortable. Moderate. **Turtle Dove Lodge,** P.O. Box 11, West End, Tortola, British Virgin Islands, tel. (809) 495-4430, U.S. tel. (800) 223-4483, fax 495-4070, overlooking Long Bay, has cabins each with twelve beds; they're spartan but clean. No credit cards are accepted. Budget.

FOOD

Brandywine Bay, tel. (809) 495-2301, near Road Town offers elegant seaside dining with Continental and Florentine cuisine for dinner only. Moderate. **The Butterfly** on Main Street in Road Town specializes in seafood and West Indian. Inexpensive-Moderate. **Fort Burt Hotel,** tel. (809) 494-2587, in Road Town serves a wide array of West Indian and traditional English dishes. Moderate-Expensive. **Pusser's Co. Store and Pub,** tel. (809) 494-2467, in Road Town has two restaurants, one with sandwiches and meat pies, the other with more formal fare. Inexpensive-Moderate. **Spaghetti Junction,** tel. (809) 494-4880, on Waterfront Drive in Road Town serves fast and full Italian. Inexpensive-Moderate. **Sugar Mill,** tel. (809) 495-4335, at the west coast's Apple Bay is one of the island's best, serving an eclectic range of creative West Indian and Continental dishes. Moderate-Expensive.

VIRGIN GORDA

Virgin Gorda is strung out over seven miles (11 km) from east to west, comprising a hilly middle section, the flatter east end, and the populated southwest end. The island's hub, **The Valley,** which incorporates the island's original center of **Spanish Town,** is in the southwest. Virgin Gorda was once a major commercial center but today is known more as an excellent anchorage for yachts. Its secluded beaches are also renowned. A road runs from the west end of the island to **North Sound,** a large bay separating the east end of the island from the offshore islets of **Prickly Pear Island, Mosquito Island, Necker Island,** and **Eustatia Island.** Prickly Pear Island has been declared a protected national park.

Transport to Virgin Gorda is by ferry or by shuttle flight from Tortola. The airstrip is located in The Valley.

BEACHES

The British Virgin Islands' most well-known beach is **The Baths,** south of The Valley, a natural formation of colossal boulders that form pools, caves, and oddly lit, shimmering grottoes. Walking trails—slogging trails, actually—are marked through the boulders and pools. This is an enormously popular attraction and is likely to be swamped with visitors most of the time, but especially during cruise ship stopovers.

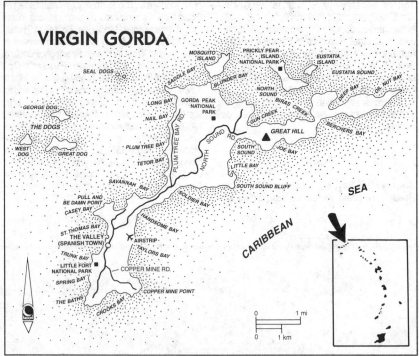

© MOON PUBLICATIONS, INC.

Still, The Baths are unlike most beaches you've seen. Plan to go early in the morning or later in the evening to avoid the crowds.

Other popular beaches on Virgin Gorda include **Spring Bay,** next to The Baths, and **Trunk Bay,** a series of secluded beaches north of Spring Bay, accessible by boat or by a hike from Spring Bay. There is a path linking the bays. **Savannah Bay,** on the narrow isthmus between the west and central sections of the island, is wide and expansive. In total, Virgin Gorda has nearly 20 beaches, many secluded. Some are easily accessed by shuttle boats.

MORE VIRGIN GORDA ACCOMMODATIONS

Rates per s, EP when applicable, winter

NAME	(809)	(800)	TARIFF
Diamond Beach Club	495-5542	N/A	luxury
Fischer's Cove Beach Hotel	495-5252	621-1270	luxury
Mango Bay Resort	495-5672	223-6510	luxury
Olde Yard Inn	495-5544	633-7411	luxury
Paradise Beach Resort	495-5871	225-4255	luxury

ISLAND SIGHTS

South of the Yacht Harbour in The Valley is **Little Fort National Park,** once the site of a Spanish fort that is now in ruins; you can, however, still see part of the old Powder House. Today the park is a 36-acre wildlife sanctuary. On the eastern shore of the western tip of the island is **Copper Mine Point,** worked by English miners from 1838 to 1867, and probably by Spanish miners 300 years before that. Remains of stone buildings, a cistern, and mine shafts can be seen.

Gorda Peak National Park, located on the central section of Virgin Gorda, encompasses 265 acres, which includes all land starting 1,000 feet (305 meters) above sea level. The peak, at 1,359 feet (414 meters), is the island's highest point. There is a small observation platform at the top, and the surrounding forest is heavy with mahogany and semi-rainforest flora.

Around the island are strings of small cays, including **Fallen Jerusalem** to the south and **The Dog Islands** to the west. Several of the islands are available for mooring and are frequently visited by nesting sea birds. Fallen Jerusalem and The Dog Islands are protected by National Park Trust regulations.

ACCOMMODATIONS

Biras Creek Estate, P.O. Box 54, Virgin Gorda, British Virgin Islands, tel. (809) 494-3555, U.S. tel. (800) 223-1108, fax 494-3557, in North Sound can be reached by boat only. This exclusive resort on 150 acres offers tennis, sailing, and individual villas. Luxury. **Bitter End Yacht Club,** P.O. Box 46, Virgin Gorda, British Virgin Islands, tel. (809) 494-2746, U.S. tel. (312) 944-5855, is also on North Sound, a retreat reached by boat only with 95 rooms and some villas. Luxury. **Little Dix Bay Hotel,** P.O. Box 70, Virgin Gorda, British Virgin Islands, tel. (809) 495-5555, U.S. tel. (800) 223-7637, fax 495-5661, one of the island's first hotels; gives you old-style elegance, tennis, water sports, and a marina. Location is south of The Valley. Luxury. **Ocean View Hotel,** P.O. Box 66, Virgin Gorda, British Virgin Islands, tel. (809) 495-5230, U.S. tel. (800) 621-1270, is near the ferry—small and simple, but clean. Budget-Moderate.

FOOD

Olde Yard Inn, tel. (809) 495-5544, in The Valley is large on old country charm, romanticism, and French Continental cuisine. Expensive. **The Bath and Turtle,** tel. (809) 495-5239, at the Yacht Harbour is a relaxed and informal pub with light fare, on the harbor. Moderate. **Chez Michelle,** tel. (809) 495-5510, in town serves French and Continental food. Moderate. **The Crab Hole,** tel. (809) 495-5307, in The Valley features West Indian savories and live entertainment. Moderate.

ANEGADA

The island's low-lying coral limestone formation and miles of white-sand coastline make it unique in the British Virgin Islands group. The atoll's reef is considerable and relatively untouched, and the diving, snorkeling, and fishing here are big attractions. An estimated 300 wrecks lie offshore and provide wide opportunities for divers searching for treasure (unlikely) or pristine environments of fish and coral formations (likely). In 1992, the government released flamingos on the island, with the aim of creating a preserve. During their nesting season, turtles can be seen on the beaches along the north shore. The entire north shore and west end is an uninterrupted beach with little shade and few facilities; bring along hats and sunscreen. Beach bars are found at **Loblolly Bay** on the north shore.

Most of the island's 300 inhabitants live in The Settlement, aptly named, near the airstrip in the south-central section of the island.

ACCOMMODATIONS AND FOOD

Accommodations
Anegada Reef Hotel, Anegada, British Virgin Islands, tel. (809) 495-8002, fax 495-9362, is the only hotel on the island and the center for diving, other water sports, bike rentals, and more. Luxury.

Food
Choices are limited here, but you won't starve. That's the beauty of Anegada anyway. It's best to make reservations for dinner. All of the following are Inexpensive-Moderate. The popular **Pomato Point,** tel. (809) 495-9466, serves local seafood and drinks on the beach. **Del's,** tel. (809) 495-8014, in The Settlement is good for lunch and local dishes. **Neptune's Treasure** serves seafood and Continental. **The Anegada Reef Hotel** serves all three meals.

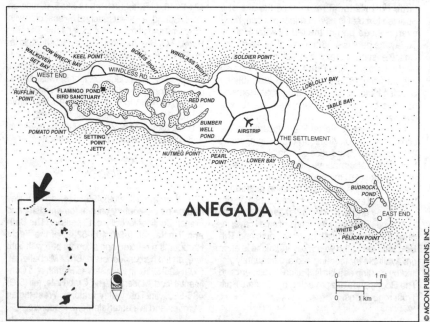

ANEGADA

© MOON PUBLICATIONS, INC.

SMALLER ISLANDS

JOST VAN DYKE

Great Harbour on Jost Van Dyke is the island's center of activity and the place to start your exploration. There you will find shops, a harbor, customs and immigration facilities, and several small beach bars and bistros. This tiny island, population about 200, received electricity in 1991 and has a few miles of paved road.

Accommodations
Sandcastle, P.O. Box 540, White Bay, Jost Van Dyke, British Virgin Islands, tel. (809) 777-1611, consists of four beach cottages. Water sports are available. Luxury. **Rudy's Mariner Inn,** Great Harbour, Jost Van Dyke, British Virgin Islands, tel. (809) 495-9282, is a small inn featuring rooms with kitchenettes. No credit cards. Moderate-Luxury. **Harris' Place,** Little Harbour, Jost Van Dyke, British Virgin Islands, tel. (809) 495-9302, fax 495-9296, is a small guesthouse on the beach in Little Harbour with just two rooms. Budget.

Food
Abe's by the Sea is a simple bar and restaurant in Great Harbour with frequent barbecues. Moderate. **Ali Baba's** in Great Harbour serves West Indian. Inexpensive-Moderate. **Harris' Place** has a midday happy hour. **Rudy's Mariner's Rendezvous** has live music and pig roasts. As a matter of fact, pig roasts are big entertainment on Jost Van Dyke and occur with frequency—keep your eye out for roasts on specialty nights.

GUANA ISLAND

Guana Island is a private 125-acre island with a nature preserve and several fine beaches, located off the north coast of Tortola. Stay at the exclusive **Guana Island Club,** P.O. Box 32, Road Town, Tortola, British Virgin Islands, tel. (809) 494-2354, U.S. tel. (800) 544-8262. Luxury.

MOSQUITO ISLAND

Mosquito Island, just off the Virgin Gorda coast, is a privately owned resort community with walking trails, water sports, and beaches. The accommodation is **Drake's Anchorage,** P.O. Box 2510, North Sound, Virgin Gorda, British Virgin Islands, tel. (809) 494-2254, U.S. tel. (800) 624-6651, consisting of villas, rooms, and suites; a French restaurant; and lots of privacy. Luxury.

NECKER ISLAND

This island to the north of Virgin Gorda is owned by Richard Branson, owner of Virgin Airways and other Virgin ventures. The island features an exclusive villa-house that sleeps up to 20 and is available for rent. Deeply luxurious. All amenities and sports are available. Call (800) 926-0636 for details.

NORMAN ISLAND

The island, south of Peter Island, is uninhabited and widely believed to be the setting that inspired Robert Louis Stevenson's *Treasure Island.* Day-trips are available for snorkeling and lolling about its beaches. The floating restaurant **The William Thorton,** converted from a 1910 Baltic Trading ship, floats off The Bight.

PETER ISLAND

Peter Island, lying south of Tortola, is an exclusive 1,000-acre island with beaches, water sports, anchorages, and the **Palm Island Resort,** P.O. Box 211, Road Town, Tortola, British Virgin Islands, tel. (809) 494-2561, U.S. tel. (800) 562-0268, fax 494-2313, a 50-room villa resort. Luxury.

M.W.A.
THE SKY IS HELD UP
BY TREES IF THE
FOREST GOES THE
ROOF OF THE WORLD
WILL COLLAPSE AND
NATURE AND MAN
PERISH TOGETHER

BOB RACE

THE BRITISH LEEWARDS
INTRODUCTION

Purists have our permission to take exception to the designation British Leewards to refer to the northern Lesser Antilles islands with British backgrounds. The term was used during the 17th century to refer to an actual political entity comprising Anguilla, St. Kitts, Nevis, Antigua, Barbuda, Montserrat, and their smaller satellite islands. The islands were then administered from the southern island of Barbados, which probably gave them their name—the islands of the northern Lesser Antilles lie, in effect, leeward of Barbados.

The Leewards became, in 1871, the British Crown Colony of the Leeward Islands and at the time included Dominica. Dominica was placed under the British Windward Islands dominion in the mid-20th century. Then as the islands began to achieve varying degrees of independence, the designations of Leeward Islands and Windward Islands became geographical rather than political—which is how we use them here.

The Leewards are generally smaller and flatter than their southern and northern Caribbean neighbors, and in that sense less dramatic. They shined, in the old days, as trading hubs rather than mass sugarcane producers, although agriculture was certainly part and parcel of their growth as colonies. Today, the Leewards are known as quiet getaways with well-developed tourism facilities that emphasize culture and beach, boating, and diving experiences rather than rugged nature excursions. Antigua, with its airport hub, can almost be termed busy, yet offers the sleepy island of Barbuda for those wishing to truly check out for a while. Montserrat's active volcano and small inland rainforest provide diversions for those interested in hiking and climbing, and low-lying St. Kitts, Nevis, and Anguilla offer some of the finest beaches in the area.

ANGUILLA

Flat, elongated, and unhurried Anguilla (an-GWI-lah) was frequently removed from the ravages of 18th- and 19th-century European wars that spread throughout the West Indies. Later, the island was mostly removed from the ravages of the plantation slave economy. Today, a visitor to Anguilla could easily feel that it is still somewhat removed—now it's from the modern tourism industry.

Yet here is an island that, in this century, has experienced enough internal political turmoil to warrant military intervention by outside forces; it amounted to a revolution. Anguillans are people not wholly given over to others' concepts of what they ought to be, either politically or culturally. This is evident in a first impression of the island. As you drive along the main roads—no highways to be found here—the absence of tourism glitz and flash is conspicuous. Several exclusive resorts can be found, yet they are isolated and set back from the main roads. Other hotels are small and unpretentious. Private homes seem to be under a constant state of construction, with iron rods poking up like spiked haircuts from the roofs of the small, concrete structures. The Valley, Anguilla's capital, is Lilliputian, and a sense of some economic struggle lingers throughout the island. Anguillans are among the most welcoming and unassuming people you'll find in the Lesser Antilles.

THE LAND

Anguilla, the northernmost of the Leeward Islands, lies 190 miles (306 km) east of Puerto Rico and five miles (eight km) north of its nearest neighbor, Saint-Martin/Sint Maarten. The open Atlantic Ocean meets its north shore, and the Caribbean Sea touches its south coast.

The island has ancient volcanic origins, but little today reminds one of the topography—sharp hills, rugged coastline, dramatic cliffs—associated with volcanic islands. Anguilla is now a low-lying and horizontal coral formation, 16 miles (26 km) long and three miles (five km) wide, with several inland depressions forming small salt ponds and valleys. The highest point on the 35-square-mile (90-square-km) island is the central **Crocus Hill,** only 213 feet (65 meters) above sea level.

The island's soil is thick with clay and nonarable in many places, and the local flora of hardy shrubs and trees is able to withstand some relatively dry conditions. No running rivers or streams cut through the countryside. The coast, a major attraction, is gently irregular, serrated by small coves and bays with powderwhite coral beaches.

Several offshore islands, used for fishing and recreation, are part of Anguilla's domain. **Dog Island, Prickly Pear Cays, Sandy Island,** and **Seal Island** lie in the waters to the northwest, **Anguillita Island** and **Blowing Rock** lie off the southwest shore, and the large **Scrub Island** lies just off the northeast's **Windward Point.**

HISTORY

The first known residents of Anguilla were Amerindians, probably Arawaks or subdivisions of that group. Remnants of their existence, dating 2000 B.C.-A.D. 1500, are plentiful on the island and are still being discovered in an archaeological dig begun in 1988 in the northeastern Island Harbour area. The Amerindian name for the island was Malliouhana, the meaning of which has been obscured by history.

In the Name of the Eel
Somewhere along the way the island acquired the name Anguilla, possibly from the Spanish *anguila* or the French *anguille.* Both words mean "eel," a reference to the shape of the island.

It's doubtful that Columbus ever charted Anguilla. The first recorded mention of the island was a 1564 reference by a French expedition under Rene Laudonniere, who, mindful of gold elsewhere, passed by the island. Various other European explorers also passed by in the late 15th and early 16th centuries, but they, too, ignored the island, thinking it contained no gold or riches; they were right.

The English claimed Anguilla in absentia—sort of a "what the heck, why not" political maneuver—but it wasn't until 1650 that the first English landing party attempted a settlement. They started small tobacco, cotton, and sugarcane farms and cultivated salt from the ponds. They also raised some cattle, but the agricultural part of the island's nascent economy failed to gain a strong foothold, and never, throughout the island's history, proved a major contributor.

In 1656, an Amerindian raid devastated the first settlement. The raid may have been conducted by Caribs from nearby islands, but there is little evidence of the Caribs having lived on Anguilla. The French raided the island several times—in 1666, 1689, and later in 1745 and

1796—but were never able to hold on to the island for any length of time. Pirate parties also took their share of booty, but the island remained a British colony throughout most of its early history.

In 1816, Anguilla was incorporated with the southern islands of St. Kitts and Nevis, and with the British Virgin Islands for administrative purposes, a move that would have a profound influence on the island over the next 150 years. At this time, the population was approximately 3,000—about 400 whites, 300 free blacks, and 2,300 slaves.

From the mid-19th century on, Anguilla was, at various times, a free port, a minor sugar producer, and a reluctant part of what the British now called the Federation of the Leeward Islands (1871). In 1872, Anguillans, feeling left out geographically and economically, petitioned Queen Victoria to dissolve their relationship with St. Kitts and Nevis. The Queen refused. An officer from the colonial administrative center on St. Kitts characterized the request as "a petition from a large number of illiterates." Clearly, diplomacy was not this officer's forte, and the statement produced some animosity on Anguilla. This animosity, further fueled by Anguilla's second-class status through its association with the successful sugarcane colonies of St. Kitts and Nevis, continued throughout the 19th and early 20th centuries.

20th Century
In 1958, the British Federation of the West Indies was formed, with the colony of St. Kitts-Nevis-Anguilla represented as a single political unit. That same year, the island legislative council petitioned the colonial governor for separation from St. Kitts and Nevis, to no avail. In 1962, the Federation collapsed under the withdrawal of wealthy Jamaica and several of the larger states. During the next several years, political parties on the island grew in strength, as did the small tourism industry.

In 1966, talks began in London with the aim of producing a constitution for a proposed semi-autonomous state of St. Kitts-Nevis-Anguilla. Anguillans were alarmed and protested the idea, supposing, with good reason, that St. Kitts and Nevis would continue to relegate the poor and relatively unproductive island to the status of an indigent country cousin. History, in that regard, had already proven them correct.

"You Say You Want a Revolution . . ."
By 1967, demonstrations to reject the state had grown into a full-fledged separatist movement. Violence flared in early February of that year, and by mid-month the British sent an extra police attachment from St. Kitts to the island. In March, Anguillan separatists burned down Government House and attacked police headquarters. By May of that year, the movement voted to expel the Kittitian police force, which they did. Then in June, a boatload of Anguillans sailed to St. Kitts and, with surprising naivete, attempted to overthrow the government. They were routed and captured, and five men went to trial.

Throughout this period, various peace-keeping initiatives originating in, among others, the U.K., Jamaica, and Barbados, were proposed and failed. By 1969 negotiations with the government of St. Kitts and Britain had broken down. Early in that year the British cut off economic aid to the island, and by February, Anguilla had declared itself an independent republic. The elected president of the republic was Ronald Webster, and the island braced itself for reprisals after its expulsion of a British junior minister and negotiator in early March. Reprisals—perhaps a stretch of the word—came on 19 March 1969, when the British invaded the island.

"Invaded" is also a stretch of the word. Troopers and parachuters were brought in by offshore frigates, and a contingent of the London Metropolitan Police Force was established on the island. It all went fairly smoothly, as these things go. President Ronald Webster flew off to the United Nations hoping to gather support for expelling the British troops; he found none. The islanders themselves were in a quandary. Most wanted independence from St. Kitts and Nevis and some form of association with Britain. Others wanted full independence. Over the next few years, minor resistance to the British occupying force was seen, but it amounted to very little. Negotiations to overcome the St. Kitts-Anguilla impasse continued, and by 1972 Ronald Webster had formed the People's Progressive Party (PPP). That same year the British government allowed the formation of the Anguilla Police Force. Elections were held for a local legislative council, and the majority of the seats went to the PPP with Webster as the island's first chief minister. Power in the Legislative Assembly later shifted to Emile Gumbs of the Anguilla National Alliance (ANA), who was named chief minister in 1977. On 19 December 1980, after years of agitation and demonstration, Anguilla was formally separated from the government of St. Kitts and Nevis. Separation Day is still celebrated as a national holiday.

In 1982, through a new constitution and island mandate, the island became a British Dependent Territory.

PEOPLE

Of Anguilla's 9,000 residents, the majority are descendants of African slaves, and a smaller group are of European descent, mostly the Irish from St. Kitts. English is widely spoken, with, of course, West Indian colloquialisms that are both colorful and descriptive. Examples: "bad rudeness"—sexual intercourse; "cut 'n contrive"—to make ends meet or make do; "kiss mi guts"—expletive used when angry; "yabba mout"—to talk too much.

Primary religions on the island are Methodist, Anglican, Catholic, Seventh-Day Adventist, Baptist, and various Protestant offshoots.

GOVERNMENT AND ECONOMY

Colony Status

Anguilla is a British Crown Colony, specifically a dependent territory, with the Queen as the head of state. The Crown is represented on the island by an appointed governor and deputy governor.

A local Legislative Assembly is elected every five years and consists of 12 members, including an assembly speaker and deputy speaker. An Executive Council consists of four assembly members, the governor and deputy governor, and an attorney general. The chief minister and his or her party are elected every five years, and that post had alternated since the late 1970s between Ronald Webster, then of the new Anguilla United Movement (AUM), and Emile Gumbs of the ANA.

A 1994 election split the available seats between two parties, the Anguilla United Party (AUP) and the Anguilla Democratic Party (ADP). The ANA won representation as well. A coalition government currently exists with Hubert Hughes of the AUP as chief minister and Victor Banks of the ADP as the finance, economic development, and planning minister.

Economy

The economy of Anguilla, once based on small farming enterprises and the salt industry, now re-

fishing boats on shore
at Island Harbour

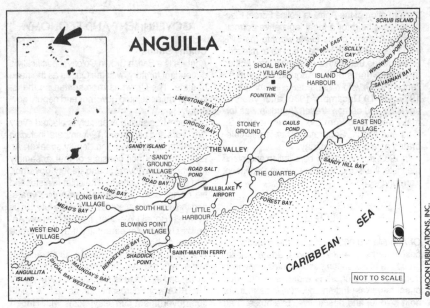

ANGUILLA

© MOON PUBLICATIONS, INC.

NOT TO SCALE

lies on tourism as the primary foreign exchange earner. The 1992 figures show 93,180 arrivals, a significant increase over the 1982 figure of 17,562. About 32,076 of the 1992 figure were overnight stays; the rest were day-trippers. Not surprisingly, more than half the island's visitors are from the U.S. and Canada. Over 900 hotel rooms are currently available, and this number is increasing gradually.

Overseas remittances and aid from the U.K. and from the Caribbean Development Bank, among others, provide Anguilla with funds for capital expenditures.

SIGHTS

Beaches
Beaches are certainly not Anguilla's sole attractions, but the island's coastline ranks among the Caribbean's best. The 12-mile (19-km) coast is lined with an estimated 45 white-sand beaches set in quiet bays and inlets. Many are protected by offshore coral reefs, making snorkeling excellent. Beaches are open to everyone, but most have few facilities outside those offered

by hotels and beachside restaurants. Topless and nude sunbathing are illegal, although there is some tacit acceptance in places. The following beaches are among Anguilla's best.

Shoal Bay, on the north coast, is a two-mile (three-km) white-sand stretch with plenty of small cafes, seaside beer joints, and chair and umbrella rental places lining the beach. This is a popular beach and may be crowded on weekends, but the snorkeling here is very good. **Limestone Bay** on the central north coast has a small beach, with rough water at times. South of Limestone Bay is first **Crocus Bay,** then **Sandy Ground,** both lined with hotels and water sports activities; both are the "places to be" at night for dancing and whooping it up. **Mead's Bay** on the far southwest Atlantic coast is also popular, the site of several of the island's luxury resorts, including Malliouhana Hotel.

On the southern Caribbean side of the island are **Shoal Bay West End, Cove Bay, Maunday's Bay,** and **Rendezvous Bay,** all with views to Saint-Martin/Sint Maarten. Several large resorts, including Covecastles, Cap Juluca, Casablanca, and the Anguilla Great House have facilities and some water sports activities. These are generally expansive and quiet, although not secluded, beaches. **Little Harbour** is less a bay than a large inlet, and is accessible either by boat or by a short walk from the end of the road. Great views and good snorkeling here.

Offshore, **Scrub Bay** and **Deadman's Bay** lie on opposite ends of on Scrub Island. **Dog Island** has a couple of coves and quiet bays, including the wide **Spring Bay** and **Savannah Bay.**

Around The Island

Beyond Anguilla's superb beaches and the galleries and shops of The Valley, not much exists of historical sites or nature attractions. A half-dozen large salt ponds recall the days of the salt industry, and several examples of turn-of-the-century West Indian architecture, primarily in The Valley, are reminiscent of the town's growth during that time.

At Crossroads, near The Valley, sits **Wallblake House,** a restored late-18th-century plantation greathouse. St. Gerard's Catholic Church currently owns the building, using it for its resident priests. Across the way is the **Devonish Cotton Gin Art Gallery,** tel. (809) 497-2405, housed in the old commercial ginnery and factory building. The building and grounds, parts of which are renovated and parts of which stand as they did years ago, can be toured by appointment.

North of The Valley, past Stoney Ground near Shoal Bay Village, is **The Fountain National Park.** The Fountain was once an important source of water for the indigenous Arawaks. Artifacts found at the nearby **Island Harbour** suggest the village was a central Arawak settlement. Pottery shards and stone and shell tools are among the area discoveries. In a cave dubbed **Big Spring,** used by Arawaks for ceremonial purposes, 37 petroglyphs have been recorded. During the ongoing archaeological dig, this cave and the surrounding area were incorporated into the national parks system, operated by the National Trust. It is not yet open to the public, and a museum is planned for the future. Contact the **Anguilla Archaeological and Historical Society,** tel. (809) 497-2727, for more information.

Elsewhere on the island are ruins of an old **Court House** at Crocus Hill, and an overgrown fortification at Sandy Hill.

Tours

Island tours and offshore cay excursions are offered by **MultiScenic Tours,** tel. (809) 497-5810, fax 497-5811, which also offers mountain bike rentals and excursions. **Malliouhana Travel and Tours** in The Valley (The Quarter), tel. (809) 497-2431, and **Bennie's Travel and Tours** in Sandy Ground Village, tel. (809) 497-2671, are both reliable tour operators.

THE VALLEY

The Valley is Anguilla's capital and main cultural and administrative center, located about

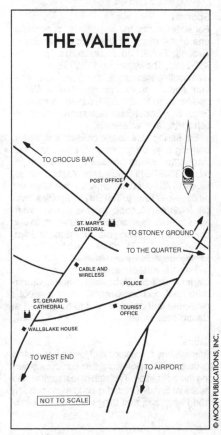

THE VALLEY

TO CROCUS BAY

POST OFFICE

ST. MARY'S CATHEDRAL

TO STONEY GROUND

TO THE QUARTER

CABLE AND WIRELESS

POLICE

ST. GERARD'S CATHEDRAL

TOURIST OFFICE

WALLBLAKE HOUSE

TO WEST END

TO AIRPORT

NOT TO SCALE

© MOON PUBLICATIONS, INC.

three miles (five km) west of the airport. It is a small town, really about a half-dozen roads, with several churches, schools, banks, a post office, police and tourism headquarters, and a few restaurants and galleries. Worth noting is **Landsome Bowl,** the island's sports stadium and center for cultural activities, including the August Carnival.

The **Anguilla Tourist Office,** tel. (809) 497-2759 or 497-2451, fax 497-3389, is located in the Social Security Building.

SPORTS AND ENTERTAINMENT

Sports

For water sports, the first stop is your hotel or one of the many facilities located at Sandy Ground. **Tamariain Watersports,** tel. (809) 497-2020, The Valley tel. 497-2798, can organize boating excursions, diving resort certification, and diving excursions. **Marine Watersports,** tel. (809) 497-2671, can do the same. At Shoal Bay, **Shoal Bay Watersports** offers sunfish sailing and water-skiing.

For sailing trips, island cruises, and trips to outlying cays on the catamaran *Wildcat,* call **Enchanted Island Cruises** at Sandy Ground, tel. (809) 497-3111. **Suntastic Yacht Cruises,** tel. (809) 497-3400, will organize cruises as well as deep-sea fishing. **Tall Boy's Big Bird Two,** tel. (809) 497-4315, organizes weekly excursions to Philipsburg and Sint Maarten, as well as charters to neighboring islands. **Princess Soya,** tel. (809) 497-2671, offers catamaran cruises to neighboring cays and islands.

Tennis is available at several hotels, including **Carimar Beach Club, Malliouhana, Cinnamon Reef,** and **Sea Grapes.** There is talk of a nine-hole golf course about to be opened at **Casablanca Hotel.**

Clubs

Anguilla has no casinos and, aside from hotels or bars, little weekday nightlife, particularly during the off season. The strip of restaurants and hotels at Sandy Ground is popular for dancing and live music, and things pick up on week-

ends. **Johno's Beach Stop,** tel. (809) 497-2728; **Lucy's Palm Palm,** tel. (809) 497-2253; and **Dragon's Disco** (no phone, best after midnight) all have music of one form or another. **Round Rock,** tel. (809) 497-2076, a small barbecue joint at Shoal Bay, has local music on Sunday evenings. **Uncle Ernie's** (no phone), also at Shoal Bay, often has live music on Sunday afternoon, as does **Gorgeous Scilly Cay** (no phone).

Malliouhana Hotel, tel. (809) 497-6111, offers nightly live lounge-lizard type music, often the "easy listening" variety.

For dancing, gambling, or general nightlife, consider taking the ferry over to Saint-Martin/Sint Maarten. There, you'll have no end of casinos, nightclubs, and fine restaurants available. Remember, however, the last ferry back departs from Marigot at 10.45 p.m.

Cultural and Folklore Performances

Make sure to see the **Mayoumba Folkloric Theatre,** a performance group that keeps the music, dance, oral storytelling traditions, and costume of pre-20th-century Anguilla alive in elaborate productions. The group can often be found at the **La Sirena Hotel** in Mead's Bay, tel. (809) 497-6827, on Thursday evenings at 9.30 p.m.

Holidays and Festivals

Anguilla's **Carnival** is celebrated in late July or early August; it's a week of calypso competitions, Prince and Princess Shows, pageants, band contests, and street dancing and festivals. Daytime activities include boat racing, which has become a national sport of sorts on Anguilla. The design of the small wooden sloops used in the races are unique to the island. Carnival activities take place all over the island, but ground zero is Landsome Bowl center in The Valley.

Anguilla observes local and British holidays, including Christmas, Boxing Day (26 December), New Year's Day, Easter, Anguilla Day (1 June), the Queen's Birthday (11 June), August Monday (first Monday in August), August Thursday (first Thursday), and Separation Day (17 December), among others.

SHOPPING

Food

For those staying in villas or in need of groceries, a good bet is **Vista Food Market** at South Hill, tel. (809) 497-2804. Open Mon.-Sat. 8 a.m.-6 p.m. Vista carries a wide selection of cheeses, vegetables and fruits, and gourmet items. **Ashley & Sons,** tel. (809) 497-2641, is a large market in South Valley. Open weekdays until 6 p.m. and Saturday until 10 p.m.

Art and Crafts

Galleries and tony boutiques are located all over the island and in hotels. The following are among the more interesting. **Anguilla Arts and Crafts Center,** tel. (809) 497-3200, a one-stop craft shop in The Valley, has a large selection, including cassette tapes by local artists. **Devonish Art Gallery** in The Valley, tel. (809) 497-4971, across from Wallblake House carries interesting local and imported items; **Cheddie's Carving Studio,** tel. (809) 497-6027, at The Cove on the West End Road, features wood and driftwood carvings by the inimitable Cheddie. The **Caribbean Style Boutique** at the Anguilla Great House has a good selection of local and imported Caribbean crafts.

ACCOMMODATIONS

The good news is that Anguilla has a fairly extensive range of accommodations, from guesthouses to villas to exclusive resorts. More good news is that prices are generally reasonable and good deals can be found. You can also find several upscale resorts with commensurate rates, but the general tenor of the island is one of medium-sized and medium-priced accommodations. So, what's the bad news? Camping is not allowed anywhere on Anguilla.

Villas and Apartments
Villas start at as little as US$100 per day for two bedrooms, to as much as US$1000 per day for luxury cottages, less by the week. Villas can be rented through **Select Villas of Anguilla,** George Hill Rd., Anguilla, West Indies, tel. (809) 497-5810, fax 497-5811; **Sunshine Villas,** Cul de Sac, Anguilla, West Indies, tel. (809)

MORE ANGUILLA ACCOMMODATIONS

Rates per s, EP when applicable, winter

NAME	(809)	(800)	TARIFF
Allamanda Apartments	497-5217	N/A	moderate
Carimar Beach Club	497-6881	382-6309	luxury
Casablanca Resort	497-6999	231-1945	luxury
Casa Nadine	497-2358	N/A	budget
Cinnamon Reef Beach House	497-2727	N/A	luxury
Cocoloba Hotel	497-6871	N/A	luxury
Ferryboat Inn	497-6613	N/A	moderate
La Palma	497-3260	N/A	moderate
La Sirena	497-6827	N/A	luxury
Milly's Inn	497-2465	N/A	moderate
Norman B	497-2242	N/A	budget
Pond Dipper	497-2315	N/A	moderate
Rendezvous Bay Hotel	497-6549	N/A	luxury
Skiffles Villas	497-6110	N/A	moderate-luxury
Spindrift Apartments	497-4164	N/A	moderate-luxury
Willie's Inn	497-6225	N/A	budget
Yellow Banana	497-2626	N/A	budget

497-6149, fax 497-6021; **Conner's Real Estate,** South Hill, Anguilla, West Indies, tel. (809) 497-6433, fax 497-6410; or **Keene Enterprises,** P.O. Box 28, The Valley, Anguilla, West Indies, tel. (809) 497-2554, fax 497-3544.

Hotels and Guesthouses

The hotels and guesthouses below are several of the many, and prices for the following categories are per person, per night, in the 15 Dec. through 15 April high season: **Luxury** US$100 or more, **Moderate** US$50-100, **Budget** US$50 or less. Add eight percent room tax in all cases and 10-15% service charge in most cases.

Malliouhana Hotel, P.O. Box 173, Mead's Bay, Anguilla, West Indies, tel. (809) 497-6111, U.S. tel. (800) 835-0796, fax 497-6011, U.S. fax (203) 656-3475, is large and super-luxurious, possibly the island's most exclusive resort. The rooms and suites are spacious, some with bathrooms that could house a small family. On the grounds are three swimming pools, four tennis courts, restaurants, a bar, boutique, exercise room, and more. The beach below, on Mead's Bay, is quiet and long. They take traveler's checks but no credit cards here. Luxury. **Cap Juluca** (P.O. Box 240 Maunday's Bay, Anguilla, West Indies; tel. (809) 497-6666, U.S. tel. (800) 323-0139, fax 497-6617, is a 179-acre resort on Maunday's Bay, composed of villas and suites and built in a strangely effective Moorish style. The amenities include tennis courts, restaurants, water sports, villas with terraces, and sunken tubs. Luxury. **Anguilla Great House,** Rendezvous Bay, Anguilla, West Indies, tel. (809) 497-6061 or (800) 241-6764, fax 497-6019, is set on Rendezvous Bay. All the West Indian-style rooms are decorated with reproduction mahogany antiques, and all face the ocean—very quaint stuff. Water sports, pool, restaurant and bar, and an art gallery on the premises. Luxury.

Less expensive accommodations include **Jeshal Apartments,** Back St., South Hill, Anguilla, West Indies, tel. (809) 497-6517, with simple and clean one-bedroom apartments. Budget. **Hibiscus House,** The Valley, Anguilla, West Indies, tel. (809) 497-5088, fax 497-5381, is a bed and breakfast 10 minutes' walk from Crocus Bay. No restaurant. Moderate. The **Inter-Island**

MORE ANGUILLA RESTAURANTS

NAME	LOCATION	(809)	CUISINE	PRICE RANGE
Amy's	Blowing Point	497-6775	West Indian	inexpensive
Brother's Cafeteria	The Valley	497-3550	West Indian	inexpensive
Capers	Mead's Bay	497-6369	West Indian/ Seafood	moderate
Cora's Pepper Pot		497-2328	West Indian	inexpensive
Jerryboat Inn	Blowing Point	497-6613	French/West Indian	moderate
La Fontana	Fountain Beach Hotel, Shoal Bay	497-3492	Italian	moderate
Mango's	Barne's Bay	497-6479	sophisticated West Indian	moderate-expensive
The Old House	George Hill	497-2228	West Indian	moderate
Que Pasa	Sandy Ground	497-3171	Mexican	moderate
Riviera	Sandy Ground	497-2833	French	expensive
Smuggler's Grill	Forest Bay	497-3728	French/Continental	moderate-expensive

Hotel, South Hill, Anguilla, West Indies, tel. (809) 497-6259, fax 497-3180, has 14 rooms and is about a half-mile walk to the beach. Moderate. **Lloyd's Guesthouse,** P.O. Box 52, Crocus Hill, Anguilla, West Indies, tel. (809) 497-2351, has a small restaurant. Moderate. **Syd-An's Hotel and Villas,** Sandy Ground, Anguilla, West Indies, tel. (809) 497-3180, fax 497-5381, has two apartments and six suites on the beach and a small restaurant. Moderate.

FOOD

Great dining is not hard to find on Anguilla; several world-class restaurants are located in hotels. Cuisines include Continental and West Indian. Stewed whelk, conch and curried conch, mutton, rice and peas, *fungi,* coconut extravaganzas, guinea corn, dumplings, and fresh fish and lobster are among the local island specialties. Several restaurants serve French or French Creole, Italian, or Chinese. Not all restaurants take credit cards, nor are all open every day—particularly during the off-season—so call ahead if possible. Categories below are based on prices per person, per entree: **Expensive** US$25 or more, **Moderate** US$10-25, **Inexpensive** US$10 or less.

For local West Indian cuisine, try **Aquarium Restaurant,** tel. (809) 497-2720, in South Hill—simple, no frills. Inexpensive. **Uncle Ernie's** (no phone) on the beach at Shoal Bay serves up burgers and beach-stand food. Inexpensive. **Lucy's Harbour View,** tel. (809) 497-6253, is reputedly the oldest restaurant on the island; you'll find it on a cliff overlooking Sandy Ground. Inexpensive-Moderate. **Fish Trap,** tel. (809) 497-4488, on the beach at Island Harbour contends for the best seafood around, a truly gourmet and sophisticated experience. Moderate. **Gorgeous Scilly Cay** (no phone) is an encounter not to be missed; it features dining (lunch only) and swimming on a small, private cay off the Island Harbour shore—wait for the free transport boat every few minutes. Closed Monday, Moderate-Expensive. **Yabba Pot,** tel. (809) 497-2820, in The Valley offers Rasta Ital (vegetarian) specialties, Inexpensive.

For sophisticated evening dining and elegant French cuisine, try **Malliouhana,** tel. (809) 497-6111. Absolutely make reservations—a day

ahead if possible—and ask for tables with views of Mead's Bay. Expensive. **Pimm's,** tel. (809) 497-6779, on the water at Maunday's Bay, also does French. Expensive. **Hibernia,** tel. (809) 497-4290, at Island Harbour features French- and Eastern-influenced seafood. Moderate. **Arlo's Place,** tel. (809) 497-6810, at Lower South Hill serves up the some of the best Italian cuisine on Anguilla. Moderate.

GETTING THERE

Anguilla's **Wallblake Airport,** tel. (809) 497-2384, is serviced by international airports in Sint

LOBSTERS

For those coming from North America, your lobster encounters in the Lesser Antilles will be slightly different than those at home. The lobster you'll see steaming in a puddle of garlic butter or slow-roasting over an open grill will be, well, missing something.

Warm water lobsters—also called spiny lobsters or rock lobsters—resemble in most ways the crustacean North Americans have come to know as crayfish. But crayfish they are not. Crayfish, which are in fact related to lobsters, are freshwater animals; the spiny lobsters of the Lesser Antilles are saltwater bound. And while North American lobsters are distinguished by their fat front-end pinchers or claws, also known as chelapeds, spiny lobsters are missing those appendages.

Lobster is a common name for the marine decapod (10-legged) crustaceans of the suborder Reptantia. The spiny lobster of the Lesser Antilles has the fanlike tail and sci-fi antennae you have come to know and expect on a lobster and, like its northern cousin, is a scavenger of the seas. The female lays eggs about every two years, and lobsters live an average 15-20 years.

Several countries in the Lesser Antilles impose restrictions on catching (usually by pots or by spearfishing) and consuming spiny lobsters during their reproductive season, April-June. Restrictions are not universal, nor are they always strictly followed or enforced; if you're concerned, check with local authorities regarding regulations.

Maarten, Antigua, and San Juan. All three international airports have direct and nonstop connections with major North American cities such as Toronto, New York, and Miami, as well as connections with European cities. From Sint Maarten, Anguilla is serviced at least three times per day by **Winair,** tel. (809) 497-2748 or 497-3748. From San Juan, take American Airlines' twice-daily American Eagle, tel. (809) 497-3500/1. **LIAT,** tel. (809) 497-5000, fax 497-5576, is the connector from Antigua or St. Kitts. Additionally, Winair, LIAT, and **Air BVI,** The Valley tel. (809) 497-2431 or 497-2348, Airport tel. (809) 497-2488, fly in from St. Thomas and St. Croix. Two air charter companies, **Air Anguilla,** tel. (809) 497-2643 or 497-2725, fax 497-2982; and **TA Tyden Air,** tel. (809) 497-2719, fax 497-3079, are available for charters and flights from and to Sint Maarten, Saint-Barts, St. Kitts, Tortola, Nevis, San Juan, and others.

Departure tax from Anguilla is US$2 (EC$5).

GETTING AROUND

Taxis

Anguilla taxis are not metered, and rates are set by the government. Typically, taxis are identified by an "H" on the license plate. Stands are located at Wallblake Airport and Blowing Point (awaiting the ferry from Saint-Martin, see "Fairy Service" below), and you can always flag down a taxi in The Valley. If you need to call a taxi, inquire at the front desk of your hotel. The taxi association has no central dispatching office. Drivers will often quote rates in U.S. dollars (see "Money, Hours, and Communication" below).

Government rates are the same for one or two persons, with US$3 added for each additional person. Taxi rates are published in the official tourism booklet *What We Do in Anguilla,* available at the tourism offices or virtually every hotel on the island.

Typical rates, from the airport to: The Valley, US$5 (EC$13.50); Shoal Bay Beach, US$10 (EC$27); Island Harbour, US$13 (EC$35); Cap Juluca, US$18 (EC$49). From Blowing Point to: airport, US$8 (EC$22); Island Harbour, US$17 (EC$46); Malliouhana Hotel, US$12 (EC$32). Island tours two to three hours in duration start at US$40 (EC$108) for one or two persons, and US$5 (EC$13.50) more for each additional person.

Car Rentals

Renting a car is less expensive than hiring a taxi for a day, and it allows you to explore at your leisure. Anguilla's roads are in fairly good shape, although some are all gravel and dust, even those leading up to luxury hotels. The roads are generally not well marked, and you are more likely to see a sign pointing toward a village rather than a route sign. Still, with a map (available at most rental agencies) you'll be fine, and you'd be hard pressed to stay lost very long on an island measuring only 16 miles (26 km) from end to end.

The speed limit in Anguilla is 30 miles (48 km) per hour. Driving is on the left, but many of the rental cars are U.S.-manufactured, meaning the steering wheel is also on the left. This leaves the driver in the odd position of being closest to the edge of the road rather than the median strip. Take care; practice a bit in the rental parking lot before pulling out.

Rental rates start at about US$35 per day for a compact car or mini-moke, which is an open-air vehicle only slightly larger than a go-cart, with tires like fat donuts. Clearly, not for large people or large parties. At any rate, with your valid driver's license you can obtain a temporary local driving license for US$6. Let the rental company organize the license for you.

Several rental companies have offices at the airport or the Blowing Point ferry docks, but to reserve ahead, call **Anguilla National Rentals,** tel. (809) 497-2065; **Apex Car Rentals,** tel. (809) 497-2642, fax 497-5032; **Avis,** tel. (809) 497-6221, fax 497-5052; **Budget,** tel. (809) 497-2217, U.S. tel. (800) 527-0700, fax 497-5871; **Concept Car Rentals,** tel. (809) 497-2671, fax 497-2901; **Conner's Car Rentals,** tel. (809) 497-6433, fax 497-6410; **Island Car Rentals,** tel. (809) 497-2723, fax 497-3723; **Roy Rogers Car Rental,** tel. (809) 497-6290, fax 497-6345; **Summer Set Car Rental,** tel. (809) 497-3778, fax 497-3037; or **Triple K Car Rental,** tel. (809) 497-2934, fax 497-2503. Make sure to inquire about free pick-up and delivery and road maps.

Bicycle Rentals

Anguilla is relatively flat and lends itself to travel by motorcycles and bicycles. Call **R&M Cycle Rental** in The Valley, tel. (809) 497-2430; **Multi-Scenic Tours** on George Hill Road, tel. (809)

INFORMATION DIRECTORY

TOURISM INFORMATION

Department of Tourism

The Valley, Anguilla, West Indies, tel. (809) 497-2795 or 497-2451, fax 497-2751.

Windotel, 3 Epirus Rd., London SW6 7UJ, tel. (01) 937-7725, fax 938-4793.

OTHER

Police, tel. (809) 497-2333.

Fire, tel. (809) 497-2333.

Ambulance, tel. (809) 497-2637.

College Hospital, tel. (809) 497-2551/2.

Anguilla Drug Store, tel. (809) 497-2738.

Paramount Pharmacy, tel. (809) 497-3836.

Baby-sitting, Clarice Hodge, tel. (809) 497-6396, or Lenore Smith, tel. (809) 497-6330.

Wallblake Airport, tel. (809) 497-2384 .

FedEx, tel. (809) 497-2719.

497-5810; or **Booth's** at The Swamp, tel. (809) 497-2075. Bicycle rentals start at about US$10 (EC$27) per day.

Ferry Service

Five miles south of Anguilla is the island of Saint-Martin/Sint Maarten, reached by a 20-minute ferry ride. Saint-Martin/Sint Maarten is lively and cosmopolitan in ways that Anguilla is not, and is an easy day trip. Casinos, duty-free shopping, an outdoor market, and fine restaurants (see the destination chapter) are all available for those who want to take advantage of the island's proximity. The ferry leaves from Blowing Point, on Anguilla's south shore, to Marigot, on the French side of Saint-Martin, every 30 minutes 7:30 a.m.-5:00 p.m. From Marigot to Blowing Point, ferries depart every 30 minutes 8 a.m.-5:30 p.m. Night ferries depart Anguilla at 6 p.m. and 9:15 p.m. The last ferry back from Marigot is at 10:45 p.m. On weekends and holidays, this one may be crowded.

Note: Before utilizing the ferry, check with the tourist office or Blowing Point Port, tel. (809) 497-6403, for changes in the schedule. Fare is US$9 (EC$24)(day) or US$11 (EC$30) (night)

one-way. Remember, you'll need your passport or travel documentation and a departure tax of US$2 (EC$5) is payable either way.

MONEY, HOURS, AND COMMUNICATION

Anguilla's official currency is the Eastern Caribbean dollar, currently exchanging at EC$2.70 = US$1. U.S. dollars, however, are used just about everywhere on the island. Traveler's checks are widely accepted, credit cards less so. Cash or traveler's checks may be changed at hotels or as you are doing business, but you will get a better exchange rate at a bank. Look for banks in the **Commercial Centre** in The Valley, including **Caribbean Commercial Bank,** tel. (809) 497-2571, and **Financial Bank, Ltd.,** tel. (809) 497-3890. Other banks in The Valley include **Barclays,** tel. (809) 497-2301, and **Scotiabank,** tel. (809) 497-3333. Banking hours vary slightly, but are generally Mon.-Thurs. 8 a.m.-3 p.m., Friday 8 a.m.-5 p.m.

Businesses are open weekdays 8 a.m.-5 p.m., with a noon lunch hour, although some grocery stores are open until 9 p.m. Some stores are open until noon or so on Saturday, grocery stores until evening, and most businesses are closed on Sunday. The **tourist office** is open weekdays 8 a.m.-noon and 1-4 p.m.

The general post office, tel. (809) 497-2528, which has a philatelic bureau, is located in The Valley and open weekdays 8 a.m.-noon and 1-3:30 p.m.

The area code for Anguilla is "809." This means North Americans dial "1-809" plus "497" and a four-digit telephone number. Dial only the last four digits for local calls. Local calls are made using telephone cards, which are purchased at **Cable and Wireless,** tel. (809) 497-3100 or 497-2210, located on Wallblake Road in The Valley. Cable and Wireless has telephones for international calls, as does the airport and Blowing Point ferry building. Hours at Cable and Wireless: weekdays 8 a.m.-6 p.m., Saturday 9 a.m.-1 p.m., and Sunday 10 a.m.-2 p.m.

For information about goings on, the tourist publications *What We Do in Anguilla* and *Anguilla Life* are available at the tourist office in The Valley, or at most hotels.

ANTIGUA AND BARBUDA

Antigua and Barbuda, officially the State of Antigua and Barbuda, comprises the islands of Antigua (An-TEE-gah), Barbuda (Bar-BEW-dah), and tiny, isolated Redonda. Barbuda lies about 27 miles (43 km) north of Antigua. The uninhabited half-square-mile (1.3-square-km) island of Redonda lies about 30 miles (48 km) southwest of Antigua.

The three islands are located at the heart of the Leewards and nearly at the midpoint of the Lesser Antilles archipelago—generally east and south of St. Kitts and Nevis, and northeast of Montserrat. Antigua's airport, V.C. Bird International, is the home base of LIAT, the regional airline. As such, Antigua has become something of a hub for interisland travelers and is a popular destination in and of itself. Tourist numbers have grown in leaps over the past dozen or so years, a 16% annual increase in recent years, and the island is one of the more tourism-conscious and developed of the Leewards. There are, at last count, 103 hotels and guesthouses on the island. Yet, for most visitors, it retains a relative simplicity of life, and provides a relaxed Caribbean experience.

THE LAND

Antigua

Antigua is, at 108 square miles (281 square km), the second largest of the Leeward Islands. The island's formation was a result of the primary wave of volcanic activity that thrust the outer islands of the Lesser Antilles through the surface of the sea. The highest point, **Boggy Peak**, is located at the southwest corner of the island, 1,319 feet (402 meters) above sea level. The area around Boggy Peak, in the St. Mary parish, is the mountainous part of Antigua; small sections of rainforest flourish here as well. The interior of the island is essentially unassuming; it's primarily flat and scrubby, with some forest cover and gentle, rolling hills. Because of infrequent and sporadic rainfall—about 45 inches (1,140 mm) per year—Antigua is one of the

Lesser Antilles' drier islands and is prone to drought. September through November are the wettest months, with daily showers lasting no longer than 20 minutes or so. There are no permanent streams or rivers, and the conservation of water is of concern to the government.

Antigua's irregular coastline features numerous small bays and outlying cays, considered by many the prime attraction of the island. Tourism hype has placed the number of Antigua's beaches at 365—one for every day of the year. While that may or may not be true, certainly an abundance of stunning white- and salmon-colored-sand beaches are found throughout the island. A barrier reef off the north coast, as well as numerous reefs and shoals, provide excellent diving opportunities.

Barbuda

If Antigua is relatively flat, then Barbuda is definitely flat. The highest point on the 68-square-mile (176-square-km) island stands a mere 145 feet (44 meters) above sea level, in the eastern coast area known not ironically as **The Highlands.**

Barbuda, a 10-minute flight from Antigua, was in the 17th century a private estate of the Codrington family. Hence, the main town of Codrington, where most of the island's population of 1,500 lives, and Codrington Lagoon, a huge body of water and mangrove swamp on the island's western side. The lagoon houses hundreds of frigate and other birds, which come to breed from August through December. Much of Barbuda is still overgrown and untamed, and domestic animals gone wild roam about. Sheep, fallow deer, pigs, ducks, and guinea fowl have found a place on the island, and all are hunted for sport. (Game hunting is allowed on Barbuda, with proper licenses and game limits required by the Secretary of the Barbuda Council.)

Barbuda is primarily coral-based and has some of the finest—and least populated—beaches in the Caribbean. Diving is spectacular. At least 73 charted shipwrecks provide ample opportunity for exploration, and an estimated

200 wrecks lie twisted and gouged on the shoals and reefs surrounding the island. Divers are also attracted by several sinkholes and underwater caves.

Redonda

Redonda is a dependency of Antigua, although today that means little in real terms. Columbus first sighted the small rock on his second voyage in 1493; he named it after a church called Santa Maria de Redonda. He did not land, however, and Redonda remained unexplored for years. Britain annexed the island, and it came under the jurisdiction of Antigua in 1869. Thanks to migrating and breeding birds, several tons of guano, rich in phosphate, made mining profitable until 1914. Today Redonda is home to gulls, goats, and the infrequent intrepid explorer.

HISTORY

Arawaks and Caribs

The original inhabitants of Antigua and Barbuda were the Stone Age Ciboney (also spelled Siboney), so-called for the stone implements they used in hunting and farming. It is likely the Ciboney inhabited Antigua at about 2000 B.C. but moved on due to the lack of a consistent supply of fresh water.

The nomadic Amerindian Arawaks arrived on the scene some 2,000 years later, just after the birth of Christ. Given the available artifactual evidence, it seems they stayed on the island until about A.D. 1200, when they were driven off by marauding Caribs—another nomadic Amerindian group with origins in South America. This was the Arawaks' lot throughout the Caribbean, always one step ahead of the Caribs and always one step behind in their capacity to defend themselves. The Caribs used the islands as bases for raiding nearby islands and were on the scene when Columbus sighted Antigua on his second voyage in 1493.

Ancient and Bearded

Columbus never set foot on the island, but he named it Santa Maria de la Antigua, after a painting of the Virgin Mary in Spain's Seville Chapel. (In Spanish, *antigua* means "ancient" and *barbuda* means "bearded.")

Having christened the islands, Columbus and the Spanish—as well as the Dutch, French, English, and other colonizers—left them in the hands of the fierce Caribs, who initially were able to defend them with characteristic vigor.

By 1632, settlement of the Caribbean was well underway, and a group of British colonizers from nearby St. Kitts landed on Antigua to claim it for the crown. Despite attacks from the Caribs, the colonizers managed to establish several tobacco and ginger plantations. Antigua has since remained in British hands, except for a few months in 1666 when the French claimed the island during one of the many skirmishes played out for Caribbean (and European) sovereignty and possessions.

In 1674, Sir Christopher Codrington arrived from the then-famed Barbados sugar plantations and established the Antigua and Barbuda sugar industry at Betty's Hope. So successful were Codrington's plantations that in 1685 he leased the entire island of Barbuda and turned it into a profitable 300-acre estate, used primarily to grow food for the burgeoning slave population. The sugar industry saw entire sections of Antigua's then-semi-forested interior razed for plantations; today many Antiguans believe that the island's continuing water problems were exacerbated by the deforestation of the island.

The growth of the sugar industry engendered the growth of slavery, and it is estimated that by 1834, the year Britain abolished slavery, there were some 30,000 Africans working the Antigua and Barbuda plantations. At the same time there were some 2,000 white planters and overseers. Sugar remained an important industry until the early 1970s, and today the remains of an estimated 140 sugar mills can be seen dotting the Antiguan countryside.

Emancipation

After the abolishment of slavery, sugar became less profitable and Antigua and Barbuda slipped into a long period of economic decline. This situation existed in many of the Caribbean islands that relied on sugar and other plantation crops as their economic bedrock. The economic decline in turn accentuated the already obvious racial (and related social and class) fissures in Antiguan society that existed well into the 20th century.

Regional discontent in the 1930s centered around poor working conditions, poor pay, and a distinctly poor quality of life. Throughout the islands, labor strikes and some violence broke out, crippling local production. The British astutely allowed the formation of labor and trade unions, the first step toward organized political parties. The first Antiguan labor union, the Antigua Trades and Labor Union, was established in 1939.

WW II and Beyond

WW II interrupted the natural flow of politics on the islands and diverted the world's attention for some time. By 1943, Vere Cornwall (V.C.) Bird became the elected president of the union and used it as a base to collect other trade unions for the formation of the Antigua Labor Party (ALP). In 1946, Bird was elected to the colonial Legislative Council. In 1951, universal suffrage was realized. By 1956, the island was granted a ministerial form of government, and Antigua and Barbuda were governed as part of the Leeward Islands associated islands until 1959. Full internal self-government as an Associated State, with foreign affairs and defense under the auspices of Britain, was granted in 1967. Full independence was granted on 1 November 1981. Except for a brief period in the early 1970s when the Progressive Labor Movement won the general elections, the ruling party has been the ALP under V.C. Bird, and, most recently, his son V.C. Bird Jr.

An arms and narcotics smuggling scandal shook up the government in 1990 and nearly brought it down. The Communications and Works Minister, Vere Bird Jr., another son of V.C. Bird, was implicated in an international scandal; allegations surfaced that Antigua was used to help smuggle Israeli arms to Colombian drug cartels. Bird resigned his post but remained a member of parliament. Further allegations of theft, corruption, and building contract irregularities plagued the government through 1993, when arson attacks and murders implied sinister dealings.

V.C. Bird Sr. declined to run in 1994's general election, citing advanced age and poor health. Another ALP victory brought leader V.C. Bird Jr. to the post of prime minister in March 1994, in his father's stead.

PEOPLE AND CULTURE

A 1991 census estimated the population of Antigua and Barbuda at 66,000. Some estimate the combined population is closer to 75,000, of which 1,500 live on Barbuda. A more significant figure, perhaps, is the racial breakdown. Descendants of African slaves account for about 95% of the population, while the remaining five percent is composed of whites, Asians, and Antiguans of mixed-race.

Culturally, Antiguans celebrate their African heritage—with a distinctly British hue. You're as likely to catch a good cricket game as you are to hear steel bands and calypso singers. Cricket is played far and wide in the Caribbean, particularly among the British islands. The West Indian cricket team has played in test matches since 1928, and since the 1970s has been one of the best in the world. Antiguans Viv Richards, who retired in 1992 as one of the four best batters of all time, and Richie Richardson, currently the West Indies' captain, rank among the world's best players. World-class matches, such as the 1993 West Indies/Pakistan Test Match and the 1994 West Indies/England Test Match, are held on Antigua and are part and parcel of Antiguan life, followed with a fervor that would put any Sunday preacher to shame.

Religions, as well, reflect the British influence. There are over 100 church structures on the island, Anglican being the most prevalent. Others include Roman Catholic, Methodist, and Seventh-Day Adventist.

At the same time, the food, carnivals (see "Sports and Recreation" below), music, and language of Antigua and Barbuda are clearly Creole. While English is the official language, the lingua franca, or local hybrid language, is a lyrical English-based Patois.

The writer Jamaica Kincaid, born in Antigua in 1949, writes novels, short stories, and essays. Her writing is descriptive of Caribbean life and, often, of the strong bonds between mothers and daughters in that context. Kincaid has published several works, including the story collection *At the Bottom of the River* (1983) and the novel *Annie John* (1985). Her autobiographical novel *Lucy* was released in 1990.

GOVERNMENT AND ECONOMY

Government
The head of government is the prime minister, currently V.C. Bird Jr. of the Antigua Labor Party. V.C. Bird Sr. has virtually monopolized the government in Antigua and Barbuda since the 1940s, serving as chief minister, premier, and prime minister. Two of his sons, Lester Bird and V.C. Bird Jr., have also been active in politics and other endeavors and have held various government posts over the years. In many ways, the Bird family is synonymous with past and present Antiguan politics.

The State of Antigua and Barbuda is a democratic republic and a member of the British Commonwealth. The British sovereign is represented on the island by a governor general. The government is legislated by two bodies; an elected 17-member Parliament, or House of Representatives, and an Upper House, or Senate, which is appointed by the governor general on the advice of the prime minister and opposition leader. Elected representatives come from the six parishes of Antigua, plus Barbuda. There are several active political parties in Antigua, including the ALP, the United National Democratic Party (UNDP), and the Barbuda People's Movement (BPM).

Economy
Antigua's economy has changed radically since the heyday of sugar production. Today's economy is primarily based on tourism, which earns more than half the gross national product and accounts for more than 60% of all economic activity. The tourism infrastructure has grown with the 1994 expansion of V.C. Bird International Airport, as well as the current development of several large resort properties. LIAT, the regional airline based at V.C. Bird International, has experienced mounting losses over the years. It is rumored, in fact, that LIAT has never had a profitable year. Its board of directors, consisting of 11 member governments, has elected to privatize the airline, and this may mean some loss of jobs or revenue for Antigua. Other economic activity takes place in the offshore banking and insurance industries, but the corruption and scandals of 1990 seem to have slowed down private sector investment.

A small amount of agricultural activity continues to take place, primarily with the production of cotton, bananas, coconuts, and pineapples. Antigua exports some petroleum products but imports most of its food, fuel, and machinery.

ANTIGUA SIGHTS

Beaches
The rallying cry of the sun-and-fun, "life is a beach" crowd has found a home in Antigua and Barbuda. Beaches are a large attraction, and, if there is a modicum of truth to the tourism department's claim that 365 beaches—a year's worth—dot the perimeter of Antigua, this may be the place to start.

Antigua's beaches are open to the public, whether they front hotel property or not. In theory, this means that one should be able to go to any beach at any time. In practice this means that beaches fronting exclusive hotels, particularly some of the all-inclusives, are difficult to get to if you must pass through hotel property to find the beach. Hotels may reserve the right to limit entry. On the other hand, many of Antigua's beaches are isolated and secluded, and often deserted. Keep in mind that most do not have lifeguards, changing rooms, or any facilities at all.

The east coast is on Antigua's windward side, facing the Atlantic, and has a more irregular and somewhat rougher coastline than the leeward side. Still, several bays and protected harbors offer excellent, quiescent beaches. Beachcombing is said to be excellent all along the coast. Head east from St. John's toward the town of Willikies where you'll find **Long Bay Beach** and the **Pineapple Beach Club.** South of Long Bay is **Nonsuch Bay,** also the site of several secluded spots. **Half Moon Bay** is nearly perfectly round, considered by many to be among the top beaches on the island. To the north near the village of Parham is **Fitches Creek Bay** and the lagoon-like beaches of **Crabbs Peninsula** (on the **Parham Harbour** side), naturally protected from the winds of the Atlantic.

On the west coast, where the water is less rough, go to **Dickenson Bay,** which is lined

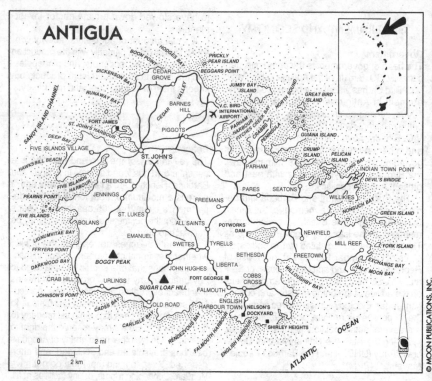

ANTIGUA

HODGES BAY
BOON POINT
DICKENSON BAY
PRICKLY PEAR ISLAND
BEGGARS POINT
CEDAR GROVE
RUNAWAY BAY
JUMBY BAY ISLAND
GREAT BIRD ISLAND
BARNES HILL
CEDAR VALLEY
V.C. BIRD INTERNATIONAL AIRPORT
FORT JAMES
ST. JOHN'S HARBOUR
PIGGOTS
PARHAM HARBOUR
FITCHES CREEK BAY
NORTH SOUND
CRABBS PENINSULA
GUIANA ISLAND
DEEP BAY
FIVE ISLANDS VILLAGE
ST. JOHN'S
PARHAM
CRUMP ISLAND
PELICAN ISLAND
LONG BAY
HAWKSBILL BEACH
FIVE ISLANDS HARBOUR
CREEKSIDE
PARES
SEATONS
INDIAN TOWN POINT
DEVIL'S BRIDGE
PEARNS POINT
JENNINGS
FREEMANS
WILLIKIES
NONSUCH BAY
FIVE ISLANDS
ST. LUKES
ALL SAINTS
GREEN ISLAND
BOLANS
POTWORKS DAM
NEWFIELD
MILL REEF
LIGNUMVITAE BAY
EMANUEL
SWETES
TYRELLS
YORK ISLAND
FFRYERS POINT
BETHESDA
FREETOWN
EXCHANGE BAY
DARKWOOD BAY
BOGGY PEAK
JOHN HUGHES
LIBERTA
HALF MOON BAY
CRAB HILL
URLINGS
SUGAR LOAF HILL
FORT GEORGE
COBBS CROSS
WILLOUGHBY BAY
JOHNSON'S POINT
OLD ROAD
FALMOUTH
ENGLISH HARBOUR TOWN
NELSON'S DOCKYARD
CADES BAY
CARLISLE BAY
RENDEZVOUS BAY
FALMOUTH HARBOUR
ENGLISH HARBOUR
SHIRLEY HEIGHTS
OCEAN
ATLANTIC
SANDY ISLAND CHANNEL

0   2 mi
0   2 km

© MOON PUBLICATIONS, INC.

with hotels, restaurants, and water sports facilities. The public beach is popular with locals.

South of Dickenson Bay and west of St. John's is **Five Islands,** a small peninsula and village with a half-dozen good beaches in the surrounding area. Here **Hawksbill Beach Resort** has four beaches, one of which is clothing-optional. The farther you get away from the hotel, the more secluded the beaches. **Deep Bay,** on which the Ramada Renaissance is located, is long enough to get out of the hotel's way. The beach at **Galley Bay** is also long and quiet, with secluded spots.

Darkwood Beach, south of **Ffryers Point** *(sic),* is a popular local hangout. On a clear day you can see Montserrat, to the west.

On the south shore, another resort area, try **Rendezvous Bay** for secluded and calm beaches. The beach at **Falmouth Harbour, Pigeon Point,** is a popular white-sand beach.

English Harbour

Antigua's rich history of colonization and development has left behind a wealth of artifacts; abandoned and decrepit sugar mills poke up from the countryside, and the remains of ancient fortifications and other defense facilities can be found along the coast. As many as 40 defense positions were manned by soldiers during the 17th and 18th centuries, one of the reasons Antigua, with its strategic location, remained in British hands throughout most of its history.

Falmouth Harbour, on the south coast, was heavily fortified; it was also the home of **Nelson's Dockyard,** one of Britain's main ship restoration facilities of the day. Admiral Horatio Nelson took charge of the Leeward Islands' fleet at age 26, and the dockyard, built around 1745, was named after him. Nelson, however, had nothing to do with its construction. It was operational until it closed in 1889 and remained unchanged until its restoration began in 1951. Now a national park (Parks Commissioner, tel. 809-460-1053), the dockyard is located in the surprisingly large town of **English Harbour.**

Here you'll find a museum and the **Admiral's Inn,** tel. (809) 460-1027, constructed in the historic pitch and tar building. The restored **Copper and Lumber Store Hotel,** tel. (809) 460-1058, is now a working hotel and features a bar and restaurant. A working masthouse, marina, several T-shirt and trinket vendors, restaurants, and gift shops are all located at the complex. Admission is EC$4 or US$1.60, free for children under 12; open daily 9 a.m.-5 p.m.

Visible from the dockyard is **Clarence House,** an official residence of the governor general and Britain's Royal Family when they visit the island. The house was built in 1787 and is open to the public in the absence of the governor general and the Royal Family.

In the hills overlooking English Harbour and Nelson's Dockyard is **Shirley Heights,** a fortification named after a General Sir Thomas Shirley, a former governor of the Leeward Islands. The view is one of the best on the island, not to be missed. Up on the bluff you'll find the remains of **Fort Shirley,** built in the late 1700s. The fortifications are spread over the hill and consist of barracks, magazines, cannon platforms, and an ancient water cistern. Also on Shirley Heights is the famous **Lookout Restaurant,** a popular place for barbecues and dancing on Thursday and Sunday.

A fork off the road to Shirley Heights leads to the **Dow's Hill Interpretation Centre,** tel. (809) 460-2777, another national park facility established in 1984. The center includes fortification ruins, an intriguing multimedia presentation in an air-conditioned room (pleasant after hiking around), and a gift shop. On a good day you can see the island of Guadeloupe to the south. Open Mon.-Sat. 9 a.m.-5 p.m. and Sunday 10 a.m.-6 p.m., admission EC$10 or US$4.

Interior

Elsewhere on the island, forts and estate ruins are plentiful. The road north from English Harbour leads to the village of **Table Gordon Hill,** east of **Liberta.** From the village, a mile's walk or ride in a 4WD vehicle brings you to **Fort George,** on **Monk's Hill.** The fort was completed in 1669 to defend Falmouth Harbour. The ruins, on about seven acres, have gone green with age and are somewhat overgrown.

Take the road east from St. John's to the village of Pares and turn south to find **Betty's Hope,** the ruins of the first sugar plantation in Antigua, established by Christopher Codrington in 1674. Betty was Codrington's daughter. Two windmill towers and a boiling house stand out among the ruins. The site, once the government seat of the Leeward Islands during Codrington's governorship, is being restored by the Antigua Historical and Archaeological Society. A visitors center is open Tuesday through Saturday.

In the village of Parham, north of Pares, you'll find **Parham Harbour,** Antigua's first port. Parham was the port used to export sugar from the island's first plantations. With the decline of the sugar industry, economic activity moved to the capital of St. John's, and Parham Harbour declined. A restoration project is currently underway, funded by the government and the Organization of American States. In Parham you'll find the striking **St. Peter's Church,** an Anglican parish church originally completed in 1755. A first structure was gutted by fire and a second shaken by an earthquake; the present one dates back to the 1840s.

For "nearly natural" attractions, the **Potworks Dam and Reservoir,** with a capacity of one billion gallons, lies north of **Bethesda,** a small town on Willoughby Bay. **Fig Tree Drive** stretches from the village of **Old Road** on **Carlisle Bay** on the south coast, to **Swetes,** near the center of the island. The drive is rough but navigable, through the lush vegetation of a small rainforest.

Boggy Peak, the island's highest point, can be reached by car from the village of **Urlings.** The road is maintained by the Cable and Wireless company, which also maintains a complex of buildings at the peak.

Devil's Bridge National Park, at **Indian Town Point** east of Willikies, is a natural bridge and several blowholes created in the limestone rocks by thousands of years of thundering surf.

ST. JOHN'S

St. John's, the island's largest town, is also Antigua's capital and economic center. Roughly one-third of the population lives here, engaged in minor manufacturing, shipping, and government work. Tourism is important in St. John's; cruise ships make their call here dozens of times each week. The shopping centers at **Redcliffe Quay** and the relatively new **Heritage Quay**

add a sleek sheen to the downtown area. Still, it's an old and rambling town, with structures and examples of West Indian colonial architecture dating back to the 17th century.

The Cathedral of St. John, between Long and Newgate streets, is Antigua's largest church. The Anglican Cathedral was first built of wood in 1681 on the orders of Governor Codrington and later replaced by a stone structure. The church was destroyed in an 1843 earthquake and rebuilt two years later. The interior is cool and quiet, ex-

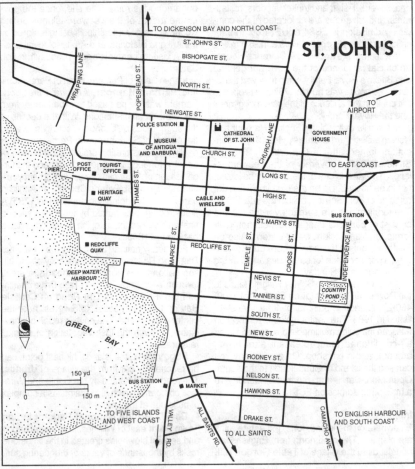

cept on Sunday, and is lined with strong pitch pine to ensure its safety in earthquakes.

The **Museum of Antigua and Barbuda,** tel. (809) 462-1469, located on Long Street across from the police station, is worth a visit. The building, built in 1750, was once the colonial courthouse. The museum is small but displays ancient Arawak artifacts, a children's section with games and hands-on displays, a gramophone, a hand-cranked telephone, and a cricket bat, courtesy of revered cricketer Viv Richards. There's a gift shop on the first floor, and a library and the national archives office are located on the second floor. The museum is open Mon.-Fri. 8:30 a.m.-4 p.m., and Saturday 10 a.m.-2 p.m. Donation is EC$5 or US$2.

The **Antigua and Barbuda Botanical Gardens,** tel. (809) 462-1007, an eight-acre garden on Independence Avenue overlooking the parliament building, was established in 1893 but deteriorated during the 1950s due to general lack of interest. A botanical society began the task of renovation in 1987, and now the garden is back in operation. Projects under development include an aviary, aquarium, orchid collection, and playground.

Fort James, northwest of town on Fort Road, was constructed in the early 18th century to protect St. John's Harbour. The ruins of the buildings date to circa 1739, and 10 of the 36 original two-ton cannons are still there.

On the south side of the harbor you'll find the ruins of **Fort Barrington,** overlooking St. John's and Deep Bay. This fort saw more action than any other in Antigua's defense. It was captured in 1666 by the French and kept for a year before the British won it back.

BARBUDA SIGHTS

Beaches

Barbuda's beaches are superb. As a matter of fact, Barbuda is just about all beach. **Low Bay,** to the west of the Codrington Lagoon, measures seven miles (11 km) of beach, with some of the best white-pink coral sand you'll find anywhere. The beach at **Coco Point,** near one of the island's two airstrips, is also popular—which, here, doesn't yet mean crowded.

Barbuda is, in a word, uncomplicated. The big thing to do is to walk the miles of beach or watch the teeming bird life on either the tiny **Man of War Island** or in the mangrove swamps of **Codrington Lagoon.** It's estimated that over 400 species of birds migrate to the lagoon yearly. Diving is spectacular on the island, with several reefs offering a plethora of corals and reef fish for observation. Serious divers can explore some of the 73 charted wrecks along the reefs.

The 56-foot (17-meter) **Martello Tower** and fort, on the south shore, was built for the defense of the island. Nine cannons were once in position, and the tower was also used as a signal station.

In the **Highlands,** Barbuda's highest point, you'll see the ruins of **Highland House,** a complex occupied by the Codrington family. Ruins of slave quarters, the main house, and a cistern are still visible.

The half-dozen-road town of **Codrington** is where most everyone on Barbuda lives. The 1743 government house and the Old Church are attractions, and you can see the entire village in a few unhurried hours. You can catch a boat at the wharf for a tour of the lagoon.

SPORTS AND RECREATION

Holidays and Festivals

The **Antigua Carnival** is considered by many to be second only to Trinidad's in style and energy. Held for 10 days in late July through the first Tuesday in August, carnival activities include street dancing, reggae bands, pan and calypso bands, contests, beauty pageants, food, costumes, "jump ups" (street marching), and, well, jumping up. The grand finale, held the first Monday night in August, is J'Overt, a huge "jump up" where bands and crowds pour into the streets at 4 a.m., dancing and becoming a bit crazy. Most carnival activity takes place in St. John's, at the open-air Carnival City.

Note: For current information about Antigua's carnival, contact the **Carnival Office,** tel. (809) 462-0194 or 462-4707.

Barbuda's smaller and more sedate, but no less intriguing, carnival is called **Caribana** and is held in June.

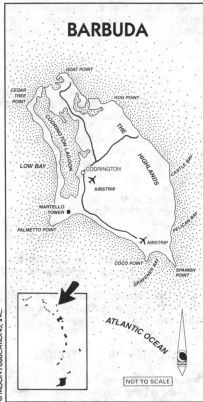

BARBUDA

GOAT POINT

CEDAR TREE POINT

HOG POINT

CODRINGTON LAGOON

THE HIGHLANDS

LOW BAY

CODRINGTON

AIRSTRIP

CASTLE BAY

MARTELLO TOWER

PELICAN BAY

PALMETTO POINT

AIRSTRIP

COCO POINT

GRAVENER BAY

SPANISH POINT

ATLANTIC OCEAN

NOT TO SCALE

© MOON PUBLICATIONS, INC.

Antigua sponsors a **Jazz Festival,** still in its infancy and held for three days in late May.

The annual **Antigua Sailing Week,** held in late April, attracts sailors from throughout the Caribbean. International tennis championship games are also held on the island, such as January 1994's Men's International Tennis Championship at Half Moon Bay.

Public holidays include New Year's, Easter and its related holy days, Christmas, Boxing Day, Labour Day (first Monday in May), CARICOM Day (or Caribbean Community Day, 4 July), and the Queen's Birthday (second Saturday in June).

Water Sports
Water sports facilities are mainly operated from hotels, and your hotel will be able to provide equipment or point you in the right direction.

Halcyon Cove Watersports, tel. (809) 462-0256, operates out of the Halcyon Cove Hotel on Dickenson Bay. **Wadadli Watersports,** tel. (809) 462-2980 or 462-4792, conducts cruises on its three catamarans and rents charters. Trips include one to Great Bird Island, a small cay off the north shore, as well as a circumnavigation cruise and snorkeling cruises. Wadadli will pick up at certain hotels on the north and west coasts. At the Jolly Harbour marina and complex, on Lignumvitae Bay on the west coast, contact **Caribbean Water Sports,** tel. (809) 460-3550.

Diving
Divers call **Jolly Dive,** tel. (809) 462-2824, fax 462-3496, at Jolly Harbour marina. **Dive Runaway,** tel. (809) 462-2626, is at the Runaway Beach Club but will pick up at certain hotels. **Dive Antigua,** tel. (809) 462-3483, fax 462-7787, is at the Halcyon Cove Hotel. **Aquanaut** diving centers are located at the St. James Club, tel. (809) 460-5000; the Galleon Beach Club, tel. (809) 460-1024; and the Ramada, tel. (809) 462-3733.

Deep-Sea Fishing
Fishing charters are available through **Obsession Deep Sea Fishing,** tel. (809) 462-2824. Game fishing off Antiguan shores is excellent.

Boat Charters
Yacht and pleasure boat charters are available through **Kokomo Catamaran Day Sails** at Jolly Harbour, tel. (809) 462-7245, fax 462-7725; or **Nicholson Yacht Charters** at English Harbour, tel. (809) 460-1530, fax 460-1531.

If you've got a desire to go on one of those fun day-cruises where you limbo and drink too much rum, then the **Jolly Roger,** tel. (809) 462-2064, is for you. Docked at Heritage Quay in St. John's, the ship is one of the largest in Antiguan waters. And, hey, you'll get to "walk the plank," pirate style.

Golf
There are three golf courses on Antigua and one on Barbuda. On Antigua, try the 18-hole, par 70 public course at **Cedar Valley,** tel. (809) 462-0161, home of the annual Antigua Open, or the nine-hole course at the **Half Moon Bay** resort, tel. (809) 460-4300. Both courses rent

equipment. At the **Jolly Harbour** complex, tel. (809) 462-6166, you can play a short 18-hole golf course.

Barbuda's nine-hole, double-tee course is at the **K Club** but is available for use by hotel guests only.

Horseback Riding

Horseback riding stables are found in Dickenson Bay or at the **Spring Hill Riding Club,** tel. (809) 460-1333, at Rendezvous Bay in the south. You can find another stable at the **St. James Club** resort.

Tennis

Most of the larger hotels feature tennis courts and fitness clubs, but a public court can be found at **Temo Sports** in English Harbour, tel. (809) 460-1781. Squash courts are also available, and the complex is open Mon.-Sat. 7 a.m.-10 p.m.

BBR Sportive, tel. (809) 462-6260, at the Jolly Harbour complex, has lighted tennis courts,

squash courts, and even a swimming pool and is open daily 8 a.m.-9 p.m.

Working Out

If you don't have a health center at your hotel, try the **National Fitness Centre,** tel. (809) 462-3681, on Old Parham Road in St. John's. You'll find a workout room, weights, and aerobics classes. Open Mon.-Fri. 6-10 a.m. and noon-8 p.m., and Saturday 9 a.m.-2 p.m. The fee is US$10 (EC$27) per day.

Hua Xia Health Centre, tel. (809) 461-6777, on All Saints Road in St. John's offers massages, reflexology, facials, and acupuncture.

Sporting Events

For major sports events, look to the **Annual Antigua Sailing Week,** now in its 28th year. There are three classes of competition yachts and nearly 200 competitors. This is a world-class regatta, and the week is filled with special events and music in addition to the races.

MORE ANTIGUA HOTELS

Rates per s, EP when applicable, winter

NAME	(809)	(800)	LOCATION	TARIFF
Admiral's Inn	460-1027	223-5695	English Harbour	moderate
Antigua Sugar Mill Hotel	462-3044	223-6510	Coolidge	moderate
Banana Cove	463-2003	223-9815	Dian Bay	moderate-luxury
Barrymore	462-4062	N/A	Fort Road, St. John's	moderate
Barrymore Beach Club	462-4101	N/A	Runaway Bay	moderate
Blue Heron Hotel	462-8564	N/A	Johnson's Point	moderate
Bougainvillea Hotel	462-3040	N/A	All Saints Road	moderate
Club Antigua	462-0061	777-1250	Jolly Beach	luxury
Half Moon Bay Club	460-4300	223-6510	Half Moon Bay	luxury
Hawksbill Beach Resort	462-0301	223-6510	Five Islands	luxury
Murphy's Place	461-1183	N/A	St. John's	budget
Pineapple Beach Club	463-2006	345-0356	Long Bay	luxury
Royal Antiguan Renaissance Hotel	462-3733	228-9898	Deep Bay	luxury
Siboney Beach Club	462-0806	N/A	Dickenson Bay	luxury
Spanish Main Inn	462-0660	N/A	St. John's	budget
Yepton Beach Resort	462-2520	361-4621	Hog John Bay (Five Islands)	luxury

MORE ANTIGUA VILLAS AND APARTMENTS

Rates per unit, EP when applicable, winter

NAME	(809)	FAX	LOCATION	TARIFF
At The Hill	461-3312	N/A	Marble Hill	moderate
Browns Bay Villas	462-0818	462-3529	Brown's Bay	moderate
Buccaneer Cove Villas	462-0959	463-3344	Dickenson Bay	moderate
Burton's Apartments	462-4268	N/A	St. John's	budget-moderate
Camp Runaway	N/A	N/A	Runaway Bay	budget
Golden Rock Apartments	462-8218	N/A	Crab Hill	budget-moderate
Harbour View Apartments	462-1762	N/A		luxury
Sunshine Cottages	460-1005	N/A	Falmouth	budget
Swifts Deluxe Apartments	462-1384	N/A	Gambles Terrace	budget
Time-A-Way	462-0075	462-2587	Runaway Bay	moderate
Trade Winds Cove	461-0111	N/A	Dickenson Bay	budget

Nightlife

For music, dancing, and nightlife, hotels are generally the best bet. The larger ones have some scheduled entertainment, from bands to limbo contests, virtually every day. Shirley Heights **Lookout Restaurant,** tel. (809) 460-1785, has a packed Sunday afternoon barbecue with a steel band 3-6 p.m., and a reggae band 6-9 p.m. The **Lime Disco** at Redcliffe Quay is small but popular.

You'll find a half-dozen casinos on Antigua, the newest and possibly largest being **King's Casino,** tel. (809) 462-1727, at Heritage Quay in St. John's. It's open every day until early morning.

SHOPPING

St. John's is the shopping center, and the modern **Heritage Quay** and more funky **Redcliffe Quay** are St. John's shopping meccas. The two mini-malls are on parallel streets down by the harbor's cruise ship dock and contain all manner of duty-free shops, including jewelry, leather, liquor, curio, art, and "beach" stores. Name brands such as Benetton, Gucci, and Radio Shack are represented. **The Toy Shop** at Redcliffe Quay is very good, and the **West Indies**

Ice Co. in Heritage Quay is recommended for its decor as well as inexpensive jewelry.

And, importantly, there are public toilets at Heritage Quay.

Elsewhere in town, try **The Map Shop,** tel. (809) 462-3993, for maps and books. The **Jolly Harbour** marina complex also features a handful of duty-free shops.

Islands Arts Galleries, tel. (809) 462-2787, is one of the island's best, at Heritage Quay. This gallery has a large branch and studio at the **Le Gourmet Restaurant** on Fort Road, tel. (809) 462-2977. **Harmony Hall,** tel. (809) 460-4120, in Freetown is also quite large and has a restaurant.

ACCOMMODATIONS

Antigua and Barbuda accommodations range from small guesthouses, of which there are few, to luxury hotels, of which there are many. At last count, 103 hotels and dozens of villa rentals were available on the islands.

Keep in mind that hotels generally add a 10% service charge to the bill, which may be regarded as a tip for the hotel staff, and a seven percent government tax.

Note: Camping is not allowed.

Antigua Accommodations

Renting a villa for a week or month be an advantage on the island, particularly if you're traveling with a group or family. Villas often come with a cook and maid service, or even a rental car tossed into the bargain. In addition to private villas you might find listed in your local newspaper or travel magazine, you can go straight to several island sources. **Caribrep,** tel. (809) 462-0818; **Jolly Harbor Realty,** tel. (809) 462-7542; and **Caribbean Properties,** tel. (809) 462-1873, all list various rental properties, time-shares, and properties for sale.

Antigua's resort hotels tend to cluster around the northwest coast, where fine beaches can also be found, as well as the quieter south coast.

The Caribbean's off-season is mid-April through mid-December, when rates may be reduced by as much as 20-40%. A comprehensive list of Antigua and Barbuda accommodations is available from the Department of Tourism (see the "Information Directory" chart, below).

Categories below refer to prices for high season, per person, per night. **Luxury** US$100 or more, **Moderate** US$50-100, **Budget** less than US$50. Top picks:

Blue Waters Beach Hotel, P.O. Box 256, St. John's, Antigua, West Indies, tel. (809) 462-0290, U.S. tel. (800) 372-1323, Canada tel. (800) 338-8782, U.K. tel. (081) 367-5175, local fax 462-0293, U.K. fax (081) 367-9949, is located on the north coast on a quiet bay and beach. Accommodation consists of standard rooms to deluxe villas, and comfortable ones at that. The restaurant here is adequate, and a very British afternoon tea is served daily. Luxury.

Joe Mike's Downtown, P.O. Box 136, St. John's, Antigua, West Indies, tel. (809) 462-1142, U.S. tel. (212) 541-4117, Canada tel. (416) 961-3085, U.K. tel. (144) 148-67073, fax 462-6056 or 462-1187, is, in fact, downtown, located on the corner of Corn Alley and Nevis Street. The hotel is clean and basic, and you'll find a small restaurant, ice cream shop, lounge, and casino downstairs. Budget.

Runaway Beach Club, P.O. Box 874, St. John's, Antigua, West Indies, tel. (809) 462-3280, U.S. tel. (800) 74-CHARMS or (212) 251-1800, fax 462-4172, is found on the Runaway Bay strip of hotels. The beach is great, rooms and villas are located on the water, and the area is jumping. The Lobster Pot restaurant, on the beach, is a treat. Moderate-Luxury.

The **St. James Club,** P.O. Box 63, St. John's, Antigua, West Indies, tel. (809) 460-5000, U.S. tel. (800) 274-0008, Canada tel. (800) 268-9051, U.K. tel. (01) 589-700, local fax 460-3015; U.S. fax (212) 308-6392, on Mamora Bay is one of the most exclusive resorts in the Caribbean. The 100-acre property features four pools, four restaurants, a half-dozen bars, casino, health club, all sports, and the ambience of elegance. The resort has rooms, suites, and villas, some privately owned. Only deep pockets need enter. Luxury.

Sandals Antigua, P.O. Box 147, St. John's, Antigua, West Indies, tel. (809) 462-0267, U.S. and Canada tel. (800) SANDALS, U.K. (071) 581-9895, fax (809) 462-4135, is located on Dickenson Bay and is everything you'd expect in a Sandals, one of the Caribbean's premier all-inclusive chains. Three bars, a pool, fine food, all

MORE BARBUDA ACCOMMODATIONS

Rates per s, EP when applicable, winter

NAME	(809)	TARIFF
Earl's Villas	462-0480	moderate
Maclean Jeffery House	460-0130	moderate
Palmetto Hotel	460-0440 or 462-0480	moderate
Pink Sands Hotel	462-0480	moderate
Selwyn Thomas' Guest House	460-0147	budget-moderate
Sunset View Hotel Apartments	460-0078	budget-moderate

sports, entertainment, and a great beach are included in the rates. We could do without the whistle-blowing activity directors. Couples (heterosexual) only. Luxury.

Barbuda Accommodations

Several private homes and villas are available for rent on Barbuda, and your first point of contact would be the Antigua and Barbuda tourism department at (809) 462-0029.

The **K Club,** tel. (809) 460-0300, fax 460-0305; and **Coco Point Lodge,** tel. (809) 462-3816, are the island's two luxury resorts, both quiet and exclusive, located on the south coast of the island.

Nedds Guest House, tel. (809) 460-0059, is clean, homey, and convenient, located above a small supermarket in Codrington. This is a good deal. Budget.

FOOD

Antigua Grocery Markets

If you're renting a villa or apartment or otherwise have a need to cook for yourself, a good place to shop is the open St. John's **Public Market,** tel. (809) 462-1216, on, not surprisingly, Market Street (and All Saints Street). The open-air public market and the **Central Marketing Corporation** are open everyday but busiest on Thursday, Friday, and Saturday. You can buy fresh fruits, vegetables, and even meat (lots of flies, maybe not so fresh) here. Try the famous "Black Pineapple," grown near Urlings, reputed to be the sweetest in the world. The market is bustling and affords an Antiguan experience you're not likely to find at your resort hotel. The market is, conveniently, located next to the **West Bus Station,** which services the southern section of the island.

Other St. John's grocery stores include the large **Bryson's Supermarket,** tel. (809) 462-2136, and **Dew's Supermarket,** tel. (809) 462-1211, both on Long Street. **The Epicurian,** tel. (809) 462-2565, on Old Parham Road sells fresh meat and produce, and some gourmet items.

In Deep Water Harbour, go to the monstrous **Food City,** tel. (809) 462-4808, open every day 7 a.m.-11 p.m.

Antigua Restaurants

Hotel restaurants are generally excellent and recommended, but keep in mind you won't be able to eat at the all-inclusives unless you're a guest there. Make reservations at hotel restaurants, and assume that dress is not extremely casual. Hotels are also useful in that they are open on Sunday, when much of Antigua shuts down.

Most restaurants add a 10% service charge and seven percent tax to the check, and many of the larger eateries accept major credit cards. It's best to call ahead to check.

In St. John's, you'll find fine restaurants as well as fast-food restaurants, pizza places, and chain restaurants such as KFC, for those in need a dose of home.

The following small sampling of restaurants specialize in West Indian Creole or international cuisine. The categories refer to average per-person entree prices, excluding drinks: **Expensive** US$25 or more, **Moderate** US$10-25, **Inexpensive** less than US$10.

Alberto's, tel. (809) 460-3007, at Willoughby Bay, serves Italian and West Indian, and is noted for its extensive wine list. You can tour the wine cellar to make your selection. The restaurant is open for dinner only, closed July-October. Expensive.

The restored **Copper and Lumber Store,** tel. (809) 460-1058, at Nelson's Dockyard in English Harbour has an old-fashioned pub ambience, and serves lunch and dinner daily. Moderate-Expensive.

St. John's

In St. John's the **Calypso Restaurant,** tel. (809) 462-1965, on Redcliffe Street is one of the island's best West Indian/local restaurants, open for lunch and drinks Mon.-Sat. 10:30 a.m.-5 p.m. In the open-air patio, try curried goat with rice and peas and top the meal off with homemade coconut ice cream. A live band plays Wednesday and Friday nights. Inexpensive-Moderate.

Chez Pascal, tel. (809) 462-3232, on Tanner Street is set in a rustic, old tin-roofed Caribbean home. The restaurant is known for some of the best French and West Indian cuisine around. Open Mon.-Fri. for lunch and

MORE ANTIGUA RESTAURANTS

NAME	LOCATION	(809)	CUISINE	PRICE RANGE
Al Porto Ristorante	Jolly Harbour	462-7695	Italian	moderate
Andes Big Bite	St. John's	462-2949	East Indian/ West Indian	inexpensive
Cacubi	Blue Waters Hotel, Boon Point	462-0290	Continental	expensive
Coconut Grove Beach Restaurant	Dickenson Bay	462-1538	International	moderate
Colombo's	Galleon Beach Club, English Harbour	460-1452	Italian	moderate-expensive
Curry House	St. John's	462-1895	East Indian	inexpensive
Kim Sha	St. John's	462-4505	Chinese	inexpensive-moderate
Le Bistro	Hodges Bay	462-3881	French	moderate-expensive
Lemon Tree	St. John's	462-1969	Continental	moderate
Lobster Pot	Runaway Bay	462-2855	International/ seafood	moderate

dinner, dinner only on Saturday; closed Sunday. Expensive. **Hemingway's,** tel. (809) 462-2763, is found upstairs in a circa 1800s building on Jardine Court, over the Sugarmill Boutique. The cuisine is solid West Indian. The open verandah overlooks St. Mary's Street and Heritage Quay. Open for breakfast, lunch, and dinner, Mon.-Saturday. Inexpensive-Moderate. The new **Commissioner Grill,** tel. (809) 462-1883, is located on lower Redcliffe Street and Commissioner Alley. The cuisine is West Indian, and the bar and open kitchen gives it the feel of a busy city diner. Open daily for breakfast until midnight. Inexpensive-Moderate.

Eating on Barbuda

Choices are limited, but you'll find plenty of snack places and several hotel restaurants (except the exclusive Coco Point, closed to nonguests) at your disposal. **The Lagoon Cafe** at the wharf in Codrington is good for light snacks, evening drinks, and entertainment.

GETTING THERE

V.C. Bird International Airport is located at the northeast corner of Antigua, about five miles (eight km) east of St. John's. The airport is the main entry point on Antigua and is serviced by several international and regional airlines.

International airlines rearrange their routes and route frequencies regularly, but those that currently serve Antigua, with local contact numbers (see the "Major Airlines Serving the Lesser Antilles" chart for toll-free numbers) are **Air Canada,** tel. (809) 462-1147; **American Airlines,** tel. (809) 462-0950/1/2; **British Airways,** tel. (809) 462-0876 or 462-3219; **BWIA,** tel. (809) 462-0262/3 or 462-0934; **Continental Airlines,** tel. (809) 462-0323/4 or 462-3195; and **Lufthansa,** tel. (809) 462-0987.

The Antigua-based regional airline **LIAT,** tel. (809) 462-0700 or 462-3142/3, services other Caribbean islands and has connections to Antigua from San Juan and the Virgin Islands.

V.C. Bird gets fairly crowded when international flights are boarding. Give yourself two hours to get through the checkout, and remember to have your departure tax on hand. Currently the departure tax is EC$25 or US$10.

Island-Hopping

For interisland travel, flying is the best way to go. LIAT serves the most destinations and in effect sets the standard in fares. LIAT's current full roundtrip fare to Barbuda is US$44 (stand-by costs less but is risky), and the numerous Antigua-Barbuda flights on the schedule can easily accommodate a day trip.

Should you choose to charter a flight, which can be cost-effective if you've got enough travelers to split the fare, try **Antigua and Barbuda Airlines,** tel. (809) 462-1124, or **Carib Aviation,** tel. (809) 462-3147, fax 462-3125.

A good source for day trips and other excursions to Barbuda is the tour operator and villa rental agency **Caribrep,** tel. (809) 462-0818.

GETTING AROUND

Taxis

Taxis and other public transport vehicles are identified by license plates featuring an "HA" or "HB." Taxis are not metered and rates are regulated by a taxi association. Rates are posted at the customs exit from V.C. Bird, and although every driver is supposed to have a copy of applicable rates in their vehicle, don't count on it. Negotiate before you get into the cab. Hotels often subcontract taxis for their guests, and you can be sure their rates are a couple of dollars higher than street taxis.

If you want to call a taxi in St. John's, try **Daylight Taxi,** tel. (809) 462-3015, or **Twenty Four Hour Taxi Service,** tel. (809) 462-5190/1. In Dickenson Bay, call **Incorporate Taxi Service,** tel. (809) 462-4325. Taxis can be hailed most anywhere in St. John's, particularly at the West Bus Station and at Heritage Quay.

Buses

The bus system on Antigua is "challenging"—or, if you're inclined to precision in your choice of words, just this side of "incomprehensible."

If you've got time to figure out the system, a bus can be an inexpensive way to travel. Generally, buses are privately owned minivans, and routes are posted in the front windows. They rarely travel by a fixed timetable and seem to depart when the drivers feel they are full.

In St. John's, catch buses at the Public Market for points south and east. Buses are, amazingly, banned from areas north of St. John's and V.C. Bird. Go figure. A typical fare from St. John's to English Harbour is EC$3.

On Barbuda, the limited road system and population will not support bus service. The best way to get around is to rent a jeep (see below).

Antigua Rental Agencies

Car rentals are probably your best bet for seeing the islands at your own pace. Most agencies are located in St. John's or at the airport. A temporary local license, good for 90 days, is needed to operate a rental vehicle. They can be obtained at a local police station, or a reputable rental agency will do it for you. The cost is EC$30, or US$12. Rental companies usually will pick up and deliver at your hotel, and most offer free mileage. Lowest daily rates for car rentals are in the US$35-50 range.

Try **Carib Car Rental,** tel. (809) 462-2062, for one of the cheapest at US$35, US$3 extra for air-conditioning. **Jonas Rent-A-Car,** tel. (809) 462-3760, also has a good reputation and may negotiate in the off-season. Others include **Avis,** tel. (809) 462-AVIS or 462-2840, fax 462-2848; **Budget,** tel. (809) 462-3009 or 462-3007, fax 462-3057; **Capital Rentals,** tel. (809) 462-0863, fax 461-2165; **Hertz,** tel. (809) 462-4114 or 462-6268, fax 462-1048; and **National,** tel. (809) 462-2113.

Street signs are virtually nonexistent outside of St. John's, so navigating around the island will be a thrill. Maps are available from rental agencies, but kindly Antiguans have long understood the plight of the lost visitor. Don't be afraid to ask, and remember to drive on the left.

A good selection of bicycles, including mountain bikes, is found at **Sun Cycles** in Hodges Bay, tel. (809) 461-0324. They will deliver and pick up for you. **Take 1 Video and Bicycle Rentals,** tel. (809) 460-2604, fax 460-1871, in English Harbour also carries a few bikes. Cost ranges US$10-20 per day.

INFORMATION DIRECTORY

ANTIGUA AND BARBUDA DEPARTMENT OF TOURISM

P.O. Box 363, St. John's, Antigua, West Indies, tel. (809) 462-0480, fax 462-2483.

610 5th Ave., Suite 311, New York, NY 10020, tel. (212) 541-4117, fax 757-1607.

121 SE 1st St., Suite 1001, Miami, FL 33131, tel. (305) 381-6762, fax 381-7908.

60 St. Clair Ave., Suite 205, Toronto, ON MT4 IN5, tel. (416) 961-3805, fax 961-7218.

Antigua House, 15 Thayer St., London W1M 5DL, tel. (071) 486-7073, fax 486-9970.

Postfach 1331, Minnholzweg 2, 6242 Kronberg 1, Germany, tel. 06173-5011.

ANTIGUA INFORMATION

Antigua Hotel and Tourist Association, P.O. Box 454, Lower Redcliffe St., St. John's, Antigua, tel. (809) 462-0374, tel. and fax (809) 462-3702.

General Emergencies, tel. 999 or 911.

Fire, tel. (809) 462-0044.

Police, tel. (809) 462-0215.

Ambulance, tel. (809) 462-0251.

Holbertson Hospital, Hospital Rd., St. John's, tel. (809) 462-0251.

American Express Representative, Antours, Long St., St. John's, tel. (809) 462-4788 (lost cards tel. 800-528-2121, lost checks tel. 800-828-0366).

Customs, tel. (809) 462-0028.

Immigration, tel. (809) 460-0050.

FedEx, Church St., St. John's, tel. (809) 462-4854/8.

The City Pharmacy, St. Mary's St., St. John's, tel. (809) 462-1363.

BARBUDA INFORMATION

General Emergencies, tel. 999 or 911.

Police, tel. (809) 460-0074.

Customs, tel. (809) 460-0085.

Barbuda Rental Agencies

The only game in town is **Thomas Car Rental,** tel. (809) 460-0047. Rental rate is US$40-50 per day.

Barbuda's limited main road system connects Codrington with the airport and the south of the island, but beyond that, you won't be driving much.

MONEY, HOURS, AND COMMUNICATION

Currency and Banks

The Eastern Caribbean dollar is official, but the U.S. dollar is widely used in Antigua and Barbuda. The official exchange rate is EC$2.70 = US$1, but when shopping or using taxis, the rate of EC$2.50 is commonly used. This makes it worthwhile to change your currency and deal in EC dollars. It's best to change some at the airport on your arrival, but the bank is not guaranteed to be open. Hotels will change currencies, but banks give better rates. Some, such as Barclays, charge a small commission.

In St. John's, several banks are found on St. Mary's Street and High Street. Among them: **Antigua Commercial Bank,** tel. (809) 462-1217 or 462-2085, fax 462-1220; **Scotiabank,** tel. (809) 462-1104 or 462-1106, fax 462-1578; **Barclays Bank,** tel. (809) 462-0334, fax 462-4910; and **Royal Bank of Canada,** tel. (809) 462-0325, fax 462-1304.

Bank branches are found all over the city and in English Harbour as well. The **Antigua Barbuda Investment Bank,** tel. (809) 462-1652, fax 462-0804, on High Street has a branch in Barbuda as well, tel. (809) 460-0162. Bank business hours vary, but most are open Mon.-Thurs. 8 a.m.-3 p.m. and Friday 8 a.m.-5 p.m.

Business Hours

As a general rule, shops are open weekdays and Saturday 9 a.m.-5 p.m., with an hour off for midday lunch. Grocery stores may stay open later on Friday. Some, but not many, are open Sunday as well. Tourist shops often remain open into the evening and on Sunday to accommodate the schedules of cruise ships. On Sunday virtually everything is closed save for a few curio shops and KFC.

Letters and Phones

The general post office, tel. (809) 462-0023, is located at Long and High streets in St. John's. You'll find a branch at the airport and a branch in Codrington, Barbuda, tel. (809) 460-0075. Hours are Mon.-Thurs. 8:15 a.m.-noon and 1-4 p.m. On Friday, the post office stays open until 5 p.m.

To make calls, telephone cards may be purchased at some tourist shops, bookstores, and even small superettes. Your best bet, however, is to go to **Cable and Wireless** on St. Mary's St., tel. (809) 462-0840. Cards are available in EC$10, EC$20, EC$40, and EC$60 denominations. C&W is also the place to send faxes and cables.

Phones that accept coins are available as well. The area code for Antigua is 809. This means direct dial is available from North America by dialing "1" plus "809" plus a seven digit number.

News

The local newspaper is the *Sentinel,* published weekly on Friday. Cost is EC$2. Another weekly paper, *The Nation* (EC$1), is available, as are several tourism newspapers and publications of political opposition organs.

ST. KITTS AND NEVIS

St. Kitts and Nevis (NEE-vis) have been linked as an entity—first as a colony, then as part of a three-island protectorate in association with Great Britain, and finally as an independent federated state—for more than a century.

St. Kitts figures prominently in the history of English colonization in the Lesser Antilles; the first settlement was established on the island in 1623, and St. Kitts was used as the base for further British colonization of neighboring islands. In fact, the island was once called the "Mother Colony of the West Indies." Yet even at that, and with a subsequent long history of sugarcane cultivation and regional affluence, St. Kitts and Nevis have not emerged in this century as highly developed tourism hot spots. All the better, in most ways.

There is an easy quality about Kittitians and Nevisians. It is the same lack of affectation found the world over in societies that live in varying degrees of paradise and find the amazement of visitors hard to fathom. This does not mean, however, that these islanders are unaware of the vagaries, the down side, of the tourism business. They are aware of unbridled and ultimately unhealthy development on neighboring islands and are keeping it in check on their own. One measure has been taken in that regard: By law, no building on the islands can be taller than the tallest palm tree.

The land has changed over the years, but only slightly. There are few large hotels; most accommodations on both islands are guesthouses and old plantation greathouses. You'll find little in the way of trendy, organized entertainment. These are islands on which to be quietly diverted and amused, and to enjoy several outstanding natural and historical sites. St. Kitts and Nevis retain a Lesser Antilles sensibility that some islands wish they could recapture.

THE LAND

While the two islands are separated by a two-mile (three-km) strait (The Narrows), they are politically linked and thought of as an entity, in the same way Trinidad and Tobago or Antigua and Barbuda are political states. Yet the two islands are distinct and separate in the psychological makeup of the islanders; you would be hard pressed to find residents of either island identifying with the other. An uneasiness exists between the two, an uneasiness not as deep as mistrust, but a bit stronger than mere rivalry. They were cast together for the sake of governance, a colonial convenience; while this arrangement has proved workable, it does not mean the Kittitians and Nevisians have always liked it.

St. Kitts is the larger of the two, with an area of 68 square miles (176 square km). Nevis is about half the size, or 36 square miles (93 square km). St. Kitts is long and thin (23 miles or 37 km), while Nevis is nearly circular, like a dollop of green floating on an azure sea. In profile the two are often likened to a cricket bat and ball.

St. Kitts and Nevis, as well as the neighboring island of St. Eustatius to the north, are really three tips of an underwater volcanic chain. These islands, as well as Montserrat to the south and Saba to the north, lie in an inner arc of Lesser Antilles islands, on all sides surrounded by the Caribbean Sea. The calmer waters of the Caribbean have created less havoc on the windward sides of St. Kitts and Nevis, compared to islands facing the open Atlantic.

The central mountainous spine of St. Kitts, towering and vivid as you see it when flying over the island, is a result of the underwater volcanic activity. The island's highest point, **Mt. Liamuiga** (lee-a-MWEE-gah), is a dormant volcanic crater in the northwest some 3,792 feet (1,157 meters) above sea level. The volcano was called Mt. Misery, obviously an unhappy place, by Kittitians until independence in 1983. It then reverted to Liamuiga, the original Carib name for St. Kitts, reputedly meaning "Fertile Land." The volcano has been dormant for years, although it did rumble and growl and cause some consternation in the 1980s.

The altitude of the central spine tapers down as it moves southeast. The mountains are surrounded by rainforest and mountain woodlands near the summits, and low-lying and fertile plains along the coast. This is the center of the island's sugarcane industry, still viable in the economic sector.

The oddly shaped Southeast Peninsula is characterized by low scrub and acacia trees, and some of the island's best bays and beaches. The peninsula was nearly unreachable for years, and was "connected" to the rest of the island with the opening of the Dr. Kennedy Simmonds Highway in 1990. The peninsula is relatively low, very different from the rest of the island, reaching heights of 150 feet (45 meters) or so. Its principal feature is several large salt ponds at its tip, including the **Great Salt Pond.**

The windward coast of St. Kitts does have some rough waters and dramatic, though not very high, cliffs. The **Black Rocks** near Belle Vue on the northeast coast are, in fact, black rocks, formed as a result of solidified lava that "froze" as it reached the sea. Past volcanic ac-

tivity has produced beaches of flinty gray volcanic sand in the north of the country. Moving toward the Southeast Peninsula, the beaches become honey-colored and clear.

Nevis was originally called Oualie by the Caribs, thought to mean "Land of Beautiful Waters." The nearly circular island is dominated by the central **Nevis Peak,** some 3,232 feet (985 meters) above sea level. Mountain rainforests and low mountain woodlands surround the peak, which tapers to low-lying plains along the shore.

In 1989, Hurricane Hugo swept through the islands, laying waste to much of the agricultural, tourism, and fishing industries, and to private property. An estimated US$40 million in damage was recorded.

FLORA AND FAUNA

Both islands are home to the vervet, or green monkey, introduced by the French in the 1600s. The estimated monkey population exceeds 50,000 (some estimates put it at 125,000— which proves either that humans tend to exaggerate or that monkeys tend to hide), greater than the human population of the two islands combined. The Southeast Peninsula is also home to a dwindling number of wild deer.

The famous royal poinciana tree, often called the flamboyant, was developed on St. Kitts by an 18th-century French governor, de Poinci (also de Poncey).

HISTORY

Stone Age peoples and later Amerindian Arawaks arrived on St. Kitts and Nevis several thousand years before Christ. They left evidence of their settlements in stone tools, pottery, and ceremonial icons.

The Arawaks were displaced, killed, or absorbed (or a combination of all three) by the warrior Caribs, who inhabited St. Kitts and Nevis when Columbus made his series of "discovery" journeys in the late 15th century. Examples of Carib petroglyphs can be found on St. Kitts, near Old Road town.

Columbus and the Spanish

During his second voyage in 1493, Columbus charted the islands but apparently did not attempt a landing. He called Nevis Nuestra Señora de las Nieves, or "Our Lady of the Snows," referring to the wispy white clouds that constantly encircled the summit of the island's highest peak, now called Nevis Peak. Columbus then named the larger island Saint Christopher after himself, evidently unencumbered by lack of hubris. (To be fair, the patron saint of travelers is also Saint Christopher.) Today the true and quasi-official name of the island remains St. Christopher. No one is sure when St. Kitts became de rigueur as the island's name, but today virtually all government documents and references use the shorter version.

The Spanish paid little attention to St. Kitts and Nevis. Columbus no doubt had bigger islands and the search for gold on his mind, and he had previously met the warlike Caribs on other islands—they seemed like the sort of people to leave alone.

Out with the Old World, In with the New

The Caribs flourished for another hundred years with virtually no contact with Europeans. A landing party headed by Captain John Smith, leader of the Virginia Colony, landed on Nevis in 1607. This landing was short-lived, and Smith used the island to simply gather water, wood, and other supplies.

In 1623 the first English landing party in the New World, led by Sir Thomas Warner, put down anchor on the west coast of St. Kitts, in the area known as Old Road. The arrival of the first French party in 1625, a small group escaping a sea battle with the Spanish, complicated the situation. Now the British, the French, and the Caribs, all mutual enemies, lived on a piece of land no larger than Brooklyn.

When in doubt, however, the Europeans stuck together. The French and British became uneasy allies with a common purpose: elimination of the Caribs. This they did, and their effort culminated in a brutal massacre of an estimated 2,000 Caribs at Bloody Point in 1626. The massacre effectively ended Carib involvement on St. Kitts.

They then, not surprisingly, turned to fighting among themselves. They united only once again, this time to repulse a Spanish attack in 1629. Afterward they promptly went back to slugging it out with each other.

Both nations used St. Kitts as a base to colonize neighboring islands. One of those islands was Nevis, which the English took in 1628 under the leadership of Anthony Hilton.

European Conflict and Resolution

For the next century the British and French intermittently fought for control of St. Kitts and Nevis. There were small treaties, and boundaries were drawn that gave the north and south sections of St. Kitts to the French and the middle section to the British. And even though the French managed to expel them in 1664, the English were back 15 years later.

Eventually the 1713 Treaty of Utrecht ended one of the ongoing European wars, and St. Kitts and Nevis were ceded to the British. The treaty, however, did little to stop the fighting in the Lesser Antilles. In 1782 the French fought and won at the British stronghold of St. Kitts, Brimstone Hill, often called the "Gibraltar of the West Indies." This fort is today one of the Caribbean's largest restored garrisons.

Finally, in 1783, the Treaty of Versailles ended the major British-French conflicts and St. Kitts and Nevis became colonies of Great Britain. The growth of the sugarcane industry proceeded in earnest from that point on. St. Kitts, and often to a greater extent Nevis, became profitable cotton-, sugar-, and rum-producing islands. Slavery was the backbone of the industry, and the importation of slaves also began in earnest during the late 18th century.

During the zenith of the plantation days, Nevis attained the reputation and status of a wealthy island. One of the first hotels in the Lesser Antilles, the Bath Hotel, was built in 1778 near the island's capital, Charlestown. Alexander Hamilton, a U.S. statesman, was born on Nevis in 1755. His family house is now a landmark and museum. Lord Admiral Horatio Nelson, Great Britain's famous admiral who was, for a time, based in Antigua, married on Nevis in 1787.

Post-Emancipation

With the emancipation of slaves in 1834, St. Kitts and Nevis entered an age of uncertainty. As in many of the British sugarcane-producing islands, indentured laborers were brought in from East India and other parts of the United Kingdom. Still, the sugar industry fell and never again reached its former eminence. During the latter half of the 19th century and the early part of the 20th century, St. Kitts and Nevis became little more than economic dependents—poor relations of England with little hope for economic viability. During that period the political makeup of the modern Lesser Antilles was created. Anguilla, another British colony some 50 miles (80 km) north of St. Kitts, was added as a dependency to the St. Kitts colonial administration. Later, in 1882, Nevis was added as well. Both moves were met with understandable consternation and alarm by the locals, who had not been consulted. They resented the move, and this feeling would simmer for about one hundred years.

St. Kitts-Nevis-Anguilla

The islanders, and the entire Caribbean, entered the 20th century with anxiety and frustration over fragile economies and racial injustices. WW I changed the face of Europe and the world, and the innocent days of isolated, tranquil Caribbean island life were over. The industrial revolution had engendered the growth of trade unions and democracies in Europe; with advanced post-war communication, these concepts found rapt audiences in the Caribbean.

Then the worldwide Depression brought increased labor and economic crises to the feet of Caribbean islanders. All local economies suffered extreme unemployment and shortages. By the 1930s, ugly labor conditions brought about strikes and riots in many of the British islands. Nominal representative internal government was granted to the St. Kitts-Nevis-Anguilla colony in 1937, and by 1952, universal adult suffrage was granted. The St. Kitts and Nevis Labour Party dominated Executive Council elections, and by 1960 the council was headed by a chief minister. Agitation for independence increased, and in 1967 Great Britain granted "associated state" status to the St. Kitts-Nevis-Anguilla government.

Bad move. Anguillans had had enough. The small island to the north, which had been lumped with St. Kitts and Nevis purely for administrative purposes, had nothing in common with the two other islands save their common status as former British colonies. Anguilla was separated from the two larger islands by miles of ocean and the four French and Dutch islands of the Leewards. Further, it had never been a sugarcane island and had different economic and social concerns. Anguillans felt, in effect, that their island would become the economic backwater of the St. Kitts-Nevis-Anguilla federation.

So they rebelled.

Anguilla Rebels

Soon after the 1967 referendum, protest movements coalesced into a quasi-armed revolution, which was more the type that might be featured in a Hollywood comedy about island life (see "Anguilla" earlier in this chapter for more on the revolution) than a threat to the greater populace. The St. Kitts police force was tossed off the island. By 1969, the situation became untenable, forcing British police and army paratroopers to drop in, literally, by parachute. They squashed armed resistance, and the rebellion evolved into a constitutional quagmire that took years to resolve. The upshot was that Anguilla pulled out of the federation, and St. Kitts and Nevis became the Federated State of St. Kitts and Nevis.

Nevis, never wholly comfortable with its status as half of the federation, nevertheless has accepted that certain aspects of association with St. Kitts are beneficial. The uneasy strain, however, was exacerbated in 1970 when a dangerously overloaded interisland ferry sank and left some 240 dead. The majority of the passengers on the Christena were Nevisians. In a population of only 10,000, the loss was devastating.

St. Kitts and Nevis Independence

St. Kitts and Nevis quietly achieved independence on 19 September 1983. The current party in power is the People's Action Movement (PAM), headed by Prime Minister Dr. Kennedy Simmonds. Simmonds has held office since 1980. The PAM has formed something of a coalition with the Nevis Reform Party (NRP). Other parties include the opposition St. Kitts-Nevis Labor Party and the Concerned Citizens Movement (CCM).

St. Kitts and Nevis were brought to world attention in early 1994 when riots broke out in the

St. Kitts capital, Basseterre. Labour Party rallies turned ugly as demonstrators threw rocks and looted downtown shops in protest over their exclusion from the ruling parliamentary coalition formed after general elections. The government declared a three-week state of emergency and restored order—no one was seriously injured—but it is clear that the long-term rule of the PAM is facing serious opposition.

PEOPLE AND CULTURE

The population of St. Kitts is 35,000, and Nevis 10,000. The majority population of the two islands is of African descent, and there are small groups of European, East Indian, and mixed-race citizens.

Culturally, the islands take their cue from Britain, with a West Indian twist. Language is English, although spoken with a dialect not unlike a rapid Patois. The predominant religion is Anglican, although Methodist, Seventh-Day Adventist, Catholic, Moravian, Baha'i, Jehovah's Witness, and several evangelical sects are found.

French influence, despite the years of French occupation, is hardly evident, although several place names such as Basseterre ("Low Land") and Molineux remind Kittitians of that aspect of their heritage.

Holidays and Festivals
Caribbean cultural traditions are strong during the annual St. Kitts **Carnival.** The Carnival takes place 25 Dec.-2 Jan. and is a weeklong extravaganza of masquerades, calypso and steel band competitions, food festivals, parades, street dancing, and private parties.

The equivalent celebration in Nevis, called **Culturama,** is held in late July and ends the first Monday of August (August Monday). Look for arts and crafts shows, talent shows, calypso competitions, and great eating.

For more information on either event, contact the tourist office, St. Kitts at (809) 465-2620, Nevis at 469-5521 (see the "Information Directory" chart at the end of this section for addresses).

The **Nevis Jockey Club,** tel. (809) 469-2481, schedules as many as eight special racing events throughout the year to coincide with the New Year's and Easter holidays, and other holidays and national festivities. The Indian Castle Race Track on Nevis is the venue.

The **St. Kitts-Guadeloupe Regatta,** held in May, is one of the year's biggest sailboat racing events. Racers from neighboring islands and the international community are invited to race from Basseterre on St. Kitts to Basse-Terre on Guadeloupe. The June **St. Kitts and Nevis Regatta** invites smaller vessels, including sunfish and people on sailboards, to race across The Narrows, from Frigate Bay on St. Kitts to Oualie Beach on Nevis.

Both St. Kitts and Nevis celebrate standard British religious holidays, including Christmas, Easter, and Boxing Day, as well as Independence Day (19 September—big day, big activities), Labour Day (first Monday in May), the Queen's Birthday (second Saturday in June), and August Monday.

GOVERNMENT AND ECONOMY

Government
The Federated State of St. Kitts and Nevis is a member of the Commonwealth, which makes the Queen the official head of state. The monarch is represented on the island by a governor general, currently Sir Clement Athelston Arrindell. A deputy governor general represents the Queen on Nevis. Power is vested in the ruling party, headed by the prime minister, currently Dr. Kennedy Simmonds of the PAM (see also "St. Kitts and Nevis Independence" under "History," above). The legislature consists of an elected National Assembly and an appointed Senate. Nevis is represented in Parliament but also supports its own internal government comprising a premier, currently Vance Armory, and a House of Assembly. Under further provisions of the federation, Nevis may elect to secede.

Economy
The economy of St. Kitts and Nevis is based largely on agriculture and tourism. Sugar represents about 55% of the state's export revenue and employs about 12% of the working population. The industry increased its output from 1991 to 1992 by 27%, and, indeed, the low-lying

Sugarcane is still a major crop on St. Kitts.

plains of the two islands are still covered by acres of pastel green sugarcane. St. Kitts produces a unique sugarcane spirit, Baron's CSR, which some say is possible on St. Kitts and only on St. Kitts due to the unique clarity of the local water. The government has recently encouraged agricultural diversification, and more small farmers are growing yams, potatoes, and other vegetables.

Tourism is gathering strength as an industry and has recently overtaken agriculture as the premier foreign exchange earner. Nearly 140,000 visitors arrived in 1992, about 24,500 of them bound for Nevis. Most tourists are from North America and the U.K., with a smaller number from South America, Europe, and neighboring Caribbean islands.

Currently, more than 1,370 rooms in 29 hotels and plantation inns, guesthouses, and cottages can be found on the islands. This number is expected to increase dramatically in the next few years. The 1990 opening of the Dr. Kennedy Simmonds Highway on St. Kitts, which in effect opened up the island's Southeast Peninsula, has put into motion several large hotel and resort development projects for that area. Included among them are plans for a large all-inclusive Sandals resort. Expansion of facilities and the airstrip at Newcastle Airport in Nevis is also planned.

More than 400 cruise ships, representing 80,000 passengers, visited the two islands in 1993-94 season (100 to Nevis, 318 to St. Kitts).

ST. KITTS SIGHTS

Out on the Island

St. Kitts is encircled by a modern coastal road, making travel around the countryside easy and pleasant. As you drive the generally non-busy roads, note the ruins of dozens of stone sugar mills, relics of 18th- and 19th-century plantation estates. In the main sections of the small towns and fishing villages, you'll see small bathhouses and public taps, also relics of a time when running water was not available in households. The bathhouses were often used by sugarcane plantation workers to wash up after a long day's toil in the fields.

North of Basseterre is the village of **Challengers** and the nearby **Bloody Point,** site of the conclusive massacre of the Carib population, some 2,000 people, in 1626. Farther along is **Old Road Bay,** site of the first settlement in the British Lesser Antilles. It was here, in 1623, that Thomas Warner and a small group landed to establish a colony. A river runs through the town and is no doubt one of the reasons Warner and his party settled here. Inland is **Wingfield Estate,** site of an old Carib settlement and site of several petroglyphs carved into rocks. Past the rocks and through a section of rainforest is **Romney Manor,** an old plantation greathouse and gardens. The picturesque greathouse itself, a good example of period architecture, is now home to **Caribelle Batik,** tel. (809) 465-6253, a

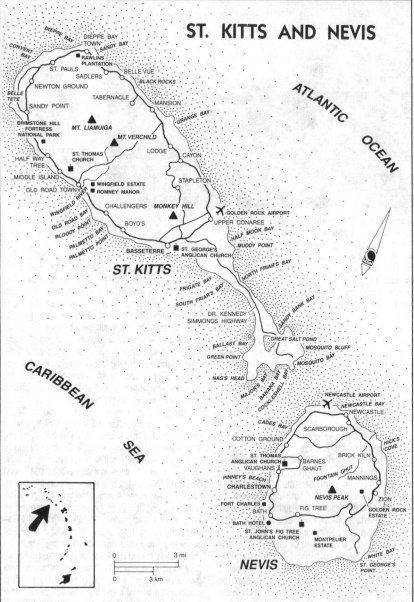

ST. KITTS AND NEVIS

fabric and clothing shop utilizing original designs executed on the property—you may watch the batikers in action. On the property note the huge 350-year-old saman tree, also called a rain tree for its capacity to hold water in its leaves and continue to "rain" long after an actual rain shower.

Farther north is the village of **Middle Island** and the St. Thomas Church. The church is the burial place of, among others, Sir Thomas Warner, who died in 1648. He is in the tomb under the canopy. The inscription identifies Warner as " . . . Generall of Ye Caribbee Ieland W Goverr of Ye Ieland of St. Chris . . . "

Brimstone Hill

Back on the coastal road, head north to **Brimstone Hill Fortress National Park.** The fort was, in its heyday, called the Gibraltar of the West Indies and has the distinction of being the second-largest pre-20th-century fort in the Caribbean (The Citadel in Haiti is largest).

The Brimstone Hill complex covers nearly 40 acres and rises 800 feet (244 meters) above the sea. Construction was begun by the British in 1690 and completed over 100 years later, most of it by the hand of slave labor. The fort saw several important battles with the French before it was captured in 1782; it was returned after the 1783 Treaty of Versailles. The British continued to build upon existing structures until the fortress comprised five bastions, including officers' quarters, a hospital, water storage tanks, and Fort George, the highest point, or citadel, of the complex. The structure is made of volcanic rock and limestone, and on a clear day the views are stunning. Saba and Statia are visible to the north, and a nearly 360-degree view shows off the rest of St. Kitts, including scars of areas where rock was mined for construction, as well as Nevis and Montserrat to the south. From the citadel it is not difficult to understand the strategic advantage of the fort.

Over the years hurricane damage and non-interest took their toll on the buildings. The fortress was abandoned in 1851 and fell into further disrepair. It was inaugurated as a national park in 1965, and restoration is ongoing. A snack bar, gift shop, and small museum are found on the grounds. Admission is EC$13; it's open daily 9 a.m.-5 p.m.

North St. Kitts

The coast road will bring you to **Sandy Point,** a small fishing and port town that seems to have more churches per square foot than anywhere but the Vatican.

To the far north is **Dieppe Bay,** a black-sand beach and small fishing town. Along the coast road is Belle Vue, where you'll see the black rock volcanic deposits looming like monoliths from the foaming surf. This is the site of the Caribbean Museum of Gems and Rocks, which seems like a good idea. Trouble is, there is no museum. Just a sign.

South and the Southeast Peninsula

South on the coastal road heads to the Southeast Peninsula, currently untouched save for a few small beach bars and unfinished hotels. If the tourism industry continues as planned, this area will host several hotels and resorts in the near future. The peninsula has some of the island's best beaches—the honey-colored sand type rather than the black sand of the north. **Frigate Bay** and **Friar's Bay** on the peninsula's "skinny" part are two of the island's best known beaches. Frigate Bay is the more quiescent of the two. In the extreme south are several good bays and beaches, although some are hard to get to by car. You'll need to walk. Among them are **Cockleshell Bay, Major's Bay,** and **Green Point.** The **Turtle Beach Bar and Grill,** operated by the Ocean Terrace Inn in Basseterre, is on the south end and faces Nevis. The best swimming, snorkeling, and diving on the peninsula is right here. They have live entertainment some evenings.

St. Kitts Tour Groups

Nature excursionists will want to hike around the Great Salt Pond, where you might run into vervet monkeys or wild deer. Several hikes, including one to the crater of Mt. Liamuiga, another through the rainforests, or a walk to the mountain lake **Dos d'Anse** on Mt. Verchild in the southern range are well worth it and can be organized through tour groups. Cost per person varies.

Call **Kriss Tours,** tel. (809) 465-4042; **Greg's Safaris,** tel. (809) 465-4121; **Kantours,** tel. (809) 465-2098; or **Tropical Tours,** tel. (809) 465-4167, all in Basseterre.

The rate for a four-hour island tour by taxi will be US$80 (about EC$215) for up to four per vehicle.

Jan's Travel Agency, with offices in St. Kitts at New St., Basseterre, tel. (809) 465-4171; and Nevis on Main St., Charlestown, tel. (809) 469-5426, can organize tours and day-trips and is one of the better full-service travel agencies on the islands.

BASSETERRE

Basseterre, the capital and chief port of St. Kitts and Nevis, was not the original capital of the is-

lands. That would have been Old Road, the site of the first British landing in 1623. Basseterre was founded by the French after their arrival in 1625 and was a small port town and base for them for more than 40 years. The town was damaged several times by earthquakes, most notably in 1689. During one of the many repossessions of the island, the British moved their administrative center from Old Road to Basseterre, where it has remained since 1727.

A devastating 1867 fire destroyed much of the town. It was again rebuilt, but the architectural styles of the city reflect layers of disaster and repair accumulated over more than two

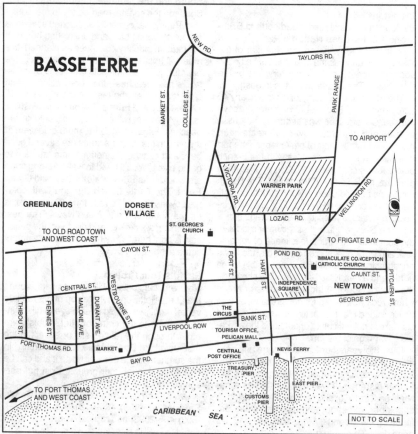

centuries. A primary style is Victorian-West Indian-Colonial, with plenty of gingerbread fretwork and wide verandas and balconies. It is a large and sprawling town, population about 17,000, and is comfortably navigated.

The central **Independence Square** is in an old section of the city. The square, once called Pall Mall Square, was constructed in 1790 for the purposes of slave auctions and public gatherings. It is now a gathering place and small park where schoolchildren can be seen lounging and goats can be seen grazing. The **Immaculate Conception** Catholic church sits on the east side of the square, dating from the early part of this century. On Cayon Street you'll find **St. George's,** the Anglican church. The original structure on the site was Notre Dame, a Catholic church built by the French. This was leveled by the British in 1706, who rebuilt it as St. George's. Fires and earthquakes destroyed it three more times. The church was last restored in 1869.

The center of Basseterre today is **The Circus,** a traffic roundabout at Bank and Fort streets and Liverpool Row. The Circus, apparently modeled after Piccadilly of the same name, features the most photographed landmark in Basseterre and possibly St. Kitts. It is the **Berkeley Memorial,** a gaudy cement structure with a clock and drinking fountains. The monument was named after Thomas Berkeley, a former colonial council president. Also on The Circus you'll find banks, taxi stands, bus stands, a hotel, a restaurant, and businesses.

In the blocks surrounding The Circus you'll find the **Treasury Building, town piers, Tourism Office,** and **Pelican Mall,** one of the town's best shopping plazas.

Good shopping, including numerous book stores—try **Walls Deluxe,** tel. (809) 465-2159—pharmacies, and gift shops, is found on Fort and Central streets.

Bay Road, south of The Circus and town, moves along the fisherman's beach. Here you'll find small markets, rums shops, grocery stores, the **central post office,** and the **public market** (open daily). Farther north along Bay Road is a **War Memorial,** dedicated to those who served in the world wars.

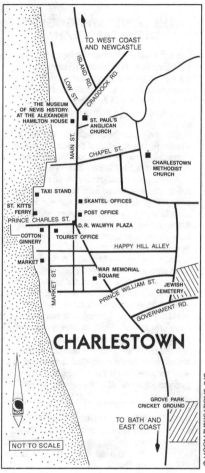

CHARLESTOWN

NOT TO SCALE

© MOON PUBLICATIONS, INC.

NEVIS SIGHTS

Nevis has much to recommend, not the least being its fine beaches and unencumbered lifestyle. You won't find much in the way of rah-rah, organized activities for tourists here, but whatever you do, you can do it in style.

Charlestown
This small, rotund island's administrative center is Charlestown, population about 1,500, a rick-

THE OLDEST SYNAGOGUE IN THE CARIBBEAN?

Near the center of Charlestown, an archaeological dig has produced evidence that the ruins of an ancient stone building, next to the town's government administration building, may be the oldest Jewish synagogue in the Caribbean. According to a team of researchers headed by anthropologist Judith Zeitlin of Brown University and supported by resident historian Dr. Vincent Hubbard, author of *Swords, Ships and Sugar: A History of Nevis to 1900,* the stone ruins may date back to the mid-17th century.

A small but intrepid group of Jews settled on Nevis after their forced exile from Brazil in the early 17th century. Other Jews, some under the cloak of anonymity, fled from Europe and South America to various parts of the Caribbean to escape persecution during the harsh years of the Spanish Inquisition.

The stone building has been in disrepair for 150 years, and no evidence exists of its original function. Yet the oldest dated tombstone in the Charlestown Jewish cemetery indicates a death in 1658, and documentation retrieved in the U.K. points to a synagogue in existence on Nevis prior to 1650. British documents also mention another synagogue on Barbados.

If research bears out the belief that the remains are in fact a circa 1650 synagogue, it would predate the 1732 synagogue on Curaçao, previously believed to be the region's oldest.

ety and tarnished town steeped in history and disaster. Earthquakes and tidal waves have taken their toll over the years, and the town has been rebuilt in and around some of the oldest buildings in the Caribbean.

Charlestown was established in 1660 on the southwest shore of the nearly circular island. It became a port town, and its principal activity was the export of cotton, the main crop on Nevis. Adjacent to the pier is the old **Cotton Ginnery,** which is still used during the harvest season of March and April. The ginnery is adjacent to the **public market,** busiest on Saturday. Along the pier are several shops and cafes, some constructed in old buildings. The **Rookery Nook** was built in an old circa 1850 livery stable.

Main Street is busy—as busy as it gets on Nevis—and here you'll find banks, the post office, shops, taxis, and businesses. The **tourist board** office is located at **D.R. Walwyn Plaza.** Tourism board employees are very helpful, and the office is open on Saturday during the high season. Nearby is the **War Memorial Square,** displaying a cannon captured from German forces in World War I.

The **Court House** is nearby. The building, circa 1825, was once government offices and the Assembly headquarters. It burned in an 1873 fire and was later restored. A public **library** (open Mon.-Sat. 9 a.m.-6 p.m.) is located on the second floor.

The **Museum of Nevis History at the Alexander Hamilton House,** on Main Street, is a mouthful. The original birthplace of Hamilton was constructed in 1680 but burned in a mid-19th-century fire. The present structure was rebuilt at Independence. The museum features memorabilia and artifacts from Nevis history, and upstairs the Nevis House of Assembly meets. Donation is US$1(about EC$2.50), and the hours are weekdays 8 a.m.-4 p.m., Saturday 10 a.m.-noon.

Turn inland (east on Chapel St.) from the museum and you'll see the **Charlestown Methodist Church,** built in 1844.

On Government Road is the old **Jewish Cemetery,** believed to date to the early 17th century.

On the southern outskirts of town is the **Bath Hotel,** built in 1778 and reputedly the oldest standing hotel building in the Caribbean. That may or may not be true, but it is old and solid, built of stone and mortar that have withstood hurricanes. A 1950 earthquake did extensive damage, but the building has been restored. It is no longer open to the public but is used as a police barracks. The nearby bathhouse has been constructed around a hot mineral spring, courtesy of underground volcanic activity. The spring is thought to have been used by the Caribs for restorative purposes, and the temperature of the water, 108° F (41° C) is said to have remained constant since the 16th century. The bath is open to the public, weekdays 8 a.m.-5 p.m., and until noon on Saturday. The admission, US$2 (about EC$5), will buy you a recommended 20 minutes maximum bathing time. Towels can be rented for fifty cents (EC$).

Nearby, the **Nelson Museum,** a tribute to Lord Nelson, contains over 600 pieces of the great admiral's memorabilia. Admission is US$2 (EC$5); the museum is open weekdays 9 a.m.-4 p.m., and Saturday 10 a.m.-1 p.m.

Out on the Island
Elsewhere on the island, several historical sites are of interest. Most prominent as you drive around the island (the road is circular, with the central Nevis Peak always in view beneath its cloud cover) are the plantation houses and ruins, many of which have been converted into small guesthouses and inns.

East from Charlestown, the **St. John's Fig Tree Anglican Church** is renowned as the church that posted the banns of marriage of Lord Nelson and his widow bride, Fanny Nisbet. At one time, the church displayed the marriage certificate of the two.

The Hermitage, now a hotel, features a well-preserved wooden greathouse on the grounds of an old plantation. The 1740 main structure is one of the Caribbean's oldest.

The northeast side of the island is curiously barren save for a few small settlements and ancient churches. The land is dry and the flora scrubby and desertlike in places. This is curious because this side of the island is the windward side, where prevailing rains would fall. Nearby is the small fishing village of **Newcastle,** which features several old buildings built in the West Indian colonial style.

On the leeward west coast are the island's hotels and better beaches. Note the **St. Thomas Anglican Church** and graveyard. This is the oldest church on Nevis, built in 1643. The present structure is an amalgam of repairs and refurbishments and is still used as a place of worship.

Nevis Tour Groups
For touring the island, the specialized group **Eco-Tours Nevis,** P.O. Box 493, Charlestown, Nevis, West Indies, tel. (809) 469-2091, fax 469-2113, will organize hikes and other excursions. One of their more popular walks is the "Eco-Ramble," a three-hour island walking tour.

Standard tours can be organized through taxi drivers, who will charge about US$50 (about EC$135) for a four-hour island tour. As

well, call **All Seasons Tours,** tel. (809) 469-5705, for your basic island tour in an air-conditioned van.

SPORTS

Sporting activities, including tennis, golf, horseback riding, fishing, and water sports, can often be arranged through your hotel. If you're striking out on your own, however, contact the following.

Golf
On St. Kitts, the **Royal St. Kitts Golf Club,** tel. (809) 465-8339, is the island's 18-hole golf course, located at Frigate Bay. A nine-hole course is located near Golden Rock Airport, tel. (809) 465-8103.

On Nevis, the **Four Seasons Resort,** tel. (809) 469-1111, complex includes an 18-hole course designed by Robert Trent Jones II.

Horseback Riding
On St. Kitts, call **Trinity Stable,** tel. (809) 465-3226.

On Nevis, call **Cane Gardens,** tel. (809) 469-5648.

Water Sports
For a wide range of water sports activities on St. Kitts, including boat rentals and deep-sea fishing, the best bet is **Tropical Watersports,** Basseterre tel. (809) 465-4167, Frigate Bay tel. 465-9649. **Tropical Surf,** tel. (809) 465-5630, at Turtle Beach rents sailboards and sunfish. Yacht charters can

Pelicans dive for fish over Pelican Bay.

BOB RACE

be arranged through **Blue Water Marina,** tel. (809) 465-1194.

On Nevis, the **Newcastle Bay Marina,** tel. (809) 469-9615, part of the Mt. Nevis Hotel organization, can provide snorkeling, water-skiing, windsurfing, deep-sea fishing, and other water activities. At **Oualie Beach** you'll find a water sports center, tel. (809) 469-9518 for snorkeling, skiing, windsurfing, and more.

Diving

An estimated 400 ships went down in the St. Kitts and Nevis waters between 1492 and 1815, some due to storms and other natural calamities, some by cannonball. Only a dozen or so wrecks have been located, and are good diving spots. Several striking coral reefs and underwater caves are also attractions.

On St. Kitts, call **Kenneth's Dive Centre,** tel. (809) 465-2670; or **Pro-Divers,** OTI Dive Center, Ocean Terrace Inn, tel. (809) 465-2754, Turtle Beach tel. (809) 465-3223, for St. Kitts dives. On Nevis, contact **Scuba Safaris,** tel. (809) 469-9518, located at the Oualie Beach Club.

NIGHTLIFE

On both islands, nightlife is often limited to hotel activities, which, in addition to live music and dancing, often include folk dancing performances, talent shows, beauty contests, and other local interest activities. Keep in mind that virtually everything shuts down on Sunday, when most dining and evening activities are limited to hotels.

On St. Kitts, the **Turtle Beach Bar** hosts an evening disco-on-the-beach, and the restaurant and bar **J's Place,** tel. (809) 465-6264, at the bottom of Brimstone Hill, hosts weekend dances. You can also find entertainment on occasion at **Fisherman's Wharf,** at the OTI Ocean Terrace. **Reflections,** tel. (809) 465-7616, an upstairs disco in Basseterre, is open every day except Tuesday.

MORE ST. KITTS ACCOMMODATIONS

Rates per s, EP when applicable, winter

NAME	(809)	(800)	LOCATION	TARIFF
Bird Rock Beach Resort	465-8914	621-1270	Basseterre	moderate-luxury
Camp's Retreat	N/A	N/A	Camps	budget
Fairview Inn	465-2472	223-9815	near Boyds	moderate
Fort Thomas Hotel	465-2695	851-7818	Basseterre	moderate
Frigate Bay Beach Hotel	465-8936	223-9815	Frigate Bay	luxury
Gateway Inn	465-7155	N/A	Frigate Bay	budget
Glimbaro Guest House	465-2935	N/A	Basseterre	moderate
Island Paradise	465-8053	N/A	Frigate Bay	luxury
Llewellyn's Haven	465-2941	N/A	Basseterre	budget
Park View Guest House	465-2100	N/A	Basseterre	budget-moderate
Rawlins Plantation	465-6221	621-1270	northwest side	luxury
Rose's Guest House	465-4651	N/A	New Pond Site, Basseterre	budget
Sun'n Sand Beach Village	465-8037	223-6510	Frigate Bay	moderate-luxury
Timothy Beach Resort	465-8597	777-1700	Frigate Bay	luxury
The White House	465-8162	223-1108	hills above Basseterre	luxury
Windsor Guest House	465-2894	N/A	Basseterre	budget

If casinos are your thing, you have one choice. The **Jack Tar Village** casino, tel. (809) 465-8651, will open its doors to nonguests.

On Nevis, be prepared for a quiet time. On weekends, live and canned music may be found at **Croney's Old Manor Estate,** or occasionally at **Pinney's Beach Hotel.**

ST. KITTS AND NEVIS ACCOMMODATIONS

Accommodation on St. Kitts and Nevis leans toward the quaint and personal, rather than the large and sprawling. You will find mega-resorts, now and in the future, but the norm is small inns, plantation houses, and guesthouses.

The **St. Kitts and Nevis Hotel Association,** P.O. Box 438, Basseterre, St. Kitts, West Indies, tel. and fax (809) 465-5304, has a complete list of island hotels and guesthouses; those listed below are recommended.

Categories used below, based on per-person, per-night prices during the mid-December through mid-April high season, are: **Luxury** US$100 or more, **Moderate** US$50-100, **Budget** US$50 or less. Many hotels will accept credit cards, but it's best to check first. Hotels charge a seven percent tax and often a 10% service charge, which is tacked on to the bill.

There are no camping facilities on St. Kitts and Nevis.

Villas and Apartments

The villa rental business hasn't hit St. Kitts and Nevis to the same degree it's hit neighboring islands. Your first and best contact for villas is the tourist board (see the "Information Directory" chart later in this chapter) or the back pages of newspapers and specialty magazines.

WIMCO, one of North America's larger villa rental agencies, lists some properties in St. Kitts and Nevis. Contact **West Indies Management Company** (WIMCO), P.O. Box 1461, Newport, RI 02840, tel. (800) 932-3222 or (401) 849-8012, U.K. tel. (800) 89-8318, fax (401) 847-6290.

Morgan Heights Condominiums, P.O. Box 536, Basseterre, St. Kitts, West Indies, tel. (809) 465-85433, fax 465-9272, is located on the windward side of the island, about 15 minutes from

Basseterre. The small complex features a swimming pool, restaurant, and one- or two-bedroom units with kitchenettes. The units are sparsely decorated but comfortable and clean, and you'll find TVs in some rooms. Budget.

St. Kitts Hotels

The Golden Lemon Inn and Villas, P.O. Box 17, Dieppe Bay, St. Kitts, West Indies, tel. (809) 465-7260, U.S. tel. (800) 223-5581, fax (809) 465-4019, is a series of rooms and villas individually decorated with antiques gathered from the West Indies and around the world. Very chichi. The restaurant is one of the island's best, and several of the villas have private pools. The black-sand beach is not particularly appealing, but the inn and villa amenities are designed to allow you to wallow in their splendor. Tennis is available as well. Luxury.

The **OTI Ocean Terrace Inn** (P.O. Box 65, Basseterre, St. Kitts, West Indies, tel. (809) 465-2754, U.S. tel. (800) 524-0512 or (800) 74-CHARMS, fax 465-1057, is one of the island's best buys. Located a short walk from The Circus in Basseterre, the family-owned hotel has two pools, three restaurants, including the Fisherman's Wharf on the water (very popular, great barbecues—go early). They offer shuttle service to their Turtle Beach Bar on the Southeast Peninsula. Some rooms have kitchenettes, all have television. The views of Pelican Bay (watch the pelicans diving for fish) are relaxing. Moderate-Luxury.

Ottley's Plantation Inn, P.O. Box 345, Basseterre, St. Kitts, West Indies, tel. (809) 465-7234, is an old plantation greathouse at the foot of Mt. Liamuiga. The 35-acre estate reeks of old-style elegance and luxury, and the air up there is fine. Many hiking trails for the energetic, and a pool for the relaxed. The Royal Palm restaurant is reputed to be very good. Luxury.

Jack Tar Village, P.O. Box 406, Frigate Bay, St. Kitts, West Indies, tel. (809) 465-8651, U.S. tel. (800) 999-9182, fax 465-1031, is an all-inclusive resort on Frigate Bay, part of a chain that has hotels in Jamaica, among other places. Great beach, casino, golf, pools, tennis, lots of water sports: This is the type of place of which there are few of on the island. Moderate-Luxury.

On The Square, 14 Independence Square, Basseterre, St. Kitts, West Indies, tel. (809) 465-

MORE NEVIS ACCOMMODATIONS

Rates per s, EP when applicable, winter

NAME	(809)	(800)	LOCATION	TARIFF
Central Cottage	469-5278	N/A	Charlestown	budget-moderate
Croney's Old Manor Estate	469-5445	223-9815	southeast Mt. Nevis	luxury
Golden Rock Estate	469-3346	N/A	east side Mt. Nevis	luxury
Headlands Cottage	469-9931	N/A	Oualie Beach	moderate
Hurricane Cove Bungalows	469-9462	N/A	Oualie Beach	moderate-luxury
Lyndale Guesthouse	469-5412	N/A	Charlestown	budget-moderate
Meade's Guesthouse	469-5253	N/A	Craddock Road	budget-moderate
Nisbet Plantation	469-9325	344-2049	Newcastle	luxury
Oualie Beach Hotel	469-9735	N/A	Oualie Beach	luxury
Pinney's Beach Hotel	469-5207	N/A	Pinney's Beach	moderate
Sylvia's Guest House	469-5775	N/A	Charlestown	budget-moderate
Tamarind	469-9549	N/A	Jones Bay	moderate
Yamseed Inn	469-9361	N/A	Newcastle	moderate

2485, is, not surprisingly, on the square in Basseterre. The small guesthouse is clean and convenient, although a bit noisy. Some rooms have private baths and some do not; most feature air-conditioning. Budget.

Nevis Hotels

The Mt. Nevis Hotel and Beach Club, P.O. Box 494, Nevis, West Indies, tel. (809) 469-9373/4, North America tel. (800) 75-NEVIS or tel. and fax (212) 874-4276, local fax (809) 469-9375, is in the north of the island, facing St. Kitts and the two-mile (three-km) Narrows Channel. The hotel is on 16 acres of gardens, elevated 275 feet (84 meters) up the slopes of Mt. Nevis. The cooling breeze of this altitude is part of the attraction. There are 32 comfortable rooms in four buildings, with suites and kitchen facilities. The restaurant is one of the island's best, and the view almost certainly is. The hotel operates a nearby (five minutes away) beach club and water sports facility. Good deal. Moderate-Luxury.

The Four Seasons, P.O. Box 565, Charlestown, Nevis, West Indies, tel. (809) 469-1111, U.S. tel. (800) 332-3442, Canada tel. (800) 268-6282, is huge, sprawling, luxurious, and everything you would expect in a Four Seasons hotel. There are 196 rooms built along the famous west coast Pinney's Beach, 18 holes of golf, 10 tennis courts, three restaurants, pools, a health club, and a pile of boutiques. It's all very tasteful, in fact. Luxury.

Others include **The Hermitage,** 129 Kelmar Ave., Malvern, PA 19355, U.S. tel. (800) 682-4025, Nevis tel. (809) 469-3477, fax 469-2481, old plantation, lovely, good restaurant. Luxury. **Montpelier Plantation Inn,** P.O. Box 474, Nevis, West Indies, tel. (809) 469-3462, North America tel. (800) 243-9420, fax 469-2932, is in the south of the island. Lush gardens, colonial antiques and elegance, very British afternoon tea and all that, with a beach nearby. Different sort of place—you'll like it. Luxury. **Sea Spawn Guesthouse,** Old Hospital Road, Charlestown, Nevis, West Indies, tel. (809) 469-5239, fax

469-5706, is clean, only 18 rooms, on Pinney's Beach on the outskirts of Charlestown, fans in rooms, good buy. Budget.

FOOD

The categories below are for per-person entree prices: **Expensive** US$25 or more, **Moderate** US$10-25, **Inexpensive** US$10 or less.

St. Kitts Restaurants

St. Kitts does not host a tremendous amount of restaurants, but several stand out. Hotel restaurants are open on Sunday, and that's an advantage. Remember, not all restaurants will take credit cards, and it's best to call ahead to confirm.

The Golden Lemon, tel. 465-7260, is located on the north coast's Dieppe Bay but is worth the drive. The hotel restaurant, on a flower-filled patio, serves up West Indian and Continental specialties and is noted for its elegant dinners and Sunday brunch. As a matter of fact, this might be a good Sunday day-trip. Bring your towels—the beach here is not wonderful, but along the drive you'll find plenty of dipping possibilities. Make reservations. Expensive.

Fisherman's Wharf, tel. (809) 465-2754, serves West Indian and seafood in an open-air bistro on the wharf across the street from the OTI. Very good deal, good service. Open for dinner only. Inexpensive-Moderate. **The Ballahoo,** tel. (809) 465-4197, on The Circus in Basseterre is upstairs in an open veranda, a great place to watch the town walk by. The food is West Indian and Continental. Open for breakfast as well. Inexpensive-Moderate. **Frigate Bay Beach Hotel,** tel. (809) 465-8935, serves elegant West Indian and Continental. Moderate-Expensive.

The Georgian House, tel. (809) 465-4049, is on Independence Square and serves West Indian and some barbecues. Occasional entertainment. Moderate.

Nevis Restaurants

Nevis is noted for fine dining at several of the luxury plantation inns and guesthouses. Among the better: The **Montpelier Plantation Inn,** tel. (809) 469-3462, will occasionally seat a limited number of nonguests for elegant West Indian/Continental specialties. Expensive. The **Nisbet Plantation Inn,** tel. (809) 469-9325, features dinner in its plantation-style dining room filled with antiques and that Old World ambience. Expensive. You can have lunch at their beachside restaurant and bar, **Coconuts.**

The **Mt. Nevis Hotel,** tel. (809) 469-9373, features fine dining inside or out on the veranda, with magnificent views to St. Kitts. Moderate. The restaurant at **Oualie Beach,** tel. (809) 469-9735, is casual. Inexpensive.

Stop in for beachside pizzas at the **Newcastle Marina** (closed off-season). Inexpensive. Also in Newcastle, on Shaws Rd., **Cla-Cha-Del,** tel. (809) 469-9640, serves authentic local dishes such as goatwater, mutton, and lamb stew. Inexpensive.

Unella's, on the Charlestown waterfront, serves local West Indian dishes and seafood. Inexpensive. **Eddy's,** tel. (809) 469-5958, on Main St. in Charlestown serves local seafood and is popular during its Wednesday 5-8 p.m. happy hour. Eddy's is closed on Thursday. Inexpensive. **Callaloo,** tel. (809) 469-5389, also on Main St., is known for West Indian cuisine. Inexpensive-Moderate. Drop in at the **Nevis Bakery,** tel. (809) 469-5219, on Happy Hill Dr. in Charlestown for fresh bread, pastries, and cakes.

GETTING THERE

Golden Rock Airport is minutes from Basseterre in St. Kitts, and **Newcastle Airport** is minutes from Charlestown in Nevis. Neither airport is large, but Golden Rock can land international flights.

BWIA, tel. (809) 465-8644, flies nonstop from New York, Miami, and Toronto. **American,** tel. (809) 465-2273, flies in via its San Juan hub or makes connections with neighboring islands such as Antigua, Sint Maarten, Guadeloupe, or the U.S. Virgin Islands. These islands, particularly Antigua, can be reached by several international airlines such as British Airways, Lufthansa, and Air Canada. **Liberty Airlines,** tel. (809) 465-5000, is a charter company that makes regular North America-to-St. Kitts runs.

Interisland connections are made by **LIAT,** tel. (809) 465-2286; **Winair,** tel. (809) 465-2186 or 465-8010; or **Air St. Kitts-Nevis,** tel. (809) 465-8571. Several charter airlines make runs between St. Kitts and Nevis, or St. Kitts and neighboring islands.

If you're flying to Nevis, **LIAT,** Newcastle Airport tel. (809) 469-5302; **Air St. Kitts-Nevis,** tel. (809) 469-9241 or 465-8751; and **Winair,** tel. (809) 469-9583, all make connections from St. Kitts. Air St. Kitts-Nevis is a charter airline, and the cost is about US$100 for a full plane (four persons).

Departure tax from St. Kitts and Nevis is EC$20 or US$8. There is no departure tax between St. Kitts and Nevis.

GETTING AROUND

Taxis

Taxis and minibuses do not have meters; rates are set by the government. Taxis are identified by the "T" on their license plates, buses by an "H." On St. Kitts, taxis are available at Golden Rock Airport, The Circus in Basseterre, and several other places around town.

Taxi fares are posted at airports on both islands and in the tourist board publication called *The St. Kitts and Nevis Traveller.* On both islands, make sure your driver knows that you know the rates. On St. Kitts, the rate for a three-to four-hour island tour will be US$80 for up to four per vehicle. On Nevis, an island tour is about US$45.

Typical fares on **St. Kitts:** Castle Rock Airport to Basseterre EC$13-16, to Frigate Bay EC$25, Basseterre to Dieppe Bay EC$45. Most hotels will be able to arrange taxis, but should you need to call one, try **Riley's Taxi Service,** tel. (809) 465-2444. Pat Riley is very knowledgeable, very efficient, and is the best man for an island tour. Also, try **NTS,** Golden Rock Airport tel. (809) 465-1719; or **The St. Kitts Taxi Association,** The Circus tel. (809) 465-4253.

Typical fares on **Nevis:** Newcastle Airport to Charlestown EC$30, Charlestown to Four Seasons EC$15, Charlestown to Montpelier EC$26. Call **Airport Taxi,** Newcastle Airport tel. (809) 469-9402; **City Taxi Stand,** Main St., Charlestown tel. (809) 469-5621; or **Fitzroy "Teach" Teacher,** tel. (809) 469-1140.

On both islands, add 25-50% to the fare after 10 p.m.

Buses

Minibuses on both islands are an inexpensive way to get around. You won't spend more than EC$3 getting anywhere on either island. The best way to discern their schedules is to talk to drivers.

Minibuses on St. Kitts are found on Bay Road in Basseterre. On Nevis, minibuses are available at the airport, the public market, and the town pier. Bus stops line the roads, but the vans can be hailed at any point.

Car Rentals

Rental cars are available on both islands, starting at about US$30 per day plus five percent tax. The driving is easy; just remember to stay on the left. You'll need to get a temporary local license, costing EC$30 or US$12, which can be arranged by the rental company.

On St. Kitts try **Avis,** (809) 465-6507, fax 465-1042; **Caines Rent-a-Car,** tel. (809) 465-2366, fax 465-6172; **Delisle Walwyn Rentals,** tel. (809) 465-8449; **Sunshine Rentals,** tel. (809) 465-2193, fax 465-7498; or **TDC Rentals,** tel. (809) 465-2991, fax 465-1099.

On Nevis call **Avis,** tel. (809) 469-1240, fax 469-5604; **Nevisian Rentals,** tel. (809) 469-5423 or 469-9583, fax 469-0487; **Nisbet Rentals Ltd.,** tel. (809) 469-9211; or **Skeete's Car Rental,** tel. (809) 469-9458.

Ferry Service

Regular passenger ferry service operates between Basseterre and Charlestown. The two boats are the *Carib Queen* and the *Spirit of Mount Nevis,* which is operated by the Mt. Nevis Hotel and Beach Club. One-way fare on the Carib Queen is EC$10 or US$4; on the Spirit of Mount Nevis, fare is EC$15 or US$6. The crossing takes 30-45 minutes. The schedule changes often, but the Basseterre-to-Charlestown ferries leave daily, sometimes three times a day, starting at 8 a.m. An exception is Tuesday, when you'll have to plan on just one trip at 2 p.m. The return Charlestown-to-Basseterre trip is also daily. Call the tourist board for current schedules.

Additionally, the Four Seasons Hotel on Nevis runs a ferry service for guests only.

MONEY, HOURS, AND COMMUNICATION

Money and Currency Exchange

St. Kitts and Nevis use the Eastern Caribbean dollar, exchanged at EC$2.70 = US$1. Most taxi drivers, shopkeepers, and businesses will accept U.S. dollars and often Canadian dollars, but your change will probably be in EC dollars. To get a better exchange rate, you'd do yourself a favor by changing your currency to EC dollars.

Banks give better exchange rates than hotels, and they are located on the main streets and malls of Basseterre and Charlestown. Among the banks on St. Kitts are **Barclays,** tel. (809) 465-2264, and **Royal Bank of Canada,** tel. (809) 465-2259, both on The Circus. On Nevis you'll find **Barclays,** tel. (809) 469-5467, and **The Bank of Nova Scotia,** tel. (809) 469-5411, both on Main Street.

Banking hours are generally Mon.-Thurs. 8 a.m.-3 p.m. and Friday 8 a.m.-5 p.m. with a few variations. The **St. Kitts and Nevis National Bank,** St. Kitts tel. (809) 465-2204, Nevis tel. 469-5244, is open Saturday morning 8:30-11:30 a.m.

Commercial business hours are Mon.-Fri. 8 a.m.-noon and 1-4 p.m., and Saturday 8 a.m.-noon. Many shops close for the entire afternoon on Thursday, and others stay open through Saturday or for cruise ship business.

Post Office and Telephone

The general post office, St. Kitts tel. (809) 465-2521, Nevis tel. 469-5221, on both islands is open Mon.-Sat. 8 a.m.-3 p.m., with the exception of Thursday, when it is open 8-11 a.m. only. Branch post office hours vary slightly.

The telephone area code on St. Kitts and Nevis in "809." Dialing is direct, and public phones use EC coins or phone calling cards. The **St. Kitts and Nevis Telecommunications (SKANTEL)** offices are located on Main Street in Nevis, tel. (809) 469-5000, and at Fort and Cayon streets in Basseterre, tel. (809) 465-1000. Hours are weekdays 8 a.m.-6 p.m. and

---

INFORMATION DIRECTORY

ST. KITTS AND NEVIS TOURIST BOARD

Pelican Mall, Basseterre, St. Kitts, West Indies, tel. (809) 465-2620 or 465-4040, airport 465-8970, fax 465-8794.

414 East 75th St., New York, NY 10021, tel. (800) 562-6208 or (212) 535-1234, fax 879-4789.

11 Yorkville Ave., Suite 508, Toronto, Ontario M4W IL3, tel. (416) 921-7717, fax 921-7997.

10 Kensington Ct., London W8 5DL, tel. (071) 376-0881, fax 937-3611.

ST. KITTS

St. Kitts and Nevis Hotel Association, P.O. Box 438, Basseterre, St. Kitts, West Indies, tel. and fax (809) 465-5304.

Emergency, tel. 911.

Joseph N. France General Hospital, Basseterre, tel. (809) 465-2551.

FedEx, Basseterre, tel. (809) 465-4155.

Jan's Travel Agency, New St., Basseterre, tel. (809) 465-4171.

Immigration, tel. (809) 465-8470.

City Drug Store, Basseterre, tel. (809) 465-2156.

American Express representative, Kantours, Palms Arcade, The Circus, Basseterre, tel. (809) 465-2098.

NEVIS

Emergency, tel. 911.

Alexandra Hospital, Government Rd., Charlestown, tel. (809) 469-5473.

Jan's Travel Agency, Main St., Charlestown, tel. (809) 469-5426.

Tourist Board, Main Street, Charlestown, tel. (809) 469-5521.

Saturday 8 a.m.-1 p.m. In Basseterre, the offices keep Sunday evening hours 6-8 p.m. Phone cards and phone and fax services are available.

MONTSERRAT

Think of an island nation where the shamrock is featured on the country's immigration stamp and is also the logo of the national airline. Where the local phone book lists names such as Cadogan, Galloway, Hogan, and O'Brien. Where St. Patrick's Day is a national holiday. Where the island itself, often referred to as the Emerald Isle, is tall and rugged with rolling green hills and deep, lush valleys.

If you're thinking of Ireland, you're close. If you're thinking of the tiny Lesser Antilles island of Montserrat, you'd be on the money.

While the Irish connection is historically strong on Montserrat, it doesn't take long to embrace the Caribbean side of the island. Sun, beach, fern-filled rainforests, and exotic people are all part of the experience. Large crowds of tourists and laden cruise ships are not, in some ways to the detriment of the island's economy. In other ways, this is a relief for those who make the effort to get here.

THE LAND

The teardrop-shaped island, some 39 square miles (101 square km) in area and about 25 miles (40 km) southwest of Antigua in the Leeward Islands group, is dominated by mountain ranges and semi-active volcanic peaks. To the north is the looming **Silver Hill ,** and at the center of island are the succinctly named **Centre Hills.**

More striking, however, is the southern range, home of the towering **Galways Soufriere** (from the French *soufre,* for sulfur). Galways, part of a 13-acre National Landmarks site, is located just below the 3,002-foot (916-meter) **Chances Peak,** the island's highest point.

Galways is not a true volcano, but rather a fault in the Lesser Antilles' volcanic chain. The chasms in the earth emit heated streams and sulfurous gases, but no lava. More fascinating, however, is its access. Hikers can walk directly into the crater to be surrounded by its thick, pungent gases and steaming vents.

Vegetation in and around the Soufriere hills consists of varying degrees of lush rainforest, high-altitude elfin woodland, and some fumarole vegetation. Areas along the coast and in the lowlands are more prone to looking scruffy; you'll find scrub grass, acacia thorn bushes, and cacti.

Montserrat's beaches are atypical of Lesser Antillean coastal regions; the striking powdery white sand of nearby islands is not the norm here. Due to the island's volcanic activity, the sand is often of crushed pumice and other volcanic jetsam, giving it a flinty gray sheen or a dark brown hue. Volcanic residue has also made the soil nutrient rich, and many Montserratans take advantage of excellent growing conditions to cultivate home gardens and larger plots.

The Montserrat coast is rugged and irregular, and the island has no deep natural harbors.

HISTORY

The Irish connection on Montserrat evolved some time after Columbus encountered the island on his second voyage in 1493.

Called Alliouagana (thought to mean "Land of the Prickly Bush") by the native Caribs, who'd displaced the Amerindian Arawaks, the terrain of the island reminded Columbus of the countryside surrounding the Barcelona abbey Santa Maria de Montserrate. Beyond that, the Spanish connection ends. Columbus bestowed the name, but bypassed the island, prudently fearing confrontation with the bellicose Caribs. Soon after, however, most of the Caribs also abandoned the island, presumably to continue their northern push toward unconquered land.

Irish Settlers
The nearby island of St. Kitts, one of the first British settlements in the New World, had been colonized in the early 17th century by mostly British Protestants and some Irish and British Roman Catholics. Historically, the religious and ethnic mix was a recipe for difficulties.

*The ruins of
Fort St. George
overlook Plymouth.*

The British colonies did not tolerate freedom of religion and even legislated against it. What's more, the Irish were proffered no political participation in the colonies. They resented this and agitated against it.

In 1632, dissident Irish were ordered off St. Kitts by governor Sir Thomas Warren and sent to colonize Montserrat for Britain. Removed from their oppression, the Catholics on Montserrat soon created a local haven of religious freedom, or at least freedom from Protestant persecution. Eventually, other Catholics arrived from nearby islands and from Europe. Their numbers included those conquered and exiled by the lord protector, Oliver Cromwell, whose hatred of the Irish and Roman Catholicism was virulent.

The island quickly became an outpost of indigo, lime, cotton, and tobacco plantations, and by 1650, African slaves were imported to work the growing sugarcane plantations. In its heyday, Montserrat hosted about 100 large sugarcane estates, although it never reached the potential of agricultural production its British leaders had hoped for; competition from the larger islands nearby and the lack of an efficient deepwater port, as well as continuing prejudicial treatment of the Irish relegated the island to the status of one of Britain's least important colonies.

The continuing European wars of the 17th and 18th centuries saw Montserrat occupied twice by the French. The 1783 Treaty of Versailles ultimately returned the island to the British, who have retained control to this day.

Meanwhile the plantations grew, as did the slave population and discontent.

Its date carefully chosen, a slave rebellion occurred on St. Patrick's Day in 1768—hence, today's national holiday, which commemorates both St. Patrick and the heroes of the uprising. The rebellion, however, was harshly put down and all the leaders executed.

England abolished slavery in 1834, signaling the end of Montserrat's small but booming economy. Today, descendants of slaves, as well as descendants of the original Irish, comprise the majority population of Montserrat.

Into the 20th Century

In 1871, Montserrat became part of the British Federation of the Leeward Islands and in 1958 joined the more encompassing Federation of the West Indies. The federation dissolved in 1962, in part due to internecine bickering between the larger islands of Jamaica and Trinidad and Tobago, which both received independence that year. Island referendums for independence were then held; yet, in 1966, Montserrat voted to remain a dependency of Great Britain. It has remained a British Crown Colony since.

PEOPLE AND CULTURE

Montserrat's population numbers approximately 12,000. The official language is English, spoken with a subtle and anomalous hybrid Irish brogue. The island's population center and capital is Plymouth (pop. 3,500), on the southwest leeward coast.

The rest of the island's population is scattered throughout the three parishes of St. Anthony's, St. George's, and St. Peter's, all no more than 12 miles (19 km) from the capital. Catholicism dominates the religious life, but other, mainly Protestant, groups are represented.

Culturally, Montserrat borrows from its African and Irish-British heritage. St. Patrick's Day is an important holiday, particularly in the village of St. Patrick's, where a three-day carnival celebrates the day. Masquerades, street theater, calypso and soca marches, and a Freedom Run mark both the commemoration of the Irish patron saint and the 17 March slave rebellion of 1768.

A popular folk dance, the "heel and toe" has Irish roots, as does one of the country's national dishes, the strangely named "goatwater," a variation of Irish stew.

Holidays and Festivals

Aside from Christmas activities, numerous festivals take place from mid-December through New Year's Day. This is Montserrat's carnival season. Calypso competitions, including the naming of the Calypso King, concerts, parades, street music, "jump ups," and food festivals culminate on **Festival Day,** or New Year's Eve day, and continue through the night into New Year's Day. More parades and calypso competitions are held through midnight on New Year's Day. Exhausting stuff.

August Monday, the first Monday of the month, commemorates the emancipation of slaves.

Folk Groups

Literature and the arts are promoted on Montserrat through the efforts of several organizations. A noteworthy one is the **Montserrat Writers' Maroon** (on Montserrat, a "maroon" is the gathering of people for a common cause), founded by, among others, the local poet and prominent historian Dr. Howard Fergus, whose latest work is the poetry collection *Calabash of Gold*. The group is a writers' collective attached to the University of the West Indies School of Continuing Studies, tel. (809) 491-2344. Look for announcements of poetry recitals and dramatizations in the local papers, or call for information.

GOVERNMENT AND ECONOMY

Government

Montserrat is a British Crown Colony with a representative ministerial form of government. A governor represents Queen Elizabeth II, who is the official head of state. A two-body legislature, consisting of a Legislative and Executive Council, is elected by popular vote, and a chief minister, currently Reuben T. Meade, is appointed head of the government. Several political parties are active, including Meade's National Progressive Party. The crown, in the form

turn-of-the-century hurricane damage in Montserrat

of the governor, is responsible for external affairs, the police, and defense.

Movements for independence have surfaced in the past, but the economic pragmatism of such a move is recognized by most Montserratans to be dicey at best.

Economy

The economy of Montserrat is reliant on foreign aid, primarily from Britain and Canada, as well as tourism, light manufacturing, offshore banking, and some subsistence farming. None of the island's industries, including tourism, are substantial, yet the infrastructure of the country is quite good, and extremes of poverty and wealth are not directly evident.

An offshore banking industry was introduced in 1978, but after 10 years of relatively unchecked growth it was found to be rife with fraud and currency laundering schemes. Strict regulations have since been instituted, and though overseas investment confidence remains somewhat shaken, Montserrat is still the third-largest offshore banking facility in the English-speaking Caribbean. Even so, if not for British and other overseas aid, Montserrat would be severely limited in developing internal resources for generating income.

In 1989, Hurricane Hugo wreaked havoc on the island, killing 12 people and destroying or partially damaging an estimated 95% of housing and much of the public infrastructure. Tourism and the small subsistence farming industry were hard-hit. Evidence of that devastation exists today, and it has only been since 1993 that the government and private sector have been able to claim full recovery. Today, more than 400 refurbished rooms in hotels and villas service the tourism industry.

SIGHTS

It won't take long to drive around Montserrat and see the sights. Even if you stop and linger, climb and hike, swim and splash, it still won't take long. This is a small and, at the risk of employing one of the more annoying cliches of travel writing, friendly island, one on which you are likely to pass the same people several times as you make the rounds. If you get lost, don't hesitate to stop and ask directions.

IRISH connection

MONTSERRAT

THE WAY THE CARIBBEAN USED TO BE

MONTSERRAT TOURIST BOARD

Good roads, though winding and dipping through the hills and valleys, make driving an easy task on Montserrat. Some of the island's hikes and climbs are easier with a guide, and this has given rise to an unfortunate situation for would-be explorers. "Official" guides, who can almost always be found at the entrance and parking areas of certain sites, or in Plymouth, are in the business for a quick buck and are apparently unimpressed by the phrase, "No, thank

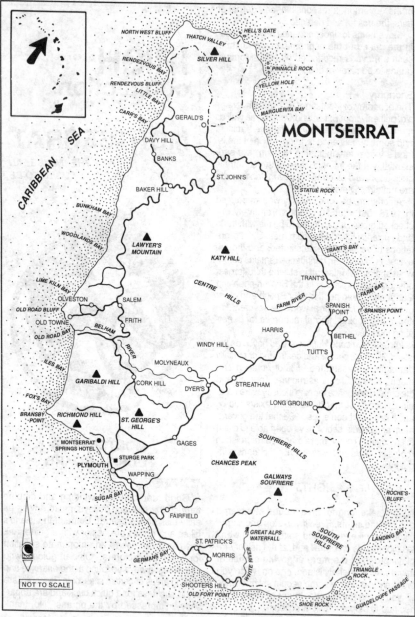

MONTSERRAT

you." Avoid these guys; they'll charge too much. By and large, you do not need a guide if you are fit and in possession of an adventurous spirit. A good map also helps.

The **Department of Tourism** (see the "Information Directory" chart, below) is in the process of compiling standard rates for qualified guides and will be able to recommend the right person for the job. Write or call ahead if you have a planned itinerary.

Beaches

The best beaches are found on the west coast of the island. Toward the south, the beaches are of dark volcanic sand, but clean. **Sugar Bay,** south of Plymouth, is long and within walking distance of town. You'll find a small yacht club here where you can grab lunch and refreshments.

The beach at the Montserrat Springs Hotel is also nice, and you can use the hotel's beach bar and hot springs bath (open seasonally). The therapeutic hot springs comes courtesy of the volcano, which emits the water at about 165° F (28° C). The water is carried down from the mountainside in an aqueduct system, where it is held in tanks for cooling.

Fox's Bay, Iles Bay, and **Old Road Bay,** just north of the Fox's Bay Bird Sanctuary, all host dark-sand beaches. You'll find a small beach hut at Fox's Bay. The Old Road Bay beach, by the Vue Point Hotel, has a beach bar, telephones, and a water sports facility.

At **Woodlands Bay** you'll find small huts for shade and caves for exploring.

On the breathtaking northwest coast, **Carr's Bay** and **Little Bay** are both popular. Some consider the island's best beach to be at **Rendezvous Bay,** which is also the island's only light-sand beach. It can be reached by a long hike from Little Bay, but the popular way to go is by boat. Trips can be arranged at the Vue Point Hotel; cost is about EC$54 (US$20) per person.

Galways Soufriere

The road south to St. Patrick's is a good place to start. **Galways Soufriere** is located about six miles (10 km) east of the town. The drive up to the volcano passes **Galways Plantation,** the hillside ruins of a circa 1750 sugarcane plantation, mill, and slave village. The plantation, first established in the 17th century, was originally 1,300 acres and is now the site of some archaeological activity. It was owned by the dynastic Blake family of Galway, who controlled several profitable plantations on other islands.

To get to Galways Soufriere involves a short and not very strenuous (about 20 minutes) hike from a parking area. Lock your car. Along the path you'll note the pungent stink of what seems to be rotten onions. At the Soufriere, you can descend a rocky path to the boiling springs, yellow and blue mineral-stained rocks, and bubbling vents. It gets hot down there. A roundtrip taxi ride from Plymouth to the Soufriere is about EC$60, and the driver will wait for you.

Chances Peak

The highest point on the island, the 3,002-foot (916-meter) **Chances Peak,** is accessible by an estimated 2,000-step-long path. The rickety steps don't help much and disappear in places, but there are ropes to help you along. The climb is arduous and will take two or three hours, depending on your comfort level. Legend has it—and this is another holdover from Irish legends—that a mermaid resides in the shallow pond near the summit of the peak. She and her friend, a snake, sit by the pond while she combs her hair, and if you're able to grab her comb and run with it down to the sea without being caught by the snake, you're said to be in for good fortune. The views from the top are astonishing. Best time for viewing is early morning.

More Hikes and Sights

Great Alps Waterfall, also near St. Patrick's, is a 70-foot (21-meter) waterfall, about a 45-minute walk from the parking area. You may need a guide for this one, although the hike through the rainforest generally follows the White River. The waterfall is a great place to cool off after the long hike. Guides are found at the carpark, and the recommended rate is EC$15 for a lone hiker, or EC$10 per person in a larger group. A return-trip taxi ride to the carpark is EC$39, and the driver will wait (the driver may even be a good guide).

North of Plymouth, the **Fox's Bay Bird Sanctuary** is worth a visit. The 15-acre preserve has mostly mangrove swamps and light woodlands and is the roosting place for dozens of local species including egrets, herons, and coots. No admission is charged. As well, the beach at Fox's Bay is one of the island's nicest.

Inland from the bird sanctuary are the overgrown ruins of **Fort St. George,** on St. George's Hill. Two cannons and a magazine, part of a French fortification built in 1782, overlook Plymouth and the ocean. Not much else is found here, but the view alone is worth the drive. Note the nearby flamboyant tree, planted by the not-so-flamboyant Queen Elizabeth in 1967. A small refreshment stand is open in season.

In the ritzy Richmond suburb of Plymouth, you'll find the tiny **Montserrat Museum,** tel. (809) 491-5443, in a restored sugar mill tower. The museum is open for the blink of an eye, only Sun.-Wed. 2:30-5 p.m. Donations are accepted.

Montserrat's 15 minutes of fame was provided by **Air Studios,** a recording studio built by former Beatles' manager George Martin. The studio has produced music by Sting, Jimmy Buffet, Elton John, and the Rolling Stones, as well as local artists. The studio suffered during Hurricane Hugo and has not been in full operation since.

PLYMOUTH

Plymouth is the small, compact, and even slightly busy hub of the island. The architecture is Georgian, the streets are clean, and the waterfront is pleasant. You'll find a busy public market on Strand Street next to the prison on Friday and Saturday. The gardens of the old 18th-century **Government House** are open to the public weekdays from 10 a.m. to noon. The **general post office** on Marine Drive has a philatelic bureau that features unique island scenes on their stamps. Next to the post office is the **War Memorial** and clock tower. The memorial honors soldiers of both world wars.

On Marine Drive, note **Arrow's Manshop.** The clothing store is owned by the famous Montserratan calypso and soca singer king Arrow, whose ubiquitous hit "Hot, Hot, Hot" is heard, well, everywhere.

SPORTS AND ENTERTAINMENT

Montserrat is a quiet island. Not much is going on in the way of exotic island entertainments, although "liming," the Caribbean pastime of hanging about and shooting the breeze, will never go out of style. It's what people do. They do it in hotels, bars, restaurants, on the street. It's easy, it's cheap, and you get to know some people.

Sports

Tennis is possible, for a fee, at the hotels Vue Point and Montserrat Springs, and at the **Montserrat Golf Course,** tel. (809) 491-5220. All have lighted courts.

Golf at the Montserrat Golf Course in Belham Valley is played on a sprawling and picturesque 11-hole course, generally approached as two courses of nine holes each. Greens fees are EC$50 per day.

Sturge Park, located just north of Plymouth, hosts regular cricket and soccer matches, some at night. Big crowds, good times.

Water Sports

Water sports, including catamaran sailing, fishing, water-skiing, windsurfing, and snorkeling, are best arranged at **Shamrock Watersports,** at the Vue Point Hotel, tel. (809) 491-5738.

Two dive centers handle Montserrat's scuba diving business. Both offer one- or two-tank dives, night dives, and are PADI-certified. Call **Dive Montserrat,** tel. (809) 491-8812, or **Seawolf Diving School,** tel. (809) 491-6859. Both maintain offices in Plymouth.

Shopping

Plymouth is the place for shopping, and several souvenir stores are found along Parliament Street and downtown. Duty-free shopping is minimal, but good bargains can be found, especially in the locally manufactured Perk's Rum Punch or Cassell's hot sauce. For local art and crafts, go to **Jus' Looking** on George Street, **The Island House Gallery** on John Street, or **Tapestries of Montserrat** on Parliament Street.

For those staying in villas or apartments, or otherwise in need of stocking a kitchen, **Papa's**

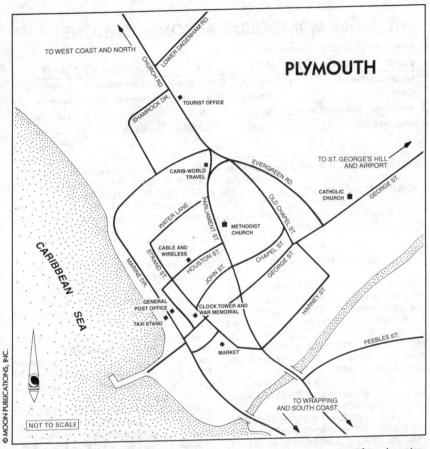

TO WEST COAST AND NORTH

LOWER DAGENHAM RD.

CHURCH RD.

PLYMOUTH

SHAMROCK DR.

■ TOURIST OFFICE

TO ST. GEORGE'S HILL AND AIRPORT

EVERGREEN RD.

■ CARIB-WORLD TRAVEL

CATHOLIC CHURCH ✝

GEORGE ST.

WATER LANE

PARLIAMENT ST.

OLD CHAPEL ST.

■ METHODIST CHURCH

CABLE AND WIRELESS ■

STRAND ST.

HOUSTON ST.

JOHN ST.

CHAPEL ST.

GEORGE ST.

MARINE DR.

CARIBBEAN SEA

GENERAL POST OFFICE ■

■ CLOCK TOWER AND WAR MEMORIAL

TAXI STAND ■

HARNEY ST.

PEEBLES ST.

■ MARKET

TO WRAPPING AND SOUTH COAST

© MOON PUBLICATIONS, INC.

NOT TO SCALE

Supermarket on Church Road is large and fairly well stocked. **Pete's 24-Hour Bakery** on George Street just outside of town sells a range of breads and pastries. The local **market,** on Strand Street next to the prison, is open and busy Friday and Saturday mornings. Get there early.

Nightlife
Festivals (see under "People and Culture" above) are a great source of entertainment in Montserrat, and they occur sporadically throughout the year. Local dance, drama, and choir groups perform at schools and other venues.

Hotels are the other source of regular entertainment and often feature steel bands, reggae bands, and shows. The Vue Point and Montserrat Springs offer live music on some weekends, mostly in high season. **La Cave** in Plymouth and **Nepcoden** in Weekes are currently the island's popular nightclubs.

The Village Place, tel. (809) 491-5202, in Salem is a restaurant, famous for its spicy chicken and its bar. You'll find live music on weekends and a sweaty, jumping crowd on Saturday night.

The **Yacht Club** in Wapping features live music on weekends. The **Inn on Sugar Bay,**

MORE MONTSERRAT ACCOMMODATIONS

Rates per s, EP when applicable, winter

NAME	(809)	FAX	LOCATION	TARIFF
Marie's Guest House	491-2745	491-3599	north Plymouth	budget
Oriole Plaza Hotel	491-6982	491-6690	Plymouth	moderate
Providence Estate Guest House	491-6476	N/A	Providence Estate	moderate
Woodlands Inn	491-5123	491-5918	Woodlands	moderate-luxury

tel. (809) 491-5067, also in Wapping, features live music several times a week. The **Belham Valley Hotel** lounge, tel. (809) 491-5553, hosts live jazz performances on Friday nights.

The island's one cinema, **The Shamrock,** is located in downtown Plymouth.

ACCOMMODATIONS

The accommodations picture of Montserrat is not one of mega-resorts; instead you'll see a few hotels and a fistful of picturesque villas and guesthouses set either in the hills or in villages with names like Frith, Bethel, and Broderick's. By and large, accommodation in Montserrat is a good buy compared to several of the larger, tourism-laden islands.

Large hotels charge a 7-10% government tax and 10% service charge; the charge is less common at guesthouses.

The following categories are based on prices per night for single occupancy in high season (15 Dec.-15 April): **Luxury** US$100 or more, **Moderate** US$50-100, **Budget** US$50 or less. Low season rates are reduced by as much as 30-50%.

Villas

As a haven for retirees from North America and the U.K., the private home market has been a boon for Montserrat's economy. Villa rentals have become big business here and represent more rooms than do all the island's hotels combined.

If you're traveling with a family or large party, villas can be the best deal going. Amenities often include a pool, maid service, and even a cook and driver if you'd like to relax completely. Off-season rates may be reduced by as much as 30-50% and are often negotiable.

The tourist board (see address under "Information Directory" chart, below) can provide a comprehensive list of the agencies that rent villas or apartments, but for starters try **Montserrat Villas,** P.O. Box 445, Plymouth, Montserrat, West Indies, Canada tel. (416) 737-5638, fax 884-1465, with two luxury villas overlooking Old Road Bay and the golf course. Brokes Palais Villa has three bedrooms, and Vista de Redonda has four. Winter rates range US$1995-2795 per week.

Shamrock Villas, P.O. Box 221, Plymouth, Montserrat, West Indies, tel. (809) 491-2431, fax 491-4660, manages 50 one- and two-bedroom units, many in the Richmond Hill area above Plymouth, that rent for US$450-550 per week in high season. Moderate.

Villas of Montserrat, 444 Castro Street, Suite 400, Mountain View, CA 94041, tel. (415) 964-3498, manages a selection of luxurious villas, most with three bedrooms, three baths, and a pool. Luxury.

Hotels

Vue Point Hotel, P.O. Box 65, Plymouth, Montserrat, West Indies, tel. (809) 491-5210, U.S. tel. (800) 253-2314, New York tel. (800) 223-9815, local fax 491-4813, is one of the island's premier hotels. The location is good—on a hill above a beach—and the hotel offers both cottages and rooms, tennis, and a pool, as well as entertainment. Luxury.

The **Montserrat Springs Hotel,** P.O. Box 259, Plymouth, Montserrat, West Indies, tel. (809) 491-2481, U.S. tel. (800) 223-9815, Canada tel. (416) 484-4864, local fax (809) 491-4070, U.S. fax (212) 545-8467; Canada fax (416) 485-8256, has been completely refurbished following Hurricane Hugo and offers simple but clean suites and rooms, a large pool, and a great view. The beach is nice, and the hotel operates a hot springs bath. Don't miss the excellent Sunday afternoon buffet (US$16 or EC$43), a tradition with Montserratans and guests. Luxury.

Flora Fountain Hotel, P.O. Box 373, Plymouth, Montserrat, West Indies, tel. (809) 491-6092, fax 491-2568, has 18 slightly ramshackle, air-conditioned rooms and is located downtown on Church Road. The restaurant specializes in Indian cuisine. Moderate.

Lime Court Apartments, P.O. Box 250, Plymouth, Montserrat, West Indies, tel. (809) 491-6985, are downtown on Parliament Street—clean, basic, good location. Budget.

The small **Niggy's Guesthouse,** Aymers Ghaut, Kinsale, Montserrat, West Indies, tel. (809) 491-7489, is located just south of Plymouth and has five clean rooms, shared baths, and a restaurant and bar. It can be noisy at times, but, at US$15 (EC$40.50) per single and US$20 (EC$54) per double, you'll get your money's worth. Budget.

Ida Moose Guesthouse, Kinsale, Montserrat, West Indies, tel. (809) 491-3146, and supermarket, in Kinsale village, offers a small restaurant and bar, and five rooms sitting on a rough, stony beach; you wouldn't want to swim there. It's neither pretty nor quiet, but at US$25-30 (EC$67.50-81), and with a name like that, you've got to take the chance. Budget.

Camping
Camping is not encouraged but is allowed in the countryside with permission from the Ministry of Agriculture and Trade. Contact the tourist board, tel. 809-491-2230, to request permission. You'll be on your own, however; as of yet no authorized camping facilities exist on the island.

FOOD

The cuisine on Montserrat combines West Indian Creole and Continental, although specialties such as Chinese and East Indian can also be found. The local dish of frogs' legs, from the large amphibian called mountain chicken, is indigenous to Montserrat and Dominica. The island's famous goatwater, a thick stew of local vegetables and goat meat, is based on an Irish dish.

Hotels often offer good deals, such as the Vue Point's Wednesday evening barbecue, where there's entertainment, as well, and the Montserrat Springs' Sunday afternoon buffet, where you're likely to encounter local families in their Sunday best, enjoying a post-church service treat.

MORE MONTSERRAT VILLAS AND APARTMENTS

Rates per unit, EP when applicable, winter

NAME	(809)	FAX	TARIFF
Caribbee Agencies Ltd.	491-7444	491-7426	moderate-luxury
Dream Home Realtors	491-2124	491-6069	moderate-luxury
Neville Bradshaw Agencies	491-5270	491-5069	moderate-luxury
Paradise Villas	491-3318	491-5466	moderate-luxury
Properties Ltd.	491-2986	491-2986	moderate-luxury
Trade Winds Real Estate	491-2004	491-6229	moderate-luxury
Woodsville Condominiums	491-5119	491-5230	moderate

MORE MONTSERRAT RESTAURANTS

NAME	LOCATION	(809)	CUISINE	PRICE RANGE
The Attic	Plymouth	491-2008	seafood/local	moderate
Brattenmuce	Belham Valley	491-7564	Continental/local	moderate
Casuarina's	Wapping	491-7289	Italian/Continental	moderate
Golden Apple	Cork Hill	491-2187	seafood/local	inexpensive
Harbour Court	Plymouth	491-2826	snacks/local	inexpensive
Inn on Sugar Bay	Wapping	491-5067	snacks	inexpensive
The Nest Beach Bar	Old Road Bay	491-5834	seafood/local	inexpensive
Niggy's Guesthouse	Kinsale	491-7489	seafood/Italian	inexpensive-moderate
The Village Place	Salem	491-5202	local	moderate

Many of the island's smaller restaurants are open only seasonally and do not accept credit cards.

The following categories are based on single entree prices: **Expensive** US$25 or more, **Moderate** US$10-25, **Inexpensive** US$10 or less.

The **Belham Valley Hotel,** restaurant tel. (809) 491-5553, overlooks the ocean and features a jazz band on Friday. The cuisine features numerous fresh seafood dishes, including a Seafood Delight of lobster, scallops, and snapper. Moderate-Expensive. **Iguana Cafe,** tel. (809) 491-2328, is in Wapping, just outside Plymouth. Seafood is a specialty, and the pizzas are the best on the island. No credit cards are accepted. The hours are odd, so call ahead. Moderate. The **Emerald Cafe,** tel. (809) 491-3821, also in Wapping, serves seafood and steaks. Also, no credit cards. Moderate.

Mrs. Morgan's, tel. (809) 491-5419, sometimes called Annie Morgan's or Mistress Morgan's (which sounds less like a restaurant than an exotic personal ad) is located in St. John's near Little Bay and serves the island's best local eats, including the famous goatwater. The unadorned, picnic-tabled joint is very popular with Montserratans, a good place to meet. The restaurant, however, is open infrequently—call ahead to confirm. Inexpensive.

The **Blue Dolphin,** tel. (809) 491-3263, in Amersham specializes in mountain chicken and seafood. Inexpensive.

For fresh bread and pastries, stop at **Economy Bakery,** tel. (809) 491-3778, on Church Road in Plymouth. The **Evergreen** pastry shop, tel. (809) 491-3514, on Marine Drive serves light snacks and ice cream and is open Mon.-Wed. 7 a.m.-8 p.m., Thurs.-Sat. until 11 p.m., and Sunday 4-8 p.m.

GETTING THERE

Blackburne Airport, tel. (809) 491-6494, on Montserrat's east coast, about 10 miles from Plymouth, is 3,400 feet (1,037 meters) long, not large enough to land major airliners. Plans are afoot to expand the airstrip, but as of yet no direct flights from North America or Europe are operating.

LIAT, tel. (809) 491-2533 or 491-2362, operates four nonstop flights per day from Antigua (20 minutes) and is the best connection. V.C. Bird International Airport on Antigua is a major destination for North American and European airlines such as American, British Airways, Air Canada, Lufthansa, and Trinidad's BWIA. LIAT connections from other Lesser Antilles islands are also made through V.C. Bird. You can find LIAT offices on Lower George Street in Plymouth.

Montserrat Airways, tel. (809) 491-5342 or airport tel. 491-6494, fax 491-6205, operates primarily as a charter outfit, but now runs a shuttle service between Blackburne Airport and V.C. Bird. The flight departs Antigua for Montserrat every hour from 7 a.m. to 7 p.m., and the fare is EC$89 one-way, half fare for children.

For visitors whose stay has been more than 24 hours, the departure tax from Montserrat is EC$15 or US$6.

GETTING AROUND

Taxis and Buses

Taxis and minibuses are easily recognized, if not by the large number of arms protruding from the windows and the colorful names such as "Mango" and "Terminator," then by an "H" on the license plate. Taxis are, in fact, usually minibuses. Rates are set by the government, and the tourist department and driver should have rate sheets.

Taxi stands are found behind the War Memorial and clock tower on Marine Drive and at the airport. All hotels have a taxi service available. Sample rates, which are based on up to four persons per car, include: Airport to Plymouth EC$29, Airport to Vue Point Hotel, EC$42, Plymouth to St. Patrick's EC$11, Plymouth to St. John's EC$34. Island tours by taxi run approximately EC$30 per hour, or you can take a day tour for EC$130. Call **James "Mango" Frith,** tel. (809) 491-2134, for reliable island tours.

Minibuses run from Plymouth to the rest of the island, leaving from the stand on Church Road. Fares are considerably less expensive than taxis, ranging EC$2-4.

Car Rentals

Rentals are plentiful; just remember to drive on the left. Driving is a pleasant way to explore the island, and the approximately 120 miles (193 km) of road affords access to many of the best sights.

Rental rates tend to be less than on many of the neighboring islands, averaging US$35 per day. You'll need a valid driver's license and a temporary local license, which can be arranged by the rental company or obtained at the Traffic Desk at the Treasury Building in town, week-

days 8 a.m.-2:30 p.m. The cost is EC$30. Most rental agencies are found in Plymouth.

Try **Budget Rent A Car,** tel. (809) 491-5778, fax 491-6066; **Ethelyne's Car Rental,** tel. (809) 492-2885; **Edith's Car Rental,** tel. (809) 491-6696; **Fenco Car Rentals,** tel. (809) 491-8200, fax 491-3891; or **Pauline's Car Rental,** tel. (809) 491-2345, fax 491-2434. **Reliable,** tel. (809) 491-6990, fax 491-8070, rents minimokes, which are smaller vehicles, sort of like elongated golf carts with bagels for wheels.

Bike Rentals

Biking Montserrat is becoming a popular way to see the countryside. With the steep hills and dips, it's also good exercise. Americans Susan Goldin and Butch Miller own **Island Bikes,** P.O. Box 266, Harney Street, Plymouth, Montserrat, West Indies, tel. (809) 491-5552 or 491-4696, fax 491-3599, and promote the annual 'Round Montserrat Road Race. They can organize tours, excursions, and rentals.

INFORMATION DIRECTORY

TOURISM

Montserrat Department of Tourism, P.O. Box 7, Plymouth, Montserrat, West Indies, tel. (809) 491-2230, fax 491-7430.

Caribbean Tourism Organization, 20 East 46th St., New York, NY 10017, tel. (212) 682-0435, fax 697-4258.

TravMark, 33 Niagara St., Toronto, Ontario M5V 1C2, tel. (416) 362-3900, fax (416) 362-9841.

Montserrat Chamber of Commerce, P.O. Box 384, Plymouth, Montserrat, West Indies, tel. (809) 491-3640, fax 491-4660.

OTHER

Police Emergency, tel. 999.

Medical Emergency, tel. 999.

Glendon Hospital, Plymouth, tel. 491-2552.

American Express Representative, Carib-World Travel, Plymouth, tel. 491-2713.

FedEx, Carib-World Travel, Plymouth, tel. 491-2713.

Piper's Drugs, Plymouth, tel. 491-2084.

MONEY, HOURS, AND COMMUNICATION

Currency and Banks

Montserrat's currency is the Eastern Caribbean dollar, currently exchanged at EC$2.70 = US$1. U.S. and Canadian dollars and some European currencies are accepted in places, but the U.S. dollar is more widely accepted.

The exchange rate on the street will drop to EC$2.50 for a U.S. dollar, so it's best to exchange your money at a bank. Several banks are located in downtown Plymouth, including **Barclays Bank,** tel. (809) 491-2501, on Church Street, and the **Bank of Montserrat,** tel. (809) 491-3843, on Parliament Street. Exchange rates vary slightly among the banks. Hours vary and are irregular but are generally Mon.-Thurs. 8 a.m.-3 p.m., and until 5 p.m. on Friday. Bank of Montserrat is open Saturday morning as well. An airport branch of Bank of Montserrat is open Mon.-Fri. 9 a.m.-5 p.m.

Major credit cards are accepted at many of the larger hotels, restaurants, and shops, but not all.

Phones, Mail, News

Telephone cards can be obtained and calls can be made from the **Cable and Wireless** building, tel. (809) 491-2112, fax 491-3599, on Houston Street, open Mon.-Sat. 7:30 a.m.-6 p.m., with extra hours Friday until 8 p.m. From North America you can call Montserrat directly by using the "809" area code plus the seven digit number. Locally, you need only dial the last four digits.

The general post office on Marine Drive is open Monday, Tuesday, and Friday 8:15 a.m.-3:55 p.m.; Wednesday and Saturday 8:15-11:25 a.m. In general, businesses and government offices are open weekdays 8 a.m.-noon and 1-4 p.m. Many shops close Wednesday afternoons, while others are open Saturday morning.

Montserrat's newspaper is the small weekly tabloid *The Montserrat Reporter*, obtainable at small shops and **Montserrat Stationery Centre.** The cost is EC$2.50.

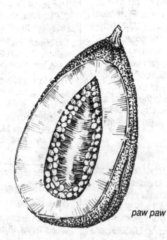

paw paw

BOB RACE

THE BRITISH WINDWARDS

INTRODUCTION

The way we've grouped our Windwards—Dominica, St. Lucia, Barbados, St. Vincent and the Grenadines, Grenada, and Trinidad and Tobago—is loosely based on the old British Windward Islands political designation applied in the 18th century to St. Lucia, Grenada, and St. Vincent, which by 1940 included Dominica as well. Today the term Windwards is confusing but mostly locative; it often incorporates all the islands south of Guadeloupe and north of Trinidad, sometimes inclusive and sometimes not, and also usually includes Barbados, but sometimes not. It's a matter of who is doing the describing.

Historical etymological conundrums aside, these large, dark, misty islands have long fascinated settlers and visitors alike. With soil rich enough to support massive sugarcane and banana estates, and hidden valleys and rainforests large enough to produce exotic species of birds and insects found nowhere else, the Windwards are a naturalist's dream. Their active volcanoes and preserved woodlands offer hiking and exploring opportunities like nowhere else in the Lesser Antilles, and their sheer size and variety of water- and land-based activity is enough to keep inquisitive minds active for much longer than the average vacation.

Due to their size as well, the Windwards have over the years attracted large cosmopolitan communities, exotic mixtures of African, French, British, and, in the case of Trinidad, East Indian cultures. Trinidad and Barbados offer unparalleled dining; St. Lucia leeward beaches and coastal fishing villages are among the finest in the Windwards; the diminutive Grenadines of St. Vincent, as well as Grenada, virtually define tropical island paradises; and the mountains of Dominica hide treasures most locals have yet to find.

DOMINICA

Dominica, the "Nature Island of the Caribbean." With a name like that, who could resist?

Well, quite a few, apparently. For all its vivid, exotic plant and animal species, towering mountains, and virtually untouched lush rainforests and jungles, Dominica remains one of the Lesser Antilles' least traveled destinations.

The reason probably lies with the mainstream touring public's taste for amenities. On Dominica you'll find sparse and rocky beaches, rustic accommodations, and little of the glitz and glamour that accompanies the preferred Caribbean vacation spots.

Preferred, that is, by some. For the rest, Dominica is everything a nature island should be; great chunks of the interior and coast exist under the protection of a national park service. With its hiking trails, waterfalls, boiling lakes, some of the best scuba diving in the Windward Islands, and a resonant Creole culture, Dominica will not disappoint an adventurous spirit.

Now, a short postal and phonetics lesson. The name of the island is Dominica (dahm-in-EEK-uh), officially the Commonwealth of Dominica. It is definitely not the Dominican Republic, a much larger country in the Greater Antilles that shares the island of Hispaniola with Haiti. Columbus is to blame for this confusion. His devotion to Catholicism apparently compelled him to name the islands he encountered after saints, abbeys, and all manner of religious icons. The "Lord's Day," or "Dominica," was one of them—twice. Today, numerous Dominica-bound letters often spend a week or two in the Dominican Republic before they are forwarded to the right place. (To avoid this confusion, letters should be addressed "Commonwealth of Dominica.")

THE LAND

Dominica lies farthest north of the Windward Islands chain and sits nearly equidistant (about 30 miles or 48 km on either side) between the French territories of Guadeloupe to the north and Martinique to the south.

The rugged, mountainous island is some 29 miles (47 km) long and 15 miles (24 km) wide, and 290 square miles (751 square km) in area, about the same size as the combined Netherlands Antilles, or, if you prefer, Bahrain.

Mountains and Parks
The descriptions "rugged" and "mountainous" hardly do the island justice. Big is a better word. Big, lush, and dramatic, Dominica's mountains, formed by ancient volcanoes, loom like monster Hershey's Kisses over small valleys, villages, and banana plantations. The island's highest point, the 4,747-foot (1,448-meter) **Morne Diablotins,** is the second highest mountain in the Lesser Antilles, just short of Guadeloupe's dormant 4,813-foot (1,468-meter) **La Soufrière.**

A spiny, mountainous ridge snakes along the center of the island from north to south, surrounded by several national parks: the **Northern Forest Reserve,** a **Central Forest Reserve,** and the magnificent **Morne Trois Pitons National Park,** which dominates the southern half of the badger-shaped island. (The word "morne" is a Creole combination of the Spanish *morro* and the French *mont*.)

A fourth and somewhat smaller **Cabrits National Park,** on the northwest coast, adds to the image and reality of a nation that takes its natural resources seriously. In fact, the national motto of Dominica is Apres Bondie C'est La Ter, a Creole expression meaning "After God, The Land."

Rainforest and Coast
The low-lying plains of the countryside and coast appear to drip off the mountain peaks like wax off candles, in cases cutting straight into the sea in sheer cliffs. The hills and mountains are blanketed by degrees of ripe and wet rainforest, including seasonal rainforest and the higher elevation mountain forest. Parts of this elevated primordial rainforest, found generally at altitudes greater than 1,000 feet (305 meters) are not easily accessed and are considered by many to be as virginal as they get in the Lesser Antilles—untouched since pre-Columbian times.

The windward (eastern, or Atlantic side) coastal region is characterized by woodlands and swamp forest, and some marshland. The windward coast is somewhat more irregular than the leeward, but this is a matter of degree—much of Dominica's coast is rough and does not offer much in the way of flat beaches and quiescent bays.

The leeward lowlands, in a rain shadow for the most part, are drier and given to scrub forest, grasslands, and rocky shorelines. The valleys of the central section of the country are covered by woodland and by many of Dominica's farms and plantations.

Water
Due to the island's overall high altitudes, rainfall is consistent and cumulative, particularly dur-

ing the July-Oct. rainy season. Rainfall reaches 75-80 inches (1,905-2,032 millimeters) per year, but the true rainfall in the mountains is estimated at three times that much. The mountains hold water, and high-altitude craters and lakes created by past and current volcanic activity provide the island with plenty of fresh, clean water. So well regarded is Dominica's water that a medium-sized industry centers around exporting bottled drinking water to neighboring islands.

Dominicans like to say that there are 365 freshwater rivers and streams throughout the country. Well, there are quite a few, at any rate, and all are put to good use for recreational swimming and bathing. The water and unusually rich soil, created by years of volcanic deposits, makes for fertile growing conditions. The island's soil produces a large variety of tropical fruits, vegetables, and cash crops, year-round. Dominica's fruits and vendors are seen in markets throughout the Lesser Antilles, as far north as the busy outdoor market in Saint-Martin.

Testament to the growing power of Dominica's combined soil and water resources followed the devastation of August 1979's Hurricane David. Winds and driving rains of 150 mph (242 kph) whipped through the island, killing 37, injuring 5,000, and destroying an estimated 75% of the country's homes. The banana and citrus fields, mainstays of Dominica's economy, were crushed. However, within two years, much of the rainforest had regenerated itself, and the banana and citrus farms had taken root once again. While the toll in human suffering lingered, the promise of quick economic recovery reassured island residents.

Fauna

Several plant and animal species found here exist nowhere else in the world. Among the 162 recorded bird species on the island, the large imperial parrot, known locally as the *sisserou,* and the *jaco,* or red-necked parrot, are endemic to Dominica. They are also endangered and protected by law. A variety of bats and frogs, including the often frying-pan-bound "mountain chicken" or *crapaud,* and five species of snakes, which include the 10-foot (three-meter) boa constrictor, or *tête chien,* inhabit the rainforests and woodlands of the island.

HISTORY

The nomadic, Stone Age Ciboney (also spelled Siboney), were Dominica's first inhabitants, as was the case on many islands of the Lesser Antilles. Not much is known of their time on the islands, and few artifacts beyond stone and shell implements have been found to give us insight into their lives.

The hunting and gathering Amerindian Arawaks followed the Ciboney, at about the time of Christ. They were in turn followed by the more aggressive Caribs, who had begun their northern push up the Lesser Antilles chain around A.D. 1000. The Caribs supplanted and absorbed the Arawak groups and were the native group on the island when Columbus sighted it on his second New World voyage in November 1493.

The Caribs had called the land Wai'tukubuli, or "Tall is Her Body." One of Columbus's caravels, hoping to find a supply of fresh water, landed on the western side of the island at the inlet now called Prince Rupert Bay. The Caribs fiercely defended the island, using arrows dipped in poison to turn back the Spanish. Columbus, never one to get too deeply into the fray while there was gold to be discovered elsewhere, moved on. No substantial colonization was further attempted by the Spaniards.

Over the years, the Caribs, who were well established in the Lesser Antilles by that point and valued Wai'tukubuli for its sources of fresh water and food and as a base for raiding neighboring islands, continued to ward off incursions. It remained so for centuries. The Caribs controlled the hills and rugged terrain of Dominica, and were well suited for the type of fighting that took place there. The British and French, in conjunction with colonizing neighboring islands, attempted to establish settlements on Dominica but were continually repulsed by the Caribs. The European wars of the 17th and 18th centuries kept the British and French at each other's throats at any rate. In the meantime, the Caribs could not be budged.

Partitioning the Island

In 1748, the French and British signed the Treaty of Aix-la-Chapelle, which promised neutrality on Dominica and basically yielded the island to the Caribs. The French however, in spite of the treaty, continued to expand their small settlements. This breach of treaty agreements didn't seem sporting to the British, who raided and captured the island in 1761. The British were officially given possession, at least in their own eyes, by the 1763 Treaty of Paris. After this treaty was signed, the British surveyed and sectioned off land parcels and left a small area of 232 acres to the Caribs, whose numbers and resources had dwindled to the point where they could offer little resistance.

The Tug of War

The French won Dominica back in 1778. It went back and forth like this for years, through the American Revolution, the French Revolution, and the Napoleonic Wars—the island changed hands nine times. The struggles between the British, French, and Caribs finally culminated in an 1805 raid, once again, by the French. They in essence held the island hostage for several days and were finally paid a ransom by the British to disappear. Thus began the long period of British rule, although, with the French islands of Guadeloupe and Martinique to the north and south respectively, the French influence on Dominica abated little.

Carib harassment had stultified the development of the island under the British, a situation that resulted in the island's status as the least developed of the British isles. Still, the British began to import greater numbers of Africans to work their plantations, and by the 1834 Emancipation, the majority population on Dominica was African. Little has changed in today's demography—Dominica is still a relatively undeveloped island with a majority African-descent population.

Carib Territory

By the late 19th century, the once-proud Caribs had been relegated to the status of little more than curious has-beens living in abject poverty on poor land. Through their leaders, they made a desperate appeal to Queen Victoria for more land and recognition. The request was granted through a governor named Henry Hesketh Bell, and in 1902 a total of 3,700 acres in the eastern section of the country were given to the Caribs; the area is today known as Carib Territory.

20th Century

By the 1930s, worldwide depression had affected the fragile economy of Dominica. New crops, such as coffee, tobacco, limes and other citrus fruits, and cocoa had been introduced, but the market dried up as the world hunkered down for war. Still, during this period local trade unions were founded, and Dominica was granted a system of internal elected representation. In the 1950s, the world seemed to discover bananas, and the countries of the Caribbean, including Dominica, found new sources of wealth. Dominica's infrastructures and towns grew, and the economy was relatively healthy.

The British colonial government granted universal adult suffrage in 1951. By 1967, Dominica was granted full internal government under an associated statehood agreement with Britain. The country became independent and a republic within the Commonwealth on 3 November 1978, with the Dominica Labour Party (DLP) and Prime Minister Patrick John at its helm.

Due to the extreme and inconsistent policies of the generally left-wing DLP, the country's situation soon degenerated into something akin to anarchy. The opposition party quickly joined with religious and civic leaders to form what they called the Committee for National Salvation and managed to usurp the government, in conjunction with DLP insiders, in what is described as a "constitutional coup." The coalition ruled until elections were called in 1980.

The winner in the 1980 election was the opposition Dominica Freedom Party (DFP), headed by—almost an irony in one of these seemingly testosterone-dominated island cultures— Prime Minister Mary Eugenia Charles. Born in 1919 and educated in Canadian law, Dame Eugenia Charles was the first woman elected head of a Caribbean government.

PEOPLE AND CULTURE

The population of Dominica is 86,000, smaller than any nation in the Windwards. The Dominican majority is of African descent, although pockets of mixed-race descendants of old and nouveau settlers are found, particularly in the capital Roseau.

On Creole Day, and for special occasions, women wear traditional madras costumes, the flowing jupe *and* la wobe douillete, *a skirt with lace petticoats, and a wide blouse and headpiece.*

Caribs

The 3,000 remaining descendants of the original Caribs represent a significant portion of the population, if not in numbers, at least culturally. Many of the high-cheekboned, light-skinned Caribs have been integrated into the general population, and Carib Territory, with village names such as Salybia and Sineku, exists as a remnant of colonial days.

The Caribs retain nominal powers vested in a chief and a six-member council, who draft by-laws with the approval of the central government. There are no markers at the territory's borders. The Caribs have of the last few years made efforts to revive their culture—1993 was, as well as the quincentennial of Columbus's arrival, the Year of Indigenous Peoples and included a Carib Month—but a general Carib revival seems unlikely. The Caribs did not have a written language and did not record their more intricate cultural customs, although a copy of a Carib dictionary compiled in 1642 by a French priest has been found.

The Caribs still practice some traditional crafts, such as fishing and carving canoes from the *gommier,* or gum tree. And Carib women still bake the staple cassava bread.

The Caribs do not celebrate Dominica's 3 November Independence Day, also the date Christopher Columbus sighted the island in 1493. The Caribs maintain that the day Europeans arrived on their shores began their slow and inexorable extinction as a once-viable culture. In Dominica, as on neighboring St. Vincent, few Caribs of pure ancestry remain.

Language

The evolution of language on Dominica mimics the evolution of its original and colonial inhabitants. English is official and widely spoken, but the dominant language is a French Creole laced with words from Carib and various African languages. A typical phrase is *ti beau doudou* ("pretty little girl"). Dominican Creole is unique but has some commonalities with Creoles spoken on the French islands and on St. Lucia.

The language amalgam is evident in all aspects of Dominican life, but perhaps most evident to a visitor looking at a map. Names such as Marigot and Roseau reflect the French influence. Concord and Scotts Head recall the British rule. Some Carib words have lost their meaning, but names such as agouti (a large gerbil-like rodent), *waiwanao* (a fish), and the endangered imperial parrot, the *sisserou,* have survived.

Due to the early French influence on Dominica, Roman Catholicism is the island's dominant religion. Anglican, Methodist, Pentecostal, Baptist, Seventh-Day Adventist, and even Baha'i churches are represented, as well as several smaller Protestant groups.

Island folklore and culture is represented in oral tales and occasionally by performances of local troupes and bands. Hotels and public venues present performances by the **National School of Dance** and the **Wai'tukubuli Dance Troupe,** or the **Dominican Folk Singers.** Check local newspapers for show information.

Literature

Dominica's fine writers have produced a small but significant body of work that offers in-depth portrayals of Dominican and other Caribbean cultures, as well as descriptions of life during and after the colonial period.

The novelist Jean Rhys (1894-1979), born in Dominica, is considered by some to be less Caribbean- than European-influenced, yet she used a Caribbean setting for one of her most famous works, *Wide Sargasso Sea* (1966). The novel deals with post-emancipation West Indian life and the colonial period. Other works by Rhys, particularly several short stories, use intricate West Indian speech rhythms.

The poet and novelist Phyllis Shand Allfrey left Dominica for education in the U.S. and England when she was a teenager. She returned in the early '50s and edited several local newspapers. On Dominica she wrote her only novel, *The Orchid House* (1953), a loosely autobiographical story of the decline of colonialism as seen through the lives of three Dominican sisters. The novel was made into a film in 1990.

Local historian and cultural chronicler Lennox Honychurch has written several excellent guides to Dominica and to the island's culture, including *The Dominica Story* and *Our Island Culture*.

HOLIDAYS AND FESTIVALS

Dominicans take great pride in their culture and in cultural displays. The French have given the country Carnival, one of the island's larger celebrations. The pre-Lenten festival starts several weeks before Ash Wednesday with calypso contests, feasts, and shows. On the Monday and Tuesday before Ash Wednesday, people take to the streets in "jump ups," masquerades, feasts, and parties.

The two Christian holidays of Christmas and Easter are important here, and *Tou Saintes* (All Saints' Day) is celebrated on 1 November, when Dominicans honor the memories of the dead

---

CARIB LIFE TODAY

On the wall outside the Carib Territory office of Chief Ervince Auguiste, you'll find the following inscription painted in bold white letters: "500 Years of Columbus Lie!!! Yet we survive."

This pithy but precise sentiment percolates like a bad wind throughout Dominica's Carib community, the largest Carib enclave left in the Lesser Antilles. The frustration felt by the once-flourishing clan is in your face not only at Chief Auguiste's office but also throughout the 3,700-acre reserve.

It is more than a little ironic that the entire Caribbean region, named after the indigenous Amerindians, was ultimately unable to sustain them. European encroachment from the late 16th century and beyond wiped out most native groups, including the Arawaks (who were already under attack by the Caribs), the Tainos (a subgroup) in the north, and the Caribs, who inhabited most of the southern Lesser Antilles at the time of Columbus's arrival. Battles, disease, and mass suicides—the Arawaks and Caribs often killed themselves rather than submit—decimated the indigenous populations. The Caribs of Dominica, who were in the late 19th century rounded up by colonial authorities and relegated to their "reserve," were viewed as lucky by some, in that they at least survived.

Today, Dominica's Caribs are in a quandary. Their power is limited to representation in parliament by a representative whose constituency includes the territory. Their chief has no real power but is allowed, with a six-person advisory council, to draft territory bylaws that must be approved by parliament. The Carib language has all but disappeared, and many ancient Carib customs, such as canoe-building and basket-weaving, are falling by the modernized wayside. True Carib culture has been eroded by intermarriage and the introduction of Western religions and ways. Farming and some fishing sustain families in the territory, but real economic block power has been lost—money is often spent outside Carib lands.

Lobbying by the Carib people themselves and by concerned outside groups has at least preserved the land and some semblance of Carib identity, even though that identity today is often associated with its own preservation. The quandary seems, for the time, to be limited to political statements. The Caribs do not celebrate Dominica's 3 November Independence Day, also the date of Columbus's "discovery." "It's a sad day for us," Chief Auguiste said in an interview in the local publication *The Tropical Traveller*. "We prefer to look forward to the declaration of Carib Day."

by visiting graves, lighting candles, and joining in public prayer.

Creole Day, usually celebrated the Friday before the 3 November Independence Day celebration, is a day when Dominicans celebrate their Creole heritage. Women dress in madras costumes, the flowing *jupe* and *la wobe douillete,* a skirt with lace petticoats and a wide blouse and headpiece. Men wear the dark trousers and white shirts of the national dress. Business that day is conducted in Creole, and restaurants make a point of serving *crapaud,* agouti, and other traditional dishes. There is much dancing and singing, accompanied by traditional *jing ping* bands (comprising a "boom-boom" bass instrument, accordion, a "shack-shack" percussion instrument, and other traditional music-and noisemakers) and some organized activities that include storytelling and folk dancing.

Independence Day celebrates 3 November 1978 with calypso competitions, speeches, and marching.

Other public holidays include **New Year's Day, May Day** (1 May), **August Monday** (first Monday in August), and **Community Service Day** (the day after Independence Day).

GOVERNMENT AND ECONOMY

Government

The Commonwealth of Dominica is an independent republic within the Commonwealth and is nominally headed by a president, although actual power is vested in the elected government, which is led by a prime minister. A 21-member House of Assembly is elected every five years from the nation's 10 parishes, and from the majority party of that assembly a ministerial Cabinet is chosen. The Carib Territory is represented by one member of the house. A nine-member Senate is appointed by the president; five members from the ruling party are selected by the prime minister, and four are selected by the opposition party. The ruling party is currently the Dominica Freedom Party led by Prime Minister Dame Eugenia Charles (see also "20th Century" under "History," above).

Not Just Bananas

The foundation of Dominica's economy is agriculture. The island is, in fact, self-sufficient in fruit and vegetable production, a claim fewer and fewer Lesser Antilles' islands are able to make today.

Even though only an estimated 10% of the land is arable, bananas, citrus fruits, and coconuts and coconut by-products are grown for export. Nearly 50% of the gross domestic product is from agricultural production, and the industry employs nearly 50% of the workforce. An estimated 32% of the workforce is employed in other industries and commerce.

Most of Dominica's banana farmers operate small farms, not the type of farm descended from massive plantations of the colonial and post-colonial period. This arrangement hearkens back to the old slavery days. Dominica's land is so fertile that many members of the slave population, who were often given small plots of land to work, were able to grow enough to eventually buy their freedom.

Despite blights and competition from Central America, bananas have managed to hold their own in the Caribbean economy. Dominica's principal trading partner is the U.K., and preferential trade agreements with the EEC have allowed the banana trade to flourish. This arrangement is due to end in 1999, whereupon Dominica, already negotiating to maintain price standards, will have several bridges to cross.

Tourism

The government has already looked to tourism to help bolster the economy. This is a delicate matter in Dominica, where the official line is that no one wants the agricultural sector contribution to be replaced by tourism. Tourist numbers, however, have steadily increased, from 24,000 in 1986 to 55,000 in recent years. Caribbean-region locals comprise about 58% of all Dominica's overnight visitors, and U.S. residents are the next most frequent visitors. Cruise ships call at the rate of about 180 per year. That number has dropped slightly in recent years even though actual cruise ship passenger arrivals have increased—the ships are getting larger.

The government is actively promoting nature-oriented tourism, not surprising given the nature, so to speak, of the island. Dominica's official tourism moniker is the "Nature Island of the Caribbean," and that rings true. This is not an island where you'll find long sandy beaches and large resorts. Rather, the virgin rainforests, waterfalls, mountain lakes, rivers, diving opportunities, and unaffected culture of the island lend themselves to exploration, hiking, and getting to know Dominicans. Most of the island's hotels are small, family owned operations. The island's capacity is about 650 rooms and is expected to increase to 1,000 rooms by 1997.

SIGHTS

Beaches

Beaches are not this island's attraction. Its best are in the northeast, near Portsmouth, Dominica's second largest town. The area is still undeveloped, and you'll have a chance to really get away from it all if you decide to explore the small bays and inlets here. The honey-colored sand beach at **Picard,** south of Portsmouth, is about two miles (three km) long and is considered to be one of the island's best. There are several small guesthouses and hotels along the water. The beach at **Douglas Bay,** north of Portsmouth, is also considered to be one of the island's best.

Central Interior

The interior trails and hikes of Dominica may be the most compelling and challenging in the Caribbean. The **National Parks Service Forestry Division,** tel. (809) 448-2401, fax 448-7999, publishes brochures and booklets dealing with the flora and fauna of the island, as well as posters and trail maps of the national parks. Cost is less than EC$15 for anything they produce. The trail map is a bargain at EC$1. Find the Forestry Division at the Botanical Gardens in Roseau.

Guides are not always necessary, but they are helpful and available at just about every attraction. The tourism department of the **National Development Corporation,** tel. (809) 448-2351, is afraid that a plethora of eager guides at the foot of every attraction will become overbearing—this has already begun to happen. Fees have not been set; if you simply show up, you'll

have to negotiate a price. Often the guides are from local villages and are very knowledgeable.

If you want to travel to a site that needs a guide, contact the tourism department first for a recommendation, or contact one of the nature tour companies listed in the chart below. In addition to those listed here, there are a dozen more in the phone book. A simple taxi tour will run about US$20 (EC$54) per hour for a car of four.

Trafalgar Falls is one of the island's most accessible sites. The twin falls are located about five miles (eight km) from Roseau. Park at the hydro station, where there is a small kiosk with drinks for sale, and walk about 10 minutes to a platform where you can view the falls. Another 15-minute hike and you're there, under 200 feet (61 meters) of cascading water. A hot spring feeds water to a natural swimming pool. You'll be glad you did this.

The **Morne Trois Pitons National Park** is accessible from various points starting about six miles (10 km) from Roseau. The name comes from the three-peaked volcanic mountain, height 4,550 feet (1,387 meters), that dominates the 17,000-acre rainforest. A half-dozen trails, some of which have shelters and picnic areas, lead to the park's sites.

The **Emerald Pool** is found off the road to **Castle Bruce.** The hike is an easy 10 minutes through rainforest to a small waterfall-fed pool surrounded by tropical flowers and plants.

Use the village of Laudat to hike about three miles (five km) to **Freshwater Lake,** a calm supply reservoir—therefore no swimming—and the source of the Roseau River. **Boeri Lake,** is found about 45 minutes farther on, and is a large and deep lake 3,000 feet (915 meters) above sea level.

Boiling Lake can be reached from Laudat. The steaming Boiling Lake is not always at a rolling boil but is pretty damn hot. Some claim it is the largest of its kind in the world; others claim it is the second-largest. The water is estimated at about 190° F (60° C) and can boil an egg. The lake sits in a crater and is kept hot by escaping volcanic gases. Don't even think about swimming here.

Below the lake is the attractively named **Valley of Desolation,** an area rendered nearly barren by sulfuric emissions. This entire hike is

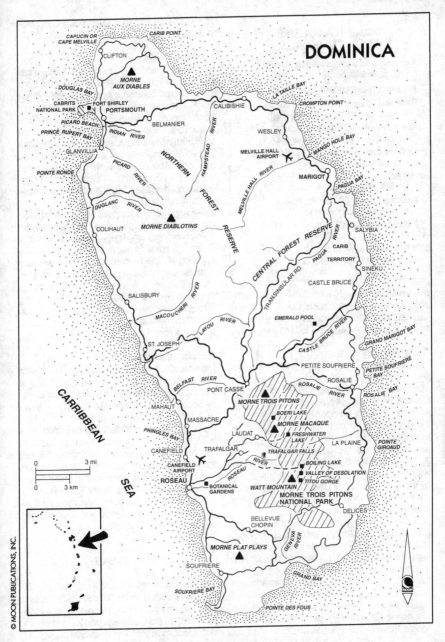

DOMINICA

CAPUCIN OR CAPE MELVILLE
CARIB POINT
CLIFTON
MORNE AUX DIABLES
DOUGLAS BAY
LA TAILLE BAY
CROMPTON POINT
CABRITS NATIONAL PARK
FORT SHIRLEY
PORTSMOUTH
CALIBISHIE
PICARD BEACH
BELMANIER
WESLEY
PRINCE RUPERT BAY
INDIAN RIVER
HAMPSTEAD RIVER
MELVILLE HALL AIRPORT
MANGO HOLE BAY
GLANVILLIA
PICARD RIVER
NORTHERN FOREST RESERVE
MELVILLE HALL RIVER
MARIGOT
POINTE RONDE
DUGLANC RIVER
PAGUA BAY
COLIHAUT
MORNE DIABLOTINS
SALYBIA
CENTRAL FOREST RESERVE
PAGUA RIVER
CARIB TERRITORY
SINEKU
TRANSINSULAR RD.
CASTLE BRUCE
SALISBURY
MACOUCHERI RIVER
LAYOU RIVER
EMERALD POOL
ST. JOSEPH
CASTLE BRUCE RIVER
GRAND MARIGOT BAY
BELFAST RIVER
PETITE SOUFRIERE
PETITE SOUFRIERE BAY
PONT CASSE
ROSALIE
ROSALIE RIVER
ROSALIE BAY
MAHAUT
MORNE TROIS PITONS
BOERI LAKE
MASSACRE
MORNE MACAQUE
FRESHWATER LAKE
LA PLAINE
POINTE GIROAUD
PRINGLES BAY
LAUDAT
TRAFALGAR FALLS
CANEFIELD
TRAFALGAR
ROSEAU RIVER
BOILING LAKE
VALLEY OF DESOLATION
CANEFIELD AIRPORT
ROSEAU
BOTANICAL GARDENS
WATT MOUNTAIN
TITOU GORGE
MORNE TROIS PITONS NATIONAL PARK
DELICES
BELLEVUE CHOPIN
GENEVA RIVER
CARRIBEAN SEA
MORNE PLAT PLAYS
SOUFRIERE
GRAND BAY
SOUFRIERE BAY
POINTE DES FOUS

0   3 mi
0   3 km

© MOON PUBLICATIONS, INC.

DOMINICA NATURE TOUR COMPANIES

Area code 809, address "Commonwealth of Dominica, West Indies."

Astaphan Tours, tel. 448-3221, fax 448-3124.

Dominica Tours and Dive, P.O. Box 34, Roseau; tel. 448-2638, fax 448-5680.

Ken's Hinterland Tours P.O. Box 447, Roseau; tel. 448-4850, fax 448-8486.

La Robe Creole Tours P.O. Box 270, Roseau; tel. 448-4436, fax 448-5212.

Nature Tours 2 Greens Lane, Roseau; tel. 448-3706.

Paradise Tours, 4 Steber St., Roseau; tel. 448-5999, fax 448-4134.

Peter Mason, Vena's Guesthouse, 48 Cork St., Roseau; tel. 448-3286.

Wilderness Tours, 81 Bath Rd., Roseau; tel. 448-2198, fax 448-3600.

only about six miles (10 km) one-way but is a difficult, all-day excursion, about four hours in and four hours to return. A guide is recommended for this hike; expect to pay about EC$40 per person.

Carib Territory

The road divides at Pont Cassé, and the Transinsular Road, a main thoroughfare that nearly bisects the island, continues straight through the **Central Forest Reserve** and on to the windward coast town of **Marigot.** A different branch at the Pont Cassé heads to Castle Bruce, also on the windward side, and the Carib Territory. There are no signs that indicate the borders of the 3,700-acre territory; you'll know you're there by a subtle change in the look of the people sitting by the roads or at small craft stands. The Caribs are mainly fishermen and farmers, and there is a small involvement in tourism here.

In Carib Territory, you can stay at a five-room guesthouse, **The Carib Territory Guesthouse,** tel. (809) 445-7256. A few minutes from the village of **Sineku,** stop at **L'Escalier Tête Chien,** a "staircase" of hardened lava that reaches from the ocean up a hillside. It resembles a frozen snake crawling up the hill, and the solidified lava has formed natural footsteps in the rock. Hence the name "Staircase of the Snake" (literally, "dog's head"—the boa constrictor's head resembles a dog's head). In **Salybia,** a Carib Museum is being developed.

Northern Coast

In the north of the country, the 1,300-acre **Cabrits National Park** (the word comes from the Creolized Spanish *cabras* for "goats," which were left to run wild in the area as sources of fresh meat for passing Spanish ships) encompasses both land and sea. Part of the park is on the Cabrits Peninsula, surrounded by Prince Rupert Bay to the south and Douglas Bay to the north. About 1,000 acres are dedicated to the marine environment. A large swamp, home to many bird species, lies between the peninsula and the mainland.

Remains of old fortifications are scattered over the property, including **Fort Shirley,** an 18th-century garrison finally abandoned in 1854. There is a small museum on the grounds. The towering **Morne Diablotins** can be seen from Cabrits. It is possible to hike to the summit of Morne Diablotins. Drive south from Portsmouth to the old Syndicate Estate, and the hike, along a rough and often vertical path, is about 3,000 feet (915 meters) to the summit. Think about hiring a guide.

Portsmouth Area

Portsmouth, population 5,000, is Dominica's second largest town. The town sits on Prince Rupert Bay, which was used as a port of call by Spanish ships on their trips to the New World. The attraction here is the beaches or maybe a trip up the quiescent **Indian River.** Guided boats will take you past mangrove swamps and thick rainforest. The guides can be aggressive, and the tours should cost about EC$20 per person.

A drive along the **Transinsular Road,** which eventually bypasses the Morne Trois Pitons National Park in the south, will bring you past banana and sugarcane fields, and small villages, the heart of rural Dominica.

ROSEAU

The population of the island's capital is 20,000. The town, located on the flat delta of the Roseau River on the southwest leeward coast, is the picture of an old Caribbean port town struggling with modernization. The orderly and generally clean streets are lined with rambling, dilapidated buildings with rusted roofs—some are downright rickety—as well as fine examples of Victorian and post-colonial wooden structures. Some parts of town, such as **Bay Front,** and features like the **New Market** and **general post office** are gleaming and new and reflect efforts to give the town a new face.

Roseau was first settled by the French in the early 1700s and takes its name from *roseaux,* for "river reeds," which were plentiful in the rivulets that ran throughout the delta. The British laid out plans for the town in the late 1700s. Several structures around town date back to that period, although many older buildings have been lost to fire, military encounters, and hurricanes.

The **Fort Young Hotel** was originally a fort constructed in 1770. The nearby **State House** dates from the mid-19th century. The **Old Market Square,** at the bottom of Church and King George V streets, was during the 18th century a center for slave auctions, executions, political rallies, and public functions. It is now a gathering place, restored in 1988, with several small craft shops and a tourism department booth, open Mon.-Fri. 8 a.m.-4 p.m. and Saturday 9 a.m.-1 p.m.

The promenade along the new **Bay Front Seawall** is a pleasant area to stroll and watch fishermen out on the water. Along the busy road you'll see the old **post office,** built in 1810. The trim on this cream-colored building is a shade of green found nowhere else on the planet. Near-

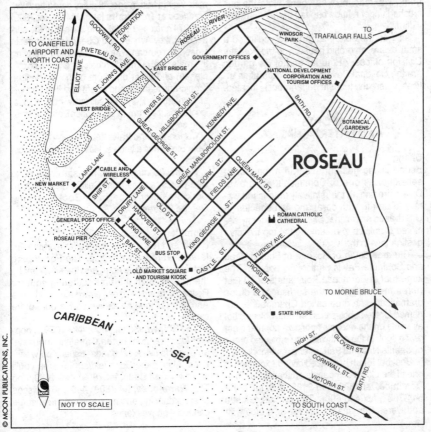

© MOON PUBLICATIONS, INC.

by is the **Court House and Registry,** and at the north end of the seawall is the busy **Roseau Pier.**

The new **general post office** sits just a few blocks north. The **New Market** is also found at the north end of town, facing the **Roseau River.** The loud and active outdoor market is the best place for fresh fruit and produce and is busiest on Friday and Saturday mornings.

The 40-acre **Botanical Gardens** are to the east of town, within walking distance from downtown. The grounds, originally established in 1890, seem curiously empty. The garden was laid low by 1979's Hurricane David but has now recovered. It is primarily trees, including the sausage tree from Africa and the ylang ylang from Asia, that you'll see here. Note the bus crushed under a huge baobab tree, a hurricane victim.

Also on the botanical grounds you'll find a small aviary, an orchid house, and the Forestry Division offices. At the far end of the garden are the National Development Corporation offices, where the tourism department is located.

SPORTS AND ENTERTAINMENT

Diving

Scuba diving has surfaced, in a manner of speaking, as one of Dominica's big draws. Divers are finding the relatively untouched waters to be rife with coral and fish species. A U.S.-based magazine, *Skin Diver,* recently declared Dominica to be among the top five dive destinations in the world.

The area south of Roseau at Scott's Head and Soufrière Bay is particularly popular. The large reef at Barracuda Point starts at 10 feet (three meters) below the surface and drops dramatically. An area called Champagne, so-named for the bubbles that rise from volcanic hot air vents on the ocean's floor, is a popular night diving spot. In the northwest, the protected areas of Cabrits National Park offer excellent diving.

Best bet for an organized diving excursion is one of the oldest companies on the island, **Dive Dominica,** tel. (809) 448-2188, U.S. tel. (800) 544-7631, fax 448-6088. The owners, Ginette and Derek Perryman, package dive trips with

their hotel, **Castle Comfort Lodge** (see "Accommodations," below for more information).

Water Sports

The **Anchorage Dive Centres,** tel. (809) 448-2638, fax 448-5680, are located on the southwest coast's Anchorage Hotel, and the Portsmouth Beach Hotel on the northwest coast. Through them you can organize diving and snorkeling trips, as well as whalewatching excursions.

Shopping

Dominican crafts are good buys. Aside from what you'll find at the aforementioned Carib Territory kiosks and the Old Market Plaza, look for mats woven from a special grass called *vertivert,* produced at **Tropicrafts Island Mats,** tel. (809) 448-2747, fax 448-7126. The shop is at the corner of Turkey Avenue and Queen Mary Street in Roseau. You can watch the women weaving the mats (ask permission before taking a photo, please) and order one from a chosen design. Tropicrafts is the island agent for UPS and will ship your mat. They also sell straw hats, spices, local rums, bay rum (a body lotion), and other island crafts.

Caribana Handcrafts, tel. (809) 448-2761, on Cork Street has a large selection of art and local crafts.

For books, magazines, and stationery go to **Cee Bee's,** across from Celia's Snackette on Cork Street, or **Paperback Books** on King George V Street.

Nightlife

Hotels and restaurants often offer evening entertainment and live music. The Fort Young Hotel hosts a happy hour, and the small bar by the pool is often the first gathering spot for Roseau's young business crowd after work. The Anchorage Hotel hosts live bands during the week.

The Shipwreck, tel. (809) 449-1059, a popular local hangout in the Canefield industrial area, hosts live local bands, usually on weekends. Also in the Canefield/airport area you'll find the **Aqua Cade,** tel. (809) 449-1489, and **The Warehouse,** tel. (809) 449-1303, discos offering dancing and music—some live, some canned—on weekends.

MORE DOMINICA HOTELS

Rates per s, EP when applicable, winter

NAME	(809)	FAX	(800)	LOCATION	TARIFF
Anchorage Hotel	448-2638	448-5680	N/A	Castle Comfort	moderate
Castaways Beach Hotel	449-6244	449-6246	626-0581	Mero	moderate
Coconut Beach Hotel	445-5393	445-5693	N/A	Picard Beach	moderate
Continental Inn	448-2214	448-7022	N/A	Roseau	budget-moderate
Evergreen Hotel	448-3288	448-6800	N/A	Roseau	moderate
Lauro Club Hotel	449-6602	449-6603	N/A	Salisbury	moderate
Layou River Hotel	449-6281	449-6713	N/A	Layou River	moderate
Portsmouth Beach Hotel	445-5142	445-5599	N/A	Picard Beach	moderate-luxury
Reigate Hall Hotel	448-4031	448-4034	223-9815	Reigate	moderate

Walk through the streets of Roseau on any weekend, and you'll hear music and mingling from the dozens of ramshackle rum shops and small bars along the main and side roads. Stop in; you won't see many tourists, and you'll get a taste of local living unavailable at the hotels.

ACCOMMODATIONS

Most of Dominica's accommodations consist of small guesthouses and family-run hotels. Large resorts are not in the plan, although more hotels are in the process of development. The government's official line is to encourage the promotion of small- to medium-sized hotels. Currently, the largest hotel on the island is the **Portsmouth Beach Hotel,** with 96 rooms, many of which are taken on a semi-permanent basis by students of the nearby Ross Medical School. The present room capacity countrywide is 650, and that is expected to increase to 1,000 by 1997.

Smaller hotels and guesthouses do not always accept credit cards; call ahead to inquire.

A more complete list of island hotels can be provided by the **Dominica Hotel Association,** P.O. Box 384, 27 Great Marlborough St., Roseau, Commonwealth of Dominica, West Indies, tel. (809) 448-6565, fax 448-2285.

Hotels and Guesthouses

Larger hotels will add a 10% service charge to your bill, and all hotels add a five percent government tax. Many retain the same basic tariffs year-round, not changing for high and low season.

The following room categories, based on prices per person per night, are used below: **Luxury** US$100 or more, **Moderate** US$50-100, **Budget** US$50 or less.

In Roseau, the **Fort Young Hotel,** P.O. Box 519, Roseau, Commonwealth of Dominica, West Indies, tel. (809) 448-5000, fax 448-5006, has been built in and among the remains of the old Fort Young, constructed in 1770. The location, just above the city next to the National Library and Government House, puts it in a historic district as well. The hotel is newly renovated and sort of cosmopolitan, with a swimming pool, attentive service, and special events on holidays and weekends. The hotel gets quite a few business travelers as well. Moderate-Luxury.

The Garraway Hotel, Place Heritage, Bay Front, Roseau, Commonwealth of Dominica, West Indies, tel. (809) 448-3247, fax 448-3962, was opened in 1993 and has that slick sheen, like a new car. Medium-sized, just 31 rooms, it's located downtown on Bay Front, with great views from the balconies. Moderate-Luxury.

The **Castle Comfort Lodge,** P.O. Box 63, Roseau, Commonwealth of Dominica, West Indies, tel. (809) 448-2188, fax 448-6088, features 10 simple but comfortable rooms, half with oceanfront exposure. The attraction here is the diving facilities; the hotel is headquarters of Dive Dominica, the island's oldest outfit. Moderate.

Vena's Guesthouse, 48 Cork St., Roseau, Commonwealth of Dominica, West Indies, tel. (809) 448-3286, is located in downtown Roseau, on the corner of Queen Mary and Cork streets. The rooms are clean but small, some share baths, and they all have fans. The place can be noisy. This guesthouse is the birthplace of writer Jean Rhys. Downstairs in a patio garden is the "World of Food, Nice Place to Eat and Drink." It is. Meals include fresh fish of the day, EC$25-50 (US$10-20). The room rates are about the same. Budget.

Cherry Lodge, Box 138, Roseau, Commonwealth of Dominica, West Indies, tel. (809) 448-2366, is an old colonial home, also downtown; clean, homey, with eight rooms, some with bath and some without. Budget.

Papillote Wilderness Retreat, P.O. Box 67, Roseau, Commonwealth of Dominica, West Indies, tel. (809) 448-2287, fax 448-2285, is a rustic, 10-room inn located inland from Roseau, just a short hike from Trafalgar Falls. If you're going to Dominica for a nature experience, the location, lush garden, open-air restaurant, and no-frills amenities of this inn will remind you why you're there. Budget-Moderate.

In Portsmouth, the **Picard Beach Resort,** Prince Rupert Bay, Picard, Commonwealth of Dominica, West Indies, tel. (809) 445-5131, fax 445-5599, features eight 18th-century-style cottages on the grounds of an old coconut plantation. Picard Beach, one of the island's best, fronts the hotel. The cottages come with kitchenettes, and you'll find a restaurant and dive center on the grounds. Luxury.

Villas

Dominica's villa rental business is not centralized, nor will you find the large number of country villas available that you'd find on some of

---

MORE DOMINICA GUESTHOUSES AND APARTMENTS

Rates per s or unit, EP when applicable, winter

NAME	(809)	FAX	LOCATION	TARIFF
Bon Marché Guest House	448-2083	N/A	Roseau	budget
Casaropa Hotel	445-5492	445-5277	Portsmouth	budget
Douglas Guesthouse	445-5253	N/A	Portsmouth	budget
Floral Gardens	445-7636	N/A	Concord	budget
Hummingbird Inn	449-1042	448-5778	Canefield	budget
Layou Valley Inn	449-6203	448-5212	Layou Valley	moderate
Mamie's	445-4295	445-4295	Prince Rupert's Bay	budget-moderate
Pringle's Apartments	448-2630		Belfast	moderate
Roxy's Mountain Lodge	448-4845	N/A	Laudat	budget
Sainte-Thérèse Guesthouse	448-4223	448-1111	Roseau	budget
Sans Souci Manor	448-2306	448-6202	St. Aroment	luxury
Springfield Plantation	449-1401	449-2160	Springfield	budget
Thomas' Guest House	4445-7264	N/A	Marigot	budget
Wykie's La Tropicale	448-8015	448-7665	Roseau	budget

MORE DOMINICA RESTAURANTS

NAME	LOCATION	(809)	CUISINE	PRICE RANGE
Castaways Beach Hotel	Mero	449-6244	Continental/Creole	moderate
Creole Kitchen	Roseau	448-6052	Creole	inexpensive
Green Parrot	Roseau	448-8944	Creole	inexpensive
Paiho	Roseau	448-8999	Hunan Chinese	inexpensive
Reigate Hall Hotel	Reigate	448-4031	Continental/ seafood	moderate
Sagittarius Reggae Restaurant	Portsmouth	N/A	Creole	inexpensive
Trends	Roseau	N/A	Creole	inexpensive

the Lesser Antilles' more tourism-conscious islands. The norm, rather, is private home and cottage rentals through individuals. The cottages tend to be simple and rustic, not the luxurious, three-maids-and-a-cook type, and their rates reflect it.

Lauro Club, P.O. Box 483, Roseau, Commonwealth of Dominica, West Indies, tel. (809) 449-6602, fax 449-6603, at the west coast's Salisbury, rents individual villas. Moderate.

Camping

Camping is not allowed in the national parks or reserves, and, in general, camping is discouraged throughout the island. This may seem like an anomalous policy given the Dominican government's desire to attract eco-conscious travelers, but, in fact, it makes sense. Dominica does not yet have the resources to provide facilities or to regulate camping activity in the parks. It makes little sense, ecologically, to simply open up the parks and let campers pitch tents anywhere they desire. However, the tourist development authorities are considering the issue, and camping may be allowed in the near future.

FOOD

Dominica's cuisine is Creole, either simple or exotic. Try the *crapaud* or "mountain chicken" (frogs' legs), nearly a national dish. *Tee tee rees,* also *titiris,* are tiny fish that live in the semi-saline environment of rivers near the sea. Fried with garlic and lime, they're a crunchy treat. Crab backs (stuffed crabshells) are an island specialty, and the stewed rodents agouti and *manicou* are also popular.

The local suds is called Piton Beer, and the island's rums are very good. For an interesting, and potentially uplifting, drink, try *bwa* (also *bois*) *bande.* The drink is brewed from the bark of the *bwa bande* (also *Richeria grandis*) tree, an illegal thing to do, and is reputedly a sexual power stimulant. *Bwa* refers to a man, and *bande* refers to the resultant, well, condition.

Hotels are a good bet for upscale dining, and many have the added attraction of being open on Sunday. Watch for Sunday barbecues and buffets. Remember, small restaurants and cafes are unlikely to accept credit cards.

The following restaurants are just a handful of the best. Per-entree price categories: **Expensive** US$25 or more, **Moderate** US$10-25, **Inexpensive** US$10 or less.

La Robe Creole, tel. (809) 448-2896, on Victoria Street across from the Fort Young Hotel, is possibly one of the finest Creole restaurants on the island. Specialties include agouti and crab backs. Moderate-Expensive. Downstairs is the **Mouse Hole Cafe,** a good place to stock up on sweets, pastries, and pies.

Cathy's Pizzeria sits across the street from the Old Market Square and serves very simple food but in hefty amounts. The service can be slow, but you get your money's worth. Rice and peas are served with everything. Inexpensive.

Callaloo Restaurant, tel. (809) 448-3386, on King George V Street on an upstairs veranda serves basic and tasty local dishes. Try their homemade fruit juices. Inexpensive.

Evergreen, tel. (809) 448-3288, is located at the Evergreen Hotel in Castle Comfort, south of town, and features nice views to the sea. Cuisine is Creole and Continental. Moderate.

La Flambeau, tel. (809) 445-5131, at the Picard Beach Resort in Portsmouth is open-air, on the beach. Moderate.

GETTING THERE

Airlines

Two airports service Dominica. **Canefield Airport** is located just five minutes from Roseau and lands smaller aircraft. **Melville Hall,** an older and larger airport, is located on the northeast coast about 32 miles (52 km), or an hour and fifteen minutes' drive, from town.

It is important to note which airport you will be using to arrive to and depart from; plan your check-in times and taxi fares accordingly.

The best way to get to Melville Hall from Roseau is to take a shared taxi, EC$42 for the seat. A private taxi would be closer to EC$130. A Melville Hall-to-Portsmouth shared taxi will run EC$30. For Melville Hall transport, call **Mally's Taxi,** tel. (809) 448-3114 or 448-3360.

No direct flights from North America or Europe service Dominica. The two airports are too small to land large aircraft. Connections can be made through main transfer points at San Juan, Sint Maarten, Antigua, Saint-Barthélémy, Guadeloupe, Martinique, St. Lucia, and Barbados, as well as many of the smaller Caribbean islands.

Main carriers that fly to Dominica from these islands are, with local numbers, **Air Guadeloupe** and **Air Martinique,** tel. (809) 448-2181; **Air Caraïbes,** tel. (809) 449-1416, Canefield Airport tel. 449-1629; and **Winair,** Trois Pitons Travel, tel. (809) 448-6977.

The regional airline, **LIAT,** tel. (809) 448-2421, Canefield Airport tel. 449-1421, Melville Hall tel. 445-7242, operates numerous scheduled flights to and from neighboring Lesser Antillean islands, with onward connections. LIAT also offers packaged day-trips from Dominica to several islands, including Sint Maarten, Antigua, and Guadeloupe, roundtrip fare US$100 (EC$270).

A Dominica-based airline, **Nature Island Express,** tel. (809) 449-2309, operates service to and from Sint Maarten, Barbados, and St. Lucia. **Caribbean Air Services,** tel. (809) 449-1748, fax 448-3124, operates mainly as a charter airline.

Ferry Service

Ferry service is available on the *Madikera,* a 352-passenger vessel connecting to Guadeloupe and Martinique daily except Tuesday and Thursday. **Trois Pitons Travel,** tel. (809) 448-6977, is the agent.

The Caribbean Express, Martinique tel. (596) 60-12-38, operates between Martinique and Guadeloupe twice per week, with stops at Dominica. Contact the local agent **Whitchurch Travel,** tel. (809) 448-2181, fax 448-5787, for information and schedules.

Caribia Ferries makes regular connections with Guadeloupe, Dominica, Martinique, and St. Lucia. The simple one-way fare from Pointe-à-Pitre to Roseau (four hours) is F150-190. There is no office in Roseau, but you can contact the local agent at Whitchurch Travel (see address above).

Departure Tax

When leaving Dominica, departure tax and airport security fees total EC$25.

GETTING AROUND

Taxis

Taxis rates are set by the government, and they, as well as rates for minibuses, are published in several places, including the tourist publication *Discover Dominica.*

Taxis are fine for around town and trips to Canefield Airport from Roseau (EC$20, or US$8 per car of four), but prohibitively priced for traveling around the island. Touring rates start at EC$45 per hour per car.

Shared taxis are also available, and most useful when traveling long distances such as to the Melville Hall airport from Roseau. Your hotel will call a taxi for you, but the most reliable Melville Hall transport is **Mally's Taxi,** tel. (809) 448-3114 or 448-3360.

INFORMATION DIRECTORY

TOURISM

Division of Tourism, National Development Corporation, P.O. Box 73, Roseau, Commonwealth of Dominica, West Indies, tel. (809) 448-2351 or 448-2186, fax 448-5840.

Dominica Hotel Association, 27 Great Marlborough St., Roseau, Commonwealth of Dominica, West Indies, tel. (809) 448-6565, fax 448-2285.

Caribbean Tourism Organization, 20 East 46th St., New York, NY 10017-2452, tel. (212) 682-0435, fax 697-4258.

Caribbean Tourism Organization, Suite 3, 15 Vigilant House, 120 Wilton Rd., Victoria, London SW1V 1JZ, tel. (071) 233-8382, fax (071) 873-8551.

OTHER

(Roseau, unless otherwise indicated)

Police, fire, ambulance emergency, tel. 999.

Princess Margaret Hospital, tel. (809) 448-2231.

American Express Agent, Whitchurch Travel, tel. (809) 448-2181, fax 448-5787.

City Drugstore, tel. (809) 448-3198.

Forestry Division, tel. (809) 448-2401, fax 448-7999.

Buses

The country's bus system works for those who've figured out the schedules. However, don't expect to travel from Roseau to far points on the island and return on the same day. The system is structured in such a way that buses—minibuses, for the most part—depart from towns and villages outside of Roseau to arrive in the capital early in the morning. The return trips, from Roseau, depart during the afternoon, and that's that until the next morning.

Having said that, buses are not difficult to use if you've got the time, and they will certainly put you in touch with the local traveling customs. In Roseau, bus stations are found at the New Market (for points northeast and north) and in town on King George V Street. Sample fares: Roseau to Portsmouth EC$7.50, Roseau to Trafalgar EC$2.25, Canefield to Roseau EC$1.50.

Vehicle Rentals

Roads throughout the country vary in quality and are not altogether well marked. Some are full of potholes, and the mountain roads wind around hairpin turns. Driving is on the left. Still, there is no danger anywhere, and renting may be the most efficient way to see the island.

Certain rental companies require the renter to be 25 years or older, and, interestingly, younger than 65 years.

Rates start at about US$35 (EC$95) per day, and most credit cards are accepted. You'll need a valid driver's license and you will have to purchase a temporary Dominica permit from the police/traffic department. Cost is EC$20, and you can ask the rental company to take you through that process.

Roseau rental companies include **Antours,** tel. (809) 448-6460, fax 448-6780; **Avis,** tel. (809) 448-2481, fax 448-0413; **Bonus Rentals,** tel. (809) 448-2650; **Budget,** tel. (809) 449-2080; **Pierro Auto Rental,** tel. (809) 448-2292, fax 448-5826; **STL Rent-a-Car,** tel. (809) 448-2340, fax 448-6007; **Valley Rent-a-Car,** tel. (809) 448-3233, fax 448-6009; and **Wide Range,** tel. (809) 448-2198, fax 448-3600. In Portsmouth, contact **CIC Car Rental,** tel. (809) 445-5847.

Small motorcycles and scooters can be rented through **Francis' Scooter Rentals,** tel. 448-5295.

MONEY, HOURS, AND COMMUNICATION

Dominica's currency is the Eastern Caribbean dollar, currently trading at EC$2.70 to US$1. Many taxi drivers and other vendors will accept other currencies, particularly U.S. and Canadian dollars, but not all will do so. If they do, exchange rates drop to EC$2.50 to US$1. It's best, particularly if you're spending more than a day on the island, to exchange your currency for EC dollars.

Banks are located in the island's three major towns, most in Roseau. The **Bank of Nova**

Scotia and the **National Commerce Bank** are both located on Hillsborough Street, **Barclays** is located on Old Street, and **Royal Bank of Canada** is on Bay Front. Banking hours are Mon.-Thurs. 8 a.m.-2 p.m. and Friday 8 a.m.-5 p.m.

In general, business hours are Mon.-Fri. 8 a.m.-1 p.m. and 2-4 p.m., and Saturday 8 a.m.-1 p.m.

You can count on credit cards being accepted in larger hotels and restaurants, but not at all guesthouses, craft stands, market stalls, and small businesses.

Dominica's telephone system uses the area code "809." To call the country from North America, dial "1" plus the area code, plus a seven-digit number. **Cable and Wireless** on Hanover Street in Roseau is open Mon.-Sat. 7 a.m.-8 p.m. for telephoning and faxing. Local calling cards are available at Cable and Wireless, the post office, or at numerous small shops in town.

ST. LUCIA

THE LAND

In outline, St. Lucia (LOO-shah) looks like a caricatured profile of, no irony intended, Charles de Gaulle. Take a look, he's facing to the west with his head tilted slightly back. Nose at Soufrière. Mouth at Gros Piton. Whatever. Perhaps it's the numerous other Gallic tendencies of this fascinating island that bring him to mind.

Lush St. Lucia, created eons ago by underwater volcanic activity, exhibits many of the same characteristics of neighboring islands St. Vincent, Martinique, and Dominica. Dramatic and sharp—therefore relatively young—mountains and peaks rise as a chain through the center of the island. The peaks and valleys are covered by degrees of rich, green woodlands. The high mountain altitudes create rain and nourishing mist, generating prolific woodland rainforests and mountain primordial rainforests.

The volcanic peaks rise toward the southwestern section of the island, culminating with the 3,118-foot (951-meter) **Mt. Gimie** and the looming landmarks **Petit Piton** and **Gros Piton,** on quiet bay. Nearby is a semi-active volcano at **Soufrière.**

The windward, Atlantic side of the island is characterized by shorter volcanic peaks and an irregular, pounding coastline. Small bays and some inlets provide shelter for small villages, fishermen, and beachgoers, but the population is, relative to the leeward side, less dense.

Mangrove wetlands and low-lying woodlands are found inland from the sea. Flat, fertile plains spread out near the base of the central mountains. This is where a great many of St. Lucia's large banana plantations are located, particularly to the north, east, and south of the highlands.

The variety of the land—from drier, scrub woodlands in the western rain shadow to the lush elevated rainforests and low-lying windward mangrove swamps—supports a disparate array of localized plants and animals, some of which are endemic.

Fauna

A variety of lizards, including the endemic St. Lucia tree lizard and the pygmy gecko, are found here. The poisonous fer-de-lance snake is found only in isolated sections of the countryside. The large and colorful St. Lucian parrot was revered by the Caribs.

The rodents agouti and *manicou* are still seen in the forests, though less frequently these days, having fallen prey to hunters. A large variety of migratory and indigenous birds, including the St. Lucian oriole and black finch, make their homes in the mangrove swamps and rainforests and outlying islets of the country.

The **Fregate Islands Nature Reserve,** off the central eastern coast, is a National Trust reserve where you can see nesting frigate birds and many others.

The triangular island measures roughly 27 miles (43 km) long and 14 miles (22 km) at its widest point and is 238 square miles (616 square km) in area, which makes it slightly smaller than Dominica. St. Lucia lies in the Windward Islands chain, separated from Martinique by the 25-mile (40-km) St. Lucia Channel in the north and from St. Vincent by the 20-mile (32-km) St. Vincent Channel in the south.

THE AGOUTI

Pity the poor agouti. The erstwhile prolific rodent, found in the forests of Mexico, South America, and the Caribbean, was hunted down during the early history of the Lesser Antilles like the near-rat it was—for it was a plump near-rat—by Amerindian Arawaks and Caribs. Later, it was hunted by frustrated colonial farmers, who sought to curb its destructiveness. Its numbers in the Lesser Antilles are today a fraction of what they were 200 years ago.

Hunted less frequently today, the rodent can still be seen but has yet to make a big comeback. With short, coarse hair, piggy pink eyes, short ears, and a practically nonexistent naked tail, the agouti resembles a guinea pig with a thyroid problem. Its relatively long legs, however, give it the swiftness of a rabbit. It—technically "they," since there are about a dozen species—feeds on green leaves, roots, fallen fruit, and the unfortunate farmer's vegetable patch.

Protected Reserves

The **Forestry Division,** tel. (809) 450-2231, and **National Trust,** tel. (809) 452-5005, organize lectures, guided tours, and—not to be missed for those interested in experiencing the island's vast natural resources firsthand—cross-island hikes.

Protected reserves cover much of the central and southern sections of the island. Large sections of the land within are still virgin rainforest, and the National Trust and forestry authorities are still in the process of developing selected portions for tourism activity. Preserves include the **Edmond Forest Reserve, Quilesse Forest Reserve, Marine National Park, Pigeon Island National Historic Park, Savannes Bay Nature Reserve,** and **Maria Islands Nature Reserve.**

HISTORY

Early Peoples

St. Lucia's early history follows a pattern similar to that of virtually all the southern islands of the Lesser Antilles. An ancient, nomadic Stone Age people, the Ciboney (also Siboney), are assumed to have existed throughout the islands, but left little in the way of artifacts save for rudimentary stone and shell implements.

The Amerindian Arawaks and related tribes migrated north in several waves from regions of South America, perhaps from 500 B.C. until the time of Christ, settling on islands along their way. Remnants of their villages have been found at Pigeon Island, in the north of St. Lucia.

Nearly 800 years later, the Arawaks were replaced by another Amerindian group, the Caribs, who were reputed to be extremely fierce and warlike and also reputed to have eaten their vanquished enemies. The Caribs either eliminated, assimilated, or drove out the Arawaks, or perhaps a combination of all three, but the recorded fact is that at the time of Columbus's late-15th-century journeys to the New World, Caribs inhabited St. Lucia, the land they called Iouanalao. The name was reputed to mean "Land of Iguanas." The word was later modified to Hiwanarau and later still to Hewanorra, which is used on the island today.

El Falcón

It was once believed that Columbus sighted St. Lucia during his fourth and last voyage, in 1502. However, most historians now believe that Columbus never landed and probably never even sighted the island. No references to it exist in his logs, and the name itself refers to St. Lucie, an Italian saint whose feast day is 13 December—a day when Columbus was nowhere near the island. A theory suggests that a Spaniard named Juan de la Cosa, who had sailed with Columbus on his first two voyages, later took up exploring himself and sighted the island, naming it El Falcón. The island pops up in Vatican maps around 1520, called St. Lucia, which gives some credence to the theory that it was at least named by a Spaniard.

Changing Hands

Over the next hundred years, several attempts were made by French and Dutch explorers to settle the island, but all were repulsed by the Caribs. In 1600 the Dutch managed to set up a small defense position, Vieux Fort, in the south of the island, but it met with calamity at the hands of the indigenes.

In 1605, a ship carrying 67 British settlers on their way to Guiana was blown off course and landed on St. Lucia. After purchasing huts from the suspicious Caribs, they apparently pushed the wrong buttons and were attacked. Several weeks later the surviving 19 settlers escaped in Carib canoes. Clashes like this continued for another 50 years, and during that time the French, because of their superior strength on neighboring islands, claimed St. Lucia.

In a 1651 transaction, the French monarch sold St. Lucia to a governor of neighboring Martinique, M. du Parquet, who, with a partner then attempted to settle the island. Nine years later, the British returned to establish sovereignty. Hostilities broke out between the two that saw St. Lucia change hands 14 times—score seven for France and seven for the British—over the next 150 years. So titanic and prolonged was this struggle that St. Lucia is often referred to as "Helen of the West Indies," in reference to the Helen of Trojan War fame.

The Caribs Meet Their End

During the lengthy British-French conflict, each group in turn used the lingering Caribs as bait, or as mercenaries. The hapless Caribs, continually playing the battered middlemen, were also set upon by missionaries, who spent a great deal of time and effort attempting to convert them from their heathen ritualistic behavior to the apparently non-heathen ritualistic behavior of Christianity. Nonconformers and nonbelievers among the Caribs were often killed. Or they killed themselves (see "Leaper's Hill" under Grenada's "History," later in this chapter).

The systematic annihilation of the Caribs continued until finally they could offer no resistance, whereupon the British, during one of their moments in power, gathered up the remaining people and shipped them off to Dominica, where they joined the Carib reservation (now called Carib Territory).

From the 18th Century to Present

Soufrière became the first town—and capital—on the island, established by the French in 1746. The French introduced sugarcane and, thereafter, the first African slaves. Continued hostilities between the British and French, however, prevented the sugarcane industry from becoming the major enterprise it was on several nearby islands.

The 1814 Treaty of Paris finally ceded St. Lucia to the British, who held onto it from then on. Again, the pattern of economics in St. Lucia mirrors the pattern throughout the Lesser Antilles. A period of prosperity, for the plantation owners at any rate, followed until the 1834 abolition of slavery. In 1838, after a period of indentured servitude by former slaves, St. Lucia became part of the British Windward Islands, with the seat of government in Barbados. St. Lucia's economy was adrift and her plantations in a state of disarray.

In the 1860s, cargo steamships used coal for fuel, and St. Lucia, with its excellent natural port, became a major coal warehousing center. Laborers were imported from East India to shore up the dwindled labor force. Then, the widespread use of oil and diesel for fuel in the 1930s and '40s rendered that industry mute and, with sugarcane on the decline, St. Lucia entered the '50s as an economic backwash. This hastened the formation of trade and labor unions, and therefore political parties, as the country agitated for more say in its government.

Universal adult suffrage was granted in 1951. In 1958 St. Lucia joined the West Indies Federation until the withdrawal of Jamaica and Trinidad and Tobago dissolved the entity four years later. A new constitution was granted in 1960, and in 1967 the island was granted full self-government. Political parties such as the St. Lucia Labor Party (SLP) and the United Workers Party (UWP) vied for power during that period.

Independence came on 22 February 1979, and St. Lucia became a state within the British Commonwealth, giving itself the official name of the State of St. Lucia. The party in power at that time was the SLP, but the UWP won the 1982 election and has held onto power since then, under the stewardship of Prime Minister John Compton. A third political party, the Progressive Labor Party (PLP), does not currently hold any seats in the House.

PEOPLE AND CULTURE

St. Lucia's estimated population is 151,000, of which 57,000 live in the capital, Castries. The majority of the population is of African descent, but noticeable numbers of descendants of East Indians, Chinese, and Europeans complete the mosaic of modern St. Lucia.

The legacy of Britain and France's 200-year tug-of-war with St. Lucia has endowed the place with a mild schizophrenia of identity; this is an island where names such as "Mount" Gimie and "Morne" Gimie can refer to the same mountain. Officially, though, the language is English. St. Lucia's government is based on a British system, and the Queen is highly regarded. St. Lucia's culture, however, is French Creole right through.

While schools, newspapers, government, and some maps conduct their business in very proper, very BBC-type English, at home and on the streets and in the rum shops, St. Lucians speak Patois, a Creole laced with French, African, and some English and Spanish grammar and vocabulary. Some St. Lucians speak only Patois. "St. Lucia," for instance, becomes "Sent Lisi." Even some public forums, such as selected court cases, are conducted in Patois.

St. Lucia is nearly 90% Roman Catholic. Saints' days are celebrated, and Carnival (*Jounen Kweyol* in Patois), the pre-Lenten round of debauchery, song, and dance, is French in origin. Even local popular music, which, much like many of the islands, is heavily dosed with calypso and reggae, features the *zouk* and beguine that are so popular in the French departments.

Traditional music, much of it springing from the harsh days of slavery, includes work songs, game songs, festival music, and dance songs. Those interested in traditional St. Lucian music might want to locate the recording "Musical Traditions of St. Lucia," compiled by the academic Folk Research Centre of St. Lucia and recorded at the Smithsonian Institute in Washington, DC.

Note: Interestingly, the Folk Research Centre has begun to disapprove of the increasing tendency of St. Lucians to celebrate Halloween in the U.S. style, which they term as distasteful and macabre. Perhaps this is some form of minor cultural xenophobia, or perhaps it demonstrates the difficulties these islands have in identifying and maintaining homogeneous, though clearly historically commingled, cultures and customs.

Nobel Prize Winners

Poet and playwright Derek Walcott put St. Lucia on the map for quite a few people when he won the 1992 Nobel Prize in Literature. Walcott was born in St. Lucia in 1930 and is recognized for his compelling, intricate, and lyrical use of the English language. He has produced to date nine volumes, including his 1990 epic *Omeros,* a broad narrative that mixes Homeric legend with West Indian themes. The collections *Selected Poems 1964* and *Selected Poems 1977* are good introductions to his greater body of work. In 1959 Walcott, who lives and teaches in Boston, established the Trinidad Theatre Workshop in Port of Spain. In St. Lucia, he's created an international writers' retreat called the Rat Island Foundation, off the coast of Castries.

Walcott is not the first St. Lucian to win a Nobel Prize. The economist Sir Arthur Lewis (1915-91), born in St. Lucia, shared the 1979 Nobel Prize in Economics with American Theodore Shultz. Lewis was a vice-chancellor of the regional University of the West Indies, developer of the Caribbean Development Bank, and a founder of the United Nations Development Project.

Holidays and Festivals

St. Lucia's **Carnival** starts up in March and is most energetic from the weekend preceding Shrove Tuesday and Ash Wednesday. It's a round of dancing, street masquerading, calypsoing (including the Calypso King contests), feasting, and general partying. It takes place in Castries.

Catholicism has brought Christmas and Easter, as well as saints' celebrations, including **La Rose** (Feast of the Rose of Lima, 30 August), **Feast of St. Peter** (also called Fishermen Day, 29 June), **La Marguerite** (Feast of St. Margaret Mary Alacoque, 17 October), and the 22 November **St. Cecilia's Day,** the Feast of Musicians.

The important 13 December **National Day** is also the Feast of St. Lucy, and island-wide cultural festivals and sports activities mark the day.

Secular holidays and festivals include the 22 February **Independence Day** celebrations, and June's **Whit Monday.**

The annual **St. Lucia International Jazz Festival** commenced in 1992 and has already attracted some of the jazz world's biggest names. The 1993 participants were, among others, Herbie Hancock, Nancy Wilson, Earl Klugh, Ramsey Lewis, and pan artist Boogsie Sharp. The 1994 participants included Julian Joseph, Stanley Clarke, Wayne Shorter, and George Benson. Look for the event in mid-May. The four-day festival is held at the **Cultural Centre** on the outskirts of Castries, and at Pigeon Island and various venues around the country. Cost for each event is US$30-35 (about EC$80-90).

GOVERNMENT AND ECONOMY

Economy

St. Lucia's economy is both historically and currently agriculture based. The first plantations were sugarcane, but due to ongoing French-British conflicts, these never reached the output of neighboring islands such as Barbados.

During the late 19th century and early 20th century, a time when the world's shipping lines were converting from sails to steam, coal was an important commodity. The ships needed good harbors within established shipping lanes to take on coal, and the Port of Castries was one of them. By 1911, three major coal companies had their fuel operations in St. Lucia. When the world converted to petroleum products in the 1930s, a once rich source of income for St. Lucians was lost.

About that time, bananas began to attract worldwide attention and St. Lucia, along with its island neighbors, stepped up production. Bananas have been the main crop since, along with some coffee, cocoa, citrus fruits, and coconuts. An estimated 80% of the island's economic activity centers around the banana industry, which accounted for US$66 million in 1992.

St. Lucia's main trading party is Great Britain. Preferential treatment and prices for bananas have been given to Commonwealth countries of the Caribbean, but with the formation of the European Community, that is due to change within the decade. The banana crop will be forced to compete on a wider open market. In 1993, a

conflict over prices between the St. Lucia Banana Growers Association (SLBGA) and farmers resulted in riots in which two farmers died. Prime Minister John Compton has since disbanded the SLBGA, but the problem appears too looming for future resolve.

Tourism

Tourism may be an answer, of sorts, to the country's economic future. Statistics show that tourist arrivals have grown threefold in the period 1982-92, and this is a trend St. Lucia hopes will continue. In 1992, 353,671 visitors spent at least one night in the country, the majority residents from other Caribbean islands, followed by residents of the U.K., U.S., and Canada. Cruise ship arrivals stand at about 320 per year, up from 88 in 1982. The number of hotel rooms available is 2,660, up from half that in 1983. The total visitor expenditure in 1992 was US$210 million, over six times that of 1982. Growth, then, has been steady, although there has been some opposition from groups such as the National Trust, who have agitated for environmental impact studies.

Government

St. Lucia is an independent member of the Commonwealth, and the British monarch, Queen Elizabeth II, is the island's titular head of state. The Queen is represented on the island by the governor general. The bicameral legislature comprises a 17-member House of Assembly, elected from the nation's electoral districts, and an 11-member Senate. The leader of the party holding most seats in the House is the prime minister, who heads the government and appoints ministers of the government. The Senate is appointed and confirmed by the governor general—six members on the advice of the prime minister, three members on the advice of the opposition party, and two members chosen by the governor general.

SIGHTS

Beaches

The farther south you drive along the coastal roads, the darker the beach sand gets, although there are exceptions. This is due to past volcanic activity of the south.

(top) Carnival, St. Thomas (Carol Lee)
(bottom) Crop Over Festival, Barbados (Manning, Selvage & Lee)

(top) stone church, Anguilla (Amanda Clement, Anguilla Tourist Board)
(bottom) street vendor's locally crafted dolls, St. Lucia (Karl Luntta)

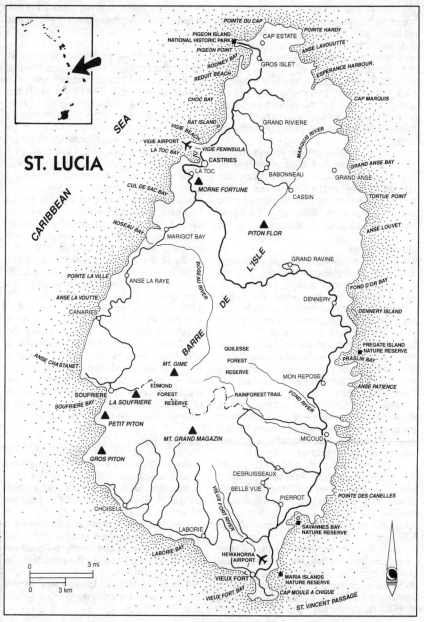

ST. LUCIA

The island's most popular beaches and bays are along the leeward coast, which is where, not incidentally, the majority of the island's resorts and hotels are located as well. The windward side of the island tends to be rough and offers few beach opportunities.

All St. Lucia's beaches are public and, in theory, accessible. This theory breaks down when they are fronted by all-inclusive hotels, but then, you may not want to be there among all that whistle-blowing and organized limboing anyway.

Among the best are the long **Pigeon Point** in the north, crowded **Reduit Beach** at Rodney Bay, **Vigie Beach** near the airstrip, **Choc Bay** just north of Vigie, and **La Toc Bay** west of Castries. Remember, though, the western side of the island is full of small, hidden bays, fishing villages, and great places to explore.

Morne Fortune

The drive south from Castries passes through rolling hills and dramatic scenery, with the ocean almost always in sight. On the south side of the town, the high-elevation Morne Fortune provides striking views of the harbor and the **Vigie Peninsula,** and the north coast beyond. You can see the island of Martinique from here, and to the south, the **Pitons.** Stop at the viewing platform with craft and snack vendors near the top. This hill's strategic position was the site of several battles between the French and British.

Farther up the road you'll find the Victorian **Government House,** the official residence of the governor general. Beyond are remnants of an old fortification, **Fort Charlotte,** which now houses Ministry of Education offices and the Sir Arthur Lewis Community College (named after the St. Lucian Nobel Prize winner). A great battle was fought here in 1776, and a monument stands to the victorious Royal Inniskilling Fusiliers, who deserve a monument just for carrying that name around. The views from here are worth the drive up.

South of Morne Fortune is **Marigot,** a small resort and fishing village and a favorite docking spot for yachts. **Anse La Raye** is a quiet little fishing village with a large, dominating church, the **Church of the Nativity of Our Blessed Virgin.** The central town green fronts a small beach, at the right time of day chock full of fishing boats and drying nets—a very colorful scene.

Soufrière

Soufrière is the oldest established town on the island, dating back to 1746, and was at one time the French capital. The architectural styles recall French colonial days. The town's bay is picturesque, and the looming half-mile high Pitons, thrusting straight out of the sea, dominate the setting. The town was used for scenes in the 1984 movie *Water,* with Michael Caine. I didn't see it either. This area, in part due to past volcanic activity, has rich soil and is known for its many small farms and plantations. There is a tourist information center on the jetty.

Nearby is the semi-active volcano and **La Soufrière,** billed as the world's only drive-in volcano. After parking, you can view the crater, which stretches across seven acres filled with bubbling, steaming, stinking pools of hot, sulfur-dense water. You can walk through with a guide from the tourist board. Admission is EC$5.

The nearby **Soufrière Estate** was part of a grant given to the Devaux family by Louis IV in 1713. The family, who was responsible for much of the development in the area, still owns the estate and allows tours. There is a mini-zoo. The **Diamond Botanical Gardens, Waterfalls, and Mineral Bath,** tel. (809) 452-4759, adjoining the estate, are worth a stop. The mineral baths, believed by many to have curative powers, were created by Louis XVI for his soldiers, but destroyed during the French Revolution. The baths were restored in the 1960s. Fee is EC$5.

South St. Lucia

Farther south, you'll find an excellent Carib craft center at **Choiseul. Vieux Fort,** the island's second-largest town and location of **Hewanorra International Airport,** is the southernmost point on the island. On a clear day, you can see St. Vincent in the south.

The two **Maria Islands** (25-acre **Major** and the four-acre **Minor**) form a nature reserve and are home to several rare species of lizards and snakes, including the *couresse,* reputedly the world's rarest snake.

The **Maria Islands Interpretive Centre** charges a small fee and is worth it. Open Wed.-Sun. 9 a.m.-5 p.m.

The nearby **Savannes Bay** is noted for its mangrove swamp and nature reserve.

East Coast

The east coast of the island is home to several small fishing villages. The **Fregate Island Nature Reserve** is closed during the breeding season of the frigate birds, May-July. Call the National Trust (see below) for information. From **Dennery,** the main road cuts northwest across the island to Castries, past the giant national **Forest Reserve.**

North

North of Castries, the coastal sand becomes lighter in color, and the resorts start to pop out like cats on mice. This is beach country, and the coast is dense with tourism activity.

The northwestern town of **Gros Islet** is set on the large harbor of **Rodney Bay,** from which, in 1782, Admiral Lord George Rodney launched his famous attack on the French forces of Admiral de Grasse at the Battle of the Saints. The battle virtually assured the British of a continued presence in the Caribbean from then on. Gros Islet is known for its large 1,000-boat capacity marina and for its popular Friday night street party, a "jump up" complete with music, dancing, fast food, and late-night goings on.

North of Gros Islet you'll find **Pigeon Point** and the **Pigeon Island National Historic Park.** A man-made causeway now connects the island to the mainland, and the beach there is long and clean. The island, administered by the National Trust, was opened as a park in 1979 after having been the site of a fort, a WW II U.S. military base, and a privately leased island. Artifacts from the Arawak involvement in St. Lucia have been found, and Pigeon Island was believed to once have been the stronghold of the

Empress Joséphine,
wife of Napoleon Bonaparte

BOB RACE

pirate François Leclerc, also known as Jambe de Bois (Wooden Leg). The 40-acre park has remains of forts, officers' mess, houses, a restaurant, and Fort Rodney, the British armament. The National Trust has opened a small museum, and entrance is EC$3. A guided 90-minute tour is available for EC$10. The park is open daily 9 a.m.-5 p.m.

The north road ends at **Pointe du Cap,** but further exploring is possible with a 4WD vehicle. The island you see from Pointe du Cap is Martinique.

A footnote: St. Lucians believe that, in a small area called Paix Bouche in the northeast, the girl who would grow up to be the Empress Joséphine, wife of Napoleon Bonaparte, was born. Martiniqueans would dispute that. The dates are unclear and proof is more a matter of national pride than fact—it has something to do with nonexistent birth certificates and the memories of priests of the late 18th century—but St. Lucians will say that Joséphine was conceived in Martinique, born in St. Lucia and lived there for seven years, and then returned to Martinique with her family.

CASTRIES

The capital city of St. Lucia burned to the ground in spectacular fires in 1796 and in 1948. Reconstruction of the town after the 1948 fire has given it a modern look, unlike many older West Indian towns. Concrete is the dominant medium, and that defines a great portion of the city. The area of Brazil Street, on the south side of downtown, contains a mix of older buildings that managed to escape the fires.

The town, population 57,000, was relocated from the nearby north peninsula of Vigie in 1768 and named Castries after a French colonial of-

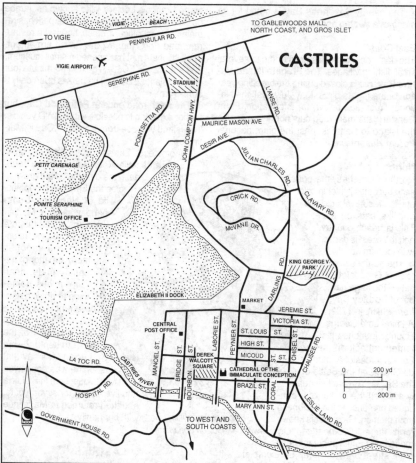

CASTRIES

ficial. The centerpiece of town is **Derek Walcott Square,** formerly Columbus Square, bordered by Brazil, Micoud, Bourbon, and Laborie streets. Here you'll find some of the town's older buildings and a monument to St. Lucia's world war dead. The huge 400-year-old *saman* tree, also known as a rain tree (its leaves are so thick and plentiful that after a rain, the tree continues to "rain" for a time) stands in the park.

At the eastern end of the square is the large **Cathedral of the Immaculate Conception.** Construction on the cathedral began in the mid-1800s but was not finished until the late 19th century. The church is large but plain on the outside. Step inside the vast, almost monolithic interior for a study in red, mahogany, diffused yellow light from ceiling portals, and detailed inlay and woodwork. The church became a cathedral in 1957 and was visited by Pope John Paul II in 1986. Note the ceiling paintings of saints, with Saint Lucie in the center.

A few blocks north from the square, across Jeremie Street, you'll find the iron-framed **public market,** constructed in 1894. The nearby

New Castries Market on Jeremie has a large selection of fruits and vegetables. The markets are busiest on Saturday morning.

North of the port and south of the airstrip is the modern Pointe Seraphine shopping and duty-free center. Built to service cruise ships from the nearby dock, Pointe Seraphine features the types of shops you'd expect passengers to be directed to. Very chichi.

A welcome store is the Sunshine Bookshop, tel. (809) 452-3222, which has a wide range of British and U.S. newspapers, including the *Miami Herald* and the *New York Times*—possibly a day late. Upstairs in the National Development Council complex is the tourist board office, and you'll find a small tourism kiosk on the ground floor as well.

SPORTS AND ENTERTAINMENT

Water Sports
For deep-sea fishing, yacht charters, and diving operations, the best place to start is the Rodney Bay Marina near Gros Islet. Most hotel operations offer water-skiing, snorkeling, windsurfing, and other light water sports activities. For specialized equipment, the following are helpful.

For yacht charters contact Tradewinds Yacht Charters, tel. (809) 452-8424; Castries Yacht Centre, tel. (809) 452-6234; Moorings Yacht Charters, tel. (809) 451-4357; Sunsail Stevens, tel. (809) 452-8648; or Via Carib Yacht Charters, Canada tel. (514) 982-6649.

Deep-sea fishing enthusiasts should call Mako Watersports, tel. (809) 452-0412.

For diving try Buddies Scuba, at Vigie Marina, tel. (809) 452-5288, or Scuba St. Lucia at the St. Lucian Hotel, tel. (809) 459-7355.

Tennis
Tennis can be found at most hotels, or the St. Lucia Racquet Club, tel. (809) 450-0551. The St. Lucia Yacht Club offers squash as well.

Horseback Riding
Call Trim's Riding Stables in Gros Islet, tel. (809) 452-8273.

Golf
Two golf courses can be found on the island, both with nine holes: the Sandals St. Lucia, tel. (809) 452-3081, in La Toc, and Cap Estate Golf Course, tel. (809) 452-8523, in Cap Estate. Greens fees start at EC$15.

Working Out
The Fitness Palace, tel. (809) 452-0882, between Castries and Gros Islet, and Jazzercise, tel. (809) 452-6853, at the Gablewoods Mall offer workout equipment and aerobics. After-

a carving in progress at Eudovic's Studio

MORE ST. LUCIA HOTELS

Rates per s, EP when applicable, winter

NAME	(809)	FAX	(800)	LOCATION	TARIFF
Anse Chastanet Beach Hotel	459-7000	459-7700	N/A	Soufrière	luxury
Daphil's Hotel	450-9318	452-4378	N/A	Gros Islet	budget
Friendship Inn	453-6602	453-2635	N/A	Choc Bay	moderate
Green Parrot	452-3399	453-2272	N/A	Morne Fortune, Castries	moderate
Harbour Light Inn	452-3506	N/A	N/A	Vigie Beach	moderate
Islander Hotel	452-0255	452-0985	223-9815	Rodney Bay	luxury
Kimatrai Hotel	454-6328	N/A	N/A	Vieux Fort	budget
Ladera Resort	459-5156	N/A	841-4145	Soufrière	luxury
Marigot Bay Resort	451-4357	451-4353	334-2435	Marigot Bay	luxury
Le Sport	450-8551	450-0368	544-2883	Cap Estate	luxury
Wyndham Morgan Bay Resort	450-2511	450-1050	822-4200	Choc Bay	luxury

ward, try out the **Isis Yoga Centre,** tel. (809) 452-3702, in Castries to work out the kinks.

Shopping
Shopping for some implies newspapers and books, and the best places for that are **The Book Salon,** tel. (809) 452-3817, on Jeremie Street, or **Sunshine Bookshop** at Pointe Seraphine.

For others it means T-shirts, crafts, art, trinkets, and duty-free items such as jewelry, cosmetics, and electronics. Best bets for those items are the Pointe Seraphine complex and **Gablewoods Mall,** which is located north of downtown Castries on the Gros Islet Highway. The shops here are open daily until evening, in some cases until 9 p.m. Some are open on Sunday as well. Castries itself is an easy place to wander around, particularly in the area of Derek Walcott Square.

Rodney Bay Marina also has numerous shops to service the large yachtie community that stops through.

For local crafts, particularly carvings, drive up to **Eudovic's Studio,** tel. 452-2747, on Morne Fortune. You can watch artisans at work and browse a small gift shop on the grounds.

ACCOMMODATIONS

Many of St. Lucia's hotels and villas are of the upscale, resort type, although a number of comfortable, clean, and inexpensive guesthouses and apartment accommodations are available, particularly in the Castries area. The greatest concentration of hotels and resorts is found on the leeward coast north of Castries to Pointe du Cap.

All rooms are subject to an eight percent tax, and many hotels will add a 10% service charge.

Rates below are based on per single per night during high season (mid-December through mid-April): **Luxury** US$100 or more, **Moderate** US$50-100, **Budget** US$50 or less.

Villas
Villas are plentiful, often the best type of accommodation for families and for those who really want to get away from the tourist stream. Villa rates often include maid and cooking services, a rental car, and other options.

For villa and apartment rentals contact **Tropical Villas,** P.O. Box 189, Castries, St. Lucia, West Indies, tel.(809) 452-8240, fax 452-8089, Canada tel. (800) 387-1201, Florida and California tel. (800) 387-2726, New York tel. (800) 387-2715, rest of U.S. tel. (800) 387-2720. Another company to try is **Preferred Properties,** Rodney Bay, St. Lucia, West Indies, tel. (809) 452-0732, fax 452-0401.

The U.S.-based **Island Hideaways,** tel. (800) 832-2302, lists several St. Lucia properties.

The local **Villa Apartments,** tel. (809) 452-2691, lists moderately priced apartments for long- and short-term stays.

Hotels and Guesthouses

For a complete list of island hotels and guesthouses, contact the **St. Lucia Hotel and Tourism Association,** P.O. Box 545, Castries, St. Lucia, West Indies, tel. (809) 452-5978, fax 452-7967, or the tourist board (see below).

Windjammer Landing, P.O. Box 1504, Castries, St. Lucia, West Indies, tel. (809) 452-0913, U.S. tel. 800-743-9609, Canada tel. 416-484-4864, U.K. tel. (044) 453-83-5801, fax 452-0907,

is a 55-acre resort built on a hill on Labrelotte Bay, about midway between Castries and Gros Islet. The accommodation consists of white-stucco, self-contained villas, some containing up to four bedrooms. The hillside location offers stunning views. On the grounds you'll find three restaurants, many pools (some private), a good beach, programs for children, and excellent service. The hills are steep and the resort is sprawling, so you're driven around in small carts. Luxury.

Jalousie Plantation, P.O. Box 251, Soufrière, St. Lucia, West Indies, tel. (809) 459-7666, North America tel. (800) 877-3643, local fax 459-7667, North America fax (305) 858-4667, is a new all-inclusive resort set between the Pitons near Soufrière. The accommodation is in luxury cottages and suites. The resort's spa-type ambience is complemented with massages, saunas, hot tubs, and pools at private cottages. Luxury.

MORE ST. LUCIA GUESTHOUSES AND APARTMENTS

Rates per s or unit, EP when applicable, winter

NAME	(809)	FAX	LOCATION	TARIFF
Alize Inn	452-1227	453-6736	Gros Islet	budget
Bay Street Guesthouse	450-8956	N/A	Gros Islet	budget
Chateau Blanc Guesthouse	452-1851	452-7967	Chaussee, Castries	budget
Genmar Apartments	452-0834	452-0165	Reduit	budget-moderate
Home Hotel	454-7318	N/A	Soufrière	budget
Islander Hotel	452-0255 (800) 223-9815	452-0985	Rodney Bay	luxury
Modern Inn	452-4001	N/A	Castries	budget
Nelson's Apartments	450-8275	N/A	Gros Islet	budget
La Panache	450-0765	N/A	Gros Islet	budget
Parrot's Hideaway Guesthouse	452-0726	N/A	Bois D'Orange	budget
Sailing Club Guesthouse	459-7194	N/A	Soufrière	budget
Seaview Apartel	452-4359	N/A	Castries	moderate
Southern Comfort Inn	454-6088	454-6284	Vieux Fort	budget
Tropical Haven	452-3505	452-5476	La Toc Bay	moderate

The Royal St. Lucian, P.O. Box 977, Castries, St. Lucia, West Indies, tel. (809) 452-0999, U.S. tel. (800) 668-1775, U.K. tel. (081) 741-5333, fax 452-6939, overlooks the popular Reduit Beach in Gros Islet. Next to its sister property, the **St. Lucian,** the hotel offers 98 luxury suites and fine restaurants. The pool, with bridges, a waterfall, and interconnecting waterways, is an attraction in itself. Luxury.

Hummingbird Beach Resort, Soufrière, St. Lucia, West Indies, tel. (809) 454-7232, North America tel. (800) 456-3984, fax 459-7033, has a colonial charm, with four-poster beds and dark mahogany in the rooms. You'll find a pool and a well-regarded Creole restaurant. The 10-room hotel offers an eclectic variety of accommodation, from simple, shared-bath rooms to luxury suites. Budget-Luxury.

Several chain-resorts are represented on the island. The all-inclusive **Sandals St. Lucia** and **Sandals Halcyon,** North America tel. (800) SANDALS, U.K. tel. (071) 581-9895, allow couples only and are located at La Toc Bay just outside of Castries. The beaches are fine and the Sandals recipe for success—meaning generic island fun—plays out no different here than it would elsewhere. Still, you'll get your money's worth if you utilize the facilities. For the best deals, look for packages offered with airlines. Luxury.

The all-inclusive **Rendezvous Resort,** tel. (809) 452-4211, North America tel. (800) 544-2883, fax 452-7419, formerly Couples, is still for couples. It's located on Malabar/Vigie Beach just by Vigie Airport. The emphasis here is on sports activity and nightlife. Here as well, look for package deals offered with airlines. Luxury.

Club Med St. Lucia, tel. (809) 455-6001, North America tel. 800-CLUBMED, is located in the south, about five minutes from Hewanorra International. The resort is semi-all-inclusive—drinks are on you. Luxury.

Camping

Camping on St. Lucia has not been developed. No facilities exist for campers, and personal security cannot be guaranteed for those who simply pitch a tent on a beach or in the forest. While no one in authority is sure if camping is actually illegal, it is definitely not encouraged.

FOOD

Hotel restaurants are generally good and open on Sunday, which helps. You can find fast-food chains such as **KFC** on Bridge Street in Castries and **Peppino's,** a local pizza chain located in Castries, Gros Islet, and the Gablewoods Mall, as well as dozens of local meat patty and burger joints.

Smaller restaurants may not accept credit cards.

The following categories, based on prices per entree excluding drinks, will help you sort out your choice: **Expensive** US$25 or more, **Moderate** US$10-25, **Inexpensive** US$10 or less.

Natural Cafe, tel. (809) 452-6241, on Chaussee Road in Castries serves vegetarian and local dishes, and creative fresh juices. They're closed Sunday and open Mon.-Fri. until 6 p.m., Saturday until 2 p.m. Inexpensive.

Rain, tel. (809) 452-3022, is located in one of the oldest standing buildings in Castries, on Derek Walcott Square. Cuisine leans toward Creole and Continental, and you can dine or snack on pizzas on the balcony overlooking the square, or in the courtyard. At least once during your trip, save room for the nightly, seven-course, four-wine "Champagne Banquet of 1885," a feast that recalls the cuisine of 1885, when the mansion-cum-restaurant was built. This is an experience not to miss. Rain serves breakfast, lunch, and dinner daily, and is closed Sunday. Moderate-Expensive.

Also in Castries, stop at **The Pink Elephant,** tel. (809) 453-2847, downtown for snacks and light Creole, or drinks. Open weekdays until 6 p.m. Inexpensive. The **Naked Virgin,** tel. (809) 452-5594, serves Creole specialties, including a famous Shrimp Creole. The "Naked Virgin" refers to a startling rum-punch drink. The restaurant is open for lunch and dinner. Inexpensive-Moderate.

In Rodney Bay try **Capone's,** tel. (809) 452-0284, for Italian, open for dinner daily except Monday. You'll find a small pizza place next door, open for lunch. **La Flambé,** tel. (809) 452-0321, overlooking the water in the lagoon, offers a French Creole touch. Open daily except Sunday, for dinner only. Both are Moderate-Expensive.

MORE ST. LUCIA RESTAURANTS

NAME	LOCATION	(809)	CUISINE	PRICE RANGE
The Bistro	Rodney Bay	452-9494	French	moderate
Bon Appétit	Morne Fortune	452-2757	Continental	moderate
El Burrito	Gablewood's Mall, Castries	451-7924	Mexican	inexpensive-moderate
Chak Chak Cafe	Vieux Fort	454-6260	Creole	inexpensive-moderate
Chung's	Choc Bay	452-4795	Chinese	inexpensive-moderate
Jimmie's	Vigie Cove, Castries	452-5142	seafood	inexpensive-moderate
Kimono's	La Toc Bay	452-3081	Oriental	moderate
The Marina Steak House	Rodney Bay	452-9800	steaks/seafood	moderate
The Mortar and Pestle	Rodney Bay	452-8756	Creole	moderate
The Still	La Perle Estate, Soufrière	459-7224	Creole	moderate

Rodney Bay's **The Lime,** tel. (809) 452-0761, is a popular hangout—the art of sitting around, talking, enjoying a few drinks, and relaxing is called "liming"—and serves up seafood and Creole specialties. Closed Tuesday, open for lunch and dinner otherwise. Moderate.

The **Charthouse,** tel. (809) 452-8115, barbecues steaks, ribs, and seafood like no one else on the island and sits overlooking the water at Rodney Bay. The restaurant is open daily except Sunday for dinner. Moderate-Expensive.

GETTING THERE

By Air

Two airports service St. Lucia. **Vigie Airport,** just north of downtown Castries, is the site for small charters and interisland flights. The small airport features a tourism booth, tel. (809) 452-2596, and a taxi stand, and that's about it. Taxi to town is EC$12 (US$5).

The larger **Hewanorra International Airport** at Vieux Fort takes international flights. You'll find a small tourism kiosk, tel. (809) 454-6644, here as well. A taxi to Castries, for instance, is EC$120 (US$48) for a car of four.

Several international airlines offer direct service to Hewanorra. **American Airlines,** local tel. (809) 454-6777, uses San Juan for connection from major North American cities. **Air Canada,** tel. (809) 452-3051/2/3, uses Barbados and Antigua for connections. **BWIA,** tel. (809) 452-3778 or 452-3789, flies direct, with a stop in Antigua, from Miami and New York, and from several European airports as well as from Trinidad. **British Airways,** tel. (809) 452-3951, connects from Europe.

Interisland

LIAT, tel. (809) 452-3051, is the best interisland connection and uses Vigie Airport as its base.

Air Martinique, tel. (809) 452-2463, connects with the French departments of Martinique and Guadeloupe. **Helenair,** tel. (809) 452-7196, operates charter flights out of Vigie.

St. Lucia Helicopters, tel. (809) 453-6950, located at Pointe Seraphine, operates a shuttle service between airports. The 10-minute flight costs US$85 (about EC$225) per person. The company also operates sightseeing tours; a 10-minute north island tour costs US$38 (EC$100) per person, and a 20-minute south island tour is US$75 (EC$200).

Ferry Service

Caribia Ferries operates a car and passenger service between Castries and Fort-de-France in Martinique, with connections on to Guadeloupe. One-way fare is about F150-190 (US$27-35).

Departure Tax

Airport departure tax is EC$27 (US$11), plus a security tax of EC$10 (US$4).

GETTING AROUND

Taxis

Taxis, which are identified by an "H" on the license plate, are not metered. A governing body sets rates and all drivers are supposed to carry rate cards in the vehicle, but don't count on it. If you're arriving at an airport, pick up a copy of the tourist board publication *Visions,* which will list selected rates.

Sample taxi fares: Vigie Airport to Hewanorra International EC$120 (US$48), Vigie to Soufrière EC$140 (US$56), Castries to Rodney Bay Marina EC$47 (US$19). Taxis charge per car of up to four people.

Your hotel can help you arrange for a taxi, but if you need a pick-up in the Castries area, call **City Taxi,** tel. (809) 452-3154; **Courtesy Taxi,** tel. (809) 452-1733 or 451-6737; **People's Choice,** tel. (809) 452-4664; **St. Lucia Taxi,** tel. (809) 452-2492; or **Vigie Taxi,** tel. (809) 452-1599.

Taxis also offer tours of the island. A tour of the northern section of the island, based on one to four people per car, would be EC$120 (US$48). A complete island tour would be about EC$300 (US$120). Per hour rates are EC$53 (US$20).

Buses

If your budget is limited or you'd like to experience travel the way St. Lucians experience it, then local bus services are the way to go. Buses, which are often minivans, are also identified by an "H" on the license plate. Very few destinations on the island will incur a fare more than EC$10. The system, however, is labyrinth-like and takes some time to master. Buses leave from points in

---

INFORMATION DIRECTORY

ST. LUCIA TOURIST BOARD

P.O. Box 221, Castries, St. Lucia, West Indies, tel. (809) 452-4094 or 452-5968, fax 453-1121.

820 2nd Ave., 9th Floor, New York, NY 10017, tel. (800) 456-3984 or (212) 867-2950, fax (212) 370-7867.

4975 Dundas St., West, Suite 457, Islington, Toronto, Ontario M9A 4X4, tel. (800) 456-3984 or (416) 236-0936, fax (416) 236-0937.

421a Finchley Rd., London NW3 6HJ, tel. (071) 431-4045, fax (071) 431-7920.

Postfach 2304, D-6380 Bad Homburg 1, Germany, tel. (06172) 30-44-31, fax (06172) 30-50-72.

53 Rue Francois I'er, 7th Floor, Paris 75008, tel. (47) 20-39-66, fax (47) 23-09-65.

OTHER

St. Lucia Hotel and Tourism Association, P.O. Box 545, Castries, St. Lucia, West Indies, tel. (809) 452-5978, fax 452-7967.

Emergencies, tel. 999.

Victoria Hospital, Hospital Rd., Castries, tel. (809) 452-2421.

Fitz St. Rose Medical Centre, Micoud St., Castries, tel. (809) 452-3333.

Williams Pharmacy, Bridge St., Castries, tel. (809) 452-2797.

American Express Office, Carib Travel Agency, 20 Micoud St., Castries, tel. (809) 452-2151.

FedEx, Bourbon St., Castries, tel. (809) 452-1320.

Castries—the market area or Jeremie Street, for example—to island points, and you'll see bus stops on the roads. You can also flag buses down.

Island Tours

If you'd like to see the island on organized tours, several organizations exist. For nature walks and other alternative tours, first contact the government **Forestry Division,** tel. (809)

450-2231. They offer a wonderful seven-mile (11-km) hike across the **Rainforest Trail** in the central 19,000-acre forest reserve, as well as other excursions.

Other tour operators include the always reliable **John Jeremie,** tel. (809) 450-5347, or at Vigie Airport tel. (452) 1599.

Barnard Travel, tel. (809) 452-2214/5/7/8, on Bridge Street will organize island tours as well as excursion to neighboring islands.

Car Rentals

St. Lucia's 500 miles (800 km) of roads, about half of them paved, provide adequate access to most of the island's sights and activities. The driving, while often on winding and dipping roads, is easy. You need to be at least 25 years old to rent a car. Remember to stay on the left.

Rentals start at about US$40 per day, but unlimited free mileage is not the norm. A temporary St. Lucian license is required, and this is best obtained through the rental company. Cost is EC$30, or US$12.

Rental companies include **Avis,** Main office Castries tel. (809) 452-2700, Hewanorra tel. 454-6325, Vigie tel. 452-2046, fax 453-1536; **Budget,** Castries tel. (809) 452-0233, fax 452-9362; **Courtesy,** Gros Islet tel. (809) 452-8140, fax 452-9566; **CTL,** tel. (809) 452-0732, fax 452-0401; **National,** Main office Castries tel. (809) 450-8721, Hewanorra tel. 454-6699, Vigie tel. 452-3050, fax 450-8577; and **SLY,** Saint Lucia Yachts, Vigie Cove tel. (809) 452-5057.

For motorcycles, try **Wayne's Motorcycle Centre,** tel. (809) 452-2059. No credit cards are accepted.

MONEY, HOURS, AND COMMUNICATION

Currency and Banks

St. Lucia's currency is the Eastern Caribbean dollar (EC$), currently exchanged at EC$2.70 = US$1. U.S. dollars are widely accepted, Canadian dollars and British pounds to a lesser extent. Your change, however, will be in EC dollars. Further, the exchange rate on the street or at small businesses will differ from that of the banks, and you'll lose. It's best to exchange money and use EC dollars during your stay.

Most major credit cards are accepted at car rental agencies, duty-free shops, larger hotels, and larger restaurants. Craft stalls and small vendors will not accept them and may not even deal with traveler's checks. You can exchange money at banks, which will always give better rates than hotels.

Banking hours vary slightly, but banks are generally open Mon.-Thurs. 8 a.m.-noon and 3-5 p.m. on Friday. Barclays and the Royal Bank of Canada are open Mon.-Thurs. until 3 p.m., and until 5 p.m. on Friday.

Several banks are found on the main streets of Castries. **Barclays** and **St. Lucia Cooperative Bank** are both located on Bridge Street. The **Bank of Nova Scotia** and **Canadian Imperial Bank of Commerce** are on William Peter Boulevard. Banks are also located at Pointe Seraphine, Rodney Bay (**Royal Bank of Canada** at the marina is open Saturday morning as well), Soufrière, and Vieux Fort.

Hours, Mail, Phones

Government business hours are Mon.-Fri. 8:30 a.m.-12:30 p.m. and 1:30-4.30 p.m.

Commercial hours are the same, with additional hours on Saturday 8 a.m.-noon. Some shops, particularly the duty-free shops at Pointe Seraphine, will remain open for cruise ship business. Most of St. Lucia, and this includes many restaurants, closes down on Sunday.

Cable and Wireless telephoning cards are sold at selected shops, banks, post offices, and the Cable and Wireless building on Bridge Street, tel. (809) 452-3301, in Castries and in Vieux Fort. The card denominations are EC$10, 20, and 40. You can phone and fax from these locations, as well as from both airports, Rodney Bay Marina, Pointe Seraphine, and other locations around Castries.

The international area code for St. Lucia is "809." Dial "1" plus "809" plus the seven-digit number. Since all telephone numbers in St. Lucia begin with "45", internal calls are made by simply dialing the last five digits of the number.

The general post office is located on Bridge Street in Castries.

ST. VINCENT
AND THE GRENADINES

The word "Grenadines" invokes for many a powerful image of tropical micro-islands scattered in a string over miles of translucent sapphire ocean. In fact, that is exactly what they are. The Grenadines of St. Vincent comprise 30-plus islands and cays ranging from relatively large pieces of land such as Bequia to the smaller uninhabited Tobago Cays. The island chain stretches like small stepping stones from the larger island of St. Vincent to Grenada, in the south. The country of St. Vincent and the Grenadines is one of the most compelling areas of the Lesser Antilles.

Because of the close proximity of the Grenadines to each other, as well as their hundreds of accessible small coves, bays, and reefs, the islands have been a favorite with yachtsmen, divers, and tourists for years. Not so with the larger island, the St. Vincent mainland. This is changing, but not so rapidly that the island and its cultures cannot be experienced in an non-hyped, natural state, without glitter or glamour.

THE LAND

The 20-mile (32-km) St. Vincent Channel separates St. Vincent from its northern neighbor St. Lucia. The Grenadines, which number 32 islands—or nearly 600, including rocks, sandbars, and islets—stretch some 45 miles (72 km) to the southwest, ending at, within the St. Vincent and the Grenadines borders, Petit St. Vincent. Barbados, a major entry point for the islands, lies some 100 miles (161 km) to the east, and Grenada sits just south of the string.

St. Vincent is approximately 18 miles (29 km) north to south and 11 miles (18 km) at its widest east-west point. The land area is 133 square miles (344 square km), which makes it about half the size of Dominica, to the north. The combined Grenadines add another 17 square miles (44 square km) to the country's total.

St. Vincent is a rugged volcanic island characterized by a high central mountain range and

a shorter range that stretches diagonally across the southeastern portion of the island. The mountains are heavily forested and experience heavy rainfall, therefore harboring numerous mountain streams and rivers.

The windward east coast is irregular and characterized by sharp cliffs, rocky and pebbled beaches, and rough surf. The quieter western, leeward coast is full of small bays and inlets and a less dramatic coastline. The northern section of the island is dominated by **La Soufrière,** a semi-dormant volcano looming 4,048 feet (1,234 meters) above sea level. St. Vincent joins its sister Windward Islands and one or two Leeward Islands in this regard—many have volcanoes and/or towns named, in some form or another, Soufrière. The word is from the French *soufre,* for "sulfur." La Soufrière last erupted in 1979, but adequate warning systems allowed for the full evacuation of the northern part of the island, and no human lives were lost. Property and crop damage, however, was extensive.

Kingstown, the capital of St. Vincent and the Grenadines, lies on the southwest coast of the island, in the large Kingstown Bay Harbour.

The Grenadines were also created by eons-ago volcanic activity but are generally low-lying and less dramatic than the mainland. Main named islands, north to south, include (but are not limited to) **Bequia, Battowia, Baliceaux, Mustique, Petit Mustique, Petit Canouan, Canouan, Mayreau, Tobago Cays, Union Island, Palm Island,** and **Petit St. Vincent.**

HISTORY

The history of St. Vincent and the Grenadines mirrors that of the Windward Islands. The first inhabitants were the Stone Age Ciboney (also spelled Siboney), whose use of stone implements gave them their name.

Next came the relatively peaceful Amerindian Arawaks, who migrated from regions of South America and inhabited the southern Caribbean is-

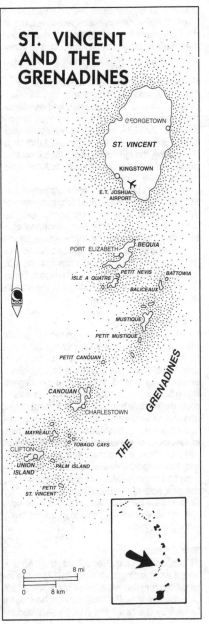

ST. VINCENT AND THE GRENADINES

GEORGETOWN

ST. VINCENT

KINGSTOWN

E.T. JOSHUA AIRPORT

PORT ELIZABETH *BEQUIA*

ISLE A QUATRE *PETIT NEVIS* *BATTOWIA*

BALICEAUX

MUSTIQUE

PETIT MUSTIQUE

PETIT CANOUAN

GRENADINES

CANOUAN

CHARLESTOWN

MAYREAU

CLIFTON *TOBAGO CAYS* *THE*

UNION ISLAND *PALM ISLAND*

PETIT ST. VINCENT

0   8 mi

0   8 km

© MOON PUBLICATIONS, INC.

lands from about 500 B.C. through the time of Christ. Some 800-1,000 years later they were followed by the Amerindian Caribs, a warlike group who conquered virtually everything and everyone in their path. The Caribs had eliminated, or assimilated, the Arawaks at the time of Columbus's third voyage to the New World, in 1498.

Youroumei

Some dispute exists regarding Columbus's relationship with St. Vincent and the Grenadines. As a matter of fact, some dispute exists regarding the Caribs' relationship with St. Vincent and the Grenadines.

Archaeologists posit the Caribs called St. Vincent Youroumei, reputedly "The Beauty of the Rainbows in the Valleys." Others claim they called it Hairoun, a word still used on the island for, among other items, the locally brewed beer.

Some historians believe that Columbus never saw the island, while others say he charted it. Whatever the case, the Spanish did not make serious attempts to settle.

Various other European explorers, who were busy settling neighboring islands, were unsuccessful in rooting out the St. Vincent Caribs from their mountain and woodland strongholds. The French made a claim in 1626, and the English claimed St. Vincent in 1672 but were not able to make any headway in routing the Caribs. The fierce tribe would hold onto the island for much longer than their unfortunate comrades in the north and south.

Black Caribs

In 1675 a passing Dutch ship sank off the coast of Bequia, and its survivors, African slaves and a few Dutchmen, made it to the mainland. The Dutch did not survive the encounter, but the Caribs seem to have been more accepting of the Africans. They let them live and ultimately commingle. Later, more Africans escaped from neighboring islands and made it to St. Vincent. They too contributed to the gene pool, adding to a growing mixed-race group called the "Black Caribs." Caribs who had been driven off nearby islands also made it to St. Vincent, swelling the numbers of their people, sometimes called "Yellow Caribs."

As the Black Carib numbers increased, the threatened Caribs felt the pressure. Friction, even battles, ensued between the two groups. The Caribs appealed to the French governor of Martinique to arbitrate their simmering and often violent rivalry. In 1700, the governor negotiated a physical division of the island, which proved to be temporary. The Black Caribs and Caribs were soon fighting once again. The original Caribs, however, allowed the French to settle and farm the island, probably as a bulwark against Black Carib incursion. The British, once again, made attempts to create their own settlements and were repulsed by both the Caribs and Black Caribs, and by the French.

Island Tug-of-War

The difficulties in colonizing St. Vincent were demonstrated by the 1748 Treaty of Aix-La-Chapelle, which in effect was a declaration of exasperation by the British and French. It pronounced the island neutral. It remained so for some time, until the British and French once again resumed hostilities, in tandem with islands-wide hostilities between the two countries and their European allies and rivals.

St. Vincent was then ceded to Britain in 1763, which caused the Black Caribs to revolt; this was known as the first of the Carib Wars. The French intervened again in 1779, but the island reverted back to English rule with the 1783 Treaty of Versailles.

The Carib Wars continued, although the island was to remain in British hands for the better part of the next century. The British had managed to get the Black Caribs to sign various agreements that in essence relegated them to small parcels of land in the northern section of the island. The Caribs were essentially pushed into a corner.

By 1795, the Black Caribs were organized and well-funded by a radical group of French rebels, who had not intended to adhere to the Treaty of Versailles from the start. The Second Carib War, also called The Brigands Wars, broke out. The Caribs gained land and fought valiantly but were dealt a crushing blow when their Chief Chatoyer, today an island hero, was killed in a battle at Dorsetshire Hill. Within a year the Caribs had been crushed, and by 1797 they surrendered. The 5,000 surviving Caribs were rounded up and shipped to the British colonies that are now Belize and Honduras,

where their descendants live still. Remaining Black Carib survivors managed to escape to the St. Vincent hills and avoid deportation, and their descendants can be found on the island today.

From Sugarcane to Arrowroot

The British were clearly in charge by 1800. Sugarcane became the cash crop, and as plantations grew more Africans were imported to work the land. By 1834, the year slavery was abolished, St. Vincent boasted several fairly large plantations, though nothing equal to the scale of plantations in neighboring Barbados and other islands to the north.

Slavery's abolition brought Portuguese and then East Indian indentured laborers, as well as British and other laborers from nearby islands. The country, however, remained economically stagnant into the 20th century. By this time arrowroot, a starchy tuber so-named for its use by the Caribs to treat arrow wounds, had surpassed sugarcane as the main crop. Today St. Vincent and the Grenadines is the world's largest producer of arrowroot.

The Big Blast

St. Vincent and the Grenadines did not go into the 20th century, however, without drama. It came via La Soufrière, the north coast's simmering volcano. The volcano's first recorded eruption was in 1718. In 1812, it erupted again, killing 56 people. But the 1902 eruption was its most destructive to date. The blast sent gases and clouds as far away as Barbados, and rock and stones were recorded falling in Kingstown, in the south of the island. Over 2,000 died. A 1971 eruption was minor, and an April 1979 eruption forced the evacuation of 20,000 people from their homes. Many of these people were descendants of the Black Caribs defeated by Britain in the Second Carib War. No lives were lost, but substantial banana and arrowroot crops were destroyed.

20th Century

St. Vincent and the Grenadines received universal adult suffrage in 1951. In 1969, the islands became an associated state within the Commonwealth. Political parties had been formed by this time. The country received independence on 27 October 1979, the same year as La Soufrière's big blast. Later that same year, the government under Prime Minister Milton Cato was forced to quell strikes and a near-rebellion that was largely due to severe economic losses suffered after the eruption.

The New Democratic Party (NDP), formed in 1975 under current Prime Minister James "Son" Mitchell, has been the dominant political entity of late. Opposition parties include a coalition St. Vincent Labour Party/Movement for National Unity (Labour/MNU Unity) and the small United People's Movement (UPM).

PEOPLE AND CULTURE

The disparate groups that settled St. Vincent and the Grenadines over the millennium have today produced a multiracial society that differs slightly from other regional islands. The majority of the 112,000 population is black, descendant from 19th-century slaves. A substantial number of people are mixed-race descendants of Africans, Portuguese indentured laborers, British laborers, and other assorted visitors. The so-called Black Caribs number about two percent of the population, and descendants of East Indians number six percent.

The long history of British involvement in St. Vincent and the Grenadines has bestowed English as the official language. A Patois is spoken by most people and it incorporates vocabulary and grammar structures from various African languages, French, and some Spanish. The French influence is also seen in place names such as Sans Souci and Chateaubelair, or Petit Vincent and Mayreau in the Grenadines. Carib names also appear on the map, such as the Grenadine island of Bequia, or Commantawana Bay on St. Vincent.

Nearly half the population practices Anglicanism, and the bulk of the rest are various Protestant religions, including Methodist and Seventh-Day Adventist. Roman Catholics number 13% of the population.

Holidays and Festivals
The French influence shows during the St. Vincent and the Grenadines **National Carnival Festival,** "Vincy Mas." The carnival is held in mid-July, removing from it any pre-Lenten religious affiliation, but in all other respects it is a Caribbean carnival in the fullest. Calypso competitions, masquerades, parades, dancing, and festivals mark the 11-day affair. The final two days of the festival, J'Ouvert and Mardi Gras, mark the biggest street party the island sees each year.

If you're on the island during the two months preceding Vincy Mas, you'll be able to hear the calypso competitions throughout the country, warming up for the big event in July.

New Year's, Easter, Christmas, and Boxing Day are celebrated, as well as St. Vincent and the Grenadines Day (22 January), May Day (first Monday in May), Caricom Day (Caribbean Community Day, 12 July), Bank Holiday (first Monday in August) and the 27 October Independence Day.

GOVERNMENT AND ECONOMY

Agriculture
The economy of St. Vincent and the Grenadines is rooted in agriculture, primarily in bananas, arrowroot, and coconuts and coconut by-products. Approximately 38% of the island's land is arable, and the soil, due to past volcanic activity, is fertile and rich. While agriculture employs many, the labor force of approximately 70,000 is nearly 19% unemployed. An estimated 90% of the population, however, is engaged in some sort of agricultural activity, whether subsistence or for profit.

St. Vincent bananas are given special market protection due to the island's Commonwealth status, but this arrangement may end with the advent of the EC. The government has given incentives to farmers to diversify to other crops such as cocoa, citrus fruits, and arrowroot. St. Vincent is the world's largest supplier of arrowroot, which is used as a food thickening agent similar to cornstarch, as well as an emulsifier and coating for industrial uses.

Tourism
Tourism is second only to agriculture as the country's economic foreign exchange earner. Tourism is concentrated in the Grenadines, although St. Vincent seems to be getting more

arrivals each year. The size of its airport, **E.T. Joshua** in Arnos Vale, limits the numbers that can arrive at any one time. A total of 155,000 visitors stopped in St. Vincent and the Grenadines in 1992, a net loss of 10% compared to 1991. However, this was due to a decrease in cruise ship arrivals. The 1992 number of stayover visitors totaled 53,000, a net gain of three percent over 1991. Most stayover visitors, 35%, are from other Caribbean countries,

with the U.S. in second place at nearly 25%. The government is encouraging tourism growth, a development that started in the heady 1980s and continues. The number of rooms have increased to approximately 1,500 to date. A new airport was opened in Bequia in 1992 and is able to land small interisland aircraft. In August 1993, construction was begun at Ottley Hall, near Kingstown, on a US$75-million luxury yacht shipyard and marina.

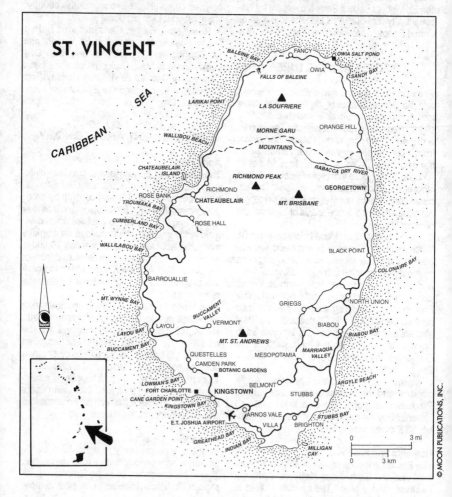

A small bridge once led from the Indian Bay beach to this small islet.

Government

St. Vincent and the Grenadines is a parliamentary democracy within the British Commonwealth. The Queen is the nominal head of state, represented on the island by a governor general. The legislature is unicameral, an elected House of Assembly that includes 15 representatives and six senators. Executive power is vested in the prime minister. Prime Minister James F. "Son" Mitchell and the NDP were returned to a third consecutive term in office in the February 1994 election, with the NDP holding 12 seats and the opposition coalition Labour/MNU Unity party holding three.

ST. VINCENT SIGHTS

Driving

St. Vincent's roads are generally good, and driving around the countryside by car is easy and recommended. The main roads, about 300 paved miles (483 km), complete a near-circle around the island. The section from **Richmond** on the leeward coast to **Fancy** on the north side is not well-paved and barely passable in sections. The Leeward and Windward highways hug the coastlines and pass by small villages, inlets, bays, forest, and often dramatic cliffs rising from the sea.

Northern St. Vincent

The Windward Highway brings you to **La Soufrière,** the island's semi-active volcano at the far north. This 4,048-foot (1,234 meters) volcano, which last erupted in 1979 and forced the evacuation of 20,000 people from the area, is a crater of one mile (1.6 km) in diameter, estimated at 1670 feet (509 meters) deep. The crater is filled with water and in 1971 sprouted a small island near the center. You can hike up to La Soufrière, a sometimes strenuous climb, in just over three hours. The trail begins after passing through **Georgetown,** St. Vincent's second-largest town, and crossing the **Rabacca Dry River** near Rabacca coconut plantation. The dry river was created from lava flow during the 1902 eruption. You'll hike and climb through a plantation, bamboo "forest," and steep inclines to the ridge. On the rim you'll be close to 4,000 feet (1,220 meters) above sea level, and you might expect some mist, cool air, even rain. Alternate access routes exist from the leeward-side villages of **Chateaubelair** or **Richmond.** These hikes are more scenic but are longer (10 miles or 16 km, still about three hours for the energetic) and rougher in places. A guide is needed for these hikes, about US$25 or EC$65. You'll find them in the villages.

North of the turnoff for La Soufrière is **Owia Bay,** site of the **Owia Salt Pond.** Owia is one of the Carib villages "given" to the group in the

18th-century relocations. A stairway leads up a short hill to a small salt pond, where swimming is allowed.

Falls of Baleine
The Falls of Baleine, also located in the north, are found past the road's end at Richmond. The usual way to get there is by boat—the views as you move up the coast are magnificent—which you can arrange in Kingstown or at **Villa Beach** near Kingstown; call **Dive St. Vincent,** tel. (809) 457-4714, or **T's Tours Ltd.,** tel. (809) 457-1433. The cost is about US$40 (EC$105) per person and includes lunch and snorkeling along the way.

After a hike through a stream you'll reach the cascade, a rush of cool, fresh water that falls about 60 feet (18 meters) into a natural bathing pool. You can also reach the falls by hiking from the northern town of **Fancy,** an area relegated to the Black Caribs two centuries ago. The hike is strenuous.

Southern St. Vincent
In the southern half of the island, several sights are worth the trip. Past the airport on the Vigie Highway, heading east, is the town of **Mesopotamia** and the **Marriaqua Valley.** The valley is the heart of the island's agricultural industry, and miles of banana plantations, arrowroot fields, forests, and streams blanket the area. The nearby gardens and natural springs at **Montreal,** tel. (809) 458-5452, offer a collection of exotic plants and trees. The view from these hills is worth the drive.

Drive north on the Leeward Highway, where you can stop at **Buccament Bay** and turn inland. Here the **Vermont Nature Trail** weaves through a rainforest. A nearby reserve has been established for the protection of the St. Vincent parrot. You may see several rainforest dwellers such as the black hawk and crested hummingbird.

Guided Tours
Island tours can be arranged through the **Taxi Driver's Association,** tel. (809) 457-1807. Cost is EC$35 per hour for a vehicle of four persons.

Other tour operators include **Barefoot Holidays,** tel. (809) 456-9334, or **Emerald Travel and Tours,** tel. (809) 457-1996.

KINGSTOWN

The nation's capital Kingstown is located in southwest St. Vincent, just a few miles north of E.T. Joshua Airport in Arnos Vale. The town is set on a natural harbor, and much of the dock and harbor area is built on reclaimed land. Downtown is easy to navigate and largely unadorned, even plain, save for several examples of colonial architecture and historic churches.

The immediate downtown area comprises a dozen blocks created by three streets parallel to the bay and to each other: Bay Street (Upper and Lower), Long Lane (Upper and Lower), and Grenville/Hallifax/Granby streets, connected by side streets. Here you'll find banks, businesses, the police station, post office, Cable and Wireless, small snack shops, large snack shops, shopping shops, taxi and bus stands, customs offices, tourism offices, and much of what Kingstown has to offer.

The busy **Kingstown Market,** open daily but bustling on Friday and Saturday, is bordered by Bedford Street and Long Lane. Here you can buy anything from clothes to peanuts to newspapers to fruits and vegetables. A block south is the also busy **New Fish Market.**

Just east of downtown is the **St. Vincent Craftmen's Centre.** The large center is the display showcase for many island craftsman, and a lot of the items are quite nice. Choose among straw crafts, woodcarvings, pottery, and dolls. As long as we're talking about shopping, try **Noah's Arkade** on Bay Street for crafts, spices, tourist books, souvenirs, postcards, and the like.

St. George's Anglican Cathedral on Grenville dates back to 1820, and its building was in part financed by the sale of Carib lands. Under the chandelier you'll find a stone memorial to the British officer who killed the Carib Chief Chatoyer in the Second Carib War. The large yellow structure features fine examples of stained glass windows, and the grounds, with a small cemetery, are well-kept.

Across the street is **St. Mary's Roman Catholic Cathedral (Assumption Cathedral),** originally completed in 1828 but renovated in the 1940s. The dark cathedral is eclectic in styles; Moorish, Georgian, and the dominant Romanesque. On the grounds are the presbytery and a school.

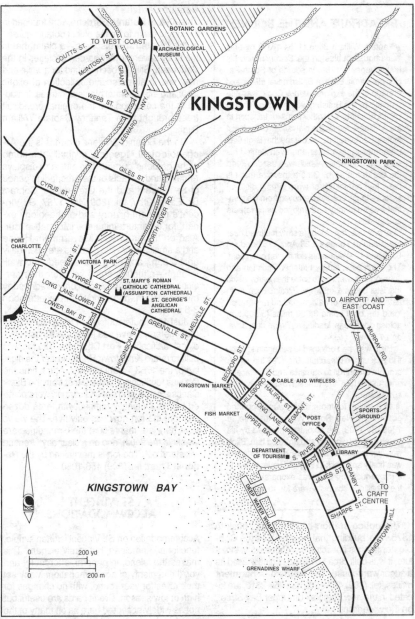

KINGSTOWN

BOTANIC GARDENS

ARCHAEOLOGICAL MUSEUM

TO WEST COAST

COUTTS ST.

McINTOSH ST.

GRANT ST.

WEBB ST.

LEEWARD HWY.

KINGSTOWN PARK

GILES ST.

CYRUS ST.

NORTH RIVER RD.

FORT CHARLOTTE

QUEEN ST.

VICTORIA PARK

TYRREL ST.

ST. MARY'S ROMAN CATHOLIC CATHEDRAL (ASSUMPTION CATHEDRAL)

ST. GEORGE'S ANGLICAN CATHEDRAL

LONG LANE LOWER

LOWER BAY ST.

HIGGINSON ST.

GRENVILLE ST.

MELVILLE ST.

TO AIRPORT AND EAST COAST

MURRAY RD.

BEDFORD ST.

KINGSTOWN MARKET

HILLSBORO ST.

HALIFAX ST.

CABLE AND WIRELESS

EGMONT ST.

FISH MARKET

LONG LANE UPPER

UPPER BAY ST.

POST OFFICE

RIVER RD.

DEPARTMENT OF TOURISM

LIBRARY

SPORTS GROUND

JAMES ST.

GRANBY ST.

TO CRAFT CENTRE

SHARPE ST.

KINGSTOWN BAY

DEEP WATER WHARF

KINGSTOWN HILL

0   200 yd
0   200 m

GRENADINES WHARF

© MOON PUBLICATIONS, INC.

BREADFRUIT AND THE *BOUNTY*

Captain William Bligh (1754-1817) met his famous troubles on the *Bounty* during his first voyage, in 1789, in search of South Pacific breadfruit. Bligh, a British naval officer and protégé of the explorer James Cook, was dispatched by the British government to Tahiti to collect breadfruit and other items for transport to the profitable sugarcane plantations of the West Indies. Some historians contend that Bligh was a heartless taskmaster and even denied his crew drinking water, which was used to keep the breadfruit alive. Others theorize that his crew just panicked, or were simply disloyal sailors—thugs one step removed from the criminal existence they had enjoyed as privateers and pirates.

At any rate, the *Bounty*'s crew mutinied near the island of Tonga on 28 April 1789 and set Bligh and 19 loyal sailors adrift in an open boat. The mutineers, led by Fletcher Christian and John Adams, went on to settle the nearby island that later became known as Pitcairn. Bligh, in an astonishing feat of navigation and raw grit, piloted the boat some 3,600 miles (5,800 km) across open seas, landing at Timor, near Java, on 14 June.

Bligh was then enjoined to sail again to Tahiti to pick up the breadfruit. The 1793 trip, which brought breadfruit to Jamaica and St. Vincent, and, ultimately, the entire West Indies, was successful.

In a telling footnote, Bligh was appointed governor of New South Wales, Australia, in 1805. By 1808, the colonists, horrified by his harsh tactics, rebelled and arrested him. Bligh was imprisoned for two years in the colony and was finally sent back to England under arrest. In a subsequent trial, he was exonerated, while the rebellious colonists were found guilty.

The **police station** building dates back to 1875. The building that now houses the **Cobblestone Inn** is not actually a cobblestone structure; it was built circa 1810 and originally used as a sugar warehouse. The **Tourism Department** offices, tel. (809) 457-1502, fax 456-2610, are located in the new complex on Upper Bay Street, on the waterfront.

Botanic Gardens

The 20-acre **Botanic Gardens** were founded in 1765 and claim to be the oldest botanic garden in the Western Hemisphere—a claim that is made by several other garden societies in the Caribbean. Still, it's been around for a while and now sports an extensive collection of exotic local and international plants and trees. Included in the collection are the original breadfruit trees brought from Tahiti by Captain William Bligh.

On the Botanic Gardens grounds is the **Archaeological Museum,** originally the home of the gardens' curator. The museum displays remains and artifacts of the Amerindian period of St. Vincent and the Grenadines. Contact Dr. Earle Kirby, tel. (809) 456-1787, St. Vincent's resident history and archaeology expert, for an entertaining and informative tour. Also on the grounds is Government House and a small aviary. The gardens are open daily until 6 p.m., and no guide is needed to walk through—although some will offer their services. The museum is open only Wednesday morning 9 a.m.-noon and Saturday afternoon 3-6 p.m.

Just 10 minutes outside of town, at 600 feet (183 meters) above sea level, sits Kingstown's oldest fortification, **Fort Charlotte.** The fort was built to guard Kingstown Harbour after the signing of the 1763 Treaty of Paris. At the time the fort was functioning, some threat from the Black Caribs existed, and several cannon were pointed inland. Originally fortified with three dozen cannon, the fort now has only five. The views from here are marvelous; the Grenadines are visible to the south, and on a clear day Grenada will stand out. The fort is maintained by the **National Trust,** tel. (809) 456-1060.

ST. VINCENT ACCOMMODATIONS

Accommodation on St. Vincent is often simple, functional, and clean, but rarely elegant. This makes the island, in general, affordable, and you'll find plenty of accommodation. Many set their rates for year-round, with no changes for high or low season. Credit cards are useful but not as widely accepted here as on many of the more tourist-developed islands.

The bulk of St. Vincent's hotels and small guesthouses are located along the south and southwest coast beach areas.

Hotels and guesthouses will tack on a 10% service charge and a five percent government tax. A more extensive list of hotels is available through the **St. Vincent and the Grenadines Hotel Association** (see below). This agency does not list every hotel on the island, but it does list those that maintain its membership standards.

The rate categories below are based on year-round rates, or high season (15 December-15 April) rates where applicable, per single per night: **Luxury** US$100 or more, **Moderate** US$50-100, **Budget** US$50 or less.

Hotels

In Kingstown, the **Cobblestone Inn** (P.O. Box 867, Kingstown, St. Vincent and the Grenadines, West Indies, tel. (809) 456-1937, has 19 rooms in a circa 1810 sugar warehouse. The rooms are comfortable, and the downtown location is excellent for exploring. You're close to the Grenadines Wharf, where ferries depart to the islands. The Creole restaurant is very popular. Moderate.

South of Kingstown, the **Villa Lodge Hotel,** P.O. Box 1191, Indian Bay, St. Vincent and the Grenadines, West Indies, tel. (809) 458-4641, fax 457-4468, is on a hill overlooking Young Island and Bequia and the Grenadines. The light-gray-sand beach at Indian Bay is fairly clean and features some good snorkeling. The rooms are simple and comfortable, and the hotel has a pool. This is a good buy. Moderate-Luxury.

The **Indian Bay Beach Hotel,** P.O. Box 538, Kingstown, St. Vincent and the Grenadines, West Indies, tel. (809) 458-4001, is small (14 rooms), basic, clean, and sits on the beach. Don't miss the weekly barbecue, all-you-can-eat seafood or chicken or whatever's on hand, with entertainment. Moderate.

Young Island Resort, P.O. Box 211, Young Island, St. Vincent and the Grenadines, West Indies, tel. (809) 458-4826, U.S. tel. (800) 223-1108, fax 457-4567, is a private island about 670 feet (205 meters) off the south coast's Villa Beach and Indian Bay. This is an elegant 35 acres of private cottages for 60 guests only, with water sports, pool, restaurant, and bar. A small ferry makes regular runs. Luxury.

MORE ST. VINCENT HOTELS AND GUESTHOUSES

Rates per s, EP when applicable, winter

NAME	(809)	FAX	LOCATION	TARIFF
Adams Guest House	458-4656	456-4728	Arnos Vale	budget
Beachcombers Hotel	458-4283	458-4345	Villa Beach	moderate
Bella Vista Inn	457-2757	N/A	Kingstown Park	budget
Coconut Beach Inn	458-4231	N/A	Indian Bay	moderate
Emerald Valley Resort & Casino	456-7140	456-7145	Penniston Valley	moderate
Grandview Beach Hotel	458-4811	457-4174	Villa Point	luxury
Heron Hotel	457-1631	N/A	Kingstown	budget
Lagoon Marina & Hotel	458-4308	457-4716	Blue Lagoon	moderate
Ratho Mill Apartments	458-4840	N/A	Ratho Mill	budget
Rick's Apartments	458-5544	456-2593	Cane Hall	moderate
Sea Breeze Guest House	458-4969	N/A	Arnos Vale	budget
Travelers Inn	456-4705	N/A	Villa	budget
Trottie's Apartments	458-4486	458-4486	Arnos Vale	budget
Umbrella Beach Hotel	458-4651	457-4930	Villa Beach	budget

MORE ST. VINCENT RESTAURANTS

NAME	LOCATION	(809)	CUISINE	PRICE RANGE
The Attic	Kingstown	457-2558	West Indian	moderate
Bounty	Kingstown	456-1776	West Indian/snacks	inexpensive
Le Cafe	Kingstown	457-2791	Continental/seafood	moderate
Chicken Roost	Arnos Vale	456-4932	barbecue/snacks	inexpensive
Chung Wua	Kingstown	457-2566	Chinese	moderate
KFC	Kingstown	457-2612	fast food	inexpensive
Jana's	Villa	N/A	snacks/bar food	inexpensive
Sugar 'n Spice	Kingstown	N/A	sandwiches/baked goods	inexpensive

Villas And Apartments

Several apartment-type accommodations may be attractive to those who're looking for self-contained or long-term accommodation. These tend to be simple and moderately priced. **Tranquillity Beach Apartments,** P.O. Box 71, Kingstown, St. Vincent and the Grenadines, West Indies, tel. (809) 458-4021, offers seven rustic one- to three-bedroom flats on the beach at Indian Bay. Budget. **Ocean Treasure,** P.O. Box 692, Kingstown, St. Vincent and the Grenadines, West Indies, tel. (809) 456-1821, rents 10 units, also on the beach at Indian Bay. The spartan rooms feature private baths and no a/c. Budget.

Others include **Belleville Apartments,** P.O. Box 746, Villa, St. Vincent and the Grenadines, West Indies, tel. (809) 458-4776, fax 456-2344; **Breezeville Apartments,** P.O. Box 222, Kingstown, St. Vincent and the Grenadines, West Indies, tel. (809) 458-4004, fax 457-4468; and Villa Beach's **Paradise Inn,** P.O. Box 1286, Kingstown, St. Vincent and the Grenadines, West Indies, tel. (809) 457-4795.

Camping

The government of St. Vincent and the Grenadines officially discourages impromptu camping, citing security problems. They know what they're talking about.

The only "camping" facility on the island is at **Petit Byahaut,** Petit Byahaut, St. Vincent and the Grenadines, West Indies, tel. and fax (809) 457-7008, an all-inclusive nature getaway on the central leeward coast. The exclusive resort features large, screened tents sitting on platforms, as well as several cabins. While this type of camping is not exactly roughing it, the experience and setting do emphasize outdoors and nature. The 50-acre secluded site can only be reached by boat, through prior arrangement, and offers hiking, diving, sailing, and water sports. Luxury.

ST. VINCENT FOOD

Dining on St. Vincent is not limited, in so much as you'll find many excellent small cafes, restaurants, and fast-food type takeout places. You won't find, however, many haute cuisine experiences. Dining at hotels is often a good bet; they may be open on Sunday. Credit cards are not widely accepted, particularly at smaller restaurants and cafes.

Note: The following are all in the moderate category, US$10-25 per entree.

In Kingstown, stop at **Basil's Restaurant** at the Cobblestone Inn for good West Indian Creole cuisine. **Aggie's Bar and Restaurant,** tel. (809) 456-2110, on Grenville features excellent Creole and seafood specialties. No credit cards.

At the Villa Beach area, the succinctly named **French Restaurant,** tel. (809) 458-4972, has a reputation for some of the best French food and seafood on the island. The seating is open air, on the beach, with pleasant breezes. **Lime N' Pub,** tel. (809) 458-4227, sits on the beach across from Young Island, with views to Bequia and the Grenadines. The cuisine is simple: rotis, grilled lobster, pizza, sandwiches. This is a great place to relax with a cold one.

BEQUIA

Bequia (BECK-way) is the largest of the Grenadines, some seven square miles (18 square km) and nine miles (14 km) off the coast of St. Vincent, with a population of 4,900. The name comes from the Carib Becouya, meaning "Island of the Clouds." A short drive to the top of the island's central, bracing, and sometimes mist-shrouded **Mt. Pleasant** will show you what they meant.

Whaling

Bequia's population is primarily involved in fishing, master ship-building, and tourism activities.

Local artisans still craft double-hulled boats and larger schooners and are known worldwide for their craft. Bequia was once a center for whaling, and local boat builders and whalers took their cue years ago from 19th-century U.S.-based whalers who sailed the Caribbean in search of their livelihood. A small industry evolved, and in its heyday the offshore cay of **Petit Nevis** became a whale processing center. The industry no longer exists, and many species of whales today are protected by international law. Bequia's residents, however, are exempted from restrictions due to their status as indigenous people. The hunt occasionally continues, often with the ancient hand-held harpoon. The island's premier whaler is the astonishing **Athneal Ollivierre,** "The Last Harpooner"; he is in his mid-70s and bagged a humpback as recently as 1992. See the small museum at his home in Paget Farm, open Mon.-Sat. 10 a.m.-5 p.m., and Sunday 9 a.m.-7 p.m., admission US$2 (EC$5). You can't miss the house; a pair of looming, bleached whale jawbones frames the entrance.

Beaches

The center of the island is forested and elevated and the coast is lined with small bays and inlets—plenty of great beaches. Best beaches: **Princess Margaret Beach,** just beyond Admiralty Bay; **Lower Bay,** which hosts the **Bequia Sailing Club** with facilities and several beach bars; **Friendship Bay,** quiet, with a beach bar at Friendship Bay Hotel and Bequia Beach Club; **Spring Bay,** with a plantation nearby, lined with palm trees, stunning views, and a beach bar that's occasionally open; and **Hope Bay,** which must be accessed by foot or boat.

Port Elizabeth

The island center is **Port Elizabeth,** a small town on **Admiralty Bay.** This is the hub of activity for locals and yachties alike, with a main street lined with shops, the **Bayshore Mall,** a **National Commercial Bank,** post office, po-

Spring Bay, Bequia

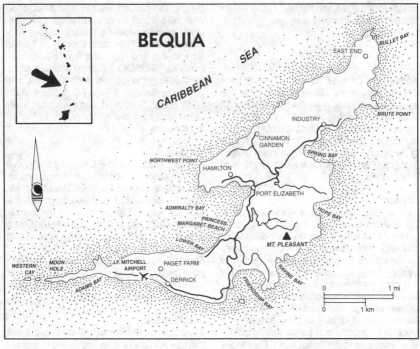

BEQUIA

CARIBBEAN SEA

BULLET BAY
EAST END
BRUTE POINT
INDUSTRY
CINNAMON GARDEN
SPRING BAY
NORTHWEST POINT
HAMILTON
PORT ELIZABETH
ADMIRALTY BAY
HOPE BAY
PRINCESS MARGARET BEACH
LOWER BAY
MT. PLEASANT
WESTERN CAY
MOON HOLE
J.F. MITCHELL AIRPORT
PAGET FARM
RAVINE BAY
ADAMS BAY
DERRICK
FRIENDSHIP BAY

0   1 mi
0   1 km

© MOON PUBLICATIONS, INC.

lice station, and an open-air market and sheltered market, taxi stand, and the ferry dock. It seems that everyone on the island ends up in Port Elizabeth at least once a day.

A **Tourist Bureau** kiosk, tel. (809) 458-3286, on the wharf is open Mon.-Fri. 9 a.m.-4 p.m., and Saturday 9 a.m.-noon.

Be sure to stop at the **Bequia Bookshop** (tel. 809-458-3905) for a wide selection of books (including many cruising guides and charts) and magazines, as well as locally crafted scrimshaw and art. Bequia may be small, but this could be the best-stocked bookstore for a hundred miles.

What To Do on Bequia

In addition to Dive Bequia and Dive Paradise, found at the Plantation House and Friendship Bay hotels (see below), **Sunsports,** tel. (809) 458-3577, fax 457-3031, at the **Gingerbread Complex** on Admiralty Bay will organize scuba diving, sailing, snorkeling, and other water sports.

For a unique and informative excursion, take a trip on the **_Friendship Rose,_** tel. (809) 458-3202 or 458-3090, fax 457-3071. The offices are located at the Local Color Boutique, next to Barclays Bank in town. You'll see the _Rose_ moored out in the bay. For many years, Captain Calvin Lewis ran the locally built schooner as a mail boat and ferry between Kingstown, Bequia, and other islands. He's now retired and takes passengers on day trips to Mustique and the Tobago Cays, and he's the one who can tell you just about everything there is to know about the Grenadines. The Tobago Cays day trip is US$65 (EC$175) per person, including lunch, drinks, snorkeling, and a flight back to Bequia.

The increasingly popular annual **Easter Regatta,** held over the long Easter Weekend, turns out to be a mini-carnival of sorts. Lots of beer drinking, amateur boat races (coconut boats and others), sports, music, dancing, and some bonafide sailing. Great fun. The **Bequia Sailing Club** is the center of it all.

Bequia Yacht Charter, Friendship Bay Hotel, tel. (809) 458-3222, fax 458-3840, will organize one- to three-day Grenadines sailing excursions, or customized charters.

Bequia Accommodations

The accommodation on Bequia consists of villas, guesthouses, and a few small but unique hotels.

For villa rentals try **Bequia Villa Rentals,** P.O. Box 23, Bequia, St. Vincent and the Grenadines, West Indies, tel. (809) 458-3393; or **Friendship Bay Villa Rentals,** P.O. Box 9, Bequia, St. Vincent and the Grenadines, West Indies, tel. (809) 458-3222, fax 458-3840. These villas lie in the Moderate-Luxury range.

Bequia's hotels include The **Plantation House Hotel,** P.O. Box 16, Bequia, St. Vincent and the Grenadines, West Indies, tel. (809) 458-3425, U.S. tel. (800) 223-9832, U.K. tel. 045-383-5801, local fax 458-3612, U.S. fax (212) 599-1755, U.K. fax 383-5525, set on 11 acres and a small beach just 15 minutes' walk along the bay from Port Elizabeth. The main house, which also houses the restaurant, is of the old greathouse plantation style. Accommodations are in the greathouse or in cottages spread over the property. The hotel used to be the "Sunny Caribbee" and was completely refurbished after a 1988 fire. You'll find a pool and beach bar, all very nice. Luxury. This is where you'll find **Dive Bequia,** tel. (809) 458-3504, U.S. tel. (800) 851-DIVE, fax 458-3886, the best place to start for your diving needs. The company offers packages with the hotel.

The **Friendship Bay Hotel,** P.O. Box 9, Bequia, St. Vincent and the Grenadines, West Indies, tel. (809) 458-3222, U.S. tel. (800) 223-1108, fax 458-3840, sits on a mile of one of the island's nicest beachfronts and bays. All 27

THE WHALE HUNT

Whaling has been a tradition among the people of Bequia since the mid-19th century though it was never a large commercial enterprise. Local whalers, including sailors, harpooners, and lookouts on land, hunted whales for meat, oil, and body parts.

Bequia's whalers hunt from February to April; they ply the warm waters of the Caribbean, looking primarily for humpbacks. Lookouts on high land use binoculars to scan the waters while boats disperse to Bequia's coastal waters and channels, ready for the chase. With their traditional double-hulled boats powered only by wind, the chase is not unlike it was at the turn of the 20th century.

When a whale is sighted, usually by its spout, lookouts signal the harpoon boats—in a past century by mirrors or smoke. As the boat closes in on the whale, harpooners get ready to "strap the iron." Thick rope is attached to the end of the harpoon and coiled in a container; in the old days this would have been a rum cask cut in half. The rope passes around a "luggerhead" at the bow of the boat, which provides resistance. The harpoon is shot from a whale gun—the days of throwing the first harpoon by hand are mostly over—and the whale dives. When, after a few minutes, it resurfaces, the killing lance is delivered.

The whalers then go overboard and sew up the mouth of the whale to prevent it from filling with water. The whale is towed—in a fallow wind, by rowboats—to Petit Nevis, a small cay and formerly busy whaling station in sight of Paget Farm, off Bequia's south coast. There the whale is processed to be distributed and sold.

Whales are profitable for their oil, meat, and bones, and for scientific research. The worldwide commercial hunt for them has greatly reduced (in some cases to near-extinction) the numbers of, among others, sperm whales, baleen whales, right whales, the smaller humpbacks, and minke whales. Only in the last few decades have conservationists and concerned indigenous people awakened to the plight of the world's whales; it has only been since 1986 that the International Whaling Commission (I.W.C.) established a moratorium on commercial whaling. This moratorium is still observed today, although violations are rife.

The I.W.C. has granted Bequians, as well as other indigenous people, Aboriginal Whaling Status, which is defined as whale hunting "for purposes of local consumption carried out by or on behalf of aboriginal families who share strong community, familial, social, and cultural ties to a continuing traditional dependence on whaling and the use of whales." Currently, the hunt is limited to three whales per year.

MORE BEQUIA HOTELS AND GUESTHOUSES

Rates per s, EP when applicable, winter

NAME	(809)	FAX	LOCATION	TARIFF
Blue Tropic Hotel	458-3573	457-3074	Friendship Bay	moderate
Dawn's Creole Garden	458-3154	N/A	Lower Bay	moderate
De Reef Apartments	458-3447	458-3484	Lower Bay	budget
The Frangiapani	458-3255	458-3824	Belmont	luxury
Gingerbread Apartments	458-3000	458-3907	Admiralty Bay	moderate
Hibiscus Apartments	458-3316	458-3103	Union Vale	budget-moderate
Keegan's Guest House	458-3254	458-3530	Lower Bay	budget
Kings Ville Apartments	458-3404	N/A	Lower Bay	moderate
Spring on Bequia	458-3414	N/A	Spring Bay	moderate-luxury

rooms look over the ocean, all have fans, no a/c, and have been recently redecorated. Beachfront bar and restaurant, good food, very casual and relaxed—a great place for families. You'll find the **Dive Paradise** dive shop here. Moderate-Luxury.

Julie's Guest House (Admiralty Bay, Bequia, St. Vincent and the Grenadines, West Indies, tel. (809) 458-3304, fax 458-3812, features 19 simple rooms on Back Street in Port Elizabeth. All rooms have fans, private baths (six with hot and cold water, 13 with cold only). A simple restaurant and bar will get you fed and watered. No credit cards are accepted. Budget.

The Old Fort, Mt. Pleasant, Bequia, St. Vincent and the Grenadines, West Indies, tel. (809) 458-3440, fax 458-3824, is a guesthouse built, in fact, in an old fort dating back to the 18th century. The fort sits on 30 acres atop Mt. Pleasant. Peacocks, donkeys, and rabbits meander about. There are six rooms only, with no phones and no television. You can walk to Hope Bay beach from

here. Ask owner Otmar Schaedle to show you his collection of antiques and artifacts he's unearthed on the property. Very unique. Moderate-Luxury.

Bequia Food

There are a half-dozen very good restaurants on the island and many takeout places. Several of the hotels, notably The Plantation Inn, offer excellent lunch and evening dining.

The Frangipani, tel. (809) 458-3255, is located at the hotel of the same name, famous for being the birthplace of Prime Minister James "Son" Mitchell. The Frangipani hosts a Thursday night barbecue and "jump up." Good Creole and West Indian. Moderate. **Le Petit Jardin,** tel. (809) 458-3318, in Port Elizabeth is elegant and serves French haute Creole. **Dawn's Creole Garden,** tel. (809) 458-3154, on Lower Bay beach has a weekend barbecue buffet with entertainment.

Getting to and Around Bequia

The **J.F. Mitchell Airport** is new, but small; it lands interisland flights only. **Mustique Airways**, tel. (809) 455-5645, operates the flight

Bequian boat

KAREN McKINLEY

from Kingstown to Bequia, EC$45 one-way. **LIAT,** St. Vincent tel. (809) 457-1821, has been contracting Mustique Airways to operate its flights and is due to begin flying its own planes by 1995-96.

The spotless airport, completed in 1992, is located at the southern end of the island, built on reclaimed land (bear to the right past the airport for a long, sometimes secluded beach). A taxi from there to Port Elizabeth is EC$25—about the most you'll pay anywhere on the island.

Taxis

Taxis on Bequia tend to be small open-air pick-up trucks outfitted with benches and canopies. The tourist booth in Port Elizabeth sometimes has the recommended rates available. Taxis and minibuses congregate at the wharf in Port Elizabeth.

For hotel pickups call **Gideon Taxi,** tel. (809) 458-3760; **Challenger Taxi,** tel. (809) 458-3811; or **Sam's Taxi,** tel. (809) 458-3868. Minibuses make regular runs to most points on the island, and bus stops with roofs are scattered along the few major roads.

Vehicle Rentals

If you've decided to rent a car to get around, it will be important to reserve it before your arrival, particularly during high season or during the annual Easter Regatta (see "What to Do on Bequia," above). Supplies are limited. Rates start at about US$40 per day.

Call **Philmore's Rentals** at Julie's Guest House, tel. (809) 458-3304, fax 458-3812, in Port Elizabeth for a limited but adequate selection of small jeeps. Philmore's will help you obtain the license at the police station.

You can hire a motorcycle from the **Bequia Art Gallery,** tel. (809) 458-3722, in Port Elizabeth.

MUSTIQUE

Most guidebooks appear to be unable to mention Mustique (Mus-TEEK) without using phrases such as "rich and famous," or dropping names like Mick Jagger and Princess Margaret. Of course, we would never do that.

It's 18 miles (29 km) south of St. Vincent and about five miles (eight km) southeast of Bequia. This is a place just three miles (four km) long and a bit over a mile (about two km) wide at its widest. The attraction? Seclusion, exclusivity, and a 12-mile (19-km) coastline with long, wide beaches. A favorite is **Macaroni Beach** on the Atlantic side. Offshore are several good snorkeling reefs and small cays, including Petit Mustique.

The island has no real town, just villas, a guesthouse, a hotel, a couple of small stores, a church, petrol station, riding stables, and a bar and restaurant.

Mustique is a semi-private island. Once owned by a private investor, the island is now owned by the Mustique Company. The prime minister of St. Vincent and the Grenadines sits on the company's board, and the government controls the island's internal affairs.

Accommodations

Villa rentals are handled locally by the **Mustique Company,** Mustique, St. Vincent and the Grenadines, West Indies, tel. (809) 458-4621/2, fax 457-2551 or 456-4565. Most will be in the luxury range. In North America, Mustique properties are handled by **WIMCO,** P.O. Box 1461,

---

MORE BEQUIA RESTAURANTS

NAME	LOCATION	(809)	CUISINE	PRICE RANGE
Bequia Beach Club	Friendship Bay	358-3248	Continental	moderate
Gingerbread	Admiralty Bay	358-3800	seafood	moderate
Mac' Pizzeria	Port Elizabeth	458-3474	light Italian	moderate
La Mezzaluna	Port Elizabeth	457-3080	Italian	moderate
Theresa's	Lower Bay	458-3802	Continental/ West Indian	inexpensive

Newport, RI 02840, tel. (800) 932-3222, fax (402) 847-6290.

The island offers two public accommodations. **The Cotton House,** P.O. Box 349, Mustique, St. Vincent and the Grenadines, West Indies, tel. (809) 456-4777, U.S. tel. (800) 372-1323, is a restored 18th-century estate house with 22 rooms, on Endeavor Bay. The hotel features tennis, a pool, and two bars and a restaurant. Luxury.

Firefly Guesthouse, P.O. Box 349, Mustique, St. Vincent and the Grenadines, West Indies, tel. (809) 456-3414 or 458-4621, is small (four rooms) and a good buy for this island. No credit cards are accepted. Moderate.

Basil's Bar and Raft Restaurant is the public restaurant on the island, which makes it famous. On the western side's Britannia Bay, the bamboo and thatched-roof bar hangs over the water.

Mustique's airstrip services flights from Barbados and St. Vincent.

CANOUAN

Canouan (CAN-oo-ahn) lies between the islands of Mustique and Mayreau in the center of the Grenadines. The small island, about 1,900 acres, has an irregular coast with excellent

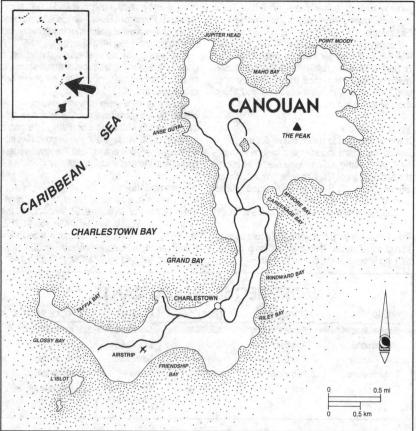

© MOON PUBLICATIONS, INC.

beaches and reefs and possibilities for exploring the nearby islands, including the Tobago Cays. This is yacht country, and dozens of boats anchor in the small inlets surrounding the island. For swimming and snorkeling, go to the popular "The Pool" beach. For **water sports,** contact **Dive Canouan,** tel. (809) 458-8234.

Canouan's small **airstrip** lands small aircraft only. Your best bet is to connect through St. Vincent. **Ferry service** to Canouan operates from St. Vincent (see "Ferry Service" under "Getting Around," below).

Accommodations

The **Canouan Beach Hotel,** P.O. Box 530, Canouan, St. Vincent and the Grenadines, West Indies, tel. (809) 458-8888, U.S. tel. (508) 788-0306, fax 458-8875, has 43 rooms on the beach, front and behind, at the southwest tip of the island, with wonderful views of the southern Grenadines. Tennis, water sports, bar, and restaurant. Luxury.

The **Crystal Sands Beach Hotel,** Grand Bay Beach, St. Vincent and the Grenadines, West Indies, tel. (809) 458-8309, features 10 cottages on the beach. The village nearby is the center of activity. Moderate.

Villa le Bijou, Friendship, Canouan, St. Vincent and the Grenadines, West Indies, tel. (809) 458-8025, is a small 10-room hotel up on a hill, great views, a walk to the beach. No credit cards are accepted. Moderate-Luxury.

MAYREAU

Tiny Mayreau (MY-row), about 35 miles (56 km) south of St. Vincent, is 1.5 square miles (about four square km, or 700 acres), with fewer than 200 residents. And, it's privately owned. You can only get here by sea (see "Getting Around," below), but this may be what you've been looking for. Ultra secluded, with the **Tobago Cays** just offshore, you can't do much other than swim, snorkel, take trips to the islands, and eat. You can't even drive, really. The island's roads are essentially paths. Hike around the island and you'll see an old schoolhouse, a stone church, and a small village. Climb the island's small "mountain," where the views of nearby islands are worth the short hike.

Saline Bay Beach and **Salt Whistle Bay,** both on the island's west side, provide the best swimming and sunning available, and the snorkeling and diving in this area and the Tobago Cays is considered by some to be the best in the Grenadines. Some snorkeling equipment is available to rent.

You'll also see yachts anchored about the island and the Tobago Cays. This is a popular stop. A cruise ship stops by once per week.

Accommodations

Stay at **Salt Whistle Bay Club,** tel. (809) 493-9609, Canada tel. (613) 634-1963, Canada fax (613) 384-6300, a 22-acre resort on the island's north side. The beach here is superb. Luxury. **Dennis' Hideaway** (tel. 809-458-8594) is a small three-room guesthouse and restaurant on Saline Bay. The separate restaurant serves West Indian. The guesthouse's spartan rooms feature private baths with cold water. Moderate.

UNION ISLAND

The three-miles-by-one-mile (approximately four-km-by-two-km) Union Island is 36 miles (58 km) south of St. Vincent, within sight of Mayreau. The population of 2,500 lives in two Lilliputian towns on the south coast, **Clifton** and **Ashton.** The latter is slightly larger. The two dramatic peaks, **Mt. Parnassus** (nearly 700 feet, or 210 meters) and **Mt. Olympus,** reveal an apparent local fascination with the ancient Greeks.

Union is a bit livelier than its neighbors, and the island is the center of the southern Grenadines. It is, however, in many ways detached, judging by its political troubles. When James "Son" Mitchell, a Bequian, won a 1979 national election, a group of about 50 Union Islanders revolted and demanded secession. They were instead arrested.

Accommodations

The following hotels are available to Union Island visitors. **Anchorage Yacht Club,** Union Island, St. Vincent and the Grenadines, West Indies, tel. (809) 458-8221, fax 458-8365, is smallish, with 21 bungalows, apartments, and rooms. The draw is that it offers all available water activities on this island and then some. Note the

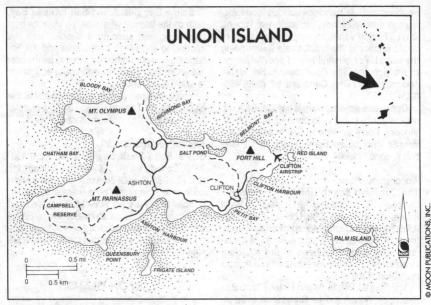

UNION ISLAND

BLOODY BAY

MT. OLYMPUS

RICHMOND BAY

BELMONT BAY

CHATHAM BAY

SALT POND

FORT HILL

RED ISLAND

CLIFTON
AIRSTRIP

ASHTON

CLIFTON

CLIFTON HARBOUR

MT. PARNASSUS

CAMPBELL
RESERVE

ASHTON HARBOUR

PETIT BAY

PALM ISLAND

0   0.5 mi

0   0.5 km

QUEENSBURY
POINT

FRIGATE ISLAND

© MOON PUBLICATIONS, INC.

saltwater pool filled with sharks. This is *not* a swimming pool. Moderate-Luxury.

The **Clifton Beach Hotel,** Clifton, Union Island, St. Vincent and the Grenadines, West Indies, tel. (809) 458-8235, is large; 25 rooms overlook Clifton Harbour, some bungalows with kitchenettes. The hotel will arrange trips to nearby cays. Budget-Moderate.

Lambi's Guesthouse, Clifton, Union Island, St. Vincent and the Grenadines, West Indies, tel. (809) 458-8549, has six small rooms, a restaurant, and occasional entertainment. No credit cards are accepted. Budget. The **Sunny Grenadines Hotel,** Clifton, Union Island, St. Vincent and the Grenadines, West Indies, tel. (809) 458-8327, fax 458-8398, has 18 rooms, some with kitchenettes, and overlooks the harbor. Simple place. Moderate.

On the Island

Minibuses service some parts of the island, particularly between Ashton and Clifton.

For local sailing day charters and customized trips, call **Captain Yannis,** tel. (809) 435-8451.

Union Island's small airstrip has an immigration facility. Flights, with stops, to and from St.

Vincent, Carriacou, Grenada, Guadeloupe, Martinique, Port of Spain, Barbados, and St. Lucia are available on the regional airline **LIAT,** tel., 458-8230. LIAT may charter airplanes from other airlines to do the flights.

The local **tourist office** number is (809) 458-8350.

PALM ISLAND

Just a mile off the Union Island shore, this was once called Prune Island. The island is a private, tranquil, secluded, one-resort getaway, and that about says it all. It's popular with some yachties whose boats you'll see anchored offshore. The walnut-sized island is a mere 130 acres, and the beach skirts completely around the island.

The owner, John Caldwell, and his family have built 24 rooms in cabanas at their **Palm Island Beach Club.** Facilities include tennis, diving, fitness path, open restaurant, bar, and tea at 4 p.m. Contact Palm Island, St. Vincent and the Grenadines, West Indies, tel. (809) 458-8824, U.S. tel. (800) 776-PALM, fax 458-8804, U.S. fax (310) 762-7283. Luxury.

To get there, sail in or fly to Union Island and they'll take you over in their launch.

PETIT ST. VINCENT

The southernmost Grenadines island within St. Vincent and the Grenadines' political sphere (Carriacou, of Grenada, is farther south), Petit St. Vincent is another private, low-key, and deeply exclusive resort.

The accommodation on 113-acre PSV consists of 22 luxury stone cottages set in tropical gardens. You raise a yellow flag on your cabana to let the staff know you'd like room service. This is considered by aficionados of this type of resort to be the most elegant private island in the Caribbean. Amenities include water sports, fine dining, and whatever you'd like, really. Contact owner Haze Richardson II, Petit St. Vincent Resort, St. Vincent and the Grenadines, West Indies, tel. (809) 458-8801, U.S. tel. (800) 654-9326, fax 458-8428. Luxury.

SPORTS AND ENTERTAINMENT

Boat Charters

Given the close proximity of the Grenadines, it's no surprise that sailing the islands is a popular activity. This area and the British Virgin Islands, which similarly comprise dozens of tiny cays and islands, have long been recognized as prime sailing spots. Most of St. Vincent and the Grenadines have good docking facilities and amenities for sailors, and the number of charter companies provide service, either bareboat or crewed. If you haven't made arrangements before you arrive, contact Barefoot Yacht Charters, tel. (809) 456-9526, fax 456-9238; or the Lagoon Marina, tel. (809) 458-4308; and CSY Yacht Charters (same phone) at the Blue Lagoon area of the south coast.

Diving

As well, given the many reefs weaving through and around the waters of the Grenadines, diving and snorkeling are excellent. In St. Vincent, contact St. Vincent Dive Experience, tel. (809) 456-9741; Caribe Divers, tel. (809) 458-7270; or Dive St. Vincent, tel. (809) 457-4714.

Nightlife

You'll find some entertainment in the hotels, most often during specialty barbecue buffet nights (check local newspapers for listings).

The Attic, tel. (809) 457-2558, in Kingstown features mellow jazz some evenings, as well as steel pan bands and other local bands. Basil's Too, tel. (809) 458-4205, in Villa stays open until the early hours and features dancing and live bands.

The **Emerald Valley Resort and Casino,** tel. (809) 456-7140, in Peniston Valley is your only bet, so to speak, for gambling. You can play blackjack, roulette, craps, and slot machines in the small casino daily except Tuesday, 9 p.m.-3 a.m.

GETTING THERE

By Air

St. Vincent's **E.T. Joshua Airport** in Arnos Vale lands only small interisland aircraft. Connections to St. Vincent and the Grenadines are made through the neighboring islands of Barbados (where you'll find a St. Vincent and the Grenadines information desk), St. Lucia, Martinique, Trinidad, and Grenada. You can fly to those islands via numerous international airlines including American, Air Canada, Air France, Air Martinique, British Airways, and BWIA. The connection to St. Vincent will more than likely be on **LIAT,** local tel. (809) 457-1821, Union Island tel. 458-8230. **Air Martinique,** tel. (809) 458-4528; **Mustique Airways,** tel. (809) 458-4380; and **SVG Air,** tel. (809) 456-5610, act as agents and carriers for LIAT, connecting to various neighboring islands and to the Grenadines, and act as charter airlines as well.

Bequia, Canouan, and Union Island have airstrips, immigration facilities, and tourist department information booths. Night-landing facilities are spotty and it is not always clear which islands are allowing or not allowing landings at night. Bequia's J.F. Mitchell Airport was opened in 1992, and the Union Island Airport was expanded in 1993. The private islands of Mustique, Mayreau, and Palm Island have small airstrips but are not entry points for St. Vincent and the Grenadines.

Departure Tax
Departure tax from St. Vincent or any of the Grenadines is EC$20.

GETTING AROUND

Taxis
On St. Vincent, taxis and minibuses operate on government-regulated fares. They have no meters. Typically, taxis are marked as such, but this is not always the case. Don't expect them to have a rate sheet in the vehicle. Pick up a copy of the government pamphlet *Discover St. Vincent and the Grenadines* at the airport or a tourist information center, and it will list some fares. Then, ask your driver to stick to it—or close to it.

Your hotel or guesthouse will be able to recommend a driver for tours or simple trips. Or call the **Taxi Driver's Association,** tel. (809) 457-1807.

Minibuses
Minibuses operate around the island and can be flagged down anywhere along the route. It is not always clear which vehicles are taxis and which are minibuses, since they can look the same, but this is half, or at least a quarter, of the fun. Look for vans with names like "Lord Is My Shepherd" or "Loves Life" emblazoned across the windshield.

Minibuses depart from the market square in Kingstown for all points. Cost for minibus transport to anywhere will rarely exceed EC$6.

Rentals
Rental cars may be your best bet for traveling St. Vincent. Average rate is US$35 (about EC$90) per day. You must have a St. Vincent and the Grenadines temporary driver's license to operate a vehicle, and the cost is EC$40. Driving is on the left. Call **Avis,** tel. (809) 456-5610; **Kim's Rentals,** tel. (809) 456-1884; or **Sunshine Auto Rentals,** tel. (809) 456-5380.

Motorcycles and scooters can be rented through J.G. Agencies, tel. (809) 456-1409, and Sailors Cycle Centre, tel. (809) 457-1712.

INFORMATION DIRECTORY

ST. VINCENT AND THE GRENADINES DEPARTMENT OF TOURISM

P.O. Box 834, Kingstown, St. Vincent and the Grenadines, West Indies, tel. (809) 457-1502, fax 457-2880.

801 2nd Ave., 21st Floor, New York, NY 10017, tel. (800) 729-1726, fax (212) 949-5946.

100 University Ave., Suite 504, Toronto, Ontario M5J 1V6, tel. (416) 971-9666, fax 971-9667.

10 Kensington Ct., London W8 5DL, tel. (071) 937-6570, fax 937-3611.

Mr Bruno Fink, Wurmberg Str. 26, D-7032 Sindelfingen, Germany, tel. (70-31) 80-62-60, fax 80-50-12.

OTHER

St. Vincent and the Grenadines Hotel Association, Box 834, Kingstown, St. Vincent and the Grenadines, West Indies, tel. (809) 457-1072.

Emergency, tel. 999.

Police, tel. (809) 457-1211.

Kingstown General Hospital, tel. (809) 456-1185.

Local information, tel. 118.

Reliance Pharmacy, Halifax Street, Kingstown, tel. (809) 456-1734.

American Express Representative, Caribbean International Travel Services, Granby Street, Kingstown, tel. (809) 457-1841.

FedEx, Halifax Street, Kingstown, tel. (809) 456-1649.

Ferry Service
Travel to and among the Grenadines by ferry is not physically difficult, but it is somewhat complicated. Schedules are subject to change at any time, so keep abreast of the situation if that's the way you decide to go. The ferries, which are inexpensive, reasonably comfortable and fun to boot, are found at the **Grenadines Wharf** in Kingstown.

(top) looking over Montserrat (Karl Luntta)
(bottom) Salt River, St. Croix (U.S. Virgin Islands Division of Tourism)

(top) Fête des Cuisinières, Guadeloupe (Michael Doneff)
(bottom) Island Harbour, Anguilla (Anguilla Tourist Board)

On Monday and Thursday the MV *Snapper* departs Bequia (6 a.m.) and arrives Kingstown (7 a.m.). The boat then leaves Kingstown (departs 10:30 a.m.) and goes back to Bequia (arrives 11:30 a.m.), Bequia (departs 11:45 a.m.) to Canouan (arrives 1:45 p.m.), Canouan (departs 2 p.m.) to Mayreau (arrives 3 p.m.), and Mayreau (departs 3:25 p.m.) to Union Island (arrives 3:45 p.m.).

On Tuesday and Friday the trip is in reverse. Union Island (departs 5:30 a.m.) to Mayreau (arrives 7:20 a.m.), Mayreau (departs 7:30 a.m.) to Canouan (arrives 8:30 a.m.), Canouan (departs 8:45 a.m.) to Bequia (arrives 10:45 a.m.), Bequia (departs 11 a.m.) to Kingstown (arrives noon).

On Saturday, the trip starts in Kingstown (departs 10:30 a.m.), and stops in Canouan, Mayreau, and Union Island (arrives 10:30 p.m.). It then makes a run from Union Island (departs 5:30 p.m.) nonstop to Kingstown, a five-hour trip.

The MV *Admiral I,* tel. (809) 458-3348, and MV *Admiral II* (same phone) make runs from Kingstown to Bequia only, a one-hour trip. Monday through Friday and on Sunday they run Kingstown to Bequia departing at 9 a.m., 10:30 a.m., and 7 p.m.; and Bequia to Kingstown departing at 7:30 a.m., 2 p.m., and 5 p.m. On Saturday they run Kingstown to Bequia departing at 12:30 p.m. and 7 p.m.; Bequia to Kingstown departing at 6:30 a.m. and 5 p.m.

Fares are also subject to change, but the following are current fares. From Kingstown to Bequia EC$10, Kingstown to Canouan EC$13, Kingstown to Mayreau EC$15, and Kingstown to Union Island EC$20.

MONEY, HOURS AND COMMUNICATION

Currency And Banks

St. Vincent and the Grenadines use the Eastern Caribbean dollar, currently exchanged at EC$2.70 = US$1. Most businesses will accept U.S. and Canadian dollars, but this is not always the case. It's easier to work in EC dollars anyway, and banks can be found at E.T. Joshua Airport (open Mon.-Sat. 7 a.m.-5 p.m.) and on the main streets of Kingstown and Georgetown.

Barclays, Scotia Bank, and **National Commercial Bank of St. Vincent** are all on Halifax Street in Kingstown. Banking hours may vary, but most are open Mon.-Fri. 8 a.m.-1 p.m. or 8 a.m.-3 p.m., and Friday 3-5 p.m.

Hours, Mail, Phones

In general, businesses are open Mon.-Fri. 8 a.m.-4 p.m., with an hour off for lunch, and on Saturday 8 a.m.-noon. Supermarkets may remain open all day on Saturday. Government offices are open Mon.-Fri. 8 a.m.-noon and 1-4:15 p.m.

The general post office is located on Halifax Street in Kingstown and is open Mon.-Fri. 8:30 a.m.-3 p.m. and Saturday 8:30-11:30 a.m.

St. Vincent and the Grenadines uses "809" as the direct dial area code. From North America, dial "1" plus "809" plus the seven digit number. Since all numbers in St. Vincent and the Grenadines start with "45," you can simply dial the last five digits when making local calls. **Cable and Wireless** is located on Halifax Street.

For local events, pick up a copy of *The News* or *The Vincentian* (both EC$1), weekly tabloids found at small shops or vendor tables at the market.

GRENADA

Grenada, the "Island of Spice," is recognized by the world in general (and by North Americans and Caribbean peoples in particular) as a bit of a legend in its own time. The island has endured some of the most radical governments and governmental changes of the Caribbean region's past 50 years; Cuba, Haiti, and perhaps Jamaica come to mind as similarly affect- ed islands. The then-U.S. President Ronald Reagan's 1983 invasion—"rescue mission" and "intervention" were the euphemisms used by the administration then, and, in fact, are the preferred nomenclature of Grenadians today—put Grenada on the map for many of us.

Tourist travel to Grenada understandably slacked off for some years, but today it has become an important income-earner for the island, signaling Grenada's acceptance of the region-wide phenomenon. The lush, rustic island has much to offer. Mountain rainforest hikes, serene beaches, exotic cuisines, a lively cultural milieu, and comfortable, affordable accommodations make Grenada a smart choice for those who want to truly get away and tread barely worn paths.

THE LAND

Grenada (greh-NAY-da), the Grenadines islands of Carriacou (CARRY-ah-koo), Petit Martinique (petty mar-tin-EEK), and about 30 smaller cays together form the State of Grenada.

The total land area of the three main islands measures 140 square miles (362 square km). Grenada itself, slightly smaller than its northern neighbor St. Vincent, measures about 21 miles (34 km) long and 12 miles (19 km) at its widest point, a land area of 120 square miles (311 square km). The island is strangely shaped like neighboring Trinidad, some 90 miles (145 km) to the south.

The 13-square-mile (34-square-km) island of Carriacou is the largest of the Grenadines chain and lies about 20 miles (32 km) to the north. Tiny Petit Martinique, less than one square mile in area, is clearly visible just across **Watering Bay,** east of Carriacou.

Grenada itself is a mountainous island, created eons ago by underwater volcanic eruptions. The island's interior is characterized by mountain ranges, some volcanic activity, high-altitude rainforests, and numerous streams and rivers. The highest point on Grenada is the north-central **Mt. St. Catherine,** at 2,757 feet (841 meters). The massive **Grand Etang,** a volcanic crater now dormant, rises 1,740 feet (530 meters) above sea level. The area surrounding Grand Etang is a national park and forest reserve with numerous trails and a government information center; it's a good start for exploring the flora and fauna of the island.

At the base of the island's central mountains are drier coastal woodlands, mangrove and other swamplands, and fertile plains, where the island's bananas, coconuts, fruits, vegetables, and famous spices, including nutmeg, are grown.

The south and southeast coasts are irregular, filled with small bays, inlets, and peninsulas. The quiet leeward west coast is characterized by a smoother coastline and several of the island's more popular beaches. In the extreme northeast is **Levera National Park,** a large mangrove swamp and offshore protected reef.

St. George's, the capital, is set on a natural harbor at the southwest end of the island. The city's harbor was partially created from the crater of an ancient volcano. The town is built among the hills at the base of Grand Etang, and its steep dips and crests are reminiscent of California's San Francisco streets.

Flora and Fauna

The topography and rainforests of the country create unique habitats for many species of plants and animals. The Grenada dove is endemic, and several species of hummingbirds, parrots, warblers, and other birds common to the Windward Islands can be found. The mangroves and lowlands host herons, coots, ruddies, and several other water species. The armadillo, which is often a local dish, is featured on Grenada's coat of arms. The opossum, called *manicou* in local Patois, is also hunted. The usual lizards and frogs are found, and imported Mona monkeys can be seen in the Grand Etang rainforest.

Carriacou and Petit Martinique

The irregular-shaped Carriacou—from a Carib word once spelled (not by Caribs) Kayryouacou, reputedly the "Land of Reefs"—is the largest of all the Grenadines. A small central range culminates in two nearly equal points: the 950-feet (290-meter) **High North** in the north of the island and **Chapeau Carré** in the south. The island's main town, **Hillsborough,** sits along a large and often calm bay on the island's leeward side. Several offshore cays, including **Sandy Island, Saline Islands, Large Island, Frigate Island,** and **Mushroom Island,** are uninhabited but visited by picnickers, anglers, or nesting birds.

Petit Martinique's one peak is a 500-foot (152-meter) hill in the center that gives the island the look of a ten-gallon hat that somebody sat on. The lowland coast is home to about 600 islanders involved primarily in boat-building and fishing.

HISTORY

First Peoples

Grenada's early history follows a pattern similar to that of many southern islands of the Lesser Antilles. The nomadic, Stone Age Ciboney (also spelled Siboney) are assumed to have existed before anyone, but left little in the way of artifacts or evidence of their lifestyles on the still-forming islands.

Amerindian Arawaks and related tribes migrated north in several waves from regions of South America, from 500 B.C. until the time of Christ. Arawak artifacts and petroglyphs have been found near Victoria on the northwest coast and Levera in the northeast.

Nearly 800 years later the Arawaks were followed, or chased, by a another Amerindian group, the warlike Caribs, who were reputed to have cannibalized their enemies. The Caribs either eliminated, assimilated, or drove out the Arawaks, or perhaps a combination of all three, and at the time of Columbus's late 15th-century journeys to the New World, the Caribs were firmly ensconced on the islands.

Early European Settlement

Columbus sailed by Grenada during his third voyage in 1498. He charted it and named it Concepción, but apparently never landed. Passing Spanish sailors began to call the island "Granada," as its hills reminded them of the eponymous Spanish city.

Early European colonization, however, was vigorously resisted by the Caribs, and it wasn't for another hundred years that adventurers were able to establish a settlement on the island. A 1609 party of English settlers was driven off, and in 1638 the French tried with the same results.

Then in 1650, the French governor of Martinique, du Parquet, sailed to the island with 200 colonists and, with trinkets and knives, purchased land from the Caribs. This proved to be a mistake for the soon-to-be-hapless aboriginals. Once the French had access to the island they took more and more, and before you could say "roast thigh," the Caribs and the French were at war.

The poison-arrow-armed Caribs proved to be ill-equipped to fight against French armaments and were virtually eliminated within months. They fled and scattered and were hunted like animals.

Leapers Hill

The Carib involvement in Grenada culminated in a dramatic mass suicide; in 1651 an estimated 40 Caribs threw their children, their women, and themselves off a precipice, now called Caribs' Leap, at La Morne des Sauteurs ("Leapers Hill") in the north of the island.

Thereafter the battle for possession of Grenada was waged between the southern Caribbean's primary European powers—the British and French—reflecting ongoing European wars as well as similar battles throughout the Lesser Antilles.

The French built forts, including the impressive Fort George, overlooking St. George's in the south. The island exchanged hands several times until the 1783 Treaty of Versailles finally ceded the island to the British. For nearly 200 years the island would remain a British possession, and that involvement laid the foundation for today's economic and demographic picture.

Slave Revolt

The British imported Africans to do hard labor on the tobacco and sugar plantations. Soon nutmeg was introduced from the Dutch East Indies and became an important cash crop. Life for the slaves was harsh, and planters' cruelty, a result of their increasing paranoia as the slave population surpassed their own numbers by four- and five-fold, resulted in a slave rebellion in 1795. Julien Fedon, a "free colored" man (see "Plantocracy and Slavery" in the "History" section of the Introduction chapter for more information on the "free colored" group) born of an African mother and French father, led a slave revolt that lasted a year and eventually saw the killing of dozens of British landowners. When reinforcements arrived and the revolt was crushed, however, Fedon had disappeared. Legend has it that he drowned while escaping.

In 1834, slavery was eliminated in the British colonies. This was the death knell for large sugar plantations, even after the importation of East Indian indentured laborers to prop up the sagging estates. By the end of the century, sugarcane took a back seat to nutmeg and cocoa as the main crop. Bananas were introduced and eventually became a major island industry.

Eric Gairy

The 1920s and worldwide depression affected Grenada both economically and politically. Throughout the Caribbean, poor labor conditions engendered the formation of labor unions, therefore political parties, therefore calls for independence. Grenada, paradoxically, was one of the first British islands to agitate for independence. Historians may say that this was the work of one man, the enigmatic Eric Gairy.

Gairy, a Grenadian who had worked as a clerk in the Aruba oil industry, organized island-wide strikes and political agitation in the late 1940s. When Britain granted universal adult suffrage in 1951 and allowed the election of a nonautonomous internal government, Gairy and his oddly named GULP (Grenada United Labour Party) were elected with ease. For years GULP vied for power with the opposition party, the Grenada National Party (GNP), led by Herbert Blaize.

By 1967 Britain had granted Grenadians a greater degree of autonomy, and Gairy led the call for independence. Many Grenadians were unclear about the necessity for independence at that point, but the charismatic and eccentric Gairy was able to rally enough support, often through unscrupulous means, to dominate the movement.

UFOs

To understand what happened later, a closer look at Eric Gairy, later Sir Eric Gairy, is in order. Gairy portrayed himself as a mystic, the destined leader of Grenada. He was brash; he once led a calypso march through an opponent's political rally. As chief minister he was accused of corruption and what amounted to theft, and he was censured and suspended. Apparently unencumbered by the appearance of conflict of interest, he had financial involvement in several large island businesses. He was fascinated by magic and UFOs and supported research in those areas. When faced with opposition he recruited a gang of armed enforcers—thugs, really—that terrorized the citizenry. The infamous group was known as the "Mongoose Gang" or "Mongoose Squad."

Independence came in 1974 with Gairy at the helm. The situation quickly deteriorated as the increasingly eccentric leader's autocracy and heavy-handedness dismayed even his followers. While he was off the island in 1979—apparently lecturing a United Nations forum on UFO research—his government was ousted in an armed coup d'état, the first in the modern British Caribbean, led by the radical New Jewel Movement (Jewel stands for Joint Endeavor for Welfare, Education, and Liberation).

Three people were killed in the coup. The head of the New Jewel Movement, lawyer Maurice Bishop, was installed as the prime minister and leader of the Marxist People's Revolutionary Government (PRG). Eric Gairy prudently remained in the United States.

U.S. Invasion of Grenada

Bishop's early rule was characterized by increased social programs and marked improvements in the lives of Grenadians. However, when Bishop, who was a protégé of Castro, began to align himself with the then-Soviet Union and import Cuban military advisors, the Caribbean, the West, and factions within his own party began to worry. The tourism industry, until then on its way to becoming a major foreign exchange earner, dropped through the floor. Grenada's economy sagged.

Then, in October 1983, a revolt within the New Jewel Movement deposed Bishop. This second coup resulted in Bishop's murder, along with several of his friends and advisors. Within days the country was in a state of anarchy. A week later a joint U.S.-Caribbean military force of about 2,000 invaded the island to restore order—and to rescue American students of the threatened St. George's University Medical School. They imprisoned Bishop's killers and ousted the Cuban military force that was, among other projects, building what was to be a military airstrip south of St. George's.

Within a year, due to increased aid from the U.S. and the West, an interim government headed by Nicholas Brathwaite had been installed, and order had been restored. Many Grenadians today speak of the intervention in positive terms, and there is a conspicuous pro-U.S. sentiment in many quarters of the country.

New Elections

In 1984 elections were held and Herbert Blaize, now head of a coalition party called the New National Party (NNP), was elected to office.

Several opposition parties, including GULP, the Maurice Bishop Patriotic Movement, and factions within the NNP have formed and reformed over the years. Blaize died of natural causes in 1989, and his party splintered. The 1990 general election resulted in the election of the National Democratic Congress (NDC), with Prime Minister Nicholas Brathwaite at the helm. In 1995, Brathwaite, citing ill health, stepped down and was replaced by George Brizan, a founding member of the NDC.

PEOPLE AND CULTURE

The populations of Grenada, Carriacou, and Petit Martinique are, respectively, 91,000, 11,000, and 600.

Culturally, Grenadians take their cues from Africa, France, and England, and to a smaller extent from East Indian and other Asian cultures. The long history of British and French contention over the island has produced a mishmash Patois that is still used, although English is the official language. The Patois includes words and grammatical structures from English and some French and African holdovers. A good number of place names, such as Grand Anse and Marigot, are French. Carriacou is Carib.

Carnival takes its precedent from the French tradition and mixes it with African and Creole imagery. Grenada's Carnival takes place the second weekend of August and involves weeks of costume and feast preparation. Calypso singers hold local competitions that culminate in the August finals and the naming of Calypso Monarch. The three days of Carnival are filled with masquerades, marches, feasts, parties, singing, and street dancing. Many of the masquerade characters are rooted in African Creole and take subtle swipes at magic and obeah beliefs. Characters such as "Jab Jab Molassi" (molasses devil) and "La Jab Bless" (she-devil) delight the crowd.

NUTMEG

Nutmeg is the common term used for the fragrant spice from the fruit of the tropical evergreen tree *Myristica*, a member of the Magnolia order. When ripe, the small fruit, native to Maluku of Indonesia, yields a red seed which is dried and crushed to form the popular spice. The fleshy orange coating of the seed is also dried and crushed to form mace—the spice, not the anti-attack chemical spray.

Nutmeg was first introduced to Grenada in 1843 and has been grown commercially on the island since the 1860s. Today, Grenada is the world's largest single producer of nutmeg and provides nearly half the world's supply.

Carriacou Festival

Carriacou's Carnival takes place in February, during the traditional pre-Lenten season. Although smaller than Grenada's Carnival, it is no less energetic. It features street parades, male/female impersonation shows, and the spectacle of "Pierrots," characters dressed in period costumes reciting Shakespeare—and "beating" each other with big sticks should a mistake be made.

Carriacou's "Big Drum" or "Nation Dances" ceremonies also recall African heritage. Big Drum dancing involves costumed dancers moving to beats provided by drums and what are called "chac-chac" rattles. The drums, often rum kegs topped with stretched goatskin, are played at weddings, funerals, boat launchings, and upon the completion of a house.

African religious beliefs are blended with established Western religions such as Anglican, Methodist, Seventh-Day Adventist, and Roman Catholic. The Anglican church dominates.

GOVERNMENT AND ECONOMY

Government

Grenada is a parliamentary democracy and member of the Commonwealth, with Queen Elizabeth the nominal head of state represented on the island by a governor general. A prime minister heads the ruling party and government.

The legislature consists of a 15-member House of Representatives, elected from the islands' parishes and districts, and a 13-member appointed Senate.

Agriculture and Nutmeg

Grenada's economy is dependant on agriculture and overseas remittances. Nearly 90% of domestic exports involve agriculture, particularly nutmeg, of which Grenada is the world's largest single producer. Record nutmeg prices and a cartel arrangement with nutmeg-producer Indonesia in the 1980s strengthened the economy, as did a relatively negligible inflation rate. The cartel arrangement faltered and prices have remained unsteady for some years. About a third of the work force is involved in some sort of agricultural endeavor, and nearly 25% of the GDP is provided by agricultural industry. Other exports include mace (a nutmeg by-product), bananas, cocoa, and some tropical fruits and other spices. Bananas are Grenada's second most important export, and farmers have enjoyed healthy trading status with the U.K. due to favorable export agreements. The introduction of the European Community will eliminate those trade agreements, and Grenada is looking toward other export markets. Some sugarcane is grown, but it is no longer a major crop.

Tourism

Tourism, the island's second industry, has grown slowly and steadily since the 1983 military intervention. Following the restoration of democracy, U.S. aid also increased. The 9,000-foot (2,745-meter) airport at Point Salines opened in 1984, increasing the opportunities for international carriers to arrive with tourists, which has happened. About 90,000 tourists arrive by air annually. Cruise ship arrivals, a popular way to visit Grenada since the turn of the century, have increased from 80 ships in 1983 to 450 ships carrying nearly 200,000 passengers in 1993.

Carriacou has recently seen a 115% rise of visitors since 1992. The total number of hotel rooms, on both Carriacou and Grenada, has increased from 588 in 1983 to nearly 1,500 in 1994. There are no hotels on Petit Martinique.

SIGHTS

Most major roads in Grenada encircle the island rather than cut across it. Exceptions are the Grand Etang Road and several others that transit the central mountains. The roads, except on Carriacou, are generally good, although stretches along the west coast are still dicey. Major repairs, paid for with assistance from the U.S. and others, were underway during the 1980s; most have been completed.

Beaches

The leeward coast, particularly the area south of St. George's, is the site of many of Grenada's hotels and beaches. There are, however, an estimated 45 beaches, all public, along the 80 miles (128 km) of Grenada's coastline.

Grand Anse, a two-mile (three-km) stretch of sand just south of St. George's, is the island's most popular beach, particularly when cruise ships are visiting. The beach is lined with guesthouses and small hotels.

South of Grand Anse is **Morne Rouge Bay,** which also has a nice beach. **Petit Cabrits** and **Magazin** beaches and several others are south of the bay. The **L'Anse aux Epines** peninsula, east of the airport, hosts several good beaches as well as hotels and cottages.

In the north part of the island, the bay at **Sauters** is long and expansive. **Levera,** the national park, has a sometimes-rough beach, but it is very appealing. The eastern windward coast has beaches at **Menere Bay** and **La Tante Bay.**

Northern Grenada

About eight miles (13 km) north of St. George's is **Concord Falls,** a series of two. The first main cascade is accessible by car or by a hike from the main road, about a 45-minute walk. There is a changing room and swimming at the first falls. The second falls is about a 30-minute walk beyond the first. Beyond the falls a trail leads to **Fedon's Camp,** the headquarters of the 1795 slave-rebellion leader Julien Fedon. The campsite is now a national historical landmark. You can, if you'd like, make the hike to Grand Etang from Concord, but it's a rough, six-hour excursion.

North of Concord is **Dougaldston Estate** and the town of **Gouyave.** This area is the center of the nutmeg industry, and the estate offers a small tour of the spice factory. Nutmeg, as well as mace, cloves, and cinnamon, are dried and processed here; you may buy samples. The tour is free, conducted weekdays 9 a.m.-4 p.m. Gouyave, called "the town that never sleeps" for some reason, is a fishing village and parish capital.

Heading north you'll come to **Victoria,** another small, quiet fishing village with a couple of hotels and restaurants. A rock marked with Amerindian petroglyphs sits just offshore.

In the far north you'll find **La Morne des Sauteurs** ("Leapers Hill") and the 100-foot (30-meter) cliff where in 1651 a group of Caribs jumped to their deaths rather than submit to French encroachment (see "Leapers Hill" under "History," above).

East of Sauteurs is **Levera Bay,** and Levera Beach, part of a national park system. This area is developed for visitors, and you'll find trails for hiking, mangrove swamps, swimming, snorkeling, and snacks. The surf and currents are rough at times, particularly between the shore and the privately owned Sugar Loaf cay.

Windward Coast

The east coast is rougher than the west, yet you'll find several good beaches and points of interest. South of Levera is the shimmering **Lake Antoine,** a lake formed in a volcanic crater, and the **River Antoine Rum Distillery.** The circa 18th-century distillery is one of the oldest in the

islands and is still powered by a waterwheel. The rum is said to be exceptional, and you're allowed to tour the estate.

Grenville, at the near midpoint of the island's windward coast, is Grenada's second town, and a busy port. Several historical buildings still stand, including the stone Anglican Parish Church and the post office. The market here is lively on Saturdays and the local spice factory is open to the public.

Nearby is the old **Pearls Airport,** not in use since the completion of Point Salines International in 1984.

Inland from Grenville is **Mt. St. Catherine,** Grenada's highest point at 2,757 feet (840 meters). The mountain can be climbed; it is rough in places but not a difficult climb overall. The starting point is the village of **Mt. Hope,** west of Grenville. The first part of the climb takes you through old plantation land and forests and past the remains of a concrete delivery truck that made it up the mountainside but didn't make it back down. The path follows a donkey trail to the summit, where you'll be able to see the Grenadines to the north.

Farther south along the east coast is **Mount Carmel,** the island's highest waterfall, and the ruins of an 18th-century fort. Still farther south you can visit the **La Sagesse Protected Seascape,** an area of protected reefs, mangrove swamps, and beaches.

Interior and South

The Grand Etang Road cuts across the island from St. George's to Grenville and is perhaps one of the island's most striking drives. The road is paved but winding and twisted in places, and it's wise to use caution while driving.

The road cuts through misty rainforest and drier woodlands and the views alone are worth it. Still, you'll end up at the **Grand Etang National Park** forestry headquarters and visitors center. The center describes the flora and fauna of

BOB RACE

La Sagesse Rum Factory

the area, as well as the origins of the park's centerpiece, the **Grand Etang,** a 13-acre lake in the crater of an extinct volcano. You'll see the lake from the visitors center and understand why it's called "grand."

Several hiking trails start out from the visitor center. The **Morne la Baye Trail** is short and not difficult. The **Mt. Qua Qua Trail** will take some time and effort; it'll take more than an hour to cover it. Off the Mt. Qua Qua Trail is another trail that circles the lake. You can also walk to Fedon's Camp and Concord Falls from here, a sometimes arduous hike of nearly six hours.

The **Forestry Headquarters,** tel. (809) 442-7425, is open weekdays 8 a.m.-4 p.m.

From Grand Etang it's a drive or hike to the 50-foot (15-meter) **Annandale Falls,** a popular swimming, picnicking, and hiking area. There is a visitors center, tel. (809) 440-2452, here as well, open daily 8 a.m.-5 p.m.

The southern section of the island, with its light-sand beaches and airport, hosts much of the island's tourist activity; hotels, guesthouses, water-sports facilities, and restaurants are found throughout the area. On the southernmost coast, where a half-dozen dramatic peninsulas jut into

GRENADA

the sea, you'll find the resort town of L'Anse aux Epines.

Guided Tours

Much of the island is accessible without guides, but if you feel you'd like an organized tour, the following offer tours of the major sights as well as off-island tours of Carriacou and Petit Martinique. Prices, which include transport, drinks, and sometimes lunch, range US$20-60 per person for groups of four or more. **Arnold's Hike Grenada** and **Tour Grenada** have the same owners, tel. (809) 440-0531 or 440-2213, fax 440-4118. **Henry's Safari Tours,** tel. (809) 444-5313, fax 444-4847, offers island tours and taxi service.

ST. GEORGE'S

St. George's has long been called one of the Caribbean's most picturesque towns. The natural harbor is deep and features the **Carenage,** an inner harbor in the crater of an extinct volcano. The town's buildings, built up, down, and around the hills at the base of the central mountains, are old and reminiscent of the colonial period of pastels and red-tiled roofs. The blend is French colonial and English Georgian and Victorian architecture.

Port St. Louis was the name of the first settlement in the area, established by the French in 1650. The town was abandoned in 1706 and was later engulfed by The Lagoon part of the harbor. The French then built Fort Royal, which was occupied in 1762 by the British; the latter renamed it St. George's.

The Carenage, shaped like a thumb, is the town's center of activity. Here you'll find the cruise ship docks, shops, the **Grentel** (Grenada Telephone) offices, the **general post office,** the **Board of Tourism** office, tel. (809) 440-2279, fax 440-6637, and a cluster of restaurants and small cafes.

It's a wonderful place to spend and hour or so and to start an exploration of the city. Note the statue *Christ of the Deep* at the head of the harbor. The statue, a bronze replica of the original, was presented to the Grenadian people by the Italy-based Costa Line for their help in rescuing passengers and crew from a cruise liner that caught fire in the harbor in 1961. The inscription reads, in part, "In Grateful Remembrance of the Fraternal Christian Hospitality Shown to Passengers and Crew of the Italian Liner *Bianca C* Destroyed by Fire in This Harbor on October 22, 1961." The liner lies in 170 feet (52 meters) of water and may soon become a marine national park. Also note the damage to several buildings that were burned in a fire on the Carenage in 1990. Water taxis are available for those who would like to cross the Carenage on water rather than walk around it. Cost is about EC$1, worth it for the view.

The **Grenada National Museum** is located in the barracks and prison of a circa 1704 French fortification to the west of the Carenage. The museum contains exhibits of Amerindian artifacts and culture, a telegraph machine installed on the island in 1871, and one of the Empress Joséphine's presumably numerous bathtubs. The museum is open Mon.-Fri. 9 a.m.-4:30 p.m., and Saturday 10 a.m.-1.30 p.m. Admission is EC$1.

The **Esplanade** runs along the ocean on the west side of town. A quick way to get to the Esplanade is through the **Sendall Tunnel,** built in 1895 to save overladen donkeys from climbing over the hill. On the Esplanade you'll find fish and meat markets and shops. On Granby Street you'll run into the large, sprawling, and oft-photographed **Market Square,** busiest on Saturday.

Fort George was a French fort built in 1705 that now houses police headquarters. Some cannons are still in place, and there are platforms from which you can view the city. Some signs describe the history of the fort. Fort George was the scene of the murders of Maurice Bishop and his followers in 1983.

Several historical buildings are found in town. Along Church Street you'll find **St. Andrew's Presbyterian Kirk,** dating back to 1830.

St. George's Anglican Cathedral was completed in 1825. **St. George's Catholic Cathedral,** built in 1884, has a church tower that dates back to 1818. **York House,** now Grenada's seat of Parliament and Supreme Court, is a circa 1800 structure. Next door is the

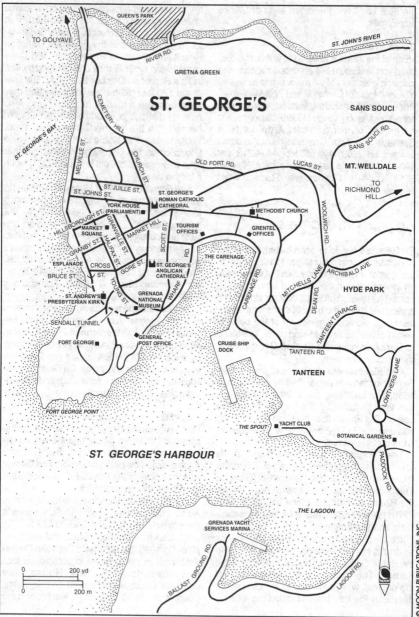

ST. GEORGE'S

Registry Building, circa 1780. The **Methodist Church** on Green Street is the city's oldest church, dating to 1820.

On Tyrrel Street is the **Marryshow House,** built early this century. This is the home of Grenada's **Folk Theatre,** which presents plays, dance, and music. For a schedule of programs call (809) 440-2451.

On the outskirts of town are several forts' ruins open to the public. **Fort Frederick** and **Fort Matthew** were started in 1783 by the French, later completed by British occupants.

CARRIACOU

The 13-square-mile (34-square-km) island of Carriacou has a population of about 11,000. Of this number, 1,000 live in Hillsborough, the capital. The rest live primarily in the windward countryside, which has a Scottish heritage, and in L'Esterre, which retains aspects of the French colonial days. The island is low-lying, dry, and green, a relaxing and easy place to explore. Attractions include several small bays and beaches, as well as interesting outlying cays. The name of the island means "Land of Reefs," and diving is also a big draw. **Tanki's Watersport Paradise,** tel. (809) 443-8406, is one of several diving outfits on the island.

Carriacou was first settled by Amerindian Arawaks and Caribs, then Frenchmen who, in the 17th century, used the island as a base for turtle hunting. Eventually the British and Scottish moved in, and plantations grew. The main crop became cotton, followed by sugarcane, coffee, cocoa, and indigo. Today's main industries are fishing, subsistence farming, and to a smaller extent, ship building and repair.

The islanders have retained aspects of their African heritage, importantly in the Big Drum dances (see "Carriacou Festival" under "People and Culture," above) that seem unique to the island. Other events include the traditional pre-Lenten Carnival and the popular annual (August) **Carriacou Regatta,** begun in 1964.

Hillsborough

The capital city of Hillsborough is a long, ramshackle town, built along Main Street on Hillsborough Bay on the leeward side of the island. Here you'll find the tourism office, banks, a supermarket, bakeries, cafes, rum shops, an outdoor market, the jetty, the police station, the post office, a small seaside park, and several guesthouses. The town is quiet and dusty, even tarnished, yet retains a turn-of-the-century West Indian charm. Hurricane Janet whipped through the island in September 1955, and, islanders

MORE CARRIACOU HOTELS AND GUESTHOUSES

Rates per s, EP when applicable, winter

NAME	(809)	FAX	LOCATION	TARIFF
Alexis Apartment Hotel	443-7179	N/A	Tyrrel Bay	moderate
Bay View Holiday Apartments	443-7403	N/A	Tyrrel Bay	moderate
Caribbee Inn	443-7380	443-8142	Prospect	luxury
Hope's Inn	443-7547	N/A	L'Esterre	moderate
Scraper Holiday Cottages	443-7403	N/A	Tyrell Bay	budget-moderate

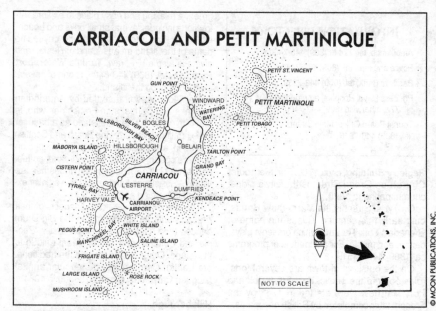

CARRIACOU AND PETIT MARTINIQUE

PETIT ST. VINCENT

GUN POINT

WINDWARD
WATERING
BAY

PETIT MARTINIQUE

HILLSBOROUGH BAY   SILVER BEACH   BOGLES

PETIT TOBAGO

MABORYA ISLAND   HILLSBOROUGH   BELAIR

TARLTON POINT

CISTERN POINT   GRAND BAY

CARRIACOU

TYRREL BAY   L'ESTERRE   DUMFRIES

HARVEY VALE   KENDEACE POINT

CARRIACOU
AIRPORT

PEGUS POINT   WHITE ISLAND

MANCHINEEL BAY   SALINE ISLAND

FRIGATE ISLAND

LARGE ISLAND   ROSE ROCK

MUSHROOM ISLAND

NOT TO SCALE

© MOON PUBLICATIONS, INC.

say, things haven't been the same since. Much of Main Street appears to be under construction.

Stop in at the **Carriacou Museum** (tel. 809-443-8288), a branch of the Carriacou Historical Society, on Patterson Street. The museum, which also houses a library, has displays of Arawak and Carib artifacts, an old telephone exchange, and photos of the hurricane damage. Curator Cassandra Cox Peters is a good source of island information. The museum is open Mon.-Fri. 9:30 a.m.-3:45 p.m.; admission is EC$5.

Island Sights
Also on the island are a scenic overlook and plantation ruins at **Belair,** historical sites at **Dumfries,** and the **Canute Calliste Art Gallery** in **L'Esterre.** Calliste is a well-known folk artist and local personality.

Island guided tours can be organized through **Carriacou Nature Tour & Trail Project,** tel. (809) 443-8064 or 443-7134, in Belvedere.

Carriacou Accommodations
A few basic but comfortable hotels and a half dozen guesthouses are found on the island, most in Hillsborough.

The **Silver Beach Resort,** Silver Beach, Carriacou, Grenada, West Indies, tel. (809) 443-7337, fax 443-7156, is on the beach with views to Union Island. The hotel has 18 units, simple but clean, some self-catering, and a bar, restaurant, and **Silver Beach Diving,** tel. (809) 443-7882. Good deal. Moderate. **Cassada Bay Resort,** Belmont, Carriacou, Grenada, West Indies, tel. (809) 443-7494, fax 443-7672, has 14 units overlooking the small White Island, Large Island, Saline Island, and Frigate Island cays on the island's south shore. Moderate.

Millie's Guesthouse, Church St., Hillsborough, Carriacou, Grenada, West Indies, tel. (809) 443-7310, fax 443-8107, is new and near the center of town. Budget. **Peace Haven Guesthouse,** Hillsborough, Carriacou, Grenada, West Indies, tel. (809) 443-7475 or 443-8365, also sits on Main Street, right on the bay. A kitchen is available for guests. Three of the six rooms share a bath and toilet. Budget. Nearby, also on Main Street, is the **Callaloo Restaurant,** tel. (809) 443-8004, known for its West Indian cuisine.

Down Island Villa Rentals, Hillsborough, Carriacou, Grenada, West Indies, tel. and fax (809) 443-8182, are agents for local apartments and villas.

Getting There and Around
Carriacou Airport, tel. (809) 443-7362, is the local airstrip, located a few minute's drive west of Hillsborough. As a matter of fact, the road from Hillsborough to the south and west crosses the airstrip; it's a small one.

You need not fly through Grenada to get to Carriacou. **LIAT,** tel. (809) 443-7362, connects the island with Antigua, Barbados, Dominica, Trinidad, Union Island, and several others, with stops. There are customs and immigration facilities at the airstrip.

Minibuses run all over the island and are found at the jetty and market in Hillsborough. You can also flag them down. Cost for a minibus from the jetty or market to all points will not exceed EC$2. There are no real routes, or schedules, but life manages to go on. Taxis are also available everywhere and will charge set rates. From the airport to Hillsborough, the fare is EC$14 or US$5, to Windward EC$27 or US$10. From Hillsborough to Belmont, the recommended fare is EC$27 or US$10.

Rental cars are available through **Barba's,** tel. (809) 443-7454, in Tyrrel Bay in Harvey Vale, or at the **Silver Beach Resort,** tel. (809) 443-7337.

SPORTS

Water Sports
Water sports are a main attraction in Grenada. The scuba diving is said to be good, and opportunities for snorkeling and sailing, particularly with the Grenadines nearby, are numerous. Most hotels can organize the usual sailboating, windsurfing, water-skiing, and other water sports.

For charter sailing, go to **The Moorings,** tel. (809) 444-4439 or 444-4549, at Secret Harbour; or **Seabreeze Yacht Charters,** tel. (809) 444-4924, in the Spice Island Marine Center on Prickly Bay, both in L'Anse aux Epines.

For deep-sea fishing, call **Evans Chartering Services,** tel. (809) 444-4422.

Divers have several options. Favorite dives include the small cay called Kick 'em Jenny, where coral and marine life is said to be plentiful, and the *Bianca C,* the Italian liner that sank in St. George's Harbour in 1961. This second dive is for seasoned divers and strong swimmers only, as the currents are apparently unpredictable and strong. Call **Dive Grenada,** tel. (809) 444-4371, fax 444-4800, at the Renaissance Hotel in Grand Anse; or **Grand Anse Aquatics,** tel.

MORE GRENADA HOTELS

Rates per s, EP when applicable, winter

NAME	(809)	FAX	LOCATION	TARIFF
Bailey's Inn	440-2912	440-4179	Springs	moderate
Calabash Hotel	444-4334	444-4804	L'Anse aux Epines	luxury
Coral Cove	444-4422	444-4718	L'Anse aux Epines	moderate
Fox Inn	444-4123	444-4177	Point Salines	moderate
Grenada Renaissance	444-4371	444-4800	Grand Anse	luxury
Hibiscus Hotel	444-4233	440-6632	Grand Anse	moderate
L'Anse aux Epines Cottages	444-4565	444-2802	L'Anse aux Epines	budget-moderate
Twelve Degrees North	444-4580	444-4580	L'Anse aux Epines	luxury
Victoria Hotel	444-9367	444-8814	Victoria	budget
Villamar Holiday Resort	444-4716	440-4124	L'Anse aux Epines	moderate

MORE GRENADA GUESTHOUSES AND APARTMENTS

Rates per s, EP when applicable, winter

NAME	(809)	FAX	LOCATION	TARIFF
Mafiken Apartments	444-4255	444-4847	Grand Anse	moderate
No Problem Apartments	444-4634	444-2803	True Blue	moderate
Palm Grove Guest House	444-4578	N/A	Grand Anse	budget
Roydon's Guest House	444-4476	N/A	Grand Anse	moderate
St. Ann's Guest House	440-2717	N/A	Paddock	budget
Wave Crest Apartments	444-4116	444-4847	St. George's	budget

(809) 444-4129, at the Coyoba Resort in Grand Anse.

Golf

Golfers have few options. The **Grenada Golf and Country Club,** tel. (809) 444-4128, is a nine-hole course at Grand Anse. The all-inclusive **LaSource,** in Grand Anse, has a private course.

ACCOMMODATIONS

Many of Grenada's 1,500 hotel rooms are found in small, unpretentious hotels and guesthouses. There are several new, large resorts, and there will be still more in the future. But for now, the trend remains to keep things simple and easily accessed by both Grenadians and tourists. The **Grenada Board of Tourism** approves and recommends hotels that comply with their standards, and the **Grenada Hotel Association** recommends members of their association. See the "Information Directory" chart at the end of this section to contact either of these organizations.

Accommodations will add a 10% service charge (in lieu of tipping, unless you feel you've received exceptional service). An eight percent tax is added to all hotels. Tax is also added to food and beverages.

Larger hotels will accept credit cards; small inns and guesthouses may not. It's best to call ahead to confirm.

The following categories refer to accommodation prices per person, per night, in high season (roughly 15 Dec.-15 April): **Luxury** US$100 or more, **Moderate** US$50-100, **Budget** US$50 or less.

Hotels

LaSource, P.O. Box 852, St. George's, Grenada, West Indies, tel. (809) 444-2556, North American tel. (800) 544-2883, fax 444-2561, is a new all-inclusive spa resort on Pink Gin Beach near Point Salines. The amenities include saunas, Swedish massages, salt loofah rubs, facials, and seaweed wraps. Sports available include golf, tennis, fencing, and archery. Luxury.

Ramada Renaissance Hotel, P.O. Box 441, St. George's, Grenada, West Indies, tel. (809) 444-4371/5, fax 444-4800, is the largest hotel on Grenada, with 186 rooms set on 20 acres. Located on Grand Anse Beach, the hotel is top-of-the-line and includes two restaurants, a pool, bars, gift shops, and a wide array of water sports. Luxury.

La Sagesse Nature Centre, P.O. Box 44, St. George's, Grenada, West Indies, tel. (809) 444-6458, fax 444-4847, has only three rooms, but the setting, an old plantation house on a bay in the southeast, is near-perfect. Facilities include a restaurant and bar, a nearby bird sanctuary, and hiking trails. Moderate.

Mamma's Lodge, P.O. Box 248, St. George's, Grenada, West Indies, tel. (809) 440-1459, fax 440-7788, is located on the Lagoon Road just outside downtown St. George's. The small guesthouse is clean, has nine rooms, and is located nearby the famous **Mamma's** restaurant and bar, tel. (809) 440-1459, easily one of the Lesser Antilles' top spots for eclectic West Indian cuisine. Here you can taste *mani-*

cou (opossum), armadillo, booby, sea urchin, and "oil down," a breadfruit in coconut milk. Mamma, alas, has died, but her tradition of fine (if bizarre to the tourist tongue) menus remains strong. No credit cards at Mamma's. Budget.

Camping
Camping in Grenada is discouraged—the lack of facilities and security make it difficult to regulate.

Villa Rentals
In the U.S., **Island Hideaways,** 1317 Rhode Island Ave. N.W., Suite 503, Washington, DC 20005, tel. (800) 832-2302, fax (202) 667-3392, lists Grenada properties.

FOOD

Grenada's restaurants are quite good, ranging from fast-food chains (the ubiquitous **KFC** is on Granby Street, St. George's) to elegant eateries. Spices, of course, and West Indian cuisine are the attraction here. Try conch (*lambi*) or the wide range of meats: *manicou,* armadillo, sea birds, goat, and even turtle are offered.

Restaurants will add eight percent tax and often a 10% service charge, and not all will take credit cards. It's best to call ahead to check. Many of the island's best restaurants are located in hotels, or in the St. George's and Grand Anse area. The following categories are based on per-person entree prices: **Expensive** US$25 or more, **Moderate** US$10-25, **Inexpensive** US$10 or less.

Nutmeg, tel. (809) 440-2539, is located on the Carenage and is very popular. Hamburgers, sandwiches, and West Indian fare are served. Moderate. **Rudolph's,** tel. (809) 440-2241, also on the Carenage, serves European and West Indian fare. Closed Sunday, no credit cards. Moderate. **The Red Crab,** tel. (809) 444-4424, is in L'Anse aux Epines and specializes in seafood, lobster, and steaks. Seating is inside or out. Very popular, with live music on Friday. Moderate-Expensive.

Morne Fendue Great House, tel. (809) 440-9330, at Sauteurs is a good place to stop for lunch when touring the north of the island. The lunch buffet includes local recipes—pepperpot soup is recommended—from owner Betty Mas-

coll. Her nutmeg-laden rum punches are renowned. The budget guesthouse, an old plantation house, is typically West Indian and features four rooms. No credit cards are accepted here, and only lunch is served. Moderate.

GETTING THERE

By Air
Point Salines International Airport is the point of entry and accepts major international airlines. **BWIA,** tel. (809) 440-3818, flies direct from New York, Baltimore, Miami, Toronto, Zurich, Frankfurt, and London. BWIA is also a connector to Barbados and Trinidad and Tobago.

British Airways, tel. (809) 444-2796, flies once a week from London. **American Airlines,** tel. (809) 444-2222, flies from San Juan, which is connected with major North American cities. **Air Canada** flies to Antigua and Barbados and connects to Grenada via **LIAT,** tel. (809) 440-

Grande Anse, one of Grenada's 45 white-sand beaches

GRENADA TOURIST BOARD

sign welcoming visitors to Carriacou

2796. LIAT is also the major connector for the rest of the Lesser Antilles' islands.

Charter flights to and from various islands, including the Grenadines, are offered by **Helenair,** tel. (809) 444-4401; **Airlines of Carriacou,** tel. (809) 444-4425; and **Aeretuyl,** tel. (809) 444-4732.

The **departure tax** from Grenada and Carriacou is EC$35 or US$13.

GETTING AROUND

Taxis

Taxis are unmetered and rates are set by the government. Typical fare from Point Salines to L'Anse aux Epines is about EC$27 or US$10. To St. George's costs about EC$32 or US$12. From St. George's to Grand Etang and Grenville and return the fare is EC$135 or US$50. If you choose to use a taxi for the day, cost will be about EC$40 or US$15 per hour. Rates are based on four persons per vehicle and are posted at hotels and the taxi stand on the Carenage. Add about one-third to all rates after 6 p.m.

A water-taxi service operates from the Carenage to Grand Anse, a nice way of making the short trip.

Buses

Buses and minibuses are inexpensive and are the typical West Indian wild ride through paradise. You'll recognize them by their personalized names ("Mannish" or "Jesus Mine"), usually painted on the front or mounted on the windshield. Buses to the outer island depart from the Market and the Esplanade in St. George's. Or you may simply flag them down. Schedules are in turmoil, so the best way to get there is to ask. Buses rarely run after 8 p.m. or on Sunday and holidays.

Car and Motorcycle Rentals

Rental cars are easy to organize, starting at EC$108-122 or US$40-45 per day, less for a week's rental, with unlimited mileage. It's not cheap, but this is the best way to tour the island. Taxis are expensive, and buses, although fun, are not very efficient. You'll need to purchase a local driving permit, which can be organized by the rental company. Cost is EC$30. Remember to drive on the left.

In St. George's call **Avis,** tel. (809) 440-3936; **Budget Rent-a-Car,** airport tel. (809) 444-1620, St. George's tel. 440-2778, fax 440-4174; **Coyaba Car Rentals,** tel. (809) 444-4129; **David's Car Rentals,** airport tel. (809) 440-2399 or 440-3038; or **MCR Car Rentals,** tel. (809) 440-5398, fax 440-6692.

Maitland Motor Rentals, tel. (809) 444-4022, fax 440-4119, rents Yamaha motorcycles as well as cars.

Ferry Service

Interisland ferries operate between the Carenage in St. George's and the Hillsborough jetty on Carriacou. The trip takes three or four hours, depending on the seas.

The following schedules have been operative for some time, but it's wise to check ahead at the docks. The *Alexia II* and *Adelaide B* depart Grenada to Carriacou Wednesday and Saturday at 9:30 a.m. The return trip is on Thursday and Monday, also at 9:30 a.m. The *Alexia III* departs Grenada to Carriacou Tuesday at 9:30 a.m., Friday at 11:00 a.m., and Sunday at 7:00 a.m. The return trips are on Wednesday and Saturday at 9:30 a.m., and 5:00 p.m. on Sunday. Fare is EC$20 one-way, EC$30 return.

The *Little Desrine, Edna David,* and the *Winnifred* sail from Grenada to Trinidad on Tuesday at 7 p.m. and return Friday at 8 a.m. The *Wisdom* departs Carriacou for Union Island on Thursday and Monday at 1 p.m.

Flying

Flights are available from Port Salines to Carriacou Airport on LIAT, which operates a daily 15-minute hop. Cost is about US$31 one-way, double that for return.

MONEY, HOURS, AND COMMUNICATION

Currency and Banks

The Eastern Caribbean dollar, Grenada's currency, currently trades at EC$2.70 = US$1. Many small businesses and taxi drivers will accept U.S. and Canadian dollars, but don't always count on it. Your change will most likely be in EC dollars. Credit cards and traveler's checks are accepted in most hotels, restaurants, and boutiques, but not at the markets and small shops.

Money can be exchanged at hotels and banks, with banks giving the best rates. Banking hours vary slightly, but are generally Mon.-Thurs. 8 a.m.-2 p.m., with extra Friday hours 2:30-5 p.m.

Banks can be found in St. George's, Grand Anse, Gouyave, Grenville, Sauteurs, and Carriacou, and include, with their St. George's telephone numbers, **Barclays,** tel. (809) 440-3232; **The Grenada Cooperative Bank,** tel. (809) 444-2111; **The National Commercial Bank,** tel. (809) 440-3566; and **Scotiabank,** tel. (809)

INFORMATION DIRECTORY

GRENADA BOARD OF TOURISM

The Carenage, St. George's, Grenada, West Indies, tel. (809) 440-2279, fax 440-6637.

820 2nd Ave., Suite 900D, New York, NY 10017, tel. (800) 927-9554 or (212) 687-9554, fax (212) 573-9731.

439 University Ave., Suite 820, Toronto, Ontario M5G 1Y8, tel. (416) 595-1339, fax 595-8278.

1 Collingham Gardens, London SW5 0HW, tel. (071) 370-5164, fax 370-7040.

OTHER

Grenada Hotel Association, Ross Point Inn, Lagoon Rd., St. George's, Grenada, West Indies, tel. (800) 322-1753 or (809) 444-1353, North America tel. (800) 223-9815, NY tel. (212) 545-8469, fax (809) 444-4847.

Police Emergencies, tel. 911.

Ambulance, tel. 434.

St. George's General Hospital, tel. (809) 440-2051/2/3.

Mitchells' Pharmacy (open until 9 p.m.), Grand Anse Shopping Centre, tel. (809) 444-4845.

Astral Travel and Tours, The Carenage, tel. (809) 440-5180.

American Express, Church St., St. George's, tel. (809) 444-2945.

FedEx, The Carenage, St. George's, tel. (809) 440-2206 or 440-1619.

444-1917. In St. George's, several banks are located on Halifax and Church streets.

Hours, Phones, News

Most businesses are open Mon.-Fri. 8 a.m.-noon and 1-4 p.m., and Saturday 8 a.m.-noon. Much of Grenada shuts down on Sunday, and this includes restaurants not attached to hotels. Some shops keep extra hours to accommodate cruise ship traffic.

Grenada uses an "809" telephone **area code.** Offices of **Cable and Wireless** and **Grentel,** tel. (809) 440-1000, are on the Carenage, and are available for phone cards, and phone and fax services, including AT&T Direct. Hours are Mon.-Sat. 7 a.m.-7 p.m. and Sunday 4-6 p.m.

Grenada's newspapers are sophisticated and contain quite a bit of editorial writing—surprising for an island of this size, perhaps not so surprising given its history over the past decade.

Among them are the weeklies *The Grenadian Voice, Grenada Today,* and *The Informer.* Cost is EC$1.25.

The general post office is located on the Carenage, open Mon.-Thurs. 8 a.m.-3:30 p.m., until 4:30 p.m. on Friday.

BARBADOS

Barbados is, in many ways, a Caribbean anomaly. The island is not technically a Caribbean island at all—it lies outside the main Lesser Antilles chain, 180 miles (290 km) northeast of Trinidad, floating alone in the Atlantic Ocean like a stray pup.

Like many of its neighbors, Barbados was settled by Amerindian Arawaks and, later, Caribs. Yet the Caribs uncharacteristically abandoned it for reasons unclear.

Even more, Barbados was never visited by Columbus, but rather by Portuguese explorers, who made no substantive claims. The island was subsequently a British possession for its entire colonial history and today retains more British customs and sensibilities—afternoon teas, cricket, formal dinners—than you'll see anywhere south of the Bahamas.

It's a relatively prosperous island, free of the pervasive, grinding poverty often seen in its neighbors. There are, of course, the haves and the have nots, yet standards set by government in education have resulted in high employment and numerous university graduates. Literature and the arts are held in high esteem, as evidenced by the country's numerous and active theater and dance companies. Yet, the ingredients that add the juice to most of our Caribbean vacations—sun, sea, sand, and vibrant cultures—are found in abundance on this popular destination.

THE LAND

The teardrop-shaped island comprises 166 square miles (430 square km) of coral limestone-capped hills and valleys. It is an ancient island, older than its volcanic neighbors in the Windwards, and flat. The highest point on the island, **Mt. Hillaby,** is only 1,115 feet (340 meters) above sea level. The hills tend to undulate rather than jut, and tame valleys offer the type of terrain perfect for growing sugarcane, which Barbados did and does in abundance.

The windward east coast is pounded by the open Atlantic—on a map it appears concave, almost gutted—and has several spots with dramatic cliffs and hidden bays, particularly at **Bathsheba.** The south and west coasts have calmer waters and host most of the island's resorts and hotels.

The central sections of the island are characterized by rolling valleys, farmland, and small settlements. Forests are dry and scrubby in places, dotted with open pastures, sugarcane fields, and few rivers and streams. The island's terrain, in a way, presents a mediocrity and sameness that may disappoint anyone interested in mountain hiking or rainforest explorations.

Barbados is about 21 miles (34 km) north to south, and 14 miles (22 km) at its widest point.

HISTORY

Due to its removed location, Barbados was disengaged from the wars and hand-changing between European powers that disrupted life in its Lesser Antilles neighbors.

Early Settlers

The island's first settlers were the Arawaks and later the warrior Caribs, and it is quite possible that the Portuguese explorer Pedro a Campos encountered Caribs when he first explored the island in 1536. Not much is recorded about early Portuguese and Carib encounters, and it appears that the Portuguese did little but populate the island with pigs intended for use as food by passing ships. And, importantly, they bestowed the name Los Barbados ("The Bearded Ones") upon the island, thought to refer to the dark, aerial, beard-like roots seen hanging from the island's fig trees.

By the time a party of 80 English settlers and their slaves landed on the island in 1627, the land was uninhabited. The English established a settlement at Holetown, on the west coast, and set about cultivating the land. It was around this time, in 1639, that the island established its first governing body, the House of Assembly.

With their feet firmly planted, the English decided to import more slaves. And indentured laborers from the working classes of Scotland and Ireland fled England for Barbados and the Caribbean, under duress of the ongoing struggles between Oliver Cromwell and King Charles I. With all the available labor and a terrain well-suited for sugarcane, plantations grew rapidly. In the eyes of many, Barbados would come to define the industry.

Rumbullion

The great plantocracies were in the hands of a few wealthy, often absent landowners. So great was the culture established around sugarcane and its by-products that the word "rum" is thought to have originated in the processing mills of Barbados. Some contend it is an abbreviation of the word "rumbullion," used to describe the effect of the alcohol on those who imbibed.

Planters were firmly entrenched by the 1650s, and the number of slaves imported to work the sugarcane plantations, by now the island's sole industry, greatly outnumbered the whites. Harsh treatment, in part due to the planters' paranoia and in part simply because that was the way blacks were treated, succeeded in producing that which the planters had hoped to suppress: slave rebellion.

Rebellion

In the late 17th and early 18th centuries, slave revolts reverberated throughout the Greater and Lesser Antilles. Jamaica, Haiti, and Martinique saw major uprisings. Barbados saw revolts in 1672, 1696, and 1702. On Easter 1816, a slave known as Bussa, from Bayley's Plantation in St. Philip, led the island's largest revolt.

The revolt grew from an ironic and tragic rumor declaring that emancipation had indeed been granted and that the plantation owners were refusing to acknowledge it. Bussa is today represented in a statue, on the outskirts of Bridgetown, honoring the true 1834 Emancipation. All the revolts were summarily and harshly squashed by the government. Sugar prevailed, and so did slavery, until the 1834 abolition.

Modern Times

For the remainder of the 19th century, freed slaves and their descendants drifted away from the sugarcane fields. Many went to work on canal construction in Panama, others went elsewhere in the Caribbean and the Americas. The Barbados economy began to rely on remittances from these expatriate Barbadians. By the early 20th century, the Panama canal was completed, and Barbados found itself in the same state as many of its neighbors—an economic backwash of diminishing importance to its colonial power, a power that was at that time dealing with the looming specter of European war.

As happened in many of the islands, the industrial revolution, then WW I, then the worldwide Great Depression, all combined to engender the growth of trade unions and political parties. Barbados's first large political party was the Barbados Progressive League, established in 1938 under the Oxford-educated lawyer Grantley Adams. Through the work of this party, and others, universal suffrage was granted in the '50s.

In 1958 Barbados joined the West Indies Federation with Sir Grantley Adams as chief minister. The federation was dissolved four years later, and agitation for independence led to elections. Independence was granted on 30 November 1966, with Errol Barrow as prime minister.

In 1985, then-Prime Minister Tom Adams (son of Grantley Adams) died in office. He was succeeded by, once again, Prime Minister Errol Barrow, who died in office two years later. Barrow was then followed by Prime Minister Erskine Sandiford.

With Sandiford's health in question, general elections were held in September 1994. The Barbados Labor Party, under economist Owen Arthur, emerged victorious.

PEOPLE AND CULTURE

The population of the Barbados is roughly 255,000. On an island of 166 square miles (430 square km), this makes for a high density rate—roughly 1,536 people per square mile.

The Amerindian influences on Barbadian (Bajan, in the local dialect) culture were not substantial. No place names and relatively few artifacts indicate their presence. Spanish and French influences also on neighboring Windward Islands were negligible. The island sensibility is a product of two primary cultures, British and African.

Nearly 80% of Barbados's citizens are descendants of African slaves. The small white population includes descendants of the "poor Whites" (in the past derisively called "red legs"), the Scottish Highlanders who fled to the island during Cromwell's purges and eventually settled in the northeast **Scotland District.**

A mixed-race group exists, as it does on all islands where slaves were kept—and it has grown. East Indians and Asians live in small communities, most in Bridgetown.

British culture and custom is evident, so much so that the country has been called "more English than England." Children attend school in crisp uniforms, white-wigged magistrates debate in court, and cricket is played with a fervor that borders on the non-secular.

Religions cover the range from Protestant to Jewish to Roman Catholic, yet 70% of the country is Anglican. The government infrastructure, the local architecture, the elaborate parade dress of the Royal Barbados Police Band, the afternoon teas, and the language, all reflect British influence. A Patois is spoken that uses English. It is very rapid English, with words picked up from around the Caribbean and from Africa.

Literature

Devotion to English, coupled with West Indian sensitivities, is exhibited by several Barbadian literary lights, who have affected regional and world literature. Novelist George Lamming, born in Barbados in 1927, often explores the dilemmas of race and culture confronting Caribbean peoples living overseas. Lamming's works include a critically acclaimed first novel, *In the Castle of My Skin* (1953), and *Season of Adventure* (1960).

Frank Collymore (1893-1980), a poet and short-story writer, was influential in the Caribbean literary scene during the heyday of 1930s nationalism. His many volumes include a posthumous collection of short stories called *The Man Who Loved Attending Funerals and Other Stories* (1993). His major legacy to writing is the Barbadian literary magazine *Bim,* which he established in 1942 and edited for most of his life. Over its long life (*Bim* is still published), the magazine has printed and promoted the work of major West Indian literary talents.

Several Bajan customs hearken back, if not directly to Africa days, at least to slave days. One is the continuing use of chattel houses, aptly named for people who were once regarded as property. Chattel houses were slave quarters, small wooden multi-roofed houses, often on stilts, that were designed to be moved from plantation to plantation as slaves were bought and sold. The design, though modified, is still used today, and it is not unusual to see an advert in the real estate classifieds: "Chattel house for sale. Must be removed by end of month."

Folk Groups

Local theater groups perform plays and dances, often depicting the vagaries of love and life in the West Indies. Check the radios and newspapers for performances by **Sistren,** an all-female theater group that performs in Bajan dialect.

The **National Cultural Foundation** sponsors cultural festivals throughout the year. One of the largest is the **National Independence Festival of the Creative Arts,** a November festival that culminates in Independence Day (30 November) performances of music, dance, art, and drama. For more information on the foundation or its festivals, call Barbados Tourism Authority at (809) 427-2623.

Holidays and Festivals

The annual **Crop Over Festival** is Barbados's nod to the sugarcane heydays. The July-August festival celebrates the sugarcane harvest and features many of the lively excesses of the pre-Lenten carnivals of Trinidad and Tobago, St. Lucia, and the French islands. From mid-

July, calypsonians perform in tents around the countryside. The week of Crop Over features the crowning of the Calypso Monarch, a large Bridgetown Market Day with local Bajan cooking, and the climactic Kadooment Day, when masqueraders and singers pour into the streets of Bridgetown for parades, dancing, drinking, and fireworks.

The **Oistins Fish Festival** takes place on Easter weekend and celebrates Barbados's links to the sea as well as the 1652 establishment of the "Charter of Barbados." The celebrations include boat racing, fishing displays, fish-boning contests, and food displays.

National holidays include Christmas, Boxing Day, New Year's Day, Easter, **May Day** (first Monday in May), **Whit Monday, United Nations Day** (October), and the 30 November **Independence Day.**

GOVERNMENT AND ECONOMY

Barbados has a high literacy rate and, subsequently, one of the highest per capita incomes in the Caribbean. The government pays tuition for all Barbadians attending the Cave Hill campus of the regional University of the West Indies. The country also has a teacher training college, a community college, and a polytechnic institute.

Tourism
Sugarcane and its by-products were once the economic bedrock of the country; now tourism has taken its place. Tourism is the country's major foreign exchange earner, contributing 12% of the GDP and employing roughly 13% of the labor force. About 450,000 people visit the island each year, not counting another 433,000 cruise ship passengers. About a third of those overnight visitors are from the U.S., about 13% from Canada. There are 150 hotels and 14,500 beds in the country, and that figure is growing. The government is currently investing US$6 million in remodeling the cruise ship port area of Bridgetown to accommodate some 20 duty-free and sundry shops.

Manufacturing
Light manufacturing of goods such as garments, furniture, and electronic products accounts for about 10% of the GDP. Agriculture, in which sugarcane is still the principal cash product, represents seven percent of the GDP. Fishing is still primarily a subsistence industry, with local fishermen providing provisions for local and hotel consumption.

Government
Barbados is an independent member of the Commonwealth. The Queen is the titular head of state, represented on the island by a governor general. Parliament comprises two houses, a Lower House of Assembly with 27 elected members, and an Upper House of Assembly with 21 appointed members. The government is led by a prime minister, leader of the majority party, currently Owen Arthur of the Barbados Labour Party (BLP). The strongest opposition party is the Democratic Labour Party (DLP).

Today Barbados has the third-oldest established government in the British Commonwealth.

SIGHTS

Beaches
South and west coast beaches tend to be less rough than windward side waters, and this is where much of the tourism industry has set up shop. All beaches are public, but some have difficult access due to hotels. Not all beaches have facilities, but many feature the ubiquitous pseudo-Rastas peddling their wares up and down the shore line. Annoying, but mostly harmless.

Note: Bardados has experienced incidents of petty theft and pickpocketing in and around beaches and tourist areas. While Barbados is not dangerous, you would be well-advised to lock your rental vehicle, watch your valuables at the beach, and avoid walking along isolated stretches of beach at night.

The west coast, north of Bridgetown, is in effect one long beach. Route 1 runs along the coast from Bridgetown to north of **Speighstown.** Stop at **Brighton, Gibbs Beach,** and **Heywoods** for good swimming.

South of Bridgetown is Carlisle Bay, another series of beaches fronted by hotels and apartment accommodations. **Needham's Point** is popular, and a favorite with locals. **Accra Beach,**

BARBADOS

ATLANTIC OCEAN

ARCHER'S BAY
NORTH POINT

ST. LUCY
CUCKHOLD POINT
ST. NICHOLAS ABBEY
GAY'S COVE

FUSTIC
BENTHAM'S

SIX MEN'S BAY
MORGAN LEWIS WINDMILL

ST. PETER
FARLEY HILL NATIONAL PARK AND BARBADOS WILDLIFE RESERVE

HEYWOODS BEACH

SPEIGHTSTOWN
BELLEPLAINE

GIBBS BAY
ST. ANDREW
SCOTLAND

ST. JAMES
MT. HILLABY
DISTRICT

MOSE BOTTOM
BATHSHEBA BAY

ORANGE HILL
BATHSHEBA

FOLKESTONE UNDERWATER PARK AND MUSEUM
FLOWER FOREST
ANDROMEDA GARDENS

HOLETOWN
WELCHMAN HALL GULLY NATIONAL PARK
HARRISON CAVE
ST. JOSEPH
BATH
CONSET BAY
CONSET POINT

PAYNES BAY
ST. THOMAS
VILLA NOVA PLANTATION
ST. JOHN
RAGGED POINT

SPRING GARDEN HWY.
CONSTITUTION RIVER
ST. GEORGE
COTTAGE VALE
ST. PHILIP

GUN HILL SIGNAL STATION
SAM LORD'S CASTLE

CAVE HILL
BULKELEY
SUNBURY PLANTATION
MARCHFIELD

BRIDGETOWN
ST. MICHAEL
THE CRANE
CRANE BEACH
CRANE BAY

WILDEY
CHRIST CHURCH
SALT CAVE POINT

CARLISLE BAY
NEEDHAM'S POINT
HASTINGS
ABC HWY.
GRANTLEY ADAMS INTERNATIONAL AIRPORT

ROCKLEY BEACH
ST. LAWRENCE
OISTINS
LONG BAY
INCH MARLOWE POINT

ACCRA BEACH
DOVER BEACH
OISTINS BAY

0   2 mi
0   2 km
·—·—· = PARISH BOUNDARY

© MOON PUBLICATIONS, INC.

or **Rockley Beach,** has some facilities, vendors, and picnic tables, and is often crowded. **Miami Beach** and **Crane Beach** are also south-coast gathering spots.

The rugged east coast has several wide-open spots and the water is often rough. You can, however, find isolated coves and inlets with quiet spots protected from the thundering surf. Bathsheba's coastline is dramatic and set against sheer cliffs. **Morgan Lewis Beach** is a short walk from the East Coast Road.

North Barbados

An excellent road system and relatively good directional signs make getting around Barbados easy. The country is divided into 11 parishes, used in the early days as administrative districts. Most roads lead to Bridgetown, passing through villages with names such as Easy Hall, Farmers, Retreat, and Byde Mill.

Driving north from Bridgetown on the **Spring Garden Highway,** you'll pass several rum refineries, the **Lazaretto Gardens** and national archives, and the **Cave Hill** University of the West Indies campus before arriving in **Holetown.** Holetown was the site of the first British landing on the island in 1627. The site apparently reminded the settlers of Limehouse Hole, on the River Thames, hence the name. Today it is a small but busy fishing village with some commerce. The landing is honored each February during the **Holetown Festival,** which features sports, races, music, and feasts.

Nearby is the **Folkestone Underwater Park and Museum.** The reef here is protected, and the park has created a fascinating underwater snorkeling trail. A Greek barge has been deliberately sunk and is home to many brightly colored, tropical fish. Glass bottom boats are available as well. A small museum and aquarium is open Sun.-Fri. 10 a.m.-5 p.m. Admission is Bds$1.

Farther north is **Speighstown,** a small harbor village used mainly during the sugar exporting days. North of the town is the **Mount Gay Distillery,** where Barbados's famous rum is produced. This distillery has been in operation since the 1800s and 500,000 gallons are produced each year. Another Mount Gay distillery is found near Bridgetown. Tours are conducted weekdays 8 a.m.-4 p.m.

Central Barbados

In the center of the island are several sites worth a stop. Along Hwy. 2 you'll pass the **Sharon Moravian Church,** originally built in 1799 by the first missionary group to work with the slave population. The church was destroyed by a hurricane in 1831 and rebuilt in 1833. Farther east is **Harrison's Cave,** tel. (809) 438-6640/1, an underground cave complex complete with lighted, ochre-tinted stalactites and stalagmites, a 40-foot (12-meter) water cascade, and underground ponds. A guided tour is conducted by electric tram. A small shop and snack bar is on the property. Tours start daily at 9:30 a.m. and reservations are recommended. Admission is Bds$15 for adults, half that for children.

Even farther north on the highway is the **Flower Forest** (tel. 809-433-8152), a landscaped botanic garden set in an old plantation's grounds. The garden features species from Barbados and around the world, all very colorful, very fragrant. The views from here are breathtaking and include the highest point on the island, Mt. Hillaby, to the west. There is a gift shop and small cafe on the grounds. The garden is open daily 9 a.m.-5 p.m.; admission is Bds$10 for adults, children half price.

Continue north on Hwy. 2 to **Farley Hill,** where you'll find the **Farley Hill National Park** (tel. 809-422-3555). The park is a botanic garden with many local and imported species and a 19th-century plantation house with great views of the east coast. Admission is Bds$3 per car, half that for motorcycles, and the park is open daily 7 a.m.-6 p.m.

Across the highway from the park, you'll see the **Barbados Wildlife Reserve** (tel. 809-422-8826), a large mahogany forest with green monkeys, exotic birds, and other animals roaming freely. Others, such as the alligator, are caged. An aviary and small natural history museum are open. Admission is Bds$10 for adults, half price for children; open daily 10 a.m.-5 p.m.

East Coast

On the southeast coast is **Sam Lord's Castle,** now part of the Marriott Hotel's resort chain. Samuel Lord was a wealthy 19th-century planter, rake, and reputed land pirate, who was rumored to have plundered ships by hanging lanterns along the shoreline, simulating the lights of a

flying fish

harbor settlement. When the ships ran aground, Lord and his crew would relieve them of their contents. The castle is somewhat of an overblown attraction, more the centerpiece of a large and flashy resort than a historical site.

Farther up the coast, on Hwy. 3, are the **Andromeda Gardens** (tel. 809-433-9261), a National Trust entity, filled with flowers from around the world. Admission is Bds$8, children half price. Open daily 8 a.m.-sunset. Just north of Andromeda is the village of Bathsheba, renowned for its crashing waves and rock cliffs.

Organized Hikes and Tours

Those interested in nature walks and hikes might start by contacting the tourism board, tel. (809) 427-2623, fax 426-4080, about the **Natural Areas Conservation Committee,** a national umbrella body incorporating members of the Barbados Environmental Association, the Caribbean Conservation Association, the Society of Caribbean Ornithology, and the International Council of Bird Protection. The committee has numerous projects on the boards, including preservation of the **Graeme Hall Swamp** in the south.

The **Barbados National Trust,** tel. (809) 426-2421, organizes weekly Sunday hikes to historic plantation houses, sugar factory yards, nature sites, and other places of interest. Hikes start at 6 a.m. and conclude at about 3:30 p.m.

The Barbados National Trust, in addition to their Sunday hikes, has created the **Heritage Passport** and a **Heritage Mini Passport,** designed to allow visitors to enter a number of historical, cultural, and ecological sites at discounted rates. The original passport allows entrance to any of 16 sites, including those mentioned above and below as National Trust entities, as well as

the **Welchman Hall Gully National Park, Gun Hill Signal Station, Codrington College, the Jewish Synagogue, Morgan Lewis Hill,** and the **Sunbury Plantation, St. Nicholas Abbey,** and **Villa Nova Plantation** greathouses. There are three types of mini passports—green, red, and blue—and each allows entrance into five selected sites. The passport's cost is US$35 (Bds$70), and a mini passport is US$18 (Bds $36). Two children under 12 per family are allowed in for free.

The **Highland Outdoor Tours** company is one of the island's newer nature excursion companies, conducting what they call "Scenic Safari Hikes" throughout the interior of the island. Full-day hikes start at 6 a.m. in their center near Bridgetown and pass through farmlands, valleys, natural springs, and working estates. Horseback riding is also available. Call the tourism authority, tel. (809) 427-2623.

BRIDGETOWN

Downtown

Bridgetown, formerly "The Bridge" after the bridge spanning the **Constitution River,** was founded in 1628 by the Earl of Carlisle. The town houses a population of nearly 100,000. The numbers belie, however, its physical size— it does not seem large. Downtown is easily seen in a few hours and is often busy and crowded with cars, taxis, and buses. In places Bridgetown displays more concrete than West Indian charm. Still, it is a pleasant and negotiable city and is the hub of government, commerce, and shopping. Eight highways emanate from the town center, the main links to the country's parishes. The outskirts and suburbs of Bridgetown are older and feature the gingerbread and stone house architecture of plantation days.

The small inner harbor is known as the **Careenage,** and this is where fishing boats and smaller pleasure craft dock along side the walkway. You can, if you time it correctly, buy fresh fish straight off the boats here.

Between the wharf walkway and **Broad Street,** the main shopping area, is **Trafalgar Square.** In the square is a statue of **Horatio Nelson,** a sore spot for the country at one time. Some Bajans feel the statue, which was erected in 1813, is reminiscent of the colonial past. Many

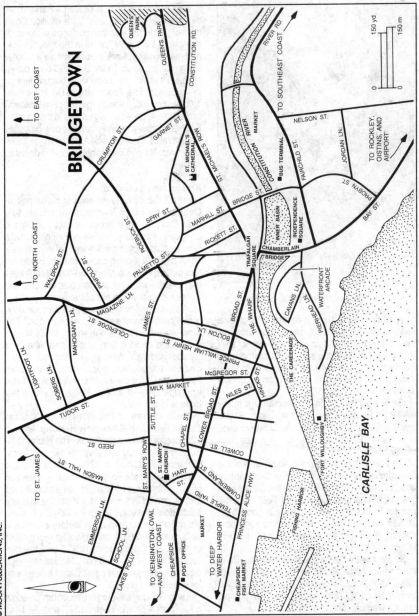

BRIDGETOWN

© MOON PUBLICATIONS, INC.

Trafalgar Square, early 20th century

have petitioned to have it replaced by a local national hero. Instead, in an odd compromise, the statue was turned so that it no longer faces Broad Street. Near the statue is a memorial to Barbados's war dead and a dolphin fountain that commemorates the introduction of running water on the island in 1861.

On Broad Street, in addition to the many banks and businesses, are the **Public Buildings,** which include the Upper and Lower House of Assembly Chambers. The buildings date back to 1871.

On Fairchild Street, on the south side of the Constitution River (feeds into the Careenage), and in Cheapside, to the west of the Careenage, are public **markets.** (Note: For fresh fish, the market in the town of Oistins is a good bet.) James Street is lined with fruit and vegetable stands, often just boxes turned upside down, laden with this and that.

St. Michael's Cathedral stands on the site of the original Anglican church first established in 1665. The structure was destroyed or damaged by hurricanes in 1780 and 1831, and the present church was completed in 1838.

East of the cathedral is **Queen's Park,** under the auspices of the National Conservation Commission. The park was the residence of the commander of the King's forces in the West Indies, and the **Queen's Park House** is now a theater and small museum (open 9 a.m.-5 p.m. daily). Note, as if you'd miss it, the large baobab tree on the grounds. The tree is estimated to be over 1,000 years old, measuring 61 feet (18 meters) in circumference—the largest tree in the country. Baobabs grow in Africa, yet this one predates the arrival of Europeans or Africans to the Lesser Antilles. No one knows how it landed on these shores.

Bridgetown Outskirts

North of the downtown area is **Kensington Oval,** one of four international cricket test grounds in the West Indies. Cricket is to Bajans as honey is to bears, and no one single activity, save perhaps politics, inflames the national passions as does a good cricket match. Barbados has placed many a player on the West Indies test team, including the famous Sir Garfield Sobers, one of the world's best.

Also north of downtown is the infamous **Baxters Road,** "the street that never sleeps." The road is filled with the one-room, dimly lit rum shops and small eating places that take on a life after midnight. Women sell fried fish cooked over open stoves, and music blasts up and down the street. Definitely the after-hours place to be in Bridgetown—a slice of Bajan life with a few tourists in the mix.

South of town on Bay Street is the National Trust's **Garrison Savannah Historic Area,** a 17th-century military complex. The grounds include forts, monuments, and military buildings. **St. Ann's Fort,** built in 1804, now houses the Barbados Defence Force. An amazing collection of cannons, some 30 in all, have been collected and displayed in front of the **Main Guard.** The **Barbados Museum,** tel. (809) 427-0201, in the old prison, features natural history exhibits, a map gallery, and African artifacts, among other exhibits. Admission costs Bds$7 and the museum is open 10 a.m.-6 p.m. Monday through Saturday. There is the small Cafe Musée here, for snacks and drinks.

Every Sunday evening the museum presents a folk-dance drama called *1627 and All That.*

The show presents aspects of past and present Bajan life through dancing, comedy, and narrative skits. The Thursday evening show is the comedy-murder mystery *Now Museum, Now You Don't.* It includes drinks, buffet dinner, and transport. Call (809) 420-3409 for show information.

Another point of interest on the outskirts of the city is **Harry Bayley Observatory,** tel. (809) 426-1317, in Clapham. The observatory is open to the public Friday evening 8:30-11:30 p.m.; admission is Bds$5. The observatory, the only one in the Caribbean, was built in 1963 and is the headquarters of the Barbados Astronomical Society.

SPORTS AND RECREATION

Water Sports
Water-skiing, windsurfing, harbor cruises, parasailing, and snorkeling are easily arranged through most hotels. The Club Mistral at the **The Barbados Windsurfing Club Hotel,** tel. (809) 428-9095, at Maxwell on the south coast offers, not surprisingly, windsurfing equipment and instruction.

Underwater excursions are offered on the **Atlantis Submarine,** tel. (809) 436-8929 or 436-8932, located in the deep-water harbor at Bridgetown. The air-conditioned submarines tour the ocean floor for about an hour each trip, making night dives and day dives, at a cost of US$68 (about EC$180) per adult, half fare for children 4-12. You'll find the offices at the Carlisle House on the wharf.

Yacht and Boat Rentals, Deep-Sea Fishing
The Barbados waters are loaded with marlin, tuna, mahimahi, and other large game fish, and if you like deep-sea fishing, you won't be disappointed. **Jolly Roger Watersports,** tel. (809) 432-7090 or 422-2335, can organize half- or full-day fishing trips. **The Dive Shop,** at the Grand Barbados, tel. (809) 426-9947, and **Blue Jay Charters,** tel. (809) 422-2098, on the west coast also arrange fishing excursions.

Sailors can charter any number of sailboats and motor boats privately. Many are also available for organized sightseeing trips, sunset cruises, and snorkeling trips. **Secret Love,** tel. (809) 432-1972, and the catamaran **Irish Mist II,** tel. (809) 436-9201, are among the many found at the Bridgetown waterfront.

Diving
Scuba diving in Barbados waters is considered by many to be excellent, though not as pristine an experience as diving the untouched waters of Dominica or Saba.

The Greek barge *Stavronikita,* at Folkestone, was deliberately sunk to create a living and feeding environment for fish and coral and now lies under 125 feet (38 meters) of water.

Dive centers can provide air and equipment and resort certification for beginners. Night dives and diving packages are also available. Serious divers should look for diving packages offered in conjunction with accommodation and flights.

Call **Dive Barbados,** tel. (809) 432-7090; **The Dive Shop** at Grand Barbados Beach Resort, tel. (809) 426-9947; **Dive Boat Safari** at the Hilton, tel. (809) 427-4350; or **Willie's Watersports** at Heywoods Hotel, tel. (809) 422-4900, for information about resort certification or diving excursions.

Golf
Golf is played at the 18-hole **Sandy Lane Club,** tel. (809) 432-1145, in St. James; or the the nine-hole **Rockley Resort,** tel. (809) 435-7873; or **Heywoods,** tel. (809) 422-4900. The newest course, still under construction, will be the Royal Westmoreland Golf and Country Club in St. James.

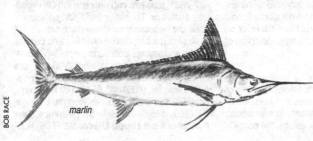

marlin

BOB RACE

Cricket

Barbados has produced many world-class cricket players, and several have played on the West Indies match teams. Barbados takes its cricket seriously. Games are held year-round, and you can catch test matches at the Kensington Oval in Bridgetown, January through April. Check the newspapers for information, or call the **Barbados Cricket Association,** tel. (809) 436-1397.

Horses

Horseracing is another popular spectator event. The **Barbados Turf Club,** tel. (809) 426-3980, hosts about 20 races per year at the Garrison Savannah outside of Bridgetown: 10 on alternating Saturdays from January to April, and 10 from August to November. The Cockspur Gold Cup, named after the famous Bajan rum, is held in March and includes horses from the Caribbean region.

Barbados also takes its polo seriously. For information regarding matches, call the **Barbados Polo Club,** tel. (809) 432-1802.

Countryside and beach horseback-riding excursions can be arranged through **Brighton Stables,** tel. (809) 425-9381.

Shopping

The airport and Broad Street in Bridgetown offer the best deals in duty-free and craft items. **Pelican Village,** on Princess Alice Highway near the harbor in Bridgetown, is a both a series of shops and an artisans' village.

Art galleries are found around the island. Among them are the **Barbados Arts Council,** tel. (809) 426-4385, at Pelican Village and **The National Cultural Foundation Gallery,** tel. (809) 427-2345, at the Queen's Park House.

Other items such as groceries, market items, stationery, T-shirts, art, and duty-free items are found around Bridgetown. Walk down Broad Street and explore. Drop in at **The Cloister** on The Wharf in Bridgetown for a large selection of books and magazines.

Nightlife

Check newspapers and hotel listings for some of the popular dinner theater presentations. In addition to the Barbados Museum's presentations on Sunday and Thursday evenings, the comedy

CRICKET

For North Americans used to fast-paced sports such as football, basketball, and hockey, cricket comes as something of a genteel endeavor. Thoroughly British in origin ("sticky wicket" is a phrase forever ingrained in the American mind as one that almost defines British understatement), the sport arrived in the West Indies during the late 1700s. Barbados had formed a national team by 1806, and the sport grew to such stature internationally that it is today *the* sport of the British West Indies current and former colonies. International test matches are today played in Barbados, Trinidad, Antigua, and Jamaica.

While early players were exclusively white, today's stars reflect the black majority throughout the islands. Star cricketeers such as Bardados's Frank Worrel and Antigua's Viv Richards have put the West Indies Team squarely on the international cricket map.

Teams of 11 members play matches that last up to five days, with scores reaching into the hundreds. The match involves flat, paddle-like bats, a ball, and the famous wicket, of which there are two. The rules of a game that can last up to five days are too complicated to explain here, but perhaps it's enough to say that skill and athleticism are important aspects of the game, as is, in the Lesser Antilles, vivid fan participation.

Look for local matches islands-wide by searching the local newspapers. In Barbados, major matches are played at Kensington Oval, near Bridgetown. For information, call the **Barbados Cricket Association,** tel. (809) 436-1397.

show *Barbados, Barbados* is offered at the old **Balls Sugar Plantation,** tel. (809) 435-6900, in Christ Church. The **Ocean View,** tel. (809) 427-7821, presents cabarets and Off Off Broadway shows on Thursday and Friday. Reservations are necessary for dinner theaters.

Nightclubs and discos offer live and canned music, and several local bands, including "Spice" and the easy-listening "Melody Makers," are very good. Among the currently hip nightspots: After Dark, tel. (809) 435-6547; **TGI Boomers,** tel. (809) 428-8439; and **The Reggae Lounge,** tel. (809) 435-6462, all in St. Lawrence Gap. Also check out **Hippo Disco,** tel. (809) 425-

1440, at the Barbados Beach Resort on the west coast and **The Comfort Zone,** tel. (809) 420-4833, in Christ Church.

After the night wanes, visit Bridgetown's **Baxters Road,** "the street that never sleeps," for late night snacks and a slice of Bajan life after dark.

ACCOMMODATIONS

The tourism authority counts over 150 hotels, apartment hotels, apartments, guesthouses, cottages, and villas on the island, for a total of 14,500 beds. Not all are recommended by the tourism people, but that ought not count out the smaller ones that haven't made the grade. Some are clean, safe, and comfortable, just a bit sparse is all. Contact the tourism authority (see below) or the **Barbados Hotel Association,** P.O. Box 711C, Bridgetown, Barbados, West Indies, tel. (809) 426-5041, fax 429-2845, for a more complete list of the country's accommodations.

Hotels and guesthouses will add a five percent tax, and some will add a 10% service charge to your bill.

The following are recommended, and fall into these categories based on prices per person,

per night, 15 Dec.-15 April high season: **Luxury** US$100 or more, **Moderate** US$50-100, **Budget** US$50 or less.

Hotels
Hilton International Barbados, Needham's Point, St. Michael, Barbados, West Indies, tel. (809) 426-0200, fax 436-8646, is one of the largest hotels on the island. It's busy with lots of activities, sports, and a good beach, just minutes from Bridgetown. Luxury.

Sandy Lane Hotel, St. James, Barbados, West Indies, tel. (809) 432-1311, is an extra luxurious resort on the west coast. Featured are five bars, two restaurants, five tennis courts, water sports on a fine beach, a golf course, and elegance, elegance. Luxury.

South of Sandy Lane is **Barbados Beach Village,** St. James, Barbados, West Indies, tel. (809) 425-1440, fax 424-0996, also on a fine beach. Simple but clean; you choose from rooms, cottages, or apartments. Moderate.

Sandy Beach Hotel, Christ Church, Barbados, West Indies, tel. (809) 435-8000, is on the crowded south shore between Bridgetown and Oistins. Here you are near dozens of restaurants and plenty of water sports. Moderate-Luxury.

MORE BARBADOS HOTELS

Rates per s, EP when applicable, winter

NAME	(809)	FAX	LOCATION	TARIFF
Accra Beach Hotel	435-8920	435-6794	Rockley Beach	moderate
Bagshot House	435-6956	N/A	St. Lawrence	moderate-luxury
Casuarina Beach Club	428-3600	428-1970	Dover	moderate-luxury
Club Rockley	435-7880	435-8015	Golf Club Road, Christ Church	luxury
Crane Beach Hotel	423-6220	423-5343	Crane Bay, St. Philip	luxury
Divi Southwinds Resort	428-7181	428-4674	St. Lawrence	luxury
Ginger Bay Hotel	423-5810	N/A	Crane Bay, St. Philip	moderate
Glitter Bay	422-5555	422-3940	Porters	luxury
Island Inn Hotel	436-6393	N/A	Aquatic Gap	luxury
Sam Lord's Castle-Marriott	423-7350	423-5918	Long Bay	luxury
Sandpiper Inn	422-2251	N/A	St. James	luxury
Southern Palms	428-7171	N/A	St. Lawrence Gap	luxury

MORE BARBADOS
APARTMENTS AND GUESTHOUSES

Rates per s, EP when applicable, winter

NAME	(809)	FAX	LOCATION	TARIFF
Bona Vista	435-6680	N/A	Rockley	budget
Crystal Waters Guesthouse	435-7514	N/A	Worthing	budget
Miami Beach Apartments	428-5387	428-5387	Oistins	budget
Nautilus Beach Apartments	426-3541	N/A	Carlisle Bay	moderate
Pegwell Inn	428-6150	N/A	Oistins	budget
Rio	428-1546	N/A	St. Lawrence Gap	budget
Rydal Waters Guesthouse	435-7433	N/A	Worthing	budget
Sandridge	422-2631	422-1965	Speighstown	moderate
Shell's Guesthouse	425-7253	N/A	Worthing	budget
Sichris Apartments	435-7930	435-8232	Worthing	moderate
YMCA Hostel	426-3910	N/A	Bridgetown	budget

Atlantis, Bathsheba, St. Joseph, Barbados, West Indies, tel. (809) 433-9445, is removed from the madding crowd, with wonderful views of the open Atlantic. Simple, with clean rooms and great buffet meals. Budget-Moderate.

Ocean View, Hastings, Christchurch, Barbados, West Indies, tel. (809) 427-7821, fax 427-7826, sits on the waterfront at Hastings, just outside Bridgetown. The rooms in the colonial-style inn vary in style and rack rate, but the overriding feeling is one of simplicity garnished with antiques. The beach here is nothing to speak of, but you'll find good swimming within walking distance. Moderate.

Villa Rentals
In addition to villas and apartment-type accommodations listed by the hotel association and tourist board, you can contact a local rental agent. **Alleyne, Aguilar & Altman,** tel. (809) 432-0840, fax 432-2147; **Bajan Services, Ltd.,** tel. (809) 422-2618, fax 422-5366; or **Exclusive Luxury Villas,** tel. (809) 432-0840, fax 432-2147, all list numerous coastal or inland properties.

In North America, one of the largest lists of Barbados villa properties exists with **WIMCO,** P.O. Box 1461, Newport, RI 02840, tel. (800)

932-3222, fax 402-847-6290. **Island Hideaways,** 1317 Rhode Island Ave. N.W., Suite 503, Washington, DC 20005, tel. (800) 832-2302, fax (202) 667-3392, also lists several Barbados properties.

Camping
Camping facilities have not yet been developed on Barbados, and it is illegal and dangerous to simply pitch a tent on a beach.

FOOD

Bajan cuisine is both like and unlike West Indian Creole found in the rest of the Lesser Antilles. A favorite is flying fish, almost a national dish. Other fish include dolphin, which is really a dorado, not the cousin of Flipper. Black pudding, a sausage made from pig's intestine, pig's blood, and spices is a popular holiday dish. *Souse* is a pickled pig's head dish. *Buljol* has French influences—it's a salted cod, onion, tomatoes, lime, and spices salad. *Conkies* are made of cornmeal, coconut, sweet potatoes, and spices, steamed in plantain leaves. *Coucou* is a side dish made from cornmeal or breadfruit, with okra, salt, and butter. *Jugjug* or *jug* is a traditional

Christmas dish made with pigeon peas, meat, and cornmeal and is believed to have originated from the Scottish dish haggis.

Cockspur rum is the island's favorite and Bank's Beer is the local suds. *Mauby* is a soft drink made from the bark of the eponymous tree that tastes like a strong sarsaparilla. Not for the weak of heart. *Falernum* is an alcoholic drink of rum, sugar syrup, and lime juice. It is similar to the *ti punch* of the French Antilles, with an extra essence of almond or vanilla.

Most hotel restaurants and larger restaurants accept credit cards. Bajans enjoy eating out, and restaurants can be crowded; reservations for evening meals are recommended, particularly during the high season.

The following restaurant categories are based on per-person entree prices: **Expensive** US$25 or more, **Moderate** US$10-25, **Inexpensive** US$10 or less.

Carambola, tel. (809) 432-0832, in St. James overlooks the ocean and offers fine French haute cuisine. Expensive. **Raffles,** tel. (809) 432-6557, in Holetown serves variations on Bajan and Continental cuisine. Very nice. Expensive.

Waterfront Cafe, tel. (809) 427-0093, sits on the Careenage in Bridgetown, and is attrac-

dolphin fish

BOB RACE

tive for its location, right in the center of things, and for its local food. Inexpensive. **Fisherman's Wharf,** tel. (809) 436-7778, also on the Careenage, upstairs, serves fish stuffed with crab and a great Bajan fish pie. Moderate.

Brown Sugar, tel. (809) 426-7684, is located at Aquatic Gap on Bay Street in St. Michael, a few minutes from Bridgetown. The Bajan menu is extensive and hearty—look for the luncheon buffet. Moderate.

GETTING THERE

By Air
The large and modern **Grantley Adams International Airport,** tel. (809) 428-7101, is located in the southeast section of the island, about 10 miles (16 km) from Bridgetown. The airport is a busy hub for the Caribbean, particularly the Windward Islands. The airport is newly renovated, with the best duty-free shopping in

MORE BARBADOS RESTAURANTS

NAME	LOCATION	(809)	CUISINE	PRICE RANGE
Chateau Creole	Porters	422-4116	Bajan	inexpensive
David's	Worthing	435-6550	Bajan/seafood	moderate
Ile de France	Hastings	435-6869	French	moderate
Josef's	St. Lawrence Gap	435-6541	Continental	moderate-expensive
Pisces	St. Lawrence Gap	428-6558	Bajan/seafood	moderate-expensive
Plantation	St. Lawrence	428-5084	French/Bajan	moderate-expensive
Reid's	Derricks, St. James	432-7623	seafood	moderate
Witch Doctor	St. Lawrence Gap	435-6581	Bajan	moderate

the Caribbean. You'll also find a bank, post office, and numerous car rental agencies in the airport.

American Airlines, local tel. (809) 428-4170, flies nonstop daily from New York and Miami, and direct from its hub in San Juan. **BWIA,** tel. (809) 426-2111, flies from Toronto, Miami, and nonstop from New York. **Air Canada,** tel. (809) 436-3835, flies in from Montreal and nonstop from Toronto. Europe is connected by **British Airways,** tel. (809) 428-0908, with a nonstop flight from London, or by BWIA with a stop in Trinidad.

Connections from other Caribbean islands are made by **LIAT,** Bridgetown tel. (809) 436-6224, airport tel. 428-0986, or BWIA, as well as a half-dozen local airlines serving the Caribbean and South America.

Departure tax is Bds$25.

GETTING AROUND

Taxis

Taxis are available everywhere and are unmetered. Rates, a bit expensive by Caribbean standards, are set by the government and are posted in both Barbados and U.S. dollars at most hotels and on a large sign as you leave the customs area of the airport.

The new **ABC Highway** (named after three of Barbados's former leaders, Tom Adams, Errol Barrow, and Gordon Cummings) connects the airport with the west coast roads and skirts Bridgetown, making travel

plantain

BOB RACE

BARBADOS CAR RENTAL AGENCIES	
Area code 809	
AGENCY	**TEL.**
A&M	424-0469
Adam's Car Rentals	436-0543
Barbados Rent-a-Car (airport)	428-0960
Blenman's Car Rentals	428-2608
Carl's Auto Rentals	429-6730
Dear's Garage	429-9277
Double J Car and Moke Rentals	427-3155
Drive-A-Matic	422-5017
Leisure Rentals	426-1452
Miramar Rentals	422-3912
National Car Rentals	426-0603
Premier Auto Rentals	424-2277
Sunny Isle Motors	435-7979
Sunshine Rentals	427-1234
Tropicar Rentals	425-5267

to that area easy and less expensive. The most expensive fare is from the airport to points north of Speighstown, at Bds$55 (US$27.50). Airport to Bridgetown is Bds$30 (US$15). In Bridgetown taxis are located at Trafalgar Square, Independence Square, and Lower Broad Street. There are stands at Accra Beach and Hastings Rock on the south coast. If you are walking, taxi drivers will slow down and ask if you want a lift, or you can flag them down if the cabs are empty.

Buses

Buses are run by the government Transport Board and are blue with a yellow stripe. Minibuses are private and are yellow with a blue stripe. Got it? Minibuses, with names like "Cobra,' "Rambo," or the ominous "Killer," are also identified by the booming reggae or calypso music resonating from them.

Buses charge a Bds$1.50 fare to any location on the island, a good deal. You can catch them at Fairchild Street, Jubilee, and Princess Alice Highway in Bridgetown, and in several places around the island. If you need a complete schedule, call (809) 436-6820.

Minibuses run from the River Bus Terminal, tel. (809) 426-3967, to points east and southeast. From Temple Yard minibuses depart for points north and northeast, and from Probyn Street they depart for points south and central.

Car Rentals

Car rentals are easily found but not always reasonably priced. More than 70 car rental agencies are listed in the phone book, and you'd think the competition would drive prices down. It doesn't. Rates start at about US$45 per day for the small, open-air Mini Mokes (sort of like a beach buggy with smaller tires), to US$70 per day for larger cars. It's cheaper to rent by the week.

You'll need a temporary local driver's license, available at any one of several Police Stations, the Ministry of Transport in Bridgetown, or your rental company. Cost is Bds$10.

The country, though small, boasts more than 800 miles (1,288 km) of paved road. Most of the roads are in good shape, although they might be winding and abrupt in places. Remember to drive on the left.

Motorcycle and Bicycle Rentals

Motorcycles and scooters are also viable means of transportation, although somewhat annoying in the rain. Rates start at Bds$60 (US$30) per day, less for a week's rental. Call **Lynn's Rentals,** tel. (809) 435-8585, in Hastings, just south of Bridgetown, or **Fun Seekers,** tel. (809) 435-8206, in Rockley.

Bicycles are also available at Fun Seekers and at **St. Lawrence Cycles,** tel. (809) 428-1335, in St. Lawrence Gap; at **Irie Mountain Bikes,** tel. (809) 424-4730, at Prospect House in St. James; or at the make-no-mistake-about-what-we-do **Bicycle Rentals,** tel. (809) 427-3995, in Hastings. Day rates range US$9-11. Three-speeds as well as three-seaters are available.

MONEY, HOURS, AND COMMUNICATION

Currency and Banks

Barbados uses its own Barbados dollar, first issued in 1973, fixed at a rate of Bds$2 = US$1. Other currencies fluctuate against the U.S. dollar rate. You may use U.S. and Canadian dollars in most transactions, but the use of Barbados dollars will garner a better rate.

Money is changed at hotels and banks, with banks providing the better rate of exchange. Banking hours are generally Mon.-Thurs. 9 a.m.-3 p.m., and Friday 9 a.m.-1 p.m. and 3-5 p.m.

Many of the country's banks are found in Bridgetown, on Broad Street. Among them are **Barclays, Barbados Mutual Bank, Barbados National Bank,** and **Caribbean Commercial**

INFORMATION DIRECTORY

BARBADOS TOURISM AUTHORITY

P.O. Box 242, Harbour Road, Bridgetown, Barbados, West Indies, tel. (809) 427-2623, fax 426-4080. (Offices as well at the airport, tel. 428-9837, and Deep Water Harbour, tel. 426-1718).

800 2nd Ave., New York, NY 10017, tel. (800) 221-9831 or (212) 986-6516, fax 573-9850.

3440 Wilshire Blvd., Suite 1215, Los Angeles, CA 90010, tel. (213) 380-2198, fax 384-2763.

5160 Yonge St., Suite 1800, North York, Ontario M2N GL19, tel. (800) 268-9122 or (416) 512-6569, fax 512-6581.

263 Tottenham Court Rd., London W1P 9AA, tel. (441) 636-9448, fax 637-1496.

Rathenau Platz 1A, 6000 Frankfurt a Main 1, Germany, tel. (069) 28 08 82, fax 49-69-294-782.

Caraïbes 102, 102 Ave. Des Champs-Élysées, 75008 Paris, tel. 45-62-62-62, fax (331) 4074-0701.

OTHER

Emergency, tel. 119.

Ambulance Emergency, tel. (809) 426-1113.

Fire, tel. 113.

Police, tel. 112.

Queen Elizabeth Hospital, tel. (809) 436-6450.

Grantley Adams International Airport, tel. (809) 428-7101.

Visitor Information Network, tel. (809) 438-2138.

Bank. The airport bank is Barbados National, which is open daily 8 a.m.-midnight—but only for arriving and departing passengers.

Traveler's checks are accepted in many places, and credit cards are almost universally used in hotels and larger restaurants. Call ahead, however, to check.

Hours, Mail, Phones
Business hours are usually weekdays 8 a.m.-4 p.m. and Saturday 8 a.m.-noon. Some supermarkets are open until 6 p.m. on Saturday, and tourist shops often remain open for cruise ships. However, most of Barbados closes up shop on Sunday.

The general post office and philatelic bureau is located in Cheapside, Bridgetown, open weekdays 7:30 a.m.-5 p.m. District post offices are found in each parish.

Barbados uses the international area code "809" for calling. Locally, phone cards are sold in denominations of Bds$10, 20, 40, and 60. **Barbados External Telecommunications,** a division of Cable and Wireless (West Indies), has offices at Wildey, in St. Michael, and is the place for calls, faxes, and telegrams. There is another public office on the Wharf in Bridgetown for the same.

The nation's press is lively and vigorous; the two daily newspapers are the *Advocate* and the *Nation*. They also publish weekend editions, and you'll find weekly tabloids such as *The Weekend Investigator*. Tourist publications include (free) *The Visitor*.

Caribbean Week, a comprehensive regional weekly news roundup, is distributed internationally and published in St. Michael.

TRINIDAD AND TOBAGO

The Republic of Trinidad and Tobago is the Lesser Antilles' wild cousin, a country of deep and abiding passion that is, in many ways, one of the most complex in the chain.

It's a nation that has produced some of the world's most recognizable cultural icons; calypso and steel-pan bands are, today, nearly universal Caribbean sounds. Trinidad's Carnival outshines other island festivals in energy and pure bombast. Several world-eminent writers, such as V.S. Naipaul, Samuel Selvon, and poet-storyteller Paul Keens-Douglas, were Trinidad-born. St. Lucian Nobel Prize-winner Derek Walcott established the Trinidad Theatre Workshop in Port of Spain in 1959 and for years has made the country his spiritual muse.

Beyond cultural exports, both islands teem with modern successes—and disparities. The country is a place of wealth and of grinding poverty, both starkly evident in Trinidad's capital, Port of Spain. Christians, Muslims, Hindus, Asians, Blacks, and Whites form a cosmopolitan population that lives, if not always side by side, at least with a degree of hopeful ethnic tolerance. Political debate is open and government is generally healthy; while a 1990 armed coup attempt by a fundamentalist Muslim group may have surprised the world, it did not surprise Trinidadians.

Culturally enigmatic, mystical, and highly stylized—like a veiled beauty, what is perplexing about Trinidad and Tobago is also enticing.

THE LAND

The sister islands of Trinidad and Tobago are the most southerly of the Lesser Antilles, and of the entire West Indies for that matter. Trinidad lies just seven miles (11 km) from the north coast of Venezuela, its nearest neighbor.

Trinidad is shaped like a small-toed boot, or for those with vivid imaginations, like a headless ghost trailing its aura behind. The island's land area, 1,864 square miles (4,828 square km), makes it the largest in the Lesser Antilles. Much of its topography resembles that of the Venezuelan mainland; the flora and fauna found on Trinidad, more so than on Tobago, are similar to species found in South America.

Approximately half of Trinidad is forested. A northern mountain range, succinctly called the Northern Range, stretches east-west and contains the island's highest point, Cerro del Aripo at 3,085 feet (941 meters). The range is thought to be part of a massive system that stretches from the Andes of South America to

North America's Rocky Mountains, which is in some ways beyond the imagination.

The center and south of the island is a flat plain, where much of the country's agricultural industry—primarily sugarcane—is located, although a central spine of relatively low hills stretches roughly diagonally from southwest to northeast. Southern Trinidad is characterized by smaller hill ranges. The northern coast is clean, serene, and hilly, host to many of the island's best swimming beaches; other sections of the coast can be rough and irregular. Massive swamps crawl along the central Atlantic coast and the western coast on the Gulf of Paria, south of Port of Spain. The west coast's Caroni Swamp is the site of a wildlife sanctuary where you can see Trinidad's national bird, the scarlet ibis.

Tobago, Trinidad's zucchini-shaped sister 21 miles (34 km) to the northeast, is roughly 26 miles (42 km) long by seven miles (11 km) wide, with an area of 116 square miles (300 square km). The generally low-lying island is dominated by a central hill range with a high point of 1,860 feet (567 meters). For the most part the central hills are protected forest reserve.

Tobago's coast is characterized by hills, bays, and stretches of sandy beach. The south of the island is flatter, home to the population centers of Scarborough, the capital, and Plymouth. The south hosts much of the island's tourism activity, as well as some of the finest beaches and hotels. The entire island is small enough to encircle in a couple of days—if you linger a few days.

HISTORY

Iere

Before its various European discoveries, before its numerous conquerings and occupations, Trinidad and Tobago was not an uncomplicated place. Various Amerindian groups, as early as 5000 B.C., had crossed the straits from Venezuela and had inhabited Trinidad, which they called Iere, thought to mean "Land of the Hummingbird." The largest Amerindian groups were the Arawaks and Caribs, who existed with several subgroups. The Arawaks inhabited the south of Trinidad and were relatively peaceful. The warrior Caribs lived in the north, and they

scarlet ibis

BOB RACE

fought a lot. This is what they were doing when Columbus happened upon the island on 31 July 1493, during his third voyage.

La Trinite

Columbus landed and named the island "La Trinite." Some say this was in honor of the Holy Trinity, to whom he had dedicated the voyage. Others believe it had something to do with the three hills he first sighted as he approached the island. At any rate, after claiming the island for Spain, Columbus sailed off and two weeks later sighted Tobago, thought to have been called Tavaco by the native Amerindian groups. The word apparently refers to the native crop the Caribs grew and smoked, which in English we call tobacco. (The island's name, "Tobago," is a Spanish corruption of the Carib word, yet is pronounced to-BAY-go.) Beyond that, there is some dispute as to what Columbus himself called the island. Some say "Concepción." Some say "Bella Forma." More for the legend gristmill. Whatever the case, Columbus did not land on Tobago—his penchant for renaming islands he charted from afar was also legendary.

The Spanish

Spanish colonization came slowly to Trinidad. Ongoing battles with native Amerindian groups inhibited landings and permanent settlements. The first substantial colony was established nearly 100 years after Columbus's first landing, in 1592. The Spaniard Don Domingo de Vera established the town of San Jose de Oruna and declared it the island's capital. A few years later, in 1595, Sir Walter Raleigh—part poet, part tobacco entrepreneur, part pirate—sacked and reduced San Jose to rubble. The town was rebuilt in the early 17th century and is now called St. Joseph. (Note that there are two St. Joseph's on Trinidad: one on the southeast coast and one west of Tunapuna, on the northern population corridor. The latter is the old capital.)

The Spanish were tenacious and hung onto their possession, seeing it primarily as a ready source of slaves. They were, as always, fired by the hope of finding vast New World gold, namely the legendary city of El Dorado. They knew it had to be somewhere and would find it somehow. In the meantime, they established mildly profitable tobacco and cocoa plantations.

Interaction between the Spanish and Amerindian groups was rife with violence, and eventually disease. The Amerindians were particularly susceptible, and their accelerated rate of death decimated the population. In the meantime, Dutch, French, and British warships raided the island with regularity and even established small settlements. They also hammered at the Amerindian groups, and, reciprocally, were attacked. By the mid-18th century, the island was already an amalgam of cultures and settlers, although nominally still in the hands of the Spanish.

By 1757, a Spanish governor had moved the capital of San Jose to the natural harbor on the northwest coast. Port of Spain was the site of Raleigh's landing and would soon become a thriving seaport town. Catholic missionaries arrived, Amerindians suffered even more because of them, and everything seemed to be taking on a New World order in 1797, when Spain and Britain went to battle during the Napoleonic Wars.

The British
An expedition under Sir Ralph Abercrombie captured the island for Britain in the late 18th century. Fighting ensued for several years, and Trinidad was finally ceded to Britain in 1802 under the Treaty of Amiens. By 1815, Tobago, which had changed hands numerous times, was also under permanent British rule. Thus began the growth of the sugarcane industry and the accelerated importation of Africans for slave work. By the 1820s, the original population of 35,000 Amerindians had been reduced to about 800. Today, a community of Carib descendants numbering 300 live in Arima, in northeast

Trinidad. There are, however, no pure Caribs or Arawaks left on the island.

20th Century
The 1834 abolition of slavery in the British colonies introduced a labor shortage that was temporarily resolved by the introduction of indentured labor from East India. This continued from 1845 until 1915. In 1846, a large number of Portuguese, fleeing religious persecution, were allowed to settle in Trinidad. Other Europeans, including Irish, Scots, and Germans, emigrated to the island seeking employment. Chinese were brought in as laborers during the late 19th century, and workers from the smaller Caribbean islands were also part of the new labor force.

Britain's industrial revolution and the changing world order brought about by WW I heightened colonial movements for political representation and some independence. Widespread worker unrest led to labor strikes, which in turn led to the formation of political parties. Universal adult suffrage was granted in 1946, and about that time the seminal figure in the modern day Trinidad and Tobago political scene emerged from the dusty libraries of academia.

Eric Williams
Eric Eustace Williams received a doctorate from Oxford University and went on to become a social and political science lecturer at Howard University in the United States. At Howard, he published four books of West Indian social and political history, including the widely respected *The Negro in the Caribbean* (1940). Williams returned to Trinidad in 1944 to serve as a member of the Anglo-American Caribbean Commission.

In the early '50s, Williams organized a series of lectures and demonstrations at Woodford Square, in front of Port of Spain's public library, which came to be known as the "University" of Woodford Square. It was during one of these lectures, in 1955, that he announced the formation of a political party, the People's National Movement (PNM); its aim was to enfranchise Trinidad's black population and to agitate for independence.

The PNM gained control of the legislative council and came to power in 1956 with Williams as chief minister. The revered Williams would remain head of government for nearly 30 years, until his death in 1981.

Trinidad joined the now-defunct Federation of the West Indies in 1958 but left in 1961 after the then-powerful Jamaica withdrew, overburdened from supporting the Federation's less wealthy members.

Riots and Oil

Trinidad and Tobago was made an independent member of the Commonwealth in 1962. Within ten years the nation faced, neither for the first time nor the last, crisis rooted in economy and ethnicism. Riots broke out in April 1970, resulting in several deaths. Prime Minister Williams declared state of emergency, and elements in the army rebelled.

The riots were seen as directed against the minority East Indian population and were in effect an expression of black frustration over the economy and perceived racism. Prime Minister Williams appointed a Commission on Racial Discrimination to hold hearing on racism in Trinidad and Tobago, but the state of emergency was extended until June 1972.

Oil reserves discovered offshore had become an important industry in Trinidad and Tobago during the early part of the century, but during the petroleum shortage years of the 1970s Trinidad's resources suddenly turned to gold. Instant and seemingly unlimited wealth catapulted the nation to heady heights, and the roads, hospitals, schools, and social services of the republic were, at the time, modern beyond comparison with other islands of the Lesser Antilles.

Of course, things change. In the late '70s the Middle East began releasing stockpiled oil again, and as world prices slipped, so did Trinidad's brightest economic prospect. The easy-flowing money of the '70s had brought allegations of heavy-handed corruption and, in turn, voter mistrust.

Jamaat al-Muslimeen

The PNM, in power since the nation's formation, lost the 1986 election to the upsurge National Alliance for Reconstruction (NAR). However, the NAR prime minister, A.N.R. Robinson, soon became unpopular by instituting cost-cutting measures and reducing social programs.

On a Friday afternoon in July 1990, a well-coordinated Muslim fundamentalist group stormed Port of Spain's Parliament building and the offices of Trinidad and Tobago Television, while simultaneously bombing nearby Police Headquarters; the hulking and overgrown shell of the headquarters, across from the Parliament building, remains much the same as it looked that day.

The group, called Jamaat al-Muslimeen and led by Bilaal Abdullah and Imam Yasin Abu Bakr, held the prime minister and several Cabinet members hostage while widespread riots and looting ensued on the Port of Spain streets. More than 20 people died and millions of dollars worth of property damage was recorded while the government negotiated with the Muslimeen. For days Trinidad was in a state of anarchy, but finally the coup leaders surrendered with a full promise of amnesty signed by the acting President. The shaken government, however, immediately threw them in jail, where most remain today, pending numerous appeals. Their leader, Abu Bakr, is no longer a member.

The PNM was returned to power once again in 1991, headed by Prime Minister Patrick Manning.

PEOPLE AND CULTURE

Population

Trinidadians like to say that their population is descended from half the world. That is as true as these types of statements get. The population of Trinidad and Tobago is 1.3 million, of which about 41% is of African descent, and 41% of East Indian descent. People of Chinese, Syrian, European, and Mediterranean descent, or mixed ethnicity, make up the remaining 18%.

In many instances, groups tend to live in ethnically homogenous areas, and mingling is done at work, in commerce, and in social situations. Calling Trinidad and Tobago a bastion of racial harmony would be an overstatement, however, particularly between the majority African-descent and East Indian populations.

More than one-quarter of the population, about 350,000 people, lives in Port of Spain and its environs. The main population corridor of Trinidad is the northern east-west strip from Port of Spain to Arima, and along the north-south coast from Port of Spain to San Fernando. Tobago's majority population is black.

Language
One look at place names on a map of Trinidad will attest to the numerous languages that have passed through the island. Spanish names such as San Fernando, Rio Claro, Port of Spain, and the derivative Trinidad reflect earliest European influences. Earlier still, Amerindian names such as Caroni, Chaguanas, and even Tobago are reminders of the islands' first settlers. The French left Trinidad with Pointe-à-Pierre, Blanchisseuse, and Roussillac, and the more recent English colonials named towns such as Claxton Bay, Flanagin Town, and, of course, Waterloo. East Indian names are less frequent, belying the numbers.

Likewise, the languages of modern Trinidad reflect these and other influences. English is official, spoken with, some say, a brogue. Dialect is fast and lyrical, peppered with bits of Spanish, French, and African languages. The majority of the East Indian population is Hindu, and some Hindi is still spoken. Urdu is spoken by some Muslims, but certainly not all. Spanish and some French Creole is spoken in pockets, particularly along the north coast.

Religion
About a third of the population practices Catholicism, not surprising given the Spanish and French influences. A quarter of the population, mostly East Indians, practices Hinduism, although many East Indians have converted to forms of Christianity. Islam is practiced by about six percent of the population, Anglicans number 15%, and the rest practice various forms of Protestantism and other offshoots. Among them are Shango Baptists and Spiritual Baptists, who are heavily influenced by African spiritualism and some African holdover practices. A small but not insignificant Jewish population exists.

Of course, magic and other forms of mystical invocation inhabit the zeitgeist of modern Trinidad as deeply as western religion. Local folklore, festivals, and, in particular, Carnival are replete with jumbies, devils in disguise, the Lagahoo (a wolfman), and various characters both sinister and cynical. Orisha, the name derived from spirits and deities of the Yorubans of southern Nigeria, is combined with spiritual Christianity to invoke spirits through drumming.

Obeah, widely practiced throughout the Lesser Antilles, has in Trinidad and Tobago appealed to the mysticism of segments of the East Indian population—Hinduism, with its multi-appendaged, elephant-headed gods and goddesses lends itself well to the imagery of magic.

Carnival
The festivals of Trinidad and Tobago have exported their fevers throughout the world. In particular, the Carnival now ranks with New Orleans' Mardi Gras and Brazil's Carnival for sheer energy and the anarchic lunacy that fuel these ancient, pre-Lenten rituals. But it distinguishes itself from the New Orleans and Brazil festivals in two ways, by incorporating the home-grown and extremely popular calypsonians and steelbands in the party.

Both locals and visitors alike get into the fray, in ways you wouldn't want to tell your mother. Music, singing, dancing, licentiousness, and bacchanalia become serious pastimes during Carnival season, and the whole thing is so deeply infused with that national character that, for many, it is the reason to visit. While this undervalues the rest of Trinidad and Tobago's attractions, a couple of days at Carnival is enough to persuade anyone that it showcases the primary cultural force of the nation.

From Christmas until the weekend before Ash Wednesday, calypso tents throughout the countryside hold competitions for the best performances. Steelbands practice, and elaborate "mas" costumes are constructed by civic groups, businesses, or other groups.

The calypso competitions, featuring singers with names such as Shadow, Black Stalin, and Calypso Rose, culminate on Dimanche Gras, when a Calypso King and Queen, or Monarch, are chosen.

On J'Ouvert (also Jour Ouvert, pronounced Jo-VAY, for "sunrise"), also called Carnival Monday, parades begin early, and this is the day of flamboyant costumes, marches, and the steel band competitions. Look to Queen's Park Savannah in Port of Spain for the start of the action. The nights are filled with local parties, or fetes, and gatherings of dancers "wining," a particularly Trinidadian form of particularly suggestive dancing, at calypso and soca venues.

On Shrove Tuesday, revelers pour back into

THE STORY OF CARNIVAL

Many trace the origins of Trinidad's Carnival to the French influences of the country's early history. In the 1700s, French settlers were allowed by the Spanish to settle certain parts of the country, no doubt due to a laissez-faire attitude on the part of the Spanish toward their possession. Soon, the French population equaled that of the Spaniards.

Beginning in the 1780s, the French celebrated their Mardi Gras ("Fat Tuesday"), a traditional but small pre-Lenten festival. The celebrations lasted from Christmas until Ash Wednesday, the first day of Lent in Roman Catholic doctrine.

For half a century the French celebrated with dinners, masquerade balls, concerts, and hunting parties, clearly a more genteel celebration than the Trinidad Carnival as it is known today. They allowed their African slaves to celebrate, surreptitiously, as well, and the slaves used the opportunity to parody their owners' mannerisms, style of dress, and dancing.

The celebration caught on and became an integral part of the culture and society of Trinidad and Tobago, lasting beyond the immediate influence of the French. Throughout the period of British occupation, the festivities grew in size and scope.

After the 1834 British declaration of emancipation, Africans openly joined the celebration. This rapidly changed the tone, tune, and character of the Carnival.

They first developed "Canboulay," caricaturing the practice of *cannes brûlees,* the routine burning of cane in the sugarcane fields. The revelry included singing, marching through the streets with lighted torches, and stick fighting between "rival" groups of *batonniers.* At one point, former slaves celebrated Canboulay as a 1 August fete (Emancipation Day), but later the Africans brought the celebration back to the Carnival. It took place on Dimanche Gras, the Sunday before Carnival's final two-day explosion.

With that, Carnival took to the streets and soon took on blatant African tones. The masquerade *(mas)* marches became more complex, with satirical and sometimes overtly sexual stock characters such as the Jab Molassi (Molasses Devil), Jab Jab (a devil character with East Indian overtones), and the Moko Jumbie (a stilt dancer, often accompanied by a dwarf) springing up from African-Trinidadian Creole lore. Singing and chanting were in French Creole and, some say, languages from Guinea in West Africa. The beat of the music, which eventually developed into accompaniment for today's calypso, was culled from African traditions and originally involved drums, "tamboo bamboo" percussion instruments, and string bands. Drums were replaced by steel pans in the 1940s due to opposition by the colonial government (see "Music and Dance" under "The Arts" in the Introduction chapter).

The late-19th-century Africanization of Carnival alarmed the Whites—the upper class—who gradually took to their homes, refusing to participate in the celebrations.

Therein, for years well into this century Trinidad's colonials and upper class heaped scorn upon the Carnival celebrations. Of course, this did not deter the libertines of the hoi polloi, who increasingly celebrated with vigorous dancing, masquerading, and, perhaps most importantly, calypsoing.

So infused is Carnival with the character of Trinidad and Tobago, then and now, that riots broke out in 1881 when local authorities tried to quell Canboulay celebrations—a rumor had circulated that authorities were trying to shut down Carnival completely. A truce was drawn, and Carnival once again took to the streets, as strong as ever.

By the 1940s, opposition to Carnival's Sunday celebrations, a nod to Christianity's Sabbath, had temporarily restricted the final days of the revelry to the last two days before Ash Wednesday. Soon, the momentum of resurgent culture pushed Dimanche Gras back into the full-blown celebration once again. As a distinct celebration, however, Canboulay has given way to the massive popular festivities of Carnival.

---

the streets in costumes, accompanied by steel bands, calypso and soca trucks, and not a small amount of rum, turning the streets of Port of Spain into what can only be described as a profoundly large party. The party lasts until midnight and beyond, when Ash Wednesday signals the beginning of Lent, ostensibly a period of atonement and cleansing for Catholics.

A word of advice: If you decide to attend Carnival, book your flight and hotel room *now*—everyone else who wants to come, including Trinidad and Tobago expatriates, is doing just that. As well, pay close attention to your personal possessions during Carnival—if there is a time when thieves and other unsavory types will look for easy targets, this is it.

Holidays and Festivals

Trinidadians complain that, due to the number of ethnic communities coexisting in the nation, the constant stream of national holidays—at least one each month—makes it hard for anyone to get work done. There is truth in the sentiment.

In October, the East Indian community celebrates **Divali** (di-WAH-li), the Festival of Lights. The religious holiday is Hindu in origin and honors Lakshmi, the goddess of light, beauty, love, and riches. Throughout the countryside, thousands of tiny candles, *deyas,* and white lights are lit in her honor—the resemblance is close to the stringing of Christmas lights. The holiday is accompanied by prayer and by exotic East Indian feasts, low-key music, and dancing.

Hindus also celebrate **Ramleema,** a holiday that honors the life and teachings of Lord Rama. The holiday is celebrated according to the lunar calendar, but it usually falls in September or October.

Hosay, a Muslim festival observed in early June, started as a religious rite honoring brothers Hussein and Hossad, who were grandsons of Mohammed. Today it is a four-day cultural festival and includes elements of Hindu life, such as tassa drumming, and also elements of African life. The ceremonies of old included firewalking and fire-eating, and singing and drumming. Today's ceremonies also consist of role-playing the deaths of the brothers.

Independence Day (31 August) and **Emancipation Day** (1 August) are accompanied by steel band competitions, parades, and various local events. The intriguing **Pan Jazz Festival** is relatively new, dating from 1986. There is some debate among purists regarding the viability of pans as jazz instruments. The fact is, the event has received enormous support and enthusiasm from international jazz musicians, and has in the past featured names such as Dizzy Gillespie, Wynton Marsalis, the Stanley Turrentine Quintet, and Trinidad's own Len "Boogsie" Sharp, the "Charlie Parker of the Pan." The festival is held in November.

Christmas is notable for its great food and festivities, which include the annual revival of *parang* music. The form is associated with the country's Spanish heritage and involves carolling and accompaniment by guitar and mandolin. *Parang* is heard throughout the season and in an annual national competition.

GOVERNMENT AND ECONOMY

Government

Trinidad and Tobago became independent in 1962 and shifted to a republican form of government, with Commonwealth ties, in 1976. A non-executive president heads the republic, but power is vested in a prime minister, head of the majority political party. The legislature is bicameral, comprising an elected 36-member House of Representatives and an appointed 31-member Senate. Tobago, which has an internally elected House of Assembly, has limited control over its internal affairs. Currently, Trinidad and Tobago's prime minister is Patrick Manning of the PNM, and the president is Noor Mohammed Hassanali.

Oil

The Trinidad and Tobago economy is deeply entrenched, so to speak, in oil and natural gas, its main natural resources. The economy is slightly diversified and includes some agricultural products and exports such as sugarcane, cocoa, and some coffee and citrus fruits. About 14% of the land is arable, and agriculture employs 12% of the labor force.

Some mineral products, such as limestone, sand, and gravel, are developed for internal use and some export. Asphalt from the amazing Pitch Lake (the world's largest known reserve of natural asphalt) at La Brea represents a significant natural resource at the local level but is less so in the world market.

Still, it is clear that oil rules. The first exploratory oil well was sunk in 1857, and the island's first successful well was drilled in 1907. Since then, substantial oil and natural gas reserves have been found at offshore sites; they provide about 75% of total production. Refineries exist at Pointe-à-Pierre and Point Fortin. Nearly 80% of the country's exports are petroleum and its by-products, which account for about 25% of the gross domestic product.

The oil economy boomed in the heady 1970s, and Trinidad and Tobago became one of the wealthiest nations in the region. Overflowing government coffers doled out cash for infrastructure development, and soon Trinidad and Tobago had modern roads, schools, and hospitals. Everyone had a car, maybe two, and the debilitating

Carib beer, manufactured in Trinidad and throughout the Caribbean, is one of the region's most popular brews.

poverty that characterizes so many small Caribbean countries seemed as if it would become a distant and ugly memory in the nation's past. Then, the OPEC nations released oil reserves and the 1980s became a time to wonder what happened to it all. The coffers were almost empty due to unmitigated spending and some sticky government fingers. This brought about changes both in government and in the way Trinidad and Tobago looked at the petroleum industry's one-sided effect on the nation's economy.

An immediate reaction to several years of economic decline was Trinidad and Tobago's decision to reschedule debts with the International Monetary Fund (IMF). This they did twice. Unemployment, however, rose to nearly 20%. So, more effort was put into promoting tourism as an industry, and that effort continues today. The government floated the Trinidad and To-

bago dollar (TT$) in April 1993, which resulted in an immediate 34% devaluation of the currency against the U.S. dollar. Good news for overseas investors. Bad news for the locals.

Tourism

Tourism is growing and is today primarily Tobago's piece of the pie. The smaller Tobago currently has more than 1,000 hotel and guesthouse rooms available, and Trinidad, which accommodates large numbers of business travelers in Port of Spain, has over 1,200 rooms. U.S. visitors account for the greatest number of overnight stays, and the two-island nation saw an increase of seven percent in its total tourism numbers in 1992. Both islands saw nearly 250,000 visitor arrivals in 1993, still a small number relative to other Lesser Antillean islands.

TRINIDAD SIGHTS

Beaches

Trinidad's best beaches are located along the northern and eastern coasts. The water on both coasts is known to be rough at times, and on supervised beaches colored flags are posted to indicate water conditions. Red means "not safe," yellow "sort of safe," and white "splash to your heart's content."

Along the North Coast Road, accessed north through Maraval in Port of Spain, are the island's most popular spots. The North Coast Road is at any rate a breathtaking drive through hills and dips and views of expansive ocean bays. The beaches mentioned below are public facilities; most have lifeguards, parking, changing facilities, showers and toilets, and food kiosks. There are generally no fees for beach use, although some charge a small fee for the changing rooms.

The north shore's **Maracas Bay Beach** is long, wide, and possibly the island's most popular beach. A small restaurant sits in the hills overlooking the bay. This beach is crowded on weekends and holidays and is about 35 minutes from Port of Spain.

A short hike into the hills south of Maracas Bay will bring you to the Maracas Waterfall, a 90-foot (27-meter) cascade and popular spot for picnickers.

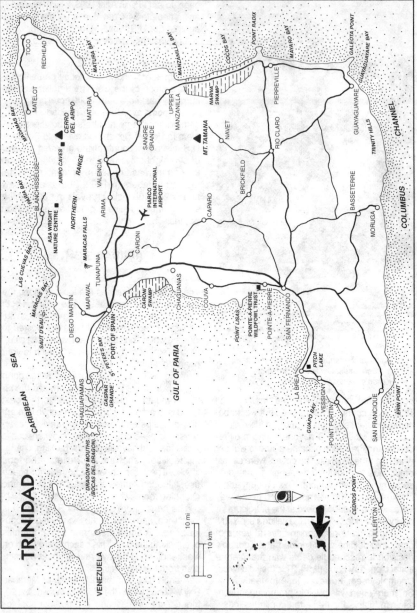

TRINIDAD

VENEZUELA

CARIBBEAN
SEA

DRAGON'S MOUTHS
(BOCAS DEL DRAGON)

CHAGUARAMAS

GASPAR
GRANDE

ST. PETER'S BAY
PORT OF SPAIN

DIEGO MARTIN

MARAVAL

SAUT D'EAU

MARACAS BAY

LAS CUEVAS BAY

MARACAS BAY

BLANCHISSEUSE

PARIA BAY

M'DAMAS BAY

TOCO

REDHEAD

MATELOT

MATURA BAY

ASA WRIGHT
NATURE CENTRE

ARIPO CAVES
CERRO
DEL ARIPO

NORTHERN
RANGE

MARACAS FALLS

TUNAPUNA

ARIMA

VALENCIA

MATURA

SANGRE
GRANDE

CARONI

PIARCO
INTERNATIONAL
AIRPORT

CARONI
SWAMP

CHAGUANAS

COUVA

POINT LISAS

POINTE-A-PIERRE
WILDFOWL TRUST

POINTE-A-PIERRE

SAN FERNANDO

GULF OF PARIA

LA BREA

PITCH
LAKE

GUAPO BAY

VESSIGNY

POINT FORTIN

CEDROS POINT

FULLERTON

SAN FRANCIQUE

ERIN POINT

MORUGA

BASSETERRE

TRINITY HILLS

GUAYAGUAYARE

GUAYAGUAYARE BAY

GALEOTA POINT

COLUMBUS
CHANNEL

RIO CLARO

PIERREVILLE

MAYARO BAY

POINT RADIX

COCOS BAY

MANZANILLA BAY

NARIVA
SWAMP

UPPER
MANZANILLA

NAVET

MT. TAMANA

BRICKFIELD

CAPARO

10 mi

10 km

0

© MOON PUBLICATIONS, INC.

A few minutes east of Maracas is **Tyrico Bay,** a smaller beach, about 300 feet (91 meters) long. Camping is allowed here. East of Tyrico is **Las Cuevas Bay Beach,** a quiet and calm beach. "Las Cuevas" refers to the many caves that are found in the area.

Farther east you'll find smaller and less crowded beaches at **Blanchisseuse, Paria, Madamas Bay,** and **Matelot.**

On the island's east coast, from **Manzanilla** in the north to **Point Radix** in the south, is **Manzanilla Bay,** which has one of the longest beaches in the country. From Point Radix to **Galeota Point,** along the Mayaro to Guayaguayare Road, is **Mayaro Bay,** which, at about 10 miles (16 km) is the longest beach on the island. This is sort of a honky-tonk area, with roadside kiosks, restaurants, hotels, guesthouses, and the usual suspects lining the road.

Beaches at **Vessigny** in the south and **Chagville** (man-made, no lifeguards) in the northwest at **Chaguaramas** are also popular. Chaguaramas, the island's northwest peninsula, was occupied by U.S. forces during WW II, and many of the old military buildings remain in place.

North Trinidad

A 30-minute drive south of Port of Spain will bring you to the **Caroni Swamp and Bird Sanctuary,** home of the national bird, the scarlet ibis. Part lagoon and part swamp, the bird sanctuary is most active at sunset, when the hundreds of scarlet ibises and other birds come home to roost. Boat tours start late in the afternoon. You can organize a trip through tour operators in hotels or in Port of Spain, or call authorized boat operators Winston Nanan, tel. (809) 645-1305, or David Ramsahai, tel. (809) 663-2207. Cost is about TT$25 per person.

The **Asa Wright Nature Centre,** tel. (809) 667-4655, is found on the North Coast Road. Turn off just past the village of Blanchisseuse, about a 90-minute drive northeast from Port of Spain. The center consists of displays, nature trails, and a small inn. One of the trails accesses **Dunston Cave,** home of a colony of the nocturnal oilbird, called the *guacharo.* Amerindian groups prized the birds for their fat, which gave them their name and gave the Amerindians oil

for lamps and fires. Dozens of other bird species can be identified. Guided tours are available, and the center is open daily 9 a.m.-5 p.m., admission TT$34 (US$6).

Central Trinidad

Chaguanas, south of Caroni Swamp, is the island's third largest city, home of writers and brothers V.S. Naipaul and Shiva Naipaul.

The **Pointe-à-Pierre Wildfowl Trust,** tel. (809) 662-4040, set on Trinoc oil refinery land, lies north of San Fernando. The conservation trust features a learning center, some trails, and a breeding area for local endangered species. It is open to the public daily 10 a.m.-5 p.m.

San Fernando, located south of Chaguanas, is the country's second largest city and industrial capital. About 30 miles (48 km) south of Port of Spain, the town was incorporated as a city in 1988. This is a population center for East Indians, and the town feels like an industrial center. The belching oil refineries and sprawling industrial plants set the tone.

Pitch Lake

Heading south—the land of sugarcane and oil fields—you'll come to the amazing **Pitch Lake** at **La Brea.** The 109-acre lake of bitumen, which is a viscous, almost solid mass of warm asphalt, bubbles and boils indiscernibly, like a rippled gray-black sea of sludge. Near the center of the "lake," the bitumen is an estimated 300 feet (92 meters) deep. You can walk on it. Whether you'd want to is your choice, but guides are available to explain the whole phenomenon—in fact, packs of guides are available, all willing to help you out for a price. Negotiate this before you set off on the lake with anyone.

A legend associated with the spot has it engulfing an Amerindian tribe called the Chimans, who had offended the Good Spirit by eating hummingbirds. The Indians called the substance *piche,* and it was here, in 1595, that Sir Walter Raleigh discovered the oozing pitch from the lake was ideal for caulking ships. The asphalt has since been used in the building of roads.

For a more thorough background on the lake, see the display at the National Museum in Port of Spain. There is a small museum at the tar pit.

PORT OF SPAIN

Port of Spain is the cultural and administrative center of the country and is unlike any city of its size in the Lesser Antilles, due only partially to the fact that there is no other city of its size in the Lesser Antilles. Still, its cosmopolitan promise and energetic street life give it a flair worth exploring for several days. This is a city of contrasts, where Christian churches, Islamic mosques, and Hindu temples stand in close proximity, and where a homeless beggar might stop a Mercedes-Benz for a handout.

The city architecture features styles from the wooden Victorian homes with classic Caribbean gingerbread fretwork, to block concrete office buildings and Gothic church towers. Port of Spain is lively, clean in places, dirty in others, and generally safe, but watch yourself at night and don't travel to outlying areas without a specific destination.

The city lies on the west coast Gulf of Paria, sheltered from northeasterly winds by the Northern Range. It is surrounded by suburbs and sloping hills, fronted by a natural harbor, and buttressed by the massive Caroni Swamp to the south.

About 350,000 people live in the metro area of Port of Spain, which became the island's capital in 1784. Downtown is laid out in blocks in a complicated one-way street system that may make driving an endeavor you'll want to leave to taxi drivers. If you do drive, you'll find numerous small parking lots downtown (Frederick Street has several) that charge TT$3 per hour or TT$10 per day.

Queen's Park Savannah

Queen's Park Savannah is the centerpiece, though not directly downtown, of the city. This sprawling 200-acre lawn is ground zero for Carnival activities and festivities year-round. Ice-cream kiosks, peanut vendors, coconut vendors, joggers, and strollers line the massive grounds, which are circumnavigated (about three miles or five km around) by busy one-way streets.

The park is lined on its northwestern edge by a group of mansions called **The Magnificent Seven,** not named for the title of a movie.

The colonial mansions, built by wealthy families between 1904 and 1906, are reminders of those days and include Queen's Royal College, the residences of the Anglican Bishop and Roman Catholic Bishop, and Stollmyer's Castle, a reproduction of the Scottish Balmoral Castle. The architecture is diverse and mystifying, an odd reminder of wealth gone awry.

To the north of the savannah is the **Emperor Valley Zoo, Botanic Gardens,** and **President's House.** The zoo, which houses examples of Trinidad and Tobago's wildlife, is open daily 9:30 a.m.-6 p.m., admission TT$3.

The gardens were established by a Governor Woodward in 1820, and garden officials claim that they're the oldest botanic gardens in the Western Hemisphere. The gardens are a good introduction to local flora and exhibit many examples from South America and around the world.

The president's official residence, as well as the prime minister's, are located on the gardens' grounds. The mansions are not open to the public.

National Museum

The **National Museum and Art Gallery,** tel. (809) 623-5941, formerly the Royal Victoria Institute, sits on Upper Frederick Street at the southwest corner of the savannah, facing the small **Memorial Park.**

The museum, the place to stop for a complete backgrounder on Trinidad and Tobago, houses displays from the coffee, coconut, sugarcane, and printing industries, as well as a large exhibition detailing the island's petroleum industry. If you've never seen Carnival costumes, you'll see them here. The display chronicling the history of the aromatic, spicy additive **Angostura Bitters,** one of Trinidad and Tobago's more well-known exports since 1824, is worth a stop.

Upstairs is an art gallery, housing local and international works of art, including examples from the 19th-century Trinidadian painter Cazabon. The museum is open Tues.-Sat., 10 a.m.-6 p.m. No photos are allowed, and admission is free.

Downtown

The downtown **Woodford Square** is at the heart of the city. This important historical site is named

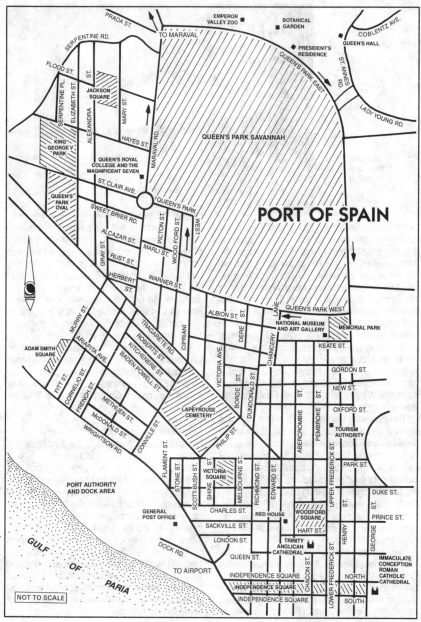

© MOON PUBLICATIONS, INC.

sign on a small cafe, downtown Port of Spain

after former Governor Woodford. This is the spot where the late Eric Williams, Trinidad and Tobago's first prime minister and political dynamo, organized the 1950s series of lectures known as the "University" of Woodford Square, and this is where he announced the formation of the island's first political party. The park is still used for public discourse, bible thumping, ranting, whatever. The square is a bustling place and residence for many of the city's homeless.

Bordering Woodford Square is Port of Spain's **National Library** (open Mon.-Fri. 8:30 a.m.-6 p.m.), as well as **Trinity Anglican Cathedral,** a circa 1820 building with architecture copied from London's Westminster Hall. **Town Hall** also borders the square.

The elongated **Red House** is, in fact, red, or at least a deep rust color, and it is the seat of Trinidad and Tobago's parliament. This is the most imposing building lining the square. The original parliament building burned down in 1903 during riots over proposed water-rate increases, and the present building dates back to 1907. Red House was the site of the 1990 coup attempt, and the burned hulk of Police Headquarters, destroyed by bombs during that attempt, is visible at the western end of Red House.

Two blocks south of Woodford Square, toward the docks area, is the busy **Independence Square.** Along one of the town's first established roads, then called Calle de Marina, the square was once called Plaza de Marina. It was refurbished in the early 1800s by Governor Woodford and named Independence Square in 1962 in commemoration of that event. Today it is home to sidewalk vendors, taxi stands, bus and maxi-taxi stands, and dozens of small shops and bars. The square is lined with examples of the old colonial-style buildings, including the massive gothic **Immaculate Conception Roman Catholic Cathedral,** at the east end. The construction of the cathedral, begun in 1816, reportedly took 16 years.

Express House occupies about a block on the south side of the square and is the home of Trinidad and Tobago's first newspaper. It was once an old cocoa storage house and now houses the Caribbean Communications Network (CCN).

Port of Spain Suburbs

Suburbs on the outskirts of town have an important role in Port of Spain's history.

Laventille, a rough, run-down neighborhood built into dramatic hills and dipping ravines, lies east of downtown. It was here that the first sounds of steel bands were popularized. In fact, many say the birthplace of the steel pan instrument is Laventille. The neighborhood is the home of the famous **Desperadoes Panyard** on Upper Laventille Road, established about 1945. This may be the epicenter of pan music today. The Desperadoes have been around since the 1960s, winning steel band competitions and traveling worldwide with the sound of Trinidad and Tobago.

North of town you'll find **St. James,** the "city that never sleeps." This is the city's neon-laden, late-night district, the place to go for a snack or drink, or whatever, after the rest of the city closes.

SPORTS AND ENTERTAINMENT

Water Sports
Call **The Surfing Association of Trinidad and Tobago,** tel. (809) 637-4533, and the **Windsurfing Association of Trinidad and Tobago,** tel. (809) 659-2457, for more information about facilities regarding those sports.

Boating
Island Yacht Charters, tel. (809) 637-7389 or 637-7100, fax 628-0437, will charter boats and organize deep-sea fishing charters, as well as snorkeling and sightseeing trips. The **Trinidad and Tobago Yacht Club,** tel. (809) 637-4260, is a good contact for yacht rentals and water sports.

Deep-Sea Fishing
Bayshore Charters, tel. (809) 637-8711, will help you set up a trip or, for general information, call the **Trinidad and Tobago Game Fishing Association,** tel. (809) 624-5304, fax 627-0391.

Diving
Diving is better on Tobago than on Trinidad, but if you're in the mood, call **Scuba Shop,** tel. (809) 658-2183, in Mirabella. **Ron's Watersports,** tel. (809) 622-0459, offers deep-sea fishing, diving, and water sports.

Golf
Check out the 18-hole **St. Andrew Golf Club,** tel. (809) 629-2314, at Moka in Maraval, and the nine-hole **Chaguaramas Golf Course,** tel. (809) 634-4349.

Nightlife
Nightlife is a way of life on this lively island, and you won't want for dancing, live music, authentic calypso and steel band shows, movies, or theater. Or, if you desire, you can find limboing and tourist-oriented shows. The best thing you can do to discover what's going on is pick up and read the local newspapers.

The **Moon Over Bourbon Street** bar, tel. (809) 637-3448, at the West Mall features live weekend entertainment and all-you-can-eat specials. **The Upper Level Club,** tel. (809) 637-1753, is also located at the West Mall.

The **Mas Camp Pub,** tel. (809) 627-8449, in Woodbrook features live entertainment most nights, usually local calypsonians and pan bands. Entertainment cover charge is TT$10. **The Attic,** tel. (809) 622-8123, and **Basement Pub,** tel. (809) 628-2705, both in Maraval, offer live entertainment.

selling coconuts in Independence Square

MORE TRINIDAD HOTELS

Rates per s, EP when applicable, winter

NAME	(809)	FAX	LOCATION	TARIFF
Chaconia Inn	628-8603	628-3214	Maraval	moderate
Hosanna Hotel	662-4593	662-5451	St. Augustine, Tunapuna	moderate
Naden's Court	645-2973	645-2973	St. Augustine, Tunapuna	moderate
The Normandie Hotel	624-1181	624-1181	St. Ann's, Port of Spain	moderate
Pelican Inn Resort	627-6271	623-0987	Cascade	budget
Royal Hotel	652-3924	652-3924	San Fernando	moderate-luxury
Royal Palm Suite Hotel	628-5086	624-6042	Maraval	moderate-luxury
Tropical Hotel	622-5815	628-3174	Maraval	luxury
Valley Vue Hotel	623-3511	627-8046	St. Ann's, Port of Spain	moderate-luxury

TRINIDAD ACCOMMODATIONS

Accommodation on Trinidad and Tobago can be a good bargain, particularly given that the floating Trinidad and Tobago dollar has rendered some foreign currencies powerful indeed. In general, Trinidad and Tobago, more so Trinidad, offer inexpensive to moderately priced accommodations.

The best bargains are found at small guesthouses and bed and breakfast homes, of which there are hundreds. Bed and breakfasts can put you in touch with Trinidad and Tobago families, which makes a good opportunity for cultural exchange.

The **Bed and Breakfast Association of Trinidad and Tobago,** P.O. Box 3231, Diego Martin, Trinidad, West Indies, tel. (809) 637-9329, fax 627-0856, lists more than 100 properties that conform to a fairly stringent set of standards.

During the slow tourist season, roughly mid-April through mid-December, room tariffs are lowered by as much as 40%. Hotel and guesthouse rates during the mid-February Carnival season do the opposite and may rise by as much as 40%. Accommodations disappear quickly during Carnival season, and bookings should be made well ahead of time, as in "as we speak."

Larger hotels add a 10% service charge plus a hefty 15% value-added tax (VAT). The VAT is also often added to guesthouse bills, but not always.

The categories below and in the Tobago section refer to tariffs during the high season, per person, per night: **Luxury** US$100 or more, **Moderate** US$50-100, **Budget** US$50 or less.

Hotels

Trinidad Hilton, P.O. Box 422, Port of Spain, Trinidad, West Indies, tel. (809) 624-3211, fax 624-6133, is functional, even elegant, and highly regarded. The location, on Lady Young Road overlooking Queen's Park Savannah, affords good views of the harbor and parts of downtown in the distance. You're within walking distance to Queen's Park Savannah and, if you've got energy, downtown. The hotel books more business travelers than tourists and has full facilities, including a large buffet breakfast. Luxury.

Holiday Inn, P.O. Box 1017, Port of Spain, Trinidad, West Indies, tel. (809) 625-3361, is located downtown on Wrightson Road, near the port and Independence Square. It's a clean, comfortable, and familiar place—hey, it's a Holiday Inn. You know what you're getting. A little pricey, but convenient. Luxury.

Kapok Hotel, 16-18 Cotton Hill, St. Clair, Port of Spain, Trinidad, West Indies, tel. (809) 622-6441, U.S. tel. (800) 333-1212, fax 622-9677, is located north of the Queen's Savannah, heading out toward the Maraval suburb. The location is good, near Port of Spain but away from the buzz. The rooms are clean and comfortable and have television, and the two restaurants, the Savanna and the Tiki, are popular with locals and tourists alike. Moderate.

Carnetta's House, 28 Scotland Terrace, Andalusia, Maraval, Trinidad, West Indies, tel. (809) 628-2732, fax 628-7717, is located in the suburban Maraval, just north of Port of Spain. Carnetta's is a small (five rooms) family-run guesthouse, comfortable, clean, very much like home. The owners, Carnetta and Winston Borrell, are flexible about schedules, meals, etc. The rooms have private baths, television, phones, and air conditioning. The location is good for exploring the north coast; a maxi-taxi from here to town costs about TT$2. Moderate.

Asa Wright Nature Center Lodge, Blanchisseuse Rd., Arima, tel. (809) 667-4655. Contact Caligo Ventures, 156 Bedford Rd., Armonk,

NY 10504, tel. (800) 426-7781. Set in the hills of the Arima Valley about 90 minutes east of Port of Spain, this small lodge attracts nature lovers and birders, in particular. The nature center itself is home to dozens of bird species, and trails offer opportunities for exploring. Meals are included in the rates. Moderate.

Camping

Camping, while allowed in designated places, is not encouraged. Security is a problem. Check with the Tourism Development Authority for current approved camping facilities.

FOOD IN TRINIDAD

Trinidadian West Indian, East Indian, Chinese, various European, and North American cuisines are represented all over the islands. Hotels generally have very good food and expect patrons to pay for it as well. East Indian restaurants tend to combine West Indies Creole-style cooking such as callaloo (leafy, green spinach stalks of the dasheen plant) and seafood with traditional items such as rotis. A roti is a flat bread rolled around a filling of mutton or goat meat, or potato and peas, always curried enough to make

---

MORE TRINIDAD
APARTMENTS AND GUESTHOUSES

Rates per s, EP when applicable, winter

NAME	(809)	FAX	LOCATION	TARIFF
The Abercrombie	623-5259	625-6453	Port of Spain	budget
Alicia's House	623-2802	623-8560	St. Ann's, Port of Spain	budget
Five Star Guesthouse	623-4006	623-4006	Woodbrook, Port of Spain	budget
Halyconia	623-0008	624-6481	Cascade, Port of Spain	budget
Monique's Guesthouse	628-3334	622-3232	Maraval	budget
Par-May La's	628-2008	628-4707	Port of Spain	budget
Pax Guesthouse	662-4084	662-5286	Mt. St. Benedict, Tunapuna	budget-moderate
Trini House	638-7550	N/A	St. James	budget
Villa Maria Inn	629-8023	N/A	Maraval	budget
Zollna House	628-3731	627-0856	Maraval	budget

MORE TRINIDAD RESTAURANTS

NAME	LOCATION	(809)	CUISINE	PRICE RANGE
Anchorage	Chaguaramas	634-4334	seafood	moderate
Chaconia Inn	Maraval	628-8603	Continental/steaks	moderate
Monsoon	Newtown, Port of Spain	628-7684	Indian	inexpensive
Seabelle	St. James	622-3594	seafood	moderate
Tiki Village	Kapok Hotel, Port of Spain	622-6441	Oriental	moderate
Veni Mange	St. James	622-7533	West Indian	moderate
Villa Creole	Woodbrook, Port of Spain	628-2209	Creole	moderate

you cry. **Pelau** is a rice and peas, and sometimes meat, dish.

Small takeout places offer good deals and let you get in touch with how the islanders eat. Don't be afraid of them. Of course you can get **Subway, KFC,** and pizzas in Port of Spain and most major towns (KFC is also one of the few places open on Sunday), but the local East Indian takeouts, such as **Callaloo Cafe** on Henry Street in Port of Spain, are recommended. Others: **Cafe Savannah,** tel. (809) 622-6441, at the Kapok Hotel in Port of Spain reputedly has some of the best Trinidadian home-style cooking in town. **Hot Shoppe** on Mucurapo Street has excellent rotis and East Indian cuisine. **Veni Mange** in St. James serves lunch only, and the cuisine is West Indian Creole, with lots of coconut bases and seafood.

GETTING TO TRINIDAD

By Air

Trinidad's **Piarco International Airport,** tel. (809) 664-5196, about 17 miles (27 km) from Port of Spain, is served by major North American, European, South American, and Caribbean airlines. **American Airlines,** tel. (809) 664-4661, one of the region's bigger carriers, has direct flights from Puerto Rico. **Air Canada,** tel. (809) 664-4065, operates service from Toronto.

ALM, tel. (809) 625-1719; **Guyana Airways,** tel. (809) 627-2753; and **Aeropostal,** tel. (809) 623-6522, connect with major South American cities.

Until late 1994, **British Airways,** tel. (809) 625-1811, and **United,** tel. (809) 627-7000, operated flights from London and from New York and Caracas, respectively. Service has been suspended, but it may resume at any time. **KLM Royal Dutch Airlines** has also recently suspended its service from Amsterdam, but it may resume in the future. Check with a travel agent.

Trinidad's own **BWIA,** tel. (809) 627-BWIA, has direct connections from Frankfurt, London, Miami, New York, Toronto, and Zurich, as well as from other Caribbean islands. The regional airline **LIAT,** tel. (809) 623-1837/8, operates the most complete schedule of connections to and from neighboring islands.

Immigration

Trinidad and Tobago has stricter immigration laws than other countries in the Lesser Antilles. To enter, everyone is required to carry a passport, not merely identification such as a license or birth certificate. Visas are also required of nationals of certain countries: Australia, India, Papua New Guinea, New Zealand, and current and former communist/socialist block countries. Check with your local authorities. Visas for stays of less than three months are not required by citizens of Canada, France, Italy, the U.K., U.S., and most of Western Europe.

For information on getting to Tobago, see "Getting to Tobago," below.

Departure Tax

When leaving Trinidad and Tobago, departure tax is TT$75. This is payable at the airport in Trinidad and Tobago dollars only. Make sure you have the cash on hand; immigration officials are serious about this.

GETTING AROUND TRINIDAD

Public Transportation

Trinidad and Tobago is a country of 1.3 million on the move, and the public transport system is sophisticated and efficient. Still, who can figure it out but a Trinidadian?

Well, it appears to work like this: Most public transport vehicles are called "taxis" in one way or another. All public livery vehicles are identified by an "H" on the license plate. "Route taxis," usually sedan cars, follow specific routes and charge each person in the vehicle. Route taxis usually operate in and about major population centers.

"Maxi-taxis," which are in fact minivans, operate along major routes between towns. These are identified by large colored stripes on their sides, which in turn indicate destinations. Green is for south Trinidad, red for east Trinidad, yellow for Port of Spain, and so on. It's all very colorful.

"Buses," which are in fact buses, are identified by their large size.

Port of Spain is the starting point, and Queen's Park Savannah or Independence Square have major taxi/maxi-taxi/bus stands. Independence Square is the best place to start your journey. When in doubt, ask around which vehicles go where.

Sample bus fares: Port of Spain to Arima TT$2, Port of Spain to San Fernando TT$3.50, San Fernando to Mayaro TT$2. You'll never pay more than TT$4 for a bus trip. A maxi-taxi from Port of Spain to San Fernando costs TT$5.

Private Taxis

Private taxis are expensive, and those that are attached to hotels are more expensive still.

Fares are set by the Tourism Development Authority, and drivers are supposed to quote the appropriate rate. Most do. For example, a ride from Piarco Airport to Port of Spain costs TT$114 (US$20).

Major city taxi stands are found at Queen's Park Savannah, Woodford Square, or Independence Square. If you need to call for a pick-up, try **Bacchus Taxi,** tel. (809) 622-5588; **Queen's Park Taxi Stand,** tel. (809) 625-3002; or **St. Christopher Taxi,** tel. (809) 624-3560 or 627-2257.

Rental Cars

Rental cars are not hard to find, except at Carnival time. Rates range US$35-60 per day, less for multiple days. Most take credit cards, but ask first, otherwise a large cash deposit is required. Several companies require drivers to be 25 years or older. For rentals, a valid driver's license or international license will be fine for up to three months. Driving is on the left.

At Piarco Airport, try, among dozens of others, **AR Auto Rentals,** tel. (809) 669-2277; **Singh's,** tel. (809) 664-5417, fax 627-8476; or **Auto Rentals,** tel. (809) 669-2277, fax 675-2258. In town, call **Toyota Rent a Car,** tel. (809) 628-5516, fax 628-6808, or **Automania,** tel. (809) 628-8503.

Motorcycle and Bicycle Rentals

Bicycles (about TT$25 per day), motor scooters, and motorcycles (about TT$80) can be rented from **Greene's General Cycle,** tel. (809) 646-BIKE, in Arouca.

TOBAGO

Tobago has become the tourism center of the two islands, both for Trinidadians as well as international visitors. The island is quiet in its own way, small and navigable, a getaway, and a good place to relax at a beach for a while.

Tobago is best seen by rental car, although taxis can do the job if you're willing to pay. The roads are generally good and, except for several of the smaller interior roads, are marked well enough to get around. You can tour the island in a day, but if you'd care to linger, and you will, three or four days is better. The best available map of Tobago is found at the **Land & Surveys Division,** 18 Abercrombie Street in Port of Spain.

TOBAGO SIGHTS

Beaches

On Tobago, the first stop is at **Pigeon Point.** This hugely popular area, minutes north of the airstrip, is where a good number of the island's hotels and other facilities are located. Area beaches include **Store Bay** and **Sandy Bay.**

The **Pigeon Point Resort's** seaside facilities are open to the public, but you'll need to pay a fee to enter the resort. Adults are charged TT$10, children ages 6-12 TT$5, and under 6 free. Remember, the beach itself is free, as are all beaches in Trinidad and Tobago. But you'll pay for the parking, changing rooms, and use of the bar and restaurant.

The town of **Buccoo,** chock full of hotels and water sports facilities, is adjacent to **Buccoo Bay** and **Mt. Irvine Bay,** two fine areas for swimming. **Buccoo Reef** is offshore, the island's best spot for snorkeling.

On the northeast shore, the beach at **Speyside** has changing facilities and showers. This beach has views to the famous bird sanctuary of **Little Tobago Island,** which can be accessed by from local hotels or by paying a local fisherman.

Other Tobago beaches include **King's Bay** near Delaford, **Man Of War Bay** (with changing facilities) near Charlotteville, and a half-dozen others scattered around the island.

Scarborough

From the small Crown Point Airport, where rental cars and taxis are available, take the **Claude Noel Highway** to **Scarborough,** the island's capital.

At population 18,000, the town is as busy as it gets on Tobago, which isn't saying much. The new Port Authority building, by the docks, is the largest structure in town. This is where island buses congregate. A few banks, guesthouses, supermarkets, a mall, and a large and busy outdoor market occupy much of the rest of town.

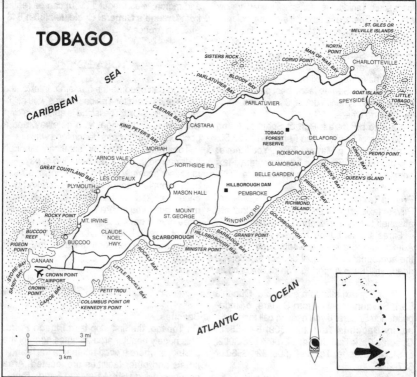

A 17-acre **Botanical Garden** is of interest, and **Fort King George,** built by the British in 1779, sits up on Fort Street in the hills above town. The fort saw battles with the French during the 18th century. It changed hands several times, and was called Fort Castries from 1781 to 1793. The fort's prison, barracks, and armament ports are still there, but the view is one of its best features. Also on the grounds is the **Tobago Museum,** located in the barracks house. The museum houses military paraphernalia, Amerindian artifacts, and documents from the slave period. The museum is open Mon.-Fri. 9 a.m.-5 p.m. Admission is TT$3, children TT$1.

leatherback turtle

BOB RACE

Around the Island

The **Windward Road** follows the south coast, through small towns, villages, and football fields, and over dramatic hills past small bays and inlets. This is a pleasant drive, and a good introduction to the island.

The **Tobago Forest Reserve,** located on the northeast side of the island, is accessible by heading north at the small town of Roxborough or via any of the dozens of trails that crisscross and enter the reserve from all directions. The Roxborough-Parlatuvier Road crosses the heart of the reserve and the heart of the island and is well worth the drive. You can stop at the **Bloody Bay Recreation Site,** a small hut with toilets, a posted map of trails, and striking views to Bloody Bay. This is a good place to begin a hike. The reserve was established in 1765 and is one of the oldest in this hemisphere.

Windward Road continues along the south coast to **Speyside,** where you'll find several nice beaches and access to **Little Tobago Island,** a 250-acre bird sanctuary.

Charlotteville is a small, isolated, and pleasant fishing town situated on the northeastern tip of the island. Some of the island's best diving is nearby. Off the Charlotteville shore is **St. Giles Island,** another bird-breeding colony. The sea surrounding the island is rough, and access is difficult.

The bays on the leeward side of the island are dramatic, and the villages seem to be built in the mountainsides.

In **Plymouth,** ask someone to direct you to the 1783 tombstone of Betty Stiven and her child. The inscription reads: "What was remarkable of her, She was a Mother without knowing it and a Wife without letting her Husband know it except by her kind indulgences to him." Clearly, Ms. Stiven led a complicated life. Nevertheless, the tombstone is a great source of mystery and local gossip.

The southwest tip of the island is the beach, guesthouse, and tourist center and is where many water sports facilities are found. **Buccoo Reef** is important not only because it is the island's best diving spot, but because it is the island's second national reserve, this one a marine reserve.

At **Turtle Beach Hotel, Grafton Beach Resort,** and other spots along the island's leeward coast, it is possible to see leatherback turtles laying eggs and nesting at night on the beaches. The season is roughly April through July and into August. The huge turtles, which lay upwards of 125 eggs at a time, are protected by law, and the hotels organize turtle-watching trips during season.

Tobago Festivals

Tobago's **Heritage Festival,** held in for two weeks in late July, is an island-wide event that celebrates the Tobago culture's African roots. Villages and towns reenact pivotal events in Tobago history and celebrate superstitions, folktales, and beliefs with storytelling, feasts, and costumed events.

SPORTS

Water Sports

Many of the beachfront hotels along Shore Bay operate their own facilities, where rentals are available. Otherwise you could try the following.

Divers have several choices on Tobago. **Dive Tobago,** tel. (809) 639-0202, is located at

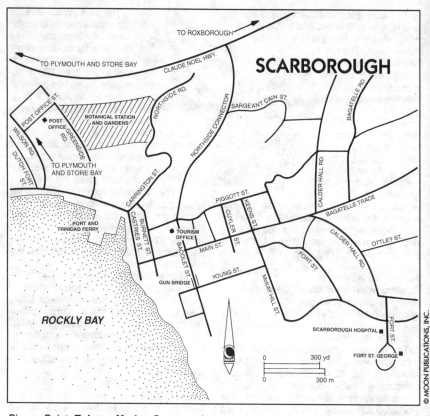

SCARBOROUGH

© MOON PUBLICATIONS, INC.

Pigeon Point; **Tobago Marine Sports,** tel. (809) 639-0291, is at Store Bay and Crown Point Beach Hotel; and **Man Friday Diving,** tel. (809) 660-4676, has facilities in Speyside and Charlotteville.

Those looking for deep-sea fishing adventures should call **Dillon's Charters,** tel. (809) 639-8765, located at Crown Point.

Boating enthusiasts can contact the *Loafer,* tel. (809) 639-8555.

Tennis
Court locations are limited to hotels. Among them, call **Blue Water Inn,** tel. (809) 660-4341, in Speyside, or **Mt. Irvine Bay Hotel,** tel. (809) 639-8871.

TOBAGO ACCOMMODATIONS

Unlike Trinidad, many of Tobago's hotels and guesthouses are located near the beach areas. For rate classifications, see "Trinidad Accommodations," earlier in this chapter.

Conrado Beach Resort, Pigeon Point, Tobago, West Indies, tel. (809) 639-0145, fax 639-0755, is located along the beach at Pigeon Point. Good location, good deal, no frills. Moderate.

Mount Irvine Bay Hotel, P.O. Box 222, Tobago, West Indies, tel. (809) 639-8871/2/3, U.S. tel. (800) 74 CHARMS, fax 639-8800, is on the grounds of a 17th-century sugar plantation and mill. It is large by Tobago standards (over 100 rooms) and located on the leeward side at Mt. Irvine Bay. The pool is huge, and two tennis courts, 16 acres of gardens, a French restaurant, and ocean views complete the picture. The golf course is a highly regarded 18-hole, 6,793-yard International Championship Quality course. Luxury.

North of Plymouth, the **Arnos Vale Hotel,** P.O. Box 208, Scarborough, Tobago, West Indies, tel. (809) 639-2881/2, fax 639-4629, has stucco cottages in pretty surroundings, a beach, pool, tennis courts, and a dive shop. Luxury.

In Scarborough, **Jacobs Guest House,** tel. (809) 639-2271, has six rooms, two that share baths, and only one with hot water. The rooms have fans and are clean, and, really, at TT$50 (about US$10) per person, there's not much to complain about. Budget.

On the north end of the island, look for rustic **Blue Waters Inn,** Batteaux Bay, Speyside, Tobago, West Indies, tel. (809) 660-4341 or 660-

4077, fax 660-5195. No television, phones, or air-conditioning— just clean rooms, some with kitchenettes, and nearly 50 acres of quiet grounds with the bay and beach outside. Moderate-Luxury.

FOOD IN TOBAGO

At the south side of Tobago you'll find several fresh seafood shacks where you can buy lobster and other delicacies. The shacks sit on the dusty road along Shore Bay. Make your choice and sit on the beach or in the cool shade of palm fronds while they cook it up. Have a beer while you're waiting. Have another.

Most of Tobago's hotels have adequate and, in cases such as the **Cocrico Inn** and **Kariwak Village,** very fine restaurants. For price categories, see "Food In Trinidad," above.

MORE TOBAGO HOTELS AND GUESTHOUSES

Rates per s, EP when applicable, winter

NAME	(809)	FAX	LOCATION	TARIFF
Cocrico Inn	639-2961	639-6565	Plymouth	moderate
Coral Inn Guesthouse	639-0976	N/A	Store Bay Beach Rd., Crown Point	budget
Coral Reef Guesthouse	639-2535	639-0770	Scarborough	budget
Federal Villa Guesthouse	639-3926	N/A	Scarborough	budget
Golden Thistle	639-8251	639-8251	Store Bay Beach Rd., Crown Point	moderate
Jimmy's Holiday Resort	639-8292	639-3100	Store Bay Beach Rd., Crown Point	moderate
Kariwak Village	639-8442	639-8441	Store Bay Beach Rd., Crown Point	moderate
Man-O-War Bay Cottage	660-4327	660-4328	Charlotteville Crown Point	moderate-luxury
Old Grange Inn	639-0275	639-9395	Mt. Irvine	budget-moderate
Plaza Guesthouse	N/A	N/A	Canaan	budget
Richmond Great House	660-4467	639-2213	Richmond Bay	luxury
Speyside Inn	660-4852	660-4852	Speyside	moderate
Tropikist Beach Hotel	639-8512	638-1110	Store Bay	moderate
Vicky's Guesthouse	660-2089 or 2087	N/A	Mt. St. George	budget

Try the **Dutchman's Cove Restaurant** across from the Port Authority in Scarborough for inexpensive, down-home cooking. Inexpensive.

Dillon's, tel. (809) 639-8765, on the road to the airport in Crown Point, serves fresh seafood. Moderate. The casual **Miss Jean's,** tel. (809) 639-0563, at Store Bay has some of the best West Indian cuisine on the island. Don't judge this book by its cover. Moderate.

INFORMATION DIRECTORY

TOURISM AND INDUSTRIAL DEVELOPMENT COMPANY

134-138 Frederick St., Port of Spain, Trinidad, West Indies, tel. (809) 623-1932/4, fax 623-3848.

Piarco International Airport, tel. (809) 664-5196.

NIB Mall, Scarborough, Tobago, West Indies, tel. (809) 639-2125, fax 639-3566.

Crown Point Airport, tel. (809) 639-0509.

25 W 43rd St. Suite 1508, New York, NY 10036, tel. (800) 232-0082 or (212) 719-0540, fax (212) 719-0988.

8A Hammersmith Broadway, London W6 7AL, England, tel. 01-4481-741-4466, fax 741-1013.

OTHER

Police Emergency, tel. 999.

Fire and Ambulance, tel. 990.

Port of Spain General Hospital, 169 Charlotte St., Trinidad, tel. (809) 623-2951.

Scarborough Hospital, Tobago, tel. (809) 639-2551.

Piarco International Airport, Trinidad, tel. 664-5196.

Crown Point Airport, Tobago, tel. (809) 639-0509.

Bhaggan's Pharmacy (open until 11 p.m.), Independence Square, Port of Spain, tel. 627-5541.

FedEx, 31-33 Abercrombie Street, Port of Spain, tel. 624-0241 or 623-4070; Piarco International Airport, tel. (809) 669-2672.

National Carnival Commission, 92 Frederick St., Port of Spain, Trinidad, West Indies, tel. (809) 623-7600 or 623-7510.

Papillion, tel. (809) 639-0275, at the Old Grange Inn in Mt. Irvine specializes in seafood. Moderate. The **Blue Crab,** tel. (809) 639-2737, in Scarborough offers up seafood and local dishes.

Most smaller cafes and takeout restaurants do not accept credit cards.

GETTING TO TOBAGO

By Air

Tobago's **Crown Point Airport,** tel. (809) 639-0509, about eight miles (13 km) from Scarborough, is large enough to land international flights as well as smaller connections from Trinidad, a 15-minute flight.

LIAT, tel. (809) 639-0484, makes connections from Piarco Airport in Trinidad and has a direct connection from Barbados. **BWIA,** Trinidad tel. (809) 627-BWIA, operates direct service to Tobago from Miami and Frankfurt. If Tobago is your eventual destination, it's best to try to book straight through to avoid Piarco altogether.

Most international roundtrip tickets to Trinidad will allow you to tack on a Tobago leg for free. However, you need to ask for it. Even if you fly over to Tobago for a day's visit, it's worth it. Value is US$45 (about TT$250).

For more information on immigration and departure, see "Getting to Trinidad," above.

Ferry Service

Say you've got an extra four or five hours to get from Trinidad to Tobago, and say you're trying to save a bit on transport. Then the ferry service is the way to go. The **Port Authority** operates ferry service between the two islands, with daily departures from Trinidad to Tobago at 2 p.m., and from Tobago to Trinidad at 11 p.m.

Call the Port Authority in Port of Spain, tel. (809) 625-4906, or Scarborough, tel. (809) 639-2181, for current schedules. The simple roundtrip fare is TT$55 (US$10), and the fare for a cabin for two is TT$160 roundtrip. More is charged for vehicles.

According to the Port Authority, a newer, faster ferry service is due to commence soon. The new service will also depart daily, but the trip will take under three hours.

Weight time and cost of ferry travel against traveling by air: A flight takes 15 minutes, with multiple daily departures either way, at a cost of US$45 (TT$250) RT.

GETTING AROUND TOBAGO

Public Transportation

On Tobago, as opposed to Trinidad, maxi-taxis are identified by stripes of just one color: blue. The place to catch buses and maxi-taxis is at the airport or in Scarborough near the public market or Port Authority. See also "Public Transportation" under "Getting around Trinidad," above.

Vehicle Rentals

Renting a car is the best way to see Tobago, and you'll find at least ten rental companies at the airport. The same rules for renting and driving apply on Tobago as apply on Trinidad.

Call **Alfred's Car Rentals,** tel. (809) 639-7448; **Hill Crest,** tel. (809) 639-5208; **Peter Gremli Car Rental,** tel. (809) 639-8400; **Thrifty,** tel. (809) 639-8507; or **Toyota Rent a Car,** tel. (809) 639-7495, fax 639-7482.

Bicycles and motorbikes can be rented through **Modern Bike Rental,** Union Village tel. (809) 639-3275; **Baird's Rentals,** Scarborough tel. (809) 639-2528; or **Blossom Enterprises,** in Canaan near the airport, tel. (809) 639-8485.

MONEY, HOURS, AND COMMUNICATION

Currency and Banks

The currency of Trinidad and Tobago is the Trinidad and Tobago dollar (TT$). The currency was floated on the international market in April 1993 and therefore fluctuates daily. Check local papers for the day's rate. On average, however,

it's been about TT$5.70 = US$1. Principal banks such as the Bank of Commerce, National Commercial Bank, Royal Bank, and others will change money at better rates than hotels.

You'll find a currency exchange outlet at Piarco Airport, open daily 6 a.m.-10 p.m.

Banking hours vary, but most are open Mon.-Thurs. 8 a.m.-2 p.m. and Friday 9 a.m.-noon and 3-5 p.m.

Hours, Phones, News

Commercial businesses are open Mon.-Thurs. 8 a.m.-4 p.m. and until 6 p.m. on Friday. Some malls remain open Mon.-Sat. until 8 p.m. Government offices are open Mon.-Fri. 8 a.m.-noon and 3-4:30 p.m. Much of Trinidad and Tobago shuts down on Sunday.

The international area code for Trinidad and Tobago is 809. From North America, you dial "1" plus "809" plus a seven-digit number. Telephones are operated by either coins or phone cards, which are available at banks, small shops, and Telecommunications Services of Trinidad and Tobago (TSTT) on Independence Square. There is a line of phones on Henry Street as well. You'll also find a TSTT office in Scarborough.

The main post office is at Wrightson Road, Port of Spain, opposite the Holiday Inn, open Mon.-Fri. 7 a.m.-5 p.m.

The country's newspapers are among the most lively and trashy in the Caribbean. The two dailies, the *Daily Express* (TT$1) and the *Trinidad Guardian* (TT$1.50), are the best bet for good news. They're found at any one of about a hundred small vendors' stands throughout the cities. The weeklies include the eye-popping, bathing-beauty-laden *Punch,* among others. The nation's three television stations and nine radio stations provide news and entertainment.

BOB RACE

THE FRENCH WEST INDIES

INTRODUCTION

France has been imported in a big way to the French West Indies. French products, fashion, cuisine, and of course language and political identity are firmly entrenched. The central Lesser Antillean behemoths Martinique and Guadeloupe—which administer as their dependencies several neighboring islands including the northern, island-sharing Saint-Martin (with Dutch Sint Maarten) and bantam-sized Saint-Barthélémy—are unmistakably bathed in the sophistication and (we had to say this somewhere) savoir faire of their European patron.

Yet these islands are unmistakably West Indian as well. With a flair that the more reserved British, Dutch, and Americans are in a sense unable to muster on their former and current island territories, the French West Indies have taken their colonial identity and thoroughly enmeshed it with island sensibilities; they've produced a vibrant, showy, and sensual culture, a culture that has managed to let surface all that is best from France and Africa.

You'll find French West Indian cuisine from Paris to London to New York, but nowhere is it better, fresher, or more innovative than at the source. If dining is your pleasure, you'll be pleasured here. Given that pre-Lenten religious festivities are historically French in origin, the Carnivals of the French West Indies are loud, lively, and unparalleled—with the exception of Trinidad's Carnival—throughout the islands.

Yet each of the French West Indies offers different experiences: Saint-Martin's beaches and bustle, Saint-Barthélémy's quiet sophistication, Guadeloupe's country French ambience and rich natural resources, and Martinique's complex history and sophisticated capital of Fort-de-France are all part and parcel of the French West Indies.

Geographically, this region presents difficulties in trying to cover it in one chapter. The Netherlands Antilles' Sint Maarten shares an island, a history, and a culture with French Saint-Martin. The two island halves are inextricable. Like an old married couple, they get along, they argue, they occasionally do things differently, but they are never apart. Therefore, in this chapter we will not separate Saint-Martin from its other half, but will rather cover Saint-Martin/Sint Maarten in the same section, as an entity, as an island.

SAINT-MARTIN/SINT MAARTEN

Saint-Martin/Sint Maarten is not, unlike its Lesser Antilles neighbors Antigua and Barbuda and Trinidad and Tobago, two islands combined to form one nation, but rather two nations combined on one island. The situation is unique in the region, to say the least. This 37-square-mile (96-square-km) island has two names, two governments, three currencies, at least four languages, and two dominant cultures.

Much on Saint-Martin/Sint Maarten can be recommended—too much, for some. This is a place thoroughly inhabited by and economically reliant upon tourism. Saint-Martin/Sint Maarten is one of the Lesser Antilles' most popular cruise ship stops, with about 180 calls per year. Some of the Lesser Antilles' best resorts, restaurants, sports activities, and shopping are found here, but at a price. It is rarely a quiet place, but rather jamming, bustling, and congested. Local cultures have been nearly buried by the onslaught of tourism; even residents you think are locals may be workers and business owners from other islands. The 1950s population of the island, in the pre-tourism-boom days, was about 5,000. Today it is estimated at over 60,000, with only an estimated 20% born on Saint-Martin/Sint Maarten.

The island's dominant cultures are derived from the French and Dutch, at least in the political sense. Hence, the unwieldy name Saint-Martin/Sint Maarten. Saint-Martin is the northern French side of the island, and Sint Maarten is the southern Dutch side. "Saint-Martin/Sint Maarten" (or its reverse) is often used on maps; in common usage, no one repeats the two names, which are pronounced the same. Other spellings such as St. Martin or St. Maarten are also used, as are variations on that theme.

THE LAND

Saint-Martin/Sint Maarten is located in the Leeward Islands of the Lesser Antilles, about 150 miles (241 km) southeast of Puerto Rico, 20 miles (32 km) north of Saint-Barthélémy, and five miles (eight km) south of its nearest neighbor, Anguilla.

The island tends to be dry, with scrubby brush and grassy plains taking up much of the lowland. Occasional rain showers briefly turn the island green, but finding potable water is generally a problem. Further, with the enormous pressure put on the island's water supply by the tourist industry, much of it is brought in by tankers.

The center of the island features some elevations, the highest being the French-side **Pic du Paradis** ("Paradise Peak"), at 1,260 feet (384 meters, easily accessible by car) more a great big hill than a mountain. The south and west coasts in particular are characterized by wide bays and long white-sand beaches. The far western **Terres Basses** region is low-lying and marshy in places, with mangrove swamps touching the shore. The southwest **Simpson Lagoon** is separated from the sea by narrow strips of land. The southern strip is the location of the island's main **Princess Juliana International Airport. Philipsburg,** the capital of the Dutch side, sits on a strip of land separating the island's largest deepwater bay and main port, from the large **Great Salt Pond,** once the domain of salt harvesters. Several small islands, including **Tintamarre** and **Pinell,** lie off the north coast and are popular recreation spots.

HISTORY

Amerindian Settlers

Several key points regarding the history of the island are in dispute. The first involves the Amerindian inhabitants of the island. Archaeologists agree Stone Age peoples inhabited the island for at least a short time circa 4000 B.C., at a time when Saint-Martin/Sint Maarten may have been joined as one with the islands today known as Saint-Barthélémy and Anguilla.

O SWEET SAINT MARTIN LAND

The national song of Saint-Martin/Sint Maarten,
composed by the late Father G. Kemps C.S. Sp.

Where over the world, say where;
You find an Island there,
So lovely small with nations free,
With people French and Dutch,
Though talking English much,
As thee Saint Martin in the sea?

Chorus:
O, sweet Saint Martin's Land,
So bright by beach and strand
With sailors on the sea
And harbours free;
Where the chains of mountains green
Variously in sunlight sheen;
Bis O, I love thy paradise,
Nature-beauty fairly nice!

How pretty between all green
Flamboyants beaming gleam
Of flowers red by sunlight seat!
Thy cows and sheep and goats
In meadow or on roads,
Thy donkeys keen can't forget.
Saint Martin, I like thy name,
In which Columbus' fame
And memories of old are closed.
For me a great delight:
Thy Southern Cross the night.
May God the Lord protect thy coast!

Columbus

Whatever the case, Amerindians of one or the other group were living on the island at the time of Columbus's second voyage in 1493. These indigenous inhabitants called the island Soualiga, meaning "Salt Island," apparently referring to the huge southern salt pond and other smaller salt sources on the island. Another legend has them calling the island Oualichi, reputedly the "Island of Women." While the latter somehow has a more exotic tenor to it, no evidence exists indicating who these women were . . . such is the stuff of legends.

An interesting footnote, and another historical dispute, involves Columbus's sighting of the island. Some researchers believe Columbus sighted the island 11 November 1493, the holy day of St. Martin of Tours, and so named the island. Others believe Columbus never sighted Saint-Martin/Sint Maarten, but rather sighted the island we today call Nevis and named it St. Martin, allowing history to later confuse the names.

Nevertheless, the Spanish made no initial attempt to settle. Nor did any of the subsequent European visitors of the 16th century, including the French, Portuguese, English, and Dutch. Yet, even though the Europeans did not settle, they did land and attempt to explore and exploit the island, often engaging the indigenous Amerindian population in battles and skirmishes. By the 17th century, the Amerindians on the island had been virtually wiped out.

Dutch and French Settlement

From 1630 to 1632, the Dutch established a small settlement in the south, determining the salt reserves there were of some economic value. At about the same time the French established a small settlement in the east coast area that came to be known as French Quarter. The two groups fought periodic skirmishes that had no lasting effects; while they did not live harmoniously, neither did they do any real damage to each other.

By 1633, the Spanish had reconsidered their diminished position in the Lesser Antilles and decided to reestablish a presence. They invaded Saint-Martin/Sint Maarten and Anguilla, driving off the French and Dutch inhabitants. Over the years the French and Dutch banded to-

Several waves of Arawak explorers and related groups from South America arrived about A.D. 800 and settled throughout the Lesser Antilles, living a relatively peaceful existence fishing, hunting, and farming. The Arawaks were followed north by another Amerindian group with its roots in South America, the Caribs. The dispute occurs here. Some historians believe the Caribs never made it as far north as Saint-Martin/Sint Maarten, and possibly no farther north than the island of Guadeloupe. They cite a lack of evidence to support Carib presence in the Leeward Islands. Others, in part supported by evidence of Columbus's sightings, believe the Caribs made it as far north as Hispaniola.

gether to repel the Spanish. Then, soon after a 1644 sea battle, the Spanish abandoned their pursuit of islands in the eastern Caribbean, and the French and Dutch moved back to Saint-Martin/Sint Maarten. There they hammered out a few treaties and, with the signing of the Mont des Accords on 23 March 1648, divided the island in near-halves.

The border was violated several times, and new treaties were drawn to divide the island; it wasn't, however, until 1772 that an actual boundary was marked.

The French and Dutch imported slaves to plant cotton, tobacco, sugarcane, and coffee. The island, however, due to its poor soil and lack of rain, never hosted the major plantations of its neighbors.

During the next century, Saint-Martin/Sint Maarten changed flags several times, including the many times when the French conquered the Dutch and vice versa. It was a time of mild schizophrenia for the island, with one hand slapping the other and in turn slapping British invaders and others. In fact, Saint-Martin/Sint Maarten changed hands 16 times until the French and Dutch established a permanent boundary in 1817. This is the boundary that stands today.

Into the 20th Century

Slavery was finally abolished by the French in 1848 and then by the Dutch in 1863. Soon after, the small plantations died and with them, ultimately, the island economy. Former slaves moved away to look for work in the large plantations of Cuba, Dominican Republic, Puerto Rico, and the United States. By the turn of the century, the sugar and cotton industries were completely gone, and a wide-scale labor exodus took place. France and the Netherlands treated the island as little more than an economic annoyance, and by the 1940s even the salt industry had dried up, so to speak. Subsistence fishing, farming, and donations from relatives abroad were all that kept locals in food and shelter. By the 1950s the population was only 5,000, as compared to double that in 1915.

Then, during the middle part of the 20th century, the economic tide of the island turned. Princess Juliana Airport was completed in 1947 as part of a U.S. military complex. Saint-Martin/Sint Maarten's first tourist hotel was built in 1955. From that point on, the history of this tiny island is inexorably linked to tourism. By 1978 the combined population had grown to 25,000. Illegal entrants poured in by the thousands to work in the new hotels and resorts. Development during the 1980s, particularly on the Dutch side, gave the island large and sprawling resort complexes and high employment.

PEOPLE AND CULTURE

The present official population is estimated at 28,000 on the French side and 32,000 on the Dutch side, with an additional 25,000 illegal immigrants working in the tourist industry. About 20% of the total population is indigenous. The rest are French and Dutch nationals and workers from around the Caribbean and the world. An estimated 80 different nationalities reside on Saint-Martin/Sint Maarten.

THE LEGEND OF THE DRUNK DUTCHMAN

A popular folktale has it that the French and Dutch settlers determined Saint-Martin/Sint Maarten's division by a foot race. According to the tale, a Frenchman and Dutchman were to circumnavigate the island, starting from Oyster Pond on the east coast. The Frenchman was to start walking north along the shore, and the Dutchman was to head south. Wherever they met would determine the other endpoint of the border.

The Dutchman headed south with a flask of gin, and the Frenchman went north with a flask of wine. The Frenchman covered more ground and ultimately got a better deal.

Whether or not this is a convoluted morality tale concerning the advantages of wine over gin, one would have to assume the tale originated with the French. At any rate, the one factual aspect is that the French side of the island measures 21 square miles (54 square km), and the Dutch side is slightly smaller at 16 square miles (41 square km).

With this Babylon of languages, it is hard to distinguish which belong and which do not. English is widely spoken on the Dutch side and is, in fact, taught in primary school. Dutch is also spoken on the Dutch side, as is Papiamento, an amalgam of Spanish, Portuguese, English, Dutch, and some African languages. Spanish is also used, mainly by those who have worked in the Dutch colonies of South America, and by workers from Spanish islands. French is used on the French side, particularly among the French nationals. English is also used although not commonly. French Creole is spoken among the African-descent locals, including those from the other French departments.

BOB RACE

woman in Carnival headdress

Religions in Saint-Martin/Sint Maarten reflect the many cultures found here and include Catholic, Anglican, Baptist, Methodist, Jehovah's Witness, Baha'i, and Seventh-Day Adventist.

Holidays and Festivals

Both the French and Dutch sides of the island celebrate variations of Carnival, but at different times. The **French Carnival** is the traditional pre-Lenten round-up of street parades, calypso contests, feasts, and masquerades. All business stops for the five days leading up to the final Ash Wednesday celebrations. The **Dutch Carnival** is celebrated during Easter week, and features parades, "jump ups," Calypso King and Queen competitions, Carnival Village (in Philipsburg, near the university) activities, and the burning of King Moumou, a stock carnival character, at the closing ceremony.

French Saint-Martin, as you might expect, celebrates various religious holidays; Christmas, Boxing Day (the day after Christmas), and the Easter holidays, as well as several Catholic saints' days, are observed. A shared national holiday commemorating the cooperation between the island's halves, **Saint-Martin/Sint Maarten Day** (11 November) is hosted alternating years on the French side and Dutch side. On the French side **Bastille Day** is celebrated on 14 July, and 21 July's **Schoelcher Day** commemorates a leading French abolitionist.

Dutch Sint Maarten celebrates New Year's, Easter, the Dutch Queen's Birthday (30 April), Labor Day (1 May), Christmas, and Boxing Day.

Folk Performances

Many of the "cultural" performances offered at local hotels and other venues are of the tourist variety, meaning heavy on fire-eating and limboing, light on historic relevance for local islanders. However, performances by folkdance groups such as **Grain d'Or** are worth finding. Check the local papers or call (590) 87-75-80. The **Fondation Historique et Culturelle,** tel. (590) 87-32-24 promotes and lists Saint-Martin cultural events.

SAINT-MARTIN/
SINT MAARTEN

© MOON PUBLICATIONS, INC.

GOVERNMENT AND ECONOMY

Today, the dual governments of Saint-Martin/Sint Maarten are no longer dueling. Trade and exchange between the two sides is for the most part congenial and efficient, although distinctions in their infrastructures such as differing currencies, postal systems, electrical systems, and telephone exchanges make logistics a bit challenging. Cooperation in airport entry regulations—one entry for both sides, no customs—as well as cooperation between tourism authorities has made life for visitors easy. The two border points between the French and Dutch sides are nominal; at Cole Bay the spot is marked by flags and a monument inscribed "1648-1948," with the sign "Bienvenue en Partie Francaise." At the western border, the sign says "Welcome to Dutch St. Maarten NA." Visitors often drive between the borders without realizing they've just crossed into another country.

Saint-Martin
French Saint-Martin is a sub-prefecture of Guadeloupe, an overseas department of

NAKED FEAR

I don't get naked much. I suppose I do as often as the next guy, say for bathing or when it has some medical purpose, but I have this hunch that most people don't get naked a lot of the time for completely understandable reasons. It is simply inappropriate for most of the working day, and sometimes it's just too damn cold.

Of course, getting naked at clothing-optional beaches—"nude" is considered tawdry—is supposed to be a different story. You go with the knowledge that someone might very well look at your body parts. Personally, I have always had a fear of sitting stitchless on a beach wondering how I'm going to make it to the water without everyone knowing as much about me as my mother does. It's a rumbling anxiety, the same gut-surge I feel whenever Roseanne is about to show us another tattoo. It is the fear of knowing a bit too much about a person.

Which is why I will never understand how, on my first trip to Saint-Martin, I was goaded into going to the famous Orient Bay clothing-optional beach by my otherwise professional colleague, whom I'll call "Steve" because if his wife knew, she would not understand that he was able to convince himself it was for reportorial purposes only and might very well kill him dead, on the spot. And I don't need that on my conscience.

So on we went, I with a mixture of reluctance and queasy curiosity, and Steve with deep enthusiasm.

When we arrived at the flesh-dense beach, it occurred to me that, in this environment, shade would be at a premium. So we found the umbrella hut and its proprietor, a young woman who was completely starkers except for an ankle bracelet and, of all horrors, a pair of mirrored sunglasses. She was French, as we found out when we tried to communicate.

The French, of course, have no shame. Several groups were playing volleyball games or were engaged in Frisbee-tossing spectacles that had them running up and down the beach, even diving into the sand. This engendered a great amount of bouncing, jiggling, and audible flapping, which looked painful and vaguely unhygienic. Yet no one seemed to care a whit. In fact, they were giddy about the whole thing. That didn't surprise me, but what did was this: I found myself admiring their freedom, their ability to be unencumbered by even the slightest degree of humiliation. Quivering and plopping, they looked less like satyrs than middle-aged, sweaty people who just happened to be naked.

Still, that didn't distract me from my own apprehensions. I broke out in a cold sweat. I have a wart on my thigh about which only two people in this world ought to admit they know, and one is me. The other is my wife, and all the rest are damn liars. In my

France. As such, it is represented in Guadeloupe's regional council, which is in turn represented in the French parliament. The subprefect is appointed by the French parliament, and a local town council and mayor take care of local affairs. The French capital is **Marigot**, on the western coast, about 20 minutes from the airport by car.

Island Economy
The economy of Saint-Martin/Sint Maarten is virtually given over to tourism. No substantial farming enterprises exist, and the little fishing done by locals is primarily for the benefit of hotels.

As early as the 1977-78 tourist season, there were nearly 2,000 hotel rooms on the island, and 200 cruise ship visits per year. Those numbers have now at least doubled, and a half-million people visit the island yearly. French Saint-

Martin has plans to expand an existing landing field in Grand Case, and plans are afoot to expand the cruise ship facilities at Great Bay in Philipsburg.

Sint Maarten
Dutch Sint Maarten is a member of the Netherlands Antilles, which includes the islands of Curaçao, Bonaire, Sint Eustatius, and Saba. Aruba is a separate entity within the Kingdom of the Netherlands.

The Netherlands Antilles are ruled by parliamentary democracy with the Dutch monarch, Queen Beatrix, as head of state. The queen is represented in the Netherlands Antilles by a governor, who is appointed by the crown. The islands have representation in the Dutch Cabinet by way of a minister plenipotentiary, who is appointed by a legislative council of the five Netherlands Antilles. Each island is allowed mind I began to pretend that this dime-size wart was the reason I did not want to get naked. It wasn't, of course. It was my fear that something else might be considered dime-size that drove up my blood pressure.

But, when in Rome, etc. Being the only guy in a swimsuit on a clothing-optional beach is sort of like being a Democrat in Congress; everyone begins to wonder who invited you along. So I took a deep breath—sucked in my gut, if you really want to know—and, casting my inhibitions and trunks to the wind, found myself sitting stitchless next to a man whom I suddenly realized I hardly knew at all.

I reacted as I knew I would. I grabbed Steve's notebook and held it purposefully over that area of my body on which I could not in good conscience nor in public slather even the least bit of sunblock without appearing to enjoy it. This moment of terror started me wondering about the human condition. More pointedly, the human body condition. Steve happens to have a pretty good body because he works out at a gym and has never eaten real food, apparently deriving nourishment via the osmosis of tanning oil. I, on the other hand, have the rugged exterior of a professional pie-eating contestant and have begun to notice the waist spread that we nearly middle-aged men call "contentment diffusion."

With that in mind, don't ever let nudists, or clothing-optionalists, tell you their sole purpose in doffing their duds is the desire to get back to nature. Nature as I know it consists of carcinogenic sunbeams, rabid poison ivy, and giant mutant mosquitoes. And all these things attack the skin, a large amount of which is available when you are stitchless.

No, publicly naked people are not always naturalists. They are something much closer to the human core, more primal.

They are nosy.

They want to compare—not always pruriently, but for the sake of old-fashioned, competitive curiosity. We compare jobs, diseases, and divorce settlements among others. Men, I have come to believe, are the worst offenders; we compare what we call our "equipment."

So there I sat in the buff (possibly from the French *ou est le boeuf,* literally "where's the beef?"), comparing and silently cursing my ancestry, which I'd begun to believe had shortchanged me, so to speak. I watched people walk by. Some were out of shape, the other side of Rubenesque. Others were buff hard-bodies, toned and tanned. They were having fun. They were free with their bodies, serene in their innocence, at one with their universe and universal exposure.

They were French, of course.

And, as I said, I'd begun to admire their freedom. Beyond this concession, however, I vowed to never again be naked in public. Sand, I thought as I caught my reflection in the umbrella vendor's mirrored sunglasses, does not make the man.

---

some self-rule, with separate responsibilities for water, electricity, land, certain infrastructures, schools, and harbors. The legislative council comprises a Council of Ministers and a 22-member elected parliament, who meet in Willemstad, Curaçao. The capital is **Philipsburg,** about six miles (10 km) from the airport.

SIGHTS

Beaches

Many of Saint-Martin/Sint Maarten's estimated 37 beaches have facilities for parking, eating, changing, and renting chairs and umbrellas. Others are remote and difficult to access. All beaches are open to the public, and few have lifeguards. There have been instances of theft from unlocked rental cars or from valuables left alone on the beach, so take care to lock up your things.

Among the best beaches: **Cupecoy Beach,** on the Dutch side near the border west of the airport, is set among sandstone cliffs and caves. The waves are often full and the surf strong, but the wind is minimized by the cliffs. There are no facilities. Park near the Ocean Club. The far end of the beach is clothing-optional. Just west of Cupecoy is **Baie Longue,** a long white-sand beach with excellent snorkeling but no facilities. On the north side of Simpson Lagoon is **Baie Rouge.** A sign on the main road points the way. Parking is a problem here, so just look for a spot along the dirt road to the entrance. A small snack stand and umbrella rental place is usually set up.

The north side's **Grand Case Beach,** in Grand Case, is a fine place to spend the day. You'll find plenty of roadside barbecue and snack places, with fires cooking up chicken, lobster, fresh fish, and West Indian delicacies.

Orient Beach (Baie Orientale) is an extremely popular—hence crowded—beach on the French east coast. Here you'll find plenty of snack huts, T-shirt and gift booths, chair and umbrella rentals, water sports, and parking. The snorkeling here is very good, and part of the outlying reef is a marine reserve. The far end of the beach, near the nudist resort Club Orient, is clothing-optional.

Other Sights

Unfortunately, outside of Philipsburg and Marigot, little stands out in the way of historical and natural sites. The villages on the French side, particularly **French Quarter,** the site of the original French settlement (also called **Orleans Quarter**), are small and quaint and feature examples of early West Indian architecture. Stop at **Colombier,** a small village and farming area between Marigot and Orleans, where you'll find several working farms, reminders of plantation days past.

A trip around the island will take the better part of a day, or, with stops for lunch and shopping, a couple of days.

MARIGOT

Quiz time! Question: How many islands in the French West Indies feature towns named Marigot? Answer: All of them. And more—Marigots

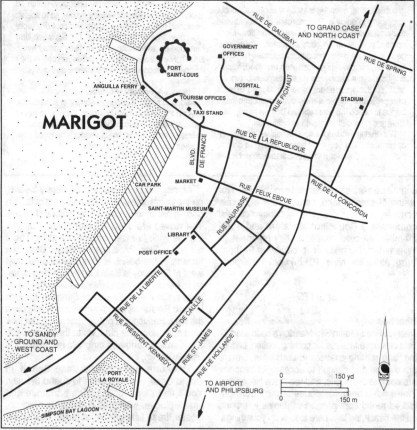

TO GRAND CASE AND NORTH COAST

RUE DE GALISBAY

GOVERNMENT OFFICES

RUE DE SPRING

FORT SAINT-LOUIS

HOSPITAL

RUE FICHAUT

STADIUM

ANGUILLA FERRY

TOURISM OFFICES

TAXI STAND

MARIGOT

RUE DE LA REPUBLIQUE

BLVD. DE FRANCE

CAR PARK

MARKET

RUE FELIX EBOUE

RUE DE LA CONCORDIA

SAINT-MARTIN MUSEUM

RUE MAURASSE

LIBRARY

POST OFFICE

RUE DE LA LIBERTE

RUE CH. DE CAULLE

RUE ST. JAMES

RUE DE HOLLANDE

TO SANDY GROUND AND WEST COAST

RUE PRESIDENT KENNEDY

PORT LA ROYALE

TO AIRPORT AND PHILIPSBURG

0   150 yd

0   150 m

SIMPSON BAY LAGOON

© MOON PUBLICATIONS, INC.

Fresh fruit, vegetables, and crafts are sold at the Marigot Market.

are found on Dominica and St. Lucia as well. The word is derived from a Creole word meaning "marsh."

Having said that, Marigot is the capital of French Saint-Martin and, with a population of about 5,500, is slightly smaller than Philipsburg. The town lies on the expansive **Baie de Marigot,** with the **Simpson Lagoon** at its south end. This is a popular yacht port, and the **Marina Port la Royale** on the lagoon is a busy center for waterfront dining and shopping. Marigot itself strains to be cosmopolitan, with dozens of sidewalk cafes, bistros, and galleries. People drive from the Dutch side just for baguettes from the many excellent patisseries. The duty-free shopping here is also very good, and a lot of time can be spent strolling the streets, stopping at mini-malls, galleries, and chichi clothiers.

The famous **Marigot Market** on the Marigot port is open daily, but Wednesday and Saturday mornings, when vendors come from nearby islands, are busiest. Produce comes in from as far away as Dominica for the 6 a.m.- 1 p.m. market. Spices, fruits, vegetables, fresh fish, crafts, T-shirts, and exotic cloth all contribute to a fairly lively scene. Small cafes surround the harbor. In front of the parking area are duty-free shops and the **St. Martin Museum,** which features Amerindian pottery, stone tools, old photographs, and artifacts from the colonial period. The museum is open weekdays 9 a.m.-1 p.m. and 3-6:30 p.m., and Saturday 9 a.m.-1 p.m.

Also at the harbor is the always helpful **Office du Tourisme,** tel. 87-57-23, fax 87-56-43, as well as a taxi stand, the ferry to Anguilla, and several duty-free shops, restaurants, and outdoor cafes. The ruins of **Fort St. Louis,** also called **Fort Marigot,** are in the hills overlooking the harbor and town. It's 91 steps to the top of the circa 1786 fort and the views are breathtaking, although there's not much left of the fort structures.

PHILIPSBURG

The Dutch Sint Maarten capital is built on a narrow strip of land between Great Bay and Great Salt Pond. The main section of the mile-long land bridge comprises two streets, Front and Back, and the Walter Nisbet Road, a main artery built on reclaimed pond land. Front Street fronts the bay and is the main shopping and duty-free center. The cobbled street is so busy it is virtually a pedestrian walkway, and parking or driving here is futile. Pick a side street to park if you have a rental car.

The beach on Great Bay looks out to the open Caribbean and is clean and fine for swimming. The bay has several marinas and will most likely have a cruise ship or two docked. Boats to Saba, St. Eustatius, and Saint-Barthélémy depart from here.

Near the center of Front Street is the town pier and **Wathey Square.** On the square, in addition to street vendors and souvenir shops, is the town hall. The white building was originally built in 1793 and renovated after a 1825 hurri-

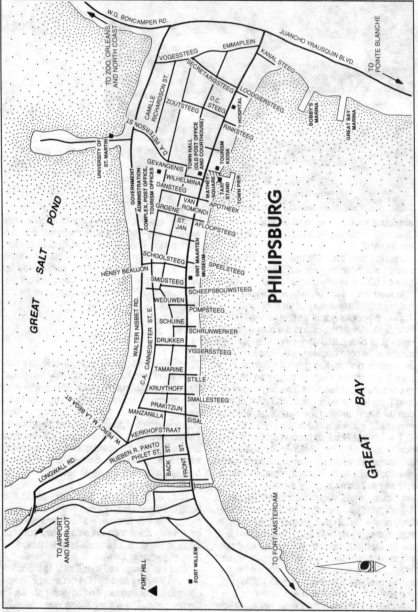

W.G. BONCAMPER RD.

JUANCHO YRAUSQUIN BLVD.

TO ZOO, ORLEANS, AND NORTH COAST

TO POINTE BLANCHE

VOGESSTEEG

EMMAPLEIN

KANAL STEEG

SECRETARISSTEEG

CAMILLE RICHARDSON ST.

LOODGIERSTEEG

ZOUTSTEEG

D.C. STEEG

BOBBY'S MARINA

GREAT BAY MARINA

UNIVERSITY OF ST. MARTIN

D.A. PETERSON ST.

RINKSTEEG

HOSPITAL

GEVANGENIS

TOWN HALL (OLD POST OFFICE AND COURTHOUSE)

WATHEY SQUARE

TOURISM KIOSK

WILHELMINA

GOVERNMENT ADMINISTRATION COMPLEX, POST OFFICE, TOURISM OFFICES

DANSTEEG

TAXI STAND

TOWN PIER

VAN ROMONDI

APOTHEEK

GREAT SALT POND

GROENE

ST. JAN

AFLOOPSTEEG

SCHOOLSTEEG

SINT MAARTEN MUSEUM

SPEELSTEEG

HENSY BEAUJON

SMIDSTEEG

SCHEEPSBOUWSTEEG

WEDUWEN

POMPSTEEG

WALTER NISBET RD.

SCHUINE

SCHRIJNWERKER

DRUKKER

VISSERSSTEEG

C.A. CANNEGIETER ST. S.E.

TAMARINE

STILLE

PHILIPSBURG

KRUYTHOFF

SMALLESTEEG

W. PERCY M. LA BEGA ST.

PRAKITZIJN

MANZANILLA

SISAL

KERKHOFSTRAAT

LONGWALL RD.

RUEBEN R. PANTO

PHILET ST.

BACK ST.

FRONT ST.

GREAT BAY

TO AIRPORT AND MARIGOT

TO FORT AMSTERDAM

FORT HILL

FORT WILLEM

© MOON PUBLICATIONS, INC.

cane and again in the 1960s. Upstairs is a courthouse and downstairs is a post office. A major taxi stand is also set up on the square.

Next to the Sea Palace is the **Sint Maarten Museum,** tel. (599-5) 24917, two upstairs rooms of artifacts, photos, old maps, a skull, Arawak *zemis,* dinner sets, and historical oddities of colonial life on Sint Maarten. The building is more than 100 years old. Books and postcards are for sale. Inquire about the museum's walking tour of Philipsburg. Entrance donation is NAF1.80 (US$1), and hours are weekdays 10 a.m.-4 p.m., extra Friday hours 7-9 p.m., and Saturday 10 a.m.-noon.

At the foot of town is the **West Indian Tavern,** with three roofs and gingerbread fretwork, typical of late 19th-century West Indian homes. Once a synagogue, the building now hosts one of the oldest restaurants on the island. Inside is the home of the island's small Guavaberry liqueur plant. The **Pasanggrahan Hotel** is one of the island's older hotels, and was once the Royal Guest House, host to Queen Wilhelmina and other Dutch royalty.

Back Street is quieter than Front Street but still features a large number of small shops and cafes. The two streets are connected by small alleys and slender streets called *steegjies.*

On the outskirts of town are the remains of **Fort Willem,** on a hill overlooking the bay. There is not much left of the ruins, and the road to the fort, from the Great Bay Beach Hotel, is rocky and irregular. However, the 300-year-old **Fort Amsterdam** is in better shape, and you'll still be able to see several cannons on the grounds. The fort is a Dutch structure built on the ruins of an original Spanish fortification. Both forts are currently being excavated and under renovation.

On the reclaimed Walter Nisbet Road running along side the salt pond you'll find the main post office, police station, a cinema, and a government administration complex, where offices of the tourism board, tel. (599-5) 22337, fax (599-5) 31159, are located. Note the stakes in the salt pond; they mark the "plots" of families who still harvest salt.

Just around the corner from the **University of St. Martin** *(sic),* at **Madame Estate,** is the small **St. Maarten Zoo,** tel. (599-5) 32030. The zoo features 35 species of animals from the

BOB RACE

Caribbean and South America. For the kids you'll find a petting zoo and small playground. The zoo is open weekdays 9 a.m.-5 p.m., and weekends 10 a.m.-6 p.m.; admission is US$4 adults and US$2 for children (NAF7.20 and NAF3.60, respectively).

OUTLYING ISLANDS

Excursions to **Ilet Tintamarre** and **Ilet Pinel** can be taken out of Marigot, but these tend to be the all-day sailing trips offering lunch and drinks. The best way to get to the islands, if all you want to do is get to the islands, is to drive to **Cul-de-Sac** on the northeast shore. From here numerous small boats (ask for Vanion) make the five-minute run to Ilet Pinel and a slightly longer run to Ilet Tintamarre for about US$5-7 per person, roundtrip.

Ilet Tintamarre and Ilet Pinel, as well as the small **Caye Verte** off the coast at Baie Orientale, offer fine swimming and snorkeling. You can find a small restaurant at Ilet Pinel.

SPORTS

Water Sports
The competition among water sports centers is fierce—any hotel on the island will have a connection with a facility that provides water-skiing, windsurfing, sailing, boating, fishing, and diving.

Divers may want to call ahead for current rates, and among the better diving shops are: **Ocean Explorers,** tel. (599-5) 45252; **Sint Maarten Divers,** tel. (599-5) 22413; **Lou Scuba Club,** tel. (590) 87-22-58; **Orient Bay Water Sports,** tel. (590) 87-33-85; and **Maho Water Sports,** tel. (599-5) 44387.

For deep-sea fishing, call **Rudy,** tel. (599-5) 42117; the **Hooker,** tel. (599-5) 42503; or **Sailfish Caraibes,** tel. (590) 87-77-46, at Port Lonvilliers.

Other Sports
Golf is available at **Mullet Bay Resort,** tel. (599-5) 42081, an 18-hole course. As courses go, it's not a bad choice—particularly since it's your only choice. A main road cuts right through the course. For horseback riding, contact **Crazy Acres,** tel. (599-5) 22061, in Cole Bay or **Caid & Isa,** tel. (590) 87-94-29, at Anse Marcel on the French side.

Three dozen tennis courts are located throughout the island, most in hotels. Try the **Tennis and Fitness Center,** tel. (599-5) 23685, in Dutch Cul-de-Sac for public courts.

ENTERTAINMENT

Major hotels are a source of entertainment, usually of the limbo/fire-eating type. The Maho Beach Hotel hosts **Coconuts Comedy Club** with regional and international acts, some well-known, US$10 (NAF$18) cover. The **Studio Seven** disco at the Grand Casino across the street from Maho Beach Hotel is very popular and rocks till the early morning hours. **Cherry's** bar is near Maho, fun for sundowners and pre-disco drinks. **L'Atmosphere** in Marigot is popular with the young French crowd. **Night Fever** in Colombier is more rustic but it rocks, and it's very popular with locals.

Gambling casinos are a big attraction on the Dutch side and are often located at resorts. You must be 18 to gamble. Among them: **Sheraton Port de Plaisance** in Simpson Bay, **Pelican Resort** in Simpson Bay, **Grand Casino** in Mullet Bay, **Great Bay Beach Hotel** in Philipsburg, **Mullet Bay Hotel** in Mullet Bay, **Casino Royale** in Maho Beach, **Seaview Hotel** in Philipsburg, and **International Casino** in Little Bay Resort).

The Dutch side's Maho Beach Hotel features an art deco motif.

SHOPPING

Saint-Martin/Sint Maarten is a duty-free port, and an estimated 500 duty free shops won't let your credit card down. Jewelry, perfumes, handbags, leather goods, electronic goods, art—the usual suspects—can be found in what appears to be a mall-a-mile density of shops throughout the island. Major shopping areas are on **Front Street** in Philipsburg, **Rue de la Liberte** and **Rue de la République** in Marigot, **Marina Port la Royale** in Marigot, and shopping malls at Mullet Bay and Maho Beach. Beyond that, smaller shopping malls are scattered along the airport-Marigot road and in the suburbs of Philipsburg.

For food shopping, the large Sint Maarten-based **Food Center** has two locations, one at Cole Bay, tel. (559-5) 22315, and the other on Bush Road, tel. (599-5) 23232. **Mammoth** is the big supermarket chain on the French side.

ACCOMMODATIONS

General

Saint-Martin/Sint Maarten may have more hotels and guesthouses per square mile than anywhere else in the West Indies. There are few miles one can drive on the island without seeing a hotel or tourist facility. The Dutch side tends to feature large mega-resorts, some with casinos, and fewer smaller hotels and guesthouses. The French side tends more toward intimate hotels and inns, although this is changing. Gambling casinos are not found on the French side.

Room tax on the Dutch side is five percent; on the French side it varies with the hotels. Both sides will tack on a service charge, usually 10-

MORE SINT MAARTEN ACCOMMODATIONS

Rates per s, EP when applicable, winter

NAME	(599-5)	(800)	TARIFF
Beach House	22456	223-9815	moderate
Caribbean Hotel	22028	N/A	budget
Cupecoy Beach Club	43219	223-1588	luxury
Divi Little Bay Beach Resort	22333	367-3484	luxury
Gracie's Mansion	70787	N/A	moderate
Great Bay Beach Hotel	22446	N/A	luxury
Holland House	22572	223-9815	moderate
Horny Toad Guest House	54323	N/A	moderate
Joshua Rose Guest House	24317	223-9815	moderate
La Vista Hotel	43005	223-9815	luxury
Oyster Pond Hotel	22206	372-1323	luxury
Town House Apartments	22898	223-9815	luxury

15%. The tourist offices of both sides print accommodation lists with rates, but these tend to feature the high-end hotels.

Categories are based on per-person, per-night prices during the high season (mid-December through mid-April): **Luxury** US$100 or more, **Moderate** US$50-100, **Budget** US$50 or less.

Villa Rentals

A large number of villas and apartments are available on the island. In the United States a good first source for information is **WIMCO**, North America tel. (800) 932-3222. As well, **Island Hideaways,** 1317 Rhode Island Ave. NW, Suite 503, Washington, DC 20005, tel. (800) 832-2302, fax (202) 667-3392, lists several island properties.

On the island, villa rental companies include **Carimo**, tel. (590) 87-57-58; **International Immobilier,** tel. (590) 87-79-00, on the French side, and **St. Martin Rentals,** tel. (599-5) 44330, on the Dutch side.

Resort time-sharing, possibly one of the tourism industry's more complex and annoying marketing creations, exists with a vengeance on the island. Time-shares are often part of the

MORE SAINT-MARTIN ACCOMMODATIONS

Rates per s, EP when applicable, winter

NAME	(590)	(800)	TARIFF
Alizéa	87-33-42	N/A	luxury
Alizes	87-95-38	N/A	budget
Blue Beach	87-33-44	N/A	moderate
Chez Martine	87-51-59	N/A	moderate
Copacabana Club	87-42-52	N/A	luxury
Coralita Beach Hotel	87-31-81	N/A	budget-moderate
Fleming's Corner	87-70-25	N/A	budget
Grand Case Beach Club	87-51-87	223-1588	luxury
Hotel du Golf	87-92-08	N/A	moderate-luxury
Hotel Marina Royale	87-52-46	N/A	moderate
Hotel Mont Vernon	87-42-22	543-4300	luxury
La Belle Creole	87-58-66	445-8667	luxury
Le Flamboyant	87-60-87	221-5333	moderate-luxury
Le Meridien-L'Habitation	87-33-33	543-4300	luxury
L'hotel Mississippi	87-33-81	N/A	luxury
Rising Sun Inn	87-33-52	N/A	budget

larger hotel complexes and are big business, particularly on Dutch Sint Maarten. While time-sharing is clearly an individual choice (and too involved to discuss here) a word for the unwary: You'll find time-share salespeople everywhere on the island selling their wares. The streets of Philipsburg and Marigot, the marinas, and even the roadsides are filled with salespeople waving their introductory offers and invitations to "just visit" a certain time-share hotel to receive a complimentary night's stay, or a meal, or whatever. The salespeople can be pushy and are definitely annoying, but mean no harm.

Hotels on the Dutch Side

The following two are recommended for those who enjoy large, sprawling, event-filled hotel life, with activities for kids. **Mullet Bay Resort and Casino,** P.O. Box 309, Sint Maarten, Netherlands Antilles, tel. (599-5) 52801, fax (599-5) 54281, is a sprawling resort with over 600 units, the island's only golf course, pools, tennis, beach, casino, and shopping. **Sheraton Port de Plaisance,** Sint Maarten, Netherlands Antilles, tel. (599-5) 45222, fax (599-5) 22323, is on Simpson Lagoon and is another sprawling complex with water sports, shops, restaurants, pools, and a fitness center—all new. Go elsewhere for a good beach, however. Both Luxury.

Pasanggrahan Hotel, P.O. Box 151, Sint Maarten, Netherlands Antilles, tel. (599-5) 23588, North America tel. (800) 223-9815, fax (599-5) 22885, was once the official guesthouse for visiting Dutch royalty. The hotel, on Front Street in Philipsburg, is small and has the feel of an old style West Indian inn. The bar is called Sidney Greenstreet. Moderate. **Mary's Boon,** P.O. Box 2078, Sint Maarten, Netherlands Antilles, tel. (599-5) 54325, North America tel. (800) 223-9815, fax (599-5) 53316, is located behind Princess Juliana Airport on the wide Simpson Bay Beach. This is an intimate guesthouse, with 12 studios that face the water. The "menu" consists of whatever the chef chooses to cook that day, and the bar is operated on an honor system. The hotel insists on several restrictions: no children under 16, no credit cards, no singles, no triples, no complaining about the airport noise. Same-sex couples are welcome, however. If you fit the criteria, this is a lovely place. Moderate.

Hotels on the French Side

Captain Oliver's, Oyster Pond, 97150 Saint-Martin, French West Indies, tel. (590) 87-40-

26, fax 87-40-84, is a bayside resort with a small marina, great for water sports. The complex straddles the border between the French and Dutch sides, on the east coast Oyster Pond. If you like marinas, this is the place. Moderate-Luxury. **La Samanna,** BP 159, Marigot, 97150 Saint-Martin, French West Indies, tel. (590) 87-51-22, overlooks Baie Longue from a hillside location and is one of the island's most exclusive resorts. Villas, water sports, pool, and fitness center are provided. Luxury. **La Residence,** BP 127, Marigot, 97150 Saint-Martin, French West Indies, tel. (590) 87-70-37, is a small 21-room inn on Rue du General de Gaulle, downtown Marigot. Great location for eating, shopping, and walking along the streets of town. No pool or beach here. Moderate.

Camping

Camping facilities are nonexistent, but it is allowed with permission from a landowner. No one, however, will vouch for your safety when camping.

FOOD

Recommending restaurants on Saint-Martin/Sint Maarten is like recommending a particular grain of sand on a beach. Well, maybe not quite like that, but it is, nevertheless, no easy task. The selection, on both the French and Dutch sides, is extraordinary, and at last count more than 200 full-service restaurants were available.

Island cuisine ranges from French to French Creole, from American burgers and pizza to Chinese to Dutch West Indian. One of the few truly indigenous foods is the sweet liqueur "guavaberry," made from a plum-like fruit (has nothing to do with guavas) which grows in the higher elevations and ripens in December, near Christmastime.

Several of the best restaurants on the island follow. Categories are based on per-person entree prices: **Expensive** US$25 or more, **Moderate** US$10-25, **Inexpensive** US$10 or less.

Grand Case is a town, not a restaurant, but it nevertheless represents the state of the culinary arts. Its restaurants are recognized throughout the Caribbean as among the region's best.

Virtually all the restaurants on Boulevard de Grand Case are exceptional and worth the trip. French, Continental, and West Indian cuisine are the norm. Among the best in Grand Case: **Cha Cha Cha,** tel. (590) 87-53-63; **Chez Martine,** tel. (590) 87-51-59; **Da Livio,** tel. (590) 87-53-63; **Hévéa,** tel. (590) 87-56-85; **Le Tastevin,** tel. (590) 87-55-45; **Rainbow,** tel. (590) 87-55-80; and **The Fish Pot,** tel. (590) 87-50-88. All Moderate-Expensive. Try the beachside barbecue huts for fun and inexpensive local food.

Marigot and its suburb Sandy Ground are also full of small French Creole restaurants and brasseries. **La Vie En Rose** overlooks the harbor and is very popular and crowded. Expensive. Stop at **Etna Ice Cream,** tel. (590) 87-72-72, on Kennedy Avenue for pastries or dessert. In Sandy Ground, a favorite is **Le Palmier,** tel. (590) 87-50-71, owned and operated by Guadeloupan Ketty Ymanette. Le Palmier serves some of the best and most authentic Creole cooking around. Inexpensive-Moderate.

In Colombier, a small settlement in the interior where you will see some working farms, try **La Rhumerie,** tel. (590) 87-56-98, for West Indian Creole. Inexpensive-Moderate. **Mark's Place,** tel. (590) 87-34-50, in Cul-de-Sac has a good reputation for inexpensive Creole West Indian. **La Samanna,** (590) 87-51-22, at Baie Longue offers elegant French. Expensive.

Philipsburg is a good feeding ground, and several of the cafes at **Maho Bay** are great for light lunches. Fast-food such as **KFC, Burger King,** and **Pizza Hut** can also be found.

The following are several personal favorites on the Dutch side. **Le Perroquet,** tel. (599-5) 54339, near the airport sits on a quiet part of the lagoon and features French-influenced seafood, sirloins, duck, veal, and much more. Expensive. **Island Bar and Restaurant,** tel. (599-5) 25162, on the Bush Road just outside of Philipsburg, serves authentic West Indian Creole. Moderate. **Grill & Ribs** has locations in Philipsburg and Simpson Bay, near the airport. The menu includes sandwiches, fajitas, and so on, but the thing to have here is the excellent grilled baby-back ribs, all you can eat, US$10.95 (or NAF20). They will bring you buckets. Literally.

GETTING THERE

Princess Juliana International Airport, tel. (599-5) 52161 or 54211, is serviced by several large North American and European carriers. **American Airlines,** local tel. (599-5) 52040, has flights from San Juan, as well as daily non-stop flights from New York and Raleigh-Durham. Other international carriers are **Air France,** tel. (599-5) 54212; **ALM,** tel. (599-5) 54230; **BWIA,** tel. (599-5) 53304; **KLM,** tel. (599-5) 54240; and **Lufthansa,** tel. (599-5) 52040.

Interisland Travel

For interisland travel, the major carrier is, as always, **LIAT,** tel. (599-5) 52403. **Windward Islands Airways (Winair),** tel. (599-5) 54210 or 52002, which is based in Sint Maarten, is a frequent flier to the Netherlands Antilles, Anguilla, St. Kitts, Nevis, Saint-Barthélémy, St. Thomas, and Tortola. **Air Martinique,** tel. (599-5) 54212, and **Air Guadeloupe** (same phone) both use Princess Juliana Airport for travel to their respective islands.

Departure tax for Princess Juliana Airport is US$5 (NAF9) to Netherlands Antilles islands, US$10 (NAF18) elsewhere.

The small **Esperance Airport** in Grand Case deals with interisland flights from mainly Saint-Barthélémy. **Air Guadeloupe** and **Air St. Barthélémy** use Esperance, and departure taxes are included in airfares. This airport is due for expansion in the near future.

Ferry and Boat Service

A regular ferry service operates to the island of Anguilla, five miles (eight km) to the north of Saint-Martin/Sint Maarten. Departure is from the harbor at Marigot, and you'll need to take your passport or other travel documents for admission into Anguilla and back to Saint-Martin. The ferry departs daily every 30 minutes from 8 a.m. up to and including 5:30 p.m., with extra trips at 7 p.m. and 10:30 p.m. The return to Marigot from Anguilla's small landing at Blowing Point is every half-hour from 7:30 a.m. until 5 p.m., plus 6:15 p.m. and 10:15 p.m. The trip is about 20 minutes. One-way fare is US$9 (NAF16 or F50), half price for children under 12. Departure tax from Marigot is US$2, and from Anguilla is US$2 (NAF3.60 or F11).

The **Pearl Line Express** operates a daily 45-minute service from both Philipsburg, tel. (599-5) 24409, and Marigot, tel. (590) 87-85-45, to Saint-Barthélémy. Call for the current schedule. The **White Octopus,** tel. (599-5) 23170, cruises daily to Saint-Barthélémy, departing from Bobby's Marina in Philipsburg at 9 a.m. and returning at 5 p.m.

GETTING AROUND

Taxis

Taxis are not metered, and governments-approved rates are posted at the airport taxi stand. Rates are also posted in the tourist newspaper *Today.* Sample fares: Airport to Grand Case US$16 (NAF29), airport to Philipsburg US$8 (NAF14.40), airport to Marigot US$8. Taxi and bus rates are the same for both sides of the island. Add 25% to taxi rates from 10 p.m. to midnight, and 50% after midnight.

You can find taxis at the airport, by the Town Hall on Front Street in Philipsburg, at the harbor and on major streets of Marigot, at Grand Case, and at virtually every major hotel on the island. You shouldn't need to call ahead for one, but if it's necessary, central dispatch numbers are (599-5) 22359 and (599-5) 54317.

Bus Service

Minibuses operate 7 a.m.-7 p.m. between Philipsburg, Marigot, and Grand Case at a flat rate of US$1.50 (NAF2.70). Buses also operate to the rest of the island, and their destinations are marked by signs on the windshield. You can flag buses down anywhere along the road or wait at bus stands.

After dark, look for a blue light in the left corner of the windshield to identify public transport vehicles.

Car and Motorcycle Rentals

Rental cars start at about US$35 (NAF63) per day, and while dozens of rental companies operate on the island, the supply seems to run out once in a while. Book ahead if possible. Driving is on the right, and all you'll need to rent a vehicle is your valid license or international license. Remember to lock your rentals when parking at the beach. Incidents of break-ins have been reported, particularly along the sometimes-isolated west coast.

Interestingly, but not surprisingly, traffic jams on Saint-Martin/Sint Maarten are common. Given the large number of taxis, buses, private cars, and tourist rentals, quite a bit of traffic is generated. There are about four traffic lights on the island, and the one at Cole Bay, which from the airport branches east over the Cole Bay Hill to Philipsburg, or north to Marigot, can be extensively jammed during morning (8-9 a.m.) and afternoon (4-5 p.m.) weekday rush hours. As well, a small drawbridge on the Simpson Bay Lagoon, just east of the airport, raises its gate at 6 a.m., 11 a.m., 4 p.m., and 6 p.m. to let boats in and out of the lagoon. Expect a 20-minute wait per opening.

A dozen rental agencies are found at the airport, and just about every hotel on the island has a contact. Rates are fairly competitive, starting at US$30-60 per day (NAF54-108 or F165-330), depending on the size of the vehicle.

At the airport, try **Avis,** tel. (599-5) 54265 or 42316; **Budget,** tel. (599-5) 54274; **Cannegie,** tel. (599-5) 52397; **Hertz,** tel. (599-5) 54314; **National,** tel. (599-5) 42168; or **Speedy Car Rental,** tel. (599-5) 23893.

On the Dutch side you'll find **Caribbean Auto Rentals,** tel. (599-5) 45211; **Opel Car Rental,** tel. (599-5) 44324; and **Roy Rogers Rentals,** tel. (599-5) 52701.

On the French side look for **Budget,** tel. (590) 87-38-22; **Continental Rental,** tel. (590) 87-77-64; **Dan's,** (590) 87-30-88; **Hertz,** (590) 87-76-69; **Island Trans Car Rental,** tel. (590) 87-91-32; **Roy Rogers,** tel. (590) 87-54-48; and **Sunny Island,** tel. (590) 87-80-21.

Motor scooters are available and inexpensive, starting at about US$20 (NAF36 or F110) per day. Call **Rent 2 Wheels,** tel. (590) 87-20-59, or **Moto Caraibes,** tel. (590) 87-25-91, both on the French side, for information.

INFORMATION DIRECTORY

DUTCH SINT MAARTEN TOURIST BUREAUS

Walter Nisbet Rd. #23, Philipsburg, Sint Maarten, Netherlands Antilles, tel. (599-5) 22337, fax 22734.

675 3rd Ave., New York, NY 10007, tel. (212) 953-2084, fax 627-1152.

243 Ellerlie Ave., Willowdale, Toronto M2N 1Y5, tel. (416) 223-3501, fax 223-6887.

DUTCH SINT MAARTEN TELEPHONE NUMBERS

Police, tel. (599-5) 22222.

Fire, tel. (599-5) 22222.

Ambulance, tel. (599-5) 22111.

St. Rose Hospital, Front St., Philipsburg, tel. (599-5) 22300.

Post Office, Front St., Philipsburg, tel. (599-5) 22289.

Princess Juliana International Airport, tel. (599-5) 52161 or 54211.

Central Drugstore, EC Richardson Rd., Philipsburg, tel. (599-5) 22321.

American Express Representative, Maduro and Sons, Emmaplein, Philipsburg, tel. (599-5) 23410.

FedEx, DeWeever Building, Simpson Bay, tel. (599-5) 42810.

FRENCH SAINT-MARTIN TOURISM OFFICES

Office du Tourisme de Saint-Martin, 97150 Port de Marigot, Saint-Martin, French West Indies, tel. (590) 87-57-21, fax 87-56-43.

"France on Call," U.S. tel. (900) 990-0040, *please note, the cost is US$.50 per minute.*

French West Indies Tourist Board, 610 5th Ave., New York, NY 10020.

French Government Tourist Office, 1981 McGill College Ave., Suite 490, Montreal, Quebec H3A 2W9, tel. (514) 288-4264.

French Government Tourist Office, 178 Piccadilly, London W1Z 0AL, tel. (071) 493-6594.

FRENCH SAINT-MARTIN TELEPHONE NUMBERS

Police, tel. (590) 87-50-06.

Fire, tel. (590) 87-72-00.

Ambulance, tel. (590) 87-86-25.

Hospital de Marigot, Marigot, tel. (590) 87-50-07.

Hotel Association, BP 622, 97510 Marigot, Saint-Martin, French West Indies, tel. and fax (590) 87-83-88.

Post Office, Rue de la Liberte, Marigot, tel. (590) 87-53-17.

Pharmacie Choisy Rita, Rue du General de Gaulle, Marigot, tel. (590) 87-54-09.

TELEPHONING SAINT-MARTIN AND SINT MAARTEN

WHEN PHONING	FROM	DIAL
Saint-Martin	North America	011 + 590 + six-digit #
Sint Maarten	North America	011 + 599-5 + five-digit #
Saint-Martin	Sint Maarten	06 + six-digit #
Sint Maarten	Saint-Martin	19 + 599-5 + five-digit #

Electricity

Even though the French and Dutch sides of the island cooperate on borders, taxi rates, and money matters, you aren't so lucky when it comes to electrical systems. The Dutch side uses 110 volts, 60 cycles, while the French side uses a 220-volt 60-cycle system. There are exceptions on the French side, particularly in some large hotels that offer 110-volt systems.

MONEY, HOURS, AND COMMUNICATION

Currency and Exchange

Currency in Dutch Sint Maarten is the Netherlands Antilles florin, or guilder, currently exchanging at NAF$1.80 = US$1. French Saint-Martin uses the French franc, which fluctuates daily against the dollar (recently F5.50 = US$1, but check your newspaper for rates). Both sides, however, use the U.S. dollar freely. Businesses on the Dutch side even seem to prefer U.S. dollars. Prices on items are often given in francs, guilders, and dollars, except in supermarkets and at the petrol pump, where the local currency is listed. Change is often given in U.S. dollars on the Dutch side and francs on the French side, but the simple fact is that you never need to exchange your U.S. dollars for francs or guilders. In some duty-free shops, U.S. dollars and only U.S. dollars are used.

To change traveler's checks, look for banks and bureaux de change located at several shopping malls and the main streets of Philipsburg and Marigot. Banking hours vary slightly, but Dutch banks are generally open Mon.-Fri. 8 a.m.-3 p.m., with extra hours on Friday 4-5 p.m. French banks are open weekdays 8 a.m.-1 p.m. Money can also be changed at the post offices. Major credit cards are accepted virtually everywhere.

Business Hours

On the Dutch side, business hours are normally Mon.-Sat. 8 a.m.-6 p.m., with an hour or two off for lunch. On the French side, businesses open Mon.-Sat. 9 a.m.-12:30 p.m. and 3-7 p.m., with slight variations. Some shops will open on Sunday and holidays to accommodate cruise ship traffic.

Telephones

Telephoning to, from, and around Saint-Martin/Sint Maarten can be a challenge. The international exchange for the Dutch side is 599, while French Saint-Martin uses 590. From North America, for Dutch Sint Maarten, dial "011" plus "599" followed by "5" and the five-digit number. When calling French Saint-Martin, dial "011" plus "590" and a six-digit number. To call the French side from the Dutch, dial "06" plus the six-digit number. When calling the Dutch side from the French, dial "19-599-5" plus the five-digit number. Got it? Neither do we. But see our "Telephoning Saint-Martin and Sint Maarten" chart for more help.

Calling either way is in effect an international phone call. Still, it's a relief that Caribbean telephone calling cards, available at post offices and many small shops, can be used on both sides of the island. Phone booths are located on Back Street in Philipsburg, the square in Marigot, and Grand Case.

Miscellaneous

Post offices are located at Wathey Pier in Philipsburg, tel. (599-5) 22289, at Princess Juliana Airport, and in Marigot, tel. (590) 87-53-17. The French side uses French stamps, and the Dutch side uses Dutch stamps. Stamps are not interchangeable on either side of the island; it's best not to apply stamps to your postcard at the post office in Philipsburg and then try to mail it from Marigot, or vice versa.

Several tourist newspapers, including Today, are available on the island. Dutch Sint Maarten publishes The Chronicle and The Guardian six days per week, as well as the regional The Caribbean Herald. Airport shops carry U.S. and European newspapers, the day's edition often arriving in the late afternoon.

SAINT-BARTHÉLÉMY

Saint-Barthélémy, more commonly known as St. Barth's or St. Barts, has for some time been regarded by outsiders as a tony enclave of the ultra-wealthy or at least ultra-hip. This has as much to do with its dominant French culture as with the attitude of the island's hoteliers and restaurateurs—small, exquisite, and mostly tasteful, it seems, has won over large and blustery.

So much the better. On an island only eight square miles (21 square km), everything naturally occurs in small doses. From the compact red-roofed French country homes to the toy airstrip to the dozen-street capital of Gustavia, the overriding impression is that an island like St. Barts would sink under extensive growth.

Of course, these same Lilliputian qualities limit that which St. Barts can ever be; it is an island with few resources beyond the natural beauty of its billowing hills and comely beaches, and this, coupled with a steady source of income from France, helps define the larger economic picture in the future of the island. It is, mostly, tourism.

Because of its understated exclusivity, St. Barts is the sort of place that has, for some time, attracted luminaries; the Rockefellers, the French Rothschilds, the King of Sweden, and today's movie celebrities and rock stars have found respite on the island. Tourism has boomed for the last 10 years. It is not always the sort of touring those on a strict budget will appreciate, but, as the market expands, the hoi polloi on holiday are finding an increasing number of good bargains. What one remembers most about St. Barts is its ability to simultaneously offer solitude and controlled boisterousness—the recipe for a good vacation.

THE LAND

St. Barts is a French West Indies island in the Leewards Islands of the Lesser Antilles, 20 miles (32 km) southeast of Saint-Martin and 125 miles (201 km) north of Guadeloupe; it is a dependency of the latter.

The hilly, boomerang-shaped island is volcanic in origin, ringed by 20-odd beaches set in small coves and bays along its uneven coast. The hills, though they often seem steep when driving the winding roadways, never reach higher than 900 feet (275 meters). The island itself tends to be dry, and several small lakes and salt ponds dot the valleys and coastline, particularly along the windward and southern coasts. **La Grande Saline** is the large, pungent salt pond on the south coast, near **Anse de Grande Saline.**

St. Barts' vegetation is low-lying and hardy, with some cactus, wild pear, manchineel, and other coastal plants dominating the flora.

Several small outlying cays, uninhabited, are homes for nesting sea birds. Common land birds found are the crested hummingbird and the green-throated carib (hummingbird), the bananaquit, the grassquit, the bullfinch, and the American kestral, a smaller bird of prey.

Among reptiles, the gecko and anole, both insect-eaters, are common. Iguanas are nearly extinct on the island but can be seen occasionally.

HISTORY

First Inhabitants

St. Barts was inhabited first by the Stone Age Ciboney (or Siboney), about 1000 B.C. Not much is known of their lives, but some evidence of their existence—primarily their stone implements—has been found throughout the Lesser Antilles. The Ciboney were long gone by the time of the arrival of the Amerindian Arawaks, a migratory group originating from the Orinoco region of South America.

A large body of evidence exists of Arawak (or related groups) settlements in Hispaniola, Jamaica, Puerto Rico, and Cuba, less so in the northern Lesser Antilles. Still, it is assumed they lived for at least some time on St. Barts or neighboring islands and were later supplanted or conquered by the Caribs, another Amerindian group that had migrated from the same regions of

South America. The Caribs, however, were aggressive where the Arawaks were not, and they were the sole inhabitants of the island, which they called Ouanalao, when it was sighted by Columbus in November 1493.

Columbus charted the island and named it after his brother, Bartolomeo. He did not land, apparently assuming, as he did of many of the smaller islands, that St. Barts had no gold to offer and no real strategic value.

The French

The next century saw numerous visits by European ships, none of which made serious attempts at colonization. The Caribs, in the meantime, became increasingly wary of the European visitors and repulsed some landings. The writing for this hapless group, however, was clearly on the wall.

In 1648, a French party of about 50, under orders from the French governor of St. Kitts, de Poincy, landed and founded a town. Under pressure from Carib attacks, the French sold the island to the powerful Order of the Knights of Malta in 1651. The Knights failed to keep order, and in 1656 the Caribs launched a massive attack against the French, massacring nearly the entire group. The few survivors fled to St. Kitts, and the Caribs had a temporary reprieve.

Under constant encroachment, the Caribs were persuaded to sign a peace treaty in 1659, and the French once again returned to the island. By 1674, St. Barts had been incorporated with the French colony of Guadeloupe, and a short period of stability followed. During this time the Caribs were eliminated, died off, or fled to neighboring islands, and little is known of them in the 18th century. In the meantime the French islanders, many from the provinces of Brittany and Normandy, started small farming activities.

Increasingly, however, the island's natural port, called Carenage, was seen by various European explorers as strategically valuable. The island attracted, among others, the infamous buccaneers, who used it as a base for raiding Spanish merchant ships. Legend has it that the WWF-esque-named Monbars the Exterminator hid treasure either in the coves of Anse du Gouverneur or in the thick sands of La Grande Saline.

The farms of St. Barts were never the size of plantations on neighboring islands, and as a result, slaves were never imported in great numbers. At any given time, the slave population was never more than a one-to-one ratio with whites and freed blacks, while on major sugar plantation islands slave levels reached as many as 10 or 15 to one.

Swedish Involvement

Through the early part of the 18th century, ongoing European wars had their effect on St. Barts. The British sacked the island in 1744, and most inhabitants escaped to other French possessions such as Martinique and St. Lucia. By 1764, the French had fought their way back to repossession of the island.

In 1785, the French government under Louis XVI traded St. Barts to Sweden's King Gustaf in exchange for the right to store goods in warehouses in the Swedish port town of Gothenborg (also spelled Goteborg). The Swedes promptly declared St. Barts a free port and renamed the harbor Gustavia, in honor of the king. The local inhabitants, then numbering 740, went on tilling their farms, and the Swedish government made a fortune from trade throughout the region. They built forts around Gustavia, including forts Karl, Oscar, and Gustave.

The island, and most importantly Gustavia, remained in Swedish hands for more than 100 years, until it was repurchased by the French in 1878. (To this day the Swedish influence is seen in architecture, in street names, and place names such as Gustavia.) In the meantime, the 1847 abolition of slavery in the French islands brought a virtual halt to agricultural production on the small plantations. When the French took over, the island's agricultural production was limited to several small cotton and pineapple farms. The conclusion of the 19th-century European wars served to widen trade agreements within the island community, and the free-port status of Gustavia was diminished in importance. When the French again took over in 1878, the economy of St. Barts was less viable than it had been 100 years before.

20th Century

During the early part of the 20th century, many of the island's inhabitants emigrated, searching for better economic shores. World War I saw hundreds of islanders drafted into the French war effort. The period between world wars was characterized by more emigration, particularly to the Virgin Islands, in search of better work. During this period France paid little attention to the island, and with the advent of the second world war, the beleaguered mother country cut off virtually all aid and even contact with its West Indies colonies.

After WW II, as France and the world recovered, the nascent St. Barts tourism industry began to grow; an airstrip was constructed, then lengthened in 1969 to 2,625 feet (800 meters). That same year the first regular airline service to the island was established. The island population in 1974 was estimated at 2,500, and a small percentage at that time were wealthy North Americans and French building villas and vacation homes. Nearly 20 years later, by 1990, the population had doubled to 5,043.

PEOPLE AND CULTURE

Of the current 5,000-plus residents, nearly 90% live in or around Gustavia, the capital. The majority population in St. Barts is white, either the *metro* French, workers and temporary residents from France, or those of Breton, Norman, and Poitevin descent who first colonized the island. A small percentage are black, either descendants of St. Barts' slave population, or workers (also slave descendants) from other islands. On the surface the two groups live with the ease of old neighbors; the slave trade on St. Barts was neither as massive nor as brutal as in most of the West Indies, and few apparent animosities have been carried down through the generations.

Much of the overt culture of St. Barts is in the hands of the French settlers' descendants. Older women still wear the nunlike ankle-

Older women still wear traditional calèches or quichenottes.

BOB RACE

length garments, reminiscent of French provincial dress with wide, shoulder-brushing sunbonnets called *calèches* or *quichenottes*. The men still take to the sea and are considered throughout the islands to be excellent sailors. Variations of the French Norman dialect are heard, as are modern French dialects. Some Creole is spoken and differs in colloquialisms from French Creole spoken elsewhere. English is not common, but, with increasing tourist traffic from North America, it has become more prevalent among hoteliers and shopkeepers.

Catholicism is the main religion, although an Anglican church in Gustavia is reminiscent of various English occupations.

A cultural note: As in most of the islands, people can be touchy about having unsolicited photos taken of them. This is true of the St. Barts women who, with their provincial attire, would otherwise make wonderful photo ops. At the very least, ask. They will probably refuse.

Holidays and Festivals
Carnival is celebrated in mid- or late February, a five-day traditional pre-Lenten festival with street parades, music contests, feasts, Mardi Gras masquerades, and partying 'til the wee hours. While the St. Barts Carnival is not as large as the carnivals of several of the larger Lesser Antilles islands, it does not lack local color.

Several Catholic saints' days, including the **Festival of St. Barthélémy** and the **Festival of St. Louis,** both in late August, commemorate the patron saint of the island and the tradition of fishing, respectively. Major Festival of St. Louis activities, including sailing races, take place in the traditional fishing village of Corossol.

All Saints' Day (early November) is a religious holiday, as are Christmas and Easter and their attendant holidays. **Labor Day** is celebrated 1 May, **Abolition Day** is celebrated later that month on the 27th, and the French holiday **Bastille Day** is marked on 14 July. **Schoelcher Day,** 21 July, honors the famous French abolitionist Victor Schoelcher. The 11 November **Armistice Day** commemorates the end of WW I and honors the war dead.

Sailing races and regattas are held throughout the year and attract sailors from throughout the Caribbean and the world. The three-day **St. Barth's Cup** is held in late January, and the **Saint-Barthélémy International Regatta** is held over a week in mid-May. The mid-December **La Route du Rosé** features a regatta of tall ships racing between Saint-Tropez and Gustavia.

GOVERNMENT AND ECONOMY

St. Barts is administered through the sub-prefecture of Saint-Martin, which is in turn a dependency of Guadeloupe, which is in turn an overseas department and region of France. The island has an elected mayor and a representative of the Sous-Prefect on Saint-Martin. All external affairs are handled through France, including the police and gendarmerie.

Economically, St. Barts is reliant both on aid from France and on its tourism industry. Some subsistence farming and fishing occupies the residents, and you are likely to see cattle and goats by the roadside. The island is still a free port and is an increasingly popular tourist destination. Most visitors still originate from France, but a substantial number these days come from North America.

According to the tourism authorities, the island had 158,306 visitors in 1991, with 75,427 overnight stays and 82,879 cruise ship or yacht visitors. This means that, on the average, the number of visitors in any given month is nearly three times the population. About 40 hotels, with a total of 700 rooms, accommodate the island's visitors.

SIGHTS

Beaches
Despite its ancient volcanic origins, St. Barts' beaches are glistening white and smooth. The number of beaches is estimated at 22; some are easy to reach, others are accessible only by sea or via hikes through the bush. All beaches are open and free to visitors and residents alike. Topless sunbathing is accepted—this is, after all, a French island—but nude sunbathing is officially against the law.

The following is a rundown of the island's best beaches. **Saint-Jean,** on the north shore crook of the elbow in Baie de St. Jean, is the island's most popular beach. The long, white beach is actually two beaches, divided by the Eden Rock promontory. The number of small restaurants, seaside cafes, bungalow hotels, and water sports outlets attests to its popularity. This is the beach at the end of the airstrip—you won't miss it as you fly in.

Anse de Lorient and, farther north, **Anse de Marigot** are smaller and more secluded. East of Marigot is **Anse de Grand Cul de Sac** on a quiet lagoon; water sports are popular here. **Anse Toiny** on the south shore is rough and stony, not recommended for swimming, but popular with windsurfers. The southern **Anse de Grande Saline,** a short walk over a small hill from the salt lake, is rougher than windward-side beaches, but is very popular, particularly with those interested in clothing-optional bathing.

On the leeward side, **Anse de Grand Galet** is popular with shell collectors—the beach is primarily made of washed up shells and almost no sand. **Anse du Public** and **Anse de Corossol** are small and popular with boaters. **Anse de Colombier,** on the extreme western tip of the island, can only be reached by the sea or by a 20-minute hike from the village of Colombier. **Anse des Flamands** is a long, expansive, yet rarely crowded beach on the northwest shore.

Around the Island
Outside of Gustavia and the beach areas, St. Barts is characterized by modest, well-kept, postcard-quaint villages, rolling hills, and valleys. The entire island is easily navigated; no village or town or recreation area is more than a few minutes from the last.

North of Gustavia is the fishing village of **Corossol,** where you'll find the descendants of the early French settlers. The women, in their sunbonnets and long skirts, sell straw hats,

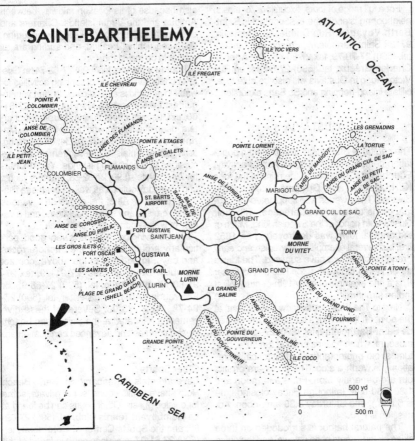

SAINT-BARTHELEMY

ATLANTIC OCEAN

ÎLE TOC VERS

ÎLE FRÉGATE

ÎLE CHEVREAU

POINTE A COLOMBIER

ANSE DE COLOMBIER

LES GRENADINS

LA TORTUE

POINTE LORIENT

POINTE A ÉTAGES

ANSE DE GALETS

ÎLE PETIT JEAN

ANSE DES FLAMANDS

FLAMANDS

COLOMBIER

ANSE DE MARIGOT

ANSE DU GRAND CUL DE SAC

ANSE DU PETIT CUL DE SAC

MARIGOT

ANSE DE LORIEN

ST. BARTS AIRPORT

COROSSOL

GRAND CUL DE SAC

ANSE DE COROSSOL

ANSE DU PUBLIC

LORIENT

TOINY

LES GROS ÎLETS

FORT OSCAR

FORT GUSTAVE
SAINT-JEAN

BAIE DE SAINT-JEAN

MORNE DU VITET

GUSTAVIA

LES SAINTES

FORT KARL

MORNE LURIN

GRAND FOND

ANSE TOINY

POINTE A TOINY

PLAGE DE GRAND GALET
(SHELL BEACH)

LURIN

LA GRANDE SALINE

ANSE DU GRAND FOND

FOURMIS

GRANDE POINTE

ANSE DU GOUVERNEUR

POINTE DU GOUVERNEUR

ANSE DE GRANDE SALINE

ÎLE COCO

CARIBBEAN SEA

0   500 yd

0   500 m

© MOON PUBLICATIONS, INC.

bags, and other products woven from *lantania* (sabal) palms. Fishing boats line the shore, and the town has the feeling of the Old World. In the village is the Ingenu Magras **Inter Oceans Museum,** tel. (590) 27-62-97, a private collection of more than 7,000 seashells. The museum is open daily 9 a.m.-5 p.m., admission F20.

North of Corossol is **Colombier,** another traditional fishing village and site of one of the island's prettiest beaches. You must walk from the village to the beach or take one of several boats operating out of Gustavia.

The Office du Tourisme, tel. (590) 27-87-27, has sanctioned and regulated three sightsee-

ing tours of St. Barts, operated by local tour conductors. The first, about one hour long, starts in Gustavia and goes to points east, including Saint-Jean, Salines, Lorient, Marigot, and Grand Fond. Cost is F200 for three persons, F250 for more than three. A second one-and-one-half hour tour covers most of the island except points south of Gustavia. Cost is F250 for three, and F300 for more than three. A shorter, 45-minute tour heads from Gustavia to Colombier, Flamands, and points west. Cost for three people is F150, and F200 for more than three. The official tour vans are located outside the tourist office at the pier in Gustavia.

For a full range of tours, excursions, or trips to neighboring islands, the best contact is **Saint-Barth Voyages,** Rue Duquesne, Gustavia, 97133 Saint-Barthélémy, French West Indies, tel. (590) 27-79-79, fax 27-80-45. The **Agence Charles Gréaux,** tel. (590) 27-64-44, on Rue Victor Hugo in Gustavia will also be able to facilitate island-hopping and St. Barts excursions.

GUSTAVIA

The capital of St. Barts is also the main population center and the island's hub of activity. Surrounding Gustavia are the ruins of the forts **Karl, Oscar,** and **Gustave,** built by the Swedes. The Swedes also supplanted the original name of the town, Carenage, with their Gustavia, in honor of the Swedish king. Much of the original town was destroyed in an 1852 fire, but several examples of Swedish and early French architecture have survived. The **Marie de St. Barth,** or town hall, on Rue de Roi Oscar II, is a fine example of early 19th-century West Indian structures.

Next to **The Wall House** (now a restaurant) at the point on the harbor's far side, is the **Musée de Saint-Barthélémy,** tel. (590) 27-89-07. The museum, which houses antique furniture, costumes, old photographs, and historical recreations, is worth a stop. The hours are erratic, but are generally Mon.-Fri. 8 a.m.-noon and 1:30-5:30 p.m. (although Friday closing time is 5 p.m.), and Saturday 8:30 a.m.-noon. Admission is F10.

The natural harbor is surrounded on three sides by the streets of downtown, and the entire area can be explored in a few hours, or a day if you linger. Several chichi shops, banks, and a dozen cafes line the streets. The tourism office is located in offices on Quai General de Gaulle on the pier and is open Mon.-Thurs. 10:30 a.m.-12:30 p.m. and 3-7 p.m., and Friday 8:30-10:30 a.m.

SPORTS AND ENTERTAINMENT

Water Sports
St. Barts is a popular yacht stop and sailing center due to its natural port and harbors, and also because of its location midway between Antigua and the Virgin Islands. Charters and equipment for diving, snorkeling, windsurfing, deep-sea fishing, boating, and surfing are all available on the island.

Loulou's Marine, tel. (590) 27-62-74, in Gustavia offers a wide range of sporting activities for water lovers and is a good place to start your inquiries. **La Maison de Mer,** tel. (590) 27-81-00, in Gustavia offers sailing, bare-boat charters, deep-sea fishing, and diving services. **Marine Service,** tel. (590) 27-70-34, offers diving, fishing, boat rentals, snorkeling rentals, and excursions to neighboring islands. **Yacht Charter Agency,** tel. (590) 27-62-38, charters yachts and offers day outings as well as deep-sea fishing excursions. All of the above offer various sunset cruises and sailing packages, and a variety of water sports.

Scuba diving on St. Barts is very good, particularly around some of the offshore rocks and cays. In addition to the above, contact **Rainbow Dive,** tel. (590) 27-91-79, fax 27-91-80; **Club La Bulle,** tel. (590) 27-68-93; or **Emeraude PADI Diving Center,** tel. (590) 27-64-78, fax 27-83-08. Several of these dive centers are located at the Saint-Jean beach. Resort courses and advanced certification are both offered.

Other Sports
Several hotels (Manapany, St. Barth Beach Hotel) have tennis courts, some private, some for outside guests. Other courts can be found at **Le Flamboyant Tennis Club,** tel. (590) 27-69-82, and the **Sports Center of Colombier,** tel. (590) 27-61-07. A squash court is found at the **Isle de France,** tel. (590) 27-80-72, hotel in Flamands.

Horseback riding is available at **La Ranch des Flamands,** tel. (590) 27-80-72, in Flamands.

If you're feeling a little anxious about having such a good time or you just want to keep up your relaxation and meditation routines, call **Yoga St. Barth,** (590) 27-80-81.

Shopping
Two words: downtown Gustavia. Due to the island's free port status, you can find good deals in many of the shops downtown. This is the is-

land's greatest single concentration of stores, so if shopping is your desire, plan to spend a few hours here. Other shops line the bay at Saint-Jean, where there is a small mall. The **La Savane Commercial Center,** located across the road from the airport, also has a dozen or so boutiques, bookstores, and trinket shops.

The island's largest supermarket, **Match,** tel. (590) 27-68-16, is also located across from the airport at La Savane and is open Mon.-Sat. 8 a.m.-1 p.m. and 3-6:30 p.m., Sunday 9 a.m.-1 p.m.

Nightlife
St. Barts is not the place to be if you're looking for wild nightlife or gambling. You won't find any casinos on the island, and your choices of discos and dancing joints are limited. On the other hand, there's no reason to be bored.

For a quiet drink at sunset, or a late-night lounge at the piano bar, try the **Hotel Carl Gustaf,** tel. (590) 27-82-83, in Gustavia. The view alone is worth it.

The popular **Le Petit Club** in Gustavia features dancing. **Gustavia's L'Hibiscus,** tel. (590)

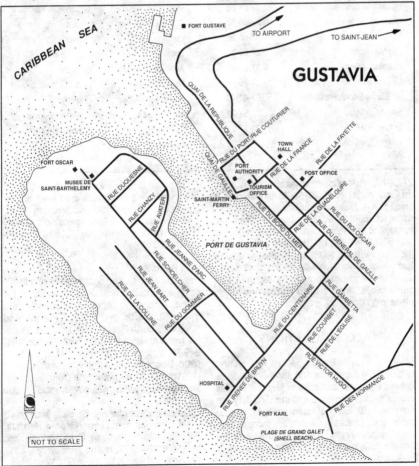

MORE SAINT-BARTHÉLÉMY ACCOMMODATIONS

Rates per s, EP when applicable, winter

NAME	(590)	LOCATION	TARIFF
Auberge Terre Neuve	27-61-93	Anse des Flamands	moderate
Eden Rock	27-72-94	Saint-Jean	luxury
El Sereno Beach Hotel	27-64-80	Grand Cul de Sac	luxury
Emeraude Plage	27-64-78	Saint-Jean	luxury
François Plantation	27-78-82	Colombier	luxury
Hostellerie des Trois Forces	27-61-25	Vitet	moderate-luxury
Hotel de la Plage	27-60-70	Grand Cul de Sac	luxury
La Banane	27-68-25	Lorient	luxury
Les Mouettes	27-60-74	Lorient	moderate
Manapany Cottages	27-66-55	Anse des Cayes	luxury
Marigot Bay Club	27-75-45	Marigot	moderate-luxury
St. Barths Beach Hotel	27-62-73	Grand Cul de Sac	luxury
Sapore di Mare	27-61-73	Morne Lurin	moderate-luxury
Sunset Hotel	27-77-21	Gustavia	moderate-luxury
Village Saint-Jean	27-61-39	Saint-Jean	luxury

27-64-82, hosts occasional jazz bands. **Autour du Rocher,** tel. (590) 27-60-73, in Lorient is a small disco, featuring canned music. **La Banane,** tel. (590) 27-68-25, in Lorient offers a live revue, and the Saint-Jean restaurant Topolino, tel. (590) 27-70-92, occasionally presents live jazz. **Le Pelican,** tel. (590) 27-64-64, also in Saint-Jean, offers Creole dining and great views, and the piano bar sometimes features live music. **Saint-Jean's Club Hurrucane** is the place to go dancing.

ACCOMMODATIONS

Most hotels on St. Barts are small, homey, and relaxed. Big high-rises and sprawling resorts are not the norm, and quite of few of the small places are family owned and run. And they are not cheap. St. Barts accommodations, restaurants, and services in general are more expensive than many of its neighbors. However, there are few guesthouses on the island, particularly in Gustavia.

Camping is not allowed.

The following categories are based on single-occupancy, per-night prices during the 15 December through 15 April high season: **Luxury** US$100 or more, **Moderate** US$50-100, **Budget** US$50 or less.

Villa Rentals

Villas are often a good deal if you have a family or large group, and dozens are available on the island. Among the better rental agencies are **Villas St. Barth,** tel. (590) 27-74-29; and **WIMCO/Sibarth Real Estate,** tel. (590) 27-62-38, North America tel. (800) 932-3222 or (401) 849-8012, local fax 27-65-02, U.S. fax 847-6290. Sibarth lists over 200 villas starting in the US$1000-2000 per week range (one bedroom) and have luxury villas with weekly rates of up to US$5000.

Other villa agencies with St. Barts and French West Indies listings: **French Home Rentals,** P.O. Box 82386, Portland, OR 97282, tel. and fax (503) 774-8977; **Island Hideaways,** 1317 Rhode Island Ave. N.W., Suite 503, Washington,

DC 20005, tel. (800) 832-2302, fax (202) 667-3392; and **St. Barth Properties,** 22 Park Rd., Franklin, MA 02038, tel. (800) 421-3396 or (508) 528-7727, fax 528-7789.

Hotels and Guesthouses

For hotels, a good first contact is the **Association des Hoteliers de Saint-Barthélémy,** Hotel El Sereno Beach, Grand Cul de Sac, 97133 Saint-Barthélémy, French West Indies, tel. (590) 27-64-80, fax 27-75-47. Their list tends to include the high-end hotels, but you can be fairly sure of high quality standards among them.

Hotel Carl Gustaf, Rue des Normands, Gustavia, 97133 Saint-Barthélémy, French West Indies, tel. (590) 27-82-83, U.S. tel. (800) 922-0276, fax 27-82-37, is a luxury hotel located on a hill near downtown Gustavia. All of the large suites have views of the harbor and town. All have a mini-bar, private pool, sun deck, television, and stereo. Very elegant. The restaurant, pool, and their views are striking. Luxury. **Christopher Hotel,** BP 571, Gustavia, 97098 Saint-Barthélémy, French West Indies, tel. (590) 27-63-63, fax 27-92-92, is a new 40-unit Sofitel hotel at Pointe Milou, with a fitness center, spacious rooms, and shuttle service to beaches. Luxury.

Le Toiny, Anse de Toiny, 97133 Saint-Barthélémy, French West Indies, tel. (590) 27-88-88, fax 27-89-30, is one of the island's more deluxe accommodations. On the far eastern end of the island, the 12 units are individual villas, each with reproduction French colonial antiques, private pools, television, raised poster beds, and kitchens. The reception area has a bar, restaurant, and pool with a great view. The beach below is rough and not for swimmers, but the hotel can arrange trips to others. This is a place for quiet relaxation, fine dining, and not much else. Here, that would be enough. Luxury.

Auberge de la Petite Anse (BP 117 Anse des Flamands, 97133 Saint-Barthélémy, French West Indies; tel. (590) 27-64-60, fax 27-72-30, is in Flamands, a great location near several beaches. The inn is small, with only 16 rooms, but it is clean and overlooks the beach. Moderate. **La Presqu'ile,** Gustavia, tel. (590) 27-64-60, fax 27-72-30, is a small 12-room inn in Gustavia with a good location and a good restaurant. Moderate. **La Normandie,** Lorient, 97133 Saint-Barthélémy, French West Indies, tel. (590) 27-61-66, fax 27-68-64, is small (eight rooms) with only a couple of air-conditioned rooms, a bar, pool, and restaurant. Reserving ahead is important. Budget.

MORE SAINT-BARTHÉLÉMY RESTAURANTS

NAME	PLACE	(590)	CUISINE	PRICE RANGE
Chez Francine	Saint-Jean	27-60-49	grilled	moderate
Chez Pompei	Petit Cul de Sac	27-75-67	French Creole	expensive
Coriandre	Gustavia	27-93-84	Thai/takeout	inexpensive
Eddy's Ghetto	Gustavia	N/A	French Creole	moderate-expensive
La Gloriette	Grand Cul de Sac	27-75-66	Creole	moderate
La Frégate	Anse des Flamands	27-66-51	French/Creole	moderate-expensive
La Langouste	Gustavia	27-69-47	French/Creole	expensive
Marigot Bay Club	Marigot	27-75-45	French Creole	expensive
Maya's	Gustavia Public Beach	27-73-61	French/Creole	expensive
Topolino	Saint-Jean	27-70-92	Italian/barbecue	inexpensive-moderate

FOOD

The emphasis is on French, French Creole, and a variety of international cuisines. Dining out can be expensive, but some inexpensive lunches can be found at beachside cafes.

Hotel restaurants are generally very good, including the above-mentioned **Carl Gustaf** and **Le Gaiac** at **Le Toiny**.

The restaurants mentioned below are in the **Moderate** category, US$10-25 per entree: **Wall House,** tel. (590) 27-71-83, on the harbor in Gustavia is elegant, with views of the boats on the harbor. **La Gloriette,** tel. (590) 27-75-66, offers beachside dining in Grand Cul de Sac, specializing in Creole; no credit cards are accepted. **Lafayette Club,** tel. (590) 27-62-51, is a bar-restaurant-boutique on the beach at Grand Cul de Sac, featuring barbecued this and that—no credit cards. **Hostellerie des Trois Forces,** tel. (590) 27-61-25, has a logo featuring the international symbol for infinity with a plus and minus sign. New Age flimflam or just good food? Good food, mostly. And large drinks, some vegetarian dishes, all in the hills with views of Vitet. **Le Pelican,** tel. (590) 27-64-64, a piano bar and restaurant on Saint-Jean Bay, serves good seafood and Creole.

GETTING THERE

By Air

On approach, the tiny airstrip on St. Barts appears out of nowhere; the plane dips sharply over a hill and there it is, right below the presumably distended landing wheels. At the far end is the beach at Saint-Jean. Good brakes are very important here.

The airstrip is convenient, just minutes from Gustavia. Connections to St. Barts are made via interisland carriers, primarily through Sint Maarten, about 10 minutes away. The Sint Maarten-based **Winair,** tel. (590) 27-61-01, is the major connector. **Air St. Barthélémy,** tel. (590) 27-61-90, connects from Princess Juliana International in Sint Maarten, and from San Juan, Guadeloupe, and the small airstrip in Grand Case, Saint-Martin. **Air Guadeloupe,** tel. (590) 27-61-90, also makes connections from Saint-

Martin, and from Guadeloupe, Antigua, and St. Thomas. **Virgin Air,** tel. (590) 27-71-76, makes connections from San Juan and St. Thomas.

Note: The airport does not yet have night landing capacity, and this may be important when scheduling your connection.

Interisland Boat Service

Several boats make regular trips between Gustavia and Philipsburg and Marigot in Saint-Martin/Sint Maarten. *St. Barth Express,* tel. (590) 27-77-24, makes the trip Mon.-Sat., leaving Gustavia at 7:30 a.m. The return from Marigot departs at 3:30 p.m., and from **Bobby's Marina,** tel. (599-5) 23170, in Philipsburg, departure is at 4:15 p.m. Cost US$35 (about F190) one-way, US$50 (F275) roundtrip. The schedule and fares are subject to change so *call ahead to confirm.* Several catamarans also make the trip, which is really a round-trip excursion rather than a ferry. Inquire at Bobby's Marina in Philipsburg.

Departure Tax

The departure tax is F12 if your destination is Guadeloupe or Esperance Airport at Grand Case, on Saint-Martin. It is F16 otherwise, including those traveling to Princess Juliana International Airport in Sint Maarten.

GETTING AROUND

Taxis

You'll find two taxi stands on St. Barts: one at the airstrip and the other in Gustavia on Rue de la République. Hotels can always arrange a taxi, or you can call a dispatching office at (590) 27-66-31 or 27-61-86 for pickups. Note that several hotels will collect you from the airport on your arrival, so inquire ahead for that service.

Taxis are not metered and not cheap. Rates are set by the government, the flat rate being US$5 (F27.50) for the first five minutes, and about the same for each three minutes thereafter. Rates go up after 8 p.m. and on Sunday and holidays. Private island tours run about US$50 (F275) for two people for three hours, and one driver indicated that he charged a whopping US$200 (F1100) for a day's tour. (See "Around the Island" under "Sights," above, for tourist office-sanctioned island tours.)

INFORMATION DIRECTORY

TOURISM INFORMATION

Office Municipal du Tourisme, Quai du General de Gaulle, Gustavia, 97095 Saint-Barthélémy, French West Indies, tel. (590) 27-87-27, fax 27-74-47.

"France on Call," U.S. tel. (900) 990-0040, *please note, cost is US$.50 per minute.*

French West Indies Tourist Board, 610 5th Ave., New York, NY 10020.

French Government Tourist Office, 1981 McGill College Ave., Suite 490, Montreal, Quebec H3A 2W9, tel. (514) 288-4264.

French Government Tourist Office, 178 Piccadilly, London W1Z 0AL, tel. (071) 493-6594.

Association des Hoteliers de Saint-Barthélémy, Hotel El Sereno Beach, Grand Cul de Sac, 97133 Saint-Barthélémy, French West Indies, tel. (590) 27-64-80, fax 27-75-47.

OTHER

Gendarmes, tel. 17 or (590) 27-60-12.

Fire, tel. 18 or (590) 27-62-31.

Police, tel. (590) 27-66-66.

Gustavia Clinic, Gustavia, tel. (590) 27-60-35.

Pharmacie Saint-Barth, Quai de la République, Gustavia, tel. (590) 27-61-82.

Pharmacie de La Savane, Saint-Jean (airport), tel. (590) 27-66-61.

St. Barts Airport, tel. (590) 27-65-41 or 27-65-33.

Car Rentals

Since only 25 miles (40 km) of paved road cover the island, it might be worth your while to rent a car. Renting a car is not difficult, except during the busy high season when the island experiences a dearth of rentals. At all times, but particularly during the winter season, it's best to reserve ahead. Some companies require a minimum of three days rental, while some hotels require that you rent through them.

The key here is to polish up your French and make some phone calls.

All you'll need to rent a car, other than a credit card or money, is a valid license. Rental rates can be as high as US$50 (F275) per day, although mini-mokes will be cheaper at about US$40 (F220)—but they are the first to be rented as well. At any rate, you can negotiate during off-season. Most rental agencies have airport offices.

For car rentals, call **Aubin Car Rental,** tel. (590) 27-73-03; **Avis,** tel. (590) 27-71-43, fax 27-69-32; **Budget,** tel. (590) 27-66-30 or 27-67-43; **Constant Gumbs Car Rental,** tel. (590) 27-75-32; **Europcar,** tel. (590) 27-73-33; **Hertz,** tel. (590) 27-71-14; **Island Car Rental,** tel. (590) 27-70-01; **Questal Car Rental,** tel. (590) 27-73-22; **Soleil Caraibe,** tel. (590) 27-67-18 or 27-65-06; or **Turbe Car Rental,** tel. (590) 27-60-70, fax 27-75-57.

Motorcycle Rentals

Motor scooters and small motorcycles can be rented through **Saint-Barth Motobique,** tel. (590) 27-67-89, and **Honda Rent Some Fun,** tel. (590) 27-70-59, both in Gustavia.

MONEY, HOURS, AND COMMUNICATION

Currency and Banks

The French franc is the official currency on St. Barts, most recently exchanging at F5.50 = US$1. This rate may fluctuate—check your local newspaper for current rates before you leave. U.S. dollars are widely accepted, as are credit cards. You will, however, get a better rate if you change your U.S. dollars at a bank or *bureau de change* rather than at a shop or taxi stand.

Island banks include **Banque Française Commercial** with branches in Gustavia, tel. (590) 27-62-62, and Saint-Jean, airport tel. (590) 27-87-75; **Banque Nationale de Paris,** tel. (590) 27-63-70; **Credit Agricole,** tel. (590) 27-89-90; and **Credit Martiniquais,** tel. (590) 27-86-57. The last three banks are all in Gustavia. Bank hours are generally Mon.-Fri. 8 a.m.-noon and 2-3:30 p.m.

Other

Regular business hours vary among shops, but figure on stores being open generally weekdays 8 a.m.-noon and 2-5 p.m., and on Saturday for a half-day. Many offices and shops are closed Wednesday afternoon as well.

To call St. Barts from North America, dial "011" plus "590" and the six-digit number. Calls to the rest of the French Antilles are direct dial.

Pay phones do not use coins, but rather telephone cards, which are available at post offices and at various businesses around town.

You'll find post offices on Rue du Roi Oscar II in Gustavia tel. (590) 27-62-00, and at La Savane near the airport and Lorient. Hours vary, but the main Gustavia office is open weekdays 8 a.m.-noon and 2-4 p.m. (except Wednesday afternoon) and Saturday 8 a.m.-noon.

GUADELOUPE

Large, dominating, and very-French Guadeloupe, nearly equidistant from its northern neighbor, Montserrat, and Dominica to the south, lies almost dead center in the Lesser Antilles archipelago.

The island is less sophisticated in infrastructure, particularly regarding tourism, than its sister French Antillean islands, and at first glance appears to have retained a French colonial sensibility.

The commercial center and harbor Pointe-à-Pitre is bustling and noisy with buses, boats, markets, and trucks loaded with cane and vegetables. Outside the main tourist areas, sugarcane and banana plantations dominate the land. Small villages and towns engaged in fishing and farming seem oblivious to the growing tourist crowds, who are often young and French. The richness and authenticity about Guadeloupe is hard to ignore; the countryside is compelling, but not always sleek; the people are preoccupied, but not necessarily with you.

Guadeloupe is itself an archipelago, an overseas department of France—in French a *département d'outre-mer*—and technically a region of France. It counts as its dependencies the small neighboring islands of Marie-Galante, the Iles des Saintes group, more commonly called Les Saintes, and La Désirade. These islands are close offshore, and can be seen from Guadeloupe.

Also counted as dependencies of Guadeloupe and in the same department are Saint-Barthélémy and Saint-Martin, which both lie over 120 miles (193 km) to the north. The island of Martinique is itself a separate department, and these islands together are the French West Indies, also called the French Antilles.

In this section, we'll deal with the islands of Guadeloupe, Marie-Galante, Les Saintes, and La Désirade as a single entity, if for nothing else because of their close proximity. The remaining islands of the French West Indies (Saint-Barthélémy, Saint-Martin, and Martinique) are each given their own sections within this chapter.

THE LAND

Guadeloupe

To make matters more confusing, Guadeloupe itself is technically two islands. The common analogy is that the two are shaped like the wings of a butterfly. This is not only poetic but true. The islands of **Grande-Terre** to the east and **Basse-Terre** to the west are separated by the narrow saltwater strait **Rivière Salée,** the backbone of the butterfly. Together they form the second largest island, behind Trinidad, in the Lesser Antilles.

The triangular Grande-Terre, about 218 square miles (565 square km), is low-lying and flat. Its eastern Atlantic coast is characterized by rough surf and dramatic cliffs, with some beaches hidden in inlets and coves. Grande-Terre's southern coast is sometimes called the "Riviera" of Guadeloupe and is host to strings of hotels and some of the island's best beaches. The soil and terrain of Grande-Terre is conducive to growing sugarcane, a major crop. The commercial center and largest town, Pointe-à-Pitre, is located on Grande-Terre's western coast, south of Rivière Salée. Three miles north of Pointe-à-Pitre is Le Raizet, the island's main airport.

A mountainous north-south volcanic ridge dominates Basse-Terre, the 312-square-mile (808-square-km) western half of Guadeloupe. At the southern portion of the ridge lies the highest point on Guadeloupe, **La Soufrière,** a 4,813-foot (1,468-meter) volcano, now dormant. Basse-Terre is lush and hilly, and much of it is part of the central Parc Naturel, a 74,000-acre protected region of rainforests, fresh-water lakes, and waterfalls.

The interior is given to banana plantations, and the coast is characterized by small fishing villages and some hotels. The administrative center of the Guadeloupe department, a small town also called Basse-Terre, sits on the southwest point of the island.

Outer Islands

The outlying islands of La Désirade, Les Saintes, and Marie-Galante are small, concerned mostly with fishing and agricultural pursuits, and relatively untouched by tourism.

Les Saintes is a group of eight islands of which two, **Terre-de-Bas** and **Terre-de-Haut,** are occupied. They are flat, somewhat barren, and feature several excellent beaches and some historical fortifications.

La Désirade is flat and dry, only eight square miles (20 square km) in area. The island is known for fine beaches but is better known as a place to truly get away from it all.

Marie-Galante is larger at 60 square miles (156 square km) and has a history of sugar plantations. The generally flat island is characterized by a central limestone plateau, which reaches a height of 670 feet (204 meters) above sea level.

HISTORY

Amerindian Arawaks were the original inhabitants of Guadeloupe, but they were driven off, as happened throughout much of the Caribbean, by the aggressive Caribs. The Caribs called the island Karukera, reportedly meaning "Island of Beautiful Waters."

Virgin of Guadalupe

Columbus sighted the island on 4 November 1493 during his second voyage and claimed it for Spain, naming it Santa Maria de Guadeloupe de Estremadura in honor of the Virgin of Guadalupe. (The Spanish word Guadalupe is derived from the Arabic *Oued-el-houb,* meaning "River of Love," which, coming full circle, sounds like it could have been French.)

Attempts to colonize the island were rebuffed by the Caribs, and the Spanish gave up any attempts to colonize the islands in 1604. For the next 150 years, no Europeans were able to settle with any lasting success.

The French

In 1635, a group of French colonists under the leadership of explorers Lienard de l'Olive and Duplessis d'Ossonville landed on the island and embarked on a series of fierce fights with the Caribs, eventually driving them from the island. Settlers were sent to outlying islands with the intent to colonize them for France and met resistance from the Caribs, or resistance from the harsh conditions on the islands themselves.

Guadeloupe (the French spelling) was officially claimed by the King of France in 1674. French colonists established settlements and introduced crops such as sugarcane—which of course later brought slavery to the island, setting the foundation for its present racial and economic makeup.

The European nations battled for possessions and sea domination throughout the 18th century. Guadeloupe changed hands, most notably during the period from 1759 to 1763, when it was occupied by the British. In 1763 France traded all French rights to Canada and repossessed her West Indies colonies. Wars, revolutions, and turnovers continued, however, and in 1815, under provisions of the Treaty of Paris, Guadeloupe was again restored to France. After several attempts, the efforts of Martiniquean Victor Schoelcher to have slavery abolished in the French colonies met with suc-

Arawak figure

cess—by 1848, slavery was illegal. Sugar production slowed, and indentured laborers, mostly from East India, were imported to shore up the plantations.

Post-Emancipation

Despite a representation in the French legislature dating from 1871, by the early 20th century Guadeloupe was little more than a backwater state, enjoying few of the fruits of French possession. Labor disputes and racial disenfranchisement rocked the entire Caribbean during this period, and radical elements in Guadeloupe and to an extent Martinique agitated for degrees of independence. In 1946, Guadeloupe was made a department of France, giving it equal status with departments of France proper. In 1974, Guadeloupe was granted the further status of region.

Autonomy movements resurfaced and became violent during the 1980s. A series of bombings in 1984 forced the French government to outlaw a radical independence group, the Caribbean Revolutionary Alliance.

La Désirade

Legend has it that La Désirade was the first island Columbus sighted on his 1493 second voyage. His name for it, La Desiderada, reflected his joy, apparently, at seeing any land at all.

The island is arid, with a long dry season and few fresh water sources, and it presented the next wave of European explorers with little in the way of economic possibilities. It was left mostly untouched until the 17th century, when French farmers migrated to the island to raise sheep and work small farms.

In the early 18th century, Guadeloupe and nearby islands began to send lepers to La Désirade. A leprosarium was built in 1930 and operated until 1954.

Today, the 1,700 inhabitants of La Désirade are engaged in boat building, sheep raising, and some minor farming of corn and cotton. Tourism is also a minor industry, and most guest facilities on the island are rustic.

Les Saintes

The eight islets that comprise Les Saintes were also named by Columbus ("Los Santos"), in honor of the feast of All Saints. The islands, including the two major islands Terre-de-Haut and Terre-de-Bas, were occupied by native Caribs and were left alone by Columbus's crew.

French settlers reached the islands in 1648 and built forts, including a major garrison on Terre-de-Haut's Morne Mire. Fort Napoleon still stands and was restored in 1973. A small museum on the grounds displays artifacts of colonial life and the history of Les Saintes.

Due to the dry climate and lack of fresh water, large plantations never took root on Les Saintes. Slaves, consequently, were never imported to any great degree. The islands were, primarily, garrisons and way stations of great strategic value for the French war efforts in the Caribbean. The French and British battled in and among the islands for the better part of the next two centuries. On 12 April 1782, the British under Admiral Rodney, engaged the French, who were commanded by Admiral le Comte de Grasse, in the Battle of Les Saintes. De Grasse lost the sea battle and Guadeloupe to the British. The 1815 Treaty of Paris once again restored the archipelago to the French.

Today Les Saintes population of 3,300 is engaged in fishing, boatbuilding, and some tourism activity. The boats of the Les Saintes builders, called *santoises,* are popular throughout Guadeloupe.

Marie-Galante

When Columbus sighted the frisbee-shaped island in November 1493, he called it "Maria Graciosa" ("Gracious Maria"), a nickname he'd coined for his flagship, the Santa María. The island was inhabited by Caribs, who repelled subsequent French efforts to colonize it.

In 1648, a group of 50 French settlers, attracted by the island's fertile soil, settled at Vieux-Fort and established tobacco and cotton plantations. The Caribs resisted the French settlers but were ultimately defeated after a series of fierce and bloody battles.

The French continued to settle the island throughout the 17th century, and during that time and well into the 18th century the island changed hands in tandem with the numerous battles fought and treaties signed by the French and their arch-rivals, the British.

Sugarcane production ruled the island economy during the 18th century, mirroring the economy of larger Guadeloupe. Slaves were imported, and the island became a thriving and successful outpost of the French, and occasionally British, empires. When slavery was abolished in the mid-19th century the sugar industry declined, and Marie-Galante settled into the economic confusion that affected the entire Caribbean through the turn of the century.

Marie-Galante today is bolstering its tourism industry with new hotels and services, but the island remains rustic and relatively untouched. Historical sites, plantation ruins, and several fine beaches are the attractions. The three major towns, Grand-Bourg, Capesterre, and Saint-Louis, host the majority of the island's 16,000 population.

PEOPLE AND CULTURE

People

The population of the Guadeloupe group is about 357,000. The majority population is black, descendants of the slave families of plantation years. East Indians, descendants of indentured laborers from, among other cities, Calcutta, represent about 10% of the population.

Guadeloupe's Europeans are either *blanc métropolitain* (the "metro" French, or temporary immigrants) or the *blanc pays* or *créole béké*, whites who are members of families long established on, or even settlers of, Guadeloupe. The so-called "coloreds," or mixed-race Guadeloupeans, have been an important social, economic, and now political class on the island from the very beginning. Racial tension is not unheard of, and some radical pro-independence movements have found strong adherents, particularly among the mixed-race and black intelligentsia and working classes.

Language

French is the official language, and French Creole is widely spoken. Creole, the unique blend of French and African grammatical structures and words, diverts widely from standard French. English is spoken at some of the larger hotels, some of the time, but do not expect it in the countryside or at smaller hotels and restaurants.

Music and Dance

Guadeloupe, much like Martinique, has managed to keep its colonial culture somewhat intact, no doubt due to the fact that the island is, in fact, French. French law and customs dominate; however, the local music and dances of Guadeloupe have a distinct flair. The lush beguine, of Cole Porter fame, invites ballroom dancing; *zouk* mixes the techno-pop of France with the beat and percussion and today's full horn arrangements of equatorial Africa.

More distinct forms of Africa's influence come out at pre-Lenten Carnival time, five days of music, dancing, and costume parades. The African-styled *gwoka*, a music form based on drumming, has resurged in recent years. The drums were originally fashioned from tree trunks and served as a catalyst for a call-and-response musical narrative.

Religion

Guadeloupe's dominant religion is Roman Catholicism, not surprising given the French influence. However, Methodist, Jehovah's Witness, Seventh-Day Adventist, Jewish, and other services can be found. Superstitions and magic, holdovers from ancient and current African roots, play a large part in Guadeloupean life. The *quinboiseur,* a traditional doctor who can be an herbalist or spell-caster, can be found in villages and towns throughout.

Holidays and Festivals

Guadeloupe's festivals are important to the life and culture of its people. **Carnival** festivities begin with weekend activities in January and end with a Mardi Gras on Shrove Tuesday and Ash Wednesday—much singing and dancing. Masquerading devils and spirits and King Carnival, as well as street marching and general rowdiness, are the order of the day.

La Fête des Cuisinières (The Festival of Women Cooks) takes place in Pointe-à-Pitre in early August, honoring Saint-Laurent, the patron saint of cooks. The festival dates back to 1916 and involves traditional costumes, parades, and what can only be described as a mega-banquet, a five-hour Creole feast featuring too much food, rum, and dancing.

Throughout the year, saints' days and Christian religious holidays are also celebrated.

Armistice Day is 11 November; Schoelcher Day, commemorating the famous abolitionist, is celebrated on 21 July; parades and feasts accompany the 14 June Bastille Day; and V.E. Day is celebrated on 8 May.

GOVERNMENT AND ECONOMY

Government

Guadeloupe is represented in the French Parliament by two senators and four deputies, as well as members in the Economic Council. Locally elected legislative bodies are called the Conseil General and the Conseil Regional. A Préfet Commissaire de la République, sort of like a governor, is appointed by the French minister of the interior and is assisted by two general secretaries. Two Sous-Préfets, one responsible for Guadeloupe and the other responsible for Saint-Martin and Saint-Barthélémy, administer the island dependencies.

Economy

Guadeloupe's economy is based mainly on agriculture, some manufacturing, and tourism. A great slice of Guadeloupe's income comes as direct aid from France.

The agricultural sector produces sugarcane, bananas, and melons, employing about 13% the island's working population. In 1989, Hurricane Hugo so damaged the agricultural sector that an estimated six months of sugarcane production and one year of banana production was lost. Close to 45% of arable land is covered by sugarcane. Related industries such as rum and sugar production employ many, but general manufacturing and light industry have seen little real growth in this century. This is due to strong overseas competition, the high cost of raw materials, and a modest local market for consumption. The result is a relatively high unemployment rate, estimated at more than 20%.

Tourism employs about 10,000 of the islands' inhabitants, and this sector has grown over the past years. The number of hotel rooms increased from about 1,000 in 1970 to currently more than 9,000 (including Saint-Martin and Saint-Barthélémy). Of the average annual 330,000 visitors to the islands, most are French (about 79%), with 12% from other European countries and eight percent from North America.

BEACHES

Guadeloupe's estimated 50 beaches are covered by fine, honey-colored sand, and most are easy to find. Some beaches charge parking fees and have facilities such as changing rooms, bistros, and picnic facilities. Others are just wide open, and yet others front hotel property. All beaches are open to the public. Take precautions and don't leave your rental car unlocked or personal items unattended.

Le Gosier, south of Pointe-à-Pitre, is at the western end of a string of beaches and hotels that stretch across Grande-Terre's popular south coast. This area is perhaps the most tourist-dense of the island, and many of the beaches are crowded on weekends and holidays. Along the beach, which is shared by the hotels Salako, Arawak, and Callinago, you'll find water sports facilities and shade.

Plage de Petit-Havre is a small but popular public beach east of Le Gosier. In the small but busy town of Sainte-Anne stop at Plage du Bourg or Plage de Bois Jolan, two long and placid beach areas. Very popular. Plage de Caravelle, accessed at one end through the Club Mediterranée (Club Med), is long, expansive, and often crowded.

Saint-François, a resort town and surrounding area on Grande-Terre given almost completely to hotels and a large marina, hosts about seven public beaches including Plage de L'Anse Tarare, a clothing-optional beach.

On Grande-Terre's easternmost peninsula, Pointe des Châteaux, you'll find jagged limestone promontories and thundering surf. Swimming here can be dangerous, but it's a good place to have lunch and to take some striking photographs. As well, you can hike up to the Pointe des Colibris calvary (it's a cross), erected in 1951. From this point you'll see the islands of La Désirade, tiny Petite-Terre, Marie-Galante, and even Dominica. Pointe des Châteaux is an entity of the National Park system.

Farther north at Le Moule, Guadeloupe's first capital, several beaches are popular. Plage de

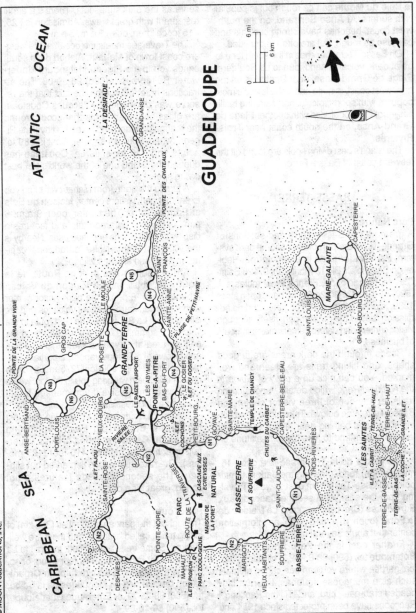

© MOON PUBLICATIONS, INC.

la Baie du Moule can be rough but is popular with surfers. At Anse Bertrand, on the northwest coast, beaches have strong currents and can also be rough, but are often uncrowded.

On Basse-Terre, beaches in the south tend to be of dark, volcanic sand, due to La Soufrière. Plage de Grand-Anse, near Deshaies on the northwest coast, is huge and is the island's most popular, with sports, picnic, and camping facilities—not to be confused with another Plage de Grand-Anse, on the south coast near Trois-Rivières.

The island's best diving spots are found off the leeward coast of Basse-Terre.

BASSE-TERRE

Parc Naturel

A great part of Basse-Terre and sections of Grande-Terre are part of the national park system, Parc National de la Guadeloupe, Habitation Beausoleil, BP 13 Monteran, 97120 Saint-Claude, Guadeloupe, French West Indies, tel. (590) 81-17-20 or 80-24-2. The park, open since 1989, is unique—there are no gates and no admission fees to the greater park itself, although visitor centers and nature centers maintain hours of business.

Roads through the park areas are in good shape, and hiking trails are clean and well marked. You can pick up a copy of Guide to the National Park, which details various hiking trails, at any one of three visitor centers on Basse-Terre (see below). Take along good hiking shoes and bathing gear, and a sweater or jacket if you intend to hike the high-altitude La Soufrière.

The Route de la Traversée is a good 16-mile (26-km) road, crossing the park and midpoint of Basse-Terre from east to west. Traveling from the east you'll see the Cascade aux Ecrevisses (Crayfish Falls) and La Maison de la Foret (open 10 a.m.-5 p.m.), an information center that abuts several hiking trails.

Further east is the Parc Zoologique et Botanique tel. (590) 98-83-52, a hillside botanical garden where you can see caged animals such as a mongoose, iguanas, the rare big-headed crab-eater bird, and "Titi the Raccoon." Raccoons have been protected since 1954 and

serve as the park's mascots. There's a small restaurant with great views. Admission is F25, F15 for children, open 9 a.m.-5 p.m.

The Traversée meets the ocean at the western coast town of Mahaut. A short drive south brings you to the Pigeon-Malendure Underwater Reserve, tel. (590) 98-89-08. The attractions here, other than the fact that the reserve was developed by Jacques Cousteau, are glass-bottomed boats that scoot around the marine park and end up at the tiny Illets Pigeon, where you can snorkel. Cost is F80 for adults and F40 for children. Cousteau has dubbed the island one of the world's ten best diving spots.

A turn to the north from Mahaut will bring you to another park visitors center, Maison du Bois at Pointe-Noire. The center, open 9 a.m.-6 p.m., is partially an arboretum and features a display of local woods and their uses. Nearby is the village of Pointe-Noire, a traditional cabinet-making and artisans village.

At the south of the park on Route de la Soufrière, you'll find La Maison du Volcan (open 10 a.m.-6 p.m.), the park visitor center where you can learn all about volcanos and the island's own La Soufrière. The best route to the volcano's summit is from Saint-Claude to the parking area at Savane a Mulets. The dome and billows of sulfurous vapor are partially visible from here, but a 900-foot (275-meter) climb on a marked path will bring you to the top, where the view is impressive if you manage to get there on a cloudless day.

East of La Soufrière, at l'Habituée and past the Grand Etang (Big Pond), you'll find Chutes du Carbet, a series of three waterfalls reaching as high as 410 feet (125 meters). The hike up the falls is marked but slippery. The second cascade features a hot spring, great for a dip.

Park Tours

Throughout the park are 188 miles (303 km) of hiking trails, called "traces," and most are well-marked. Some trails are difficult; the trail to La Soufrière, for instance, takes four hours or so. Guides are available for hire through Organisation des Guides de Montaigne de la Caibe, tel. (590) 80-05-79, or Emeraude Guadeloupe, tel. (590) 80-16-09.

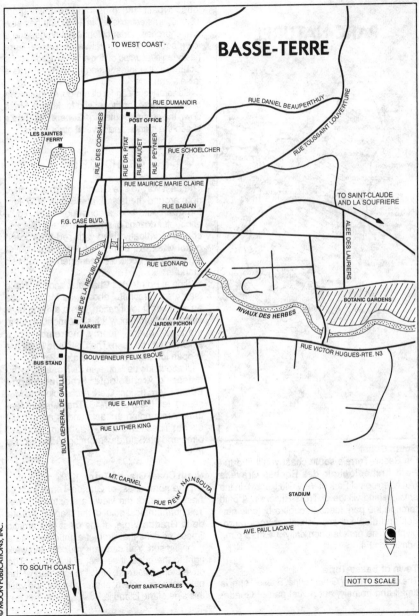

BASSE-TERRE

TO WEST COAST

RUE DANIEL BEAUPERTHUY

RUE DUMANOIR

POST OFFICE

LES SAINTES FERRY

RUE DES CORSAIRES

RUE DR. PITAT

RUE BAUDET

RUE PEYNIER

RUE SCHOELCHER

RUE TOUSSAINT LOUVERTURE

RUE MAURICE MARIE CLAIRE

RUE BABIAN

TO SAINT-CLAUDE AND LA SOUFRIERE

F.G. CASE BLVD.

RUE DE LA REPUBLIQUE

RUE LEONARD

ALEE DES LAURIERS

BOTANIC GARDENS

RIVAUX DES HERBES

MARKET

JARDIN PICHON

BUS STAND

GOUVERNEUR FELIX EBOUE

RUE VICTOR HUGUES-RTE. N3

BLVD. GENERAL DE GAULLE

RUE E. MARTINI

RUE LUTHER KING

MT. CARMEL

RUE REMY NAINSOUTA

STADIUM

AVE. PAUL LACAVE

TO SOUTH COAST

FORT SAINT-CHARLES

NOT TO SCALE

© MOON PUBLICATIONS, INC.

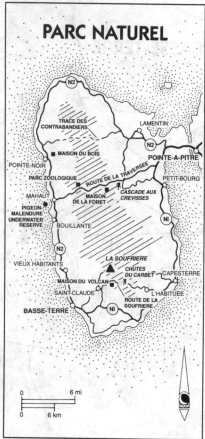

PARC NATUREL

N2

TRACE DES
CONTRABANDIERS

LAMENTIN

MAISON DU BOIS

N2

POINTE-NOIR

POINTE-A-PITRE

PARC ZOOLOGIQUE

ROUTE DE LA TRAVERSEE

PETIT-BOURG

MAHAUT

MAISON
DE LA FORÊT

CASCADE AUX
CREVISSES

PIGEON-
MALENDURE
UNDERWATER
RESERVE

BOUILLANTE

N1

N2

LA SOUFRIERE

VIEUX HABITANTS

CHÛTES
DU CARBET

CAPESTERRE

MAISON DU VOLCAN

SAINT-CLAUDE

L'HABITUÉE

ROUTE DE LA
SOUFRIERE

BASSE-TERRE

N1

© MOON PUBLICATIONS, INC.

0   6 mi

0   6 km

MOON

South Coast

On Basse-Terre's south coast you'll find the
Parc Archéologique des Roches Gravées
(Archaeological Park of Very Old Rocks), in the
small fishing village of **Trois-Rivières**. A path
through the park leads through a botanic garden and displays pre-Columbian rock petroglyphs. The park is open daily 9 a.m.-5 p.m.,
admission F4.

Town of Basse-Terre

The capital town of Guadeloupe, Basse-Terre, is
small and homely, but a vital part of Guade-

loupe's past and present. The town (pop.
16,000) was established in 1640 and has several churches, forts, colonial buildings, and a
town square of historical value. Basse-Terre
has been evacuated during a few eruptions of La
Soufrière, the latest being in 1976—it was a
false alarm.

Generally quiet and a bit run-down, the town's
charm is there for those who look for it. Head
down the central **Boulevard General de Gaulle**
to see the market and several other sights.

GRANDE-TERRE

The best way to see Grande-Terre is to drive
right around the island, an 85-mile (137-km)
trip that could take a couple of days. You'll
encounter dozens of small towns and villages,
characteristically filled with red-tile-roofed
country homes, colonial-style wooden buildings, brightly decorated cemeteries, and fish
markets.

Stop at **Pointe des Châteaux** and **Le Moule**
(see also "Beaches," above). Le Moule, once
an east coast fortification, has a striking neo-
classical church (now a historic monument) at
the town square. Nearby, the remains of a
small fort can be seen. The **Distillerie Bellevue**
is open for tours Mon.-Fri., 8 a.m.-2 p.m.

Just outside Le Moule, in **La Rosette**, is the
**Musée d'Archéologie Precolumbienne
Edgar Clerc** (Edgar Clerc Archaeological Museum), tel. (590) 23-57-43. The museum features Amerindian artifacts and is open daily
except Tuesday 9 a.m.-12:30 p.m. and 2-5
p.m., and on Saturday morning. Admission is
free.

North Coast Grande-Terre

On the north coast of Grande-Terre, east of
Anse Bertrand, the views are extraordinary.
The northernmost point of the island is **Pointe
de la Grande Vigie,** at the crest of dramatic
limestone cliffs that drop straight down into a
rumbling surf. You can park your car and walk
right to the edge, it seems, of the world. The
drive along this road, which is also part of the
national park system, shows how flat and vast
this side of the island is.

POINTE-À-PITRE

Pointe-à-Pitre is Guadeloupe's main commercial and shipping center, with a population of about 80,000. Located just south of Le Raizet airport (taxi here for about F60), this is the place for shopping, business, and some sightseeing. The outskirts of the town, particularly toward the Rivière Salée bridge to Basse-Terre, is characterized by concrete high-rise apartment buildings and small malls. Downtown is slightly tarnished, noisy, and congested, but its charms are evident as well. An 1834 earthquake destroyed some of the old colonial structures, but the remaining buildings with their iron balconies retain some of the ambience of the old town. Hurricanes in 1979, 1980, and 1989's Hugo further damaged the city.

The **Place de la Victoire** is the central square, surrounded by historic buildings, markets, and cafes. The square was once the site of a guillotine. At its southern end, opposite Rue Duplessis, is **La Darse** harbor, where ferries depart for outlying islands, and taxis and buses cram for space.

At the southwest corner of the square, on Rue Bebian, you'll find the tourism office, where you can pick up a copy of *Bonjour Guadeloupe* (in English and French). The small magazine contains a good amount of island practical information.

The tourism building is surrounded by vendors who sell everything from wigs to pantyhose to sandals. Turn right out of the tourism office and you'll find several boisterous open-air (but covered) markets bordered by rues Saint-John Perse, Peynier, Schoelcher, and Frebault. The market women carry vegetables, exotic fruits, spices, and meats. Most of the market vendors don't speak English but are very helpful nonetheless.

The **Musée Saint-John Perse,** tel. (590) 90-01-92, a restored 19th-century colonial house dedicated to the famous Guadeloupean poet and Nobel Laureate (see "Caribbean Authors" under "Literature" under "The Arts" in the Introduction chapter), sits on Rues Norzières and Achille René-Boisneuf. The museum houses a complete collection of Perse's poetry and memorabilia. The museum is open Mon.-Sat. 9 a.m.-5 p.m., and the admission is F10. Saint-John Perse is pervasive in the city; a new commercial complex on the town pier, with a hotel, shops, a tourism information booth, and cafes, is called **Centre Saint-John Perse.** Perse's birthplace, at 54 Rue Rene-Boisneuf, is marked with a plaque.

On Rue Peynier, the **Musée Schoelcher,** tel. (590) 82-08-04, is dedicated to the abolitionist Victor Schoelcher and features books and memorabilia. The museum is open weekdays 9 a.m.-12:30 p.m. and 2-4:30 p.m., Saturday 9 a.m.-12:30 p.m. The entrance fee is F10.

Don't miss the astounding **Cathedrale de Saint-Pierre et Saint-Paul,** north of Place de la

the small harbor at Port-Louis, on Grand-Terre's west coast

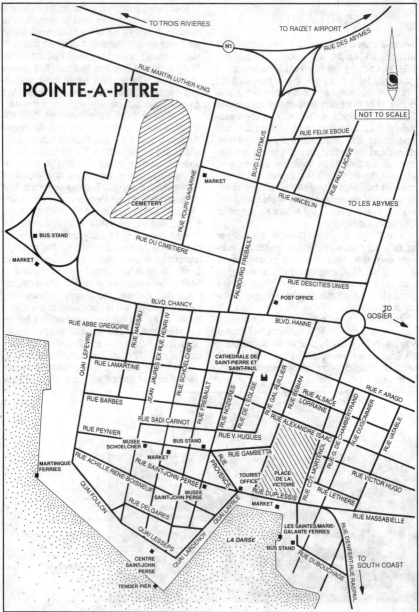

POINTE-A-PITRE

TO TROIS RIVIERES

TO RAIZET AIRPORT

N1

RUE DES ABYMES

RUE MARTIN LUTHER KING

RUE FELIX EBOUE

BLVD. LEGITIMUS

RUE PAUL LACAVE

NOT TO SCALE

MARKET

RUE YOURI GAGARINE

RUE HINCELIN

TO LES ABYMES

CEMETERY

BUS STAND

RUE DU CIMETIERE

FAUBOURG FREBAULT

MARKET

RUE DESCILIES UNIES

POST OFFICE

BLVD. CHANCY

TO GOSIER

BLVD. HANNE

RUE ABBE GREGOIRE

QUAI LEFEVRE

RUE NASSAU

JEAN JAURES EX RUE HENRI IV

RUE SCHOELCHER

RUE LAMARTINE

CATHEDRALE DE SAINT-PIERRE ET SAINT-PAUL

RUE GAL FRULLIER

RUE BEBIAN

RUE ALSACE LORRAINE

RUE F. ARAGO

RUE BARBES

RUE FREBAULT

RUE NOZIERES

RUE DE L'EGLISE

RUE ALEXANDRE ISAAC

RUE G. DE CHAMBERTRAND

RUE DUGOMMIER

RUE SADI CARNOT

RUE PEYNIER

RUE V. HUGUES

RUE VATABLE

MUSEE SCHOELCHER

BUS STAND

RUE GAMBETTA

RUE CDT. MORTENOL

RUE VICTOR HUGO

MARKET

RUE SAINT-JOHN PERSE

RUE PROVENCE

RUE LETHIERE

MARTINIQUE FERRIES

RUE ACHILLE RENE-BOISNEUF

TOURIST OFFICE

PLACE DE LA VICTOIRE

MUSEE SAINT-JOHN PERSE

RUE DUPLESSIS

RUE MASSABIELLE

QUAI FOULON

RUE DELGARES

QUAI LAYRLE

MARKET

QUAI LESSEPS

QUAI LARDENOY

LES SAINTES/MARIE-GALANTE FERRIES

RUE DENFERT-RUE RASPAIL

LA DARSE

BUS STAND

RUE DUBOUCHAGE

TO SOUTH COAST

CENTRE SAINT-JOHN PERSE

TENDER PIER

© MOON PUBLICATIONS, INC.

Victoire, a structure dating to the 1840s. Over the years the cathedral has been weakened by hurricanes, but it is now propped up by huge, bolted metal columns that give it the appearance of being in jail.

SPORTS AND ENTERTAINMENT

Tennis
Tennis courts are found at many of the hotels, and some allow nonguests to play, including the **Marina Club,** tel. (590) 90-84-08, in Pointe-à-Pitre and the **Centre Lamby-Lambert,** tel. (590) 90-90-97, in Le Gosier. Squash courts can be found at **Vive Forme,** tel. (590) 90-98-74, at the Villa Viva hotel in Bas-du-Fort.

Working Out
Fitness clubs are located at the Villa Viva hotel's **Viva Forme** (see above) in Bas-du-Fort and in many of the island's hotels. **Espace Tonic,** tel. (590) 82-88-34, in Pointe-à-Pitre offers aerobics and weights.

Horseback Riding
Horseback riding stables are **Le Criolo,** tel. (590) 83-38-90, in Saint-Felix or the **Poney Club,** tel. (590) 24-03-74, in Le Moule. They can arrange picnics, mountain rides, and tailored rides.

Golf
The island's ultimate golf course is the 18-hole, 6,755-yard, Robert Trent Jones Sr.-designed **Golf International de Saint-François,** tel. (590) 88-41-87, fax 88-42-20, in Saint-François. Greens fees are F250.

Water Sports and Boat Charters
A wide range of yacht and boat charters can be arranged at the marina at Bas-du-Fort. This is one of three on the island, in fact the largest. For advance information, contact **ATM Yachts,** tel. (590) 90-92-02, or in the U.S. call. (800) 634-8822. The **Marina de Saint-François** is also large and you'll find dozens of charters for hire.

Deep-sea fishing is gaining popularity, and, again, the place to go is the marina at Bas-du-

Fort. **Caraibe Peche,** tel. (590) 90-97-51, and **Evasion Exotic,** tel. (590) 90-94-17, offer half-day or full-day outings.

Surfing information is available through **Comite Guadeloupeen de Surf,** tel. (590) 91-77-64. Sailboats, glass-bottomed boats, windsurfing, snorkeling, and pedal-boats are easily arranged through any beachfront hotel, whether you are staying there or not.

Diving
In general, Guadeloupe waters do not provide the Lesser Antilles' best diving, but several spots are excellent. Island scuba schools will provide tailored programs for beginners or advanced divers, resort certification, night dives, and multiple-dive packages. Look to your travel agent for dive packages offered with hotels and airlines.

Scuba diving is popular off Pigeon Island, on Basse-Terre's west coast. The area is also where several diving outfits are found. Contact **Les Heures Saines,** tel. (590) 98-86-63; **Chez Guy,** tel. (590) 98-81-72; or the **Nautilus Club,** tel. (590) 98-85-69.

Aquafari, tel. (590) 90-46-46, in Le Gosier will also arrange diving trips, specializing in trips to the tiny Ilet du Gosier, just off the coast.

Adventure Tours
Several companies specialize in adventure tours of the kayaking, canoeing, 4WD, biking, or hiking variety. Contact **Guadeloupe Decouvertes,** tel. (590) 84-29-32, fax 26-80-10, in Le Gosier; or **Espace Losiers,** tel. (590) 88-71-93, fax 88-44-01; and **Parfum d'Aventure,** tel. (590) 88-47-62, both in Saint-François.

Cockfighting
For something completely different and, frankly, odd, go see a cockfighting match. It's sanctioned and there's a season for it, November through April. Matches are flamboyant and loud, and the betting is frenetic. Sometimes a mongoose is pitted against a snake. Check local newspapers for schedules. Matches are usually held Saturday and Sunday afternoon.

Nightlife
For bloodletting of a different sort, two casinos can be found on Grande-Terre. **Casinos de Gosier,** tel. (590) 84-18-33, is open from 9 p.m.

to the wee hours every day except Sunday. **Casino de Saint-François,** tel. (590) 88-41-31, is closed on Monday. Neither have slot machines, but they do have roulette and blackjack. An admission fee (currently F69) is charged, and you'll need a photo ID to get inside. Minimum age is 21.

ACCOMMODATIONS

Accommodation on Guadeloupe and its outlying islands ranges from inexpensive guesthouses, apartments, or villas (*gîtes*) to small, moderately priced and often family-owned hotels (col-

MORE GUADELOUPE AND ISLANDS ACCOMMODATIONS

Rates per s, EP when applicable, winter

NAME	(590)	FAX	LOCATION	TARIFF
GRANDE-TERRE				
Bouganvillée	90-14-14	91-36-82	Pointe-à-Pitre	moderate
Callinago	84-25-25	84-24-90	Le Gosier	moderate
Club Med Caravelle	88-21-00	88-06-06	Sainte-Anne	luxury
Ecotel (Best Western)	90-60-00	90-60-60	Le Gosier	moderate
Hotel Marissol	90-84-44	90-83-32	Bas-du-Fort	luxury
La Creole Beach	90-46-46	90-46-66	Le Gosier	luxury
La Toubana	88-25-78	88-38-90	Sainte-Anne	luxury
Le Hamak	88-59-99	88-41-92	Saint-François	luxury
Les Flamboyants	84-14-11	84-53-56	Le Gosier	moderate
Mini-Beach	88-21-13	88-19-29	Sainte-Anne	moderate
Plantation Ste-Marthe	88-72-46	88-72-47	Saint-François	luxury
Relais du Moulin	88-23-96	88-03-92	Châteaubrun, Sainte-Anne	moderate
Saint-John Anchorage	82-51-57	82-52-61	Pointe-à-Pitre	moderate
Serge's Guest House	84-22-22	84-48-14	Le Gosier	budget
Villa Viva	90-46-46	90-46-66	Bas-du-Fort	moderate
BASSE-TERRE				
Auberge de la Distillerie	94-25-91	94-11-91	Rte. de Versailles, Petit-Bourg	moderate
Club de Fort Royal	25-50-00	25-50-01	Deshaies	moderate-luxury
Coucou des Bois	95-42-25	N/A	Montebello, Petit-Bourg	moderate
Rocher de Malendure	98-70-84	98-89-92	Bouillante	moderate
LES SAINTES (TERRE-DE-HAUT)				
Auberge des Anacardiers	99-50-99	99-54-51	La Savane	moderate
Bois-Joli	99-50-38	99-55-05	Anse-à-Cointe	luxury
Village Créole	99-53-83	99-55-55	Pointe Coquelet	moderate-luxury
MARIE-GALANTE				
L'Arbre-à-Pain	97-73-69	N/A	Grand-Bourg	moderate
Le Salut	97-02-67	N/A	Saint-Louis	moderate
Soledad	97-75-45	N/A	Grand-Bourg	moderate

lectively called *Relais Créoles*). As well, several of the Caribbean's most exclusive and expensive hotels are found on Grande-Terre's south coast "Riviera."

An estimated 4,300 rooms can be found throughout the Guadeloupe archipelago. Most hotels are run on the European Plan (no meals) or Continental Plan (breakfast), but other plans are available. All-inclusive hotels can be found, but they are not as popular here as on several of the English-speaking islands.

Categories are based on per person per night during high season (15 December-15 April): **Luxury** US$100 or more, **Moderate** US$50-100, and **Budget** US$50 or less.

Gîtes de France
Gîtes can be defined as anything from small inns to apartments to rooms in private homes and are creative alternative accommodations, as well as good ways to get to know some people. And they can be inexpensive. Unit rates average F1000-2000 per week to as much as F5500 per week. On Guadeloupe, more than 400 accommodations are designated as *gîtes*.

However, choose a *gîte* carefully: ask questions and know what you want. Some leave much to be desired. Do you need hot water, or is cold fine? Your own bathroom, or would you share? Air conditioning or fan? How much privacy? Many of the *gîtes* are located off the beaten path, and some offer few of the amenities you'd be accustomed to at larger hotels.

For a full listing, contact Gîtes de France, French West Indies Tourist Board, 610 5th Ave., New York, NY 10020, tel. (212) 315-0726. Or you can write directly to the Office Départemental du Tourisme, 5 Square de la Banque, BP 1099, 97181 Pointe-à-Pitre Cedex, Guadeloupe, French West Indies, tel. (590) 82-09-30, fax 83-89-22.

Villas
Many private villa and apartment rentals are handled centrally through the tourism office and Gîtes de France (see address above). The **Association des Villas et Meublés de Tourisme,** BP 1297 97186 Pointe-à-Pitre Cedex, Guadeloupe, French West Indies, tel. (590) 82-02-62, fax 83-89-22, is the tourism office's reservation service.

The **ANTRE Association,** tel. (590) 88-53-09, handles short- and long-term condo and apartment rentals, and the U.S.-based **French Home Rentals,** P.O. Box 82386, Portland, OR 97282, tel. and fax (503) 774-8977, lists several Guadeloupe properties.

Camping
Camping is allowed in designated areas and at some beaches. It usually involves areas on which you can park a rented camping van or pitch a tent. In general, camping outside designated areas is not encouraged by the government (for your own security), and if you just want to pitch your tent on an inviting beach, you'll have to get permission from the local authorities, usually the mayor's office.

Les Sables d'Or, tel. (590) 28-44-60, on the expansive Plage de Grand Anse in Deshaies, features bungalows as well as tent and vehicle sites. Rates for tent rental run about F85 per night, and you get a good deal and a good beach. More sites are found at **Camping la Traversée,** tel. (590) 98-21-23, at Pointe-Noire on Basse-Terre.

Camping vans, small RV-like vehicles, accommodate four to six people and can be rented for about F600 per day. Call **Antilles Locap Soleil,** tel. (590) 90-95-72, in Gosier or **Vert'-Bleu,** tel. (590) 28-51-25, in Deshaies.

Grande-Terre Hotels
Hotels will often add a service charge of 10-15% to your bill. Hotels will also tag on a *taxe de séjour* (room tax), which varies from establishment to establishment.

The majority of Grande-Terre's resorts and hotels are found along the south coast beach areas between Bas-du-Fort and Saint-François, which includes the resort towns of Le Gosier and Sainte-Anne. The following hotels are among the islands' best.

Le Meridien, tel. (590) 88-51-00, fax 88-40-71, in the resort town of Saint-François is a large four-story complex with over 260 rooms, set on a large beach. All the bells and whistles, including water sports and tennis, are included. Top of the line. Luxury.

Hotel Salako, tel. (590) 88-22-22, fax 84-38-15, is soon to become a Holiday Inn, albeit a very nice Holiday Inn. In Le Gosier, the hotel shares three beaches with nearby hotels and has a pool, aerobics, water sports, tennis, and a kids' club, all included in the rate. Moderate-Luxury.

La Maison de Marie-Galante, tel. (590) 90-10-41, fax 90-22-75, on the Place de la Victoire

FRENCH CREOLE CULINARY GLOSSARY

accras—deep-fried codfish fritters

blaff—boiled stew of fish or shellfish

boudin Créole—spicy blood sausage

calalou—vegetable and herb soup or gumbo

chatrou—squid

chiquetaille—grilled or shredded fish, served with a tart vinaigrette

colombo—preparation of meat, usually goat, lamb or chicken, in a spicy curry sauce

christophine—vegetable with white, pulpy flesh

coco—coconut

crabe—crab

crabes farcis—stuffed land crabs

féroces d'avocat—avocado and salted codfish salad, with manioc (cassava) and hot chili pepper

fruit-à-pain—breadfruit

goyave—guava

lambi—conch

mangue—mango

manicou—opossum

maracudja—passion fruit

ouassou—crayfish

papaye—papaya, or paw-paw

patate douce—sweet potato

pistache—peanuts

planteur—rum drink with fruit juices and spices

ragout—spicy meat-based stew

rhum blanc—white rum

rhum vieux—dark rum

shrubb—traditional Christmas drink made from rum and orange peels

soudon—clam

ti punch—a traditional and popular drink of rum, sugarcane syrup, and a dash of lime

titiri—small fish, deep-fried and eaten whole

in Pointe-à-Pitre is small, only nine rooms, but clean, with air conditioning, television, and a central location. Budget-Moderate.

Basse-Terre Hotels

Accommodation on Basse-Terre is a bit limited, but the **Hotel Grand Anse,** tel. (590) 92-90-47, in the southeastern town of Trois-Rivières has good reports. It's basic but offers a pool, some kitchenettes, air conditioning, and a beach. Moderate. The **Relais de la Grand Soufrière,** tel. (590) 80-01-27, fax 80-18-40, at Saint-Claude is inland, on the hillside of the volcano, a good place to base yourself for exploration. Moderate.

Accommodations on the Islands

You'll find hotels and guesthouses on the islands, and, again, the **Gîtes de France,** tel. (590) 91-64-33, will have information on accommodations in apartments and private homes.

On La Désirade your choices are limited to the aptly named **L'Oasis du Desert,** tel. (590) 20-02-12, Moderate, and the small guesthouse **Guitoune,** tel. (590) 20-01-22. The island, only eight square miles (21 square km), can be covered fairly quickly, so you may not need an overnight stay here.

On Les Saintes, Terre-de-Haut is the place to stay. The small **La Saintoise,** tel. (590) 99-52-50, at Bourg has 10 rooms and is moderate. **Hotel Kanoa,** tel. 99-51-36, offers simple rooms, a no-frills hotel. Moderate.

On Marie-Galante there are several hotels, including **Hajo,** tel. (590) 97-32-76, Moderate, and **Le Soleil Levant,** tel. (590) 97-31-55, fax 97-41-65, Moderate, in Capesterre. **Le Touloulou,** tel. (590) 97-32-63, fax 97-33-59, in Capesterre has rooms and bungalows and a good restaurant.

FOOD

Guadeloupe's cuisine begins with French, but spicy—exotic Creole is the result. The island's fresh seafood, island spices, fruits, and local vegetables, mixed with the traditional sauces and the flair of French cooking are showcased in Guadeloupe's finest haute cuisine restaurants as

MORE POINTE-À-PITRE RESTAURANTS

NAME	LOCATION	(590)	CUISINE	PRICE RANGE
Krishna	Rue A.R. Boisneuf	N/A	Indian	inexpensive
Le Moundélé	Rue Jean Jaurè	91-04-30	African	moderate
Le Normandie Hotel	Place de Victoire	82-37-15	Italian/Creole	moderate
L'Oasis	Rue A.R. Boisneuf	82-02-70	Creole	moderate

well as smaller roadside and beachside bistros. With the exception of several four-star restaurants found elsewhere in the Lesser Antilles, it would be hard to top the overall eating experience you'll find on Guadeloupe.

As well, the nearly 400 island restaurants feature the cuisines of France, Italy, Vietnam, China, Germany, and more. The beach areas, particularly the stretch between Bas-du-Fort and Saint-François, and towns are lined with cafes and patisseries and open-air bistros.

Credit cards are not accepted everywhere; it's best to call ahead. Since it's rare to find an English-speaker on the other end of the phone, here's how to ask in French: "Acceptez-vous les cartes de crédit?" Check, too, to see if the restaurant is open evenings. Beachside bistros do a brisk lunch business but may not be open for dinner. In French: "Êtes-vous ouvert pour le dîner?"

The following are only a few of the dozens of recommended restaurants. Categories are based on per-person per-entree prices: **Expensive** US$25 or more, **Moderate** US$10-25, **Inexpensive** US$10 or less.

Pointe-à-Pitre Restaurants
In Pointe-à-Pitre, try the restaurant at **La Maison de Marie-Galante,** tel. (590) 90-10-41, for a great location on the Place de la Victoire and simple Creole. Inexpensive. Try **La Gargantua,** tel. (590) 90-97-32, at the marina between Bas-du-Fort and Pointe-à-Pitre for good bar food and drinks, and for its name if nothing else.

MORE GRAND-TERRE RESTAURANTS

NAME	LOCATION	(590)	CUISINE	PRICE RANGE
Chez Prudence	Anse Bertrand	22-11-17	Creole	moderate
Escale à Saigon	Le Gosier	90-95-75	Vietnamese/Chinese	moderate
Espace Tropical	Le Moule	93-97-97	French/Creole	moderate
La Baboucha	Saint-François	88-51-16	French	expensive
La Grand Pizzeria	Bas-du-Fort	90-82-64	Italian	inexpensive
La Plantation	marina, Bas-du-Fort	90-84-83	French/Creole	moderate
La Mouette	Pointe des Châteaux	88-43-53	Creole/snacks	inexpensive-moderate
La Route du Rhum	marina, Bas-du-Fort	90-90-00	Creole	moderate
Le Balata	Le Gosier	90-88-25	French	moderate-expensive
Le Koukouly	Port-Louis	22-89-10	Creole	moderate
Relais du Moulin	Châteaubrun, Sainte-Anne	88-13-78	Creole	moderate

MORE BASSE-TERRE RESTAURANTS

NAME	LOCATION	(590)	CUISINE	PRICE RANGE
Chez Paul	Matouba, Saint-Claude	80-29-20	Creole	moderate
La Louisiane	Saint-Claude	88-44-34	Creole	inexpensive-moderate
La Touna	Bouillante	78-70-10	French/Creole	inexpensive-moderate
Le Rocher de Malendure	Bouillante	98-70-84	French/Creole	moderate
Le Ti'Racoon	Parc Zoologique	98-83-52	French/Creole/snacks	inexpensive-moderate

Moderate. **Le Côte Jardin,** tel. (590) 90-91-28, also at the marina, features fine Creole dining. Expensive.

La Canne à Sucre, tel. (590) 82-10-19, is one of Pointe-à-Pitre's renowned French and Creole restaurants. Recently relocated to the town pier, the restaurant offers elegant dining; reserve a table upstairs for the views of the harbor. Jackets are required for upstairs seating in the evening. Expensive.

Grande-Terre Restaurants
A drive along the beach road from Bas-du-Fort to Pointe des Châteaux passes through Le Gosier, Sainte-Anne, Saint-François, and a fistful of smaller resort areas. The dining and snacking along this stretch is superb.

La Toubana, tel. (590) 88-25-78, in Sainte-Anne overlooks the Club Med from a hill; the view is the draw. Moderate. Also in Sainte-Anne is **L'Amour en Fleurs,** tel. (590) 88-23-72, a small roadside Creole bistro. Inexpensive.

In Saint-François, **La Pecherie,** tel. (590) 84-48-41, is popular for good seafood. Inexpensive. **L'Oursin Blanc,** tel. (590) 88-66-02, serves fresh seafood and overlooks the ocean. Inexpensive.

Basse-Terre Restaurants
Le Karacoli, tel. (590) 28-41-17, located on the Plage de la Grand Anse in Deshaies, serves an excellent *boudin créole* (blood pudding) and *colombo de poulet* (hot and spicy chicken). The setting is at beachside, under the cool shade of almond trees. The chef and owner, Lucienne

Salcede, has won awards for her creations. Open for lunch only, daily noon-5 p.m. Moderate.

Chez Jacky, tel. (590) 98-06-98, on Anse Guyonneau at Pointe-Noire, creates Creole and exotic African dishes. Moderate.

Food Markets
Match is the big chain supermarket, with branches throughout the islands. There are dozens of other large supermarkets around the island. In them you will not suffer for food but may want for freshness in produce. The wide wine selections feature fine and inexpensive French wines.

All fair-sized towns and villages will have a marketplace, usually the best place to buy fresh fruits, vegetables, and fish. The lively open markets of Pointe-à-Pitre are the busiest and best on the island.

GETTING THERE

From North America
Guadeloupe's main entry point is **Aeroport du Raizet,** tel. (590) 82-80-80 or 90-32-32 or 90-34-34, about three miles (five km) north of Pointe-à-Pitre.

American Airlines, with local contacts at Raizet and Pointe-à-Pitre, tel. (590) 83-62-62 or 82-99-48, is the biggest and most frequent U.S. carrier, with direct flights from New York and Newark and connections from San Juan.

Air Canada, tel. (590) 83-62-49, operates flights from Montreal and Toronto at least once per week. **Air France,** tel. (590) 82-50-00 or 82-11-11, operates flights directly from Paris, and once per week from Miami. The Miami flight has been, in the past, through charter companies. Other Air France flights come in from Martinique, Dominican Republic, Haiti, and several European cities.

Regional Airlines

Air Guadeloupe, tel. (590) 82-28-35, operates a number of flights from other French Antillean islands, as well as from Miami on Thursday and Saturday. It is also the best service to La Désirade, Les Saintes, and Marie-Galante.

The regional airline **LIAT,** tel. (590) 82-12-26, has regular service through Guadeloupe to the rest of the Caribbean, including San Juan. **Air St. Barths,** tel. (590) 27-71-90, handles daily connections between Saint-Barthélémy and Pointe-à-Pitre and connects to the Grand Case Airport in Saint-Martin, as well as other Caribbean islands. **Winair,** tel. (590) 83-89-06, connects to Princess Juliana International Airport in Sint Maarten.

There is no departure tax when leaving Guadeloupe.

GETTING AROUND

Taxis

Most, but not all, taxis are unmetered. This makes for fascinating conversations regarding appropriate rates, more so if there is a language barrier. Most taxis drivers speak French and Creole, but some also speak English. Fares are posted at taxi stands, at the airport, and at some larger hotels.

A typical fare from the airport to Pointe-à-Pitre is F60, to Le Gosier F80. Taxi rates are 40% higher at night, in effect 9 p.m.-7 a.m., and on Sunday. Hiring a taxi for island touring is expensive—you might pay as much as US$100 (F550) for a trip around the island, or US$25 (about F135) per hour. Better to rent a car, unless you need a guide or your time is limited (see "Car Rentals," below).

Taxis are found at the airport, at the pier in Pointe-à-Pitre, and in the town of Basse-Terre. Taxi stands can also be found on the main streets of Sainte-Anne and Saint-François.

If your hotel isn't able to recommend a taxi, the following numbers can be used for pickups: in Pointe-à-Pitre, tel. (590) 82-13-67 or 90-00-00; in Le Gosier, call Serge, tel. (590) 90-84-44 (Serge is also one of the better island tour guides, but practice your French); in Saint-François, tel. (590) 88-75-85; in Basse-Terre, tel. (590) 81-79-70.

Buses

The public bus system is not difficult, but language may be a problem. If you don't speak French, at least try to pronounce where you want to go. Or, carry a map and point. Buses operate from about 5 a.m. to 7 p.m. and traverse Grande-Terre and Basse-Terre. You can wave the driver down anywhere or use bus stops marked "**arret-bus.**" Pay the fare when you get off.

On Grande-Terre, buses from Pointe-à-Pitre to the south coast (as far as Saint-François, F12) depart from the **La Darse Station** on the

---

GUADELOUPE CAR RENTAL AGENCIES

Country code is 590. If two numbers appear airport number is first.

Avis	82-33-47 or 90-46-46
Azur Auto	84-30-56 or 90-14-24
Budget	82-95-58
Carmax	83-37-11
Chris Auto	88-54-00
Citer	82-10-94
Europcar	82-50-51 or 84-45-84
Euro Rent	91-42-16 or 88-48-96
Garage Zami	82-03-86
Guadeloupe Car	83-22-88
Hertz	82-00-14 or 82-88-14
Jumbo Car	91-42-17
Kabwa Location	88-32-68
Kurakera Car	83-78-79
Montauban Cars	90-79-94
Nad' InCar	91-60-06 or 88-19-17
Thrifty	91-42-17 or 90-86-32
Tropic Car	84-07-25 or 91-84-37
Varglod-Car	81-48-08
Victory Car	84-18-57

pier. Buses to the north and east coast depart from **Mortenol Station,** located at the northern end of Rue Vatable. Buses to the airport (about F5) depart from Rue Peynier.

Car Rentals

When all is said and done, a rental car is perhaps the best way to get around. The 1,200 miles (1,920 km) of roads on the islands are excellent and well marked—in French, that is. The competition among rental companies is strong, and this helps keep the rates down. Still, they are not inexpensive. A basic Citroen goes for F150 per day, a Peugeot about F170 per day. Typically, you can get a car with unlimited mileage, or a cheaper rate with about F1.50 per km, or about 40 cents (US$) per mile. Several companies offer certain cars that, for some inexplicable reason, require the driver to be 25 years of age. Still, 21 is the norm. All drivers must have a valid license. Credit cards are widely accepted, otherwise substantial cash deposits are required.

Almost every major international, French, or local rental company is represented at Le Raizet Airport. Still, in Pointe-à-Pitre, Le Gosier, Sainte-Anne, and Saint-François you'll find plenty of rental companies. Beware, they're usually closed on Sunday. In most cases, your hotel will be able to point you toward car rentals. See the "Guadeloupe Car Rental Agencies" chart.

Motorcycles

Seeing the islands by scooters and motorcycles is popular, and you'll see plenty of locals and tourists alike traveling by bike. However, Guadeloupe's drivers, though generally law-abiding, tend to be drive like they've got places to be, *right now.* On the highways around Pointe-à-Pitre, this could be a problem.

In Pointe-à-Pitre, call **Vespa Sun,** tel. (590) 91-30-36. In Saint-François, try **Dingo Location,** tel. (590) 88-76-08, or **Rent a Bike,** tel. (590) 88-51-00. In Sainte-Anne, call **Rent A Car,** tel. (590) 88-91-43.

Mopeds can be rented through **Velo-Vert,** tel. (590) 83-15-74, in Pointe-à-Pitre. The day rate for a scooter ranges F100-170.

Bicycle Rentals

Bicycling is a major and fast-growing sport on Guadeloupe, especially on flat Grande-Terre, and bikes are easy to find. Try Velo-Vert (see

above) or **Cyclo-Tours,** tel. (590) 84-11-34, in Le Gosier. In Saint-François, **Rent-a-Bike,** tel. (590) 84-51-00, is at the Hotel Meridien. **Rent A Car** (see above) in Sainte-Anne also rents bicycles. Bikes go for about F50-70 per day.

Note: For information regarding biking tours and excursions, contact **Association Guadeloupeen de VTT,** tel. (590) 82-82-67. The "VTT" is *velo tout terrain,* or "all-terrain bike."

Outer-Island Rentals

For outer-islands car and bike rentals on La Désirade call **Loca 2000,** tel. (590) 20-02-65; **Eurodollar,** tel. 20-01-11; or **Villeneuve Lacation,** tel. 20-02-65.

On Les Saintes, scooters are all that are needed. Call **Archipel Rent Service,** Terre-de-Haut, tel. (590) 99-52-63.

On **Marie-Galante,** contact **Caneval,** Grand-Bourg, tel. (590) 97-97-76; or **Le Touloulou,** Capesterre, tel. (590) 97-32-63, **Magauto,** Grand-Bourg, tel. (590) 97-98-75; or **TSL,** Saint-Louis, tel. (590) 97-01-01.

Interisland Ferries

Guadeloupe's extensive boat service to nearby islands is handy, and in cases boats may be able to transport bikes and cars. The ferries are high-speed, generally comfortable, and a bit less expensive than flying—but not that much. Weigh the relative time and effort (rough seas, some crowds) it takes to travel by ferry, and make your choice.

Ferry schedules and fares, *always subject to change,* are available at the tourism office in Pointe-à-Pitre. Some departures to outlying islands are early in the morning.

From Pointe-à-Pitre: Ferries departing from La Darse in Pointe-à-Pitre to Marie-Galante, an hour's journey, are about F160 roundtrip. Your choices are *Trans Antilles Express,* tel. (590) 83-12-45 or 91-13-43, fax 91-11-05, and the car ferry *Amanda Galante,* tel. (590) 83-12-45.

From Pointe-à-Pitre to Les Saintes, the roundtrip fare is F160. Call **Transports Brudey Freres,** tel. (590) 90-04-48, fax 82-15-62. Departure is at 8 a.m.

From Pointe-à-Pitre to Dominica, Martinique, or St. Lucia you can take *Caribbean Express* or *Trans Antilles Express,* tel. (590) 83-04-45 or 91-13-43. *Trans Antilles* also connects to Saint-François, and goes on to La Désirade.

INFORMATION DIRECTORY

OVERSEAS TOURISM OFFICES

French West Indies Tourist Board, 610 5th Ave., New York, 10020, tel. (212) 315-0726.

Service Francais du Tourisme a Montreal, 1981 Ave., MacGill College, Suite 490, Montreal, Quebec H3A 2W9, tel. (514) 288-4264.

GUADELOUPE TOURISM OFFICES

Office Départemental du Tourisme, 5 Square de la Banque, BP 1099, 97181 Pointe-à-Pitre Cedex, Guadeloupe, French West Indies, tel. (590) 82-09-30, fax (590) 83-89-22.

Basse-Terre, Maison du Port, tel. (590) 81-24-83.

Saint-François, Ave. de l'Europe, tel. (590) 88-48-74.

OTHER

Pointe-à-Pitre Police, tel. 17 or (590) 82-00-17.

Basse-Terre Police, tel. (590) 81-11-55.

Pointe-à-Pitre Emergency Medical, tel. 89-11-20.

Pointe-à-Pitre Emergency Fire, tel. 18 or (590) 82-00-28.

Centre Hospitalier de Pointe-à-Pitre, tel. (590) 89-10-10.

Parc National de la Guadeloupe, Montéran, 97120 Saint-Claude, Guadeloupe, French West Indies, tel. (590) 80-24-25.

Weather Forecast, tel. (590) 90-22-22.

Raizet Airport, tel. (590) 82-80-80.

FedEx, tel. (590) 26-85-44.

The relative newcomer **Caribia Ferries,** tel. (590) 89-42-67, fax 91-91-66, transports passengers to Roseau in Dominica for F150 one-way and features sleeping cabins and car transport facilities.

From Saint-François: Several ferries operate directly from Saint-François to La Désirade, 45 minutes one-way and F100 roundtrip. They are *Sotromade,* tel. (590) 20-02-30; *Socimade,* tel. (590) 88-47-28; and *Le Mistral,* tel. (590) 88-48-63.

From Basse-Terre: From Basse-Terre and Trois-Rivières to Les Saintes, check schedules at the tourism office. *Princess Caroline,* tel. (590) 96-95-83, departs Pointe-à-Pitre for Les Saintes via Trois-Rivières daily.

MONEY, HOURS, AND COMMUNICATION

Currency and Banks

The French franc is Guadeloupe's currency, and the current exchange rate is F5.50 = US$1. Exchange rates of major currencies change daily; check your local newspaper for current rates. Dollars are widely used, but the franc is easiest to use in markets or with taxi drivers and small businesses. It's best to exchange your currency for francs.

Banks and *bureaux de change* are located throughout Pointe-à-Pitre and major towns. Hours are weekdays 8 a.m.-noon and 2-4 p.m. Some are open on Saturday. *Bureaux* are occasionally open on Sunday mornings as well. Exchange booths at the airport are open during flight arrivals and often crowded. Hotels will change money, bank rates are better, but *bureaux de change* rates are best.

General business hours are weekdays 8 a.m.-noon and 2:30-5 p.m., with some variations. Many businesses are open Saturday morning as well.

Telephones

The country code for Guadeloupe is 590. This is not an area code where you dial "1" first. For North Americans, this means dialing the international access code (U.S. is "011") plus "590," then the six-digit number.

MARTINIQUE

Martinique. The word would roll well off the tongue of Maurice Chevalier—it's that kind of word. This sophisticated, stylized, and complicated island is deeply immersed in the ways of modern France and the Caribbean, yet it's defined by its history of colonization and by its various settlers. The Carib Indians called the island Madinina, reputed to mean "Island of Flowers." Columbus was said to have called it "the most beautiful thing I have ever seen."

THE LAND

The island's shape strikes me as that of a large-headed, dancing tadpole. Approximately 50 miles (80 km) long by 22 miles (35 km) wide, the 425-square-mile (1,100 -square-km) island covers the same area as Phoenix, Arizona. Martinique is in the Windward Islands, lying between Dominica and St. Lucia at about the same latitude as Dakar, Senegal.

The northern central section of Martinique is characterized by a volcanic mountain range that includes the still-active volcano Mont Pelée, the highest point on the island at 4,660 feet (1,421 meters). The central part of the island is covered by the low-lying Lamentin plain, where most of the island's agricultural activity takes place. Smaller hills and sweeping valleys connect the plains areas to the mountainous southern region.

The Atlantic-facing east coast is irregular and characterized by dozens of small bays, coves, and the large Caravelle Peninsula. The western windward side and southern coast are major population centers, including the capital of Fort-de-France. The natural harbor at Fort-de-France is large and picturesque and the center of commerce on the island.

HISTORY

Martinica

It is speculated that Columbus sighted Martinique in 1493, but it wasn't until his disastrous fourth voyage in 1502 that he landed at the point now known as Le Carbet, on Martinique's northwest coast. He named the island Martinica in honor of St. Martin, and that about sums it up for Spanish involvement in Martinique.

The Amerindian Caribs, a warlike group who had driven the Arawaks from the island, did not welcome the newcomers, and after several rude awakenings on the battlefield, the Spanish abandoned the island.

French Arrivals

French explorers and settlers, under the leadership of Pierre Belain d'Esnambuc, founder of the St. Christopher Company, arrived in 1635. In 1636 King Louis XIII authorized the introduction of slaves to France's West Indies possessions. For the next 25 years, the French fought the Caribs for the island's control.

In 1660, the Caribs, defeated by superior weaponry, signed a treaty that promised them half the island. Instead, the French killed or captured and enslaved the Caribs, until those remaining fled to nearby islands or died under French domination.

The French needed more workers for their growing plantations, so the first African slaves were imported during the 17th century. The heirs of d'Esnambuc sold trading rights to their king, and France officially annexed the island in 1674. Martinique then became one of the many pawns in the ongoing European battles of the 17th and 18th centuries. From 1762 to 1814, the British occupied the island. In 1815, European treaties restored Martinique to France, and accelerated sugarcane production made that crop the economic staple of the island.

Slave Revolts

While the French revolution of 1789 diverted attention in Paris, a chain-reaction surge of unrest throughout the French colonies made planters and colonialists uneasy. Slaves outnumbered planters by the tens of thousands. Eventually the British were invited to occupy Martinique again, essentially as a strong-arm security force, from 1794 to 1802. By 1804, a slave revolt in Haiti led by Toussaint l'Ouverture had succeeded in turning the colony into the New World's first Black republic, and nearby islands took heed. Agitation and revolts plagued the Caribbean plantocracy, and calls for abolition of slavery became louder. Slavery, which had been made illegal several times in the French West Indies' past, only to resurge again (notably with Napoleon's late 18th-century rise), was officially and finally outlawed in 1848. Thereafter, thousands of indentured laborers from East India were brought in to work Martinique's diminishing plantations.

20th Century

Martinique entered the 1900s with a weakened economy, labor unrest, and its mother country, France, wondering what to do about it.

In May, 1902, the eruption of Mont Pelée in the northwest killed nearly 30,000 people, casting a bit of a pall on the island and on France. When WW I broke out in 1914, more than 50,000 islanders left to fight for France. During WW II, with the collaborationist Vichy government in control of unoccupied France, many French West Indians left for nearby Allied-government islands.

In 1946, Martinique was given the status of an overseas department of France, and later in 1974 was deemed a *région*. In 1983 a Conseil Régional was established.

PEOPLE AND CULTURE

Within the first years of slavery, a mixed-race group, called *gens de couleur* or "free colored" (most often produced by forced miscegenation) emerged in Martiniquean society. They occupied a peripheral—and confusing—social and economic position between the slave class and the ruling whites. Their presence, in one of the ironies of racial intolerance, served to emphasize and exacerbate racial differences rather than bridge the gap. Gradations of color were defined in the infamous Code Noir of the late

18th century, which outlined nearly 130 classifications or degrees of color between white and black. Because of the associations of white skin with enhanced wealth and social status, this led to some scrambling among the free black population to be classified "up" and some scrambling among the whites to keep their population "pure." To varying extents this situation existed throughout the West Indies and has had ramifications in society felt even today.

The mixed-race group plays a significant part in Martinique's middle and upper-middle class economic structure and are evident throughout the population. Still, the majority of the population is black, and this group has only recently (as early as the 1920s) become accustomed to political recognition and a stronger societal position.

Much of the emergent Black pride of that era can be attributed to the *négritude* movement of the 1920s, which was first articulated among black expatriates in Paris, and for which the Martiniquean scholar and poet Aimé Césaire (see "Caribbean Authors" under "Literature" in "The Arts" in the Introduction chapter) was largely responsible. *Négritude* called for the recognition and advancement of black cultural values and black heritage worldwide—black humanism—and further rejected the French colonial influences.

A smaller but not insignificant group are the Whites, both descendants of settlers (*békés*) and long-term residents, and the so-called "metro" French or short-term workers. Whites have controlled great chunks of the economy in the French Antilles since colonial days, and the situation remains, in many ways, unchanged. East Indians, descendant of post-emancipation indentured laborers and other Asians also contribute a significant presence to the population.

Martinique's culture is African-based with strong French influence. The dress, food, music, and dance, as well as belief systems and world view, are uniquely Creole. The island is in some ways

a bakoua, or fisherman's straw hat

the sophisticated sister of Guadeloupe, and the two islands share characteristics of culture. Religion is primarily Roman Catholic, with others represented. The practice of magic is also pervasive.

The dance of Martinique is particularly sophisticated, and is represented by **Les Grands Ballets de la Martinique,** one of the Caribbean's most respected dance companies. The popular beguine and zouk are denizens of Fort-de-France's nightclubs. On festivals and during carnivals, people will wear the traditional checkered madras cloth and women's headdress called tete, sort of a turban. Men may be seen wearing the tall bakoua, a fisherman's straw hat.

The population of Martinique is 400,000, of which 102,000 live in Fort-de-France, the capital.

Holidays and Festivals

Martinique's festivals are, as is the case in many of the Lesser Antilles islands, colorful, loud, and rife with history. The famed **Carnival** begins on the day after New Year's, with weekend events, and culminates in a bash for five days before Shrove Tuesday and Ash Wednesday, complete with dances, marches, balls, singing contests, beauty pageants, and feasts.

Several smaller carnivals and cultural festivals are held in Fort-de-France and Sainte-Marie in July. In March, the **International Sailing Week** is held. The April **Aqua Festival du Robert** takes place in the town of the same name and involves regattas, boat races, feasts, and nautical exhibits.

The Catholic tradition has given each town a patron saint. Each town celebrates their **Saint's Day,** generally held January through July. Saint's Day is very popular with local sailors who race traditional gommier fishing boats. The name is taken from the word for gumtree, the tree that traditionally provided the oversized canoes' hollowed-out hulls. Today the sleek, 30-foot (nine-meter) boats are fashioned from lumber and other materials.

Other holidays are **Le Mai de Saint-Pierre,** a monthlong festival of music, dance, and theater, commemorating the town that once was; Slavery Abolition Day on 22 May; the 14 July Bastille Day; Armistice Day on 11 November, commemorating the end of WW I.

GOVERNMENT AND ECONOMY

Government

A Préfet, appointed by the French minister of the interior, administers the island. A 45-member Conseil General and 41-member Conseil Régional are the elected legislative bodies in Martinique, and the island sends four deputies and two senators to the French Parliament. The system is multi-party and includes established parties agitating for independence or greater measures of autonomy from France.

Economy

The primary contributor to Martinique's economy is France, in the way of direct aid. France supplies more than half of the island's gross income, and the roads, hospitals, and social programs of the island are modern and reflective of this input.

turn-of-the-century banana merchant in Martinique

Tourism is playing a greater part in Martinique's economy today than it did 20 years ago but is still not the primary industry. Agriculture and agricultural products drive the economy, accounting for the largest export block; yet the industry employs less than 10% of the working population. Main agricultural products are sugarcane, bananas, rum, and pineapples. Of these, bananas are the main export, accounting for 55% of all agricultural exports. Others are spices, vanilla, some fruits and vegetables, and a growing exotic flowers export industry. Nearly 32% of the labor force work in the service industry, which includes tourism. Cruise ships, which account for nearly 400,000 visitors per year, bring in a significant portion of tourism income. Overnight visitors number about 345,000. Most are from France (68%) and other European countries (13%). North America accounts for a small seven percent of all visitors.

SIGHTS

Beaches

As on most Lesser Antillean islands, the windward Atlantic side of Martinique is irregular and rough in places, while the south and leeward coasts are quiet and less frothy. Excellent beaches, however, can be found right around the island. All beaches are open to the public, and many have free picnic, shower, toilet, and other facilities.

On the south coast, from **Trois-Ilets** to **Grand Anse des Salines,** the famous beach south of **Sainte-Anne,** you'll find more than a dozen fine but often crowded beaches. This is a popular strip, especially crowded on weekends. Anse des Salines is featured in many a postcard, with palm trees lunging over the sand of the 1.5 mile (2.4-km) crescent beach. This is the southernmost tip of the island, from which you can often see St. Lucia. There is only one road to Salines from Sainte-Anne, and you may experience traffic jams on holidays and weekends.

Stay on the road past des Salines for **Anse-Trabaud,** an often-deserted but lovely beach on the Atlantic coast. Sainte-Anne itself has a beach, which stretches north to the large beach at the Club Med. North of Sainte-Anne is a beach at **Pointe Marin** in the town of **Le Marin,** site of a large marina.

Le Diamant is a popular resort town that boasts the island's longest beach at 2.5 miles (four km), although the water is somewhat murky and rough. Note the volcanic rock, Rocher du Diamant, about a mile from shore.

There are good beaches west of Le Diamant, **Petit Anse, Les Anses-d'Arlets,** and **Grand Anse.** Les Trois-Ilets and the nearby **Pointe du Bout,** on the bay at Fort-de-France, are small villages and probably the center of large resorts, hotels, marinas, cafes, shops, and beaches. Still, this is where it's happening. The beaches at the **Meridien** and **Bakoua** hotels are nice but small. The beaches at the **Meridien** and **Bakoua** hotels are nice but small. The beach at **Anse-à-l'Ane** also features the nearby **Musée de Coquillages,** a shellfish museum and gallery. Regular ferries connect Trois-Ilets and Pointe du Bout to Fort-de-France.

North of Fort-de-France, the beaches become less crowded and the sand becomes darker with volcanic matter, due to Mont Pelée. Small, picturesque fishing villages are the norm here, and dark mountains loom from the center of the island.

North Martinique

In some ways, the modern history of Martinique starts in the north. Along the coastal road from Fort-de-France, the first town you'll encounter is **Schoelcher.** Originally called Case-Navire, the town is now named after Victor Schoelcher, the well-known French abolitionist of the 19th century. Schoelcher is really a suburb of Fort-de-France and looks it. The **University of the French West Indies** is located here.

Farther north you'll find **Case-Pilote,** a small fishing village, and one of Martinique's oldest, given the (French) name of a Carib chief. The church here dates to the 17th century.

Bellefontaine, another small fishing village with a public beach, is notable for the odd boat-shaped house you'll see up on the hill. It is also notable for the roughly 11 million cubic feet (308,000 cubic meters) of earth that fell to the road during a 1981 earthquake.

A quick side trip from Bellefontaine to **Le Morne-Vert** will bring you into the hills, at an altitude of about 1,200 feet (366 meters).

Saint-Pierre

Le Carbet is purported to be the site of Columbus's 1502 landing. A marker on the pier notes the event. The fishing village is one of the oldest on the island; its church was built in 1645. The town has a carny, honky-tonk ambience, with thin streets and local restaurants stretching along the beach. In town, the **Jardin Zoologique Amazona,** tel. (596) 78-00-64, has a small garden and zoo featuring wildcats and snakes from Africa, South America, and the Caribbean. Admission is F20, and the zoo is open daily 9 a.m.-6 p.m.

Just north of Carbet is the **Musée Gauguin,** tel. (596) 78-22-66, which features tormented artist Paul Gauguin's work, letters, and memorabilia of the five months in 1887 he spent with friend Charles Laval in Anse Turin. Admission is F10, and the museum is open daily 10 a.m.-5:30 p.m.

Saint-Pierre is legendary in the annals of Caribbean history. The town was first established at the site of a fortification built by Pierre Belain d'Esnambuc and his company after their arrival in 1635. It soon became a flourishing town, and the capital of the colony. By 1902, it was a sophisticated and bustling city of 30,000, often called "Little Paris of the Antilles." Then, in late April 1902, residents began to feel the rumbling of Mont Pelée, the 4,660-foot (1,421-meter) volcano to the north.

They were doomed. On 8 May, the volcano exploded, and everyone, save for a town drunk named Cyparis who was in jail during the blast, was killed. The town was completely destroyed.

Saint-Pierre never recovered its former eminence, and its residents today number about 6,000. Remains of the old town, including a church, theater, and the cell that saved Cyparis, can be seen. Two museums, both on the main Rue Victor Hugo, record the life of that time. The small **Historical Musée Sainte-Pierre,** on the road's west side, houses artifacts and photos of the town, post-eruption, and is open Mon.-Sat. 9:30 a.m.-5:30 p.m., and on Sunday 9:30 a.m.-1 p.m. Admission is F10 for adults and F3 for children. The larger **Musée Franck A. Perret,** tel. (596) 78-15-16, is dedicated to the study of the volcano and ruins. The photographs are fascinating, and on display are melted glass, porcelain, a crunched church bell, and even carbonized kitchen items such as honey and spaghetti. Tours in English are available. The museum is open daily 9 a.m.-5 p.m., admission F10.

Mont Pelée itself is accessible if you are determined. Turn inland from Saint-Pierre to **Le Mourne Rouge,** a long town, distinguished for its natural water springs. Bottled water from Le Mourne Rouge is sold throughout the island. The carpark here is the starting point for the climb. The hike up is close to three hours, and rest stops are along the way—a map at the carpark shows the route. From the carpark, you can see the Atlantic Ocean and Saint-Pierre.

The coastal road continues north from Saint-Pierre to **La Precheur,** the northernmost vil-

MARTINIQUE

lage and, literally, the end of the road. Hikes to a hot spring, courtesy of the Mont Pelée, or to the village of **Grand' Rivière** can be undertaken; there is no direct road to Grand' Rivière and the hike is about five hours one-way.

Atlantic Coast

The Atlantic coast is characterized by rough surf and a few picturesque fishing villages. In the north, **Basse-Pointe** is notable for being the

---

THE BIG BLOWOUT

In late April 1902, the residents of the northwest coastal town of Saint-Pierre, the "Little Paris of the Antilles," began to feel odd rumblings. Mont Pelée, the 4,660-foot (1,421-meter) volcano to the north, sputtered and coughed. Over the course of several days, fires were spotted leaping from its dome and the smell of sulfur filled the air. Frightened animals followed their instincts and hightailed it out of the area.

On 5 May, the volcano spewed hot mud and steaming underground effluvium, and people began to pack their bags. In a tragically ironic twist, however, an order came from the colonial government: the residents were to remain in Saint-Pierre to participate in a forthcoming election. On 8 May, the volcano exploded with a blast estimated at 40 times more powerful than that of the atomic bomb over Hiroshima, excoriating the town with hot ash and deadly, noxious steam. The nearly 30,000 town residents, save for one, were vaporized, crushed, and burned to death in, according to a museum guide, 47 seconds. While one wonders how anyone could arrive at such a figure, the destruction of life was nonetheless estimated to be absolute within three minutes.

The town's sole survivor, a town drunk named Cyparis, was in jail recovering from a binge during the blast. The thick walls of his underground cell saved him, though he was severely burned. In later years, Cyparis met with a modicum of notoriety and success as a sideshow act with the Barnum & Bailey Circus, exhibiting his scars.

The volcano erupted several more times that year and had its last major eruption in 1929. Today the town's population of 6,000 lives among the ruins of the old town.

---

birthplace of the poet and advocate of *négritude* Aimé Césaire. The area is covered with pineapple and banana plantations, and the restored **Plantation de Leyritz** features a hotel and fine restaurant, as well as a unique museum of doll sculptures made from plant leaves.

In the relatively large town of **Sainte-Marie,** you can visit the **Distillerie Saint-James** and **Musée du Rhum,** tel. (596) 69-30-02. You'll get a good history of the sugarcane and rum industries here. Admission is free, as is the rum-tasting. The works are open Mon.-Fri. 9 a.m.-1 p.m. and 2-4:30 p.m., and weekends 9 a.m.-noon.

Farther south is **La Trinité,** a small town at the foot of the **Caravelle Peninsula.** Much of the peninsula is protected land of the Parc Naturel, and there are opportunities for hiking and swimming at **Anse l'Etang.** Stop at **Château Dubuc,** the ruins of a 1773 castle of one of the island's settlers. It is now a park entity, open Mon.-Fri. 8:30 a.m.-12:30 p.m. and 2:30-5:30 p.m., Saturday 8 a.m.-noon. Admission costs F5.

Farther south is the vast Lamentin plains area, where much of the island's arable land is located. **Le Vauclin,** the southernmost coastal town on the windward side, is at the base of **Mont Vauclin,** at 1,654 feet (504 meters) the highest point in the southern mountain range. This is an important fishing village and a good place to buy fresh seafood.

South Martinique

Aside from the coastal and beach attractions, the southern part of the island has several interesting historical and natural sites worth stopping for.

In **Trois-Ilets,** the small village across the bay from Fort-de-France, you'll find, among dozens of tourist attraction, the **Musée de la Pagerie,** tel. (596) 68-34-55, where Napoleon's Empress Joséphine (her given name was Marie-Josephe Rose Tascher de la Pagerie) was born in 1763. A garden, the main buildings (partially destroyed by fire), and ruins of a sugar plantation comprise the museum; here you'll see Joséphine's bed, love letters from Napoleon, and antique furnishings. Open Tues.-Fri. 9 a.m.-5:30 p.m., weekends 9 a.m.-1 p.m. and 2:30-5:30 p.m. Admission is F20 for adults, F5 for children.

The cockfighting "pitt" at Clery near Rivière-Pilote also features snake and mongoose battles.

Also in Trois-Ilets is the **Musée de la Canne,** tel. (596) 68-32-04, a sugarcane museum in the restored buildings of an old distillery. The museum takes you through the process of growing and curing the cane. It's open every day except Monday 9 a.m.-5:30 p.m.; admission is F15. Stop at **The Pottery,** tel. (596) 68-17-12, a working artisan center.

In **Rivière-Pilote,** inland from the coastal town of **Sainte-Luce,** is another rum museum at **Le Mauny Distillery,** tel. (596) 62-62-08, tours at 10 a.m. and 11 a.m., and 12:30 p.m., 2 p.m., and 3 p.m. Rivière-Pilote is also known for one of the island's more popular cockfighting "pitts," at **Clery,** tel. (596) 62-61-69, open Sunday at 2:30 p.m.

FORT-DE-FRANCE

Fort-de-France, with a population of more than 100,000 (nearly one quarter of Martinique's total population), is a large city by Lesser Antillean standards. The downtown area, fronting the **Baie des Flamands,** has an Old World feel, with narrow streets, iron-balustraded buildings, and markets, cafes, banks, taxis, and people competing for space. Congested suburbs are visible in the hills surrounding town, and nowhere is the striking view more complete than when crossing the bay by ferry from Pointe du Bout, in the south.

Located on a large natural harbor, Fort-de-France is the economic and cultural center of the island and became the capital after Mont Pelée's obliteration of Saint-Pierre in 1902. The town was originally called Fort Royal and was developed around the large **Fort Saint-Louis,** which dominates the waterfront. The fort is still used by the French navy, but it's occasionally open for tours.

Downtown is easily covered by foot, and the 12-acre **La Savane** is a good place to start. Located across from Fort Saint-Louis, the park is filled with palms, gardens, fountains, and benches and is often the site of public gatherings and concerts. A bronze statue of d'Esnambuc, leader of the island's first European settlers, and a white marble statue of native daughter Empress Joséphine, are located on the western side. As of this writing, the Empress had suffered an unfortunate accident or dark practical joke—her head was missing.

East of the park is the **Baie du Carenage** and the cruise ship pier. At the height of the season, Fort-de-France hosts an average of three cruise ships per day, which inevitably adds a sort of frenzied quality to the town. A market, adjacent to La Savane, sells T-shirts, art, wraps, and other items and is particularly busy during cruise ship stopovers.

There are three other markets in town. A walk west along **Rue Lamartine** will bring you to a large fruit and vegetable market; a right and

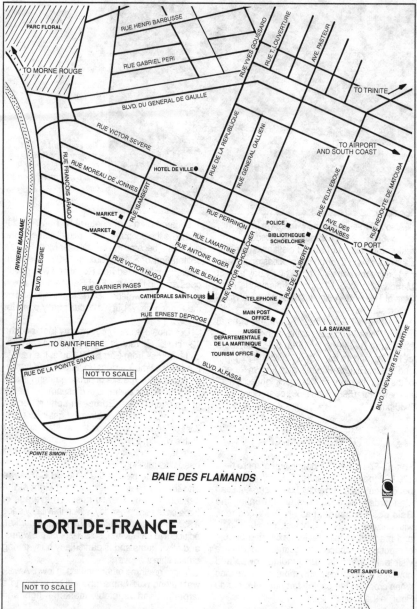

PARC FLORAL

RUE HENRI BARBUSSE

RUE GABRIEL PERI

TO MORNE ROUGE

RUE YVES GOUSSARD

RUE T. LOUVERTURE

AVE. PASTEUR

TO TRINITE

BLVD. DU GENERAL DE GAULLE

RUE VICTOR SEVERE

TO AIRPORT AND SOUTH COAST

RUE FRANCOIS ARAGO

RUE MOREAU DE JONNES

RUE ISAMBERT

RUE DE LA REPUBLIQUE

RUE GENERAL GALLIENI

HOTEL DE VILLE

RUE FELIX EBOUE

RUE REDOUTE DE MATOUBA

MARKET

MARKET

RUE PERRINON

POLICE

AVE. DES CARAIBES

BIBLIOTHEQUE SCHOELCHER

TO PORT

RUE LAMARTINE

RUE ANTOINE SIGER

RUE VICTOR SCHOELCHER

RUE VICTOR HUGO

RUE BLENAC

RIVIERE MADAME

BLVD. ALLEGRE

RUE GARNIER PAGES

CATHEDRALE SAINT-LOUIS

RUE DE LA LIBERTE

TELEPHONE

RUE ERNEST DEPROGE

MAIN POST OFFICE

LA SAVANE

TO SAINT-PIERRE

MUSEE DEPARTEMENTALE DE LA MARTINIQUE

RUE DE LA POINTE SIMON

TOURISM OFFICE

NOT TO SCALE

BLVD. ALFASSA

BLVD. CHEVALIER STE. MARTHE

POINTE SIMON

BAIE DES FLAMANDS

FORT-DE-FRANCE

FORT SAINT-LOUIS

NOT TO SCALE

© MOON PUBLICATIONS, INC.

two-block walk north on **Rue François Arago** will bring you to a fish market. Fish are unloaded right from boats on the **Rivière Madame.** Markets are open daily, but Friday and Saturday are busiest.

Rue Ernest Deproge runs perpendicular to the park; this is where you will find the tourism office, tel. (596) 63-79-60, fax 73-66-93. The office is very helpful and can provide brochures and information in English and French. The Air France building is located in the same complex.

A walk up **Rue de la Liberté,** along La Savane's west side, will bring you past the main post office and the telephone company. Across from the post office, facing the park, is—take a deep breath before you say this—the **Musée Départementale d'Archéologie Precolombienne et de Prehistoire de la Martinique,** tel. (596) 71-57-05. The museum features pottery, beads, bones, maps, and artifacts from Martinique's Arawak and Carib periods, as well as exhibits exploring slavery and colonial days. Hours are daily 9 a.m.-1 p.m. and daily except Saturday 2-5 p.m., admission F15.

Turn west on **Rue Blénac** to the central square **Place Labat** to see the **Saint-Louis Cathedral.** The Romanesque church, complet-

VICTOR SCHOELCHER

Throughout the French West Indies, you'll find streets, museums, and even, in the case of Martinique, suburbs bearing the name Schoelcher. The reference is to Victor Schoelcher (1804-93), the French abolitionist, writer, and politician.

As a colonial administrator, Schoelcher spent time in the French West Indies between 1836 and 1847, where he witnessed firsthand the plight of hapless slaves in the plantocracy system. His opposition to the practice was strengthened by early abolitionist movements in the British West Indies (slavery was illegal in the British colonies by 1834), and in 1840 he published his influential *Abolition of Slavery.* Through that and his other books, and lectures, Schoelcher became, along with religious groups, a figurehead of the French abolitionist movement. In 1848, while an administrator in the Navy Department, Schoelcher helped draft that year's emancipation proclamation.

With the advent of Napoleon III's Second Empire (Napoleon III was a nephew of Napoleon Bonaparte), Schoelcher was forced into exile. After the empire's collapse in 1870, Schoelcher returned to France. After his death, his books and papers were returned to Martinique where they are housed in Fort-de-France's **Bibliothèque Schoelcher.** The ornate library, trimmed with iron and majolica tiles, was created for the 1889 Paris Exposition. It was later dismantled and shipped to Martinique, where it was reassembled.

Downtown Bibliotheque Schoelcher (Schoelcher Library) was named in honor of the French abolitionist.

ed in 1895, was designed by architect Henri Pick, a contemporary of Gustave Eiffel, architect of the Eiffel Tower.

At the corner of Rue de la Liberté and **Rue Victor Severe** is the stunning and extravagantly baroque **Bibliothèque Schoelcher,** tel. (596) 70-26-67, another Henri Pick creation. The Byzantine-domed library, trimmed with iron and majolica tiles, was created for the 1889 Paris Exposition. It was later dismantled and shipped to Martinique, where it was reassembled in 1893. Named for the abolitionist and writer Victor Schoelcher, the now-public library holds an extensive collection of his books.

Farther west on Rue Victor Severe is the ornate **Hotel de Ville,** once a city hall and now a municipal theater. Even farther west, just north of the fish market, is the **Parc Floral et Culturel,** tel. (596) 71-66-25. The gardens and galleries document many of the 2,800 plant species found in Martinique. Open 9 a.m.-noon and 2-5 p.m. daily, except Sunday.

Shopping in Fort-de-France

Main shopping areas, offering duty-free shops, curio shops, banks, and some of the Lesser Antilles' finest patisseries and cafes, are found in the city blocks bordered by **Rue Victor Hugo** and **Rue de la Liberté.** The central **Rue Victor Schoelcher** is the heart of the shopping district.

Organized Tours

You can hire a taxi for a full-day, half-day, or customized tour of the island. Taxis charge by the carload (one to four persons), which makes it best to go with a small group to cut down your costs. Rates start at F800 for a tour of north Martinique, about F600 for a tour of the Atlantic coast, and about F700 for a tour of the south. Contact the tourism office (see the "Information Directory" chart at the end of this section) for a list of recommended guides. **Annie Merlande,** Route de L'Union, Residence Mahoganies #8, Didier 97200 Fort-de-France, Martinique, French West Indies, tel. 596-64-35-13, is one of the island's better guides; she's knowledgeable, fun, and her English is probably better than your French Creole. Annie also rents cars and rooms at reasonable rates.

The island's big touring company, **Mandinina Tours,** tel. (596) 61-49-49, offers excursions to all major sights and beaches.

SPORTS

Water Sports

Water sports, including diving, snorkeling, waterskiing, and glass-bottom boat excursions, can be found at major hotels and marinas. Otherwise, the Pointe du Bout Marina and the marina at the Meridien hotel in Trois-Ilets are good places to start.

Diving

Bathy's Club, tel. (596) 66-00, at the Meridien organizes scuba diving and deep-sea fishing excursions. **Planete Bleue,** tel. (596) 66-08-79, at Pointe du Bout is a scuba-diving outfit.

In Diamant, call the **Okeonos Club,** tel. (596) 76-21-76.

Sailing and Boat Charters

Call **Caraibe Evasion,** tel. (596) 66-02-85; **Soleil et Voile,** tel. (596) 66-09-14; or **Star Voyages,** tel. (596) 66-00-72, at the Pointe du Bout Marina. Those who seek boat charters can also try **Antilles Loisers,** tel. (596) 62-44-19, in Sainte-Luce; **Bambou Yachting,** tel. (596) 62-46-57, in Marin; **Outre Mer,** tel. (596) 74-87-41, in Sainte-Anne.

Horseback Riding

Horseback riders can contact **Ranch Jack,** tel. (596) 68-63-97, at Anses d'Arlets, or **Black Horse Ranch,** tel. (596) 66-03-46, in Trois-Ilets.

Tennis

Try hotels first—the Meridien, Bakoua, Plantation Leyritz, and others all have courts. Many private clubs allow day players. The **Golf de l'Imperatrice Joséphine,** tel. (596) 68-32-81, has three lighted courts. For more information, call the regional tennis organization, **La Ligue Régionale de Tennis,** tel. (596) 51-08-00, in Lamentin.

Golf

The queen of Martinique's golf courses is the **Golf de l'Imperatrice Joséphine,** tel. (596) 68-

32-81, fax 68-38-97, also called the Empress Joséphine Golf Course. The sweeping course is 18-holes, designed by Robert Trent Jones Sr., in Trois-Ilets. You'll find a fully equipped pro shop and lighted tennis courts.

Hiking and Biking

Trips of this nature are best organized through the **Parc Naturel Régional,** tel. (596) 73-19-30. The park department publishes a guide, *Guide de la Randondée,* which outlines the island's trails and hikes. Cost is about F30.

Biking tours are organized by **VT Tilt,** tel. (596) 66-01-01—the VT is from the French *velo tout terrain,* meaning "all-terrain" bike—in Pointe du Bout.

NIGHTLIFE

Nightlife is the domain of hotels, and activities run the gamut from mellow jazz bars to steel band and limbo-fueled rev-ups. The bands are often very good. Several clubs in Fort-de-France and larger towns are popular. The **New Hippo** on Boulevard Allegre is currently a happening place. **Swing Club** is on Rue François Arago, and **Le Coco Loco** on Rue Ernest Deproge has a piano bar.

The Hotel Meridien hosts the island's big casino, open 9 p.m. until about 3 a.m. Picture ID is needed to enter, and admission is F70.

Several hotels, including Bakoua and Meridien, feature regular performances by the astonishing **Les Grands Ballets de la Martinique,** thought by many to be one of the Caribbean's finest folk-dance troupes. The repertoire of this polished and professional group includes singing, drumming, and energetic dancing. Not to be missed.

ACCOMMODATIONS

Martinique's range of accommodations is wide and varied. Several four-star hotels are at hand, primarily in the tourist-dense Pointe du Bout area south of Fort-de-France. About 50 small hotels, in the US$100 (F550) or less range, are grouped under the umbrella name **Relais Créoles.** These can be good bets, even though the designation itself is in fact a marketing tool.

MORE FORT-DE-FRANCE ACCOMMODATIONS

Rates per s, EP when applicable, winter

NAME	(596)	FAX	LOCATION	TARIFF
Hotel Balisier	71-46-54	N/A	Rue Victor Hugo	moderate
Hotel Central	71-53-23 or 70-02-12	N/A	Rue Victor Hugo	moderate
Hotel Tortuga	71-53-23	63-80-00	Rue de la Liberté	budget
La Batelière	61-49-49	61-62-29	Schoelcher	luxury
Le Blénac	70-18-41	N/A	Rue Blénac	budget
Le Gommier	71-88-55	73-06-96	Rue Jacques Cazotte	budget
Le Lafayette	73-80-50	60-97-75	Rue de la Liberté	moderate
Le Palasia	60-32-60	N/A	west end	budget-moderate
L'Impératrice	63-06-82	72-66-30	Rue de la Liberté	moderate
Squash Hotel	63-00-01	63-00-74	Blvd. de la Marne	moderate-luxury
Un Coin de Paris	70-08-52	N/A	Rue Lazare Carnot	budget
Victoria	60-56-78	60-00-24	Didier	moderate

Hotel reservations may be made through **Centrale de Réservation,** BP 823, 97208 Fort-de-France Cedex, Martinique, French West Indies, tel. 596-71-56-11, fax 73-66-93.

Several overseas companies handle a substantial number of hotel bookings in Martinique. Among them are New York's **International Travel and Resorts,** tel. (800) 223-9815 or (212) 251-1800, fax 545-8467; and **Bounty Resorts,** tel. (800) 462-6868 or (203) 266-0100, fax 266-0188, in Connecticut.

Categories are based on prices for single occupancy per night during high season: **Luxury** US$100 or more, **Moderate** US$50-100, **Budget** less than US$50. A 10% service charge is often added to the bill.

Gîtes de France

Gîtes are defined as small villas, apartments, or studios and are often located in private homes. Over 200 *gîtes* are designated so in Martinique. These can be inexpensive and may even put you in touch with a local family, certainly a good way to experience Martinique. Contact Gîtes de France Tourism Office, 610 5th Ave., New York, NY 10020, tel. (212) 315-0726, or in Martinique, tel. (596) 73-67-92, or Centrale de Réservation (see above) for a complete list of *gîtes*.

Camping

Camping on Martinique is inexpensive and popular, but allowed only in designated areas. In general, rates start at about F75 for campsites. Bring your own tent if you've got the space, or, for about F25 more per night you can often rent a tent (see below).

Good spots are **Tropicamp,** tel. (596) 62-49-66, in Sainte-Luce or **Vivre & Camper,** tel. (596) 76-72-79, fax 76-97-82, in Sainte-Anne, both on beaches.

Courbaril Campsites, tel. (596) 68-32-30, at Anse-à-l'Ane also rents bungalows. **Le Nid Tropical,** tel. (596) 68-31-20, is also located on Anse-à-l'Ane, and offers small apartments as well.

MORE TROIS-ILETS ACCOMMODATIONS

Rates per s, EP when applicable, winter

NAME	(596)	FAX	LOCATION	TARIFF
Alizés 2000	66-05-55	66-01 04	Anse Mitan	moderate-luxury
Hotel de la Baie	66-06-66	63-00-70	Anse Mitan	moderate-luxury
Bambou	66-01-39	66-05-05	Anse Mitan	moderate-luxury
Carayou	66-04-04	66-00-57	Pointe du Bout	luxury
Hotel Camelia	66-05-85	66-05-85	Anse Mitan	moderate
Davidiana	66-00-54	66-00-70	Pointe du Bout	moderate
Eden Beach	66-01-19	66-04-66	Anse Mitan	moderate-luxury
Impératrice Village	66-08-09	66-07-10	Anse Mitan	luxury
La Bonne Auberge (Chez André)	66-01-05	66-04-50	Anse Mitan	budget
Le Karacoli	66-02-67	66-02-41	Pointe du Bout	moderate
Les Alamandas	63-13-72	N/A	Anse Mitan	moderate-luxury
Rivage Hotel	66-00-53	66-06-56	Anse Mitan	moderate

MORE SOUTH COAST ACCOMMODATIONS

Rates per s, EP when applicable, winter

NAME	(596)	FAX	TARIFF
ANSE-À-L'ANE			
Frantour Trois-Ilets	62-31-67	68-37-65	luxury
Hotel Maharadja	68-36-70	68-37-51	moderate
Hotel Tamarind Plage (Anse d'Arlets)	68-67-88	N/A	moderate-luxury
DIAMANT			
Diamant Bleu	76-42-15	N/A	moderate
Diamant-Novotel Evasion	76-42-42	76-22-87	luxury
Hotel Calypso	76-40-81	76-40-84	moderate
Marine Hotel	76-46-00	76-25-99	luxury
Palm Beach	62-53-82	78-29-98	moderate-luxury
Relais Caraïbes	76-44-65	76-21-20	moderate-luxury
Village du Diamant	76-21-89	63-53-32	moderate
Plein Sud	76-26-06	76-26-07	moderate-luxury
SAINTE-LUCE			
Aux Délices de la Mer	62-50-12	N/A	budget
Brise Marine	62-46-94	62-57-17	moderate
La Corniche	62-47-48	62-57 64	moderate
Les Amandiers	62-32-32	62-33-40	luxury
Les Moubins	62-58-65	N/A	luxury
Résidence Deville	62-50-64	62-58-78	budget
Résidence Grand Large	62-54-42	62-54-32	moderate
SAINTE-ANNE			
Anchorage	76-92-32	76-91-40	moderate-luxury
Anse Caritan	76-74-12	76-72-59	moderate-luxury
La Belle Martinique	N/A	N/A	budget
La Dunette	76-73-90	76-76-05	moderate
The Last Resort (Marin)	74-83-88	74-76-41	budget
L'Orangerie	51-51-51	76-90-13	moderate

Renting Camping Equipment

For camping van rentals, call **West Indies Tours,** tel. (596) 54-50-71. Prices start at about US$600 (F3300) per week.

The National Forest department, tel. (596) 71-34-50, allows camping in designated areas June through September. Those areas are rustic as rustic can be, and you'll find no facilities.

Some towns allow overnight camping on beaches during holidays, but you'll have to check with local authorities at the mayor's office. If you'd like to rent a tent and traipse the countryside, call **TS Autos,** tel. (596) 63-42-82, or **MAB Location,** tel. (596) 71-98-85, in Fort-de-France. Cost is F30-40 per day.

Villas

Villas, available throughout the countryside, may be the best deals for families or large parties. Typically, villas accommodate two to eight people or more, and the rates vary with the size and villa location. Apartment and condo-type accommodation is also available. Rates for

MORE NORTH SIDE ACCOMMODATIONS

Rates per s, EP when applicable, winter

NAME	(596)	FAX	TARIFF
BASSE-POINTE			
Plantation de Leyritz	78-53-92	78-92-44	luxury
CARBET			
Le Christophe Colomb	78-05-38	N/A	budget
Marouba	78-00-21	78-05-65	moderate
FRANÇOIS			
Frégate Bleue	54-54-66	54-78-48	luxury
La Riviéra	54-68-54	54-30-43	moderate-luxury
Les Brisants	54-32-57	54-69-13	budget
Prairie Bungalows	54-34-16	50-55-20	moderate-luxury
Lamentin			
Martinique Cottages	50-16-08	50-26-83	moderate
Victoria Airport Motel	56-01-83	60-00-24	moderate
MORNE ROUGE			
Auberge de la Montagne Pelée	52-32-09	73-20-25	moderate
MORNE VERT			
Bel-Air Village	55-52-94	55-52-97	moderate
Chez Cécilia	55-52-83	75-10-74	moderate
SAINT-JOSEPH			
Habitation Créole	50-64-61	50-60-42	moderate
SAINT-PIERRE			
La Nouvelle Vague	78-14-34	N/A	budget
TRINITÉ			
Saint-Aubin	69-34-77	N/A	moderate
Primereve Hotel	64-49-75	64-49-73	luxury
TARTANE			
La Caravelle Studios	58-37-32	58-67-90	moderate
La Village Tartane	58-46-33	63-53-32	moderate-luxury
Le Madras	58-33-95	58-33-63	moderate
Paradiles	58-66-90	58-29-67	moderate

villas and apartments, during high season, will range US$500-2000 (F2750-11,000) per week.

The tourist office operates a rental service that will help locate villas; contact **Office Départementale du Tourism, Service de Location de Villas,** BP 520, 97206 Fort-de-France Cedex, Martinique, French West Indies, tel. (596) 63-79-60, fax 73-66-93. English is spoken.

As well, the **Centrale de Réservation** (see address above) on Rue Ernest Deproge lists apartments and villas as well as hotels.

In the U.S., contact **Villas International,** 605 Market St., San Francisco, CA 94105, tel. (800) 221-2260 or (415) 281-0910, fax 281-0919, for Martinique villas and condos.

Hotels

One of Fort-de-France's better deals is **La Malmaison,** tel. (596) 63-90-85, on Rue de la Liberté. The 20-room hotel overlooks La Savane and is comfortable and spotless. Budget-Moderate.

In the Trois-Ilets (Pointe du Bout/Anse Mitan) area, you'll find nearly three dozen hotels, from large to small. **La Bakoua,** tel. (596) 66-02-02, U.S. tel. (800) 221-4542 or (212) 575-2262, local fax 66-00-41, U.S. fax (213) 719-6763, takes its name from the traditional straw hat worn by fishermen. It's located at Pointe du Bout, and the view across the bay to Fort-de-France, especially at night, is worth lingering over a *ti punch* or two. The hotel is four-star and offers tennis, water sports, sailing, a swimming pool, shops, and entertainment. Standard rooms are not large and neither is the beach, but you won't be disappointed. The hotel is located in the thick of the tourist center. Luxury.

Le Meridien Trois-Ilets, tel. (596) 66-00-00, U.S. tel. (800) 543-4300 or (212) 245-2920, fax 66-00-74, is located next to La Bakoua and shares beachfront. This is a big, imposing hotel, but you won't lack for things to do, both day and night. The hotel is a bit run down for the money, but the Pointe du Bout location compensates. Luxury.

La Pagerie, tel. (596) 66-05-30, U.S. tel. (800) 221-4542, fax 66-00-99, is another Pointe du Bout hotel. It's built in the colonial style with the rooms surrounding a central courtyard and pool. Some rooms offer kitchenettes. The hotel is not on beachfront, but it's central, cozy, minutes from the water, and minutes from the Fort-de-France ferry. Moderate.

In Diamant, the **Hotel Diamant les Bains,** tel. (596) 76-40-14, fax 76-27-00, has 24 rooms and bungalows set on a garden overlooking the beach, the longest beach in the country. The place is homey, simple, and local—you will encounter fewer tourists here than other places. The restaurant is superb. Moderate.

In Sainte-Anne, the **Club Med,** tel. (596) 76-72-72, U.S. tel. (800) CLUB-MED, fax 72-76-02, is busy, busier at night, and popular with young people. The beach is a big attraction. This Club Med is semi-all-inclusive, meaning drinks are extra. Luxury.

For a quieter experience, **Chez Julot,** tel. (596) 74-40-93, in Vauclin is a modest, 10-room hotel on a thundering beach. Budget-Moderate.

FOOD

The Creole and French cuisines of Martinique have long been recognized as some of the best in the Caribbean. Hotels generally serve fine food and are open on Sunday when most of the rest of the country shuts down. Still, it's worth finding a small cafe or seaside restaurant; the quality of the food often belies the appearance. In Fort-de-France, you'll find fast-food restaurants such as McDonald's and Pizza Hut.

MORE FORT-DE-FRANCE RESTAURANTS

NAME	LOCATION	(596)	CUISINE	PRICE RANGE
Chez Gaston	Rue Felix Eboue	71-45-48	Creole	inexpensive
El Chico Chico	Rue Garnier Pages	72-48-92	Creole	inexpensive
La Mouïna	Rte. de Redoute	N/A	French	expensive
La Privilège	Rue Perrinon	60-27-32	French	expensive
Le Chandelier	Didier	70-20-32	Asian	expensive
Le Coq Hardi	Rue Martin Luther King	71-59-64	French	moderate
Le Coucoussière	Rue Perrinon	60-06-42	French North African	moderate
Le King Creol	Ave. des Caraïbes	70-19-18	Creole	inexpensive-moderate
Le Tea Garden	Rue Victor Hugo	73-09-52	French/Italian/Creole	moderate
Marie-Sainte	Rue Victor Hugo	70-00-30	Creole	inexpensive

MORE RESTAURANTS NORTH

NAME	(596)	CUISINE	PRICE RANGE
FRANÇOIS			
Chez Milo	54-65-70	Creole	moderate
Club Nautique	54-31-00	seafood	moderate
La Riviéra	54-68-54	French/ Creole	moderate
LAMENTIN			
La Plantation	50-16-08	French/ Creole	moderate
Le First	52-79-80	Creole	inexpensive
TRINITÉ			
Le Don de la Mer	58-26-85	Creole	moderate
Le Dubuc	58-60-81	Creole	moderate-expensive
TARTANE			
Chez Titine	58-27-28	Creole	moderate
Le Dubuc	58-60-81	Creole	moderate-expensive
Le Madras	58-33-95	French/ Creole	moderate
SAINT-PIERRE			
La Factorerie	77-12-53	French/ Creole	moderate
Le Cyparis Station	78-36-73	Creole	inexpensive-moderate
CARBET			
Grain d'Or	78-06-91	seafood	moderate
Le Trou Crabe	78-04-34	French/ Creole	moderate
O-Ra-La Lanme	78-08-48	French/ Creole	moderate

The tourist office in Fort-de-France will have copies of *Ti Gourmet,* a more complete guide to the restaurants of Martinique.

The categories below are based on per-person entree prices: **Expensive** US$25 or more, **Moderate** US$10-25, **Inexpensive** US$10 or less.

A 1992 *Ti Gourmet* prizewinner was the restaurant at the **Hotel Diamant les Bains** (see "Hotels," above). Lunch here is a treat. Try their *accras* (fritters made from vegetables or fish) or the curried red snapper fillet. The restaurant is closed Wednesday. Moderate.

Le Fromager, tel. (596) 78-19-07, in the hills overlooking Saint-Pierre and the bay, is the place to stop while taking an island tour. The view and breeze alone are worth it. This place is very popular with Martiniqueans and is likely to be crowded on weekends. Give yourself some time. The *feroce d'avocat,* a spicy avocado and saltfish appetizer, is a wonder. The restaurant is open daily for lunch and open for dinner Thursday through Saturday. Moderate-Expensive.

Several restaurants sit on the dock at the Pointe du Bout Marina. **Davidiana,** tel. (596) 66-00-54, has a pub feel to it, and serves tasty seafood and Creole dishes. Inexpensive-Moderate.

In Fort-de-France, the sheer number of restaurants and sidewalk cafes may keep you busy for a long while. Try **Le Lafayette,** tel. (596) 63-24-09, at the hotel of the same name. The upstairs restaurant overlooks the Savane. Expensive. **La Case,** tel. (596) 63-04-00, serves French, Italian, and Creole, and is nice for an elegant night out. Moderate-Expensive.

GETTING THERE

The central **Lamentin Airport,** tel. (596) 51-51-51, located about 20 minutes by taxi from Fort-de-France, is a large and modern airport and accommodates dozens of international flights daily.

American Airlines, local tel. (596) 51-12-29, connects North American cities to San Juan with hundreds of weekly flights. From there the connection to Martinique is on American Eagle (same airline). **Air Canada,** tel. (596) 51-29-81, operates connections from Montreal and Toronto.

MORE RESTAURANTS SOUTH

NAME	(596)	CUISINE	PRICE RANGE
DIAMANT			
Coin Tranquille	76-41-12	seafood	moderate
La Quenette	76-41-47	French/Creole	moderate
Le Diam's	76-23-28	French/Creole	inexpensive-moderate
Le Poisson Rouge	76-43-74	Creole	moderate
SAINTE-LUCE			
La Corniche	62-47-48	French/Creole	moderate
La Petite Auberge	62-59-70	Creole	moderate
Le Bounty	62-57-65	French/Creole	moderate
SAINTE-ANNE			
Athanor	76-97-60	French/Creole	moderate
Le Peuplier	76-92-87	Creole	moderate
Le Sunny	76-76-74	Creole	moderate

Air France, tel. (596) 55-33-00, operates daily flights from Paris and several French provincial towns, as well as a weekly connection from Miami and other connections from San Juan. Air France also connects to Guadeloupe, Haiti, and the Dominican Republic.

Air Martinique, tel. (596) 51-09-90 or 60-00-23, connects to and from selected neighboring islands, including Trinidad, Barbados, St. Vincent, Guadeloupe, and Sint Maarten. **Air Guadeloupe** operates flights to and from Guadeloupe. The regional carrier **LIAT,** tel. (596) 51-10-00, is the best Caribbean connection.

GETTING AROUND

Taxis

Taxis are not metered and rates are determined by a regulating agency. Rates are posted at the airport and in various tourist brochures. Does this mean your driver will heed this important information? No. He or she will probably try to charge more—not ten times more, just a bit more. But by arming yourself with the information and polishing up your French, you can keep the damage to a minimum.

Sample fares, at press time: Airport to Fort-de-France, F70; Airport to Trois-Ilets, F160; Trois-Ilets to Sainte-Anne, F270; Pointe du Bout to Fort-de-France, F210; Pointe du Bout to Diamant, F160; Pointe du Bout to Anse-à-l'Ane, F50.

After 8 p.m. and on Sunday, about 40% is added to fares. Most taxis offer touring excursions, for one to four persons, at about F800

MORE TROIS-ILETS RESTAURANTS

NAME	LOCATION	(596)	CUISINE	PRICE RANGE
Au Poisson D'or	Anse Mitan	66-01-80	Creole	moderate-expensive
Bambou	Anse Mitan	66-01-39	French/Creole	moderate
Chez Jojo	Anse-à-l'Ane	N/A	Creole	inexpensive-moderate
La Matador	Anse Mitan	68-05-36	French/Creole	moderate
L'Amphore	Anse Mitan	66-03-09	French/Creole	moderate-expensive
La Villa Créole	Anse Mitan	66-05-53	French/Creole	moderate-expensive
Ti Calebasse	Anse-à-l'Ane	68-38-77	Creole	inexpensive-moderate

for a tour of the north, about F600 for a tour of the Atlantic coast, and about F700 for a tour of south Martinique. Bottom line: Negotiate with the driver.

Taxis are found virtually everywhere—in Fort-de-France on Boulevard Alfassa, Rue Ernest Deproge, and elsewhere—but if you need to call try **Radio Taxis,** tel. 63-10-10, or **Radio Tele,** tel. 63-63-62. Both maintain 24-hour services.

Buses

Taxis collectif (collective taxis or minibuses) are identified by a "TC" on the license plate. These function as buses and are inexpensive, the best bet for up-country trips. The main bus station is found at Pointe Simon, Fort-de-France. The inter-city bus station is on Boulevard General de Gaulle. Buses run until about 6 p.m.

Car Rentals

Renting a car is an easy, relaxed way to see the island; the 190 miles (306 km) of roads are in good shape and well marked—not, however, in English—and car companies are plentiful. Rental companies will provide you with adequate maps, but detailed maps are available either at the tourist office or you can pick up one of the country's best, the *Carte Routiere,* at most bookstores.

Rental agencies are located at the airport and Fort-de-France, Trois-Ilets, and along the south coast resort towns. You can often count on the company delivering the car to your hotel or having a car ready at the airport should you call ahead. Credit cards are generally accepted. Rates start at about US$30 (F165) per day for the smallest car, but the average is closer to US$50 (F275) per day. Minimum age is generally 21.

Motorcycle and Bicycle Rentals

Motor scooters and bicycles are available from **Funny,** Fort-de-France tel. 63-33-05, or Pointe du Bout tel. 66-04-57; **Discount,** Pointe du Bout tel. (596) 66-54-37; **Scootonnere,** Diamant tel. (596) 76-41-12; and **Tropicamp,** Sainte-Luce tel. (596) 62-49-66. Rates start at US$20 (F110) per day.

Ferries

Ferries run regularly from the marina at Point du Bout, and Anse-à-l'Ane and Anse Mitan to the Quai d'Esnambuc on the waterfront in Fort-de-France. The crossing takes about 25 minutes and runs nearly every thirty minutes during peak time, from early in the morning until evening. The trip is faster and much more pleasant than driving or hiring a taxi to go to town—cheaper, too. Return fare from Pointe du Bout is F25 for adults and F11 for children. Schedules are available at all hotels.

Some ferry service to neighboring islands is also available. *Caribbean Express,* tel. (596) 63-12-11, fax 70-50-75, operates weekly connections to Guadeloupe and Dominica during summer, when demand is low, and five-times-weekly departures in winter. The new and fast **Caribia Ferries** (31 Rue Lamartine, no phone) carries automobiles and up to 1,200 passengers. Very comfortable, and sleeping cabins are available. The basic route connects Guadeloupe, Dominica, Martinique, and St. Lucia. Simple single one-way fare is F150-190. Fares for children 4-11 years old are reduced 50%.

MARTINIQUE CAR RENTAL COMPANIES

Country code is 596. When two numbers are given, the airport number appears first.

Avis	51-17-70 or 51-45-62 or 70-11-60
Budget	51-22-88 or 63-69-00
Caribe	51-19-33 or 51-43-13
Citer	51-65-75 or 72-66-48
Eurodollar	51-66-21 or 63-54-54
Europcar	51-20-33 or 51-01-96
Hertz	51-01-01 or 60-64-64
Inter-Rent/Dollar	51-28-22 or 60-00-77 or 50-01-02
Mattei	51-66-21 or 63-54-54 or 63-99-46
Milleville	51-51-51 or 71-64-58 or 73-51-24
Moucle	73-35-15 or 60-20-21
Pop's Car	51-02-72
Sunset	66-04-27 or 66-00-53
Thrifty	51-03-73 or 66-09-59

MONEY, HOURS, AND COMMUNICATION

Currency and Banks

The French franc is the legal tender, but U.S. and Canadian dollars and some European currencies are widely used. Still, it's best to use francs, if only for the favorable exchange rate you'll get at banks or *bureaux de change.* At the current exchange rate, US$1 will buy F5.50. Exchange rates change regularly, so it's best to check your local newspaper for current rates before you leave.

Banks are found at the airport, all over Fort-de-France, in Trois-Ilets, and in major towns. *Bureaux de change,* which only change money, give better rates than banks. Banking hours vary, but banks are generally open 8 a.m.-noon and 2-5 p.m., and many are closed Wednesday and Saturday afternoon.

In Fort-de-France, **Credit Martiniquais,** tel. 59-93-0, on Rue de la Liberté, and **BNP,** tel. 63-82-5, on Avenue des Caraïbes are among the many. **Change Caraibes** has an office on Rue Ernest Deproge (open Mon.-Fri. 8 a.m.-6 p.m. and Saturday 8 a.m.-1 p.m.) and a smaller branch at the airport.

Hours, Phones, News

General business hours include a midday lunch closing and some Wednesday afternoon closings. Much of Martinique closes down on Sunday.

Public telephones utilize the phone-card system, although some coin phones are available.

INFORMATION DIRECTORY

TOURISM

Office Départementale du Tourisme de la Martinique, Blvd. Alfassa, 97206, Fort-de-France, Martinique, French West Indies, tel. (596) 63-79-60, fax 73-66-93.

French West Indies Tourist Board, 610 5th Ave., New York, NY 10020, tel. (212) 315-0726, fax 247-6468.

Martinique Tourist Office, 1981 Av. McGill College, Montreal, Quebec H3A 2W9, tel. (514) 844-8566, fax 844-8906.

OTHER

Police emergency, tel. 17.

Police, Fort-de-France, tel. 55-30-00.

Fire emergency, tel. 18.

Ambulance, tel. 71-59-48.

Lamentin Airport, tel. 51-51-51.

FedEx, tel. 75-56-56.

Phone cards may be bought at cafes, some bookstores, and small shops. The international country code for Martinique is 596. From the U.S., dial "011" plus "596" plus a six-digit number.

Newsstands and bookstores are well stocked, and just about everything is in French. British and U.S. newspapers and magazines can be found at the airport newsstand. The "Presse" newsstand in Pointe du Bout stocks a wide selection of French, German, and English magazines.

BOB RACE

THE NETHERLANDS ANTILLES

INTRODUCTION

The Dutch have a long history of New World activity, from their 16th-century explorations of North America and the West Indies, to 17th- and 18th-century shipping and trading enterprises throughout the Americas. Today, the Dutch government has the enviable task of associating with several of the more unique islands in the Lesser Antilles.

The Netherlands Antilles (in Dutch *De Nederlands Antillen*) once formed a Dutch colony comprising two groups of three islands each, adding to the confusing nomenclature that today attempts to define the islands. Tiny Saba, the slightly larger Sint Eustatius, and Sint Maarten, which shares island space with French Saint-Martin, were called the Netherlands Windward Islands, even though they lie squarely in what is known today as the Leeward Islands. Their names are derived from the fact that they lie windward of the three Dutch Leewards—Aruba, Bonaire, and Curaçao—which sit off the north coast of Venezuela.

Today the Netherlands Antilles—for the purposes of our book, Sint Maarten, Saba, and

Sint Eustatius—offer some of the region's best dining, diving, and accommodations. Busy Sint Maarten, which maintains one of the region's major airports, Princess Juliana International, is known for its luxurious resorts, some of which host the Lesser Antilles' premier gambling casinos. Bulbous Saba's tiny Dutch villages offer homestyle accommodations, and the island's expansive marine park is known throughout the region as a natural and pristine diving destination. Sint Eustatius is steeped in mercantile history, and in its old town, Oranjestad, you can savor the architecture and styles of a time when the island dominated the West Indies trade routes.

Please note: As the Netherlands Antilles' Sint Maarten shares an island, a history, and a culture with French Saint-Martin, we felt it would be a disservice to attempt to detach the essentially inseparable two here. Sint Maarten has been covered, along with its French twin sister Saint-Martin, in the chapter "French West Indies."

SABA

Saba holds few ambiguities for a visitor. The island's main road winds through steep moun-

tains from one village to another and is simply called The Road. It is the only road. The volcanic pinnacle of Saba is called Mt. Scenery, another appropriate name. The village of Windwardside is on the windwardside of the island, and the capital, The Bottom, is, well, at the bottom. In a way, it all sounds like something from a child's fairy tale. In other ways, it makes an unequivocal statement about the quality of life here: Few frills and simple adornments define the island sensibility.

Saba is not the sort of place you'd usually expect in the Lesser Antilles. Palm-lined beaches, gourmet restaurants, and fire-eating limbo dancers are not part of the picture; diving, hiking, simple accommodation, and outdoorspeople are.

It has been difficult for Sabans to carve their lives, sometimes literally, out of this rock. Yet they have continued to do so over three centuries. Still, this is one of the few islands in the Lesser Antilles where visitors are sincerely invited, without reservation, to make themselves at home—home, that is, as the Sabans know it.

THE LAND

Saba (SAY-buh) is in fact a rock—and a big rock, to be sure. The 2,855-foot (871-meter) **Mt. Scenery** dominates a series of smaller hills and slopes, all part of an ancient volcanic chain in the "inner arc" of the Leeward Islands (from Nevis in the south to Saba in the north). The volcano on Saba has been extinct for more than 5,000 years, and no one is even sure where the crater is or was.

Sheer cliffs roll off mountains and plop into the sea, and a rugged, thrashing surf is the norm along the island's perimeter. There are no true beaches to speak of, save for an inaccessible patch of black sand at Rum Bay.

At only five square miles (13 square km), the rock is home to the island's 1,200 residents, who all live in the four major settlements along its east and south sides. The seven-mile (11-km) road that connects the villages and airport took 20 years to carve out of the mountainside; it is, for good reason, the only road. There are few views in the Caribbean comparable to approaching the looming monoliths of Saba by airplane. While on the island, from most any point, the views to the open Caribbean and

neighboring islands such as Statia, St. Barts, St. Kitts, and Sint Maarten are absolutely breathtaking.

The terrain around Mt. Scenery is rugged and varies with altitude. Low woodlands are replaced by secondary tropical rainforest, which is in turn replaced by clouded rainforest. The vegetation is thick and lush, featuring the dominant towering mountain mahogany (not related to West Indian mahogany), mountain palm, trumpet wood, cashews, elephant ears, lilies, ferns, oleander, and orchids, to name a few. The Saban national flower is the black-eyed Susan.

Lizards and tree frogs inhabit the forests, and over 180 species of birds, including the pearly thrasher, bananaquit, green-throated carib hummingbird, booby, and other sea birds have been recorded on the island. The harmless racer snake lives in the hills.

Before the advent of The Road in 1947, Sabans walked or rode donkeys to get from one village to another. The result of that legacy is miles of walking trails that crisscross hills, mountains, and valleys, creating a network both practical and recreational.

HISTORY

During his 1493 voyage to the West Indies—his second—Columbus sighted Saba. He did not land, presumably judging there were no riches to be found and wary of the impenetrability of the coast. It is not clear which name Columbus used when he charted the island, but later reports cite that the Amerindian word Siba, thought to have meant "Rock," was used by the island's first inhabitants, the Arawaks. Other reports claim the Amerindian name was Amonhana, a word of unknown meaning.

Early European Exploration
The island was uninhabited when Sir Frances Drake happened upon it in 1595 and when the Dutch explorers Pieter Schouten and Piet Heyn encountered it again in 1624 and 1626, respectively. Shortly thereafter, an English ship was wrecked off the coast in 1632, yet by all reports the survivors spent as little time as possible on the island.

In 1635 the French, under the explorer Pierre d'Esnambuc, made a half-hearted claim; yet they, too, did not settle Saba. In 1640 intrepid Dutch explorers established settlements on the southwest coast in the areas known as Tent Bay and The Bottom. The Bottom, which lies in a low valley between several hills, was derived from the Dutch word *botte,* meaning "bowl." The Tent Bay settlement was destroyed by a landslide in 1651.

Over the years, European powers, mainly the Dutch, Spanish, French, and English, fought over control of the island. *Why* they fought over it is not always clear. No substantial minerals were ever found, the coast was rugged and dangerous, and no flat land existed for any sort of plantation production. A good defense position was Saba's only real asset, yet no substantial forts were ever built due to the tremendous difficulties in building and settling any part of the island. From the old landing pier at The Ladder, for example, one would ascend 800-900 stone steps to get to, paradoxically, The Bottom.

Regardless, the European powers did constantly fight over the island—a favorite military tactic that worked well was to bury opponents in landslides—probably due more to the momentum of their other European and West Indian battles than to any real desire to hold onto Saba. The island changed hands 12 times before reverting to the Dutch in an 1816 treaty.

The 20th Century

From the mid-19th century into the 20th century, Saba existed as a lonely outpost of the Netherlands empire. Sabans scratched out livings by fishing and hiring out as seamen. A small shoemaking business flourished for a while in the village of Crispeen, named after St. Crispin, the patron saint of shoemakers.

Construction of The Road, an astonishing feat of engineering and pure physical labor, was not begun until the 1940s. The architect of The Road was local carpenter Josephus Lambertus Hassell. When professional Dutch engineers said a road could not be built, the tenacious Hassell took a course in engineering through correspondence school and proceeded to build it by hand, with local help. The feat took twenty years.

The island's first automobile did not appear until 1947, a jeep that was floated to the pier lashed to two rowboats and then lifted to dry land by four dozen men. The tiny airstrip, one of the world's shortest at 1,312 feet (400 meters) was completed in 1959, and regular air service to Sint Maarten was instituted in 1963. Around-the-clock electricity was not available until the 1970s.

PEOPLE AND CULTURE

Saba's population, about 1,200, is nearly evenly split between descendants of European settlers (including Dutch, Irish, Scottish) and descendants of African slaves who were brought in to work small farms and help in construction. Names such as Hassell, Peterson, and van den Berg are common.

The island's architecture is almost universally modern West Indian and Dutch; clean white homes with red-tiled roofs, stone or picket fences, and small country gardens are the norm—you'd expect to see tulips, but you don't. The language is officially Dutch, but everyone speaks English. Saba's dominant religion is Catholicism, a legacy of European settlement.

Some ancient and time-honored customs are still practiced. Women, even young women, still hand-embroider the famous, delicate **Saban Lace,** sometimes called Spanish Work, imported to the island in the 1870s from Venezuela. An island drink called **Saban Spice,** made with 151-proof rum, anise, cinnamon, orange peel, cloves, nutmeg, and an assortment of spices, is still a local favorite. These items are sold in several shops around the towns, or straight out of people's homes. Ask your taxi driver where to buy the items.

Stop at the **Saba Artisan Foundation,** tel. (599-4) 63260, in The Bottom for local hand-screened items, dolls, books, and other handmade gifts.

Holidays and Festivals

Saba celebrates **Saba Days,** an early December weekend of parties, dances, and donkey races. The July **Saba Summer Festival** is the island's answer to Carnival, a week of street dances, hill races, calypso contests (imported performers), talent shows, and a Grand Festival Parade.

Saba officially celebrates religious festivals such as the Christmas and Easter holidays, as well as Boxing Day (26 December), and the Dutch Queen's Birthday (30 April).

GOVERNMENT AND ECONOMY

Saba is a semi-autonomous member of the Netherlands Antilles, which also includes the islands of Curaçao, Bonaire, Sint Eustatius, and Sint Maarten (see "Saint-Martin/Sint Maarten" in the French West Indies chapter). Aruba is a separate entity within the Kingdom of the Netherlands.

The Netherlands Antilles are ruled by parliamentary democracy with the Dutch monarch, Queen Beatrix, as head of state. The queen is represented in the Netherlands Antilles by a governor, who is appointed by the crown. The islands have representation in the Dutch Cabinet by way of a minister plenipotentiary, who is appointed by a legislative council of the five Netherlands Antilles. Each island has a modicum of self-rule, responsible for water, electricity, land, certain infrastructures, schools, and harbors. The legislative council comprises a Council of Ministers and a 22-member elected parliament, who meet in Willemstad, Curaçao. The council is responsible for police, defense, taxation, foreign exchange, health, and major foreign affairs decisions.

The economy of Saba relies on remittances from the Crown and tourism. About 25,000 visitors were recorded in 1992, 65% of whom made overnight stays. The rest were day-visitors from the nearby islands of Sint Maarten, Sint Eustatius, Saint-Barthélémy, and others. Of the 25,000, about 4,000 visited Saba for diving and related activities. Approximately 440 yachts per year visit Saba.

SIGHTS

You won't have to worry about which are the best beaches on Saba; there are none. The closest you'll get to ocean bathing is using the ramp at Fort Bay's **Leo Chance Pier.** Otherwise, you might consider a boat trip to get out on the water. There was talk some time ago of building a hotel called the Saba Beach Resort, proposed for the south side of the island, that would, judging by its name, have a beach. This is not yet reality.

From **Juancho Yrausquin Airport,** the small field on the island's only flat spot (creatively named **Flat Point**) a road winds over 15 hairpin turns up to the village of **Hell's Gate.** Given the Sabans' penchant for truth in advertising, you might be tempted to worry, but this is not an ominous sign. **Hell's Gate** (Upper and Lower) is a small village, full of typical Saban cottages. Beyond are several small banana farms.

The road winds to **Windwardside,** a slightly larger village and Saba's commercial center. On the thin streets you'll find several hotels and guesthouses, a supermarket, post office, and the tourist board offices, tel. (599-4) 62231. The Saba tourist board is extremely helpful with maps, brochures, and information and is in fact a contact point for many of the island's villa and cottage rentals. Call the energetic assistant director Wilma Hassell or director Glenn Holm for information.

In Windwardside you'll also find a few restaurants, galleries, two banks, and a dive center. The small **Harry L. Johnson Memorial Museum,** the former home of a sea captain, features antique furniture, a safe, a four-poster bed, and a bust of Simon Bolivar, a 1983 gift from the Government of Venezuela. The museum is under renovation and has been closed for long periods in the past; otherwise it is open weekdays 10 a.m.-noon and 1-5 p.m., admission US$1 (NAF 1.80). On Sunday afternoon, Sabans and visitors gather on the grounds of the museum for a few rounds of croquet, now apparently an island tradition. The fun and games are spiked with mimosas, and everyone is invited to wear their whites and meet a few locals and visitors.

From Windwardside, a path leads up to the summit of Mt. Scenery (see "Mt. Scenery," below). This is a wonderful climb, difficult in only a few places, and well worth the 90 minutes it takes to get to the top.

The road from Windwardside passes through and over several huge hills, with spectacular views all around, to the village of **St. John's.** From St. John's, the road drops down to **The**

SABA

DIAMOND ROCK
GREAT POINT
CAVE OF RUM BAY
GREEN ISLAND
TORRENS BAY
GREY HILL
FLAT POINT
TORRENS POINT
OLD SULPHUR MINE
JUANCHO YRAUSQUIN AIRPORT
MARY'S POINT WALK
WELL'S BAY
MARY'S POINT
COVE BAY
MARY'S POINT MOUNTAIN
HELL'S GATE
SPRING BAY
SANDY CRUZ WALK
MT. SCENERY WALK
MT. SCENERY
ENGLISH QUARTER
OLD BOOBY HILL
LADDER BAY
THE LADDER
LITTLE RENDEZVOUS
CORE GUT BAY
LADDER POINT
THE GAP
WINDWARDSIDE
THE BOTTOM
BIG RENDEZVOUS
THE LEVEL
GREAT HILL
BOOBY HILL
THAIS HILL
ST. JOHN'S HILL
ST. JOHN'S
JOHNNIE'S GROUND
CORNER POINT
TENT POINT
FORT HILL
TENT BAY
FORT BAY
GREAT LEVEL BAY

0   100 yd
0   100 m

© MOON PUBLICATIONS, INC.

Bottom, Saba's capital. The Bottom, population about 400, is situated in a valley nestled among several large hills and is considered to be the "warm" town of Saba. Everything, of course, is relative, but the indication here is that the breeze factor is diminished in the valley. In The Bottom you'll find a small inn, a guesthouse, several villas, a few car rental agencies, a bank, and a post office.

The Road continues from The Bottom and descends 800 feet (244 meters) to **Fort Bay,** where a small pier is the base for the island's dive operations. Cruise ships—small ones such as Windjammer Cruises—and private yachts moor in the area. Also found here is a small pub, a gift shop, an electricity plant, and Saba's petrol station.

Hiking is one of Saba's more popular activities, and trails are maintained by the **Saba Conservation Foundation,** The Bottom, Saba, Netherlands Antilles, tel. (599-4) 63348, fax (599-4) 63299. Before they imported the island's first car in 1947, Sabans got around on foot and by donkey. Many of the trails, which connect villages and coastal sites, were well worn and fitted with stone steps. The foundation has placed rest stops and informational signs along the trails, and has detailed them in a publication called *Saba Nature Trails.* Most of the trails, which vary in difficulty, do not require a guide. Among the named trails are **Tent Point, The Boiling House, Booby Hill, Mary's Point,** and **Mt. Scenery.**

Mt. Scenery
The 2,855-foot (871-meter) Mt. Scenery is accessible from Windwardside by a steep trail of 1,064 steps. The walk will take 90 minutes, more if you linger, and trail signs and rest areas along the way keep you informed and comfortable. Ascending the trail, you'll be led through several layers of rainforests, palm forests, and elfin woodlands. Birds will flit about throughout the climb. The trail can be slippery and wet, and near the summit the constant patter of small raindrops is heard. It is not raining, necessarily; the high-altitude dew is condensing and falling. Bring a sweater; it can get cool up there. From the summit, which has been cleared, Windwardside appears as a series of small specks below. On a clear day you will see Saint Martin/Sint Maarten, Sint Eustatius, St. Kitts, and Nevis. As one local put it, "It's like going to heaven without having to die." Bird viewing is best in early morning or late afternoon.

Saba Marine Park
The Conservation Foundation is also responsible for maintaining and regulating the **Saba Marine Park,** tel. (599-4) 63295. The marine park was established in 1987 to preserve and manage Saba's reefs and marine resources. The reserve is underwater and encircles the island (plus two outlying sections) and includes waters and seabed up to 200 feet (61 meters) in depth. The park maintains 26 dive sites as well as zones for diving, fishing, anchoring, or combinations of all three. Basically, the park is there to manage what has become known as one of the Caribbean's best diving environments and to preserve the fishing and other natural sea habitats for Sabans.

Visibility can be as good as 100 feet (30 meters) in places. The park, which is funded by various sources including the Netherlands World Wildlife Fund and the Saban government, charges a nominal use fee for upkeep. The fee was recently "a dollar a dive," but we've heard it's gone up to two dollars a dive. We can live with that. The marine park also administers a hyperbaric facility at Fort Bay, donated by the Royal Netherlands Navy. The office is located at Fort Bay. See below for information on local diving operations.

SPORTS AND ENTERTAINMENT

Miscellaneous Sports
Several hotels have pools (including Captain's Quarters and Scout's Place, see "Accommodations," below) they'll open to the public, and the **Sun Valley Youth Center** in The Bottom offers a tennis court, also for public use. Beyond that, look to the ocean for sports and recreation.

Diving
Three dive shops operate on Saba. **Sea Saba,** P.O. Box 530, Windwardside, Saba, Netherlands Antilles, tel. (599-4) 62246, fax (599-4) 62362; **Wilson's Dive Shop,** P.O. Box 50, Windwardside, Saba, Netherlands Antilles, tel. (599-4) 63410, North America tel. (800) 883-SABA, fax (599-4) 63334; and **Saba Deep,** P.O. Box 22, Fort Bay, Saba, Netherlands Antilles, tel. (599-4) 63347, fax (599-4) 63397, offer a full range of equipment rentals and excursions to the Marine Park dive sites. Among them they operate a range of boats able to carry large or small groups and offer deep dives, shallow dives, and night dives. All three collaborate with island hotels and cottages for hotel/dive packages. All offer resort certification and will be able to customize dives, snorkeling trips, photography trips, fishing trips, and sunset cruises.

Nightlife
Nightlife on Saba will consist of small gatherings in the pubs and bars around the island, a bit of canned music here and there, and live music on occasion. In the evening hours, Captain's Quarters and Scout's Place in Windwardside are popular with both Sabans and visitors. The **Lime Time** pub, tel. (599-4) 63351, in The Bottom features weekend dances.

ACCOMMODATIONS

Saba's infrastructure, while it may sound rustic, is well developed for Sabans and for the small number of visitors the island takes in yearly. The island offers no large resorts, just a half-dozen hotels, inns, and guesthouses, universally spic-and-span, comfortable, and quaint—

SABA APARTMENT AND COTTAGE ACCOMMODATIONS

Rates per unit, EP when applicable, winter

NAME	(599-4)	LOCATION	TARIFF
Arrindell's Apartments	62473	Windwardside	moderate
Blue Horizon	62261	Windwardside	moderate
Casa Elderina	62313	The Level	moderate
Crispeen Apartments	63244	St. John's	moderate
Effie's Cottage	62254	Windwardside	moderate
Garfunkel's Cottage	62230	Windwardside	moderate
Greengate Apartments	62282	Booby Hill	moderate
Jerry's Cottage	62441	The Bottom	moderate
Renz Apartment	62316	Windwardside	budget
Sea Scape Apartments	62236	Windwardside	moderate
Sunrise Apartment	62347	Booby Hill	moderate
Tudda's Apartments	63212	St. John's	moderate

remember, this is an island where a bad hotel will stick out like a sore thumb. Don't worry about air-conditioning, or fans for that matter. The cool breezes and altitudes will let nature take care of the heat (in fact, pack a sweater for even cooler night breezes). If you are a diver, inquire about hotel/diving package discounts.

Camping is not allowed on Saba.

The categories below are prices per single, per night in high season (15 December through 15 April): **Luxury** US$100 or more, **Moderate** US$50-100, **Budget** US$50 or less.

Villas and Cottages

Dozens of cottages and small villas are available for rent island-wide, ranging US$50-100 (NAF90-180) per day. Call Wilma Hassell at the tourist board, tel. (599-4) 62231; or **Saba Real Estate**, P.O. Box 17, Windwardside, Saba, Netherlands Antilles, tel. (599-4) 62299, fax (599-4) 62415, for information. Renting one's own home is, so to speak, a cottage industry here.

Hotels

All hotel rates are subject to a five percent government tax and 10-15% service charge.

In Hell's Gate, the new **The Gate House,** Hell's Gate, Saba, Netherlands Antilles, tel. (599-4) 62416, U.S. tel. (708) 354-9641, fax (599-4) 62415, features six rooms, two with kitchenettes, and a small cafe. Moderate.

In Windwardside the following hotels are recommended. **Juliana's,** Windwardside, Saba, Netherlands Antilles, tel. (599-4) 62269, North America tel. (800) 223-9815, fax (599-4) 62389, sits on the hill 1,500 feet (450 meters) up, with cool breezes and great views, a pool, and restaurants. The hotel is neat as a pin, like your grandmother's sitting room. Moderate. **Captain's Quarters,** Windwardside, Saba, Netherlands Antilles, tel. (599-4) 62201, North America tel. (800) 223-9815, fax (599-4) 62377, has that hotel feel, with a pool with a nice view and an outdoor patio restaurant. The bar and restaurant are popular gathering places for locals and visitors alike. Geraldo Rivera has stayed here, but don't hold that against the place. Moderate. **Scout's Place,** Windwardside, Saba, Netherlands Antilles, tel. (599-4) 62205, U.S. tel. (800) 365-8484, fax (599-4) 62388, is a 15-room bed-and-breakfast with great views, a pool, and restaurant. Budget-Moderate.

The new **Willard's of Saba,** P.O. Box 515, Windwardside, Saba, Netherlands Antilles, tel. (599-4) 62498, North America tel. (800) 883-SABA, fax (599-4) 62482, is the island's sole luxury "resort," although it has only seven rooms. Located 2,000 feet (610 meters) up on the side of Booby Hill, the hideaway hotel is indeed ornate, and features huge VIP, Luxury, or Bungalow rooms. You'll find a tennis court, pool, hot tub, and restaurant on the grounds, and the view captures both the sunrise and sunset. No children or pets. Luxury.

In The Bottom look for **Cranston's Antique Inn,** The Bottom, Saba, Netherlands Antilles, tel. (599-4) 63203, fitted with antiques, not surprisingly, and a restaurant and pool. Budget-Moderate. **Caribe Guesthouse,** The Bottom, Saba, Netherlands Antilles, tel. (599-4) 63259, has five rooms and a kitchen for guests. Budget.

FOOD

The hotel restaurants are all good, with special kudos to **Captain's Quarters,** which offers some interesting Dutch-Indonesian Creole dishes, and **Scout's Place,** which serves a highly recommended goat curry (see "Accommodations," above). The choices are otherwise limited, but you'll find plenty to eat.

If you're staying in a villa or cottage, the island's best supermarket is **Big Rock Market** in Windwardside. Since visitor business on Saba is often at a lull, all restaurants may not be open every day. As well, not all take credit cards. Call ahead to check.

The following are all priced in a Budget-Moderate range, under US$25 per entree. **Brigadoon Restaurant,** tel. (599-4) 62380, is located in a 19th-century house in Windwardside and serves fresh fish and island and Continental specialties. It's one of the island's best restaurants.

Saba Chinese Restaurant, tel. (599-4) 62268, in Windwardside has 100 choices of inexpensive Cantonese food; no credit cards. **Guido's Pizzeria,** tel. (599-4) 62230, in Windwardside serves pizzas and sandwiches and is also a disco; no credit cards. **Tropics Cafe,** tel. (599-4) 62469, is part of Juliana's and serves breakfast, lunch, and snacks; no credit cards are accepted. Great views.

In The Bottom, stop at the **Serving Spoon,** tel. (599-4) 63225, up on the mountainside for owner Queenie Simmons's famous peanut chicken or other Creole dishes; no credit cards. **Lollipop's Bar and Restaurant,** tel. (599-4) 63330, specializes in seafood and local dishes.

In Two Deep in Fort Bay, tel. (599-4) 63347, attached to the Saba Deep Dive Center, is popular for breakfast, brunch, and lunch.

The road from tiny Saba's equally tiny Juancho Yrausquin Airport winds up to the village of Hell's Gate.

GETTING THERE

By Air

Saba's Juancho Yrausquin Airport measures 1,312 feet (400 meters), one of shortest in the world. The approach is exhilarating, to say the least; if there is one place in the world you might want to leave your safety belt buckled until the plane has completely stopped, this is it. **Winair** operates at least six flights daily from Sint Maarten. The flight is 15 minutes, making it possible to go for a day-trip and return, either way, with plenty of time to relax before dinner; currently US$66 round-trip. Winair often posts special rates for day-trips; contact agent F. Johnson, Windwardside, tel. 599-4-62255, for Winair flights. Sint Maarten is served by major airlines from North America and Europe (see "Saint-Martin/Sint Maarten," in the French West Indies chapter). Winair also operates flights to and from the neighboring island of Sint Eustatius.

Ferry Service

A ferry once operated between Sint Maarten and Saba, but as of this writing has been discontinued. The boat sank. Check with the tourist office for details about renewed service.

GETTING AROUND

Walk, hitchhike, rent a car, or take a taxi; those are the choices. Taxis charge about US$40 (NAF72) per vehicle (for four persons) for a two-hour tour of the island. Several taxis will be at the airport when you arrive, and you might want to make touring arrangements on the spot with them. Otherwise, your hotel or guesthouse will call a taxi for you.

Vehicle Rentals

Rental cars start at about US$40 (NAF72) per day. You'll need only your valid license from home or an international license. Contact **Hardiana NV Car Rental,** c/o Scout's Place, tel. (599-4) 62205; **Doc's Car Rentals,** tel. (599-4) 62271; **Johnson Rent A Car,** tel. (599-4)

INFORMATION DIRECTORY

SABA TOURIST BOARD:

P.O. Box 527, Windwardside, Saba, Netherlands Antilles, tel. (599-4) 62231, fax (599-4) 62350.

OTHER

Medhurst & Associates, 271 Main St., Northport, NY 11768, tel. (516) 261-9600, fax 261-9606.

62269; or **Steve's Scooter Rentals,** tel. (599-4) 62507.

Driving is on the right—and take care. The Road is, for the most part, in good shape but is also full of twists and sharp turns. Drive slow. Here's a fun fact: Saba has no traffic lights.

Hitchhiking

Hitchhiking is not something we frequently recommend or encourage in the Lesser Antilles, but on Saba it is safe and common among locals and tourists. As a matter of fact, Saba is one of the Lesser Antilles' safest islands, no doubt in part due to its small population.

Departure tax from Saba is US$2 (NAF3.60) to other islands of the Netherlands Antilles, and US$5 (NAF9) anywhere else.

MONEY, HOURS, AND COMMUNICATION

Saba's currency is the Netherlands Antilles florin, or guilder, exchanged at NAF$1.80 = US$1. However, U.S. dollars are used widely and frequently. Two banks operate on the island: **Barclays** and **Commercial Bank.** Barclays is located in Windwardside, open weekdays 8:30 a.m.-1:30 p.m.

Businesses are generally open weekdays 8 a.m.-noon and 1-5 p.m. and Saturday 8 a.m.-noon. Most businesses close on Sunday.

To call Saba from North America, dial the international access code "011" plus the country code "599," then "4," then the five-digit number.

SINT EUSTATIUS

The tourist boards of Lesser Antilles islands are fond of sobriquets; "The Island of Spice" for Grenada or "The Nature Isle" for Dominica are among several that attempt to describe the best the island has to offer. For the tiny island of Sint Eustatius, called Statia (STAY-shuh) by just about everyone, "The Undiscovered Isle" would be an appropriate moniker, and would be truer for Sint Eustatius than for most of the Lesser Antilles.

Yet the island, then called "The Golden Rock," was once bustling with people. Its streets and pubs swelled with sailors, traders, merchants, and pirates—as much as four times the population of today. It was, in its heyday, one of the Caribbean's most important free ports and transfer points, profiting from trade and the smuggling of goods from the French, English, and Spanish islands. In its golden days, before the abolition of slavery collapsed the sugar industry, as many as 200 ships on any given day were stacked outside its harbor, waiting to load or discharge cargo. So strategic was the island that it changed hands 22 times as European powers vied for dominance of the Caribbean trade routes.

THE LAND

Statia is a miniature pinch of a volcano in the "inner arc" of Lesser Antilles. All the islands from Saba in the north to Montserrat in the south are believed to be pinnacles of the same volcanic ridge. Saba, Statia's political and cultural first cousin, lies 17 miles (27 km) to the northwest. Sint Maarten, the probable gateway for getting to the island, lies 38 miles (61 km) to the north, and 15 miles (24 km) to the south is St. Kitts.

Statia itself is a mere eight square miles (21 square km) dominated by a southern volcanic peak called **The Quill,** a long-extinct crater rising 1,980 feet (604 meters) above the sea. The slopes of the hill and inside of its crater are covered with a lush tropical rainforest. The green forest is a haven for a wide array of flora and fauna, including hummingbirds, lizards, hanging vines, mosses, and towering mahogany trees. The Quill is accessible by trails and is one of the more popular excursions on the island.

Conversely, the central part of the island is characterized by low-lying plains and grassy scrub land. The land here has never been particularly fertile, and plantations on Statia never achieved the output or status of those on neighboring islands. The north part of the island is again hilly and is largely deserted of any population.

Several small beaches are found on the leeward side of the island, near the capital of Oranjestad. The island measures roughly five miles by two miles (eight km by three km) and is crisscrossed by several roads and a dozen walking trails.

HISTORY

Early History

Statia was once inhabited by Amerindian Caribs, and Arawaks before them, as evidenced by artifacts displayed in the local museum. It is not clear whether the warlike Caribs ever defended the island with any vigor; it certainly was not the sort of island that provided strategic hiding places.

Columbus sighted Statia on his second voyage in 1493. He charted it, named it, then left it alone. Columbus's name for the island was reputedly St. Anastatia, later changed to Sint Eustatius by the Dutch, then colloquially shortened. Another theory has the Caribs calling it something that sounded like *eustatius,* which was corrupted by the Spanish and later the Dutch-French-British contingents who occupied the island throughout the next several centuries.

At any rate, the Spanish passed on Statia. The first attempted colonization occurred in 1625, when then-rivals France and Britain landed explorers who established settlements. The colonies fell prey to pestilence, Carib opposition, and finally Dutch invasion. In 1636 the Dutch built Fort Oranje, which became the first permanent settlement on the island.

A Mercantile Port

During the late 17th century and into the 18th, the Dutch West India Company bankrolled development in Statia. Plantations sprang up on the land, numbering about 76 in their heyday. Slaves were brought in from Africa, and trade grew. Goods from the French, Spanish, and British islands—some smuggled, some stolen, some under legitimate trade conditions—found their way to a growing number of warehouses in the Dutch port. Fine silver, pewter, silks, cloth, crystal, cotton, tobacco, sugar, rum, and, importantly, slaves, helped establish Statia as the primary mercantile port in the Lesser Antilles. Sensing profit, and a somewhat easy mark, the British, French, and Spanish invaded and occasionally occupied the island 22 times over the years.

In the meantime, the port had continued to prosper. By 1790, the island's population had reached 8,124, consisting of 5,140 Whites, 2,341 slaves, 43 freed slaves, and assorted drifters. This, compared with today's population of 1,860, attests to Statia's former affluence.

A Reckless Salute

A not insignificant side note in Statia's mercantile history occurred after the War for Independence in the soon-to-be United States. During the 1700s, Statian merchants had made a large profit dealing arms and supplies to rebellious colonies.

On 16 November 1776 (a day still celebrated on Statia) the brig Andrew Doria, flying the Grand Union flag of the Continental Navy, approached the harbor. She saluted and the Dutch commander Johannes de Graaff returned a 13-gun salute of recognition. This was a customary thing to do at the time and was probably not intended as a formal recognition of the newly formed state. In fact, there is every indication that the salute was intended to welcome the Andrew Doria as a merchant vessel and not a ship of war. Nevertheless, it was the first recorded recognition of the American colonies' sovereignty, and this action brought the ire of the British. De Graaff was forced to resign under formal protest, and the British felt forced to save face by taking more drastic action.

The British Take Statia

This they did by ordering the seizure of Statia. The British commander Admiral Sir George Brydges Rodney sailed with his fleet into the harbor in December 1781. The British took the island without a shot fired from Fort Oranje.

Rodney proceeded to confiscate the next 130 ships that sailed into the harbor over a period of a month. He sacked the town and island and reputedly made off with nearly five million pounds sterling (which was in turn recaptured by the French and Dutch while in transit to Britain). Yet he left the infrastructure of Oranjestad intact, taking only timbers from a warehouse to refurbish his ships.

This non-destruction of Oranjestad helped in the quick recovery of Statia, which was soon once again, for a brief time, a thriving mercantile port under the British and the French. However, several events would follow and lead to the downfall of trade throughout the islands.

The French Revolution and subsequent Napoleonic Wars disrupted Europe on a massive scale. In the early part of the 19th century, the Caribbean slave trade became increasingly disreputable, and the sugar boom had begun to wind down. The forts of Statia fell into disrepair, and the island's defense status was no longer important. The British almost eagerly turned Statia back over to the Dutch in 1816, but by then the days of trade and plantocracy in the Caribbean were over. From 1834 to 1863, the sugar industry collapsed almost entirely after the abolition of slavery in the British, French, and Dutch islands. Thereafter Statia's economy all but died. Merchants and former slaves left in droves, searching for a better life elsewhere. Statia has never recovered the glory of its boom days.

Statia in Modern Times

Six territories were remitted to the Dutch in 1816: Statia, Saba, Sint Maarten, Aruba, Bonaire, and Curaçao. They all became Dutch colonies.

In 1954 the Dutch government granted the islands the status of autonomy, wherein they became, as a single entity called the Netherlands Antilles, a member of the Kingdom of the Netherlands. Aruba separated from the Netherlands Antilles in 1986 and became an autonomous member of the Kingdom in and of itself.

Today Statia is in effect supported by the Dutch government. Recent efforts by the government and the Historical Society have helped to restore many of the historic buildings in Oranjestad and around the island. Tourism is the chief, although small, industry. Government actually employs the largest number of workers.

The Statia-U.S. Connection

Statians have a historical and curious affinity for the United States. This started with the Statian arms and supplies smuggling business, which aided colonists in their War for Independence effort of the 1770s. An official state holiday, the 16 November Sint Eustatius Day (often called "Statia-America Day"), is celebrated on the anniversary of the day the Dutch commander saluted an American brig, inadvertently making Statia the first government to recognize the independence of the colonies. That this act brought down the wrath of the British government and the subsequent sacking of the island is not a fact lost on Statians, who seem to have taken it in stride. A verse of the Statia national anthem declares: "Statia's past you are admired / though Rodney filled his bag. / The first salute fired / to the American flag."

Apparently, Statians are nothing if not ironic, and they celebrate the day by dressing in colonial garb and staging reenactments of the event. Parades, feasts, and contests are also part of the celebrations. Another result of the *Andrew Doria* incident is the somewhat disturbing nickname for the island, "America's Childhood Friend."

The airport is called the Franklin Delano Roosevelt Airport in honor of the U.S. president, who in 1939 presented the island with a plaque inscribed: "Here the sovereignty of the United States of America was first formally acknowledged to a national vessel by a foreign official." Presumably Roosevelt was a better president than grammarian, yet his sentiment was nevertheless important to Statians. Later, in 1976, Statia honored the U.S. Bicentennial with the restoration of the island's first bastion, Fort Oranje.

PEOPLE

The population of Statia is 1,860. Statian workers have traditionally found better employment elsewhere, a trend that has only recently abated, and only somewhat at that. The population is almost wholly descended from African slaves. Others, mostly Dutch and some North American retirees, make their homes on the island. Oranjestad, which is the island's sole town, hosts the majority of the population.

The official language of Statia is Dutch. Most everyone, however, speaks English. Dutch is taught in schools and used on most government documents. Street signs are in Dutch and English. Dutch influence is also shown in the Dutch Reformed Church. Other, mostly Protestant religions exist.

GOVERNMENT AND ECONOMY

Government

Statia is a semi-autonomous member of the Netherlands Antilles, which are ruled by parliamentary democracy with the Dutch monarch, Queen Beatrix, as head of state. The queen is represented in the Netherlands Antilles by a governor, who is appointed by the crown. The islands have representation in the Dutch Cabinet by way of a minister plenipotentiary, who is appointed by a legislative council of the five Netherlands Antilles. Each island has a modicum of self rule, responsible for water, electricity, land, certain infrastructures, schools, and harbors. The legislative council comprises a Council of Ministers and a 22-member elected parliament, who meet in Willemstad, Curaçao. The council is responsible for police, defense, taxation, foreign exchange, health, and major foreign affairs decisions. Statia's major political party is the Democratic Party (DP).

Economy

The economy of Statia is reliant on remittances from the Crown and from overseas relatives. Government on the island employs about 20% of the working population. Some subsistence farming and fishing feeds the local economy, but is no longer significant. An oil-storage facility employs several dozen Statians.

Tourism has emerged as the bright light on the island's economic dashboard. Nearly 18,000 visitors were recorded in 1992, and there are currently over 90 total guest rooms. The Dutch government has pledged US$5 (NAF9 million) million in a 10-year project to restore historical buildings and sites around the island, which they hope will attract tourists. The cruise ship dock at Gallows Bay will be expanded in hopes of bringing in more traffic.

In 1989 Hurricane Hugo swept through the island, eliminating a third of all homes and damaging just about every building left standing. The island has recovered through large input from the Dutch government and relief agencies.

SIGHTS

Keep in mind that euphemisms employed by tourist brochures, words such as "unspoiled" and "natural," are often drawing the thin line between reality and enticement. "Natural" can mean "tattered," or "barely visible," which is true of some of the old Dutch forts on Statia.

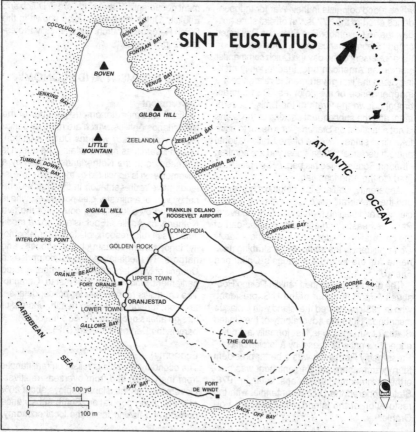

More than a dozen small forts were built around the perimeter of the island during its days of requiring heavy defense, and many are today in a "natural" state. Granted, the island is a tourism destination still in progress, and that ought not cast a shadow on its true qualities, that is, large doses of natural beauty, history, and opportunities for relaxation, and not much else.

Beaches

Oranje Beach, also called Smoke Alley Beach, is a dark-sand beach in places and stretches north along the coast from Lower Town. This is a popular beach with Statians, although it was severely damaged during Hurricane Hugo. Several beaches on the windward side of the island, including those at **Corre Corre Bay** and **Zeelandia Bay,** are rough and have strong undertows. These are better for wading and beach-combing rather than swimming.

Oranjestad

Statia's capital is **Oranjestad,** located on the southwest leeward side of the island. The town is partially built on a cliff that overlooks the sea. Upper Town is built on the 130-foot (40-meter) cliff, and Lower Town is on the water. **Fort Oranje** overlooks the town and is one of the island's major attractions. The fort was built in 1636 by the Dutch and was partially restored in 1976 in honor of the U.S. Bicentennial. It now houses some government offices, a post office (closed), and a **tourist office** booth, tel. (599-3) 82433. At the tourist office you can pick up a number of brochures, including the Historical Foundation's *Walking Tour Guide* to Oranjestad and a guide to the island's 12 hiking trails.

Tourist office booths are also located at Lower Town and the airport.

In the center of Upper Town is the **Sint Eustatius Historical Foundation Museum,** tel. (599-3) 82288. The restored red-roofed building, called the Doncker-de Graaff House even though the ill-fated Dutch commander never lived there, housed Admiral Rodney during his profitable looting of Statia in 1781. The museum includes Amerindian artifacts and a skeleton, as well as furniture, money, and artifacts from the island's heyday. Note the strings of blue glass beads still occasionally found around the island by beachcombers. The beads were manufactured by the Dutch West India Company and were used in the trade of goods, including rum, tobacco, land, and slaves. Some speculate that these were the same type of beads the Dutchman Peter Minuit used in 1625 to purchase Manhattan Island from the natives. The museum is open weekdays 9 a.m.-4 p.m. and until noon on weekends. Admission is US$1 (about NAF1.80).

Also in Upper Town is the **Dutch Reformed Church,** built in 1775. The building, with a square tower housing a Historical Society info center, is now partially restored. Climb the tower for a good view of town. Nearby, the ruins of the **Honen Dalim Synagogue** can be found. At one time Statia was a refuge for Jews escaping persecution in South America and Europe. This synagogue, built in 1738, is the second-oldest in the Western Hemisphere. Both churches were abandoned during the general exodus of the post-Rodney-pillage of the island. Both have interesting and revealing historical cemeteries. Elsewhere in Upper Town is **4 Fort Oranjestraat,** a house built early in this century and typical of the architecture of the time. Behind it is the 18th-century house complex called **Three Widows Corner,** featuring a cookhouse and garden.

Lower Town was home to docks, warehouses, taverns, and slave quarters during the Statia glory days. Much of it has been restored and now hosts hotels and shops.

Out on the Island

Elsewhere on Statia are remnants of the 16 or so small forts built for defense during the island's 22 flag-changes. Many are so completely ruined and buried by sand, scrub, and time that they are no longer discernible. Statia is an archaeologist's dream and several organized digs are ongoing, including frequent visits by students of the U.S. William and Mary College of Archaeology and the Netherlands' University of Leiden.

The tourism department has designated 12 island nature trails, ranging from easy to difficult. The trails are old slave paths or goat and donkey paths and are marked and easy to follow. Guides are available through the tourist office, starting at about US$20 (NAF36) per hike.

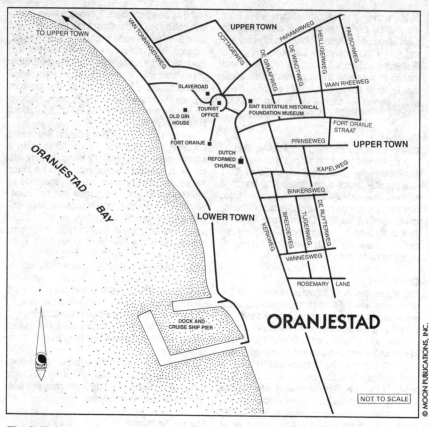

UPPER TOWN

TO UPPER TOWN

VAN TONNINGENWEG

COTTAGEWEG

PARAMIRWEG

DE GRAAFWEG

DE WINDTWEG

HEILLIGERWEG

FAESCHWEG

SLAVEROAD

OLD GIN HOUSE

TOURIST OFFICE

SINT EUSTATIUS HISTORICAL FOUNDATION MUSEUM

VAAN RHEEWEG

FORT ORANJE STRAAT

ORANJESTAD BAY

FORT ORANJE

DUTCH REFORMED CHURCH

PRINSEWEG

UPPER TOWN

KAPELWEG

LOWER TOWN

BINKERSWEG

KERWEG

BREEDEWEG

TJUGERWEG

DE RUYTERWEG

VANNESWEG

ROSEMARY LANE

DOCK AND CRUISE SHIP PIER

ORANJESTAD

© MOON PUBLICATIONS, INC.

NOT TO SCALE

The Quill

A hike to the summit of The Quill is the island's most popular excursion. The Quill, a corruption of the Dutch word *kuil,* for "pit," is the crater of an extinct volcano. The mountain is now covered by a lush rainforest on its upper slopes and crater interior. Damage by 1989's Hurricane Hugo made parts of the hike around the rim impossible, but experienced guides can get you to the best bits, not the least of which is the highest point, called the **Mazinga.** The view from several points on the hike are alone worth the effort. The path to the inside of the crater is accessible. Allow two to three hours for the hike.

SPORTS AND ENTERTAINMENT

Sports

Sports activities other than hiking on Statia are limited. Tennis and basketball are available at the **Oranjestad Community Centre,** which has a lighted tennis court and changing rooms.

Diving

Other than the above, diving is the thing. Statia's diving sites are unique and regarded by some as way above average. Talk is afoot of turning part of the surrounding reef into a marine protected area, but even beyond that there are currently some

200 wrecks to explore. The 16 charted sites include The Supermarket, two downed ships about 60 feet (18 meters) underwater and 150 feet (46 meters) apart off the shore of Lower Town. The area is replete with coral, sponges, exotic fish, the works. A dozen other sites are just as pristine.

The one dive operation on the island is **Dive Statia,** tel. (599-3) 82435, fax (599-3) 82539. Owners Judy and Mike Brown will organize open water certifications, snorkeling, boat charters, and deep-sea fishing excursions.

Nightlife

Things go quietly in the Statia night, but you'll be able to find entertainment, dancing, and music, both live and canned. Weekends are the best bet for finding evening activities. Franky's, the Chinese Restaurant, Sonny's, and the Golden Era (see "Accommodations" and "Food," below) all offer entertainment.

On Saturday night, look to the Oranjestad Community Centre for occasional music and dances. The **Lago Heights Disco** (no phone) features dancing and some live music.

ACCOMMODATIONS

Statia currently has about a dozen small hotels and guesthouses/apartments. You won't find a large resort or mega-hotel anywhere on the island, so much the better for those who like simplified vacations.

On Statia, most hotels don't complicate matters with on-season or off-season rates. For most, one rate applies year-round, although several may close down in the slow September/October season.

Add a seven percent government tax and 10-15% service charge to room charges. Credit cards are accepted in most hotels. As always, call ahead for current information.

The rates below are based on single occupancy per-night tariff, during high season where applicable (15 December-15 April): **Luxury** US$100 or more, **Moderate** US$50-100, **Budget** US$50 or less.

Hotels and Guesthouses

The Old Gin House, P.O. Box 172, Oranjestad, Sint Eustatius, Netherlands Antilles, tel. (599-3) 82319, is located in Lower Town in a reconstructed 18th-century cotton ginnery and warehouse that was built using the ballast bricks of Dutch ships. The hotel is smallish, with 20 rooms, but finely decorated with period antiques and furniture. The pool is freshwater and the small beach is worth walking. This is where Queen Beatrix stays when she visits the island. Luxury. **La Maison Sur la Plage,** P.O. Box 157, Zeelandia Bay, Sint Eustatius, Netherlands Antilles, tel. (599-3) 82256, U.S. tel. (800) 845-9405, is located on the windward side of the island on a small, rough, but pretty beach. The 20 rooms are in cottages, and the restaurant serves fine French cuisine. Moderate.

The **Golden Era Hotel,** P.O. Box 109, Oranjestad, Sint Eustatius, Netherlands Antilles, tel. (599-3) 82345, North America tel. (800) 365-8484, fax (599-3) 82445, has a brochure that says: "Welcome on our island in our hotel!" With a greeting like that, who could resist? In Lower Town, the hotel is small and comfortable. Moderate.

The **Talk of the Town,** tel. (599-3) 82236, a simple, unassuming hotel with clean rooms and no view, is located just outside of Upper Town on the way to the airport. The restaurant here is a good deal as well. Budget-Moderate.

Henriquez Apartments, tel. (599-3) 82299, has two locations, one near the airport (Airport View Apartments, tel. 599-3-82474) and the other in Upper Town. The apartments have kitchenettes and private baths. Budget.

MORE STATIA ACCOMMODATIONS

Rates per unit, EP when applicable, winter

NAME	(599-3)	TARIFF
Alvin Courtar Apartments	82218	moderate
Cherry Tree Villa	(tel. 800-325-2222)	luxury
Lens Apartments	82226	moderate
Richardson Guesthouse	82378	moderate
Sugar Hill Apartments	82305	moderate

FOOD

Most restaurants are located in Oranjestad and the choices are somewhat limited, but you won't go hungry. Many of the smaller businesses do not take credit cards; don't eat first, then find out later. Categories below are based on per-person entree prices: **Expensive** US$25 or more, **Moderate** US$10-25, **Inexpensive** US$10 or less.

Hotels have some fine eating places, including the **Mooshay Bay Publik House** in the Old Gin House and **La Maison Sur la Plage**'s French restaurant. Moderate-Expensive. Hotel restaurants are also convenient in that they are open on Sunday.

King's Well Restaurant, tel. (599-3) 82538, near the water at Lower Town, serves seafood and northern European meat dishes; no credit cards are accepted. Moderate.

Franky's, tel. (599-3) 82575, in Upper Town serves sandwiches and West Indian cuisine, including bullfoot soup, grapefruit soup, and whelk stew. Occasional entertainment. No credit cards at Franky's. Inexpensive. **Stone Oven,** tel. (599-3) 82543, serves West Indian and is a popular bar and gathering spot, with occasional entertainment. No credit cards. Inexpensive-Moderate. The succinctly named **Chinese Restaurant,** tel. (599-3) 82389, in Upper Town serves, well, you know. Tasty Indonesian and some West Indian delicacies are also offered. No credit cards. Inexpensive. **Super Burger,** tel. (599-3) 82142, in Upper town also serves its eponymous dish, with sandwiches and snacks as well. Inexpensive.

GETTING THERE

Winair, tel. (599-3) 82362 or (599-3) 82381, makes at least five daily connections from Sint Maarten, a 20-minute flight, US$31 (about NAF56) one-way. Check with your travel agent about the possibility of ticketing yourself through Sint Maarten and bypassing immigration there; given the large numbers of flights and people that pass through Sint Maarten immigration, you'll save time by avoiding that scene. Sint Maarten is a major entry point from North America and Europe. Winair also makes a 10-minute connection to Statia from St. Kitts.

Departure tax, when departing for places not in the Netherlands Antilles, is US$5 (NAF9). Departure tax to other Netherlands Antilles islands is US$2 (about NAF3.60).

GETTING AROUND

Statia has no more than a dozen taxis, and all can provide an island tour for about US$40 (NAF72). Best thing to do is find one at the airport, and, if you like the driver, make plans for a tour. Negotiate the price.

Hiring a car is the best way to see the island. This can be done in a day or two, depending on your inquisitiveness. The roads are fair, although you'll discover potholes and debris. Cow and goats roam with impunity, and it's better to refrain from a lot of cross-island night driving. Or, just drive slow. All you need is a valid license from home to get a car. Cost averages US$35-40 (NAF63-72) per day. Driving is on the right.

MORE ORANJESTAD RESTAURANTS

NAME	(599-3)	CUISINE	PRICE RANGE
Enriquillo Restaurante	N/A	West Indian/Spanish	moderate
Cool Corner	82523	snack bar	inexpensive
L'Etoile	82299	West Indian/snack bar	inexpensive
Sonny's Place	N/A	snack bar	inexpensive

Note: These restaurants do not take credit cards.

Rental cars available at F.D.R. Airport include **Avis,** tel. (599-3) 8-2421, U.S. tel. (800) 331-1084, the island's major rental agency. **Lady Ama's,** tel. (599-3) 82451, rents jeeps and cars. **Rainbow Rentals,** tel. (599-3) 82586, and **Brown's,** tel. (599-5) 82266, also rent vehicles.

MONEY, HOURS, AND COMMUNICATION

Statia's currency is the Netherlands Antilles florin, or guilder, exchanged at NAF1.80 = US$1. However, U.S. dollars are used widely and frequently. The one bank on the island, **Barclays,** is open Mon.-Fri. 8:30 a.m.-1 p.m., with extra afternoon hours Friday 4-5 p.m.

Businesses are open generally weekdays 8 a.m.-noon and 1-5 p.m. and Saturday 8 a.m.-noon. Most businesses close on Sunday. Some are not open at all on weekends. There is a cruise ship dock just to the south of Lower Town,

---

INFORMATION DIRECTORY

TOURISM

Sint Eustatius Department of Tourism, 3 Fort Oranjestraat, Oranjestad, Sint Eustatius, Netherlands Antilles, tel. (599-3) 82433.

Medhurst & Associates, 271 Main St., Northport, NY 11768, tel. (516) 261-9600, fax 261-9606.

OTHER

Police, tel. (599-3) 82333.

Queen Beatrix Medical Centre, tel. (599-3) 82211.

---

and a shop or two may remain open odd hours to accommodate ship schedules.

To call Statia from North America, dial the international access code "011" plus the country code "599," then "3," then the five-digit number.

BOOKLIST

The recommended readings represent a small portion of a large and fascinating body of work about the Caribbean region and its people. Titles have been briefly annotated.

A good source for new, used, and first edition books about Caribbean issues and by Caribbean writers is West Indies Books Unlimited, P.O. Box 2315, Sarasota, FL 34230, USA, tel. (813) 954-8601.

BIBLIOGRAPHY

Dance, Daryl Cumber, ed. *Fifty Caribbean Writers: A Bio-bibliographical Critical Sourcebook*. Westport, CT: Greenwood Press, 1986. Presents English-language Caribbean writers from 1700 until the 1980s; Spanish, French, Dutch, and writers of other nationalities are not represented.

Desnoes and Edmundo. *Literatures in Transition: The Many Voices of the Caribbean Area*. Minc, Rose S., ed. Gaithersburg, MD: Ediciones Hispamerica, 1983.

Fenwick, M.J. *Writers of the Caribbean and Central America: A Bibliography*. 2 vols. New York: Garland Publishing, 1992. Recent and thorough collection of titles.

Gordon, R. *The Literature of the West Indies*. 20 vols. Gordon Press, 1977. One of the largest critical and bibliographical works in existence.

Miller, E. Willard and Ruby M. Miller, eds. *The Third World - Lesser Antilles: A Bibliography*. Monticello, IL: Vance Bibliographies, 1990. A brief (25 pages), concise list.

BIOGRAPHY

Kennedy, Gavin. *Bligh*. London: Duckworth, 1978. The life and times of Captain William Bligh, adventurer, dispossessed commander of the fated *Bounty*, and transporter of the life-saving breadfruit to the West Indies.

Wilford, John Noble. *The Mysterious History of Columbus: An Exploration of the Man, the Myth, the Legacy*. New York: Alfred A. Knopf, 1991. Treatment of the often harsh, vain, and enigmatic man who, through one of the greatest mistakes ever, brought European involvement to the West Indies and changed the course of world history.

CULTURE AND CUSTOMS

Horowitz, Michael, ed. *Peoples and Cultures of the Caribbean*. Garden City, NJ: Natural History Press, 1971. Some of the observations ring true today in this only slightly historically accurate work.

Kurlansky, Mark. *A Continent of Islands: Searching for the Caribbean Destiny*. Redding, MA: Addison-Wesley, 1992. Well-regarded treatise on the future of the Caribbean states and their cultures.

MacKie, Christine. *Life and Food in the Caribbean*. New York: New Amsterdam Books, 1991. Life, food, and the Caribbean—a winning combination.

Walton, Chelle K. *Caribbean Ways: A Cultural Guide*. Westwood, MA: Riverdale Co., 1993. More than a list of "dos" and "don'ts," the work discusses the background of cultures and customs.

DESCRIPTION AND TRAVEL

Anthony, Michael and Andrew Carr, eds. *David Frost Introduces Trinidad and Tobago.* Deutsch, 1975. Eighteen essays on life and culture in the sister islands.

Bastyra, Judy. *Caribbean Cooking.* New York: Exeter Books, 1987. Recipes, terminology, and background information on the cuisines of the West Indies.

The Cambridge Encyclopedia of Latin America and the Caribbean. 2nd edition. New York: Cambridge University Press, 1992. Essential reference work for Caribbean region aficionados.

Cameron, Sarah and Ben Box, eds. *Caribbean Islands Handbook.* 5th edition. Chicago: Passport Books, 1994. Solidly packed with practical information.

Carrington, Sean. *A-Z of Barbadian Heritage.* London: Heinemann (Caribbean), 1990. Concise, easy-to-read Barbados primer.

Dawood, Richard. *Traveller's Health, How to Stay Healthy Abroad.* London: Oxford University Press, 1992. Vaccinations, common ailments, and everything you wanted to know and worry about while traveling.

Dyde, Brian. *Caribbean Companion, the A to Z Reference.* London: Macmillan, 1992. Mini-encyclopedia; a good, practical guide to Caribbean terms, issues, history, and personalities.

Ellis, G. *Saint Lucia: Helen of the West Indies.* London: Macmillan, 1988. This series tends to present their destinations as undiscovered utopias and can read more like travel brochures than travel guides. Good maps, however, and photos.

Fergus, Howard A. *Montserrat: Emerald Isle of the Caribbean.* London: Macmillan, 1986. Ditto—see above.

Foree, Rebecca, ed. *Caribbean Access.* New York: Access Press, 1992. Good photography but light on practical and background information for Caribbean travelers.

Haberfeld, Caroline, ed. *Fodor's Caribbean.* New York: Fodor's Travel Publications, 1994. Mainstream travel information, accurate and frequently updated.

Honychurch, Lennox. *Dominica: Isle of Adventure.* London: Macmillan, 1991. See description of G. Ellis's Macmillan guide, *Saint Lucia,* above.

Hunte, George. *The West Indian Islands.* New York: Viking, 1972. The author, a former Time/Life writer, is a Barbadian and describes cultures and life in the West Indies as only an insider can.

Jeffrey, Nan. *Best Places to Go, Vol. I.* San Francisco: Foghorn Press, 1993. Highlights of popular vacation spots, with an emphasis on culturally sensitive family travel.

Lanks, Herbert C. *Highway Across the West Indies.* New York: Appleton-Century-Crofts, 1948. A man travels through the West Indies from Cuba to Trinidad by car, a distance of more than 12,000 miles. An interesting and somewhat alarming endeavor.

Rodman, Selden. *The Caribbean.* New York: Hawthorne, 1969. A bit dated, but a good backgrounder on the history and geography of the region.

Schwab, David, ed. *Insight Guide: Caribbean, The Lesser Antilles.* Hong Kong: APA Publications, 1993. Splashy photos, good travel writing, very few practicalities.

Showker, Kay. *One Hundred Best Resorts in the Caribbean.* Old Saybrook, CT: Globe Pequot, 1992. Good journalism for an esoteric guide. If resorts are what you want, this is the book.

Zellers, Margaret. *Fielding's Caribbean.* New York: Morrow, 1991. Chatty, personal, informative guide.

FICTION, POETRY, ESSAYS

Abrahams, Peter. *Lights Out.* New York: Mysterious Press, 1994. A tale of false imprisonment and skullduggery set against a Caribbean backdrop.

Allfrey, Phyllis A. *The Orchid House.* Colorado Springs, CO: Three Continents, 1985. Tale of three sisters growing up in colonial Dominica.

Anderson, John L. *Night of the Silent Drums.* New York: Scribner's, 1975. The story of the 1733 St. John's (now part of the U.S. Virgin Islands) slave rebellion.

Barton, Paule. *The Woe Shirt: Caribbean Folk Tales.* Great Barrington, MA: Penmaen Press, 1980. A collection of regional folk tales from a Haitian goatherd and folklorist.

Bissoondath, Neil. *Digging Up the Mountains.* New York: Viking, 1986. A collection of 14 short stories from a Trinidadian expatriate writer.

Brathwaite, Edward. *The Arrivants, A New World Trilogy.* London: Oxford University Press, 1973. This collection of the lyrical and often stark poetry of the Barbadian writer/university lecturer explores issues in the lives of Africans in the West Indies and the cities of Europe and North America.

Burnett, Paula, ed. *The Penguin Book of Caribbean Verse in English.* New York: Viking Penguin Books, 1986. Writers of and from the Caribbean.

Carpentier, Alejo. *The Harp and the Shadow.* San Francisco: Mercury House, 1990. The Cuban writer's novel of the life and times of Christopher Columbus.

Césaire, Aimé. Eshelman, Clayton and Annette Smith, translators. *The Collected Poetry.* Berkeley, CA: University of California Press, 1983. Poetry from the famous Martiniquean poet, politician, and proponent of the *négritude* movement.

Césaire, Aimé and Charles Calixte. *Poems From Martinique.* Millwood, NY: Kraus, 1952. More collected poems, in English.

Collymore, Frank. *The Man Who Loved Attending Funerals and Other Stories.* 1993. A posthumous collection of short stories from the well-known Barbadian writer who died in 1980.

Cooper, Susan. *Jethro and the Jumbie.* New York: Atheneum, 1979. A children's ghost tale.

Greene, Graham. *The Comedians.* New York: Viking, 1981. Greene's famous novel of the Haiti of notorious dictator Papa Doc.

Joseph, Lynn. *Coconut Kind of Day: Island Poems.* New York: Lothrop, Lee & Shepard Books, 1990. Poetry for young adults.

Joseph, Lynn. *A Wave in Her Pocket; Stories from Trinidad.* New York: Clarion Books, 1991. A collection of short stories from Trinidad.

Kincaid, Jamaica. *Annie John.* New York: Farrar Straus Giroux, 1985. Novel of a young Antiguan girl's life and relationships, particularly with her mother.

Kincaid, Jamaica. *At the Bottom of the River.* New York: Farrar Straus Giroux, 1985. Collected short stories by the Antiguan writer.

Kincaid, Jamaica. *A Small Place.* New York: Farrar Straus Giroux, 1988. Tales of islanders and tourists.

Kincaid, Jamaica. *Lucy.* New York: Farrar Straus Giroux, 1991. Familiar theme for followers of Jamaica Kincaid's work—a young girl's life, loves, and travails in the islands.

Lamming, George. *In the Castle of My Skin.* New York: McGraw-Hill, 1954. The Barbadian writer's first novel, a powerful description of island youth and life in the wake of colonialism and pre-independence social awakening.

Mais, Roger. *Black Lightening.* Portsmouth, NH: Heinemann Ed., 1983. One of the last novels from the Jamaican poet and short-story writer.

Markham, E.A., ed. *Hinterland: Caribbean Poetry from the West Indies and Britain.* Chester Springs, PA: Dufour Editions (Bloodaxe, U.K.), 1990. Collected poetry from Caribbean-based and expatriate writers.

McDonald, Ian and Stuart Brown, eds. *The Heinemann Book of Caribbean Poetry.* Portsmouth, NH: Heinemann Ed., 1992. Text-book treatment of Caribbean poetry.

McKay, Claude. *Banana Bottom.* This out-of-print work by the Jamaican poet was first published in 1933 and is considered by many to be one of the first classic West Indian novels.

Michener, James A. *Caribbean.* New York: Random House, 1989. Michener's epochal and exhausting tale of the settling of the Caribbean from pre-Columbian to modern times.

Murray, John A., ed. *Islands and the Sea: Five Centuries of Nature Writing from the Caribbean.* New York: Oxford University Press, 1991. Collected literature and essays, some turgid and florid, others written by masters.

Naipaul, Shiva. *The Chip-chip Gatherers.* New York: Alfred A. Knopf, 1973. Chips-chips, tiny shellfish, are gathered by inhabitants of a small town in Trinidad; novel of village life, futility, and class.

Naipaul, V.S. *Finding the Center.* New York: Alfred A. Knopf, 1984. Essays by the Trinidadian/British writer, including one concerning his family in Trinidad.

Naipaul, V.S. *A House for Mr. Biswas.* New York: Alfred A. Knopf, 1983. Reprint of Naipaul's classic tale of Trinidadian society and life as seen through the experiences of an East Indian family.

Naipaul, V.S. *The Mystic Masseur.* New York: Viking Penguin, 1964. Comic novel of a failed Trinidadian schoolmaster and writer turned mystic masseur, or healer; Naipaul's first book, published in 1959.

Ramchand, Kenneth, ed. *Best West Indian Stories.* Surrey, U.K.: Nelson Caribbean, 1982. An brief anthology of lesser-known but admirable Caribbean short story writing.

Ramchand, Kenneth. *An Introduction to the Study of West Indian Literature.* Surrey, U.K.: Nelson Caribbean, nd. The writer is an authority on Caribbean literature and lecturer in English at the University of the West Indies.

Ramchand, Kenneth. *West Indian Narrative.* Surrey, U.K.: Nelson Caribbean, 1966. The origins, structures, and rhythms of West Indian writing.

Reid, Victor. *The Leopard.* Madison, NJ: Chatham Bookseller, 1972. Originally published in 1958, the novel of Africa was one of the first that brought Caribbean writing to world attention.

Rhys, Jean. *Wide Sargasso Sea.* New York: Norton, 1967. The novel presents the early life and marriage in the post-Emancipation West Indies of the mysterious madwoman in Charlotte Bronte's *Jane Eyre.*

Saakana, Amon S. *The Colonial Legacy in Caribbean Literature.* Trenton, NJ: Africa World Press, 1988.

Selvon, Samuel. *Brighter Sun.* Chicago: Dearborn Trade, nd. Originally published in 1953, Selvon's tale concerns a 16-year-old Trinidadian bridegroom, Tiger, and Urmilla, his younger bride, as they piece together the puzzle of married life.

Selvon, Samuel. *Turn Again Tiger.* Portsmouth, NH: Heinemann Ed., 1980. Picks up the tale of Tiger, the Trinidadian protagonist of Selvon's novel *Brighter Sun.*

Shacochis, Bob. *Easy in the Islands*. New York: Viking, 1985. Collection of short stories of life in the islands; winner of the American Book Award.

Shacochis, Bob. *Swimming in the Volcano*. New York: Scribners, 1993. Novel of political intrigue, expatriate lust, and life on the fictional island of St. Catherine.

Spillane, Mickey. *The Day the Sea Rolled Back*. New York: Windmill Books, 1979. The master of the potboiler Spillane turns his talents to children's tales in this story of boys lost at sea.

Trillin, Calvin. *Travels With Alice*. New York: Ticknor & Fields, 1989. Collection of travel essays from the quirky humorist, including several that deal with Lesser Antilles islands.

Walcott, Derek. *Collected Poems 1948-1984*. New York: Farrar Straus Giroux, 1986. Important introduction to the Nobel-prizewinning poet and playwright's work.

Walcott, Derek. *Omeros*. New York: Farrar Straus Giroux, 1990. Omeros, Greek for Homer, is one character in this ambitious narrative of exile, spiritual travel, and the redemption of place. Considered by many to be one of Walcott's most important works.

Waugh, Alec. *Hot Countries*. New York: The Literary Guild, 1930. Collection of travel essays.

Waugh, Alec. *Love and the Caribbean: Tales, Characters, and Scenes of the West Indies*. New York: Paragon, 1991. Reissue of classic essays on West Indian life.

HISTORY

Bourne, Edward G. *Spain in America (1450-1580)*. New York and London: Harper & Bros., 1904. History of Spanish influences in North, South, and Central America, as well as the Caribbean.

Burg, B.R. *Sodomy and the Pirate Tradition; English Sea Rovers in the 17th Century Caribbean*. New York: New York University Press, 1984. Male bonding in the pirate tradition reflects the tolerance and attitudes of 17th-century society. Raises questions rarely asked.

Course, A.G. *Pirates of the Western Seas*. London: Muller, 1969. Pirate fun, fact, and fiction.

Cripps, L.L. *The Spanish Caribbean from Columbus to Castro*. Cambridge, MA: Schenkman, 1979. In view of imminent changes in Cuba, parts of the work are outdated, but important nonetheless.

Dunn, Richard S. *Sugar and Slavery: The Rise of the Planter Class in the English West Indies (1624-1738)*. Chapel Hill, N.C.: University of North Carolina Press, 1972. Details the link between slavery and the sugar economy and culture of the West Indies.

Durham, Harriet Frorer. *Caribbean Quakers: History of Quakers in the Caribbean since 1650*. np., 1972. Esoteric but engaging history of the religious group in the tropics.

Friends of English Harbour. *The Romance of English Harbour*. Antigua: The Friends of English Harbour, 1969. History of Antigua's English Harbour, site of the famous Nelson's Dockyard.

Goldberg, Mark H. *Going Bananas: 100 Years of Fruit Ships in the Caribbean*. Kings Point, NY: American Merchant Marine Museum Foundation, 1993. Banana boats also brought the first tourists from North America to the Caribbean.

Gosse, Dr. Philip. *The History of Piracy*. New York: Tudor, 1934. Gosse was considered one of the world's foremost experts on the pirates of the Americas.

Gosse, Dr. Philip. *The Pirate's Who's Who*. London: Dulan, 1924. Biographical sketches of major and minor pirates and adventurers.

Klein, Herbert S. *African Slavery in Latin America and the Caribbean*. New York: Oxford University Press, 1986. Sociological study of slavery in the New World.

Knight, Franklin W. *The Caribbean*. London: Oxford University Press, 1978. Basic introductory history of the region.

Marx, Jenifer. *Pirates and Privateers of the Caribbean*. Malabar, FL: Krieger, 1992. One of the many chronicles of the history of these famed malcontents.

Naipaul, V.S. *The Loss of El Dorado: A History*. New York: Alfred A. Knopf, 1970. Trinidad history from the Spanish exploration to modern society.

Naipaul, V.S. *The Middle Passage; Impressions of Five Societies: British, French, and Dutch in the West Indies and South America*. New York: Macmillan, 1963. Trenchant observations by the essayist/novelist/travel writer.

Parry, J.H. and P.M. Sherlock and Anthony Maingot. *A Short History of the West Indies*. London: Macmillan, 1987. Accessible and concise, this is one of the best histories of its kind.

Pitman, Frank Wesley. *The Development of the British West Indies, 1700-1763*. Hamden, CT: Archon Books, 1967. Follows the history, influences, and consequences of the heyday of British West Indies plantocracy.

Ragarz, Lowell Joseph. *The Fall of the Planter Class in the British Caribbean, 1763-1833*. New York: Octagon Books, 1971. Compelling, if somewhat academic, investigation of the crash of the wealthy British landowner class. Good companion to Richard Dunn's book, above.

Thomas, Gordon and Max Morgan Witts. *The Day the World Ended*. New York: Stein and Day, 1969. The 1902 eruption of Mt. Pelée, at Saint-Pierre, Martinique, was in fact the end of the world for thousands of people. A well-regarded history of an event that changed the history of Martinique.

Van Sertima, Ivan. *They Came Before Columbus: The African Presence in Ancient Ameica*. New York: Random House, 1976. Thought-provoking theories of Africans exploring the New World before Columbus.

Williams, Eric. *From Columbus to Castro: The History of the Caribbean 1492-1969*. New York: Harper and Row (HarperCollins), 1970. Not-so-recent, but well-regarded regional history by the first leader of independent Trinidad.

Williams, Eric. *History of the People of Trinidad and Tobago*. London: Deutsch, 1964. Williams not only wrote this history of the sister islands, he was a major part of it. The work is more than 30 years old, but holds well.

Wright, Irene A. *Early History of Cuba—1492-1586*. New York: Macmillan, 1916. "Somewhat" dated, in light of mid-20th century events.

MUSIC AND ARTS

Burgie, Irving, ed. *Caribbean Carnival: Songs of the West Indies*. New York: Tambourine Books, 1992. Includes music and words.

Ekwene, Laz E.N. *African Sources in New World Black Music*. Toronto, 1972. Traces African influences in black music past and near-present, much of which still holds true today.

Hamelecourt, Juliette. *Caribbean Cookbook*. Melrose Park, IL: Culinary Arts Institute, 1987. Recipes and references.

NATURAL SCIENCES

Allen, Robert Porter. *Birds of the Caribbean*. New York: Viking, 1961 edition. One of the most comprehensive bird guides.

Bond, James. *Birds of the West Indies*. London: Collins, 1960 edition. Author Ian Fleming took the name of this famous naturalist for his super-agent, 007.

Bourne, M.J., G.W Lennox, and S.A. Seddon. *Fruits and Vegetables of the Caribbean*. London: Macmillan, 1988. Short pamphlet describing major Caribbean species, vivid photographs are its best feature.

Greenberg, Idaz, and Jerry Greenberg. *Guide to Corals & Fishes of Florida, the Bahamas* and the Caribbean. Miami: Seahawk Press, 1977. Waterproof book perfect for carrying to the beach, with illustrations of warm-water coral and sealife.

Greenberg, Idaz, and Jerry Greenberg. *Sharks and Other Dangerous Sea Creatures.* Miami: Seahawk Press, 1981. The authors have photographed sharks for the National Geographic Society, and many startling photos appear here. Excellent illustrations and knowledgeable text.

Hargreaves, Dorothy, and Bob Hargreaves. *Tropical Trees.* Lahaina, HI: Ross-Hargreaves, 1965. Picture guide to tropical trees from Hawaii to the Caribbean.

Honychurch, Penelope N. *Caribbean Wild Plants and Their Uses.* London: Macmillan, 1986. Uses of wild plants in island folklore, from medicine to magic, with illustrations by the author.

Kaplan, Eugene. *A Field Guide to the Coral Reefs of the Caribbean and Florida.* Princeton, NJ: Peterson's Guides, 1984. This fact-packed guide covers a wide area and is well-regarded.

Seddon, S.A. and G.W. Lennox. *Trees of the Caribbean.* London: Macmillan, 1987. The roots, so to speak, of Caribbean rainforests, landscapes, and gardens.

Stilling, P.D. *Butterflies and Other Insects of the Eastern Caribbean.* London: Macmillan. Photographs and descriptions of buzzing fauna in the Lesser Antilles.

SOCIAL ISSUES

Abrahams, Roger D. *After Africa.* New Haven: Yale University Press, 1983. Chronicle of Africans as slaves, citizens, and leaders in the West Indies.

Black, George. *The Good Neighbor: How the United States Wrote the History of Central America and the Caribbean.* New York: Pantheon, 1988. Is the Caribbean's Big Neighbor to the north guilty of wanton adventurism or simple benign regional interest? This is one theory.

Davis, Kortright. *Emancipation Still Comin': Explorations in Caribbean Emancipatory Theology.* Maryknoll, NY: Orbis, 1990. The author is an Antiguan priest who offers an insider's look at African and other influences in regional religious thought and practice.

Davison, Robert Barry. *Black British: Immigrants to England.* Boca Raton, FL: Florida Atlantic University Press, 1972. Explores the impact of West Indian emigrants on the society of the United Kingdom.

Ferguson, James. *Far from Paradise, An Introduction to Caribbean Development.* New York: Monthly Review Press (Latin American Bureau, U.K.), 1990. A regional reality check.

Hamshire, Cyril. *The British in the Caribbean.* Cambridge, MA: Harvard University Press, 1972. Historical analysis of the British presence in the Caribbean, to modern times.

Lewis, Gordon K. *Main Currents in Caribbean Thought: The Historical Evolution of Caribbean Society in Its Ideological Aspects.* Baltimore: Johns Hopkins University Press, 1983.

Paget, Henry and Carl Stone, eds. *The Newer Caribbean: Decolonization, Democracy, and Development.* Philadelphia: Institute for the Study of Human Issues, 1983. Some island situations have changed since 1983, but issues raised in this work ring true today.

Patterson, Orlando. *Sociology of Slavery.* London: 1967. Slavery was the beast that pulled the West Indies economic cart, and its resultant race and class problems are alive today.

Perkins, Whitney T. *Constraint of Empire: The United States and Caribbean Interventions.* Westport, CT: Greenwood, 1981. A history of

U.S. interventions, political and otherwise, in the Greater Antilles.

Thomas, Clive Y. *The Poor and the Powerless, Economic Policy and Change in the Caribbean.* New York: Monthly Review Press (Latin American Bureau, U.K.), 1988. Investigates some of the disturbing causes of trouble in paradise.

Vallette, Jim, and Heather Spalding, eds. *The International Trade in Wastes; A Greenpeace Inventory.* 5th edition. Washington, D.C.: Greenpeace, 1990. An alarming expose on the trade of simple rubbish and toxic waste among countries worldwide.

PERIODICALS

The Affordable Caribbean. 8403 Colesville Rd., Suite 830, Silver Spring, MD 20910. Published as an adjunct of Caribbean Travel and Life magazine, this newsletter lists value-oriented travel destinations throughout the region.

Caribbean Newsletter. Friends of Democracy, Box 8838, Kingston C.S.O., Jamaica, W.I. A 12-page newsletter covering current and controversial Caribbean issues.

Caribbean Travel and Life. Box 6229, Syracuse, NY 13217-7921. A bimonthly glossy magazine devoted solely to travel in the Caribbean.

Caribbean Week. Lefferts Place, River Rd., St. Michael, Barbados, W.I. Monthly newspaper covering Caribbean issues.

Condé Nast Traveler. Box 57018, Boulder, CO 80322. Another glossy monthly, featuring fairly candid reporting and very good photography.

Consumer Reports Travel Letter. Box 53629, Boulder, CO 80322-3629. Unbiased travel reportage, covering the world. The monthly report is not inexpensive (more than US$35/year), but it is highly regarded for honest, nuts and bolts reporting.

GLOSSARY

agouti—small guinea-pig-like rodent indigenous to the Caribbean and South and Central America, once widely used as a food source, now depleted in number

Anansi (also Anancy, Ananci)—chief character, usually a spider, of West Indian folk tales, thought to have originated in West African traditional stories

Angostura Bitters—a tonic made from the bark of the tree native to South America and the West Indies, used in flavoring drinks and as a febrifuge (to reduce fever). Since the mid-19th century, the tonic has been manufactured in Trinidad.

Antilles—the islands of the West Indies, including the Greater and Lesser Antilles, but excluding the Bahamas and Turks and Caicos

Arawak—refers to several Amerindian groups from South America, the first known inhabitants of many Lesser Antilles islands. No ethnic Arawaks remain in the Caribbean.

archipelago—a group of islands

arrowroot—starchy flour made from the roots of the plant of the same name; in the Caribbean, the species is *Maranta arudinacea* and is used in baking and other foods. Arawaks were said to have used it to draw poison from wounds of poisoned arrows, hence the name.

asiento—"contract" in Spanish; at the end of the War of Spanish Succession in 1713, England was awarded France's Asiento for supplying slaves to Spain's Caribbean possessions

Babylon—in Rastafarian creed, non-believers and institutions that obstruct or simply are not of the faith

Bajan—colloquial term for Barbadian

balm—from the English balm, also from the Twi *abam*, or name of a fetish, it refers to natural folk-medicine herb treatments administered by balmists

bamboo—a member of the grass family originating in the Far East. The fast-growing plant is resilient, prolific, and has had myriad uses in Lesser Antilles life.

bananaquit—ubiquitous yellow-breasted, dark-plumaged Lesser Antilles humming-bird of the tiny Honeycreeper family

bay rum (also bay rhum)—fragrant spirits, used in cosmetics and some folk medicines, made from distilled rum and the leaves of the West Indian bayberry

beguine—energetic dance form popular in the French Antilles, resembles the rumba

Big Drum—drumming and dancing festival with African origins surviving, in its purest form, on the Grenadines island of Carriacou

Bim—the literary magazine of Barbados and the Caribbean, now published irregularly, founded in 1942 by poet Frank Collymore; nickname for a native of Barbados

Black Caribs—name used for the descendants of intermarried Caribs and escaped slaves in 18th-century St. Vincent

breadfruit—imported to the West Indies from Polynesia in 1793 by Captain William Bligh. The starchy fruit helped overcome food shortages among slave populations and today remains a popular food source.

British West Indies—Inclusive term once used to refer to British possessions in the West Indies, which, at one time, were the Bahamas, Jamaica, Cayman Islands, Turks and Caicos Islands, Leeward Islands, Windward Islands, Barbados, and Trinidad and Tobago; today the term is rarely used.

buccaneers—bands of thieves, pirates, and adventurers nominally employed by various European governments to harass Spanish possessions and ships throughout the Caribbean during the 17th and 18th centuries. The name comes from the French *boucan*, referring to wooden racks upon which meat was dried.

bulla—small, hard, flat sweetcake made with molasses and ginger

BWIA—British West Indian Airlines International, a regional and international airline based in Trinidad

calabash—tree native to South and Central America that produces a gourd used for food storage and as an eating utensil

callaloo (also calulu, kallaloo)—green, spinach-like vegetable used in, among other foods, the Caribbean's famous pepperpot soup

calypso—popular West Indian music form originating in Trinidad, in its original form thought to have been a type of rebellious call-and-response song originating in the slave fields. The name itself is a source of debate, but many believe it has its roots in *kaiso*, derived from a West African word meaning "well done." Today the stream-of-consciousness lyrics laced with political commentary and ribald sexual innuendo have spawned aficionados throughout the Caribbean and the world.

Canboulay—antecedent of Trinidad's Carnival celebration. The ceremony takes its name from the French *cannes brûlées*, for burned cane, and is a music- and dance-filled harvest celebration

Carib—Refers to the peripatetic and bellicose Amerindian group that conquered and inhabited many of the West Indian islands before Columbus's arrival. So fierce were Carib warriors that today's English term "cannibal" is probably derived from the Spanish word for them, *caribal*, for "savage." The few ethnic Caribs left in the Caribbean are found on Dominica and St. Vincent.

Caribbean—In popular usage, the land areas touched by the Caribbean Sea as well as the Bahamas, Turks and Caicos, and Barbados. The term also refers, rightly, to the north coast of South America and the coastal regions of Central America.

Caribbean Sea—one-million-square-mile body of water encompassed by the Greater and Lesser Antilles islands in the north and east, the South American coast in the southeast, and Central America to the west

Caribbee (Caribbees, Caribbee Islands, Caribbee Sea)—popular 17th-century name for the Caribbean region

CARICOM—Caribbean Community and Common Market, a collective regional organization that promotes trade and services within the region and abroad

Carnival (also Carnaval, Vaval)—The popular festival originated with French Catholic pre-Lenten extravaganzas, now expanded throughout the Caribbean to include festivals called by different names and held at times other than prior to Lent (a pre-Easter religious observance). Some elements of Carnival remain the same, no matter where they are held: Calypso and soca competitions, masquerade parades, street dancing, feasts, and private fetes are the mainstays. Trinidad's Carnival, held in Port of Spain, is famous throughout the world.

cassava—starchy tropical root crop of the manioc family used to make fried cakes and other foods

cay—bank, reef of sand, or small island, from the Spanish word *cayo*, or "shoal" (pronounced "KAY" or "KIE")

CDB—Caribbean Development Bank

Ciboney (also Siboney)—the first reputed inhabitants of the West Indies islands, a prehistoric people who left scarce but significant evidence of their existence

CITES—Convention on International Trade in Endangered Species

cocoa—the tree from which the cocoa bean is cultivated

coolie—deprecatory reference to a person of East Indian ancestry

coral—calcified skeletons of tiny marine animals called polyps, which often grow as colonies into larger structures along ocean reefs

crapaud—"mountain chicken," an enormous frog related to the South American Bullfrog and found on several of the Lesser Antilles islands, the legs of which are considered a delicacy

Creole—a person of European blood born in the West Indies. The term also refers to mixed-race persons, languages spoken, Caribbean cooking, or, in general, blending of cultures in certain areas, particularly Spanish America, Louisiana, and the U.S. Gulf of Mexico states. In the Lesser Antilles, the reference is most popular in the French islands.

Crop Over—Barbadian festival, stemming from the days of sugarcane harvest, now similar to Carnival

CTO—Caribbean Tourism Organization

dasheen—also called *eddoe,* a starchy tuber native to West Africa now grown throughout the West Indies, the leaves of which are used in various soups and stews

départements d'outre-mer—overseas departments of France, referring to, in the Lesser Antilles, Guadeloupe (which includes in its sphere Saint-Martin, Saint-Barthélémy, Marie-Galante, Les Saintes, La Désirade, and several smaller island off the southern Guadeloupe coast) and Martinique

dread—shortened from the term "dreadlocks," referring to a Rastafarian or person wearing their hair in the Rastafarian style

duppy—spirit of the dead, believed to be on earth to influence lives of the living, therefore figuring prominently in folk tales and obeah or other ritualistic practices

eddoe—see *"dasheen,"* above

El Dorado—the mythical and elusive place, said to contain vast amounts of gold, that was the object of Spanish exploration in the West Indies during the 16th and 17th centuries

endemic—restricted or unique to a particular area

escoveitch—Spanish method of cooking fish with vinegar and other spices

Federation of the West Indies—collective term used to describe what was, in effect, a country created in 1958 comprising the British colonies of Jamaica, St. Kitts-Nevis-Anguilla, Antigua and Barbuda, Montserrat, Dominica, St. Lucia, St. Vincent and the Grenadines, Barbados, Grenada, and Trinidad and Tobago. Its collapse in 1961, due to disagreements between, primarily, Jamaica and Trinidad and Tobago, hastened independence for many British possessions in the region.

fer-de-lance—venomous snake found in St. Lucia and Martinique

festival—cornmeal sweet cake commonly served with fried fish or seafood

fig banana—species of small, sweet banana

"free colored"—term used to describe former slaves or persons of mixed race who had been given freedom, or bought their freedom, from slavery

fungi—popular music form in the Virgin Islands with bands consisting of guitars, bass and drums, and bamboo instruments

ganja—East Indian word for marijuana, which was imported to the West Indies during the influx of indentured laborers to the British West Indies after the abolition of slavery

gecko—a small insect-eating lizard known for its ability to walk upside-down utilizing small adhesive pads on its toes

ghut (also *gut, ghaut*)—a dried river bed

ginger—The plant is native to Asia, but the spice is widely cultivated in the West Indies and used in a variety of ways, from flavoring—the strong ginger beer is a good example—to medicine.

goombay (also *gombay, gombah*)—drum made from wood and covered with animal skin, often used in religious ceremonies; also the rhythm of the drum

greathouse—refers to the large and sometimes elegant home of the plantation owner or overseer of 17th and 18th century sugar plantations in the British West Indies. Many of these houses remain standing, some dilapidated and others well kept, and are used as private residences, hotels, and bed and breakfasts.

guava—small tropical tree which produces a gritty, succulent fruit that is eaten fresh or used to make jelly or nectar

guinep (also *genip*)—small green fruit that grows in clusters on a tree, thought to be native to Surinam, but now seen throughout the islands

gungo **peas**—popular pea found in traditional dishes such as rice and peas; also known as congo or pigeon peas

hibiscus—a genus of shrubs that produce highly colorful, full-bodied ornamental flowers, native to tropical areas, thought to have originated in China

hurricane—A large, swirling high-pressure storm that revolves around a placid, low-pressure center, or eye. Caribbean hurricanes, known as cyclones or typhoons in other parts of the world, often originate off the west coast of Africa and travel west, generating destructive winds of 100 miles per hour or more. The word is thought to have derived from the language of the Tainos, a subgroup of the Amerindian Arawaks.

iguana—large, herbivorous, tropical lizard, extinct on many islands due to hunting for its prized flesh and to the introduction of the mongoose (name derivation is Spanish, from the Carib language)

indigenous—originating in the locality; not imported

Irish moss (also sea moss)—gelatinous drink prepared from edible seaweed, sometimes combined with milk or rum or various combinations, considered health food

jackfruit—a relative of breadfruit, originating in India, that produces a yellowish, edible fruit and seeds that resemble chestnuts

jerk meat—a method of seasoning meat, usually chicken, pork, or fish, with a multi-spice mixture heavy on pimento and roasting slowly it over a wood fire. The method originated with the Maroons of Jamaica, when cooking and preserving pork was a method of survival.

Jonkanoo (also Jonkonnu, Jonkunnu, John Canoe)—post-Christmas festival originating during slavery days, when groups of masqueraders dressed as animals, kings, and other mythical and comical figures parade through the streets of towns and villages. The festival is practiced primarily in Jamaica and the Bahamas.

J'Ouvert (also Jour Ouvert, J'Ouverte, Jouvay—from the French *le jour est ouvert,* pronounced "JOO-vay," referring to sunrise. In many of the islands, particularly those with French ties, it is the name given to Carnival Monday, the start of the two days of festivities before Ash Wednesday.

jumby (also *jumbi*)—spirit, often of a family member, that directly affects the events of the living in either a benign or injurious manner. The existence of jumbies is widely accepted throughout the West Indies, and many children are given the names of spirits, a jumby name, to curry favor with the entity.

June plum (also jew plum)—a large plum, introduced from the South Pacific, eaten raw or stewed in desserts

kaiso—the apparent root of the word "calypso," referring to a West African language term for "well done" (see Calypso, above)

leeward—the direction of the sheltered side, opposite to that against which the wind blows, called the "windward" side

Leeward Islands—Some confusion exists as to which islands are considered the Leewards. This has much to do with archaic political designations such as the old British Colony of the Leeward Islands, a group of British colonies administered from Barbados during the late 17th century. The designation also depends on the nationality of the designator—the French, for instance, do not use the term. Most often, however, the Leewards are today considered to be Anguilla, Saint-Martin/Sint Maarten, Saba, Sint Eustatius, Saint-Barthélémy, St. Kitts and Nevis, Antigua and Barbuda, Montserrat, Guadeloupe, and their dependencies.

LIAT—Leeward Islands Air Transport, a large regional carrier jointly owned by several island nations and based in Antigua

lignum vitae—"the tree of life," a tall tropical tree native to the Caribbean that has wood so dense and strong it sinks in water and has been used as ship's propeller shaft bearings

lime—as well as the tropical fruit, a verb used to describe the singular West Indian activity of sitting, talking, drinking, chatting, and passing some time—loosely, to hang out

mace—spice produced from the outer covering of the nutmeg seed

madras—brightly colored, checkered cotton cloth known worldwide that has become integral to the national dress of Martinique, Guadeloupe, and Dominica

manatee—large, herbivorous marine mammal, also called sea cow or dugong, threatened with extinction. Columbus's crew is rumored to have seen the animals and, remarkably, mistaken them for mermaids.

mangrove—genus of tropical trees and shrubs growing in swamps and marsh land which, when left unchecked, will create new land masses by trapping soil between its roots, eventually building it above the water line

manicou—an opossum-like rodent common to the rainforests and semi-rainforests of the Lesser Antilles.

Mas' (also "De Mas'")—shorthand for Masquerade, a popular Carnival activity; also refers to Carnival itself

mauby (also *mawby*)—sometimes bitter health drink made from the bark of a tree, said to be particularly useful in restoring energy to pregnant women and sexually nonenergetic men

mento—popular folk and dance music, antecedent to the Jamaican ska and reggae, nowadays performed by specialists at cultural events

Mocko Jumby (also Mokajumby, Mokajumbie)—stock character in Carnival masquerades and other festivals, seen with exaggerated headgear and high stilts

mongoose—small carnivorous mammal resembling a weasel, first introduced to the islands to help control rat damage in sugarcane fields. The mongoose, a relentless breeder, has since become a nuisance and contributed to destruction on farms and the near-extinction of the iguana on several islands.

naseberry—Known as sapodilla elsewhere, the sweet, pulpy fruit grows on a low bush and is popular throughout the islands.

New Jewel Movement—"Jewel" is for Joint Endeavor for Welfare, Education, and Liberation. The political movement inspired the 1979 coup in Grenada that installed Prime Minister Maurice Bishop, a lawyer, as the leader of the Marxist People's Revolutionary Government. Bishop was murdered in 1983 by rival factions within the group, an act that moved the U.S. President Ronald Reagan and several Caribbean nations to send troops to the island to restore order.

négritude—The term, attributed to the Martiniquan poet, playwright, and politician Aimé Césaire, describes a Paris-based literary movement of the 1930s. *Négritude* called for the recognition and advancement of black cultural values and black heritage worldwide—black humanism—and further rejected French colonial influences in the Lesser Antilles and throughout the world.

nutmeg—The spice, native to Indonesia, was brought to the West Indies in the mid-19th century and is grown commercially on Grenada, which produces nearly half the world's supply.

obeah—Also called "black magic" and "blackheart," the cult is based on the manipulation of herbs, *duppies,* and quasi-religious practices, and, though it enjoys widespread acceptance, its practice is illegal on most islands

OECS—Organization of Eastern Caribbean States, a regional organization created to promote similar interests in economic and foreign affairs. The members are St. Kitts and Nevis, Antigua and Barbuda, Montserrat, Dominica, St. Lucia, St. Vincent and the Grenadines, and Grenada. Anguilla is an associated state. The member nations use the Eastern Caribbean Dollar as their currency.

opia—in Arawak culture, a spirit of the dead

otaheite apple—Brought over by Captain Willaim Bligh in the same cargo in which breadfruit arrived, the otaheite apple tree produces both striking blooms and succulent fruit.

PADI—Professional Association of Dive Instructors

pan (also "steel pan")—The dented, grooved, and tuned tops of oil drums that later became the instruments of the steel bands of Trinidad and, now, the rest of the world. Trinidadians today claim that the pan is the only musical instrument to have been invented in this century.

Papiamento—a language spoken in the Dutch islands, based on an amalgam of Spanish, Dutch, English, Portuguese, and various African and Amerindian languages

parang—music form heard most often in Trinidad at pre-Christmas festivals, sung in Spanish and incorporating guitars, mandolins, and tambourines

Patois—a language taking different forms on, primarily, the English-speaking islands, incorporating English, some African and Amerindian words, and various European languages; the generic term for dialects of English in the West Indies

pawpaw (also "papaya")—tree common to tropical areas that produces a large orange or yellow fruit high in vitamins and *papain,* an enzyme that is particularly useful as a meat tenderizer

pear—avocado, also called avocado pear

pepperpot—traditional soup made with callaloo and other greens, beef or pork, and spices

pimento—island spice indigenous to Jamaica, combining the flavors of pepper, nutmeg, clove, and cinnamon, marketed as allspice in other parts of the world

pineapple—Introduced from South America, the fruit became so successful it was exported to Hawaii, which is now the world's leading producer.

plantain—looks like a large banana, but is not exactly. It must be cooked prior to consumption.

poinciana—a large flowering tree that produces bright red or orange blossoms in December, hence its common names Christmas Tree or flamboyant

quadrille—traditional European dance that, in the West Indies, combines with African influences and is widely seen today at cultural festivals

Rastafarianism—A religio-cultural group with members called Rastas or Rastafarians, whose tenets are based on the belief that Ethiopian Emperor Haile Selassie was the reborn savior, and who believe that redemption will occur through repatriation to Africa. The movement originated in the 1930s, partly springing from the teachings of Jamaican black nationalist Marcus Garvey. Rastafarianism enjoys great influence in Caribbean cultures today.

reggae—widely appreciated Jamaican music form, characterized by choppy rhythms, lilting melody, and somewhat politicized lyrics, often associated with Rastafarianism, and popularized by Bob Marley and The Wailers

Revivalism—compendium of syncretic religious cults, blending large doses of African, European, and Jamaican influences

rhumba box (also "rumba")—the box is a musical instrument constructed with metal strips over a hollowed core, which provide bass rhythm for string bands

rock-steady—musical form considered to be the precursor of reggae, and credited with originating the bass beat that reggae adopted

roti—East Indian flat bread, popularly served with curry dishes

rum—Liquor derived from sugarcane, originally developed on a wide scale in Barbados and originally called "rumbullion" for its propensity to inspire reckless behavior in imbibers. Rum is *the* drink of the Lesser Antilles and is used socially and ceremonially, for example, in obeah rituals.

salt fish—salted cod

sea grape—shrub found near coastal regions that produces a grape-size, sweet fruit

Shango—syncretic cult found in Trinidad that combines aspects of animism and African beliefs with Christian tenets

Siboney—see "Ciboney"

sisserou—the large imperial parrot, endemic to Dominica

ska—onomatopoeic name of Jamaican music popular in 1950s and 1960s, a hybrid of U.S. R&B and lush, jazz-oriented horn arrangements, named after the scratch sound of the rhythm guitar

soca—a form of calypso music, popular throughout the islands. The word comes from the combination of "soul" and "calypso," and the form is derived from the marriage of calypso with an American rhythm and blues backbeat. Soca originated with a younger generation of calypsonians who were exposed to R&B.

sorrel—plant native to temperate regions that produces sour juice which, in the West Indies, is spiced and sugared to create a popular Christmas drink

souse—popular island dish that combines pig's head with lime juice, vegetables, and spices

soursop—The tree, native to the tropics, produces a large, green, rough-skinned fruit that yields white, pulpy flesh that is sweet, not sour.

steel band—band utilizing pans, or steel drums

sugarcane—the West Indies' most widely successful cash crop, a grass, responsible for the colonization of the islands and introduction of slave labor large plantations

sweetsop—a tree that produces a fruit similar to, but smaller than, soursop (see above), also called the sugar apple

syncretic—syncretistic; conciliation of several often disparate concepts, particularly in religion, to form an amalgamated belief

Taino—Amerindian Arawak subgroup that inhabited, primarily, the Greater Antilles at the time of Columbus's arrival

tamarind—tropical tree which bears the pod from which acidic, sour fruit is eaten and a relish-like syrup is made

tinpanny—steel band (see above)

Tortuga—island off the coast of Hispaniola, infamous during the 17th century as a buccaneer and pirate lair

ugli—self-descriptive name of a hybrid citrus fruit, a cross between a grapefruit and tangerine, discovered and developed in Jamaica in the early 1900s and now seen throughout the West Indies

UWI—University of the West Indies, a regional institution established in 1948 and headquartered at Mona, Kingston, Jamaica. UWI branches are found throughout the English-speaking Lesser Antilles.

West Indies—When Columbus sighted land in the New World, he began a chain of events that eventually saw the term West Indies tagged to the region. The West Indies is an archipelago some 1,500 miles in length, comprising the Greater and Lesser Antilles and the Bahamas and Turks and Caicos, that roughly divides the Atlantic Ocean and the Caribbean Sea.

Winair—Windward Islands Airways, a regional airline based in Sint Maarten

windward—the side facing the prevailing winds, as opposed to "leeward" side

Windward Islands—locative term used to describe a group of islands in the southern Lesser Antilles, comprising Dominica, Martinique, St. Lucia, St. Vincent and the Grenadines, Grenada, and adjacent islands

yabba—large earthenware bowl used to carry water and food, of African origin

yam—starchy tuber of a plant native to tropical areas

yard—reference to slum dwelling; tenement

yuca—cassava; the starchy tropical root crop that was the staple of the Arawaks and remains popular today

zemi—Arawak stone idol in which the personal spirit of the owner was believed to dwell

Zion—in Rastafarian parlance, the homeland, usually in reference to Africa; Ethiopia; heaven, utopia

zouk—lush music and sensual dance form popular in the French Antilles

INDEX

Page numbers in **boldface** indicate the primary reference. *Italicized* page numbers refer to information in captions, charts, maps, or special topics.

MOON
TRAVEL HANDBOOKS
THE IDEAL TRAVELING COMPANIONS

Moon Travel Handbooks provide focused, comprehensive coverage of distinct destinations all over the world. Our goal is to give travelers all the background and practical information they'll need for an extraordinary, unexpected travel experience.

Every Handbook begins with an in-depth essay about the land, the people, their history, art, politics, and social concerns—an entire bookcase of cultural insight and introductory information in one portable volume. We also provide accurate, up-to-date coverage of all the practicalities: language, currency, transportation, accommodations, food, and entertainment. And Moon's maps are legendary, covering not only cities and highways, but parks and trails that are often difficult to find in other sources.

Below are highlights of Moon's Central America and the Caribbean Travel Handbook series. Our complete list of Handbooks covering North America and Hawaii, Mexico, Central America and the Caribbean, and Asia and the Pacific, are listed on the order form on the accompanying pages. To purchase Moon Travel Handbooks, please check your local bookstore or order by phone: (800) 345-5473 Monday-Friday 8 a.m.-5 p.m. PST.

MOON OVER CENTRAL AMERICA
CENTRAL AMERICAN AND THE CARIBBEAN
TRAVEL HANDBOOK SERIES

> "Solidly packed with practical information and full of significant cultural asides that will enlighten you on the whys and wherefores of things you might easily see but not easily grasp."
>
> *—Boston Globe*

BELIZE HANDBOOK by Chicki Mallan, 300 pages, **$14.95**
"Indispensable for those wanting to explore the Mayan ruins and other attractions of the interior." *—Islands Magazine*

CARIBBEAN HANDBOOK by Karl Luntta, 384 pages, **$16.95**
Famous for white beaches and crystal water, the islands of the Caribbean include such popular tourist destinations as the Virgin Islands, Barbados, and Guadeloupe. Author Karl Luntta covers these well-known spots, along with many not-so-famous island get-aways in *Caribbean Handbook*. Travelers may choose among 38 Caribbean islands, including the volcanic craters of Montserrat, Saba's scuba diving, and the tropical rainforest of Sint Eustatius.

COSTA RICA HANDBOOK
by Christopher P. Baker, 574 pages, **$18.95**
"There are numerous Costa Rica books on the market; but if only one comprehensive guide were to be chosen, this compact and thick paperback should be the item." —*Reviewer's Bookwatch*

JAMAICA HANDBOOK by Karl Luntta, 228 pages, **$14.95**
"Positively—without a doubt—the best guide book on Jamaica for the independent traveler. No other guide even comes close."
—*The Shoestring Traveler*

STAYING HEALTHY IN ASIA, AFRICA, AND LATIN AMERICA
by Dirk G. Schroeder, ScD, MPH, 200 pages, **$11.95**
"Your family doctor will not be able to supply you with this valuable information because he doesn't have it." —*Whole Earth Catalog*

"Read this book if you want to stay healthy on any journeys or stays in Asia, Africa, and Latin America"
—*American Journal of Health Promotion*

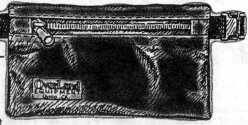

MOONBELT

A new concept in moneybelts. Made of heavy-duty Cordura nylon, the Moonbelt offers maximum protection for your money and important papers. This pouch, designed for all-weather comfort, slips under your shirt or waistband, rendering it virtually undetectable and inaccessible to pickpockets. It features a one-inch high-test quick-release buckle so there's no more fumbling around for the strap or repeated adjustments. This handy plastic buckle opens and closes with a touch, but won't come undone until you want it to. Moonbelts accommodate traveler's checks, passports, cash, photos, etc. Size 5 x 9 inches. Available in black only. **$8.95**

TRAVEL MATTERS

Travel Matters is Moon Publications' free quarterly newsletter, loaded with specially commissioned travel articles and essays that tell it like it is. Recent issues have been devoted to Asia, Mexico, and North America, and every issue includes:

Feature Stories: Travel writing unlike what you'll find in your local newspaper. Andrew Coe on Mexican professional wrestling, Michael Buckley on the craze for wartime souvenirs in Vietnam, Kim Weir on the Nixon Museum in Yorba Linda.

Transportation: Tips on how to get around. Rick Steves on a new type of Eurail pass, Victor Chan on hiking in Tibet, Joe Cummings on how to be a Baja road warrior.

Health Matters: Articles on the most recent findings by Dr. Dirk Schroeder, author of *Staying Healthy in Asia, Africa, and Latin America.* Japanese encephalitis, malaria, the southwest U.S. "mystery disease" . . . forewarned is forearmed.

Book Reviews: Informed assessments of the latest travel titles and series. The Rough Guide to *World Music,* Let's Go vs. Berkeley, Dorling Kindersley vs. Knopf.

The Internet: News from the cutting edge. The Great Burma Debate in rec.travel.asia, hotlists of the best WWW sites, updates on Moon's massive "Road Trip USA" exhibit.

TRAVEL MATTERS

MOON PUBLICATIONS

ISSUE 12   FOCUS ON U.S.A.   SPRING 1995

BLACKJACK, BLUES, AND BALES OF COTTON
Travels and Tangents in the New Mississippi Delta
by Jeff Perk

At night, the first you see of Tunica, Mississippi are the searchlights. Coming down Highway 61 from Memphis, or west on Route 304 from the Interstate, you see the swirling circles of light against low clouds, long white beams cutting through the humid night air, clearly visible even through the spattering rain of bugs against your windshield. All around in the darkness is a rural landscape of farms, fields, and wood lots: the Mississippi Delta.

Technically speaking, the Delta begins around Cairo, Illinois, a full thousand river miles from the Gulf, but nobody pays attention to technicalities here. The Delta, as cotton historian David Cohn wrote, "begins in the lobby of the Peabody Hotel in Memphis and ends on Catfish Row in Vicksburg." The Delta is history and culture, as deep and fertile as the alluvial soil. The Delta is a century of King Cotton, from which a few reaped enormous wealth while everyone else was yoked with backbreaking labor. The Delta is field hands tilling and picking and praying and creating a musical tradition of hymns and hollers that begat blues, jazz, country, gospel and even, eventually, that hip-slinging white boy who rolled it all together, Elvis Aaron Presley.

The Delta is the memory of slavery and secession and a chorus of ghosts as poignant and garrulous as they ever were alive, for here in the Delta, the dead aren't allowed to rest: Robert Johnson, Tennessee Williams, and old Sam Grant (General Ulysses S. to you) still exist in the present tense, as if they just stepped out for a drink or piss and might yet return. Past and present are swirled together like the bourbon and water in a frosty mint julep: you might be able to tell 'em apart to start, but after a few swigs, why try?

This, then, is the countryside through which you drive: old skeletons rattling around, fat brown moths stabbing your radiator, loose tufts of white cotton swirling beside the road in your wake, and, up ahead, dancing white beams of light. Lights that promise a dramatic change for the Delta, on par with Grant's armies, the Corps of Engineers, or the mechanized cotton harvester. Because behind those lights is money—lots of money, all just itching to build as much tackiness as traffic will bear.

Welcome to the new Delta: the land that gave us the blues now gives us blackjack, progressive slots, and lounge entertainers like Gary Puckett and Suzanne Somers. The land that exhausted the mule of many a poor sharecropper, that filled the inkwell of Faulkner's pen, now clamors to the sound of quarters dropping in slot trays and cards slapping felt. The change is dizzying: two-lane farm roads being turned into four-lane highways, mini-marts and motels and an endless parade of casino billboards sprouting like kudzu. Stand still and you're likely to be paved over.

Tunica County in the northwest corner of Mississippi is the scene of greatest transformation, but it isn't the only game along Old Man River. There are riverboat casinos up and down the Mississippi, from

continued on page 3

There are also booklists, Letters to the Editor, and anything else we can find to interest our readers, as well as Moon's latest titles and ordering information for other travel products, including Periplus Travel Maps to Southeast Asia.

To receive a free subscription to *Travel Matters,*

call—(800) 345-5473

write—Moon Publications
P.O. Box 3040
Chico, CA 95927-3040,

e-mail—travel@moon.com

Please note: subscribers who live outside the United States will be charged $7.00 per year for shipping and handling.

MOON TRAVEL HANDBOOKS

CENTRAL AMERICA AND THE CARIBBEAN
Belize Handbook (0307). $14.95
Caribbean Handbook (0277) $16.95
Costa Rica Handbook (0358). $18.95
Jamaica Handbook (0129) $14.95

MEXICO
Baja Handbook (0528). $15.95
Cabo Handbook (0285) $14.95
Cancún Handbook (0501). $13.95
Central Mexico Handbook (0234) $15.95
*Mexico Handbook (0315) $21.95
Northern Mexico Handbook (0226) $16.95
Pacific Mexico Handbook (0323) $16.95
Puerto Vallarta Handbook (0250) $14.95
Yucatán Peninsula Handbook (0242). $15.95

NORTH AMERICA AND HAWAII
Alaska-Yukon Handbook (0161). $14.95
Alberta and the Northwest Territories Handbook (0676) . . . $17.95
Arizona Traveler's Handbook (0536) $16.95
Atlantic Canada Handbook (0072) $17.95
Big Island of Hawaii Handbook (0064) $13.95
British Columbia Handbook (0145) $15.95
Catalina Island Handbook (3751) $10.95
Colorado Handbook (0137). $17.95
Georgia Handbook (0609) $16.95
Hawaii Handbook (0005) $19.95
Honolulu-Waikiki Handbook (0587). $14.95
Idaho Handbook (0617). $14.95
Kauai Handbook (0013). $13.95
Maui Handbook (0579) $14.95
Montana Handbook (0544) $15.95
Nevada Handbook (0641). $16.95
New Mexico Handbook (0153). $14.95
Northern California Handbook (3840) $19.95
Oregon Handbook (0102). $16.95
Texas Handbook (0633). $16.95

Utah Handbook (0684) $16.95
Washington Handbook (0552) $15.95
Wyoming Handbook (3980) $14.95

ASIA AND THE PACIFIC
Bali Handbook (3379) $12.95
Bangkok Handbook (0595) $13.95
Fiji Islands Handbook (0382) $13.95
Hong Kong Handbook (0560) $15.95
Indonesia Handbook (0625) $25.00
Japan Handbook (3700) $22.50
Micronesia Handbook (3808) $11.95
Nepal Handbook (3646) $12.95
New Zealand Handbook (3883) $18.95
Outback Australia Handbook (3794) $15.95
Philippines Handbook (0048) $17.95
Southeast Asia Handbook (0021) $21.95
South Pacific Handbook (3999) $19.95
Tahiti-Polynesia Handbook (0374) $13.95
Thailand Handbook (3824) $16.95
Tibet Handbook (3905) $30.00
*Vietnam, Cambodia & Laos Handbook (0293) $18.95

INTERNATIONAL
Egypt Handbook (3891) $18.95
Moon Handbook (0668) $10.00
Moscow-St. Petersburg Handbook (3913) $13.95
Staying Healthy in Asia, Africa, and Latin America (0269) . . $11.95

* New title, please call for availability

PERIPLUS TRAVEL MAPS
All maps $7.95 each

Bali	Hong Kong	Penang
Bandung/W. Java	Jakarta	Phuket/S. Thailand
Bangkok/C. Thailand	Java	Sarawak
Batam/Bintan	Ko Samui/S. Thailand	Singapore
Cambodia	Kuala Lumpur	Vietnam
Chiangmai/N. Thailand	Lombok	Yogyakarta/C. Java

WHERE TO BUY MOON TRAVEL HANDBOOKS

BOOKSTORES AND LIBRARIES: Moon Travel Handbooks are sold worldwide. Please write to our sales manager for a list of wholesalers and distributors in your area.

TRAVELERS: We would like to have Moon Travel Handbooks available throughout the world. Please ask your bookstore to write or call us for ordering information. If your bookstore will not order our guides for you, please contact us for a free title listing.

Moon Publications, Inc.
P.O. Box 3040
Chico, CA 95927-3040 U.S.A.
Tel.: (800) 345-5473
Fax: (916) 345-6751
e-mail: travel@moon.com

IMPORTANT ORDERING INFORMATION

PRICES: All prices are subject to change. We always ship the most current edition. We will let you know if there is a price increase on the book you order.

SHIPPING AND HANDLING OPTIONS: Domestic UPS or USPS first class (allow 10 working days for delivery): $3.50 for the first item, 50 cents for each additional item.

EXCEPTIONS:

Tibet Handbook and *Indonesia Handbook* shipping $4.50; $1.00 for each additional *Tibet Handbook* or *Indonesia Handbook.*

Moonbelt shipping is $1.50 for one, 50 cents for each additional belt.

Add $2.00 for same-day handling.

UPS 2nd Day Air or Printed Airmail requires a special quote.

International Surface Bookrate 8-12 weeks delivery: $3.00 for the first item, $1.00 for each additional item. Note: Moon Publications cannot guarantee international surface bookrate shipping. Moon recommends sending international orders via air mail, which requires a special quote.

FOREIGN ORDERS: Orders that originate outside the U.S.A. must be paid for with either an international money order or a check in U.S. currency drawn on a major U.S. bank based in the U.S.A.

TELEPHONE ORDERS: We accept Visa or MasterCard payments. Minimum order is US$15.00. Call in your order: (800) 345-5473, 8 a.m.-5 p.m. Pacific Standard Time.

ORDER FORM

Be sure to call (800) 345-5473 for current prices and editions or for the name of the bookstore nearest you that carries Moon Travel Handbooks • 8 a.m.-5 p.m. PST.
(See important ordering information on preceding page.)

Name: _____ Date: _____

Street: _____

City: _____ Daytime Phone: _____

State or Country: _____ Zip Code: _____

QUANTITY	TITLE	PRICE

Taxable Total_____

Sales Tax (7.25%) for California Residents_____

Shipping & Handling_____

TOTAL_____

Ship: ☐ UPS (no P.O. Boxes) ☐ 1st class   ☐ International surface mail
Ship to: ☐ address above   ☐ other _____

_____

Make checks payable to: **MOON PUBLICATIONS, INC**. P.O. Box 3040, Chico, CA 95927-3040 U.S.A. We accept Visa and MasterCard. **To Order**: Call in your Visa or MasterCard number, or send a written order with your Visa or MasterCard number and expiration date clearly written.

Card Number: ☐ **Visa**   ☐ **MasterCard**

☐ ☐ ☐ ☐   ☐ ☐ ☐ ☐   ☐ ☐ ☐ ☐   ☐ ☐ ☐ ☐

Exact Name on Card: _____

Expiration date:_____

Signature:_____

S/95–A

THE METRIC SYSTEM

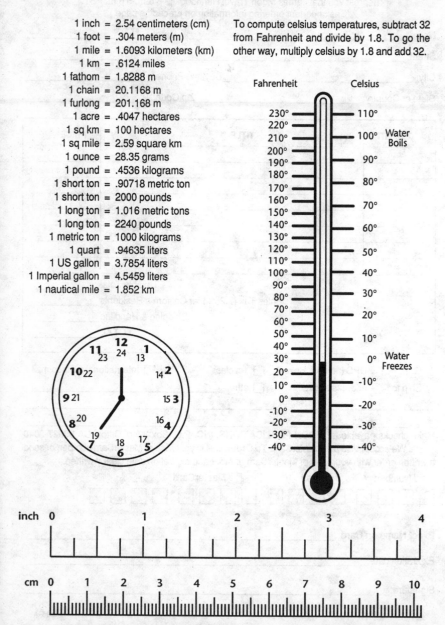

1 inch = 2.54 centimeters (cm)
1 foot = .304 meters (m)
1 mile = 1.6093 kilometers (km)
1 km = .6124 miles
1 fathom = 1.8288 m
1 chain = 20.1168 m
1 furlong = 201.168 m
1 acre = .4047 hectares
1 sq km = 100 hectares
1 sq mile = 2.59 square km
1 ounce = 28.35 grams
1 pound = .4536 kilograms
1 short ton = .90718 metric ton
1 short ton = 2000 pounds
1 long ton = 1.016 metric tons
1 long ton = 2240 pounds
1 metric ton = 1000 kilograms
1 quart = .94635 liters
1 US gallon = 3.7854 liters
1 Imperial gallon = 4.5459 liters
1 nautical mile = 1.852 km

To compute celsius temperatures, subtract 32 from Fahrenheit and divide by 1.8. To go the other way, multiply celsius by 1.8 and add 32.

Fahrenheit   Celsius

230° — 110°
220°
210° — 100° Water Boils
200°
190° — 90°
180°
170° — 80°
160°
150° — 70°
140°
130° — 60°
120° — 50°
110°
100° — 40°
90°
80° — 30°
70°
60° — 20°
50°
40° — 10°
30° — 0° Water Freezes
20°
10° — -10°
0°
-10° — -20°
-20°
-30° — -30°
-40° — -40°

inch 0   1   2   3   4

cm 0   1   2   3   4   5   6   7   8   9   10

ABOUT THE AUTHOR

Karl Luntta lived and worked in Africa, the South Pacific, and the Caribbean before settling in Massachusetts with his profoundly lovely family. He is the author of Moon's *Jamaica Handbook* and other travel guides and has published fiction and nonfiction in national magazines and newspapers.